THE BEGINNINGS OF CIVILIZATION

Part II of Volume I of the *History* begins with the dawn of culture in the Bronze Age and goes up to the splendid civilizations of Mesopotamia and the Nile at the end of the thirteenth century B.C. The author describes the gradual urbanization of society in Sumer, Egypt, Phoenicia, Crete, India, and China. He relates the development of religion, languages, writing systems, education; the growth of social and economic institutions such as law and taxation; the rise of a professional class—officers, priests, artists, merchants—who did not hunt or farm, but who were supported by the products of the community.

Beautifully illustrated with plates, drawings, and maps, Sir Leonard's account takes us to the point where many ancient societies had collapsed, when Babylonia had become a second-rate power, India was in the hands of the Aryans, and all civilization stood poised on the brink of a new advance.

"Sir Leonard Woolley . . . tells [*his*] *story in a spirit at once imaginative and objective, sophisticated and sensible, always humane."* —Herbert J. Muller

"A splendid global history of the evolution of man . . . a monumental work."

—Charleston News and Courier

Other MENTOR Books Published in Cooperation with UNESCO

HISTORY OF MANKIND: Cultural and Scientific Development Volume One, Part I, Prehistory by Jacquetta Hawkes

This first volume in the UNESCO history describes primitive man from his beginnings in Africa to the Neolithic Age. (#MY632—$1.25)

THE EVOLUTION OF SCIENCE: Readings in the History of Mankind edited by Guy Metraux and Francois Crouzet

Essays from the *Journal of World History,* a UNESCO publication, by leading scholars including V. Gordon Childe, Bertrand Gille, Francois Russo, Clyde Kluckhohn. (#MQ505—95¢)

THE NINETEENTH CENTURY WORLD: Readings in the History of Mankind edited by Guy Metraux and Francois Crouzet

Essays on the nineteenth century from UNESCO's *Journal of World History,* by such scholars as R. R. Palmer, Werner Conze, Henri Gouhier, and others. (#MQ506—95¢)

HISTORY OF MANKIND

Cultural and Scientific Development

Volume I, Part 2

THE BEGINNINGS OF CIVILIZATION

by Sir Leonard Woolley

A MENTOR BOOK

Published by The New American Library, New York and Toronto
The New English Library Limited, London

For information, address Harper & Row, Publishers, Inc., 49 East 33rd Street, New York, New York 10016.

Published as a MENTOR BOOK by arrangement with George Allen and Unwin, Ltd.

FIRST PRINTING, AUGUST 1965

Prepared under the auspices and with the financial assistance of the United Nations Education, Scientific and Cultural Organization and published for the International Commission for a History of the Scientific and Cultural Development of Mankind.

Consultant for Volume I, Part 2
Professor Jean Leclant
(University of Strasbourg, France)

A hardcover edition of *History of Mankind*, containing Volume I, Parts 1 and 2, is available in the United States from Harper & Row, Publishers, Inc.

MENTOR BOOKS are published *in the United States* by
The New American Library, Inc.,
1301 Avenue of the Americas, New York, New York 10019,
in Canada by The New American Library of Canada Limited,
295 King Street East, Toronto 2, Ontario,
in the United Kingdom by The New English Library Limited,
Barnard's Inn, Holborn, London, E.C. 1, England

PRINTED IN THE UNITED STATES OF AMERICA

FOREWORD

Director-General of UNESCO

At a time when man is preparing to launch out from this planet into space, it is well that History should hold him in contemplation of his trajectory through the ages.

Never before, indeed, has he shown so searching a curiosity about his past or such jealous care to preserve its vestiges. It is as though in some mysterious way a balance were now maintained in his thought between the exploration of space and that of time, the extroversion of the one being offset by the inwardness of the other.

Be that as it may, never more than now, when man finds himself hurtling at vertiginous speed towards a wondrous future, has there been a great need for the function of memory to ensure for mankind the appropriation of its creative actuality. If consciousness were not thus rooted in such reflection on its own process of becoming, many of the inventions we hail as conquests and advances would be no more than the uncontrollable workings of an alienated destiny.

To evoke this retrospective awareness is the first thing that this work which we now have the honour of introducing to the public sets out to do; it is an attempt to sum up the heritage of civilization to which we owe our present élan.

The ambition to write a universal history is a very old one indeed. Many have tried their hand at it before, particularly in the classical epochs—not without merit, nor without success. The present work belongs to that noble line of great syntheses which seek to present to man the sum total of his memories as a coherent whole.

It has the same twofold ambition, to embrace the past in its entirety and to sum up all that we know about that past. And it adopts the same intellectual approach—that of the interpretative as opposed to the descriptive historian—reducing events to their significance in a universal frame of reference, explicit or implicit.

However, this *History of Mankind* parts company with its

predecessors on several essential points. In the first place, it deliberately confines itself to shedding light on one of mankind's many aspects, its *cultural and scientific development.*

In so doing it departs from the traditional approaches to the study of history, which, as we know, attach decisive importance to political, economic and even military factors. It offers itself as a corrective to the ordinary view of man's past. And those who initiated the enterprise may well have thought at first that this was, in itself, sufficiently useful and original for them to dispense with any further aim.

Admittedly, it rests with the science of history to decide objectively, *a posteriori* and according to the case, on the relative importance of the different elements and factors in particular situations. To that extent the approach deliberately adopted in this History may well be said to be an *a priori* postulate. This is the very postulate on which UNESCO itself is based, namely, the conviction that international relations, in their ultimate reality, are determined not merely by political and economic factors and considerations but spring as well, and perhaps even more surely, from the capabilities and demands of the mind.

Nevertheless, even from the strictly scientific point of view, this History, deliberately partial though it be, may well claim that, in restoring to the achievements of culture and science their full reality and significance, it has made an essential contribution to that sum of factual knowledge and right understanding which a complete history aspires to offer.

But the originality of the enterprise does not stop there. In point of fact, that is where it begins. For the facts of which this History treats are no ordinary ones. To put them back in their proper place is not merely to fill a long-standing gap and thus complete the sum, restoring its balance to the whole. It is to discover a new dimension of the historical object, perceptible only when approached from a particular intellectual angle.

Cultural or scientific facts, whatever their subject-matter, means, cause, pretext or circumstances, are essentially thoughts of man about man.

This is obvious in the cultural sphere, every value being a human ideal. But it is no less true of science; for apart from the fact that truth, too, is a value, the essence of science is not knowledge, but the method by which knowledge is gained, the rule the mind prescribes itself in order to attain it; and every rule is a form of reflection and self-discipline; that is, doubled consciousness.

Thus, the history of what has no doubt been too simply

described here as 'the cultural and scientific development of mankind' is, strictly speaking, the story of how, through the ages, men—individually and collectively—have conceived of humanity. Or, to be more correct, have conceived of *their* humanity, that is, the universal aspect of their experience. In short, the subject of this work is the gradual development, in its most expressive manifestations, of the consciousness of the universal in man.

As will be seen, great care is taken to describe the exchanges and influences which link the different foci of civilization across space or time. We are shown how this web of reciprocal influences is becoming more closely woven as spatial communications grow more numerous and rapid and relations in time more intensive.[1] Indeed by no means the least interesting feature of this work is the stress it lays upon this still too little known aspect of historical reality in which the 'intellectual and moral solidarity of mankind' referred to in the Preamble to UNESCO's Constitution can really be seen at work.

Yet even this is not the decisive discovery. That lies not so much in the evidence of interrelation between the many and varied civilizations as in the fact, manifest in all forms of culture and science, that every civilization implies, produces or invokes an image of man in terms of the universal.

This immanence of the universal in every cultural and scientific experience is what gives its essential character to the spiritual solidarity of mankind. And it is in this form that that solidarity can serve as the foundation for the true peace described in UNESCO's Constitution, whereas the effect of intercultural relations upon the interplay of the forces conducive, in a given situation, to peace is, as well we know, extremely complex and indirect, and therefore contingent. In fact it is because the object of this History, as already pointed out, is the development of the consciousness of this solidarity that UNESCO regards such an undertaking as both vital and necessary.

But straightway we are faced with another fact, no less rich in implications. In the actual experience of science and culture, sense and style, which constitute the universal element, remain indissolubly bound up with the singular act of invention or creation from which they derive. It may truly be said both of science and of culture, regarded as experiences, that 'the more one concentrates on the particular, the more universal

[1] Even in time, relations are reversible—not, of course, through any real causation, but owing to the perpetual reappraisal of the significance of events that takes place in the course of man's constantly renewed, and renewing, retrospection.

one becomes'. And it is only by repeating the various operations of the act of creation, reduced to their objective characteristics—which make up what we call method—or by subjective communion with the mental atmosphere of that act—which is what we call intuition—that another person can understand and assimilate this sense and style.

It follows that for a history which aims to keep in constant touch with experience and restore it in its contingent truth, scientific and cultural facts have significance only for certain individuals, namely those who are capable of applying these methods and of exercising this intuition which give access to the secrets of creativeness in its unique aspects. However, to possess this ability, there is no doubt that one must belong to the particular context of civilization in which such unique phenomena occur. Accordingly a concrete history of science and culture can only be written from a plurality of viewpoints corresponding to the variety of civilizations.

To acknowledge the fact that there is more than one civilization is not to deny in any way the continuity or solidarity of human development. On the contrary, the study of the interrelations, across time and space, of ideas, values and techniques restores this sense of continuity and solidarity, which have never before been so definitely and convincingly established as in this History. Similarly, to be aware of the originality of the works and symbols which make up each civilization is not to gainsay the universality of the human mind. As we have seen, true universality is no more than a dimension of this consciousness of a sense or style, which opens out to the potential totality of mankind only by rooting itself in the particularity of its initial emergence.

The classical rationalism of the West conceived the history of the human mind as a process of development in which all scientific and cultural facts are arranged in order with reference to a single, constant subject that is universal by nature. There is no need to plunge into a philosophical discussion on ontological humanism in order to expose this myth. It would be only too easy, now of all times, to show how into this allegedly universal subject has been projected, out of pride or sheer naïveté, the subjectivity, in more or less sublimated form, of certain personalities eminently representative of their epoch, civilization or race.

The work you are about to read represents the first attempt to compose a universal history of the human mind from the varying standpoints of memory and thought that characterize the different contemporary cultures.

But in doing so, its main purpose was not to banish all subjectivity of interpretation. Indeed, such a pretension could not be entertained in a history which seeks to assess the significance of events and which takes as its starting points the positions adopted by the various cultures. For there is a kind of subjectivity, co-substantial, as it were, with culture, which causes the perspective opened by each culture on the universal in man to be a projection of that culture's humanity in its own particular circumstances. The originality of this attempt at a universal history lies in its having taken for its frame of reference the multiplicity of contemporary cultural perspectives and projections. For the first time an attempt has been made to present, with respect to the history of consciousness, the sum total of the knowledge which the various contemporary societies and cultures possess and a synthesis of the conceptions which they entertain. For the first time an attempt has been made to offer a history of human thought which is the product of the thought of mankind in every aspect of its present complexion. A universal history indeed, and doubly so—in both its object and its subject.

This aspiration, which is the essence of the whole undertaking, has determined the choice of method.

The History is the work, not of a team with a homogeneous cultural background, but of an International Commission which, by its very composition and even more by the spirit pervading it, embraces all the varied cultural traditions and modern ideologies which form the spiritual framework of our present-day world. What is more, the International Commission made it a rule that the contributions of the many scholars whose services it enlisted be submitted to the scrutiny of the National Commissions which, in the Member States of UNESCO, group together persons particularly qualified to represent the fields of education, science and culture. Subject always to the overriding considerations of scientific truth, the observations received in the course of these extensive consultations were scrupulously taken into account in drawing up the final text. Never before has what I may call the decentralization of viewpoints and interpretations been carried so far in the science of history.

Accordingly the work is also an act; for this historical study is itself a cultural achievement calculated to influence, by its spirit and its methods, the present trend of culture. And that, no doubt, is its ultimate end. For just as the awareness of mankind's intellectual and moral solidarity to which it leads stems less from the discovery of the interrelations of the past than from the effort of synthesis by which mankind seeks to apprehend the whole compass of its scientific and cultural heritage, so the essential feature of this effort is not so much the complete restitution of the object which it is designed to achieve as the fact that the whole of the subject as it exists today is taking part in it and thus affirms its own unity in the process of achieving it.

In this humanism, whose universality springs not from a unique abstract nature but is being gradually evolved, on the basis of a freely acknowledged diversity, through actual contact and a continuous effort at understanding and co-operation, UNESCO recognizes both its own *raison d'être* and its guiding principle. The unity of mankind, we believe, has to be patiently built up, through mutual respect for the cultures which diversify it without dividing it, and by the establishment of more and more centres of science which spread man's technological power throughout the world, fostering equality of opportunity for progress and for the genuine preservation of his dignity.

Such, then, are the principal ideas and essential features of this work; they are, at the same time, the very reasons which led UNESCO, as the educational, scientific and cultural organization of the United Nations, to conceive the project and assist in its execution.

The author of this History is not UNESCO; it is the International Commission which, since 1950, has directed this venture in complete intellectual independence. It is to the Commission, therefore, and to it alone, that the full credit for this work is due. And at the same time—allow me to state—it also bears the sole responsibility for its scientific worth.

UNESCO is, however, proud to have organized this work and to have made possible its accomplishment by providing the necessary funds, administrative machinery and international background. In that sense this great venture, without precedent in many respects, is also in some measure its work, too.

It is, therefore, my pleasant duty to express the Organization's gratitude to all those who have, to whatever degree, participated in this undertaking and contributed to its success. Above all its thanks are due to the distinguished members of the International Commission and to its eminent Chairman, Professor Paulo E. de Berrêdo Carneiro, who for thirteen years have given unsparingly of the wealth of their knowledge and talents, with a devotion and selflessness equalled only by the nobility of their thought. In this concept of scientific and cultural development in which consciousness is an act and all reflection a creation, it may be said without fear of exaggeration that, in presenting this vast panorama of the past history of the human mind, such as never was before, they have made a powerful contribution towards the advent of a consciousness of civilization on a scale encompassing the whole of mankind. With all my admiration, I wish to express to them UNESCO's gratitude.

RENÉ MAHEU
Director-General

UNITED NATIONS EDUCATIONAL, SCIENTIFIC
AND CULTURAL ORGANIZATION

Paris, 1962.

PREFACE

PROFESSOR PAULO E. DE BERRÊDO CARNEIRO
President of the International Commission
for a History of the Scientific and Cultural Development of Mankind

Among the great tasks assigned to UNESCO by its Constitution is the duty to promote and encourage mutual knowledge and understanding throughout the world. While many of the divergencies which divide peoples date from a distant past, an analysis of their historical antecedents discloses links which draw them nearer to one another, brings to light their contributions to a common patrimony of humanity, reveals the ebb and flow of cultural exchanges and emphasizes their increasing tendency to become integrated into an international community.

Beyond differences of race, climate, economic structure and systems of ideas, history shows the fundamental identity of the various human groups, making it possible to discern, in many cases, profound analogies among the transformations they have undergone from the Palaeolithic era down to the present time. If we consider the human species as a whole, we perceive that the course of its evolution has been accomplished from one region and one people to another by way of a series of oscillations, greater or lesser in extent, longer or shorter in duration. The different civilizations which have arisen in the course of the ages correspond to distinct phases and patterns of this general movement. Almost every one of them is to be found somewhere in the world of today. Contemporary society appears as a mosaic in which the most widely-differing cultures adjoin and confront each other.

It was, I think, in order to know them better and to strengthen their solidarity that UNESCO took the initiative of entrusting to historians, men of science and of letters, recruited from all parts of the world, the task of preparing and of publishing this work. This, at least, is how I have understood the mandate of the International Commission over which I have the honour to preside. Our task was not to draw up a philosophy of history in the light of the economic, intellectual and moral laws which may govern social development, but to describe, from a universal standpoint, the contribution of each age, each region, each people to the scientific and cultural ascent of humanity.

In the official reports which I have presented since 1951 to the General Conference of UNESCO, will be found a detailed account of the steps taken in implementing this project which originated in a resolution submitted to the second session of the General Conference held in Mexico City in 1947. The idea had been put forward in 1946 by Dr Julian Huxley, then Executive Secretary of the Preparatory Commission for UNESCO:

'The chief task before the Humanities today would seem to be to help in constructing a history of the development of the human mind, notably in its highest cultural achievements. For this task, the help of art critics and artists will be needed as well as of art historians; of anthropologists and students of comparative religion as well as of divines and theologians; of archaeologists as well as of classical scholars; of poets and creative men of letters as well as of professors of literature; as well as the whole-hearted support of the historians. Throughout, of course, the development of culture in the various regions of the Orient must receive equal attention to that paid to its Western growth. Once more, UNESCO can help by being true to its many-sidedness, and by bringing together from all these various fields to help in one or other facet of this huge work.' (UNESCO: *Its Purpose and Its Philosophy* [London, 1946].)

Several preparatory meetings were held and preliminary studies made in 1947 and 1948 with the participation of Professors Carl J. Burckhardt, Lucien Febvre, Joseph Needham, Georges Salles, Taha Hussein, and UNESCO officials, among whom

Dr Julian Huxley, then Director-General, Mr Jean Thomas and Professor Pierre Auger. In 1949, Professors Lucien Febvre and Miguel Ozorio de Almeida were asked to prepare general reports on the basis of which the General Conference, at its fourth session, recommended that the work should proceed immediately.

In the same year a committee of experts was called to draft the plan to be submitted to the General Conference for the elaboration of a scientific and cultural history of mankind. It included the following scholars: R. Ciasca, L. Febvre, M. Florkin, J. Needham, J. Piaget, P. Rivet and R. Shryock. In opening the proceedings, Dr Jaime Torres-Bodet, at that time Director-General, evoked the spirit in which he considered the work should be accomplished:

'Through UNESCO, humanity must come to realize its common past and understand the significance of the sum total of endeavour, invention and enlightenment which have gone to make up the heritage we seek to serve today. If we can regard this moment in the world's history as UNESCO's hour, it is thanks to the slow and often unnoticed growth of an outlook shared by all men, which is now beginning to take shape as the outlook of Mankind. . . .'

'We seek only to draw up the table of the major cultural events which have shaped Man's existence and slowly brought civilization into being. . . .'

'The important thing is to embark on it with the will to succeed and in a spirit of serene and dispassionate objectivity. . . .'

'Nevertheless, by publishing today a synthesis of our present knowledge of *humanity's scientific and cultural history*, UNESCO, far from lulling the critical spirit to sleep, will spur it to new and eager research. It is my profound conviction that there is nothing in the nature or the present state of historical science precluding the making of such a synthesis; indeed all circumstances invite us to it.'

In accordance with a resolution of the General Conference of 1950, consultations were held with the International Council of Scientific Unions (ICSU) and the International Council for Philosophy and Humanistic Studies (CIPSH) as to the appointment of an international commission to undertake, on behalf of UNESCO, full responsibility for the preparation and execution of the work. The following experts nominated by these two councils were invited by the Director-General to become active members of the Commission: Professors Homi Bhabha (University of Bombay), Carl J. Burckhardt (Switzerland), Paulo E. de Berrêdo Carneiro (University of Brazil), Julian Huxley, FRS (United Kingdom), Charles Morazé (University of Paris), Mario Praz (University of Rome), Ralph E. Turner (Yale University), Silvio Zavala (University of Mexico), and Constantine K. Zurayk (University of Damascus).

The International Commission met for the first time in December 1950 and again in March 1951 in Paris. It decided during these two meetings to invite a number of distinguished persons to become Corresponding Members, and to set up an Editorial Committee, under the chairmanship of Professor Ralph E. Turner, with Professors Constantine K. Zurayk and Charles Morazé as members. The Commission did me the honour of electing me as its President, with Dr Julian Huxley and Professor Carl J. Burckhardt as Vice-Presidents. A Bureau was created comprising the President, the Vice-Presidents and the Chairman of the Editorial Committee. Dr. Armando Cortesao, a member of the Department of Cultural Activities of UNESCO, initially responsible for the secretariat of the Commission, was unanimously elected Secretary-General. In 1952 he was succeeded by Dr Guy S. Métraux.

Between 1952 and 1954 new members were added to the International Commission to enlarge its geographical, cultural and philosophical representation. The following scholars were appointed in agreement with the Director-General of UNESCO: Professors E. J. Dijksterhuis (Netherlands), Jacques Freymond (Switzerland), Mahmud Husain (Pakistan), Hu-Shih (China), Erik Lönnroth (Sweden), R. C. Majumdar (India), Percy E. Schramm (Federal Republic of Germany), Ali A. Siassi (Iran), and J. Pérez Villanueva (Spain).

As early as 1952 the International Commission approached scholars of countries which, at the time, were not members of UNESCO but which represented important cultural areas. Invitations were sent to national academies of sciences and arts, but met with no response. It was only in 1955 that the International Commission was able to welcome as new members historians and scientists from the Union of Soviet Socialist Republics and the People's Republics of Czechoslovakia, Hungary and Poland.

Since 1954 the Bureau, acting as delegate of the International Commission with additional responsibilities placed on it by the General Assembly, has been enlarged to comprise the President and six Vice-Presidents as follows: Sir Julian Huxley (United Kingdom), Professor R. C. Majumdar (India), Professor Ralph E. Turner (United States of America), Professor Gaston Wiet (France), Professor Silvio Zavala (Mexico), and Professor A. A. Zvorikine (Union of Soviet Socialist Republics). Professor Louis Gottschalk (United States of America) was unanimously elected as a further Vice-President in 1961.

The first publication which the International Commission initiated, on the proposal of Professor Charles Morazé, was a quarterly review, the *Journal of World History*. Professor Lucien Febvre was the Editor until his death in 1956, when it came under the supervision of the Bureau, with Dr François Crouzet and Dr Guy S. Métraux as its editorial staff.

The main function of the *Journal of World History* has been to provide the International Commission with material for the final compilation of the History—documentary or bibliographical details about problems which have so far remained obscure; translations of documents which may have appeared desirable; contributions to the History itself. This review has also enabled scholars in all countries to take part in an exchange of views on questions of interpretation and the actual presentation of the History.

The *Journal of World History* represents a considerable contribution on the part of the International Commission to historical knowledge and towards a better understanding of historical processes. Composed of articles of the highest scientific quality which bear the signature of scholars from every country and which express the most diverse ideological trends, it foreshadows to some extent the great work for which it has furnished basic materials.

The preparation of the History was examined in detail during the first and second meetings of the International Commission. Several courses of action presented themselves: the Commission could draft the final text, or it could be entrusted to a single editor, or to independent authors. It was decided that, while the Commission would retain the full authority conferred upon it by the General Conference of UNESCO, the wisest course would be to select individual author-editors for each of the six volumes. The author-editors would be fully responsible for the text, but they would work under the supervision of, and in collaboration with, the Editorial Committee and the Commission; they would benefit by the assistance of scholars, designated by them, to deal with certain chapters; and, if necessary, sections could be referred to specialists.

On the recommendation of the Editorial Committee, author-editors for five of the six volumes were at this time appointed. For Volume I, Parts 1 and 2, Jacquetta Hawkes and Henri Frankfort, both of the United Kingdom. On the death of Professor Frankfort in 1954, the late Sir Leonard Woolley (United Kingdom) was appointed to write Volume 1, Part 2. For Volume III, René Grousset (France), with two co-authors, Vadime Elisséeff and Philippe Wolff (France). Professor Gaston Wiet (France) took over the author-editorship of this third volume in 1953 on the death of Professor Grousset. For Volume IV, Louis Gottschalk (United States of America); for Volume V, Jorge Basadre (Peru), who afterwards resigned and was replaced later by Professor Charles Morazé (France); and for Volume VI, K. Zachariah (India), who was succeeded in 1956 by Dr Caroline F. Ware (United States of America), H.E. Dr K. M. Panikkar (India), and the late Dr J. M. Romein (Netherlands).

In 1953 the late Professor Luigi Pareti (Italy) was appointed author-editor of Volume II, with Professors Paolo Brezzi and Luciano Petech of Italy as assistants.

By the spring of 1952 a first draft plan of the History was in circulation. Through the active interest of the author-editors, the members of the International Commission, and scholars consulted throughout the world on the initiative of the International Commission, this plan was slowly revised to constitute a general guide for the elaboration of the six volumes.

At a meeting of the International Commission in February 1954 it was decided, on my proposal, to include in its membership the author-editors of the six volumes and the editor of the *Journal of World History*. This measure was designed to enable those primarily responsible for the text of the volumes to take part in discussions and so to make a more effective contribution to the direction of the activities of the International Commission. In addition it was decided that one single body—the Bureau of the Commission—should be made entirely responsible for the co-ordination of the Commission's work. To ensure the unity of style and presentation essential to a work of such high intellectual standing and covering so wide a field, Professor Ralph E. Turner was entrusted with the task of editing the English texts.

In the course of the execution of its programme the International Commission benefited by the co-operation of UNESCO and of the General Conference which, at several of its sessions, had the opportunity to examine the work plans prepared for the History, and on two occasions took decisions which markedly influenced our work. The Ninth General Conference held in New Delhi in 1956 recommended that the texts of all volumes be submitted to the National Commissions set up in the Member States. The objective was to assist the International Commission in obtaining for each volume additional critical materials to enable the author-editors to revise and to perfect their texts. While not all National Commissions responded, the comments which were received proved most useful. All the author-editors have conscientiously noted the criticisms received and have taken them into account, wherever possible, when revising their texts. Furthermore, the International Commission has sought the advice of experts on several points.

Again at the invitation of the General Conference, following its tenth meeting held in Paris in 1958, the International Commission decided to appoint a number of historians to advise the Bureau and the author-editors on possible modifications of the text of each volume of the History, in the light of comments and criticisms received, and to suggest editorial notes on controversial issues. This step had become necessary as Professor Turner's illness had prevented him from accomplishing the editorial work. In pursuance of this policy, and in agreement with the members of the Bureau and with the author-editors, I selected a number of eminent historians, of different nationalities, particularly qualified to act as special consultants. Thus, at the end of each chapter of all volumes the reader will find grouped together editorial notes and bibliographical references that will provide him with summaries of historical opinions on those questions which can be variously interpreted.

The International Commission plans to issue a supplement

to Volume VI, *The Twentieth Century*. While the first part treats of the History of our age in the same way as the history of previous periods was considered in all the volumes, this second tome will be devoted to an open debate on the main trends in scientific and cultural development at mid-century.

The six volumes include line drawings prepared by Mrs. Stella Robinson at the request of the author-editors, photographic plates assembled by the Secretariat of the International Commission in co-operation with the author-editors and their assistants, and maps drawn specially by the Swiss firm, Hallwag, A.G.

At the time of publication I must recall with gratitude and regret the memory of those scholars whom the International Commission had the misfortune to lose in the course of its work and who contributed so much to the achievement of its task: Professor René Grousset, Henri Frankfort and K. Zachariah, Sir Leonard Woolley, Professors Luigi Pareti, Lucien Febvre, and J. M. Romein.

I must hereby express, on behalf of the International Commission, by gratitude to the General Conference of UNESCO which made this project possible, to the Director-Generals, Messrs. Julian Huxley, Jaime Torres-Bodet, Luther Evans, Vittorino Veronese and René Maheu, and to the Secretariat of UNESCO which, through ten years, has extended assistance and guidance on every possible occasion.

The International Commission is greatly indebted to the author-editors who, often under difficult circumstances, fulfilled their task with the highest competence and devotion; to its Vice-Presidents, who constitute the Bureau, for assuming with me full responsibility for every phase of the execution of this project; and in particular to Professor Ralph E. Turner, Chairman of the Editorial Committee, for the elaboration of the general plan of the History and for his whole-hearted dedication to the success of the work to which he brought his own personal outlook of an integrated world history. I am particularly happy to acknowledge herewith the co-operation of the Corresponding Members, the consultants and the translators, whose work proved invaluable for the completion of this project.

The International Commission benefited throughout its work by the advice of the official Observers of the

International Council of Scientific Unions, Professor R. J. Forbes; of the International Council for Philosophy and Humanistic Studies, Sir Ronald Syme; and of the International Social Sciences Council, Professor F. H. Lawson.

Lastly, I would like on behalf of the International Commission to thank the Secretary-General, Dr Guy S. Métraux, and his staff for their active and faithful collaboration which has contributed so much to the success of this scientific and cultural history of mankind.

International Council of Scientific Unions, Professor [illegible] of the International Council for Philosophy and Humanistic Studies, Sir Ronald Syme, and of the International Social Sciences Council, Professor W. H. [illegible].

Lastly, I would like on behalf of the International Commission to thank the Secretary-General, Dr Guy S. Métraux, and his staff for their active and untiring collaboration which has contributed so much to the success of the scientific and cultural history of mankind.

[illegible]

ACKNOWLEDGEMENTS

The UNESCO International Commission, the authors and the publishers wish to thank all those who have kindly given permission for the reproduction of the plates in this book. Acknowledgements are made under each illustration and abbreviated as follows:

Archaeological Museum, Ankara ANKARA
Archaeological Museum, Antakia ANTAKIA
Ashmolean Museum, Oxford ASHMOLEAN
British Museum, Oxford B M
Professor J. M. Casal and the French Archaeological Mission CASAL
J. D. Chen, Hong Kong CHEN
Department of Antiquities of Egypt DAE
Department of Archaeology, Government of India DAI
Direction générale des Antiquitiés et des Musées, Syria DAMS
Egypt Exploration Society, London EES
Calouste Gulbenkian Foundation, Lisbon CGF
Heraclion Museum HM
Institute of Archaeology, London IA
Iraq Directorate-General of Antiquities IDA
Metropolitan Museum of Art, New York MMA
Museo Egizio, Turin ME
Musée Guimet, Paris MG
Musée du Louvre, Paris LOUVRE
National Museum, Athens NM
Ny Carlsberg Glyptotek, Copenhagen CARLSBERG
Oriental Institute, University of Chicago OI
Professor André Parrot PARROT
C. F. A. Schaeffer, *Ugaritica* I and II SCHAEFFER
Smithsonian Institution, Freer Gallery of Art, Washington, D. C. SMITHSONIAN
Capt. G. E. Spencer-Churchill, London SPENCER-CHURCHILL
W. Thesiger, Esq., DSO THESIGER
University Museum, University of Pennsylvania, Philadelphia PENN
Vorderasiatisches Museum, Berlin VM

British Museum, [illegible]

Calouste Gulbenkian Foundation, Lisbon: GULBENKIAN
Heraklion Museum: HERAKLION

Museo Egizio, Turin: [illegible]
Musée Guimet, Paris: GUIMET

CONTENTS

LIST OF ILLUSTRATIONS

FIGURES*

* Unless otherwise indicated, drawings were supplied by Sir Leonard Woolley.

All line drawings were executed especially for this work by Stella Robinson in collaboration with R. G. Hadlow.

FIGURES

33 Ground plan of the school at No. 1 Broad Street, Ur — 98

34 [illegible] from the tomb of [illegible], from a photograph — 324

34 Starving peasants from the tomb of Unas, from a photograph — 329

35 Cypriote white slip ware, after H. B. Walters, *Catalogue of the Greek and Etruscan Vases in the British Museum* (London, 1912), Vol. I, Part II, *Cypriote, Italian and Etruscan Pottery*

36 The Battle of Kadesh, after H. Frankfort [illegible] *Space and Time in Representational Art of the Ancient Near East* (Chicago, 1951)

All line drawings were executed especially for this work by Stella Robinson in collaboration with [illegible]

MAPS

The maps of Vol. I, Part 2, were drawn by Hallwag, A. G., Berne, on the basis of original sketches prepared by Sir Leonard Woolley

INTERNATIONAL COMMISSION FOR A HISTORY OF THE SCIENTIFIC AND CULTURAL DEVELOPMENT OF MANKIND

	MEMBERS	
H.E. Professor Paulo E. de Berrêdo Carneiro	*Brazil*	PRESIDENT
Professor Louis Gottschalk	*United States of America*	Vice-President
Sir Julian Huxley, FRS	*United Kingdom*	Vice-President
Professor R. C. Majumdar	*India*	Vice-President
Professor Ralph E. Turner	*United States of America*	Vice-President Editor
Professor Gaston Wiet	*France*	Vice-President
Professor Silvio Zavala	*Mexico*	Vice-President
Professor A. A. Zvorikine	*Union of Soviet Socialist Republics*	Vice-President
Dr Jorge Basadre	*Peru*	
Professor Eduard J. Dijksterhuis	*Netherlands*	
Professor Jacques Freymond	*Switzerland*	
Professor Karel Krejčí	*The Socialist Republic of Czechoslovakia*	
Professor Mahmud Husain	*Pakistan*	
Professor Witold Kula	*The Polish People's Republic*	
Professor Erik Lönnroth	*Sweden*	
Dr Eric Molnár	*The Hungarian People's Republic*	
Professor Charles Morazé	*France*	
H. E. Dr. K. M. Panikkar	*India*	
Professor Mario Praz	*Italy*	
Mrs J. B. Priestley (Jacquetta Hawkes)	*United Kingdom*	
Professor Percy E. Schramm	*Federal Republic of Germany*	
Professor Ali A. Siassi	*Iran*	
Professor J. Pérez Villanueva	*Spain*	
Professor Caroline F. Ware	*United States of America*	
Professor C. K. Zurayk	*Syria*	
Dr Guy S. Métraux	*Switzerland*	Secretary-General

CORRESPONDING MEMBERS

Argentina
Dr R. Frondizi

Australia
Professor R. M. Crawford

Austria
Dr Karl Jettmar

Belgium
Professor Marcel Florkin
Professor Charles Manneback

Brazil
Professor Fernando de Azevedo
Professor Gilberto Freyre
Professor Sergio Buarque de Hollanda
Dr José Honorio Rodrigues

Burma
Dr Htin Aung

Canada
Professor Wilfred Cantwell Smith

Chile
Dr Ricardo Donoso

China
Professor Tso-ping Tung
H.E. M. Chang Chi-yun

Colombia
Professor German Arciniegas
Professor Luis Martinez Delgado

Cuba
H.E. Dr J. Remos y Rubio

Denmark
Dr Kaj Birket-Smith

Egypt
Professor Aziz S. Atiya

France
Monseigneur Blanchet
Professor Julien Cain
Professor J. B. Duroselle
Professor C. Lévi-Strauss

Federal Republic of Germany
Dr Georg Eckert
Dr Hermann Heimpel
Dr Ludwig Dehio

Honduras
H.E. Prof. Rafael Heliodoro Valle

India
Professor J. N. Banerjea
Dr Humayun Kabir
H.E. Sir Sarvepalli Radhakrishnan
Professor K. A. Nilakanta Sastri

Indonesia
Dr S. T. Alisjahbana
Professor M. Sardjito

Iran
Professor Ali-Asghar Hekmat

Iraq
Dr Abdul Aziz al-Duri

Israel
Professor B. Mazar

Italy
Professor Domenico Demarco
Professor Giacomo Devoto
R. P. Antonio Messineo

Japan
Professor Shigeki Kaizuka
Professor Suketoshi Yajima
Dr Seeichi Iwao
Professor Daisetso Suzuki

Lebanon
Emir Maurice Chehab
H.E. Dr Charles Malik

Mexico
Dr Alfonso Caso
Professor Samuel Ramos
Professor Manuel Sandoval Vallarta
Professor Daniel Cosio Villegas

Nepal
Professor Gókal Chand

Netherlands
Professor Dr R. Hooykaas
Dr Maria Rooseboom

New Zealand
Dr J. C. Beaglehole

Norway
Professor Alf Sommerfelt

Pakistan
Dr A. Halim
Dr I. H. Qureshi
Dr S. Suhrawardy

Philippines
Professor Gabriel Bernardo

Senegal
H.E. M. L. S. Senghor

Spain
Professor Claudio Sanchez Albornoz
Professor Antonio Garcia Bellido
M. Ciriaco Pérez Bustamante
M. F. Cantera
Professor Emilio Garcia Gomez
Duke of Maura
Professor R. Menendez Pidal
Professor José Pijoan

Sweden
Professor Axel Boëthius

Switzerland
Dr Werner Kaegi
Professor Jean Piaget

Syria
H.E. Khalil Mardam Bey

Thailand
Prince Dhani Nivat

Turkey
H.E. Mehmed Fouad Köprülü

Union of South Africa
Professor A. N. Pelzer

Union of Soviet Socialist Republics
Professor A. V. Artsikhovski
Professor N. A. Figourovsky
Professor Guber
Professor B. Kedrov
Professor D. V. Sarabianov
Professor N. A. Sidorova
Professor Vinogradov
Professor V. P. Zoubov

United Kingdom
Sir Ernest Barker
Dr Joseph Needham
Bertrand Russell

United States of America
Professor Eugene Anderson
Professor Salo W. Baron
Professor Norman Brown
Professor J. K. Fairbank
Professor Harold Fisher
Professor G. Stanton Ford
Professor R. H. Gabriel
Professor Oscar Halecki
Dr C. W. de Kiewiet
Professor A. L. Kroeber
Professor Martin R. P. McGuire
Professor H. W. Schneider
Professoı Richard Shryock
Professor John A. Wilson

Uruguay
Professor Carlos M. Rama

Venezuela
H.E. C. Parra-Perez
Professor Mariano Picon Salas

NOTE ON THE EDITORIAL TREATMENT OF VOLUME I, PART 2

The original text of Sir Leonard Woolley was submitted to all the National Commissions for UNESCO and to a number of specialists selected by the International Commission for a History of the Scientific and Cultural Development of Mankind.

All the comments which were made available to the International Commission on the original text were communicated to the author-editor, who used them widely in revising the manuscript, occasionally redrafting material or making additions. The specialists responsible for the most important of these modifications are indicated in the footnotes appended to the relevant passages.

It had been Sir Leonard's intention to reserve certain contributions for incorporation as separate footnotes, either because they seemed to him to warrant separate presentation, or because they could be considered only marginal to his own study. Sir Leonard had also prepared the elements of a discussion on certain points at issue. Having reviewed as a whole both the comments of scholars consulted and the relevant arguments advanced by Sir Leonard Woolley, Professor Ralph E. Turner, Vice-President of the International Commission, then indicated the observations which, in his opinion, particularly justified retention.

Sir Leonard Woolley died before the work could be completed. The critical comments submitted by scholars, together with the notes of Sir Leonard Woolley and of Professor Turner, were entrusted to Professor Jean Leclant of the University of Strasbourg.

Thus, Part 2 of Volume I of the *History of Mankind: Cultural and Scientific Development* includes the notes originally designed by Sir Leonard Woolley to accompany his own text, the observations and discussions of the scholars consulted by the International Commission, and lastly the additions made by Professor Leclant who was responsible for the compilation and editing of all notes and comments with the co-operation of the Secretary-General of the International Commission.

The greatest possible care has been taken to ensure that the reader should always be able to identify immediately the type of note concerned. The difficulty of achieving a coherent presentation of extremely heterogeneous material, without the benefit of Sir Leonard Woolley's guidance, should, however, be borne in mind.

The comments of the following scholars were used in elaborating the notes:

Dr D. C. Baramki, American University, Beirut.

Professor J. M. Casal, Musée Guimet, Paris.

Professor A. Caquot, Ecole des Hautes Etudes, Paris.

Professor I. M. Diakonoff, Oriental Institute, Leningrad, on behalf of the Commission of the USSR for UNESCO.

Professor S. J. Gasiorowski, University of Cracow, on behalf of the Polish National Commission for UNESCO.

Dr G. F. Ilyin, Institute of Oriental Studies, Academy of Sciences of the USSR, on behalf of the Commission of the USSR for UNESCO.

Professor Shigeki Kaizuka, Corresponding Member of the International Commission, Institute for Humanistic Science, Kyoto University, on behalf of the Japanese National Commission for UNESCO.

Professor E. Laroche, University of Strasbourg.

Professor R. C. Majumdar, Vice-President of the International Commission, Calcutta.

Professor J. Maluquer de Motes, University of Salamanca.

Professor D. J. Mulvaney, Lecturer in History, University of Melbourne, on behalf of the Australian National Advisory Committee for UNESCO.

Professor F. Schachermeyr, University of Vienna, on behalf of the Austrian Commission for UNESCO.

Professor A. Sommerfelt, Corresponding Member of the

International Commission, University of Oslo, on behalf of the Norwegian National Commission for UNESCO.

Dr W. C. Sturtevant, Bureau of American Ethnology, Smithsonian Institution, on behalf of the United States National Commission for UNESCO.

Professor R. E. Turner, Vice-President of the International Commission, Yale University, New Haven, Conn.

Dr A. A. Vaiman, Moscow, on behalf of the Commission of the USSR for UNESCO.

Dr L. V. Vasilyev, Institute of Sinology, Academy of Sciences of the USSR, on behalf of the Commission of the USSR for UNESCO.

Professor B. L. van der Waerden, Zurich.

Professor John A. Wilson, Corresponding Member of the International Commission, University of Chicago.

Professor A. P. Yushkevich, Institute of the History of Science and Technique, Academy of Sciences of the USSR, on behalf of the Commission of the USSR for UNESCO.

The International Commission would also like to thank the following scholars for their comments and suggestions on the original manuscript:

The late Professor F. S. Bodenheimer, Corresponding Member of the International Commission, Hebrew University, Jerusalem.

Professor Martin R. P. McGuire, Corresponding Member of the International Commission, The Catholic University of America.

Dr K. M. Panikkar, Member of the International Commission, Co-author of Volume VI of a *History of Mankind: Cultural and Scientific Development*.

The following scholars made their observations available at the request of the National Commission for UNESCO in their own countries:

Professor M. Almagro Bach (Spain), the University of Madrid.

Professor G. R. Castellino (Italy), the University of Rome.

Dr Vaclav Cihar (Czechoslovakia), Oriental Institute, Prague.

Dr Hugh Hencken (United States of America), Peabody Museum, Harvard University.

Dr J. Klima (Czechoslovakia), Oriental Institute of the Academy of Sciences, Prague.

Professor K. Majewski (Poland), the University of Warsaw.

Professor Tahsin Ozgüz (Turkey), the University of Ankara.

Professor Timoteus Pokora (Czechoslovakia), Oriental Institute of the Academy of Sciences, Prague.

Dr H. H. Roberts (United States of America), Bureau of American Ethnology, Smithsonian Institution, Washington, D.C.

Professor E. Sangmeister (Federal Republic of Germany), the University of Freiburg.

Dr Jirina Sedlakova (Czechoslovakia), Charles University, Prague.

Professor Kiyoski Yabuuchi (Japan), Institute for Humanistic Science, Kyoto University.

Finally, the International Commission would like to thank the scholars whose comments and suggestions were forwarded by the National Commissions for UNESCO in Afghanistan, India and Israel, and by the Ministry of Education of Pakistan.

GUY S. MÉTRAUX,
Secretary-General

Paris, March 1962

AUTHOR'S PREFACE

BECAUSE in the following chapters it is claimed that the Bronze Age saw the birth of civilization as contrasted with the barbarism of the Neolithic period, it were well to start with a definition. This is the more necessary because the term has too often been loosely used of cultures which, while remaining essentially primitive, have developed arts or aptitudes that invite comparison with the achievements of more advanced peoples. Some criterion is obviously needed to fix the distinction between them.

The very word 'civilization' by its etymology implies an urbanized society. This is generally acknowledged: but because the word 'urbanization' is itself loosely used it is insufficient as a definition of anything else; the most convenient and easily recognizable criterion of civilization is the knowledge of the art of writing. As Professor Gordon Childe has put it in an admirable article entitled 'Civilization, Cities and Towns',[1] writing 'not only represents a new instrument for the transmission of human experience and the accumulation of knowledge, but is also symptomatic of a quite novel socio-economic structure—the city'. And here again definition is called for if the stages of human progress are to be clearly envisaged. We have in English the three words, 'village', 'town' and 'city'. The meaning of 'village' is tolerably precise and the term is rightly applied to the Neolithic settlement; the village is based mainly upon agriculture, though some of its inhabitants may be not food-producers but craftsmen; its affairs are likely to be directed by a headman or a council of elders; it may comprise a temple or church, and it may be walled. The village, growing in size, in population and in its social organization, may in the course of time develop into a town. But it does so by imperceptible degrees, and there is no point at which we can say that it has ceased to be a village and has become a town, for the simple reason that in the English language the word 'town' has never had any definite connotation; we use the word freely but vaguely, we mean something by it but, if pressed, cannot say in positive terms precisely what we do mean. On the other hand, between 'town' and 'city' there is a clear-cut distinction, because the essential characteristics of a city are lacking in a town. To quote again from Professor Gordon Childe, 'In English this untranslatable word [city] implies a cathedral, a bishop's palace, a body of canons and other clergy, and a large number of laymen who are neither farmers, fishers nor hunters. I have taken this as the essential character of a city (we might add that the term further implies a recognized form of municipal government, as regards England, and a royal charter confirming the city's status); a community that comprises a substantial proportion of professional rulers, officials, clergy, artisans and merchants who do not catch or grow their own food, but live on the surplus produced by farmers or fishermen who may dwell within the city or in villages outside its walls. These professional and full-time specialists represent a new class of persons, an absolute addition to the population that could be included in, or supported by, any barbarian community. This increment is my justification, or at least excuse, for speaking of an "Urban Revolution" on the analogy of the Industrial Revolution or the Neolithic Revolution.'

It was during the Bronze Age that this Urban Revolution gradually took place, and in the Bronze Age we can for the first time speak of civilization. Now, in certain areas of the earth, men were living not in groups or hordes but in organized communities, submitting to the disciplines and profiting by the opportunities of the city, intent upon the quality of living rather than upon mere existence, enjoying (some of them) that degree of leisure and wealth that makes possible the pursuit of learning and the cult of art, and stabilized by the possession of the written word which could enlarge the individual horizon by the experience of the past and preserve for the future whatever of value man might invent.

Only of a limited number of areas is this true, and then in varying degrees; moreover, the evidence that we possess regarding them is unevenly distributed and often sadly deficient; this must serve as the explanation, or the excuse for a certain lack of consistency in my treatment of the subject. Where the development of some particular branch of culture was peculiar to one country, or in different countries followed different or even divergent lines, there the subject was best treated regionally. Where advance was more uniform, with local differences less marked, or where progress in one area was well documented while the evidence from others gave only supplementary detail, there the regional treatment could be abandoned and interest be concentrated on progress as made by man generally, the record drawing its illustration from different areas in turn. Our theme is not the history of this or that people or nation, and, although the regional treatment was often dictated by circumstances, stress has been laid throughout upon the degree of common effort that has gone to the making of the world. No people has lived for itself alone. Sometimes we can see how, by the catalysis of war or of trade or of migration, disparate elements of different cultures were, even in those early days, amalgamated into something new and of value; sometimes the combination was to occur only after the date at which our volume ends, but even then our knowledge of what was to be makes worth while an understanding of the elements so to be resolved.

The Bronze Age was indeed the formative period in man's cultural advance, and in the course of it the greater part of what constitutes modern civilization visibly begins to take shape; the headings of the chapters and sections in this volume cover almost every branch of human activity and might, with but few additions, serve as headings for a cultural review of our own time. Admittedly the contents of the sections show that the sciences were still in their infancy—man was not yet interested in speculation and theory; but he understood already the art of living and, on the practical side at least, was developing with skill and intelligence the opportunities for the good life which nature offered to him.

The field to be covered here is therefore very wide, far too wide for a single writer to have first-hand knowledge of all its varied features, any one of which may be the life-time study of a specialist. Since I figure on the title-page as sole author I may well be thought guilty of intellectual arrogance in that I have ventured to write on so many subjects lying outside my own experience and knowledge, and I confess—or rather, I protest—that I was at first daunted by the complexity of the task before me. My reason for attempting it is that in this far-reaching study of civilization's progress unity of view is more important than detailed analysis, and a volume of essays by different specialists could hardly fail to lack just that balance and harmony demanded by the whole, of which each of these subjects is but a part. The whole was therefore drafted by me to the best of my unaided powers, and then sections, as required, were submitted to the judgement of kind friends who have ungrudgingly placed at my disposal a wealth of learning to which I could make no pretension; the result is that such sections combine in their final version the form and treatment which I had thought most fit with a content approved by scholars of undisputed authority. I would therefore record here my deep gratitude to those who have helped me in their different spheres and have given to my work in those spheres whatever value it may possess. On the Egyptian side, Professor Sir Alan Gardiner has spared no pains, and on the Sumerian, Professor C. J. Gadd; on mathematics, astronomy and the calendral systems Professor B. L. van der Waerden has corrected and re-corrected with minute care everything that I have written; in the section on Law I have had the advice of Dr O. R. Gurney and of Professor W. F. Leemans; in the section on Medicine and Surgery that of Professor Lindeboom; throughout I have profited much by the criticisms and suggestions of Professor I. M. Diakonoff, Professor V. V. Struvé, Father Vast van Bulk, SJ, and Dr R. J. Forbes, and not least by the constant help of Sir Julian S. Huxley; and I am indebted to my friends Mr Shui Chien Tung, for material on the calendar of ancient China which I could not have obtained otherwise, and Mr Teulon Porter for general criticism of the text. To all of these I wish to render my heartfelt thanks; and to readers who may, not unnaturally, hesitate to accept what I say on matters so far from my competence I would plead that 'the voice is Jacob's voice, but the hands are the hands of Esau'.[2]

NOTES TO PREFACE

1. In *Antiquity*, No. 121, March 1957, p. 36.
2. Genesis xxvii. 22.

CHAPTER I

THE BRONZE AGE

THE CONDITIONS OF CIVILIZATION AND THE GROUPING OF MANKIND

AT the beginning man, like every other animal, has been forced to adapt himself to his environment; that was the condition of his survival, and such species as failed to fulfil that condition died out. But alone of the animals man in time adopted a different solution to the problem of existence, that of adapting his environment to himself; by the control of fire, by the use of shelters and clothing, by the use of tools fabricated by himself, he could to some extent disregard the changes of climate, and instead of having to live where food abounded he made it abound where he lived. That revolution had been effected during the Neolithic period. There were still vast areas wherein it was incomplete—as it was to be for many centuries—where hunting and food-gathering continued to be the rule of life, but those were the backward areas; by the end of the first part of our story we have seen great parts of Asia, Europe and Africa sparsely peopled by farmers living in small but largely self-sufficient settlements. They were in possession of a considerable body of knowledge; flint-knapping, pot-making, weaving, agriculture and stock-breeding were commonly practised. Sedentary and self-contained, the various communities tended to develop, in response to their several environments, local peculiarities in their arts and crafts and, even more, in their speech, their customs and their beliefs; long before the Late Stone Age came to an end the main branches of the human race had become differentiated physically and, to some extent, mentally; but in spite of this it remains true that throughout the vast stretch of the Old World wherever evidence of Neolithic culture has been found their mode of life was essentially the same.

Out of this homogeneous and more or less static condition of barbarism was now to be evolved the complex picture of the modern world. The change, portentous in its ultimate effects and almost bewilderingly rapid in its operation, began in the fourth millennium before Christ. Far from being general, it was confined to a few areas where conditions were favourable; and whereas in those areas the whole manner of man's life was quickly transformed, elsewhere, over the greater part of the world's surface, the ancient barbarism was to persist for centuries and for millennia. The revolution started in Mesopotamia and very soon afterwards spread to Egypt, and in those two countries we can trace its course from the outset; it took place in the Indus valley also, and in China, on the banks of the Yellow River, but in both these cases we are faced with a civilization already full-grown whose genesis is a matter of conjecture. While therefore our story must deal primarily with all four centres, Mesopotamia and Egypt are those which give us the detailed and factual evidence required by the historian (Map I). But before discussing the nature of their contribution to progress we should note the reasons for which they played so much more spectacular a part than did the rest of the ancient world.

If hitherto change had been painfully slow it was because Neolithic man was hard put to it to live. All his efforts were necessarily devoted to getting sufficient food for his family out of an unpromising and a thankless soil; only when the struggle for existence ceased to absorb all his time and energy could he find leisure for the amenities of life. The first requisite for civilization was a wide extent of rich soil easily worked.

That condition applies to a good many regions wherein in fact cultural advance was none the less negligible. To get the best out of life man requires not only good soil but also a climate that permits and encourages him to work out of doors, in moderation, all the year round. A lotus-land existence in which nature supplies a livelihood without the need of effort applies no spur to initiative, and a climate which exhausts man with unceasing toil for half the year and for the other half immobilizes him in cold or sodden misery equally disinclines him from any effort of invention. Only where soil and climate alike were favourable could man produce in excess of his actual needs and yet have leisure to enjoy the surplus; and hitherto he had found no region which satisfied both conditions.[1]

Then, apparently at more or less the same time, two new lands came into being. The vast marshes through which the Tigris and Euphrates made their way to the Persian Gulf, bringing with them the silt from their upper reaches, began to dry up, and the water gave place to an alluvial plain more fertile than any other man had known. Similarly in Egypt the delta became for the first time habitable: the Nile waters were confined to definite channels, and the yearly inundations so far from being destructive only added to the richness of the soil. In both regions (and possibly the same was true of the Indus valley) it would seem that nature suddenly[2] provided, in a part of the world where the climate was best suited to living conditions of the time, a land where agriculture was rewarded without stint and with little risk of failure; what was no less important, the new territories were so extensive that they could support such a population as under the conditions of the Neolithic Age had been impossible. It was not a case now of small and isolated hamlets; families and clans congregated in villages, some of which might grow into towns, and the towns might be in touch with one another. With the settlement of these two river valleys we see the emergence of civilized society. Political entities of unprecedented complexity arose; occupations became specialized, involving divisions of class, trade was organized, writing was invented, monumental architecture expressed the symbolic significance of public buildings and representational art tended to replace the largely decorative art of Neolithic times.

But while the impetus was the same and the revolution that resulted from it was similar, the process of change in the Nile valley and in the valley of the Tigris and Euphrates differed in important respects. In both of them corporate existence took an entirely new shape in that the simple social life of the old days was reconstituted on a fresh basis; but in Mesopotamia civilized society crystallized into a number of separate nuclei, each city forming a small state jealous of its autonomy, whereas in Egypt the whole Nile valley was united in a single realm under one king. We shall see later that this contrast in political organization is but one aspect of a profound difference in the spirit of the two civilizations.

Egypt

In Egypt the high desert which had been the hunting-ground of Palaeolithic man had long since become the desiccated waste which we see today,[3] unfit for human occupation, though the side *wadis* were still filled with jungle growth and supported animal life. The Nile valley proper was still, in Badarian times, marshy and waterlogged, and the delta was but a reed-covered swamp; settlement was necessarily confined to the limited areas wherein agriculture was possible, to the great depression of the Fayum, to the valley borders and to the lower reaches of

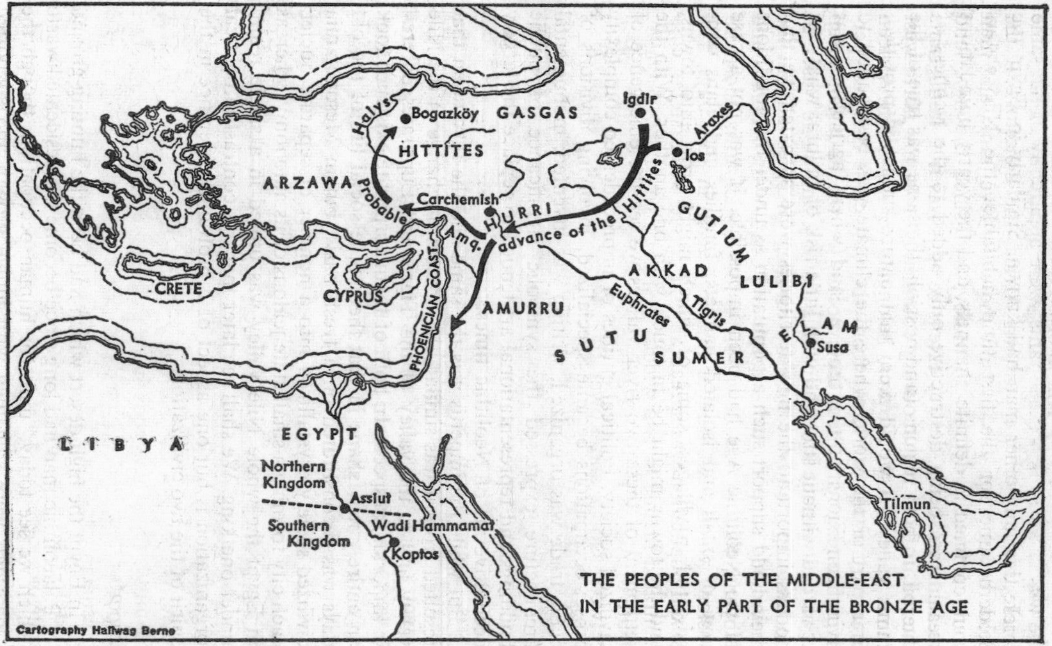

THE PEOPLES OF THE MIDDLE-EAST
IN THE EARLY PART OF THE BRONZE AGE

Halys
Bogazköy
GASGAS
HITTITES
ARZAWA
Probable
Carchemish
HURRI
Amq.
advance of the Hittites
Igdir
Araxes
Ios
GUTIUM
AKKAD
LULIBI
ELAM
Susa
Tigris
Euphrates
SUTU
SUMER
AMURRU
PHOENICIAN COAST
CRETE
CYPRUS
LIBYA
EGYPT
Northern Kingdom
Assiut
Southern Kingdom
Wadi Hammamat
Koptos
Tilmun

Cartography Hallwag Berne

MAP I

the *wadis*. These first inhabitants[4] were apparently of the same stock as the peoples of eastern Africa, the ancestors of the modern Bega and Somali. Now the water-level sank, and man could move down into the valley, and since the new land created by the Nile was as extensive as it was rich immigrants filtered in from neighbouring countries. From the north-west came in, probably, Libyans, belonging to the north African branch of European man; from the east came Semites, perhaps bringing with them their flocks, for the Badarian sheep is of west Asiatic stock, and the pottery and stone vases of Badarian Egypt have affinities with those of Palestine; but the main body came from the south and south-west, Nubians and Libyans, thus at the dawn of history anticipating those invasions which were to recur time and again in after days. The mixed population was spread along the river's course but concentrated mainly in two widely separate areas, the Nile valley south of Assiut, and the Fayum,[5] so that already the distinction between Upper and Lower Egypt was a reality, so much so indeed that the development of two independent states was inevitable. Then at the beginning of what is called the Naqada II period, probably in the second half of the fourth millennium BC, there arrived a new wave of immigrants, Semites from Asia, bringing with them a higher culture and at least an elementary knowledge of metal. These settled first in the south country, not, it would seem, as conquerors but as peaceful newcomers, and ushered in there the Chalcolithic phase; later they colonized Lower Egypt also. By the end of the fourth millennium the disparate elements of the population had amalgamated so thoroughly that the physical characteristics which had differentiated them can no longer be distinguished: the Naqada skulls are neither Semitic nor Libyan but Egyptian; some of the pottery resembles that still made by the Kabyles of north Africa, but the language of the people has, especially in its vocabulary, Semitic elements combined with the native Hamitic; some new gods have appeared, and may have been imported, but the religion as a whole is definitely Nilotic and presumably inherited from the Badarian farmers. In our survey therefore we shall have to deal with a hybrid people who, in spite of geographical or political divisions, none the less formed a consistent unity and had already begun to develop a character of their own; that hybridization[6] may be held to account for the intellectual energy which enabled the Egyptian to take advantage of the favourable conditions of the land and to develop one of the great civilizations of the ancient world.

Mesopotamia

In Mesopotamia the process of nature was different. The delta of the Tigris and Euphrates, instead of being formed from north to south as one might expect, started in the south. Two other rivers, the Karun running from the Persian mountains in the east and the now dry Wadi al Batin which drained the heart of Arabia, emptied into the Persian Gulf almost directly opposite one another, and in due time the vast amount of silt carried by them formed a bar across the gulf; from that moment the silt of the Tigris and Euphrates, instead of being borne out to sea and scoured by the tide, was deposited in the lagoon behind the bar and raised the level until what had been deep water turned to marsh and eventually to dry land. But it was against the bar that the dry land formed first, and therefore the earliest immigrants settled in the extreme south; according to Sumerian tradition Eridu, the southernmost of all their cities, was the oldest of them. The south country, then, was taken over by a wave of immigrants coming from the east —on the evidence of their painted pottery we can associate them with Elam; as the apex of the delta formed in the north a wholly different people, this time of the Semitic stock, moved down into it from the north so as in the course of time to form in the upper part of the country the majority of the population; the new land was divided therefore between two unconnected peoples, and its title in later times, the Land of Sumer and Akkad, records a duality that goes back to the beginning of its history. But the division was not absolute in any geographic sense. Some of our earliest documents attribute Semitic names to individuals and even to kings of the southern cities, while, on the other hand, not only the dispersion of the earliest (al'Ubaid) pottery but also the royal records of the Dynastic period prove that the southerners extended their power to the north-west as far as Mari on the middle Euphrates. There was indeed a considerable overlap, but it remains generally true that in the north-east the population was predominantly Semitic while in the south and west it tended to be mainly of the other stock.

The southerners, whom for the sake of convenience we may call the Sumerians, although the name should properly apply only to the mixed stock which eventually evolved what is rightly called the Sumerian civilization, were an eastern people about whom very little is known. Their language was agglutinative, like Turkish or Mongolian, but has no recognized affiliation to any other language. They were still in or were but beginning to emerge from the Neolithic stage of culture, but they had advanced it to a rare height of excellence. Their painted pottery shows close affiliation with that of the people of Susa, in southern Persia, and would appear to be a locally specialized branch of the Neolithic painted wares whose vogue extended as far eastwards as Baluchistan and as far northwards as Mongolia. Primarily farmers—their flint hoes and sickles of burnt clay are found in astonishing numbers on all sites of the al'Ubaid period—they were none the less founders of cities, and several of the great urban centres of historic times traced their origin back to these first settlers. As traders they must have been active, for their pottery occurs freely on northern sites in the Semitic sphere and travelled westwards as far afield as the Amq Plain on the lower Orontes. Since excavation at Eridu has brought to light the superimposed ruins of no less than sixteen temples all belonging to the al'Ubaid period and since at Warka there are found eleven superimposed building-levels of exclusively al'Ubaid culture, giving a total depth of 15 metres (and the al'Ubaid pottery continues in use, side by side with the Uruk ware, for another 9½ metres), it is certain that the period must have been a very long one; and if we may judge by the material remains that survive, the original culture developed on its own lines without any serious admixture of foreign elements except that in the later days at least copper began to come into use. Then, as Sumerian historians of after times were to record, 'then came the Flood'.

This literary record is substantiated by the results of archaeological excavation. At Ur there is found material evidence of a great inundation which occurred towards the close of the al'Ubaid period, thus agreeing with the sequence-date vaguely assigned to it by Sumerian tradition. The city of Ur itself, standing as it did on a mound already fairly high, survived; but numerous village sites of the al'Ubaid period show no signs of later occupation and must have been completely destroyed; the mass of silt deposited against the Ur mound implies a flood of a depth sufficient to drown the entire delta, and it is easy to believe that the bulk of the population perished.[7]

Naturally the land was too valuable to be left untenanted, and a horde of immigrants flocked into it from the north and settled down side by side with the survivors of the old stock.[8] They brought with them new arts. They were skilled in the working of metal; they introduced the potter's wheel, and their plain wares, grey or black or red, soon displaced the now degenerate painted pottery of al'Ubaid. If, as the excavators at Warka believe, the great palace there with its mud-brick columns and walls overlaid with elaborate mosaic (Pl 1, a) really goes back to the 'Uruk' period, then under the guidance of the newcomers the south country achieved a prosperity unparalleled hitherto; and if, as seems probable, the invention of writing dates to this period then the contribution of the Uruk people to civilization was great indeed. The earliest written documents are in the Sumerian language, and it has been urged by some scholars (e.g. S. N. Kramer[9]) that the real Sumerians were the Uruk people, migrants and barbarians who conquered the more civilized Irano-Semitic al'Ubaid stock. But, judging by the archaeological evidence, the Uruk people were not barbarians (they were a metal-using folk, and they introduced the wheel) and so much of the later Sumerian civilization can be traced back to the al'Ubaid people that they can scarcely be regarded as a crushed and suppressed class.[10] It is more likely that the two stocks amalgamated (as seems to be implied by the long cultural overlap in the stratification at Warka) and that by the time writing was invented, late in the Uruk period, the Uruk people had adopted the al'Ubaid language;[11] that is something for which history provides many parallels.

But shortly before 300 BC another invasion, this time again from the east, brought a fresh change. We find no evidence of war and destruction; quite possibly things started with 'peaceful penetration', but undoubtedly in course of time the 'Jamdat Nasr' people made themselves masters of the country. For the most part they carried on faithfully its cultural traditions, as indeed would be but natural if they had been acclimatized to them during the period of their gradual incoming; but they themselves were by no means savages. Their pottery, with its polychrome decoration, is of a high order; they were admirable carvers in stone as had been the Uruk people before them; they were good builders and they adorned their walls with painted designs; moreover, under their régime the art of writing was further developed and came into common use. Although, after a century or two, their government was overthrown by the older elements of the population, they had certainly made their contribution to the culture of the country, and presumably they had also by intermarriage added something to its breeding. When they fell from power, and the Early Dynastic period of Sumer started, Sumerian civilization properly so called was fully formed and the Sumerian people, who will figure largely in our history, was an amalgam of three racial elements whose identity was now merged in the common stock; but when we attempt to trace that civilization back to its source we find that while each of the three partners played an essential part in its development an unbroken tradition links the historic age with the primitive farmers of al'Ubaid.

To the north of Sumer, along the middle reaches of the Tigris, lies the country which in later times was to be called Akkad. It had been inhabited by Neolithic men long before the delta was formed, and here, on such sites as Jarmo and Hassuna, we can see the first beginnings of agricultural village life in Mesopotamia. But by the time when the al'Ubaid people were developing the south country, the north, for all that it had had the earlier start, seems to have been lagging behind in progress. Progress of course there had been, and Nineveh may even at that time have ranked as a town rather than a village, but it is noticeable that such objects of luxury as its inhabitants enjoyed were for the most part imports, not of local manufacture. According to Assyrian tradition, the early people of the land were Subaraeans, whose country lay to the north and east of Assyria proper and included at least part of Assyria itself; these Subaraeans seem to have been related to if they were not actually identical with the Hurri. But mixed with them there was a Semitic element—Amurru—akin to those earliest Semites who had come into northern Mesopotamia at the same time as the al'Ubaid people came into the south. This element was in course of time to preponderate and to spread southwards so that when in the twenty-fourth century BC Sargon set up a new kingdom in the north and established his rule over the entire delta, his dynasty and his government were Semitic and his capital city was Akkad.

Up to nearly that date the north country could boast no real culture of its own. There is no reason to think that it formed a united realm governed by a single ruler; the towns, if we may judge from Assur, were held by the Sumerians with a Sumerian governor and a garrison, and though the handicrafts might follow local traditions the arts were those of the south country and even the gods were largely those of the Sumerian pantheon. From very early days there had been constant wars between south and north; the Subaraeans were no match for the well-organized armies of Sumer and were held in subjection, but they could appreciate the superior civilization of their conquerors and were quick to imitate it; by the time of Sargon they had assimilated practically all that Sumer had to teach, and amongst other things had learned the art of war. It was as a military power that Akkad, and afterwards Assyria, was to play so prominent a role in Middle Eastern history, but it initiated little else, so that up to the end, whether Nineveh or Babylon was in the ascendant, it made hardly any difference to the character and the course of Mesopotamian civilization.

Westwards from Akkad, along the middle Euphrates and almost to the shores of the Mediterranean, was the land of the Hurri.

North Syria

The original home of the Hurri seems to have been in the general region of Armenia, where they would have been neighbours of the Hittites, and, as has been said above, they are scarcely to be distinguished from the Subaraeans. At what date they spread westwards across northern Mesopotamia we cannot say with any precision, but it was early in the Bronze Age, certainly long before the time of Sargon and Akkad, when Hurri documents were already being written in the cuneiform script. The earlier inhabitants were presumably Amurru, Western Semites, but it would be unwise to claim any one ethnical name for the authors of the very different local cultures which the exploration of the area has brought to light.

From the outset the country was thickly inhabited. The settlements were naturally most dense in the well-watered land along the Euphrates and in the valley of the Khabur, then on the north Syrian plateau and in the Amq plain by the Orontes, stopping short only at the foothills of the Amanus range; much of the area, open steppe covered in spring-time with lush grass, was more suitable for the pasturing of flocks and herds, and its sparse population would be dwellers in tents rather than in houses; but even so the *tells* that dot the plain, sometimes far from any source of water existing at the present day, bespeak a region of no small importance.

At the beginning of the Chalcolithic Age, or perhaps rather earlier, there was developed here a type of painted pottery which is one of the most remarkable in the ancient Middle East (Fig. 1). It is a hand-made ware magnificently decorated with polychrome designs (red, black, white and purple on a pink or cream ground) built up for the most part from geometrical elements elaborately combined but including flower rosettes and more or less schematized bucrania, this last suggesting a religious motif. Called Tell Halaf ware after the place where it was first discovered, it was widely dispersed; there was a centre of manufacture at Tell Arpachiyah (Arpachia) in the valley of the Upper Zab, another at Carchemish on the Euphrates; evidently it was not all manufactured at a single centre, and there are local differences in the shapes and decoration of the vessels, but the family resemblance is unmistakable. The finest of the ware comes from the Upper Zab valley, which may have been the main productive area, but it occurs in Nineveh and as far west as the Amq plain, though there it is certainly an import brought in by the way of trade. It was an original and a gifted people that produced the Tell Halaf pottery but evidently not one equipped to hold its own in the struggle for existence, for the settlements all bear the marks of violent overthrow. In the east it was replaced by people using a late northern variant of the al'Ubaid ware—suggesting just such Sumerian conquests as we have noted in the case of Assyria. At Carchemish a barbarous Neolithic folk squatted on the ruins of the Tell Halaf village, to be replaced later by Bronze Age invaders. In the Amq plain the indigenous population began to import northern al'Ubaid pottery instead of that of Tell Halaf and then proceeded to evolve from the pattern of the two foreign fabrics a painted ware of their own—the Tell esh Sheikh ware—which if it could not rival that of Arpachiyah yet possessed considerable artistic merit and originality (Fig. 2). While it would appear to have been evolved in the Amq, it enjoyed a fairly wide dispersion, for it is found in Cilicia, at Mersin, and specimens of the ware, or at least of a derivative of it, are reported from Hacilar in western Anatolia, i.e. it occurs along the overland trans-Anatolian route which leads on ultimately to south-east Europe and Thessaly. In the Amq it is ousted by the black burnished pottery of Kherbet Kerak concerning which more will be said hereafter.

Even when the Hurri came upon the scene there was no cultural uniformity throughout the whole region occupied by them. Like the Subaraeans in Akkad, they were an imitative people, ready to be impressed by a superior civilization, and they had that of Sumer constantly before their eyes. In the eastern part of their country bordering on Akkad, which for a long time was subject to the early dynasts of Sumer, Sumerian influence was so strong that its capital city, Mari,[12] must, so far as its material remains go, be reckoned as an outpost of Sumer—so strong indeed that Mari itself could produce a royal family deemed not unworthy of a place in the list of Sumerian dynasties. Farther to the west Sumerian connections were less intimate, though thanks to the trade route passing up river to the cedar forests of Amanus there was an exchange of ideas, so that a successful ruler of Alalakh could build himself a palace on the model of those of his Mesopotamian clients. But the region was too wide—and perhaps, in the west, the population too mixed in blood—for anything like political

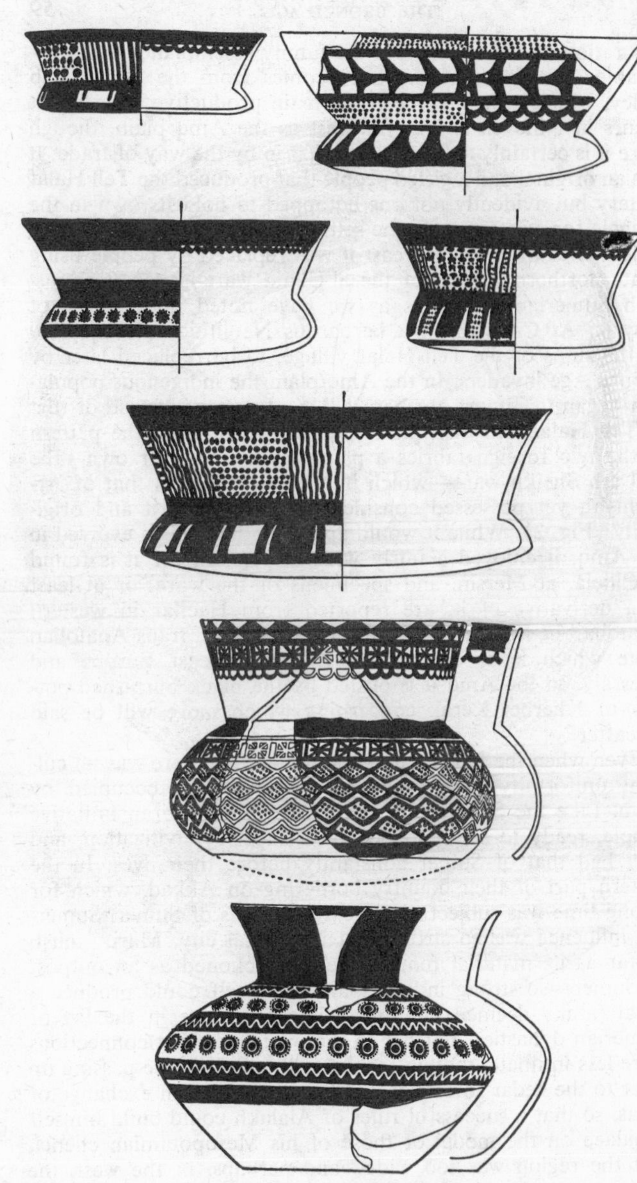

FIG. 1A. *Tell Halaf pottery.*

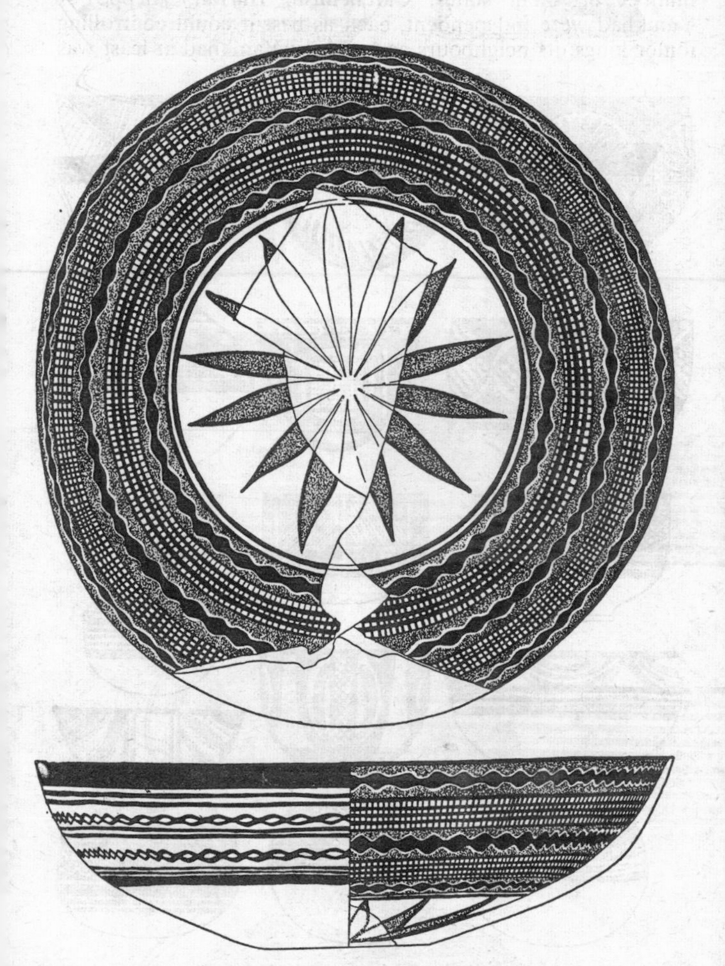

FIG. 1B. *Tell Halaf pottery.*

unity. When historical records begin we find it split up into a number of small states; Carchemish, Harran, Aleppo or Yamkhad were independent, each as best it could controlling minor kings, its neighbours and vassals; Yamkhad at least was

FIG. 2. *Tell esh Sheikh pottery.*

almost as closely in touch with Syria as with Sumer, and its southern boundary ran with that of the purely Amurru kingdom of Damascus.

The Hurri seem to have been imitators rather than initiators of culture, but for that very reason they played an important part in cultural history. Mixing freely as they did with other peoples (we find Hurrian names on tablets in southern Mesopotamia at the time of the Third Dynasty of Ur, and there were Hurri in southern Palestine before the patriarchal period) they were admirable middlemen in the traffic of ideas. Themselves thoroughly imbued with Sumerian traditions, they handed those on to the Hittites, and it was almost certainly through them that the Hittites learned the art of writing and adopted the cuneiform script invented by the Sumerians.[13] If they did not invent, at least the Hurri spread far afield and so perpetuated much of the highest civilization that man had yet evolved.

Anatolia

North of the Fertile Crescent the broken mountainous country and high-lying plateaux of Asia Minor were inhabited by peoples of whom, in the Neolithic Age, we know little or nothing; but this wild region was to play a pre-eminent part in the development of ancient civilization. The land is extremely rich in mineral ores, and when some accident had shown that from the gaily coloured stones of the hill-sides there could be got malleable copper which made tools infinitely more convenient than chipped or polished flints, the primitive Asiatic was quite ready to exploit his discovery and to barter his produce with his neighbours in the south. Here, then, emerged a culture of which the primary basis was not agriculture but industry and commerce. At a later date we shall recognize in the east of Anatolia the important kingdom of Urartu with its traditions of skilled work in metal, in the centre the warrior race of the Hittites and in the west the people of Arzawa; but at the beginning of the Copper Age there was no such definite pattern and the Hittites certainly had not yet entered upon the scene.

The historic Hittites were not, strictly speaking, a race but a confederacy some of the elements of which we may assume to have been indigenous; but the more important were immigrants of Indo-European-speaking stock; it is agreed by most authorities that they must have originated in the Caucasus, and according to their own account they came into Anatolia from the south,[14] establishing one capital centre after another until at last—towards the close of the third millennium BC—they reached Boǧazköy in the Halys basin and made that the seat of empire.

The Russian excavator B. A. Kuftin, working in the Caucasus area, has found at Igdir (in the upper Araxes valley) the stratified remains of a culture which, starting in the Neolithic stage, lasted into the Chalcolithic and was then, towards the end of the fourth millennium, characterized by pottery of a very individual sort, generally black, highly burnished, and decorated with patterns both impressed and in relief, and also by curious horseshoe-shaped terra-cotta hearths adorned with human figures and heads (Fig. 3.) There is no later development; the sites were deserted.[15] Well on in the Chalcolithic Age, in the Amq plain on the middle Orontes, the villages of

FIG. 3. *Igdir: hearth or pot stand (after Hood)*

the people using the local type of painted pottery are found to have been destroyed and in the buildings which replaced them we find the black burnished relief ware (Pl. 2, a) and the horseshoe-shaped hearths which had been developed by the people of Igdir. At a still later date, in the Early Bronze Age, the same Araxes pottery suddenly appears in Syria and Palestine, above the burnt ruins of the houses of the earlier population. A few shreds of the pottery have been found in central Anatolia; one complete vase of the sort occurs in each of the 'Royal' tombs of Alaca Höyük, and a degenerate version of the Araxes hearth was still in use in the nineteenth century BC at Kultepe, 150 miles south of Boḡazköy. If we may connect the archaeological evidence with tradition, as is probably justifiable, then we can follow one of the early 'mass migrations' which play so important a part in the history of the Middle East. Displaced for some reason from their original home an entire people (how numerous we cannot say) set out in search of a new. They could not travel due west, partly because of the natural difficulties of the mountain chains, more because of the opposition of the wild mountaineers (even in historic times these were a constant thorn in the flesh of the Hittite kings, who could never conquer them) so they pushed south and once on the steppes turned westwards across Upper Mesopotamia; when at length they came to the rich Amq plain, held only by poor villagers, they put those to the sword and settled down on their lands. After many generations they in their turn were expelled, this time by their Syrian neighbours on the east, and while some fled down into Syria and Palestine others went eastwards and northwards into Anatolia and very gradually, defeating opponents or making allies as they went, advanced to their final resting-place on the Halys.

Syria and Palestine

Another folk-migration, of the details of which we know nothing, affected the coast of Syria and Palestine. That coast is cut off from the interior by the Amanus and Lebanon mountain ranges for the northern part and by the Judean hills in the south; the mountains, then thickly wooded, were an effective barrier isolating what is at best a narrow belt of maritime plain, with the result that while the interior—whether we think of the Aleppo plateau stretching down the Orontes to Hama, or of the Damascus oasis, or of the desert steppes south of Damascus, haunted by Beduin nomads—is typically Asiatic, the Syrian coast is purely Mediterranean. The Neolithic inhabitants were indeed a branch of Mediterranean man—actually some of their pottery finds its closest parallel in Crete—but at a very early date, presumably in the Chalcolithic period but perhaps towards its close, a Semitic people, the Phoenicians, came into the country and, wherever the natural features of the coast offered the chance of a harbour, founded cities. According to their own traditions the Phoenicians had originally lived on the shores of the Persian Gulf[16] and it is tempting to believe that that is true, although there is an almost complete lack of material evidence to support it; in any case they had already arrived by the time when we first got any real knowledge of Syria. Phoenicia never formed a political unit. Each of the cities along the coast was an independent state under a king (usually with a Council of Elders at his side)[17] who was really a merchant prince, for the cities were founded for and lived by international trade. From the outset their relation to Egypt was close, for they alone could supply the cedar and hardwoods which were needed for the temples and palaces of Egypt but did not grow in the Nile valley, but still more important for our purposes was the traffic in ideas. The Egyptians themselves traced not a little of their religion back to the Syrian coast; later on, Plutarch quotes the story of the body of Osiris being brought back by Isis[18] from Byblos; whereas then the Phoenicians throughout their history did much as middlemen to help the growth of Mediterranean civilization on its material side, at the beginning they may have made to it a moral contribution of lasting value.

Crete

The island of Crete, like that of Cyprus, received its first Neolithic inhabitants as immigrants from the south coast of Asia Minor. But whereas Cyprus was never able to boast of more than a derivative culture whose progress was due to successive borrowings from Asia Minor, Crete was to develop a brilliant civilization of its own which a little later spread to the mainland of Greece. Naturally this advance was not made on the sole initiative of a small country isolated 'in the midst of the sea' (as the Egyptians described it); in very early days immigrants from Egypt driven out, perhaps, by the civil wars that led to the establishment of the First Dynasty there, brought new ideas to the island; the Cretans themselves were a seafaring people and their ships, visiting Asiatic and Egyptian ports, kept them in touch with mainland progress; but it was the native genius of the Cretans that transmuted all that they learnt from abroad into something original and peculiar to themselves, so that in the first half of the second millennium Cretan civilization was in many ways the finest of the old Mediterranean world.

BRONZE-AGE HISTORY

Such was the grouping of the Middle Eastern peoples when towards the close of the fourth millennium BC the introduction of metallurgy established new demands and brought into new relations the hitherto self-contained and isolated regions in which Neolithic man had been content to live. It happened that the two potentially most wealthy and powerful stocks, the Egyptians and the Mesopotamians, inhabited areas in which metal was almost or entirely lacking, so that it had to be imported from abroad. Moreover, the same two countries produced no good timber, and as urban civilization began in both to replace the village culture of primitive times the public buildings that symbolized the importance of governments called for just those hard woods that native resources failed to supply; so these too had to be imported. International trade therefore flourished and brought into contact lands that had heretofore not known each other. Mining prospectors travelled far and wide overseas; and since at home fuel was too rare and expensive a thing to allow of smelting, it was not worth while to import raw ore; the ore had to be smelted in the lands wherein it was mined, and therefore the natives of those lands had to be instructed in the technique and had to be paid for practising it; [10] and payment could best be made in manufactured goods from the home country. Just because trade meant barter, because the cedar wood of Lebanon and the frankincense of Arabia, the gold, the ivory and the semi-precious stones had to be exchanged for the finished works of Egyptian or Mesopotamian craftsmen, fashions and ideas circulated freely. The countries which produced the raw materials but, until those came into demand, had lagged behind those blessed with a more fertile agricultural soil, now derived not only riches but mental stimuli from the network of barter that connected them with the main centres of progress. By the end of the third millennium BC Palestine and Syria, Persia and Anatolia, had to some extent caught up with the great river valleys. Already in the Chalcolithic period sea traffic had brought the eastern Mediterranean into touch with the eastern part of the European mainland; the Danube valley served as a natural trade-route and thence contacts could be made with the north and east also; in southern Russia and the eastern Ukraine the megalithic stone burial-cists of the Neolithic Age had been replaced by hut-graves which witness to Aegean influence. But the alternative route was not less important. Soon after 2000 BC the hut-graves were in their turn replaced by catacomb-graves, a type which seems to have originated somewhere to the east of the Sea of Azov; they are the graves of a people whose wealth consisted in sheep, horses, cattle and camels, who were not tied down to a sedentary village life but were nomadic. In their earlier home, living close to the centre of metallurgy in the northern Caucasus, they had learnt the art of metal-working, and they now introduced it to the regions north of the Black Sea; the Bronze Age begins now in that area, and the uniformity of type of the awls and daggers found in the graves of the Ukraine is proof that all were derived from a single source. But the wandering smiths did not stop there. For them the open steppe country was but a corridor facilitating east-by-west movement; they went on beyond it, and beyond the loess-land of the western Ukraine; and their cultural influence can be traced into central Europe. In the course of the second millennium BC the knowledge of how to win metal from the ore by smelting, of how to alloy copper with tin and make ductile bronze, and of the shapes of tools, weapons and ornaments that could be cast in it, was widely diffused over the dark continent.

The international trade in metal was to have far-reaching consequences. Prospectors were impressed by the possibilities of the lands seen in their wanderings, and reports were spread abroad of countries which might make the fortune of settlers or could offer shelter and home to displaced peoples. Thus the Italian peninsula was invaded by a Latin race which descending through the north-eastern passes drove before them, or assimilated, the old Chalcolithic stock and exploited the rich copper-mines of Tuscany. Far-off Britain had in about 1900 BC received a wave of immigrants, the so-called 'Bell Beaker' people, who came in from Brittany and from the Lower Rhine; stories of the copper, the tin and the gold of the British Isles reached the Continent, and two centuries later a second wave of immigrants from the same areas, metal-workers trained in the traditions of Bohemian Aunjetitz and of northern Italy, brought the Bronze Age proper into Britain. The immediate results of these folk-movements was of local rather than of general significance —the huge megalithic monuments of Carnac in Brittany and Stonehenge in Wessex have had little direct influence on the history of man. But already the foundations were being laid, in Britain and in Italy, of the great cultures with which later volumes will have to deal at length.

In tracing the history of human progress it is easy to point to a limited number of centres, or societies, where the advance was most marked and the standard attained was highest. But it is impossible to attribute the origin of civilization to any one region or people. No single region provided all the material elements requisite for civilization; no single people invented all the techniques essential to civilized life. The raw materials that were lacking in one country had to be imported from another, and with them came the knowledge of techniques; because of the need for international trade of this sort, new ideas originating in one area spread quickly and easily, to be adopted and improved upon by the independent genius of different peoples. Civilization is indeed due to diffusion, but to the diffusion more of ideas than of models, and not from a single source but from many. Undoubtedly in this exchange of knowledge the individual played a very great part. To recognize the value of a new idea and to adapt it to the peculiar character of his own culture is the work of individual imagination, and it is where natural conditions guarantee the necessities of life and afford that leisure which encourages individuality that the best advantage is likely to be taken of imported inventions. This is why the fertile river valleys of Egypt and Mesopotamia outstripped their neighbours in cultural progress, and the same must be true of the Indus valley and of that of the Huang Ho, though we are unable, through lack of documentation, to follow the process there with the detailed assurance that is possible in the nearer east; there too trade contacts and the resultant traffic in ideas must have enriched the resources of a primitive but gifted people.

The two countries for which material evidence is reasonably abundant are Mesopotamia and Egypt, and it is precisely there that the 'traffic in ideas' is best illustrated; it is to their record that we must look if we are to understand the growth of civilization generally.

Egypt

As we have seen, Egypt, divided into two areas and later organized into two kingdoms lying to the south and the north of the Fayum basin, had entered the Chalcolithic phase of culture at the beginning of the Naqada II period; that phase was one of astonishing progress. At its beginning Egyptian culture could be described as an advanced barbarism; before it ended, at the close of the proto-Dynastic age, irrigation of the fields had been introduced, towns founded and temples built, a system of writing had been developed, a calendar had been devised, the basis of which was to endure to the present day, and art was already taking the form which was to be characteristic of Ancient Egypt so long as Ancient Egypt lasted.

The Egyptians of later times attributed much of this change to 'the Followers of Horus' who, coming from the east, introduced new arts to the Nile valley. The tradition refers to the incoming of those Asiatic Semites of whom mention has already been made, and it is well founded; what the Egyptians did not remember but the archaeological evidence makes quite clear is that the immigrants brought with them the knowledge of what had been achieved by the superior civilization of Mesopotamia. That there was direct intercourse between the two countries cannot be asserted. In any case it could not have been by land, for the barrier of the Syrian desert which throughout history forced land transport to make the long detour by way of the Fertile Crescent rules out any such possibility, and the evidence of early settlements proves that the strangers came first to southern Egypt, landing on the Red Sea coast and following the Wadi Hammamat to Koptos. But even so they need not have been Sumerians—indeed they certainly were not if we are correct in calling them Semites. It is more likely that they were middlemen, seafarers of the Persian Gulf, who were in close touch with Sumer: there is reason to think that there did exist such a people, that from which the Phoenicians claimed descent, the people who supplied Sumer with bronze from the Oman mines and made out of the local stalagmitic calcite stone vases which the Sumerians bought and the Egyptians imitated in their native alabaster. But whoever were the carriers, Egypt did get the Mesopotamian goods and ideas. Stone carvings such as the famous slate palettes (Pls. 19, a and 21, b) (the oldest belong to the close of the pre-Dynastic period and the series continues into the First Dynasty) are unmistakably Sumerian in inspiration, and the stone mace-heads are of a type borrowed from Mesopotamia; clearest evidence of all, the cylinder seals, which are a hallmark of Mesopotamia and were used there for over two thousand years, now for a brief space make their appearance in Egypt, where they are obviously incongruous. But one loan was of permanent importance. In Sumer the art of writing was already known. Egypt did not copy the Sumerian characters but did borrow the idea behind them, the wonderful invention whereby pictures of things could be made to stand not for the things themselves but for the sounds of their names, so that by their aid you could translate human speech into something concrete and enduring; she elaborated her own syllabary, and with the standardization of the script Egyptian civilization properly so called began.[20]

Connection with Mesopotamia broke off and was not to be renewed, except for casual diplomatic missions, until the armies of the two countries met in war more than two thousand years later; but its effect upon Egypt had been incalculable. Of the two proto-Dynastic kingdoms the northern was under strong Libyan influence (reliefs in the pyramid-temple of Sahure of the Fifth Dynasty actually show Libyan princes wearing the uraeus frontlet of the Pharaohs) and was probably therefore less civilized and less well armed; and it was the southern kingdom that, thanks to the use of the Red Sea–Koptos route, benefited most from the wisdom of the Sumerians. Perhaps as a result of this, the southern kingdom under 'Menes'[21] was able to conquer its neighbour and to unite the crowns of Upper and Lower Egypt. 'Menes' and his successors, the kings of the First Dynasty, were not mere raiders, out to destroy an enemy's country; they were 'Lords of the Two Lands'; they assumed the double crown, the Red and the White; to the northern royal symbol of the bee they added the southern symbol of the papyrus tuft, and they shifted their capital north (to Thinis near Abydos) so as to preserve a due balance between the two realms; in theory at least the delta was allowed to keep its identity in spite of amalgamation with Upper Egypt. In the opening years of the third millennium BC the fusion was complete and Egypt had become a unity. The different elements of its population made each its own contribution to the national consciousness, the lessons to be learnt from abroad had been absorbed, and the country was equipped for the shaping of its own destiny; there is scarcely any feature of later Egyptian civilization that is not adumbrated in the First Dynasty period. On the lines thus laid down Egyptian civilization, art, religion and thought developed throughout the Old and Middle Kingdoms, attaining its height in the Twelfth Dynasty;[22] then, in the eighteenth century BC, progress was suddenly arrested by the invasion of the Hyksos. What is really most important during this period is not what happened in Egypt but the influence exercised by Egypt on the Near East. The powerful Pharaohs of the Twelfth Dynasty, Sesostris III and Amenemhet III, instead of contenting themselves as their predecessors had done with extending their dominions to the south, thus emphasizing the position of Egypt as an African power, faced about and invaded Syria, overrunning the entire coastal country from Gaza in the south to Ugarit in the north and probably even beyond that to the Amq plain.[23] Nor was this merely a military promenade or a raid undertaken for the sake of booty. Certainly a vast amount of booty was taken from the wealthy cities of Palestine, but Amenemhet III at any rate seems to have aimed at a permanent overlordship of Syria, reducing the local kings to vassalage and appointing Egyptian commissioners to control their politics. It was a new political departure, to apply to an alien people the scheme of government which was traditional in the Nile valley; it involved Egypt in an imperialistic venture which brought it into contact and would eventually bring it into conflict with the other imperial states of the Middle East. Egypt was no longer isolated, as it had been for many centuries, but was open to foreign influences of thought and fashion while, on the other hand, Syria, whether its rulers welcomed or chafed against Egyptian suzerainty, could not but assimilate some measure of Egyptian culture.

The first repercussion was as violent as it must have been unexpected; the Nile valley was invaded by the Hyksos with such success that for a short time Hyksos chiefs bore rule as Pharaohs, their royal capital being established at Avaris in the eastern delta. It is difficult to say who these 'Hyksos' were. The name itself tells us nothing—it is not a patronymic and is probably a corruption of a phrase meaning perhaps 'Ruler of Countries'. The tradition preserved by Manetho, that they were Arabians and Phoenicians, is not likely to be far from the truth, but it does not imply that they were a single race or the people of a single country. That they were Semites does seem to be certain, and certainly they came into Egypt from the

East. Since, after they were driven out of the Nile valley by Ahmose I, they were able to hold out in Palestine and south Syria for no less than six score years we may assume that the base of their power was there; the choice of a site for their capital on the extreme eastern border of Egypt agrees with that; the fact that their capital was defended by a *glacis,* a characteristically Syrian type of fortification, is further evidence; Hyksos scarabs occur frequently on Palestinian sites, and an alabastron lid engraved with the name of the Hyksos king Khyan, which was unearthed at Knossos, may well have been taken to the island in a Phoenician ship. The probability is that the anti-Egyptian elements in the Phoenician cities which Sesostris and Amenemhet had subdued took advantage of the weak rule of the Thirteenth Dynasty Pharaohs to raise the standard of revolt and, calling in to their aid the desert Beduin, made themselves masters of Egypt. It was a short-lived triumph, for in 1580 BC, perhaps little more than a generation after their incoming,[24] they were driven back into Asia by the founder of the Eighteenth Dynasty and are no more heard of under a common name—i.e. the confederacy broke up, the Beduin retired to their deserts and the Syrian townsmen to their several city states. But the invasion was not unimportant. Under the Hyksos Egypt and Syria were still subject to the same king, though the old relations between them were reversed; in that the Hyksos rulers aped the state of the former Pharaohs, the Egyptian civilization won yet a firmer hold on the south Syrian towns, but at the same time they overthrew many of the Egyptian temples and introduced what seems to have been the exclusive worship of their own god, identifying him with Set-Sutekh, the god of Upper Egypt who was later to become the favourite of Ramses II and patron deity of the royal city. Of much more far-reaching consequences was the fact that the Hyksos taught the Egyptians the use of the horsed chariot,[25] an innovation which revolutionized military tactics, made possible the creation of the Egyptian empire, and by introducing into the army a *corps d'élite* to which only the rich aristocracy could afford to belong accentuated the class distinctions in Egyptian society.[26]

Revenge for the barbarian invasion came with the great Syrian expeditions of Thutmose I and III. Already Amenhotep I had invaded the country and pushed as far north, possibly, as the Euphrates; but his was little more than a punitive raid, and it was left to his successors to effect a permanent conquest.[27] Thutmose I met with little resistance in the south and he fought his main battle in the extreme north, in

Naharain, and set up his trophy on the bank of the Euphrates, making the boundary of Egypt 'as far as the circuit of the sun'; undoubtedly he organized some form of provincial government in all the principal cities.

The powerful state of Mitanni, which had been established in the Hurri lands of northern Syria (see pp. 79–80), was naturally not pleased to find a new and great empire establishing itself as an immediate neighbour on the west; the most obvious means of defence was to encourage a buffer state between Mitanni and the armies of the Pharaoh. Political intrigues started at once, and when the death of Thutmose I gave the signal, revolt broke out over the whole country from northern Palestine to the Great River. The domestic troubles that ensued between Thutmose III and his queen Hatshepsut afforded the rebels a welcome respite of some twenty years, and by the time the Pharaoh was in a position to assert his claims on Syria, the king of Kadesh—the chief town, it would seem, of the surviving Hyksos—was at the head of a confederacy which included all the northern cities and disposed of forces not unevenly matched with those of Egypt. In the spring of his twenty-second year, about 1480 BC,[28] Thutmose III led his army across the Egyptian frontier; less than a month later he won the hard-fought battle of Megiddo; he beleaguered and finally received the surrender of Megiddo and before the campaigning season ended he had recovered the country as far as the southern slopes of Lebanon. Kadesh however was still unconquered, and four years were spent in consolidating the south country before Thutmose ventured against his chief enemy. Then Kadesh fell; but more time was needed to reduce the towns on the northern coast, and it was only in his thirtieth year that Pharaoh could lead his army down the Orontes; Aleppo fell, then Carchemish, and the warriors of Mitanni 'fled like a herd of mountain goats', and with the capture of Niya the recovery of the Naharain province was an accomplished fact. Before this, the newly-risen power of Assyria had sent presents to the king of Egypt; now, while he hunted elephants in Niya, envoys from Babylon brought him gifts of lapis lazuli, and from the heart of Asia Minor the great king of the Hittites sent silver and precious stones. The adventure of imperialism had plunged Egypt into world politics of which in her sequestered days she had never dreamed.

The mention here of Babylon and Assyria, of Mitanni and the Hittites, implies great changes since the beginning of the third millennium in all the Middle Eastern lands.[29]

Sumer and Akkad

We have seen that in southern Mesopotamia by about 3000 BC Sumerian civilization was fully formed, and very soon after that date it may be said to have reached its zenith. The overthrow of the alien rule of the Jamdat Nasr people was at once the symbol and the cause of a nationalist resurgence which brought out all that was best in the mixed population which now called itself Sumerian.[30] For some time the spirit of independence manifested itself in a centrifugal policy. Now that the overlord who had forcibly united the country was removed the old city states reasserted themselves and Sumer was divided up into a number of petty kingdoms, each under the patronage of its local god. The fact that they were extraordinarily prosperous did not obviate, more probably it encouraged, war between neighbours, generally due to quarrels over water-rights or to rival claims to some fertile territory irrigated by the elaborate system of canals different states might hold in common. At last, about 2600 BC, the kings of Ur who were very wealthy and had been enabled by their wealth to form and equip an army which as a fighting force must have been well above the standard of its contemporaries, subdued all the other states and set themselves up as rulers of the whole of Sumer. The First Dynasty of Ur lasted for five generations, then the suzerainty passed to a number of other states in succession, but while these constant wars must have weakened the morale of the people they seem not to have interfered greatly with their material prosperity. But they paved the way for foreign conquest.

The Semitic and Semitized peoples of northern Mesopotamia, whose history from this time onwards suggests that they were more virile than the southerners but less original and less imaginative, had readily absorbed the superior culture of their neighbours; on the material side they were completely Sumerianized, but they preserved their own language (though they wrote it in Sumerian script) and they preserved their own ethnic spirit. About 2385 BC Sargon,[31] an energetic king of Akkad, took his part in the inter-dynastic feuds that rent the south country, overran the land and established himself and his sons as kings of Sumer and Akkad. It did not mean the end of Sumerian civilization, for the Akkadians kept its traditions faithfully; but in very few respects were they able to carry them any farther, and the admixture of the Semitic element and its ultimate preponderance were to result in cultural stagnation.[32]

The traditions were indeed so firmly rooted that even the invasion and occupation of the country by a barbarous tribe failed to eradicate them. From somewhere in the mountainous area of the north-east there came down the Guti (about whom we know really nothing); they overthrew the dynasty of Akkad but were too uncivilized to set up any regular form of government in its stead, and so lax was the administration that local governors of the old stock were able, after the first shock of war, to carry on the rule of their city states in comparative independence. When, after more than a century and a half of foreign tyranny and disorder, Sumer and Akkad regained their freedom and the Third Dynasty of Ur ushered in an era of material prosperity greater than had been known hitherto, the amalgamation of the north and south countries appeared to be complete; official posts were distributed impartially between Semites and Sumerians, and the same laws applied equally to all. But while the civilization, which was essentially southern, was crystallizing into stereotyped forms, the more energetic northern race was now taking the lead; business, even in the old cities of Sumer, was passing into Semitic hands and the Semitic language was beginning to oust the Sumerian.[33] Shortly before 2000 BC the Third Dynasty of Ur was overthrown by an invasion of the Elamites and the Amorites. Some of the cities which resisted, Ur in particular, were savagely destroyed, but the conquering Amorites were aiming at sovereignty and, having given their subjects this salutary lesson, were quite ready to repair the damage they had done and to pose as beneficent rulers. So Sumer, though it had lost its independence, was allowed to follow the old paths and, since trade flourished as much as ever, was perhaps content, the more so because government control over the bankers[34] and merchants was relaxed and individualism was allowed freer play. The northerners on the other hand, farther removed as they were from the seat of Amorite sovereignty, established first at Isin and later at Larsa, were not prepared to accept permanent subordination. At Babylon a local dynasty set itself up and gradually secured the adhesion of the Akkadian Semites, with the result that the city now for the first time acquired the leading position which it was to boast for many centuries. In 1783 BC Hammurabi, the sixth king of this Babylonian line, turned his attention to the south. There a fresh Elamite invasion had installed an Elamite, Warad-Sin, upon the throne of Larsa; his son, Rim-Sin, though old, was a formidable adversary, but after prolonged warfare Hammurabi defeated him and succeeded to the imperial title 'King of Sumer and Akkad' which Rim-Sin, following Sumerian tradition, had adopted after his capture of Isin and of Nippur. Actually Hammurabi's empire extended from the Persian Gulf to north of Nineveh, from the Elamite mountains to the borders of Syria on the west. His title of 'King of the Amorites' and his ascription of his victories to the god Dagan 'his Creator' illustrate the pride that he felt in his West Semitic blood; but culturally he was a descendant of the Sumerians, and in the Prologue to his famous Code of Law the holy cities of Nippur and Eridu are placed above Babylon itself. Sumer and Akkad had little love for one another—Ur was to head a revolt against Hammurabi's son and to be destroyed in consequence—but the Semite in Babylon showed himself to be an adaptor, not a creator; he was the prophet of Sumerian culture and in the sphere of intellect and art merely perpetuated the achievements of the race which politically he displaced and in the end absorbed.

The dynasty of Hammurabi came to an inglorious end. His son Samsuiluna was able—though hardly—to cope with rebellion within the empire, but he had no strength to deal with foes from abroad. A raid by Kassite tribesmen from the east was followed by others, until by constant infiltration the Kassites had secured a firm footing in the northern country. But the crushing blow fell from elsewhere. In some year between 1600 and 1580 BC the Hittites of Boğazköy under their king Mursilis marched down the Euphrates and stormed and sacked Babylon and carried off the image of Marduk. The Babylonian empire broke up, and while the south country passed under the control of the 'Kings of the Sea Lands' who found security in the impenetrable marshes of the lower delta, the Kassites, who probably were of Indo-European stock,[35] installed themselves in the cities of the north as the aristocratic caste and the country's rulers.

The Hittites

The Hittites had now become an important kingdom. If, as has been suggested, their original trek from the Caucasus was by way of the steppe country of northern Mesopotamia and was interrupted by a long sojourn in the Amq plain we should be able to understand some of the problems which otherwise must baffle us. They must have mixed a good deal with the older inhabitants: and when they moved on into Anatolia some of them must have stopped behind. This would explain the fact that from a very early date Carchemish seems to have had a strongly Hittite character, and that in the Amq plain there was always a pro-Hittite party opposed to the north Syrian or the pro-Egyptian factions. A later tradition, perhaps authentic, says that Naram-Sin, son of Sargon king of Akkad, fought against a coalition of seventeen kings, one of whom was a king of Hatti—and in 2200 BC the Anatolian Hatti had not reached Bogazköy and were in no position to wage war in north Syria. Another of the seventeen allies was a king of Amurru whose name is supposed to belong to the 'hieroglyphic' language of the (later) Syro-Hittites; this again may bear witness to the passage of the Hittites through the Amurru land.

For some time after their entry into Anatolia the Indo-European tribes (not all of whom had as yet adopted the collective name 'Hatti') were occupied in carving out for themselves by their conquest of the Asiatic 'proto-Hatti' separate principalities, at least ten in number, which were virtually independent although the chief of one of them was distinguished as 'The Great Prince', a title which was always to be preserved as that of the head of the confederacy. Naturally there was rivalry for the honour, and rivalry might lead to civil war. We hear first of the 'Great Prince' of the city of Puruskhanda; later on two kings of the city of Kussura, Pitkhanas and his son Anittas, subdued all the other cities, including Hattusas, and transferred their capital to Nesa, apparently thus advancing northwards. If, as is probable, King Anittas was responsible for the destruction of the colony of Mesopotamian merchants that had long been established just outside the walls of the city of Kanish in Cappadocia (a dagger inscribed with his name has been found there[36] in the town ruins) then his reign should be dated to about 1900 BC. A later king, Labarna, claims to have extended his frontiers to the sea, conquering the kingdom of Arzawa. His son Hattusilis I moved his capital northward from Kussura to Hattusas (Boğazköy)—the move may have been connected with the unification of the clans under the common name 'Hatti'—and for the first time led a Hittite army beyond the frontiers of Anatolia; he invaded Syria and reduced to vassalage the kingdom of Yamkhad, of which Aleppo was the capital city and Alalakh in the Amq plain a subject state. The next king, Mursilis I, overthrew Babylon and put an end to the First Dynasty; this was in about 1585 BC.

The victory of Mursilis was of far-reaching importance. In the first place it laid the foundations of the Hittite power in Syria, the maintenance of which was to be the settled policy of future kings and brought them into direct conflict with Egypt. In the second place by eliminating Babylon as a military force it made possible the Kassite invasion of Babylonia and the rise of Mitanni. A period of weakness which set in in the latter days of the Hittite 'Old Kingdom' postponed the first of these results but facilitated the other.

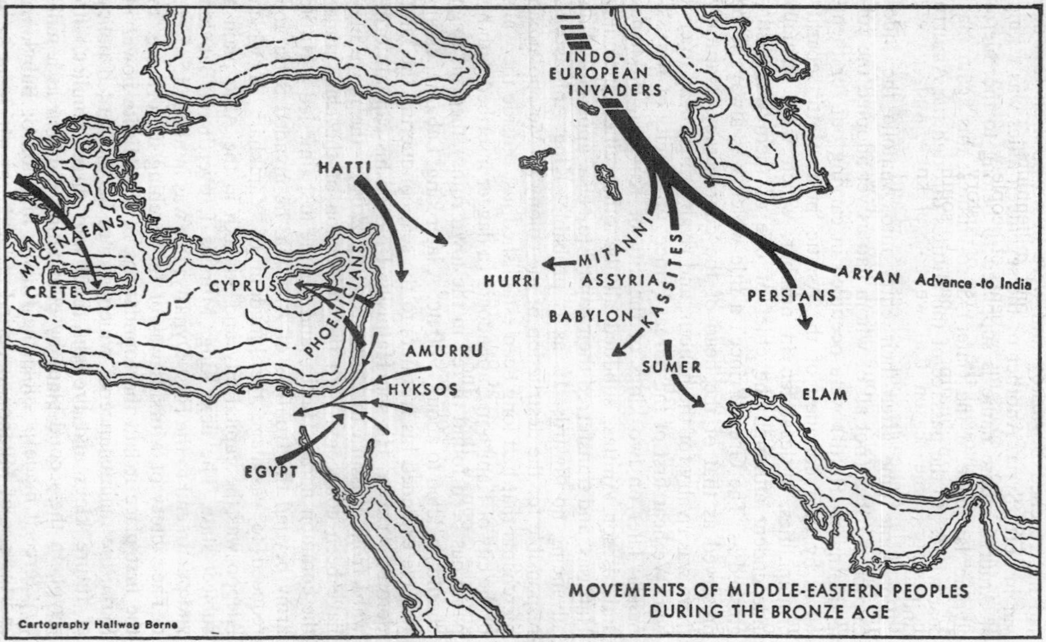

INDO-
EUROPEAN
INVADERS
HATTI
MYCENAEANS
CRETE
CYPRUS
PHOENICIANS
MITANNI
HURRI
ASSYRIA
KASSITES
BABYLON
ARYAN Advance -to India
PERSIANS
AMURRU
HYKSOS
SUMER
ELAM
EGYPT
MOVEMENTS OF MIDDLE-EASTERN PEOPLES
DURING THE BRONZE AGE
Cartography Hallwag Berne

MAP II

The Aryans

In the early part of the second millennium BC there took place one of those mass movements of people which every now and then have changed the course of history. Tribes of Indo-European stock, originating probably in south Russia, left their homes for some reason that we do not know and, passing through the Caucasus, poured eastwards and westwards (Map II), an armed host accompanied by their wives and children, in search of new places wherein to live; and they were determined to live not as outcast settlers in an alien land but as masters in a land of their own. In the view of many scholars one branch, perhaps the advance party, whom we know as the Kassites, penetrated into Akkad, and in due course their leader seated himself upon the throne of Babylon, founding a régime that was to endure for five and a half centuries; one branch came to a halt in northern Persia. One wave of the 'Aryan Invasion' in time broke through the mountain barrier of northern Baluchistan into India; there they found still existing (this is generally assumed to have been round about 1500 BC) the great cities of the Indus valley whose merchants had up till now maintained their touch with Mesopotamia, and they overwhelmed them—the *Rigveda*[87] is the epic of the destruction of one of the great cultures of the ancient world.[88] Yet another group of these Indo-European adventurers—who may have entered the country originally by means of 'peaceful penetration', for we have no hint of any warlike conquest and their numbers do not seem to have been so great as to make conquest probable—succeeded in establishing themselves as the ruling aristocracy of the Middle Hurri region. These 'Mitanni' supplied just that energy and initiative which their new subjects in that area had lacked hitherto, and with their advent a new Great Power arose in the Middle East. In the fifteenth century BC the Mitanni kingdom extended from Nuzi beyond the Tigris to the Mediterranean, from the head waters of the Khabur to the Syrian borders of Egypt; it could menace the authority of Pharaoh and fight on equal terms with the Hittite rulers of the New Empire. The Mitanni, like their brethren the Kassites and the Aryan wreckers of the Harappā civilization, seem to have been a semi-barbarous people culturally far inferior to the nations which they vanquished; they did indeed introduce the worship of the 'Aryan' gods, and (what was more immediately important) they introduced the horse to Asia Minor and popularized the breeding of it there; but apart from this they could contribute but little to progress. The success of the Mitanni as an independent power in northern Mesopotamia did not last very long; but even the temporary unification of the 'Fertile Crescent' and its exploitation meant that the long-established culture of the Hurri received a greater authority and could impress itself more directly on the neighbouring states. The Hittite kings of the New Empire invariably took to themselves Hurri wives; Hurrian scribes and magicians frequented the Hittite court, and the Hurrian gods were admitted to the Hittite pantheon, so that the deities represented on the famous rock reliefs of Yasilikaya are called by Hurri instead of by Hittite names.

Egypt ana Syria

We have seen that the victorious campaigns of Thutmose III had brought the greater part of northern Syria under the control of Pharaoh and that it was thanks to the active intrigues of the Mitanni king that Egypt had had to withdraw; the natural result was that the north Syrian states which had been vassals of the Hittites took the prudent course of changing masters; Hattusas lost all its Syrian possessions. Rebellion is infectious, and the Anatolian states in their turn were encouraged to turn upon the Hittites; the Gasgas, the wild mountaineers east of the Halys basin, sacked Hattusas itself; Arzawa invaded the western regions and occupied the Hittite frontier towns with at least the moral backing of Pharaoh; the position of the Hittite empire seemed desperate, while the upstart kingdom of Mitanni could now ally itself to Egypt as an equal and seal the alliance with a royal marriage.

The different characters of two individuals reversed the situation. Akhenaton of Egypt, engrossed in religious reforms and in the distractions of court life at his new capital Akhetaton (Tell el Amarna), had no interest at all in imperial politics or military adventures. In Hattusas arose a king, Suppiluliumas, whose ambition was equal to his generalship. After one set-back at the hands of the Mitanni he renewed his attack, captured their capital, installed his sons as kings of Aleppo and Carchemish, extended his frontier southward to Lebanon and set a puppet of his own on the Mitanni throne. The kingdom of Kizzuwatna made peace and an alliance with him. He reconquered the kingdom of Arzawa. By the end of his reign he was in possession of an empire more extensive than any ruler had yet boasted, stretching from the Tigris to the Mediterranean, from Syrian Kadesh to Hattusas and perhaps beyond Hattusas to the Black Sea. The sun of Egypt was for the time being in eclipse; the rising power of Assyria was as yet scarcely a danger and in any case was kept at a distance by the buffer state of Mitanni; the Hittites were the Great Power of the Middle East.

Apart from politics the effects of these conquests were of lasting importance. The Hittite element which seems always to have existed in northern Syria was undoubtedly strengthened by the Hittite rule, which was never very onerous provided that people submitted to it. In the principal temples of north Syrian towns Hittite gods were now worshipped and dedications were made by Hittite kings; the Kassites had introduced the horse into Mesopotamia and the Hittites had been quick to profit by this and to develop the new tactics in war which chariotry made possible, and now the Syrian kinglets (as well as the Pharaoh of Egypt) followed their example; the Hittites again were users of iron and although even for them it was still a rare and costly thing, brought in by trade from the Armenian highlands, the knowledge at least of this strange metal spread from them southwards to the Levant and the way was thus paved for its regular adoption. The commerce of ideas between the Anatolian rulers and their subjects in north Syria was to have no small part in a later epoch when the Syro-Hittite civilization was to fill the gap left by the obliteration of Hattusas; but in the meantime it helped much towards that intellectual and artistic union which was to link together the peoples of the eastern Mediterranean in the immediately succeeding age.

Cyprus

When Thutmose III organized his newly won Syrian province, General Thutiy, appointed governor of the north countries, had included in his jurisdiction 'the isles in the midst of the sea'. It is true that thanks to the sea power which Pharaoh enjoyed by reason of his mastery over the Phoenician cities on the Syrian coast he could overawe the king of Cyprus and reduce him to vassalage; but the same cannot have been true of Crete. Cyprus, with its fertile soil, its timber-forests on Mount Troodos and its precious copper-mines, was a rich country, full of possibilities; but its people were singularly unimaginative. They initiated nothing. Their cultural history, of which we can speak with confidence seeing that it is illustrated by a wealth of archaeological material, divides itself into a series of well-defined and disconnected phases the characteristics of each of which are imported from abroad, and each phase is in itself static. The Cypriots, time after time, adopted an alien fashion and imitated it with an adequate amount of technical skill, but they did not progress beyond their model, repeating it until a new model was imposed upon them. They may have helped to spread ideas and inventions westwards, but those ideas and inventions were borrowed by them from the east. Even their trade with the Syrian coast (which is within sight of the island) was carried for the most part at least in Phoenician bottoms, and the business side of it was in the hands of a Phoenician merchant colony who had their own city on the island and their own king. Except as a metal-producing country, Cyprus played little part in early history.[89]

Crete

Exactly the reverse is the case in Crete. The natural resources of the island were relatively small—it possessed no minerals, and only the centre of it was really fertile, the mountains at its eastern and western ends being rugged and inhospitable; but its inhabitants had just that genius and energy which the Cypriots lacked. Coming originally from the Anatolian coast they seem to have been even in Late Neolithic times in contact with the marsh-dwellers of the northern delta of the Nile; there is some evidence to show that when Egypt was unified under 'Menes' some refugees from the delta fled and settled in Crete, and this may have given to the native population the impetus that was needed to start them on the road to civilization. There have been found on Cretan sites imported Egyptian objects dated to the Third, the Sixth and the Thirteenth Dynasties, so it is clear that trade connections with Egypt were maintained throughout the early period; but the Cretans, even if they borrowed, did not merely imitate but transmuted their borrowings into something new and peculiar to themselves. Being islanders they were mariners, too, and could freely visit other countries for the exchange of goods and ideas. But their island lay far beyond the reach of the great land-powers, Mesopotamia, Egypt and Hatti, so they could develop on their own lines without interference, and whatever they brought home they improved. In this remote island they built up a civilization which from many points of view was the most magnificent of the ancient world. They derived their architecture from Asia, but no Asiatic building could vie with the palace of Minos at Knossos; they had their own system of writing; as workers in metal they were unequalled, and their potters produced painted vases of a quality and a beauty elsewhere unknown. Naturally such objects of art were exported, and examples of them are found in Egypt (Pl. 2, b) and on the Syrian coast; but the Cretans were not content merely to trade with the markets of the established kingdoms and empires of the east; their ships sailed westwards and northwards to the Cyclades and farther still, to the Greek mainland, and there they founded colonies of their own. By the middle of the fourteenth century BC cities such as Mycenae and Tiryns were flourishing centres in which Minoan art was gradually being adapted to suit the taste of a subject population. Judging from the signs of destruction at Phaestos and other Cretan sites the kings of Knossos had before this time made themselves masters of the whole island, and that by violent means. The same imperialistic spirit may have turned against them their Greek vassals; in any case the fate that normally overtakes imperialism put an end to the dynasty of Minos. About the middle of the fifteenth century 'Mycenaeans' from the mainland, who had for some time been infiltrating into Knossos, finally gained the mastery of the city; then, about 1400 BC, possibly with their connivance, a wave of invaders seems to have overthrown and destroyed Knossos and the other Cretan cities. From that moment Crete lost all its old importance and became merely an outlying province of Mycenaean Greece.

The first Mycenaean immigrants were a people alien from the Cretans by race, speaking a Greek tongue; but they adopted and perpetuated the Minoan traditions, at least up to a point, though they were quite incapable of the artistic triumphs of the old Minoan 'Palace Style'. But they, and the later invaders also, were admirable craftsmen of the second-rate, and whereas the luxury of Knossos may have made the Minoans rather indolent, the Mycenaeans were full of energy and keen business men; favoured by their geographical position they, and their kinsmen in Cyprus, plunged headlong into the trade of the eastern Mediterranean. Bands of Mycenaean workmen came into Egypt to decorate the new capital that Akhenaton built at Tell el Amarna; a colony of Mycenaean merchants established themselves in the harbour town of Ugarit on the north Syrian coast; Mycenaean pottery is found in the Phoenician coastal cities, in the Amq plain and as far inland as Damascus; even the Palestinian potter was obliged by his clientele to copy the painted vases that came from Crete; Egyptian wall-reliefs and paintings show us 'Keftiu' works of art which may come from Crete itself or from Mycenaean colonies such as Ugarit but in either case prove the popularity and the ubiquity of Mycenaean goods. The Mycenaeans, by reason of their commercial activities, entered fully into what seemed likely to become the common civilization of the Middle East, so much so that figures of Oriental gods such as the Syrian Resheph[40] are found in Crete, in Tiryns and Mycenae. The Asian element that plays so important a part in Greek religion and mythology is probably due to the Mycenaeans who, themselves a Greek-speaking people instructed in Cretan art, laid the foundation of classical Hellas.

Egypt and the Hittites

Suppiluliumas the Hittite, who had been careful to send his diplomatic congratulations to Akhenaton when the latter ascended the throne of Egypt, had soon taken advantage of the Pharaoh's weakness to win for himself the whole of Syria from Kadesh northwards—and that without any overt breach with Egypt. But that was not the sum total of Egypt's losses. The Phoenician coast and the entire south country down to the Negeb were before long in a state of utter chaos. The Amorite princes fought against each other and against Pharaoh indiscriminately, each trying to secure for himself loot and dominion; from the eastern desert the Khabiri[41] came to take part in the game; some entered the service of the warring princes as mercenaries, others formed bands and raided on their own account. Appeals to Akhenaton fell on deaf ears; one by one the cities were stormed or went over to the enemy, Simyra, Byblos, Berytus, Tyre and Sidon, Jerusalem and even Gaza were lost, and by 1350 BC the Asiatic empire of Egypt had ceased to exist.

The loss of Syria was a blow not only to the prestige but to the economy of Egypt; the king of Babylonia writes to complain that his merchant caravans have been plundered and cannot get through to the Nile valley. When 'the criminal of Akhetaton' died and in time an orthodox and powerful dynasty secured the throne of Egypt, the recovery of the lost provinces was an obvious necessity. In 1310 Seti I invaded Palestine, overcame the Amorite kingdom of the south, but failed to capture Kadesh; he had opened the caravan route, but had done nothing to dislodge the Hittites. Muwatallis of Hattusas recognized, however, that a trial of strength between the two empires was inevitable, and during the next twenty years of uneasy truce he fortified Kadesh to make it the southern bulwark of his realm; it was at Kadesh that in 1285 BC the imperial armies clashed. In spite of the boasts of Ramses II that he won a glorious victory it is quite clear that the battle was undecisive and if anything went in favour of Muwatallis, who was even able to advance his frontier towards Damascus, while Ramses marched straight home to celebrate a triumph. For the next fifteen years the war continued with varying success for either side, but Pharaoh claims to have subdued peoples as far north as Naharain and the Orontes valley. Probably both parties were by that time tired of fighting; probably both were rendered uneasy by the rising power of Assyria which threatened their eastern flank; at length, in 1269 BC, a new Hittite king, Hattusilis III, made peace with Egypt; the position in the Levant was stabilized and a royal marriage set the seal on a treaty of friendship.

Egypt and Libya

Trouble was to come from an unexpected quarter.

In the last years of Ramses II (he was about ninety when he died) the Libyans began to push their way into the western delta. Possibly Hittite intrigue was in part responsible for this. The Hittite king, observing the terms of his treaty with Ramses, outwardly kept the peace with Ramses' son Merneptah and even called on the latter in the first year of his reign for shiploads of corn to relieve a famine in Anatolia. Nevertheless he certainly was behind a rebellion against Egyptian rule which broke out in Syria about a year later, a rebellion so serious that Askalon, Gezer and the tribes of Israel (now for the first time mentioned by name as being in Palestine) had to be crushed before anything could be done on the western border, and it was not until his fifth year that Merneptah could turn to deal with the Libyan king, who had advanced deep into Egypt with a regular army of occupation. The invaders were defeated with enormous loss and the danger was over for the moment.

But what is interesting is the fact that the Libyan army was largely composed of allies, or mercenaries, who were northerners from overseas, Sherden, Shekelesh, Turshu, Ekwesh—Sardinians, Sicilians, Etruscans and (perhaps) Achaeans—from Asia Minor and the islands. Clearly these were warriors and seafarers who could not find scope for their activities at home; they could sail the sea as merchants or pirates (the two trades running together), or they could lend or hire their services for any enterprise that sounded profitable; like the Norsemen of a later day they went in search of adventure.

We may connect with this Libyan interlude the unrest that was showing itself in Anatolia. There the Hittite king began to have trouble with his neighbour on the west, the king of Ahhiyawa, who was perhaps an Achaean; he was reckoned one of the four great kings who divided the Middle East between them, and though a mainland ruler he included some at least of the Ionian islands in his dominion. Whether he was in part the cause or himself one of the victims of what was to come we have as yet no means of knowing.

The Peoples of the Sea

In the fifth year of Ramses III of Egypt, 1194 BC, a fresh attack on the western delta was made by the king of Libya, again supported by allies or mercenaries from the north, and was defeated. But a far greater danger threatened from the north. A vast host was on the march. The movement began in Anatolia, or at least its first effects were felt there. It can only be supposed that the country had been invaded and it was pressure from behind that drove the entire population from their homes and forced them to seek some new land to be won by violence. For this was not an army but a congeries of peoples; some came by sea, skirting the coast; others marched overland with their womenfolk and children, travelling in heavy two-wheeled ox-carts, prepared to settle down in the conquered land; wherever they came they ravaged and burned and slew, and those that escaped the sword were enrolled in their ranks to swell the numbers of the fighting men. They sacked Hattusas, and we never again hear of Hittites in Anatolia; they sacked Carchemish and Aleppo, Alalakh and Ugarit and the Amorite kingdom of southern Syria; their fleet went across to Cyprus and wasted it; always they pressed on southwards, leaving destruction in their track, and so they came to the borders of Egypt. They were a mixed crowd, Danauna or Danaans (from Cilicia) and Peleset or Philistines, and the Sherden and Shekelesh, Turshu and Ekwesh, Lycians and many others. What drove them from their homes is not known, but their objective is clear enough. They all knew—it did not need the mercenaries returned from Libya to tell them—of that fabulously wealthy land that was irrigated by the Nile's flood, and deliberately, as Ramses rightly said, they advanced on Egypt, 'their hearts relying on their arms'; if they could not stop at home only the world's best land was good enough for them. The victory of Ramses saved Egypt. But just because the invasion failed it was one of the most important happenings in ancient history. The Peleset settled down where they had fought, in the coastal plain of Palestine; the remnants of the Hittites entrenched themselves in northern Syria, where they had long borne rule and had many friends, and gave a new impetus to the Syro-Hittite civilization. The breakdown of two colonial empires opened the gates of Syria and Palestine to the Assyrians and Babylonians. The other allied tribes made their way overseas and as Etruscans[42] and Sicilians introduced a new element and a new age into Italy, and it was perhaps now that the 'Dorians' came into Greece. The epic of Troy deals with one incident of the wars that shook the Asiatic and the Aegean world; but the real drama was set upon a far wider stage and had consequences that Homer could not guess.

INDIA: THE INDUS VALLEY CIVILIZATION

In the present state of our knowledge it is not possible even to sketch in outline the political history of those eastern peoples whose contribution to world culture rivalled that of the Mediterranean races. In the cases both of India and of China civilization confronts us as an accomplished fact and literature throws no light upon its genesis or upon the political relations which may have influenced its growth. In the Indus valley we have a culture which is not without some contacts with the village cultures which are proved by archaeological stratification to be of older date, but it is so infinitely in advance of such and so markedly individual that it would hardly seem to have been evolved entirely from them; moreover, it is directly superimposed upon the remains of the older cultures in a way which suggests that it was introduced suddenly, and in the form which it was to preserve with no perceptible modification for the entire period of its existence. The skeletal evidence proves that the population of the Harappā cities was of mixed stock. Three of the skulls from Mohenjo-daro belong to the Proto-Australoid group and represent the type which forms the main element in the south and central Indian aboriginal tribes of the present day; these are the true Indians, and just because they were of the old native stock, whereas the Harappā culture seems to have no local precedents but is introduced as the result of the violent destruction of the old settlements, it can fairly be assumed that they constituted the lower classes in the social system of Harappā.[48] About 50 per cent of the skulls are of the dolichocephalic Mediterranean type very similar to those of al'Ubaid in Sumer, also to some from Baluchistan; with these are a few brachycephalic Alpine-type skulls and one which is typically Mongolian; disregarding the last as being foreign—and one would expect to find a few immigrants from the north-eastern hill countries—we may conclude that Mediterranean man played the predominant part in building up the Harappā civilization. A certain number of features in that civilization are common to it and to Sumer—e.g. the burnt-brick architecture and the use of bitumen—but in spite of that fact and of the skeletal evidence it cannot be maintained that the Harappā civilization originated in Sumer and was imported thence into India ready made. The archaeological evidence makes it tolerably certain that it was not developed locally in the Indus valley but arrived there already mature. The presence of Mediterranean man certainly suggests a western origin, as also does the fact that from the outset the Harappā people were familiar with the working of copper and of bronze, for that knowledge must have been derived from a country in which copper ore was available. Although, when once they were settled in the Indus valley, they may well have exploited the mineral resources of Rajputana—and discoveries in Gujerat supply evidence of their connections with that southern area—yet, before that, they are more likely to have got their material and their technique from the west, from the ore deposits in Baluchistan or in Persia; already one site in Baluchistan and one in Afghanistan (see pp. 94–95) have given proof of direct contact between Sumer and the Indus valley. But this does not at all justify us in attributing the Harappā culture as a whole to any Sumerian tradition. We have seen that Sumerian civilization was in part at least due to people who came into the Euphrates valley from the east; the source whence the seeds of progress were brought into Mesopotamia may have inspired also the eastern civilization which was ultimately to establish itself in the valley of the Indus; and something in the nature of a common origin might account for the later contacts traceable in the two countries. It is quite impossible to say where the Harappā civilization grew up; but by the time it took over the river-land and the cities of Harappā and Mohenjo-daro were built it had acquired a character of its own, essentially different from that of Sumer and, indeed, essentially Indian.

And of its subsequent history we know nothing. It is fully mature on its arrival and thereafter it stagnates; its buildings are destroyed by floods and rebuilt time after time, but 'from top to bottom of the accumulated layers of debris no change can be detected in the content of the material culture'; primitive features persist unimproved, and the technological advances made by Sumer in, for instance, the casting of socketed metal weapons have no influence upon India in spite of the commercial ties between the two peoples. Those ties were closest, it would seem, in the time of Sargon of Akkad, in the twenty-fourth century BC, but two hundred years later the signs of contact become few and far between; the growing isolation of Harappā may be the cause, or the effect, of the gradual impoverishment of the people to which the buildings of the upper levels bear eloquent witness. The civilization endured for the greater part of a millennium; its character is illustrated by a vast collection of monuments of every sort; but of its history no more can be said than that decadence set in some time before its complete destruction at the hands of the Aryan invaders, probably towards 1500 BC.

CHINA

As in the case of India, so in China also we are confronted with a civilization which has already attained a very high level and is concentrated in a relatively small area of northern China comprising the provinces of Hopei, Shantung, Anhwei, Shansi, Shensi and Honan. Throughout this area excavations and casual discoveries have brought to light bronze vessels and pottery of the Shang period and some, especially those from the Honan province, seemingly older than those of Anyang, the main site. But even if we can recognize, tentatively, an earlier phase of the Shang civilization we are still unable to explain its origin; it is surrounded by peoples still in the stage of barbarism, and its antecedents remain unknown. It is true that orthodox Chinese tradition tells of a Hsia Dynasty of seventeen or eighteen kings supposed to have ruled over China from 2205 BC till 1765 BC, when it was overthrown by T'ang the Successful, a Shang ruler who founded the Shang Dynasty, which continued in power until it in its turn was overthrown in 1122 BC by the Chou.[44] But there is no material evidence whatsoever to prove the existence of a Hsia Dynasty. The earliest literary evidence that we possess is that provided by the excavations at Anyang, and it dates from the latter part of the Shang Dynasty. Anyang can confidently be identified as the site of 'the great city Shang' (later, by the Chou people, called Yin) to which the capital was removed by P'an Kêng, 1401–1374 BC. Therefore we cannot expect to find anything earlier than his reign, and in fact we do not; of the thousands of bone inscriptions none, apparently, goes back to the days of P'an Kêng, and even his two immediate successors are but doubtfully represented, the earliest dated texts being of the reign of Wu Ting; the written history of China as given by contemporary documents begins only in the fourteenth century BC.

But those documents do confirm the orthodox tradition regarding the names and genealogy of the later Shang rulers. When then the bone inscriptions cite, as they do, the names of earlier kings known to us from the traditions we are justified in assuming that the orthodox view regarding the dynasty as a whole may be accepted and its history be taken as going back to *c.* 1750 BC (see pp. 107–08, note 44) although we have no actual knowledge and no recognizable monuments for its initial three and a half centuries. The case of Hsia is less simple. Although the Chou kings had a good deal to say about the Hsia Dynasty they were speaking of something very far removed from themselves in time and, because they were exploiting the story for purposes of political propaganda, they may well have distorted it not a little. In the Shang tradition Hsia seems to have been not so much a dynasty as a state which down to the time of T'ang the Successful controlled the rulers of the Shang tribe; but that its power even over its professed vassals was limited is shown by the fact that Hsiang T'u, the twelfth Shang prince before T'ang, is described as a conqueror who spread his dominions beyond the seas. Consistent with this is the fact that in the list of T'ang's conquests Hsia appears merely as one of a number of states incorporated by him in his dominions, and there is no reference to any former overlordship.

In later times, in the eighth to sixth centuries BC, the term Hsia is used to mean not a dynasty or a state, but 'Chinese', and is applied generally to the various states lying north of the territory of Ch'u. Ch'u, which occupied both banks of the Yangtze and reached half-way up to the Yellow River, was not 'Chinese', but was gradually coming into the sphere of Chinese culture. Hsia therefore was a cultural term. Nor was this a novel gloss upon the word. It has been remarked that the old Chou people used it for propaganda purposes; they were themselves by origin part of the Jung and Ti barbarians, and when they were 'converted' they called their new western territories part of 'the Hsia region', adopting the term because it implied a cultural and traditional justification of their domination—and it is in precisely that sense that it persists into Chou times. The theory that barbarians could be amalgamated into the Hsia group by adopting Chinese culture is wholly consistent with the view that Chinese culture had originated with the Hsia people in pre-Shang times. 'That there was a culture which could properly be called Chinese, even on a linguistic basis, at the early date assigned to Hsia is altogether probable, for the Chinese writing system as we find it on the Shang bones of the fourteenth century BC is amazingly complex, embodying almost every principle of the formation of characters which is in use today; it must have been preceded by many centuries of development.' Creel,[45] from whom the above paragraph is quoted, summarizes the question by saying, 'The evidence warrants us in concluding that while there was not a Hsia dynasty, in the traditional sense, there was a state by this name. And the fact that the term Hsia was later used so persistently to mean "Chinese" and "the Chinese states" in a cultural sense leads us to infer that this state was the leading exponent of Chinese culture in its day. As such it may have exercised political sway over a fairly large territory, and its cultural prestige may have given it a certain hegemony even beyond its proper borders. We have an example of this in the case of the Chou people, whom we know to have admired Shang culture and considered it superior to their own before and even after they conquered the Shangs. In a cultural sense, then, it is perhaps not completely erroneous to look upon Hsia as a Chinese dynasty. The term has perhaps this much basis of truth, that the torch of Chinese culture was passed from Hsia to Shang to Chou.'

The historical existence of Hsia is a matter of prime importance if we are to explain the origins of Chinese civilization.

The district in which Anyang lies is formed of the rich loess plain on the north-west bank of the Huang Ho, some 200 miles south of Peiping; protected on two sides by the river and on the west by a long mountain chain whose slopes provided heavy timber for building and wild game for the hunt, whereas the level valley was ideal for the growing of grain and for pasturage, it was admirably adapted to the development of a wealthy city. But it was not the birthplace of a civilization; the monuments of a highly developed and long-established culture are imposed upon the wreckage of a Neolithic settlement; obviously the development had taken place elsewhere.

Excavations at Chengchou and Loyang have produced material which is held to illustrate an earlier phase of the Anyang civilization—thus, the bronze ritual vessels are identical in type, as are the arrows and spear-heads, but the oracle bones are not inscribed, the buildings are similar but smaller in scale, and the pottery is generally similar but has none of the white kaolin decoration characteristic of Anyang. Such differences might possibly mean no more than that these were provincial sites, but may well indicate an earlier date, as suggested by the excavators. But even so, the civilization is already well developed, and in the crucial matter of metallurgy is as mature as it is seen to be in the Anyang phase. Its genesis therefore is still to seek.

The Chinese tradition which states that Anyang (Yin) was selected by P'an Kêng as his capital—a tradition which the archaeological evidence amply confirms—says further that the Shang people were not natives of this region but immigrants who after various wanderings settled in it, but tells us nothing as to whence they came. Because no local origin has yet been discovered for the Shang civilization, it has been suggested that it was introduced ready made by an aristocracy of immigrants from the far west, i.e. from the Mediterranean area, who imposed themselves on and ruled by force over the Chinese natives of the region. That theory, however, while purporting to explain the Chinese tradition, disregards the very serious difficulties of chronology and derives virtually no support from the archaeological material—on the contrary, the bronze vessels, which represent the finest art of the workers in metal (which is *ex hypothesi* an imported art) show a decoration which is purely Chinese, and their forms can be traced back to the pottery of Neolithic China (Pl. 2, c). Were the theory true, the supposedly earlier sites of Chengchou and Loyang might have been expected to produce some evidence of the invaders, but in no single object from those sites has there been detected any indebtedness to Mediterranean influences. It is true that Dr Li Chi[46] would relate the designs upon a Yin *tao-tieh* mask to Mesopotamian art of a thousand years earlier and finds an astonishing resemblance between an Anyang clay vessel and similar vessels discovered at Mohenjo-daro in the Indus valley and at Jamdat Nasr in Mesopotamia; but it would be rash to deduce an invasion from what need not bear witness to anything more than the passing of stray goods by way of barter through many hands and over great distances; in all other respects the uniform evidence of the tomb objects would seem to be decisive. Still more conclusive is the fact that the skeletal remains from the Anyang cemetery—and such are so numerous that some of the skulls must be those of the Shang aristocrats—uniformly belong to the Mongoloid branch of mankind and forbid the suggestion of any invasion by people of any other type.

Faced with this indisputable evidence some scholars have, not unnaturally, regarded the Shang civilization as indigenous, the result of the complex interaction of many elements, amongst which the most important were the autochthonous proto-Chinese cultures.[47] Certainly, to underestimate the part played by those autochthonous cultures would be to misrepresent the whole character of the Shang civilization, which is essentially Chinese. But what differentiates it from them is, first and foremost, the fact that it is a Bronze Age civilization, and it is hard to believe that those Stone Age cultures could have been responsible for that momentous change. Metallurgy must originate in a country where metal is easily obtainable—which is not the case for most parts of northern China; but even so, the mere presence of ore is not enough for, as we shall see hereafter (p. 267) the smelting of the ore requires a degree of heat unobtainable by the simple means at the disposal of most primitive peoples. The art of working metal must have reached China from the west, where it was invented; if the first centre was, as we believe, in eastern Anatolia, the line of advance eastwards would have followed the oriferous deposits of the mountain chain through Khorassan and Bokhara to the Kizil Kum desert; directly or indirectly, the Chinese borrowed their metallurgical technique from the Middle East. If the Anyang bronzes are in every respect purely Chinese it is because Chinese craftsmen were using the technique of metallurgy in their own way; if by that time they had developed a school of metallurgy not only completely individual but also so well established that it was to dominate the whole future art of China, that can only mean that development had been going on for very many generations. This is where the Hsia tradition is of value. If the Shang people were indeed the cultural heirs of the Hsia, and if the emergence of the Hsia, as a dynasty or as a tribe, is rightly put at something like 2200 BC, then we arrive at a date consistent with that of the spread of metallurgical knowledge in the west and one which allows reasonable time for the growth of an idiosyncratic Chinese school.

But side by side with the marvellous bronze vessels, weapons and tools of Anyang we have the oracle-bones bearing a syllabic script which also is fully developed and must have resulted from the labours of very many generations. Chinese writing may indeed be almost as ancient as Chinese metallurgy—in fact, some scholars would deduce from 'Yao's Calendar', preserved in the Canon of Documents of Confucius, that it was already known by the beginning of the second millennium BC. Although our existing material is late, belonging to the latter half of the second millennium, it is at least possible, if not probable, that the Chinese took over the technique of metal-working and the art of writing not so very long after both had been invented in the west. Now to suggest that arts so complicated as these two were invented independently and at more or less the same time by two different branches of the human race having absolutely no connection one with the other would be stretching coincidence too far. There can be no question of 'conquest' or 'immigration' by Sumerians or any other west-Asian people; but the difficulty can be solved by assuming a spread of ideas, not necessarily of imported patterns, but of the basic principles or processes of the arts. Bearing in mind that the search for metal ores, suddenly become so precious, sent prospectors wandering far and wide, and that goods might travel in the way of barter very far afield, we may imagine that a tribe in western China, having even indirect contacts with the Middle East, might learn the possibility of using pictorial signs to represent sounds and invent its own set of characters accordingly, just as they would learn, perhaps at much the same time and possibly from the same source, the technique of melting and casting metal.[48]

Chinese civilization was certainly not imported wholesale from the west, but, on the other hand, none of the various civilizations of the Old World was produced in isolation. If we look at the New World we shall see in the central American civilizations of the pre-Columban period a lop-sidedness which has no parallel in the lands with which this volume deals. There a magnificent achievement in the arts (which spring from individual intuition in response to social conditions) accompanies a technological ignorance almost as abysmal as that of the Palaeolithic painters of Lascaux. In the Old World advance was far more balanced for the reason that the various centres of man's activity were sufficiently in contact, direct or indirect, for the knowledge of new inventions and techniques to spread from one to another; the brief sketch of the political history of the more creative communities which has been given above is primarily intended to suggest the possibility of the cross-fertilization of ideas which trade and conquest could effect.

THE MIDDLEMEN

For the countries of the Middle East, bordering as they do one upon another, direct contacts were easy and the exchange of goods could introduce new models and new methods. Where greater distances are involved, as in the case of the Far Eastern countries, we may have to postulate middlemen concerning whom we may have little knowledge or none.

In southern Afghanistan, on a site called Mundigak, some thirty miles north of Kandahar, French excavators have discovered remains which, when fully published, should throw much light upon this question of international contacts. In the upper part of the mound, in a level provisionally dated to *c.* 1600 BC,[49] there are huge granaries, with raised floors ventilated from below, which certainly seem akin to those of Harappā; in a lower level, attributed to the latter part of the third millennium, a great building in mud-brick with a façade of half-columns reproduces a type familiar in Mesopotamia and suggests Sumerian connections in the Uruk or the Jamdat Nasr period (Pl. 1, b). Again, farther south, superficial exploration at Mehi has shown that in Baluchistan in and before the time of Harappā there was a culture, the Kulli culture, which was in touch both with Mohenjo-daro and with Sumer; 'There is good evidence that trade exchanges did take place, and goods and even people found their way from the Baluchistan hills to the Indus plain', and not only are stone vessels of Mehi make fairly common on such sites as Ur and Erech, but the painted pottery manufactured in the Diyala region (near Baghdad) in about 2800 BC reproduces the Kulli style and motifs with such accuracy that one suspects the arrival of Kulli potters in Mesopotamia. Similarly, when we find at Ur and other Sumerian cities, and again in Egypt, 'alabaster' vases so exactly alike in form that they might be products of the same workshop, but those from Egypt are of the veined calcite from deposits on the edge of the western desert whereas the Mesopotamian examples are of stalagmitic calcite from the southern end of the Persian Gulf, it is difficult to avoid the conclusion that somewhere on the shores of the Gulf there was a settlement of skilled workers in stone who exported their vases by sea northwards and westwards, finding a ready market in Sumer and supplying Egypt with models which could be copied in the local stone.

Those countries which in the course of the Bronze Age made the most notable advance were not the only ones to contribute to civilization; indeed, their advance was only made possible by discoveries due to peoples of whom we know nothing whatsoever. The chief discovery, which gives to the period its name, was that of mining and working copper, and since no copper ore is available in the silt-formed valleys of the Nile, the Euphrates, the Indus and the Huang Ho, the dwellers in those valleys must have acquired the art from abroad. In historic times Egypt exploited the copper-mines of Sinai, her main source of supply, but that was because the value of metal had already been realized. The Neolithic agriculturist of the Nile valley, hating and fearing the desert, would never have dared the dangers and the terrors of the journey to Sinai to look for a kind of stone that was no use to him when he found it; before he did that, he had to be convinced that copper was worth having. The Sumerian imported his copper and bronze; the latter came from Oman on the Persian Gulf, but the Sumerians did not exploit the mines themselves and, so far as we can tell, never owned them; themselves masters in the technique of metal-working they owed the technique and the metal to a people of whom no record is preserved. When, in the time of Sargon of Akkad, Mesopotamia was cut off from the source of supply in Oman, copper had to be brought in from the north, and, if one may judge from the Maikop treasure, a profitable trade began with the hill peoples west of the Caucasus; later on, the kingdom of Urartu was to rise into prominence there, but for the early period and for the beginnings of metal-working there is no history. The Harappā people brought the knowledge of metal with them into the Indus valley and there is nothing to show when or where they learned it, and so too with the Shang people of China. As soon as any one of the old agricultural groups, settled in the rich riverine plains and stocking their granaries with surplus foodstuffs, had discovered from the objects which barbarous mountaineers bartered for their grain the nature and the use of metal, mining prospectors scoured the known and the unknown world in search of independent sources of supply. The early traffic in metal opened up new countries, but it also brought the old countries into closer contact in that the traffic involved the spread of ideas and techniques as well as of actual metal; from now on, a new discovery made in one land could quickly become the common property of all, not necessarily by imitation but by adaptation. The exchange of goods by international trade could spur the imagination to novel achievements. Thus at Tell esh Sheikh, the site of a village lying on the route of the Amanus timber trade, people received payment for their wood in kind, and amongst the goods came the fine painted pottery of Tell Halaf and, later, as we have seen above (p. 59) that of the northern al'Ubaid type; very soon the local potters found that the plain black wares which had satisfied their clients in the past could not compete with the decorated wares coming in from abroad, and in self-defence they set to and produced a local painted pottery which while it utilized the technique and the motifs of both the foreign varieties copied neither but possessed a character altogether its own.

But while the import of foreign products contributed so much to the advance of civilization the part played by the carriers of those products was not less important; a great deal that was not for export could none the less be spread abroad by word of mouth—*volitat vivu' per ora virum.* Inventions such as that of the principle of phonetic writing, religious beliefs and mythological tales would be carried far afield by itinerant merchants, and together with the bartering of material things there went the commerce of the mind.

Amongst the carriers who helped to link together centres of culture geographically so far removed from each other that they might well be thought mutually inaccessible, some part must have been played by the inhabitants of the northern steppes. We know as yet very little about those peoples, and what we know would not warrant us in claiming for them credit for making any direct contribution of importance to the early stages of civilization except, indeed, the domestication of the horse, which is probably due to them; it was the nature of the country rather than the genius of its occupants that aided progress.

A vast belt of open steppe extends from Roumania across the Ukraine and the Chersonese area to Kuban, eastwards by Astrakhan and Uralsk, and far beyond that to Mongolia. It is a pastoral, not an agricultural land, and its population was necessarily nomad, men living in tents or booths and constantly moving on as their flocks and herds exhausted the nearby pastures. To whatever race the population might belong—and they differed widely—the conditions of environment imposed a similar manner of life upon all alike, and their enforced wanderings brought them into contact and induced a degree of uniformity in their culture. Thus in the second millennium BC burials of the Andronovo type extend uniformly from the Yenisei to the Ural mountains; in the southern Urals cemeteries of this type present a series of peculiar traits indicating the impact of both western and eastern cultures; in the Late Bronze Age funerary barrows in Uzbekistan, near Tashkent, closely resemble those of the Ukraine, and bronze buckets found in the Ukraine graves are well known in the Kuban area and reappear in a columbarium at Igdir in Erivan, thus showing contacts with the metal-working centre of Urartu. Later in history we find the Scythians at the western end of the steppe zone making a lavish use of Greek works of art. And at the same time in western Siberia, between Biisk and the Altai mountains, the astonishing tombs of Pazyryk yield Chinese mirrors, Han chariots, Persian embroideries and carpets which may be either Persian or (less probably) Anatolian, while the actual bodies in the tombs show that in these nomad tribes the Indo-European element from the west and the Mongoloid from the eastern extremity of the steppe meet in a single household, just as the intricately stylized animal forms characteristic of Scythian art are equally at home in Mongolia and in the Crimea.

From one end of Asia to the other, along the northern fringe of the settled lands where cities were built and civilization flourished, the clans of fierce horsemen were always on the move; nothing was permanent for them except the one secret spot where were the tombs of their chiefs. But they were not out of touch with the civilized world. They coveted the objects of luxury which they had not the skill to make, and they could always obtain such by trade, selling their horses and their felts, embroidered by the womenfolk with their own animal designs; or they could raid the settled lands and carry off the spoil; and, because their forces were a standing menace, the rulers of the great countries to the south, emperors of China and Persian kings, would buy peace from them by sending rich gifts or giving their daughters in marriage to the tribal chiefs. In such ways the men of the steppe got to know what the city craftsmen could do, and that knowledge was passed along from clan to clan; some new invention, a novel type of weapon or ornament, learnt from neighbours at one end of the chain might ultimately reach neighbours at the other end and inspire the workers of a city very far from the place of its discovery. It is quite certain that throughout the Bronze Age new ideas spread widely and sometimes very quickly in spite of the great distances involved and of the difficulties of transport across country; direct evidence for the early periods is lacking, but in view of what we can learn about later times it is reasonable to suppose that in some cases the steppe-dwellers were the middlemen for the dissemination of knowledge.

Our account began at the point at which man was emerging from his primitive savagery and with the invention of metal embarked upon the adventure of progress. In a brief factual sketch we have defined the main groups whose different characteristics and conditions of existence gave rise to different cultures and have emphasized not their individual contributions to civilization—that is to be our principal study hereafter—but rather their interrelations, trying to see what contacts of war and trade, of travel or of race migration, would make possible the interchange of cultural goods, and therefore of ideas, which promotes growth. Some of those original groups have flourished and endured, some have made their contribution to the common cause and have disappeared; new races, unconsidered at the beginning, have come to the fore, inheriting the traditions and sometimes usurping the territories of those that went before. Now the dawn of the Iron Age comes to a Middle East peopled for the most part by races which were to hold their own throughout history.

AUTHOR'S NOTE AND DISCUSSION

(Note 38, p. 79)

Sir Leonard Woolley

Since there are differences of opinion on this subject something should be said regarding the alternative views. Some Indologists hold that the Rigvedic literature, and *a fortiori* the

Rigvedic Age, go back beyond the twelfth century BC, and that the Aryan Indians were by that time at least a highly civilized people, as is shown by the character of their literature and religion. It is historically true that southern India was, by the third century BC, conquered by Aryan Indians and dominated by Brahmanical culture, and that the conquest had been preceded by a religious infiltration which resulted in the establishment of Vedic schools in the south. The earliest hymns of the *Rigveda* show the Indo-Aryans as established exclusively in the north-west of India and in eastern Afghanistan; it is argued therefore that, assuming the Vedic schools in the south to have been established in the seventh century (which is a pure assumption), five hundred years is a ludicrously short time to allow for the extension of Aryan domination over the rest of northern and central India, so that the Aryan occupation of the north-west must go back far beyond 1200 BC. The many different strata in the Rigvedic hymns prove that the period in which they were developed must have stretched over very many centuries, and reckoning back from the earliest Buddhist literature (which presupposes the *Veda*) and allowing for the vast lapse of time required by oral tradition for the earliest hymns to have taken shape in the Vedic schools and to have been compiled into a *Samhitā* or 'Collection', those hymns must be assigned to a date before 1200 BC. Further, since the grouping of the Aryan gods in the Mitanni texts from Bogazköy, with their particular forms of names, can be traced elsewhere only in the *Veda,* it is argued (*a*) that these are Indian Vedic deities, and (*b*) that the Mitanni leaders were immigrants from India, from which it follows that the Aryans had been established in north-western India considerably earlier than 1500 BC. In view of this overwhelming evidence that eastern Afghanistan and north-west India were occupied by the Rigvedic Aryans from about 2500 BC either their civilizations was for a long time contemporary with the Harappā civilization or those Aryans, instead of having destroyed the Harappā civilization, were actually its authors.

The view adopted in this volume is that the Rigvedic hymns (regardless of the late date at which they assumed their present form) do embody early elements, as early as 1200 BC probably, in which the Aryan invasion of north-west India is rather vaguely remembered, and that the actual invasion took place somewhere around 1500 BC; the 'Vedic Age' may be said to have started at that time, the literature comes later, and the type of literature represented by the early elements in the hymns does not imply any high degree of material culture. The Harappā civilization was non-Aryan and was destroyed by the Aryans (there is indeed no other possible explanation of its destruction) who were a non-urbanized people and semi-barbarous.

That the Hindu civilization resulted from a mingling of that of Harappā and the Aryan culture seems certain; but that fact does not mean that the two flowed parallel for a long time; the Harappā element is due to the survival of Harappā people as slaves or serfs of the Aryan conquerors. The religious parallel between the Mitanni and the Indo-Aryans implies no more than that both came from a common stock, and that at no great interval of time. The length of time postulated for the Aryan conquest of (or infiltration into) central and southern India is greatly exaggerated—the conquest of the north-west need not have taken more than a few years, though that was a well-organized land with walled cities, whereas the rest of the country was probably easier to overrun; to speak of 'many centuries' is to strain all historic probabilities in support of a theory. Even if we grant (as we should) that the Aryans spent a long time consolidating their power in the north-west before embarking on further conquests, and accept for the conquest of the south a date 'perhaps as early as the seventh century BC' which is purely hypothetical, there is nothing in this to support an earlier date than 1500 for the incoming of the Aryans: 1500 BC is approximately the date given by archaeological evidence for the destruction of Harappā and Mohenjo-daro and if these were not the 'walled cities' destroyed by the Aryans to what can the Rigvedic hymns refer? For they are almost certainly the earliest walled cities of the Indus valley.

Dr R. C. Majumdar

The Aryans imbibed the pre-existing culture and assimilated much of it, the result being the growth of what we usually called Hindu culture. But this does not mean that the Aryan culture was insignificant. The *Rigveda* is the earliest manifestation, in a permanent and intelligent form, of the ideas and beliefs of mankind and their gradual evolution, and the culture reflected in it should find a prominent place in the history of the period 1500–1200 BC. The idea that the authors of the hymns of the *Rigveda,* or the people among whom they gained currency, were barbarous or semi-barbarous is not supported by M. Winternitz in his *History of Indian Literature,* I (Calcutta, 1927), pp. 63–75. See also my 'L'Antiquité et l'importance du Rigveda', *Journal of World History,* VI, 2 (1960), pp. 215–22.

Sir Leonard Woolley

Had my period gone down to 500 BC, I should have treated the *Rigveda* at length; but with 1200 BC as the terminus, that would have been wrong. The *Rigveda* was certainly not composed in its present form until much later, and it is impossible to say what stage of culture had been reached by the Aryans at 1200 BC; a description based on the *Rigveda* and applied to the period 1500–1200 BC would be an anachronism unsupported by any evidence whatsoever; the culture reflected in the *Rigveda* is itself that of a later period, and of the 'gradual evolution' of that culture we can speak only in a summary (which would be most in place if given for the fourth–third century BC); the poem does not help us to trace its evolution in dated steps.

Professor Ralph E. Turner

The *Rigveda,* according to Stuart Piggott, *Ancient India* (Penguin ed.), pp. 255–6, was composed 1400–1500 BC (Piggott accepts the dating of Max Müller). While accepting the *Rigveda* as a genuine document on archaeological grounds, Piggott points out that the archaic Sanskrit in which it is written makes it an imprecise and limited source. Within these limits the *Rigveda* gives us a general impression of the life of the Aryans, a pre-urban, and in this sense barbarian people. Theirs was an agricultural economy which includes the growing of a grain crop, but in which herds of cattle and flocks of sheep and goats are of prime importance. The Aryan society was formally divided into a threefold grading of warriors, priests, and artisans—*Ksatriyas, Brahmans* and *Vaisyas*—but the concept of caste was not yet known. The Aryans were among the first to introduce the idea of rapid transport made possible by the domesticated horse. Ox-drawn four-wheeled carts were used for farm work, and light two-wheeled chariots drawn by specially bred horses were used for sport or warfare.

NOTES TO CHAPTER 1

1. Professor I. M. Diakonoff suggests that climate is not a primary factor in encouraging work. In Neolithic times man had to work hard enough to survive in any climate. The tools and means of survival he had developed by that time could yield him surplus production under certain conditions (in the alluvial lowlands); but not in others (dense woodlands) where his stone implements were

not adequate to clear a sufficient area of arable land or get a sufficient harvest.

In support of Sir Leonard Woolley's position, see Ellsworth Huntington, *The Climatic Factor* (Washington, 1914), *Civilization and Climate* (New Haven, 1915), *Mainsprings of Civilization* (London, 1945) and S. F. Markham, *Climate and the Energy of Nations* (London, 1942).

2. Both Professor John A. Wilson and Professor I. M. Diakonoff feel that the process was not as sudden as suggested by Sir Leonard Woolley. Sir Leonard takes the view that while the process of evolution was progressive, its final phase, and the results achieved, can be considered relatively sudden, particularly if we bear in mind the extremely lengthy span of this evolution as a whole.
3. The desiccation of Egypt and, more generally speaking, of the present desert zone surrounding it, began as early as the end of the Pleistocene (Palaeolithic) Age [see K. S. Sandford, 'Palaeolithic Man and the Nile Valley in Nubia and Upper Egypt', University of Chicago, Oriental Institute, *Publications,* No. 17 (Chicago, 1933); G. W. Murray, 'The Egyptian Climate, an Historical Outline', *Geographical Journal,* Vol. 117 (December, 1951), pp. 442–3].
4. Professor J. Leclant stresses the still highly theoretical character of the hypotheses put forward concerning the earliest settlement of Egypt. Anthropological analysis of the very earliest tombs is still at a very early stage; see Andrzej Wiercinski, 'Introductory Remarks Concerning the Anthropology of Ancient Egypt', Société de Géographie d'Egypte, *Bulletin,* XXXI (1958), pp. 73–84.

   The various migration charts put forward remain hypothetical and based on speculation, rather than on true archaeological observation.
5. Professor John A. Wilson points out that the approach of the desert to the Nile valley has destroyed the evidence on which this statement rests.
6. Professor I. M. Diakonoff feels that any people placed in the same conditions would achieve similar results. There are no ways of checking what a non-hybrid people might have done—if indeed the Egyptians were a non-hybrid people, which is by no means certain.
7. The theory of a single 'flood' cannot be accepted without discussion. The flood was not a cosmic disaster. Certain archaeologists have, moreover, reported other floods dating from different periods and in different locations.
8. Professor F. Schachermeyr doubts that there was another invasion at the beginning of the Uruk Age. The changes in pottery are due rather to the introduction of the potter's wheel and the production of metal vessels imitated by the potters. Sir Leonard Woolley feels, however, that his own position is supported by archaeologists who have specialized in Mesopotamia.
9. See S. N. Kramer, 'Sumerian Mythology: A Study of Spiritual and Literary Achievements in the Third Millennium BC', American Philosophical Society, *Memoirs,* XXI (Philadelphia, 1944).
10. Professor I. M. Diakonoff refuses to apply the word 'class' to a conquered people or tribe when speaking of pre-urban times. Class division, in the sense of the place of a given group in the system of production and in relation to property, did not exist until the 'Urban Revolution'.
11. Dr D. C. Baramki considers it purely hypothetical to presume that the people of Uruk adopted the language of the people of al'Ubaid, since we are completely ignorant of the latter's language.
12. According to Professor I. M. Diakonoff, there is little proof that

Mari was ever a Hurrian city. It does, however, appear that the Hurrians were sufficiently numerous in Mari to have warranted the inclusion in the local archives of a number of texts in their own language; see Fr. Thureau-Dangin, 'Tablettes hurrites provenant de Mari', *Revue d'Assyriologie et d'Archéologie Orientale*, Vol. 36 (1944). Later on, Hurrian material becomes more abundant; see E. S. Speiser, 'The Hurrian Participation in the Civilization of Mesopotamia, Syria and Palestine', *Journal of World History*, I, 2 (1953), pp. 318–19.

13. Professor Diakonoff considers it probable that the Hurrians and the Hittites adopted the cuneiform writing of the Semites of Syria and northern Mesopotamia. Reference may also be made to the bibliographies in V. Istrine, 'L'écriture, sa classification, sa terminologie et les regularités de son développement', *Journal of World History*, IV, 1 (1957), p. 15; and David Diringer, 'Problems of the Present Day on the Origin of the Phoenician Alphabet', *Ibid.*, pp. 57–8. Professor Diakonoff refers to the paper read by Th. V. Gamkrelidze at the XXVth International Congress of Orientalists, Moscow, 1960, in support of his position.

14. Any reconstitution of the very earliest history of the Hittites must be based exclusively on the examination of pottery. As has been pointed out by Professor E. Laroche, there exists no written Hittite tradition pointing to their place of origin. Attempts have been made (e.g. F. Sommer, *Hethiter und Hethitisch*, Stuttgart, 1947), to prove that they retained memories of some eastern, Caspian, origin.

15 Recent exploration (C. A. Burney, 'Eastern Anatolia in the Chalcolithic and Early Bronze Age', in *Anatolian Studies*, Vol. VIII, 1958) has shown that this ware is far more widely distributed than had been assumed. The sites on which it has been noted range from the middle Araxes northwards to the Kura basin and southwards to the western shore of Lake Urmia and are very numerous to the west of Lake Van, while there is a further group in the neighbourhood of Malatya. Kuftin's excavations seemed to show a local development of the ware, and since the other sites are known from surface remains only, his views should hold good pending proper excavations elsewhere. So too his chronology is not upset by the fact of wide dispersion, for the type may have been elaborated in its original homeland some centuries before it was imitated far afield. In the text Kuftin's views are adopted, with the *caveat* that they may have to be slightly modified by discoveries yet to be made.

16 The tradition according to which the Phoenicians came from the Red Sea (and perhaps also from the Persian Gulf) has little foundation beyond the references in Herodotus, I, 1; VII, 89, and in Justin, XVIII, 13, and is therefore of debatable value. While still accepted by O. Eissfeldt ('Phoiniker', in Pauly-Wissowa, *Realencyclopaedie* XX, 1, col. 353–5) it is rejected by the majority of scholars, and by W. F. Albright in particular.

17 This elaboration was suggested by the remarks of Professor Diakonoff.

18. Professor John A. Wilson and Professor Jean Leclant both stress that no Egyptian text states explicitly that Isis came to Egypt from Byblos. Modern commentators base themselves mainly on the famous text of Plutarch and on new interpretation of older evidence in the light of this text. See S. Herrmann, 'Isis in Byblos', *Zeitschrift für Aegyptische Sprache und Altertumskunde*, Vol. 82, 1 (1957), pp. 48–55.

19. According to Professor I. M. Diakonoff, evidence that ore was found by mining prospectors and not by local people is scanty; and

evidence for the employment of hired labour is also slight, it being more likely that the mines were worked by slave labour. Sir Leonard Woolley's contention that there were mining prospectors from the more advanced cultures is, however, supported: see C. F. Hawkes, *The Prehistoric Foundations of Europe* (London, 1940) and T. A. Rickard, *Man and Metals* (New York, 1922), p. 202. Slave labour appears to have been extensively utilized on ancient mining projects. For work in Egyptian mines in Sinai and in Nubia, see H. Kees, *Kulturgeschichte des alten Orients,* I, *Aegypten* (München, 1933), pp. 126 sq., and Professor J. Cerny, *The Inscriptions of Sinai,* II (London, 1955), pp. 14 sq.

20. Sir Leonard Woolley's reasons for attributing to Sumer priority in the invention of writing are given in detail in Chapter VI, p. 366 sq. The question of the priority of Egyptian or Sumerian writing is still far from settled. It is possible only to note that both were in use at the end of the fourth millenary. See D. Diringer, *The Alphabet: A Key to the History of Mankind* (2nd ed., London, 1948), pp. 58–9. As suggested by Sir Leonard Woolley and supported by Professor Ralph E. Turner, there may have been 'idea diffusion', a concept developed by the anthropologist A. L. Kroeber, 'Stimulus Diffusion', *American Anthropology,* Vol. 42 (1940), pp. 1–20.
21. Scholars are not agreed as to whether Menes is an actual historical figure or whether he is a later legendary composition. See John A. Wilson, *The Burden of Egypt* (Chicago, 1951), pp. 43–4; E. Drioton, J. Vandier, *Les Peuples de l'Orient Méditerranéen,* II, *l'Egypte,* (3rd ed., Paris, 1952), pp. 160–2; W. Helck, *Zeitschrift der deutschen Morgenländischen Gesellschaft,* 103 (1953), pp. 354–9.
22. Some authorities set the summit of Egyptian civilization back into the Old Kingdom. See John A. Wilson, *The Burden of Egypt* (Chicago, 1951), and E. Otto, *Aegypten: Der Weg des Pharaonenreiches* (2nd ed., Stuttgart, 1955).
23. It is permissible to raise questions, as does Professor John A. Wilson, as to the true nature of the political aims in Asia of the rulers of the Middle Empire. The military expeditions into Nubia, and the establishment of powerful fortresses, will, of course, be contrasted with the single campaign of Sesostris III against Sekmen. There is no doubt that the Egyptian contribution to Byblos was of considerable importance. The treasure of Tôd testifies to the existence of close relations between Egypt and Asia. Statues of Sesostris II and Amenemhet III have been found at Ras-Shamra. It appears, however, that Egyptian influence in Asia was primarily cultural and economic and that, strictly speaking, there was never any politico-military empire.
24. The opinion that the Hyksos were expelled after a rule of little more than a generation is based on the work of R. Weill, 'XIIème dynastie. Royauté de Haute-Egypte et Domination Hyksos dans le Nord', Institut Français d'Archéologie Orientale, *Bibliothèque d'Etude,* Vol. XXVI (1953). These conclusions, however, have by no means met with general acceptance. The prevailing opinion is that the intermediary period between the Middle and New Empires lasted from about 1730 to 1580 BC and the Hyksos domination from 1680 to 1580 BC. See, e.g., E. Drioton and J. Vandier, *Les Peuples de l'Orient Méditerranéen,* II, *L'Egypte* (3rd ed., Paris, 1952).
25. That the horse was introduced in the time of the Hyksos is generally assumed [see the bibliography in *Syria,* XXXVII (1960), pp. 17–18]. We have no record of horses in Egypt prior to the Hyksos invasion;

but Ahmose I, at the siege of Avaris, used a chariot. Since a senior officer, Ahmose, son of Ebana (from whose tomb at El Kab we get our information) fought on foot, it looks as if the horse was still a great rarity.

26. Professor J. Leclant emphasizes that in addition to its strictly technical and military effects, the introduction into Egypt of the horse and chariot had considerable political and social consequences. The importance of the officers, particularly of chariot officers, was constantly on the increase. New guilds arose—cartwrights, saddlers, metal-workers. Even aesthetics took on a new aspect, Egyptian art showing henceforward not only new motifs but also new forms of expression: the speed, movement, variety and elegance of line, together with the vivacity of the great compositions becoming the hallmarks of the art of the New Empire.

27. There exist no known texts concerning any campaign by Amenophis I in Asia. All that is known is that in the year II of the reign of Thutmose I, the empire extended from Tombos (in the Sudan) to the Euphrates: cf. the Tombos stele 1. 13–14; this inscription refers to the Euphrates as 'the water which runs backwards [i.e. in the opposite direction to that of the Nile] and which descends towards the South'.

28. It is impossible to determine with absolute certainty the chronology of the New Empire. There persists a margin of error of some ten years See in particular M. B. Rowton, *Iraq,* VIII (1946), pp. 94–110, and *Journal of Egyptian Archaeology,* 34 (1948), pp. 57–74. The date most commonly assigned to the beginning of the reign of Thutmose is 1504 BC, and that for the death of Hatshepsut 1482 BC. On the controversial and difficult question of the reigns of Thutmose III and Hatshepsut, see W. E. Edgerton, 'The Thutmosid Succession', Oriental Institute of Chicago, *Studies in Ancient Oriental Civilization,* No. 8 (1933).

29. Egypt, an African land, an oasis created by an African river on the border of the great Sahara desert, as Professor J. Leclant points out, offers an opportunity of throwing some light on the earliest history of the African continent, still so obscure. We should, at all events, keep in mind the substratum common to the culture of Africa and to that of the Egypt of the Pharaohs. [See the work of H. Frankfort, in particular 'The African Foundation of Ancient Egyptian Civilization', Congresso Internazionale di preistoria posthistoria e mediterranea, *Atti* (Florence, Naples, Rome, 1950), pp. 115–16; and *The Birth of Civilization in the Near East* (3rd ed., 1954), pp. 42–3.] In order to understand the history of Egyptian civilization it is, in any case, essential to take into account the main lines of the history of the Sudan, the land of Kush, a convenient summary of which is to be found in A. J. Arkell, *A History of the Sudan to A.D. 1821* (London, 1955).

30. Professor I. M. Diakonoff refuses to recognize the existence of a nationalist sentiment as early as 3000 BC. In his opinion, nations as such did not exist. The Sumerians did not even have a common name; 'the black-headed' was a term used of the Sumerians as well as of the Akkadians; people were called by the name of the city to which they belonged. Sir Leonard Woolley, however, considers that 'nationalism' is the only expression that corresponds to what we know of the facts; it was perhaps hardly conscious except in so far as all the people thought and felt alike, in face of foreigners.

31. The final chronology of the early period of Mesopotamian history is still subject to further examination and possible revision. The tendency in recent years has been to advance to a considerable ex-

tent the dates previously accepted. See the works of S. Smith, W. F. Albright, A. Goetze and of Sir Leonard Woolley.

32. It might perhaps be preferable to speak of a slackening in the rhythm of progress rather than of actual stagnation. Professor Diakonoff suggests that this is due to the establishment of despotism. Commentators on behalf of the National Commission of Israel are opposed to the establishment of a relationship of cause and effect between cultural lag and the preponderance established by the Semitic element.
33. Professor I. M. Diakonoff refuses to consider the history of southern Mesopotamia in the third millennium as a social conflict between the Semites and the Sumerians. The position adopted by Sir Leonard Woolley was based on the study of the tablets of Ur. See also Th. Jacobsen, 'The Assumed Conflict between Sumerians and Semites in Early Mesopotamian History', American Oriental Society, *Journal,* LIX (1939) pp. 485–95.
34. Professor I. M. Diakonoff considers it misleading to call ancient moneylenders 'bankers', a term denoting an institution of much later date.
35. Both Professor I. M. Diakonoff and Professor Alf Sommerfelt draw attention to doubts recently cast on the validity of including the Kassites among the Indo-European races; see Kemal Balkan, 'Kassitenstudien I, Die Sprache der Kassiten'. German translation by F. R. Kraus, *American Oriental Series,* Vol. 37 (New Haven, 1954). It is possible that the Kassite rulers were Indo-Europeans, but certainly not the majority of the Kassite people; see S. A. Pallis, *The Antiquity of Iraq* (Copenhagen, 1956), p. 615. Professor Diakonoff doubts that even the rulers of the Kassites were Indo-Europeans. Their names were certainly not Indo-European.
36. Tahsin Ozgüc, 'The Dagger of Anitta', *Belleten,* XX (January 1956), p. 77.
37. Some Indian scholars have advocated a theory on the indigenous origin of the Aryans; see R. C. Majumdar, ed. *The History and Culture of the Indian People,* I, *The Vedic Age* (London, 1951), pp. 215–17. The National Commissions of India and Pakistan, as well as Professor I. M. Diakonoff and Professor G. F. Ilyin, draw attention to the fact that there is more than one theory regarding the fall of the Harappā civilization. R. E. M. Wheeler, 'Harappā, 1946: the Defenses and the Cemetery R.37', *Ancient India,* No. 3 (1947), pp. 81–3, supports the point of view given above, as does Stuart Piggott, *Prehistoric India* (London, 1950), p. 244. M. R. Sahni, *Man in Evolution* (Calcutta, 1952), pp. 153–4, holds that floods were responsible for the destruction, while A. Ghosh, 'The Rajputana Desert: Its Archaeological Aspect', National Institute of Sciences of India, *Bulletin,* No. 1 (1952), pp. 37–42, discovered a gap between the end of the Indus valley civilization and the incoming of the 'Painted Grey Ware People'. For a good summary cf. B. B. Lal, 'Proto-historic Investigation', *Ancient India,* No. 9 (1953), pp. 80–102.

Sir Leonard Woolley, however, considers that these different theories are not of equal value. That of a flood being responsible for the destruction of the great Indus valley cities is inconsistent with the fact that citizens were killed in the streets. The overthrow of the cities would result in the neglect of the canal banks and therefore in the flooding of the sites *after* the war.

According to Sir Leonard, a gap between the fall of Harappā civilization and the settlement (not the incoming) of the 'Painted Grey Ware People' would be inconclusive as an argument for or against the view that they were responsible for the destruction of that civilization; if they were the Aryans, they were still in the pre-urban stage and would take time to settle down. The fact of the gap is still non-proven. Rupar, in the Punjab, showed two levels, (*a*) Harappā, and (*b*) Painted Grey Ware, with no overlap but a distinct break between them. Hastinapura showed three levels, (*a*) crude ochre-coloured pottery, (*b*) Painted Grey Ware, (*c*) (after a break caused by a flood) Northern Black Polished Ware, with iron; Harappā was not represented here. A. Ghosh, in his summary of the Hastinapura excavations (*Ancient India,* No. 10, 1954) points out that the Painted Grey Ware is widespread in north-west India in the first half of the first millennium BC with a possible extension into the last part of the second millennium; Lal's date for the ware at Hastinapura is *c.* 1100–800 BC. Ghosh says 'this ware is probably a relic of the Aryan-speaking people, or a branch thereof; its distribution corresponds with the holy land of Aryan literature, and the date agrees, for if the conventional date for the entry of the Aryans into India, viz. 1500 BC, be accepted (and evidence about their movements in the Near East does not contradict this date), they would have reached the Gangetic plain a few centuries later'. Lal agrees that the ware represents the Aryans, though he admits that not all Indian archaeologists share that opinion. Ghosh concludes that 'it is doubly premature to say that the Aryans had nothing to do with the disappearance of the Harappāns'.

38. cf. Author's note at the end of chapter, pp. 98–101.
39. As Professor J. Maluquer de Motes observes, the ideas of mining and metallurgy reaching the Iberian Peninsula by the end of the third millennium may very possibly be traced to Cyprus.
40. Sir Arthur Evans, *Palace of Minos,* III, p. 477, has spoken of Resheph in connection with statuettes found at Knossos and Tiryns portraying a figure in 'a valiant posture'. It does not, however, appear that these necessarily represent a god and there is, in any case, no evidence to justify the assumption that they represent Resheph in particular.
41. Sometimes read 'Khapiri'. See J. Bottero, 'Le problème des Habiru à la 4ème Rencontre Assyriologique Internationale', Société Asiatique, *Cahiers,* XII (Paris, 1954).
42. There are divergent views regarding the origin of the Etruscans. Sir Leonard Woolley accepts the traditional account of their immigration from Anatolia after the fall of Troy, for which important support, if not complete confirmation, comes from recent studies of Etruscan tomb objects [e.g. 'Urartian Bronzes in Etruscan Tombs', by K. R. Marxwell-Hyslop in *Iraq,* XVIII, 2 (1956), p. 150], and of physical anthropology [e.g. 'Sur les origines des Etrusques', by Sir Gavin de Beer in *Revue des Arts,* No. 3 (1955)]. The admitted difficulty of the time gap between the twelfth century and the first appearance of the Etruscans in Italy is in course of solution as the dates assigned to the tombs are shown to have been unduly late. See also *History of Mankind: Cultural and Scientific Development,* Vol. II, by Luigi Pareti, with the assistance of Paolo Brezzi and Luciano Petech.
43. According to Professor G. F. Ilyin, one cannot, on the basis of the Australoid skulls, found among others in Mohenjo-daro, infer that the old native population constituted the lower classes.
44. The Bamboo Books reduce these dates by as much as two centuries, i.e. to 1989, 1558 and 1050 BC (or even 1027 BC). Some modern scholars adopt this shorter chronology, but in the present text the author has adhered to the 'orthodox' chronology. Professor L. S.

Vasilyev recommends reference to W. M. Hawley, *Chinese Chronology* (Los Angeles, 1953) and to Cheng Mengchia, *On the Question of the Chronology of the Chang-Yin and Hsia-Chou* (Shanghai, 1955).

45. See H. G. Creel, *Studies in Early Chinese Culture* (Seattle, 1938), pp. 120, 130 sq.
46. See Li Chi, *The Beginnings of Chinese Civilization* (Seattle, 1957), p. 29.
47. See, for instance, Chêng Tê-k'ung. 'The Origin and Development of Shang Culture', in *Asia Major*, New Series, Vol. VI, Pt. 1 (1957), pp. 80–98.
48. Professor I. M. Diakonoff stresses the hypothetical character of this point of view. He considers that similar conditions—in this case urban civilization—create similar needs and stimulate similar inventions. The invention of an identical technique may take place in two different places. Professor Diakonoff and Professor L. S. Vasilyev call attention to the fact that the tribes living on the vast expanse of the plains and in the mountains stretching between Mesopotamia and China were all illiterate.
49. Professor J. M. Casal feels that this dating may be too high: 'As I have pointed out [*Illustrated London News* (May 7, 1955), p. 832] these late levels seem to go back to the first half of the first millennium BC and this dating still holds. As for the "great building in mud-bricks with a façade of half-columns" referred to a few lines farther down, attributed to the latter part of the third millennium, more extensive excavations carried out up to 1958, and a better knowledge of finds coeval with it, have convinced me that this monument, now identified as a Palace, should be contemporary with the Early Dynastic of Mesopotamia, which still better fits with Sir Leonard Woolley's conclusions.' See J. M. Casal, Délégation archéologique française en Afghanistan, *Mémoires*, XVII (Paris, 1961).

CHAPTER II

THE URBANIZATION OF SOCIETY

It is an axiom of economic history that real civilization can begin only in regions where the character of soil and climate makes surplus production possible and easy; only so is man relieved from the necessity of devoting all his energies and all his thought to the problem of mere survival, and only so is he enabled to procure from others by means of barter those things which minister to well-being and promote advance but are not naturally available in his own land; moreover, such conditions must prevail over an area large enough to maintain not merely a small group of individuals but a population sufficiently numerous to encourage occupational specialization and social development. So does civilization begin. Most of the community continue to devote their energies to actual food-production, but men whose gifts or tastes are of another sort become artisans, specialists in production of a different but scarcely less necessary kind, making those things without which the agricultural worker cannot get on. Increasing wealth and the uneven growth of private property lead to the development of technical knowledge, of art and of government, and the respected elders of the old days, now free to devote themselves to the ever more complicated task of government, evolve an apparatus of law which is calculated to maintain order within the community and to defend it from outside aggression. The higher progress is the direct outcome of acquired skills and techniques, but those skills and techniques can be developed only where natural conditions make possible the surplus production of foodstuffs.

In two countries of the Middle East, in Mesopotamia and Egypt, these conditions were amply fulfilled and in those two countries Middle Eastern civilization accordingly began. Great emphasis has been laid by many writers on the fact that in them, as in none of the neighbouring lands, nature supplied precisely what was requisite for progress; in both there is a long valley of vast extent filled with water-borne silt which as agricultural soil is of amazing richness; in both a great river running through the centre of the flat plain brings the water that is essential in a sun-scorched land, floods it and leaves behind a silt that further enriches the soil, and can be tapped by canals to secure fertility throughout the year. So described, Mesopotamia and Egypt would appear to be exactly parallel in the opportunities that they afforded to early man, and therefore one might have expected early man in the two countries to develop along parallel lines, especially when, as we have seen, the two were in contact and Mesopotamia exercised a considerable influence upon the beginnings of Egyptian civilization. But in point of fact the two peoples progressed along lines wholly divergent. Nothing could be more unlike the mosaic of city states that divided between them the valley of the Euphrates and the Tigris than the unified kingdom of Egypt in which the city was really non-existent. The whole basis of society is radically different in the two countries, and the historian cannot ascribe this to 'the different mentality' of the two peoples because we know nothing of their respective mentalities so far as they had been formed at the outset of our period; and when later on they had been formed and we can fairly contrast them, they must be considered as the results just as much as, if not more than, the possible cause of the opposing conditions of life. The course of history can only be properly understood when it is realized that the similarity in the physical conditions of Egypt and Mesopotamia is only partial; actually the two valleys differ fundamentally, and in such a way as to impose upon their inhabitants quite different modes of life, and widely divergent religious views.

EGYPT

The valley of the Nile, lying between hills of sandstone and limestone, is in profile slightly concave and slopes towards the sea with an average fall of 1:13,000. The annual flood, depositing the heavier silt close to the stream's course, raises the banks a little above the level of the bottom of the hollow through which the river runs, and at normal times the surface of the water is well below that of the ground on either side, the channel being deeply cut and the amount of sediment deposited on the river bed being negligible. At flood time the river rises slowly, spreading over the valley, or at least over the lower part of it, and falls slowly, draining away, thanks to the ground contours, and leaving behind it no stagnant water but a fairly uniform deposit of silt (clay with up to 20 per cent of sand) which is free of salt and an excellent fertilizer; and again, because of the gentle rise and fall and because of the ground's slope, which ensures the draining-away of the flood water, the sediment does very little in the way of silting up canals. But the most important feature of the Nile is that its flood in the first place is remarkably regular, so that its coming is predictable and—since it is gradual—can be observed in the river's upper courses in good time to give exact warning to the inhabitants of the valley downstream; and in the second place it occurs in the autumn, lasting from about August 15th into early October. This means that the flood comes long after the harvest has been gathered and, when the ground is parched and hard, irrigates it, covers it with fresh sediment and withdraws as winter sets in and gives the signal for sowing; the soil holds enough moisture for the winter-sown crops to come to maturity, and for later sowings a very simple system of short canals tapping the stream higher up will assure a summer harvest.

All that the earliest settlers had to do was to sow their seed along the riverside as soon as the flood waters receded and wait for the crop to grow and ripen; by such a simple means a single isolated homestead would obtain more than enough foodstuff to support itself. As the population increased, the relatively small area of naturally irrigated soil would no longer suffice and had to be expanded artificially; but to do so was an easy task. The primitive farmer had made the obvious discovery that the effects of the flood could be supplemented if necessary by cutting through the natural dyke of the river's bank a channel that would lead fresh water on to the growing crop, and when the ground had been thoroughly saturated the gap could be closed and the surplus water drained off by cutting the bank lower downstream. On this simple process was based the whole economy of after times, i.e. the basin irrigation of the Nile valley. The principle is that the land along the river is divided into compartments—basins—by embankments thrown up at right-angles to the river's course; a canal started from upstream conducts water from the river to the basin, where smaller canals and ditches spread it evenly over the compartment; another canal drains the excess water off to a second basin or to the river downstream. Basin irrigation can produce only one crop in the year because when the river sinks below a certain level the lead-off canals dry up; but with the rich soil of Egypt one crop is sufficient, and the system has the advantages of short canals, simple upkeep and very slow silting-up of the channels. This means that every village was economically independent in that the labour necessary for the surplus production of food was well within the scope of a small social unit, left indeed a fair amount of leisure and allowed for the specialization of handicrafts. Obviously there was an interest in having some kind of market where the produce of different villages could be exchanged, and this would lead to the growth of market towns, the existence of which would imply a certain amount of local administration; but with that the requirements of the village would be satisfied. Egypt in the pre-Dynastic period must be envisaged as a land of village communities each primarily concerned with the cultivation of its own fields by its own efforts; it is possible and indeed likely that the existence of particularly holy centres of worship acted to some extent as a centralizing influence and served to divide the country into major groupings, but these 'nomes', though they might supply a rallying point and leadership in times of crisis, had not, so far as we know, developed into administrative capitals. It is safe to say that there were no pre-Dynastic cities. With the unification of Egypt the king was at pains to regularize the happy-go-lucky irrigation system of the old days; Nilometers were built and observers attached to them to give due warning of the coming of the annual flood; the king himself performed the ceremony of cutting the dykes, as is shown on the mace-head of Khasekhamui (Pl. 3); a land-registry office in the interests of government taxation measured and counted the fields whose boundaries might have been obliterated by the mud of the inundation; forced labour was imposed on the peasants to dig canals on a more ambitious scale so as to bring into bearing the higher land beyond the reach of the flood waters. But though the once free farmer was now the drilled and regimented serf of the divine Pharaoh, his basic manner of life was but little changed and for him at least social conditions remained the same; Egypt was still an agricultural country of villages and market towns wherein, apart from the temporary capital arbitrarily set up by the dynasty of the time, there were no cities overshadowing the countryside.

MESOPOTAMIA

To Egypt Mesopotamia affords a striking contrast (Map III). Between hills of marl containing salt and gypsum lies a wide plain which in cross-section is absolutely flat and has a seaward slope (1:26,000) only half that of the Nile valley. Of the two rivers which run through the length of the plain the Tigris,

MAP III

on its eastern marge, is of relatively little use for irrigation because it has a deeply-cut bed and the normal level of its waters lies too low beneath that of the surrounding country for the stream to be tapped by any simple system of canalization. The Euphrates it is that makes agriculture possible in a land where the rainfall is as scanty as in Egypt and the climate even less equable, with greater extremes both of heat and of cold.

From its source in the Anatolian mountains down to the rocky barrier below Hit the Euphrates has a violent current (at Carchemish, for instance, it flows at a rate of five miles an hour), and in consequence its turbid waters carry about five times as great a content of sediment—loam mixed with a large proportion of lime—as does the Nile. When it enters the flat alluvium of the delta the current is naturally slowed up and much of the sediment is dropped on to the bed of the river and especially along its edges where the main force of current is less; the bed is raised thereby and high banks are formed on either side, and in time the whole river runs above the level of the plain.[1] Clearly this high-running water can be tapped for the benefit of the fields alongside, and clearly also the natural banks of the river must be maintained and strengthened if those fields are not to be submerged at the wrong time. To cut the bank is only too easy, and the Euphrates' water, like that of the Nile, will not only irrigate but with its silt will enrich the soil; the difficulty in this flat plain is rather to get rid of the superfluous water, which is prone to lie in pools and stagnant swamps and, if it be merely dried out by the sun, impregnate the earth with salts and alkaline compounds which in time will make it barren. Drainage in Mesopotamia is as essential as irrigation.

But the chief difference between the Euphrates and the Nile is in the date of the annual floods. No one can foretell precisely when the Euphrates flood is to be expected, because that depends upon weather conditions in the far-distant mountainous regions of Anatolia, the flood being caused by the melting of the winter snows there. It comes in the late spring, at some time between the beginning of April and early June, and the rise of the waters is sudden. Now from the farmers' point of view no time could be worse than this. Crops must be sown according to the climate, and by April the winter-sown crops are well advanced and the summer crops are in; if at this stage the fields were to be drowned beneath two or three feet of water all hope of a harvest would vanish, and after the flood waters had dried it would be too late for a fresh sowing. In Egypt, Hapi, the god of the inundation, was a beneficent deity by whose help man was able to eat bread; in Mesopotamia the flood was the enemy of man and Nin-Girsu and Tiamat who ruled over the chaos of waters were to that extent malevolent powers. The flood had to be fought, to be kept in check at all costs; some of its waters might indeed be led off to fill the reservoirs or natural depressions on the edge of the higher desert, but the fertility of the country—and it was wonderfully fertile—depended on the river's normal flow when it could be profitably tapped by irrigation canals, and was only endangered by its rise.

The Mesopotamian agriculturalist was compelled by nature to adopt the system of perennial irrigation. Because the river bed was high above the cultivated plain, water could be brought to the latter all through the dry season and he could therefore count on having two harvests in the year ripened by the torrid sun. But against this tremendous advantage was set the colossal amount of labour involved. Because the river ran at a high level, the canals leading from it had also to be high, so as to obviate a too-sudden rush of water, seeing that such would tend to destroy the canals, built as they were of fine light silt (sometimes it was thought worth while to strengthen the canal banks with layers of reed matting, as was more often done in the case of the river banks); and since distances had to be great and the wastage of water was considerable, size was an important consideration, and the main canals therefore might be as much as 25 yards in width, navigable channels making inland voyages possible and so facilitating transport as well as irrigating the soil. From the main channels smaller canals and ditches distributed the water; but again there had to be drainage canals which served the further purpose of cleaning the soil by washing out the superfluity of salt deposited with the silt.

All this meant not only a vast amount of manual labour but also an elaborate organization. It was not a case of a peasant watering his own smallholding; individual work of that sort was possible only in the immediate vicinity of the river and would have limited agriculture to a narrow strip of soil doomed to be destroyed by the flood. If any reasonable area was to be cultivated, water had to be carried far inland, and only communal labour could achieve the task. A network of subsidiary canals had to be planned which would ensure an equal distribution of water over the largest possible extent of arable land. Constant supervision was necessary to prevent one landowner exploiting the canal-borne water to the detriment of his neighbours. There had to be due authority for enforcing and directing labour (the *corvée*) to build the canals in the first place, to clean them when, as happened very quickly, they were choked with silt, and, above all, to prevent the breaching of the Euphrates' banks in flood-time. The Mesopotamian delta held out to early man the promise of a better and a richer life than could be found in any neighbouring land, but it was a conditional promise; its fulfilment required a co-operative effort and a centralization of control quite beyond the scope of a village community. The very nature of the country and of the river forced the inhabitants to make common cause throughout a territory whose size was decided by the limits of an interdependent canalization system, and the planning and upkeep of the canals required the direction of a regional authority enjoying absolute powers. By the mere logic of circumstances the Euphrates delta was from the outset parcelled out into a number of agricultural-irrigational units each having its own centre of administration, and the development of the city state was due not to the peculiar mentality of the Sumerian people but to the physical character of Sumer.

The surplus production of foodstuffs leads almost inevitably to occupational distinctions, the non-agriculturalist following his natural bent in manufacturing something that is in general demand and exchanging his handiwork for the food produced by others, and this specialization leads to distinctions of class. In the most primitive communities we are likely to find an 'intellectual' minority enjoying a more or less privileged ascendancy over the 'labouring' classes, and as the 'professions' become more sharply differentiated from each other and from the workers on the soil there must result a social organism in which functions are regularized and there is an admitted system of government.[2] But while such development is essential to the urbanization of a society, it is not the sole condition; by itself it does not necessarily lead to the growth of cities or the birth of the civic spirit. In Egypt class distinctions were at least as sharply defined as they were in Mesopotamia, but in the manner and degree of urbanization the contrast between the two countries is profound.

SUMER

The Elamitic farmers who, as immigrants into the drying delta of the Euphrates, introduced there the al'Ubaid culture, brought with them a common religion. But each family or clan seems to have selected from the general pantheon one particular god or goddess to be its patron deity. As in ever greater degree the conditions of agricultural life in the valley enforced co-operation and centralization within each irrigation unit, there developed a non-labouring intellectual class to assume the direction of the communized body; something in the nature of an official hierarchy took shape, and the particular deity under whose protection the leaders of the community rose to power became *ex officio* the god of the community. The Sumerian mythology makes this perfectly clear when it says that the supreme council of the gods parcelled out the land into states each of which was assigned to one of the gods as his kingdom, and these in turn selected each a mortal ruler to be his representative; although this might seem to reverse the actual order of things yet it does in fact emphasize the underlying truth that different gods accompanied the groups of immigrants and that the area chosen for the settlement of each was the seat of its god's rule. The fact that all the gods belonged to a pantheon recognized by all the settlers alike guaranteed a uniformity which entitles us to treat of Sumer, from the cultural point of view, as a whole. On the other hand, the fact that individual gods of the pantheon were the divinely appointed owners of their territories guaranteed the autonomy of the Sumerian city states. A god might temporarily be reduced by the armies of a neighbouring god to a condition of vassalage, but he could not be deprived of his kingdom; for his own subjects he was still the city's lord.

If then the rise of the Sumerian city states was the logical outcome of economic conditions, their identity was perpetuated by the sanction of religion. As they all shared common traditions and conformed to one general pattern the establishment by an ambitious and warlike ruler of a dynasty claiming suzerainty over all alike did not seriously affect their individuality; such conquest involved no cultural change, and nothing would dispossess the local god of his authority, neither did enforced submission call for any wider loyalty. From first to last the Sumerian was essentially a citizen; he was not a Sumerian national but a citizen of this or that capital city, owing allegiance only to the city's divine lord and, in due measure, to his human representative; his entire way of life and his outlook were dictated by the conditions of a city state.

A Sumerian city state might include various townships, but these, however important in their own eyes, were politically but the satellites of the capital city. Thus Eridu, which claimed to be the earliest Sumerian foundation and, as the centre of the cult of Ea, enjoyed peculiar sanctity, formed part of the domains of Ur and had no separate political existence; indeed, if we may judge from its remains, it survived only as a religious institution. The political and economic administration of the state was centred in the capital.

It is only against the background of the city itself that the culture and character of the citizens can be understood. While the later chapters of this history will have much to say regarding the religion that formed the basis of Sumerian citizenship, the type of government and the system of law under which the Sumerian lived and the professions and industries that he followed, his material surroundings must also be taken into consideration.

The most detailed and accurate picture of a great Sumerian city is given by the ruins of Ur. As a capital city, at one time the headquarters of a dynasty, Ur answers our purpose better than would a provincial town such as Eshnunna; excavations there have been on a larger scale than elsewhere and so give more material for judgement. The Isin-Larsa period (*c.* 1700 BC), to which belong the remains most consistently preserved, still kept the tradition of the Third Dynasty of Ur and was a time of great prosperity though no longer of imperial power; and work upon other sites makes it clear that Ur was in all essentials typical of the Sumerian state capitals from the Persian Gulf right up to Mari on the middle Euphrates.

Ur consisted of three parts, the Temenos or Sacred Area, the old walled city, and the outer town.

The walled city (Fig. 4) stood on the mound formed by the ruins of successive buildings set up on the site of the original settlement of al'Ubaid days; along its western wall ran the river Euphrates, along its eastern wall a broad navigable canal which led off from the Euphrates just above the city, so that this in fact occupied the northern tip of a land promontory, and at its extreme northern end, inside the line

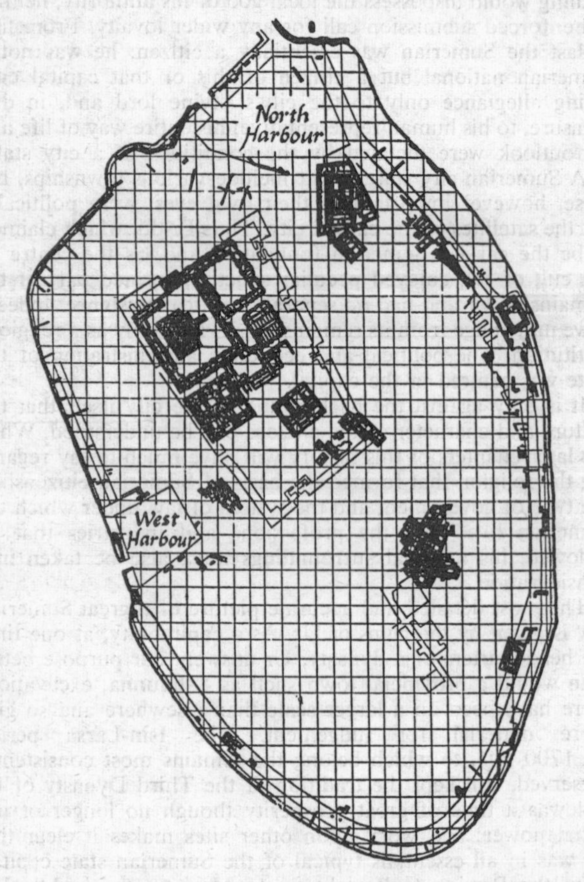

FIG. 4. *Ur: the walled city.*

of its walls, there was a harbour serving both canal and river; it is possible that in the time of the Third Dynasty of Ur a smaller canal ran right through the city from the harbour and turned westwards to rejoin the Euphrates. The city was in shape an irregular oval, with a maximum length of approximately three-quarters of a mile and a width of half a mile; it was surrounded by a huge rampart of mud-brick some 25 feet high, with a steeply sloping outer face, and along the top of this *glacis* King Ur-Nammu of the Third Dynasty built in burnt brick a great wall of defence 'like a mountain'; that wall had been razed when the Elamites destroyed the city and, in the eighteenth century, had been replaced by a continuous line of temples and private houses whose blank outer walls made a more normal bulwark.[3]

In the north-western quarter of the city was Temenos. The whole of this was really the palace complex of Nannar, the Moon god who was the owner of the city state. It was a rectangular enclosure which in Ur-Nammu's day (it was enlarged subsequently) measured about 270 yards by 190; it was raised as an artificial terrace above the general ground-level of the city and was girt with a massive wall of mud-brick; in its west corner, on a higher terrace also heavily walled, rose the Ziggurat, the huge staged tower, 68 feet high, capped by the shrine which was the holy of holies, the dwelling-place of Nannar himself. In front of the Ziggurat, at a lower level, stretched a great courtyard surrounded by storerooms and offices to which were brought the offerings for sacrifice and the rents due from the tenants who farmed the god's lands; the rest of the Temenos was entirely filled with temples—each furnished with its offices and magazines—dedicated to Nannar and his wife Nin-gal, to Nin-gal alone and, again, to Nannar as the supreme judge. This walled complex was the core of the city. Inasmuch as the state was a theocracy, the Sacred Area was the administrative centre, and its tax offices and court of law would directly influence the lives of the individual citizens, but much more important was its psychological effect. The Ziggurat, with its terraces planted with trees to give point to its name 'the Hill of Heaven', dominated the entire city, and 15 or 20 miles away across the dead level of the plain the farmer looking up from his work in field or garden would see that towering shrine which was the actual dwelling-place of the god his master. It was impossible not to be continually aware of the divine presence. It was true that the temples owned a vast proportion of the land and engaged in business of all sorts, and that the priesthood formed a large part of the personnel of government, and these and like material proofs of theocracy might at times seem oppressive, aimed at human aggrandizement rather than at religious service; but such impatience and such doubts could not stand against the assurance given by the Temenos sky-line, where the stepped-up roofs of temple and government office seemed to be but a pedestal designed to support the unique glory of Nannar's house;

God's in his heaven,
All's right with the world.

This is the sentiment that finds expression in the hymns and lamentations of the Sumerian poets, and nothing less will explain the fervent patriotism of the state's citizens.

The palaces of the earthly king, judging from what was true at Ur in the days of the Third Dynasty, lay outside the Temenos proper, on a somewhat lower platform built against the Temenos wall. When that dynasty came to an end the site, together with that of the royal tomb chapels, was soon usurped for private houses, because ground-space in the walled city was far too valuable for a large central area to be left unoccupied for long.

While the Temenos was strictly reserved for the service of the city's patron god, other deities of the pantheon had temples set up in their honour both in the walled city and in the outer town. These might be large and imposing buildings, but they lacked altogether the dignified seclusion of the Sacred Area; they were closely hemmed about by the houses of the townsmen. The congestion within the walls was indeed remarkable. If the residential quarters excavated at Ur give, as presumably they do, a fair sample of the city as a whole, we see something that has grown out of the conditions of the primitive village, not laid out on any system of town planning (Fig. 5). The unpaved streets are narrow and winding, sometimes mere blind alleys leading to houses hidden away in the middle of a great block of haphazard buildings; large houses and small are jumbled together, a few of them flat-roofed tenements one storey high, most of them of two storeys and a few, apparently, of three. Lanes sheltered by awnings and lined with open booths correspond to the bazaars of a modern Middle Eastern town. Wedged in between the houses there were little public chapels dedicated by pious citizens to the minor deities.

The houses themselves (Fig. 6), however much they might differ in size, were built to a plan which, though it might be modified to adapt it to the irregularities of the ground-plot, was

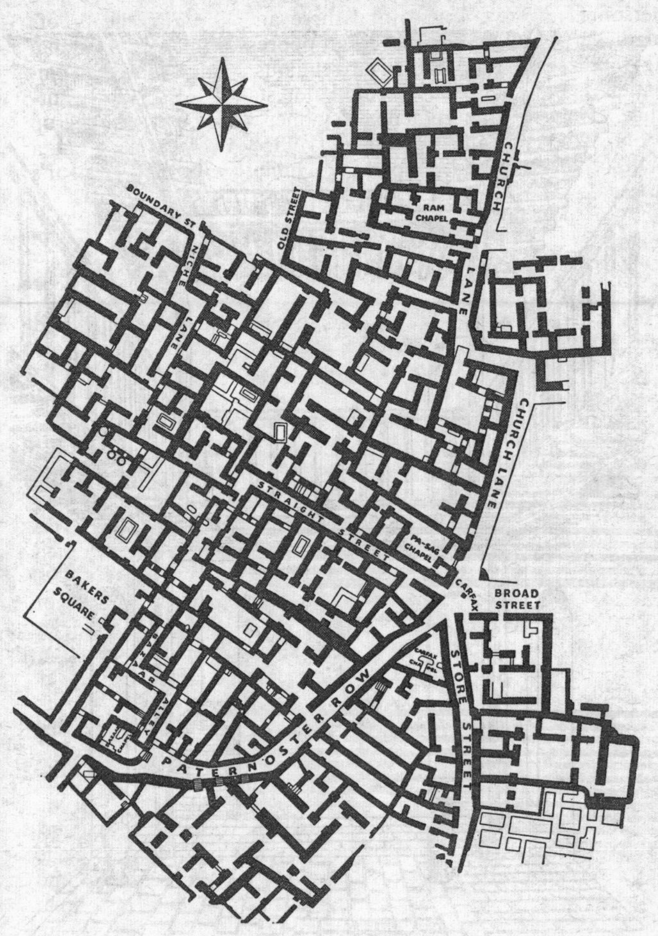

FIG. 5. *Ur: plan of residential area.*

in all essentials uniform. The façades were generally of burnt brick up to the height of the first-floor ceiling, and above that of mud-brick; for interior walls the proportion of burnt brick was optional, reduced sometimes to a mere damp-course, sometimes carried up to a height of five or six feet; doorways were most often topped with flat lintels but were occasionally arched. The basic plan was that of a house built round a

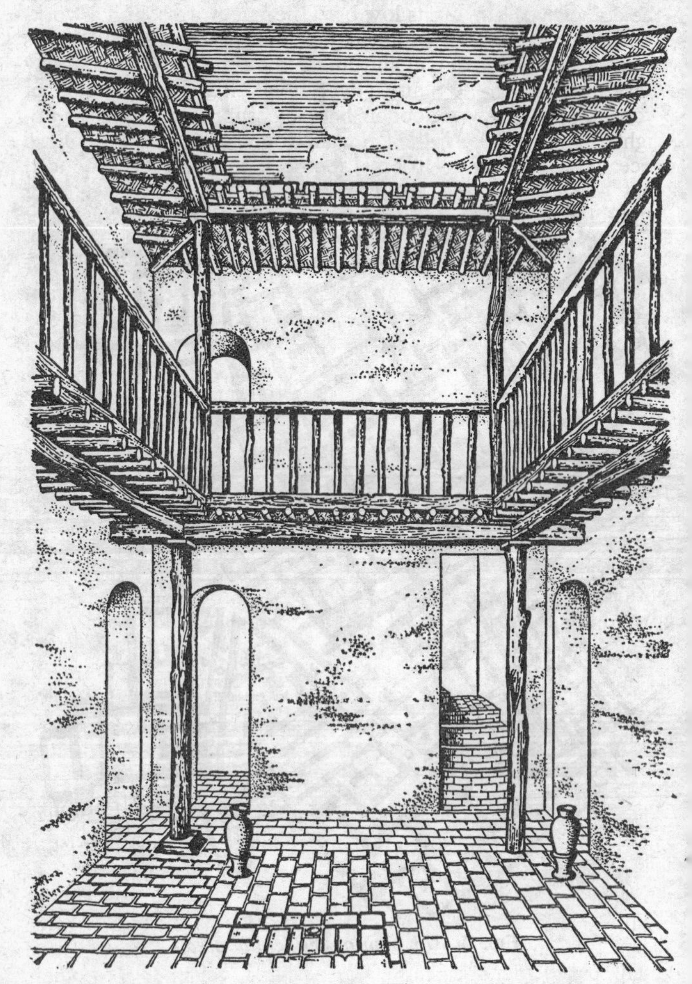

FIG. 6. *Ur: reconstruction of a private house.*

central courtyard. The street door led into a small lobby through which one passed into the court. On to this opened the ground-floor rooms, the guest-room at the back of the court, the kitchen and service-room, the sleeping-room for the domestic staff with its low brick bed-platforms, and a work-room; one doorway contained the bottom flight of the stairs going to the upper floor, and under the return of the stairway was a lavatory. The stairs (their upper flight constructed of wood) gave on to a wooden balcony, supported by four uprights at the angles, which ran all round the court and gave access to the first-floor rooms, whose arrangement reproduced that of those on the ground floor; the house roof, sloping slightly inwards, projected from the walls sufficiently to shelter the balcony, and left in the middle a large opening that gave light and air to the house; gutters projecting from the roof shot rainwater into the centre of the court, where was a drain intake and a sump-pit. At the back of the house proper was the domestic chapel and burial-vault of which a description is given in Chapter VIII.

Houses like these, very much more sophisticated than the one-storeyed houses of a provincial town such as Eshnunna in the Sargonid period (Fig. 7) are quite obviously the result of a long process of urbanization in which the interests of the individual citizen were never unduly subordinated to the discipline of the state. If the ground-plan is more or less stereotyped that is not because the government dictated a norm but because this was the plan best adapted to the climatic conditions of the country and to the ideals of family life of the people—as is amply proved by the fact that an identical plan, even in its details, is followed by the better-class Arab houses of Baghdad and Basra at the present day. Documents found in the houses showed that they were the homes not of wealthy aristocrats but of people in the middle and lower middle classes, merchants, shopkeepers, tradesmen of all sorts, and occasionally a priest or scribe; clearly the material benefits of a fairly advanced civilization were shared by a far greater proportion of society in Sumer than was the case in Egypt. Undoubtedly there were slum quarters; to the north-west of the Temenos there were one-storey houses of a very shoddy type, but these may quite possibly have been for the slaves attached to the temple services; excavation in one area of the outer town seemed to show that there were there artisans' quarters where men practising the same trades lived together: but their houses were little if at all inferior to those of the walled city.

Regarding the population of Ur only a rough estimate is possible. The old cities of Aleppo and Damascus, at the beginning of the present century, counted about 160 persons to the acre; in both there were included large open spaces, and

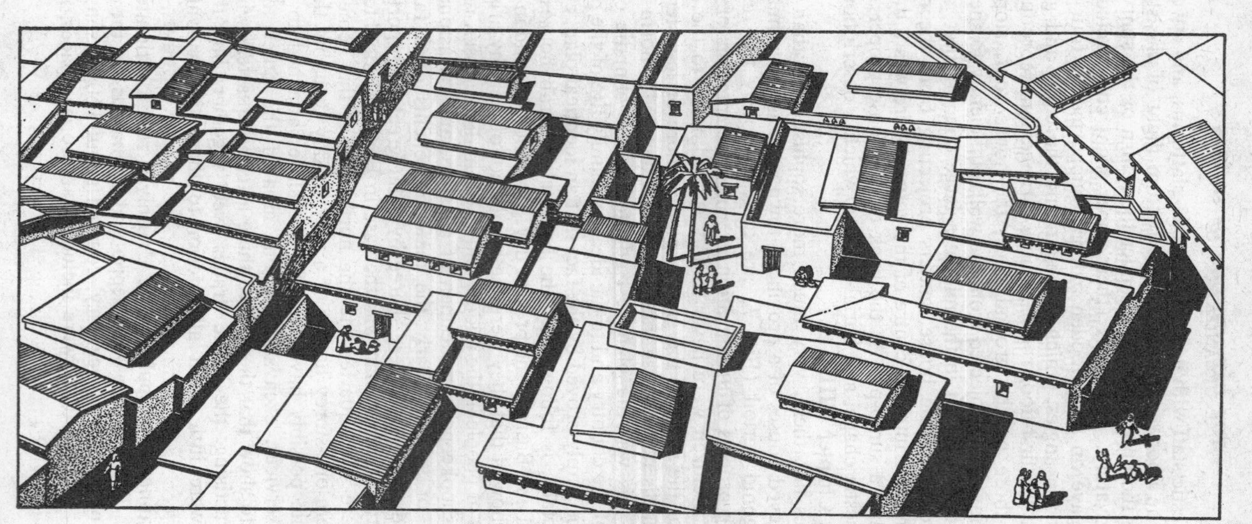

FIG. *1. Restoration of Eshnunna in the time of Sargon (after Frankfort).*

the great majority of the houses were of one storey only and often took up a liberal ground-space. Professor Frankfort found that at Khafaje, in the time of Sargon of Akkad, the one-storey houses (the rooms built round not an open court but a central room rising above the rest and lit by clerestory windows) averaged about 2,750 square feet in area and were about twenty per acre; allowing six to ten occupants for each house he arrived at a figure of 120 to 200 persons per acre and a total population of 12,000; a similar calculation gave him a population of only 9,000 for Eshnunna in the Isin-Larsa period. Both of these were small provincial towns.[4] When, in the ninth century BC, Assur-nasi-paí celebrated the completion of his new royal city of Calah by a banquet to all the residents, the number of guests (including officials and foreigners) was 69,574, of whom the residents proper would be no less than 65,000; although some women were invited (presumably those who had been employed on the palace building) we must add to this number the bulk of the women and all the children and the slaves in domestic service, which would, roughly speaking, more than double the number of the guests. The area of Calah is about 884 acres, which would give some 150 persons to the acre, a very close approximation to the figures for Aleppo and Damascus; but it is known that the walls of Calah included open spaces, gardens and farms and orchards; moreover, as an artificial and non-commercial city it could hardly be expected to have a very large population. The approximate area of the really built-up part of Ur, excluding wide stretches where there are signs of occupation but occupation of a scattered sort, is 1,450 acres, which on the analogies cited above would give a population of about a quarter of a million. On the other hand, open spaces at Ur seem to have been few; in the excavated parts of the residential area the density of houses works out at about 44 to the acre, two-storey houses predominating; and an allowance of six persons (including slaves and children) per house would give more than 250 to the acre, i.e. a total for the city of 360,000 souls.

Although Ur, like the other Sumerian cities, started as the administrative centre of an irrigated district, no purely agricultural economy could have led to the growth or maintained the existence of anything like the population which even our more modest estimate suggests. The farming of the rich delta plain was, of course, more important than ever when so many mouths had to be fed, and the ultimate dependence of the city upon its home-grown food was proved when, at a much later date, the river Euphrates changed its course, the whole elaborate system of irrigation was hopelessly dislocated and, in consequence, Ur was abandoned by its citizens. But in the prosperous days of the Third Dynasty, and in the Larsa period, industry and commerce played a bigger part than agriculture and occupied a greater number of people; the owners of the houses excavated at Ur may, some of them, have had a garden or an orchard out in the country, but they were business men first and foremost. Some of the capitals of Sumerian city states, less well situated than Ur for trade and manufacture, may have retained rather the character of the market town; but the Sumerian civilization was pre-eminently an urban civilization and, since commerce and industry were the concern of the ordinary citizen and called for individual enterprise, that civilization permeated society far more deeply than was the case in Egypt and assumed a democratic complexion of which the Nilotic civilization showed no trace at all.

EGYPT

The city states of Sumer had no analogy in Egypt; nothing of the kind was ever known there. The nomes or administrative areas into which the country was divided in historic times undoubtedly had their origin in the pre-Dynastic period, when they were distinguished by standards which seem to imply that they were territorial divisions corresponding to the localized worship of different gods. The nature of the Nile valley and the type of irrigation used there did not lead to the formation of such economic units as explain the development of the Sumerian city state; it is more likely that the existence of temples possessing wide estates and the emergence of a limited number of wealthy landowners tended to give to different areas a certain measure of individuality; and it can safely be assumed that those areas, the nomes, were adopted, if not created from the first, for purposes of government administration. When Egypt was unified by Menes the delta was already 'the Northern Kingdom' and the conqueror took over from his rival the badge of the papyrus tuft and the Red Crown which were the symbols of Lower Egypt as a whole; he had in fact acquired not a congeries of small states but an organized kingdom of which the nomes were but the provinces. Naturally, he maintained the old system. He built a new capital, the White Wall, probably at Memphis, as the seat of the central government, but for the control of the provinces his officials had to be installed in provincial areas, and the market towns which each nome must have possessed would again serve the purpose. But this was not a step towards urbanization. The provincial governments were merely branches of the central government, and this very fact ruled out the possibility of any political and civic development. Even when the central power lost control, as when the collapse of the Sixth Dynasty involved the whole land in anarchy, the internecine wars were waged not by cities asserting their freedom but by ambitious monarchs and landed nobles seeking their private advantage.

Again, although the nucleus of each nome may have been a temple and the temple estates, religion did not operate in Egypt, as in Sumer, towards the creation of a local loyalty; the local god might and did own territory, but he was in no sense a king. Egypt's theocracy was of a totally different sort from that of Sumer; instead of the earthly ruler being but the chosen representative and the 'tenant farmer' of the sovereign deity, Pharaoh was himself a god, and his government was divine simply because it was Pharaoh's. The other gods did not and could not dispute his authority. To whatever deity of the Egyptian pantheon the local temple might be dedicated yet Pharaoh's statues adorned it and, as likely as not, the reliefs on its walls celebrated Pharaoh's exploits; the religious motive therefore tended to promote centralization rather than to assert local individuality or autonomy.

Egypt was one and indivisible. The government of the divine Pharaoh legislated for the country as a whole, indiscriminately and arbitrarily. The Egyptian, in consequence, as a creature of Pharaoh, was consciously an Egyptian—this comes out very clearly in, for instance, the story of Sinuhe[5]—but he was never a citizen. The lack of any civic tradition is shown by the manner in which the capital was shifted from one place to another to suit the tastes or the habits of a new dynasty; but not even in the capital, for all its magnificence, was there any real civic life.

The Egyptian towns (Map IV) were normally unwalled. Amenemhet III built a great wall round the old city of el Kab (it is still standing) but this seems to have been an innovation; it was possibly after the pattern of the Syrian cities that the Pharaoh thus singularly honoured what had been the capital of the southern kingdom before Menes united Egypt. Professor Flinders Petrie thought that he found remains of a town wall on the old site of Naqada, and on a pre-Dynastic vase there is painted the picture of a wall manned by soldiers—but this is as likely to be a fort as a town. Civil war was rare in Egypt, and armed invasion by foreigners was rarer still, so

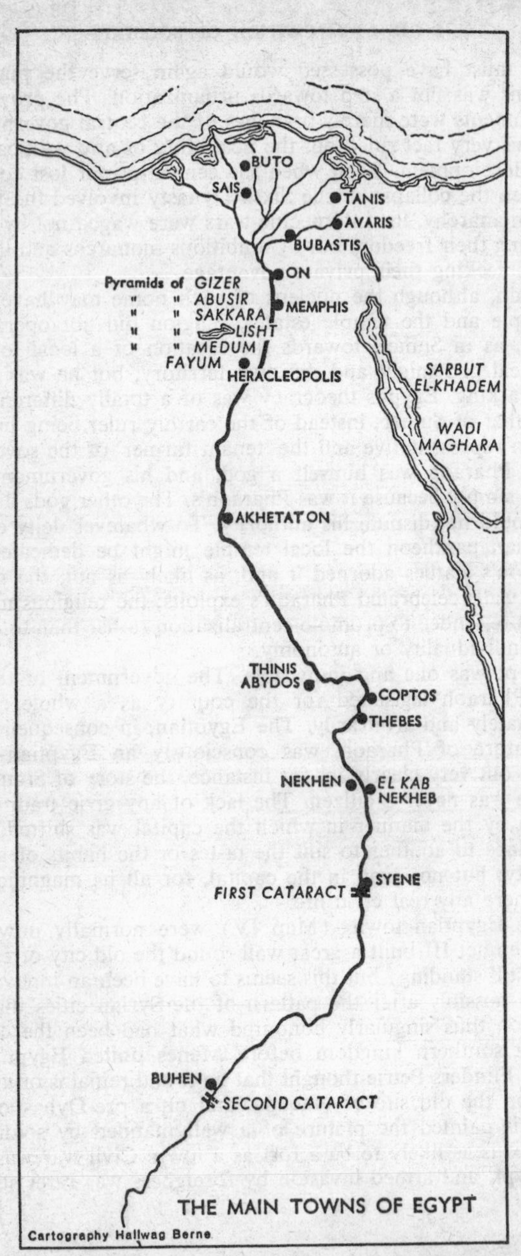
BUTO
SAIS
TANIS
AVARIS
BUBASTIS
ON
Pyramids of GIZER
" " ABUSIR
" " SAKKARA
" " LISHT
" " MEDUM
MEMPHIS
FAYUM
HERACLEOPOLIS
SARBUT
EL-KHADEM
WADI
MAGHARA
AKHETATON
THINIS
ABYDOS
COPTOS
THEBES
NEKHEN
EL KAB
NEKHEB
SYENE
FIRST CATARACT
BUHEN
SECOND CATARACT
THE MAIN TOWNS OF EGYPT
Cartography Hallwag Berne

MAP IV

(a) [U.M.

1 (a) *Warka, the Palace, mosaic columns. Berlin, Vorderasiatisches Museum*

(b) *Mundigak, Afghanistan: the Palace showing the half-columns and the stepped merlons*

(b) [Casal

(a)

(b)

(c)

2

(a) *Kherbet Kerak pottery. Ankara, Archaeological Museum*

(b) *Cretan Kamares pottery found in Egypt. Oxford, Ashmolean Museum*

(c) *Shang ceremonial vessel in bronze, twelfth century B.C. Washington, D.C., Freer Gallery of Arts*

[Smithsonian

3 *Khasekhamui opening a canal. Mace-head. Oxford, Ashmolean Museum*

[E.E.S.

4 *Tell el Amarna: interior of a house, central hall, (reconstruction)*

(a) [D.A.E.

5 (a) *Sudanese troops of the Egyptian army*
(b) *The 'standard' of Ur. London, British Museum*

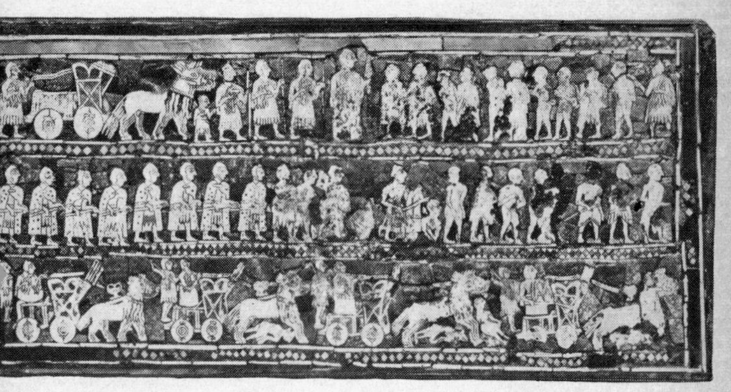

(b) [B.M.

[photo Chuzeville

6 (a) *The 'Stele of the Vultures.' Paris, Louvre*

(b) *The Naram-Sin stele. Paris, Louvre*
[*photo Chuzeville*

(a) [Thesiger

7 *Reed hut building in Southern Iraq*

(a) *the basic structure*
(b) *the completed building*

(b) [Thesiger

(a) [B.M.

8

(a) *Warka: stone trough, London, British Museum*
(b) *Khafajeh, Iraq: Mehi-type vase*
(c) *North Syrian half-timber and brick construction*

(b) [O.I.

(c) [I.A.

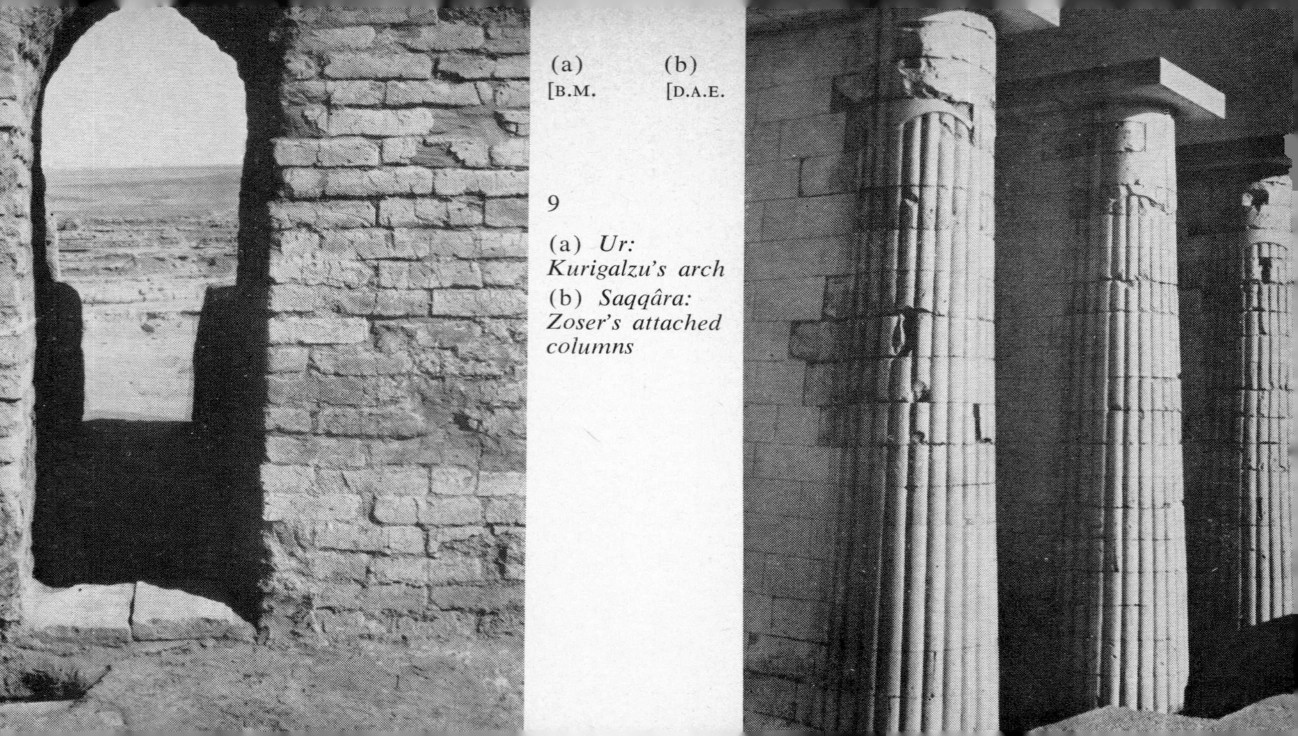

(a) [B.M. (b) [D.A.E.

9

(a) *Ur: Kurigalzu's arch*
(b) *Saqqâra: Zoser's attached columns*

(c) [H.M.

(c) *Crete: Palace of Minos, tapered columns*

(a)

[I.D.A.

10 *Sumerian goldsmith's work:*

(a) *dagger discovered at Ur, Third Early Dynastic Period*

(b) *gold tumbler and bowl. Philadelphia, University Museum*

(b)

[Penna

(a) [B.M.

(b)

[D.A.E.

11

(a) *Al'Ubaid: recumbent copper heifer. c. 2600 B.C. London, British Museum*

(b) *Dahshur, Egypt: pectoral of Amenemhet III*

(c) *Egyptian polychrome glass bottles of the Eighteenth Dynasty. London, British Museum*

(c) [B.M.

[H.M.

12 *Cretan pottery*

photo Josephine Powell

[E.H.M

[B.M.

[H.M.

13

Indus Valley civilization: painted pottery. Burial jars from Mohenjo-daro Cemetery H

that the need for walled defences would be little felt—the walled city of Avaris was, of course, a Hyksos and not an Egyptian foundation. Generally speaking, the Egyptian town was open, and also small in size. It must be remembered that from first to last the Egyptian economy was based on agriculture. The vast bulk of the people lived and worked on the land. They required a market where they could barter their produce for what they could not themselves make; the town must have shopkeepers and craftsmen of the humbler sort, and there would be the government officials and the priests attached to the local temple; but there were no big industries and no large-scale commerce to swell the population or to give rise to a responsible middle class; there was nothing that called for the urban organization proper to a city.

Although based on entirely different economic principles, social conditions throughout the Egyptian countryside must have been very much the same in the second millennium BC as in the nineteenth century AD, with an essentially rural population content to stagnate in villages and small towns, the administration being entirely in the hands of functionaries appointed by and responsible only to the central government. But even in the capital, where were concentrated all the elements of Egyptian civilization, there seems to have been little in the way of a municipal organization to attract the loyalty of the inhabitants or to give them the personal interest in the running of affairs which is essential to the civic spirit. The capital was the home of Pharaoh, and everything led up to him. The gradual hierarchy of officialdom culminated in the person of the ruler; that, of course, was but natural. But the artists also and the skilled craftsmen of all sorts were literally in the service of Pharaoh; the best of them, together with the minor officials, did form a middle class such as was virtually non-existent in the provinces, but it was a middle class entirely dependent upon the royal court.

Excavation has told us very little about any Egyptian capital other than Akhetaton (Tell el Amarna), and conditions were not necessarily always the same. Thus we know that at Thebes, where ground-space was valuable, there were buildings of two storeys, whereas at Akhetaton, built *ab initio* on a virgin site, houses were laid out on a generous scale (Fig. 8) and had no upper storeys, no more than a light loggia on the flat roof; but as men's ideals of domestic comfort are shaped largely by tradition Tell el Amarna may well illustrate the Egyptian norm.

The unwalled town straggles for about five miles along the Nile bank, with a width varying from half a mile to a mile.

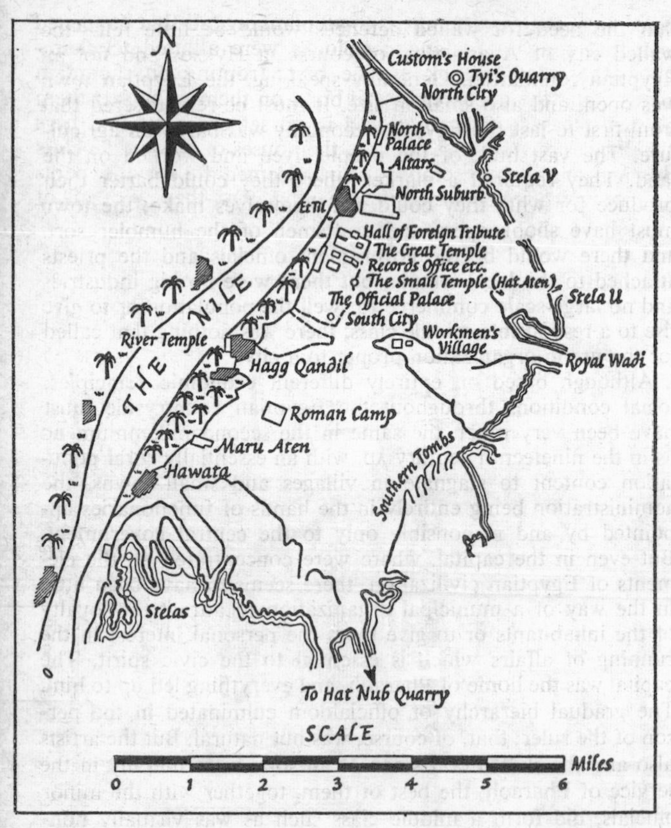

FIG. 8. *Tell el Amarna: plan of the city (after Pendlebury).*

There is no wall, no 'inner city' and no sacred Temenos. The temples, royal palaces and offices of state, which together take up a large proportion of the town's area, are not concentrated in a single quarter but are sited almost at random, so that, while there is a main central group which includes the vast Temple of the Sun's Disk, the official Palace, the Hall of Foreign Tribute and the Secretariat, the Northern Palace is a mile and a half away from it and the pleasure park of Maru-Aten is three and a half miles to the south. Apart from the fact that there were two main streets running parallel to the river there was no attempt at town planning; all that happened was that roughly rectangular blocks were allotted to claimants—the wealthy took up the best, fronting on the main roads—and the occupiers could build on them or sub-let them as they pleased; juxtaposed and in no set order we find here the palaces of the court nobility, the houses of the middle-class burgher and the miserable cabins deemed fit for the poor.

The typical middle-class house (Fig. 9)—they were all of

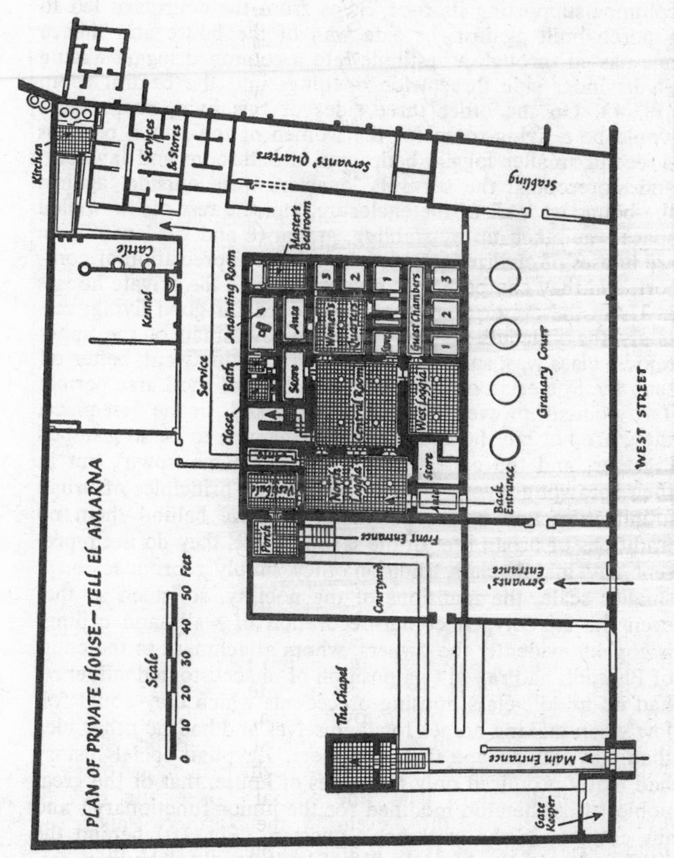

FIG. 9. *Tell el Amarna: restoration of a typical house plan (after Pendlebury).*

one general type—lay in the centre of a walled enclosure entered by a single gateway on the street. Facing the entry there would be a small domestic chapel in which might be placed a stele showing Akhenaton worshipping the sun's disk —a guarantee of the family's orthodoxy. The house proper, built throughout of mud-brick except perhaps for a stone frame for the front door, was built round a central living-room whose walls rose well above the roofs of the surrounding chambers and had clerestory windows to light it and four wooden columns supporting its roof. Steps from the courtyard led to a porch built against the side wall of the house and thence one passed through a vestibule into a columned loggia having on its inner side three wide openings into the central room (Pl. 4). On the other three sides of this living-room there would be a living-room for the women of the house, perhaps a second smaller loggia, bedrooms, a bathroom and lavatory, and storerooms; the servants' quarters were outside, against the boundary wall of the enclosure, and the rest of the walled space was taken up by stabling, granaries and gardens. These are houses of civilized people with a keen appreciation of comfort, and they compare very favourably with the private houses at Ur in the opportunity that they afford for good living; certainly the sixteenth-century Egyptian townsman of the upper middle class was, so far as his domestic setting went, better off than the Sumerian or Akkadian merchant of the Larsa period. Two points, however, have to be remarked. In the first place, these are not city houses at all; they happen to be so grouped together, and the collection justifies the name 'town', but in their sprawling layout they violate the first principles of urban architecture and it is clear that they have behind them no traditions of urban life. In the second place, they do not represent any middle-class tradition; they simply reproduce, on a smaller scale, the mansions of the nobility, so much so that even the stereotyped colour-decoration of walls and ceilings is copied; evidently the owners, whom attachment to the court of Pharaoh had raised to a position of unaccustomed affluence, had no middle-class housing precedents which they could follow when making homes for themselves and had no other idea than slavishly to ape their superiors. Egyptian social history had really produced only two types of house, that of the great noble (at Akhetaton modified for the junior functionary) and the cottage. In the workmen's quarters (Fig. 10) behind the big houses, in the 'model village' built for the labourers employed upon the tombs to the east of the town, and again in

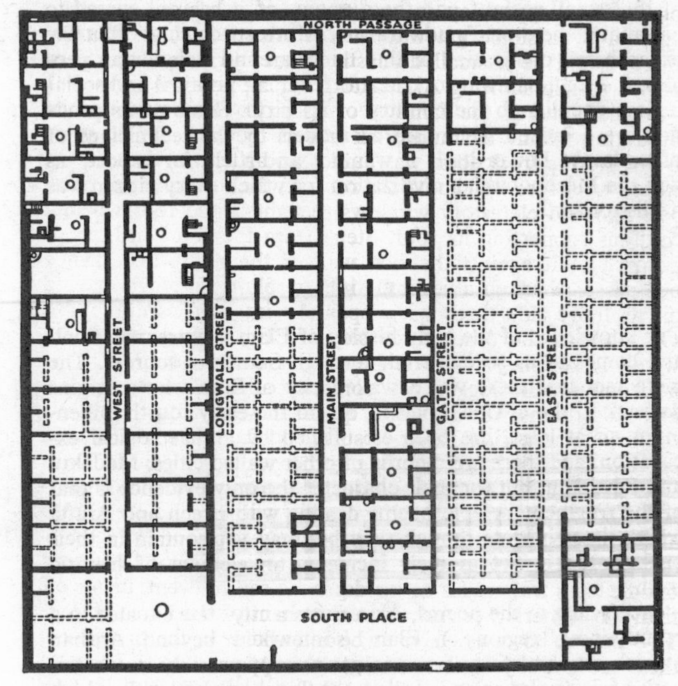

FIG. 10. *Tell el Amarna: workmen's quarters.*

the houses of the clerks near the Records Office there are monotonous rows of identical hovels containing each an entrance-hall, a living-room, a bedroom and a kitchen which the working man shared with his wife and children and perhaps with his animals also; they are like slave lines, and since they reproduce almost exactly the quarters provided for workmen at Lahun in the Twelfth Dynasty it would appear that five centuries of civilization had done nothing to ameliorate the living conditions of the Egyptian proletariat.

Civilization in Egypt did not result from any process of urbanization properly so called, for Egypt was never urbanized, never developed the material city or the civic life; it was a court civilization. The regimentation of the entire populace for the benefit of a limited social class, that of the Pharaoh and his favoured circle, produced the conditions in which the arts could flourish and find ample scope within the confines of that small society, and the outcome of it has not ceased to command the world's admiration. More spectacular than the broad-based civilization of the Sumerian and Babylonian peoples, the Egyptian was inseparable from the political and social régime peculiar to the country of its birth. Some of its products were indeed welcomed as models by the technicians of other lands, but in itself it was not an article for export,[6] as was the Mesopotamian civilization for which every citizen was a missionary.

ELAM

Our knowledge of the early history of Elam is extremely small and comes to us secondhand, through Sumerian sources. The mere fact that there was a walled city of Susa whose origins go back to the al'Ubaid period, i.e. to the early fourth millennium BC at least, has been established by archaeological excavation, and there are records of other walled cities, Madaktu and Khaidalu; but for their character the only evidence is that of the fragmentary epic poems dealing with Erech and Aratta which, later in date though they be, may yet contain in their background if not in their incidents an element of historic truth.

According to the poems, Aratta was a city state situated in a mountainous region of Elam, somewhere beyond Anshan (which one had to traverse to get there), possibly in what is now Láristan. Its ruler is called not 'king' but by a title which may mean 'high priest', and we hear of an assembly of Elders and of 'knights' and 'supervisors', but the real monarch of the city is the Sumerian goddess Inanna who 'has placed the crown on the head of the Lord of Aratta'. This certainly suggests a theocratic government organized on much the same lines as the city states of Sumer; moreover, the people are represented as worshipping the gods of the Sumerian pantheon, and, yet more surprising, the king of Erech claims political suzerainty over this far-off Elamite state. Even if the fact that one of the epics gives to the Lord of Aratta the Sumerian name Ensurkushsiranna does not warrant the conclusion that the ruling caste consisted of Sumerians, yet it seems safe to assume that Elam was early, in the third millennium, divided into city states formed on the Sumerian model, and that these were, culturally and sometimes politically, very much under the influence of Sumer. Sargon of Akkad, and his son Manishtusu, fought against Elam and reduced it to subjection, but an Elamite governor of Susa, who had been appointed to his post by Naram-Sin, started by aggrandizing himself through the conquest of northern Iranian tribes such as the Guti and finally revolted and made himself independent. The northerners, the Guti and the Lullubi, then asserted themselves; but the few monuments left by their kings—rock reliefs—show that their culture was largely derivative, inspired by Sumerian or Akkadian models, and their written language is Akkadian. In the middle of the third millennium the Guti sacked Babylon and made themselves masters of the delta country and also, it would seem, of Elam; but they were barbarous masters, quite incapable of organizing the territories which they overran. Indeed, the city states appear to have retained their individual identity up to the close of the millennium, for the kings of the Third Dynasty of Ur dealt with them piecemeal and make no mention of a united Elam; on the contrary, there are records of rulers of different Elamite cities, Susa, Ashnunnak, etc., who had the title of *patesi* (*ensi*) and must therefore have held office from the kings of Ur of the Third Dynasty,[7] and Bur-Sin is shown by tablets found at Susa to have been in undisturbed possession of that city while other Elamite cities—presumably city states—had to be forcibly subjugated. But that the dynastic principle which prompted so many attempts to unify Sumer operated in Elam also appears to be proved by what is narrated of the downfall of the Third Dynasty; the destruction of Ur is attributed not to this or that Elamite state but to 'the Elamites'; the cult statue of Nannar was carried off to Anshan, but the victor (probably Kudur-nankhundi) was king not of Anshan but of Elam. Hammurabi of Babylon, after a long series of campaigns, defeated the Elamites, but when, a hundred years later, Shutruk-nakhkhunte re-established the kingdom of Elam there is no sign of originality other than a revival of the Proto-Elamitic script. Of the history of the following centuries nothing is known, but when, towards the end of the period dealt with in this book, a vigorous dynasty revived the glories of the past, the cultural dependence of Elam on Mesopotamia was still evident; the bronze statue of Napirasu, queen of one of the first rulers of the thirteenth-century dynasty, is technically a fine piece of work, but so far as style is concerned it might as well have been made at Babylon as at Susa.

Granted that the al'Ubaid culture was largely derived from Elam it must yet be acknowledged that the early promise given by painted pottery of Susa seems to have found no fulfilment in the country's later history. Our knowledge is certainly slight and discontinuous; there are long periods of utter darkness, so far as archaeology is concerned, and literary evidence is seldom

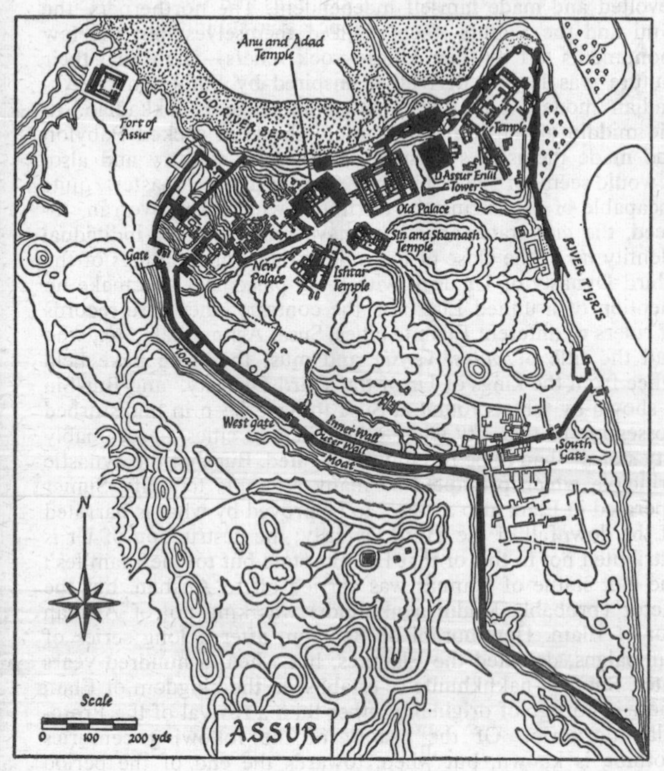

FIG. 11. *Assur: general plan (after Andrae).*

forthcoming. On the whole it would seem that social conditions in Elam were not unlike those of Sumer and Babylon, and that, in general, the part played by Elam in promoting advance in hither Asia was that of a middleman for Mesopotamian cultural exports rather than that of an originator. But the detailed evidence necessary for any firm conclusion is lacking, and even the tentative suggestions here put forward are disputable.

THE NORTHERN SEMITES

More than any other people, the Akkadians and the Assyrians who later settled in northern Mesopotamia submitted to the

FIG. 12. *Assur: a land gate (after Andrae).*

influence of the superior civilization of their southern neighbours. Themselves of a different stock and with different traditions, they assimilated an alien setting of life gradually and they preserved to the end a character quite unlike that of the Sumerians; the Assyrian autocratic monarchy, exercised by ambitious warrior kings, resulted in a purely military state which could not but find expression even in the material aspect of their cities,[8] but, for all that, it is only in the light of Sumerian traditions that the north can be understood.

This mixed culture is well illustrated by the excavations at Assur, the old Assyrian capital. Here we have what is really a contour fort, built on a promontory, secured on two sides by the waters of the Tigris, running at the foot of rocky cliffs, and on the landward side protected by a moat and massive walls of defence (Fig. 11). Only two gates, and those strongly fortified, gave access through the land wall (Fig. 12), and one water-gate opened on a quay on the north side of the promontory; the city is designed as a stronghold, not grown up from simple beginnings as a market town or open village but planned by a military architect who has taken advantage of all the accidents of terrain to make his fortress impregnable.

The whole of the northern side of the city is given over to temples and palaces (Fig. 13); the priest-king as the earthly Power is housed side by side with Assur, the god-king who is the heavenly Power, and the temples of the other gods, Anu and Adad, Sin and Shamash, Ishtar and Nabu, cluster round the royal palaces. There is no formal Temenos. The oldest of the temples, that of Ishtar, which dates from the Early Dynastic period, is 'wholly un-Babylonian and un-Sumerian' in ground-plan; judging from the clay model shrines found here the building was in fact of the type of the more or less contemporary temple at Alalakh with its low flat-roofed fore-chamber and lofty sanctuary lit by windows; of a 'northern' type, therefore, which was characteristic of the Amoritic or Hurri[9] peoples. In building the Ishtar temple (*c.* 3000 BC) the king of Assur (and later kings followed his example for nearly two thousand years) adopted the form traditional with his own

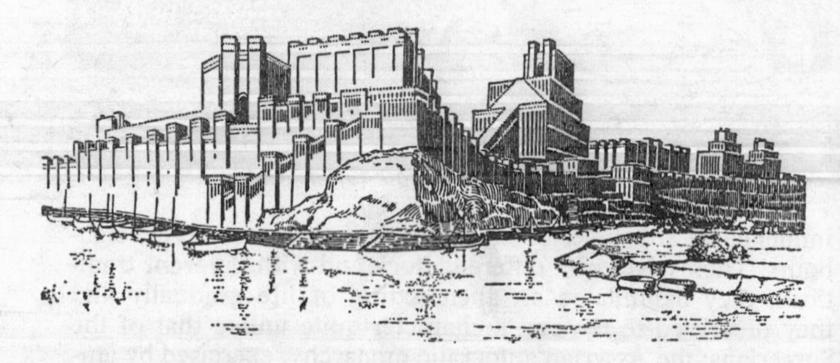

FIG. 13. *Assur: temples and palaces (after Andrae).*

people; but the statues which were dedicated in it are purely Sumerian. Other temples of later date are of the southern type and, with their ziggurat towers, might have been transplanted from Babylonia.

Very little is known about the residential quarters of Assur, but in view of the artificial character of the city's foundation it is at least probable that here, as in the smaller and less important town of Tepe Gawra in northern Assyria, 'the town planning is orderly, streets are well distributed and there is a good drainage system'. Early private houses are of 'northern' type (Fig. 14), the open houses of people who in simple village communities had not been trammelled by ideas of domestic privacy; but as time goes on first the richer citizens began to imitate their southern neighbours, building for themselves the secluded type of homes which are the rule in such a city as Ur in the second millennium BC, and in due course the rest follow their example. A further proof of the close relations between north and south is the fact that when, under the Third Dynasty of Ur, the Sumerians began for the first time to bury their dead not in outlying cemeteries but in brick vaults underneath the houses of the living, the same revolutionary change takes place in Assur also. It is, of course, true that at this time Assur, and the whole of the north country, had been brought into subjection by Ur-Nammu of Ur, and conquest may well have led to a settlement of Sumerian merchants and others, in addition to the officials appointed to carry on the government of the Sumerian overlord, so that the exchange of ideas was the more easy; but an innovation in anything so conservative as burial customs must mean the practical unification of the northern and southern cultures.

In the following age Assur regained its independence and a measure of importance; Shamshu-Adad I, an elder contempo-

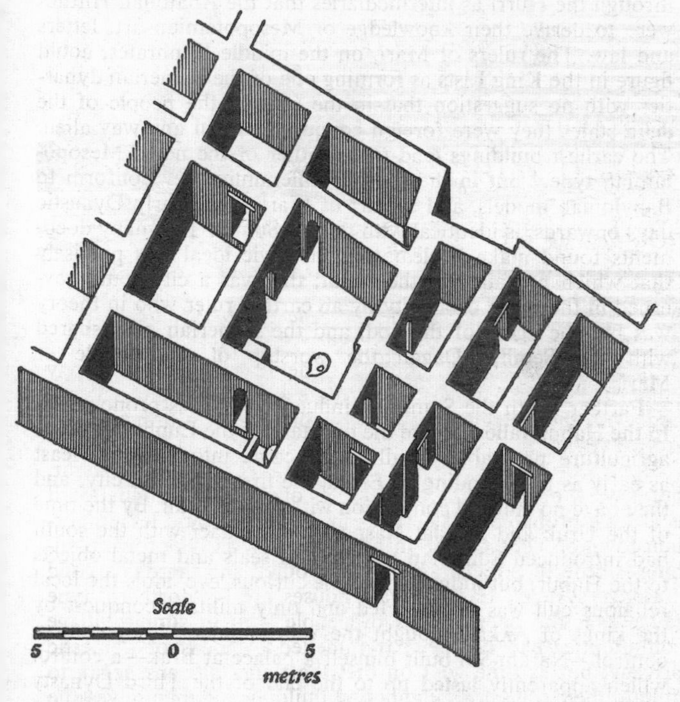

FIG. 14 *Northern type of house (after H. Frankfort)*

rary of King Hammurabi of Babylon, seems to have ranked almost as his equal; but a few years after Shamshu-Adad's death Hammurabi attacked Assur and added it to his dominions. In the Kassite period the connection was largely broken off and the warlike rulers of Assur emphasized more and more the military character of their kingdom, moulding Assyria into the form in which we know it best in the first millennium BC. At that time the difference between Assyria and Babylon is perhaps more striking than the resemblance; but in its early days Assyria must be reckoned a cultural dependency of Sumer.

THE HURRI AND THE AMORITES

To the north-west and west the Hurri and the Amorites of Syria alike fall within the orbit of Sumerian culture. It was through the Hurri as intermediaries that the Anatolian Hittites were to derive their knowledge of Mesopotamian art, letters and law. The rulers of Mari, on the middle Euphrates, could figure in the King Lists as forming one of the Sumerian dynasties with no suggestion that in the eyes of the people of the delta states they were foreign conquerors or in any way alien. The earliest buildings tend to be rather of the north Mesopotamian type,[10] but in the second millennium they conform to Babylonian models, and the art of Mari, from Early Dynastic days onwards, is identical with that of Sumer. The many documents found make it clear that the civic ideal was precisely that which prevailed in the south; this was a city state, governed in the name of a deity by an earthly ruler who in theory was but the agent of the god, and the Sumerian gods shared with the Semitic Dagan the worship of the people of Mari.

Farther north the Sumerian influence was less pronounced. In the Habur valley, where the tributary of the Euphrates made agriculture profitable, small towns came into being at least as early as the founding of Eridu, the first Sumerian city, and they have no cultural connection with Sumer at all. By the time of the Uruk and Jamdat Nasr periods contact with the south had introduced Sumerian pottery and seals and metal objects to the Habur, but judging from the curious 'eye' idols the local religious cult was not affected and only military conquest by the kings of Akkad brought the valley under Mesopotamian control—Naram-Sin built himself a palace at Brak—a control which apparently lasted up to the end of the Third Dynasty of Ur.

These Habur towns lay off the main lines of communication and there was no valid reason for Sumerian activity in their sequestered retreat, but where the westward trade-routes ran commerce brought the higher civilization of Mesopotamia to bear upon the culture, the politics and the religion of the Syrian peoples.

Harran, as a centre of the worship of Nannar, was almost a sister city of Ur; and although practically nothing is known of its history and character it would seem to have maintained its Babylonian connections right down to the days of Nabonidus in the sixth century BC. More details are available about the little city state of Alalakh on the lower Orontes. Commanding as it did the road along which hard timber went from the Amanus mountain forests to Mesopotamia, it was peculiarly open to Sumerian influence, so much so that in the Early Dynastic period the architecture of the royal palace is borrowed from that of the Euphrates valley. One of the many little city states which parcelled out between them all north and central Syria, Alalakh may be taken as typical. In the eighteenth century BC the town proper was enclosed in a heavy wall (Fig. 15) rising from a *glacis* about 20 feet high, this being a military feature characteristic of north Syria; the only gate found was defended by a massive gate-tower, but there was probably a second similar gateway at the south-east end of the town, and on its south-west side a small postern gate giving on the river bank. The walled enclosure was an irregular oval rather more than 700 yards long and some 200 yards wide, lying north-west by south-east; at the north-west end, where it had the benefit of the cool winds blowing from the Taurus mountains, were the royal palace and the temple of the city's god, and next to the palace, immediately within the town gate, was a fortress housing the royal troops and commanding the rest of the city. The remainder of the walled area seems to have been densely occupied by private houses; built of mud-brick upon stone foundations and sometimes at least of two storeys, many of them covering a considerable area, they were generically of the open 'northern' type, but far from uniform in plan, as if each householder had his own ideas as to what constituted comfort. But the general layout appears to have been fairly regular, with straight streets running at right-angles except where they were deflected by the direction of the town wall. It is probable that the walled city, set high on the mound formed by the ruins of older buildings, was really an acropolis and that there was an outer town on the low ground at its foot; in that case it would conform to the pat-

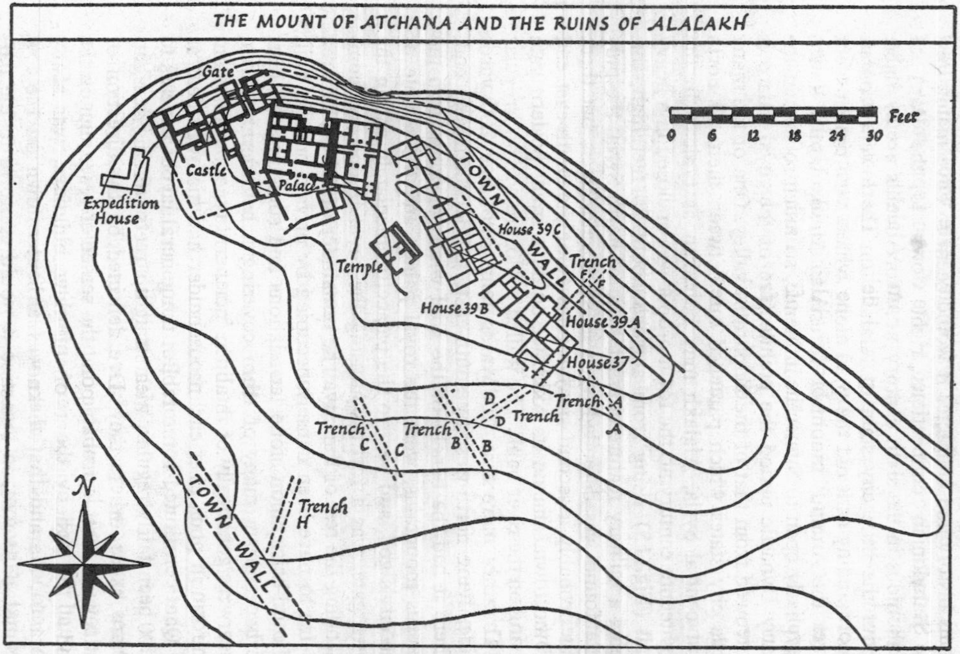

FIG. 15. *Alalakh: the walled city.*

tern of Carchemish, where there was an acropolis, an inner walled city and an outer town also with its lines of defence, as well as to that of other (unexcavated) towns in the Amq plain where the remains of built-up areas at the foot of the *tell* are quite obvious. Alalakh undoubtedly depended upon its trade, in cedar-wood primarily and also in ivory. As a small state it preserved its autonomy with difficulty and was at various times a vassal of Mitanni, or of Hattusas, or of Yamkhad, but essentially it was a city state whose king, like the Sumerian kings, governed as the chosen representative of the city's god—actually the very name 'Alalakh' seems to be derived from that of the patron deity. There is a certain amount of evidence to show that the Syrian conquests of the Twelfth Dynasty Pharaohs brought Alalakh, like Ugarit, under Egyptian control, but if the king of Alalakh professed allegiance to Pharaoh it was a political façade which affected the state but little; the prevalent cultural influence was that of Mesopotamia. Thus, of some 160 seals and seal-impressions found on the site, eleven are Hittite, ten are Egyptian or Phoenician imitations of Egyptian, and all the rest cylinder seals (and therefore of Mesopotamian type) with designs which may be Hurri or Amorite but often go back to Mesopotamian originals; moreover, the inscriptions on them are in cuneiform, as are the many tablets found, and the writing shows a local dialect of Akkadian to have been the language in ordinary use.

Throughout Syria it was Mesopotamia, not Egypt, that set the pattern. Thus at Qatna on the upper Orontes, although much of the material culture—the pottery and so on—is Syrian, as one would expect, yet all written documents are in Akkadian, and side by side with the local king, who has a north Syrian or Hurri name, there appears a Babylonian official, a *sakkanaku,* who was presumably installed by the king of Ur; moreover, it is the Sumerian goddess Nin-Gal (of Ur) who is 'Lady of the City', and it is noteworthy that Nin-Gal, perhaps because she was the goddess of the Mesopotamian suzerain, ranks high above all the other deities, who are called 'the king's gods', i.e. the native gods of Syria. The temple at Qatna from which the tablets come is dated to just before 2000 BC; it is therefore clear that up to the time when the Pharaohs of the Twelfth Dynasty invaded Syria, Egyptian influence there—except upon the sea-coast—was negligible, and all the higher elements of culture were derived from Mesopotamia. Admittedly, we know but little of the character of the inland towns of Palestine. The ruins of Megiddo, the stronghold commanding the fertile valley of Esdraelon, are imposing in themselves, but tell us nothing of its constitution during the Bronze Age; Hazor shows us a provincial, not to say barbaric, culture, a poor relation of the north Syrian; the fact that the little hill town of Jerusalem was under the rule of a king who was also the High Priest of Aleyn-Bel at least removes Jerusalem from the sphere of Egyptian influence. On the whole the generalization probably holds good that these petty kingdoms or states, while essentially Canaanite and not necessarily under Mesopotamian control, were both by trade and by politics oriented rather towards the east.

PHOENICIA

With the Phoenician coastal cities (Map V) the case is entirely different. The sites of the Syrian cities were dictated by the fertility of the soil and their economy was ultimately based on agriculture. Even Alalakh, for all its interest in international trade, had its share of the rich Amq plain; Harran had both irrigated land and wide pastures; Aleppo was the centre of the steppe cornlands; Kadesh commanded the upper Orontes valley; Qatna's great ramparts, a square measuring a thousand yards either way, rose from the fertile plain of Homs, and Damascus was set in its fabulous oasis watered by twin rivers. The contrast afforded by the Phoenician cities is illuminating. Ugarit with its 'White Harbour' lies on one of the very few bays on the Syrian coast that give even relative shelter to small ships; Arvad is a tiny rock island heavily walled except on its eastern side which faces the roadstead between it and the mainland; so small is it that the Arvadites were obliged to have an outpost, Amathus, on the mainland to assure their food supply. Tripoli was a promontory fort girt on three sides by the sea, and although there is a fertile plain behind it the site of the city was evidently determined by the easily defended rocky harbour. Byblos also has a harbour protected by reefs at the stream's mouth; Berytus occupies a headland, again with its harbour, which in the second millennium BC may well have been virtually cut off from the hinterland by a lagoon now filled with the silt deposited by the Nahr Beirût; Sidon lay partly on a promontory, partly on an island, and Tyre was an island city cut off from the nearby coast. It must be quite obvious that these towns do not represent the urbanization of a primarily agricultural people; their sites were chosen as affording facilities for shipping, and they were founded for commercial ends.[11] Their

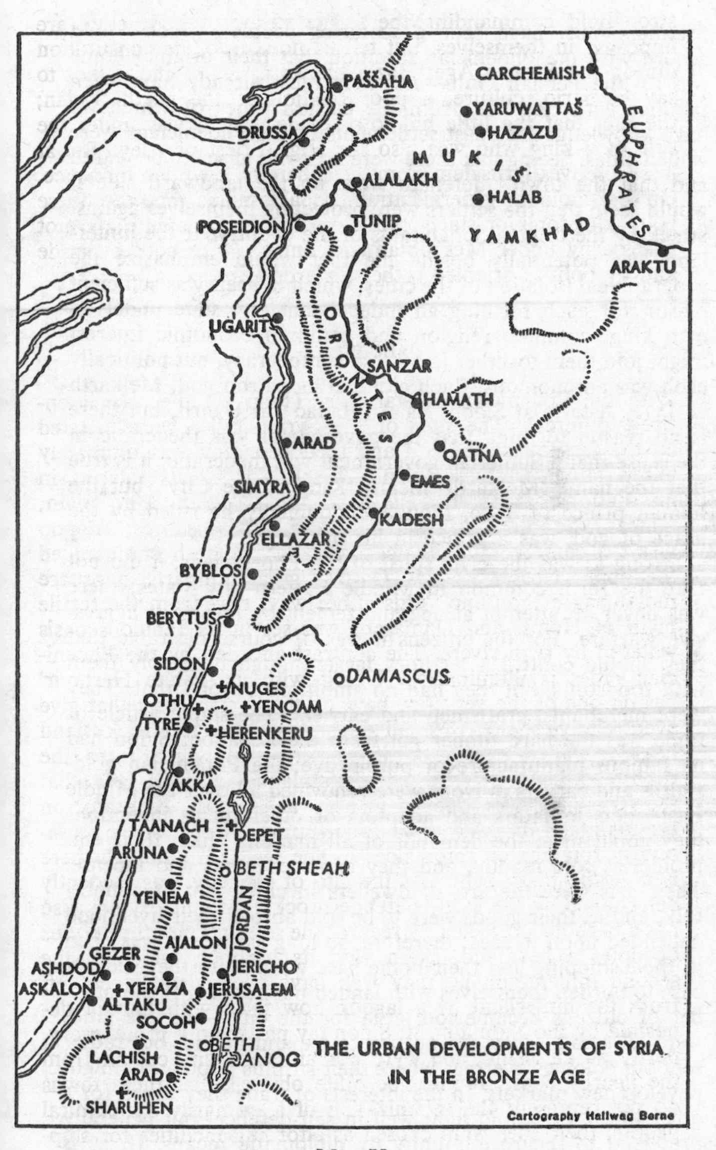

PAŠŠAHA
CARCHEMISH
YARUWATTAŠ
HAZAZU
EUPHRATES
DRUSSA
MUKIŠ
ALALAKH
HALAB
POSEIDION
TUNIP
YAMKHAD
ARAKTU
UGARIT
ORONTES
SANZAR
HAMATH
ARAD
QATNA
EMES
SIMYRA
KADESH
ELLAZAR
BYBLOS
BERYTUS
SIDON
DAMASCUS
NUGES
OTHU
YENOAM
TYRE
HERENKERU
AKKA
TAANACH
DEPET
ARUNA
BETH SHEAH
YENEM
JORDAN
AJALON
GEZER
AŞHDOD
JERICHO
AŞKALON
YERAZA
JERUSALEM
ALTAKU
SOCOH
BETH ANOG
LACHISH
ARAD
SHARUHEN
THE URBAN DEVELOPMENTS OF SYRIA IN THE BRONZE AGE
Cartography Hallwag Berne

MAP V

founders must have been a seafaring people—which would accord with the Phoenician tradition that their original home was on the Persian Gulf—and they must already have been familiar with city life; from the earliest times of which we have knowledge the coast settlements of the Phoenicians were walled cities. Seeing that there were no rivals at sea to be feared and that the town's defences were on the landward side it would seem that the settlers were protecting themselves against attack by the original inhabitants of the country. If the hinterland was potentially hostile the fact would emphasize the geographical isolation of the cities, which in itself was sufficient reason for each forming an independent city state under its own king; common religion and common economic interest might join them together in a loose confederacy, but politically each was autonomous. Each city had its patron god, Melkarth at Tyre, Astarte at Sidon, Ba'al (Hadad) at Ugarit, but there is no reason to think that the government was theocratic in the sense that a Sumerian government was theocratic; it is true that the name 'Melkarth' means 'King of the City', but the human prince of Tyre, though undoubtedly he ruled by the grace of god, was a prince in his own right.

Strong as was the civic spirit of the Phoenicians, it did not take the form common in Middle Eastern city states; there was never an attempt at aggrandizement by means of aggressive warfare. For the citizens it was of course desirable that they should control a territory large enough to supply them with foodstuffs, but they had no ambitions beyond that. They were merchants, craftsmen and carriers. The staple article of trade was the hard timber got from the Lebanon; Sidon had its famous manufacture of purple dye; the Phoenician goldsmiths and carvers in ivory were renowned all over the Middle East—deft imitators and adaptors of other men's inventions they could meet the demands of all markets alike; their embroideries sold readily, and they exported gums and incense. Their arts were the arts of dwellers in cities, not of country folk, and as their goods were to be sold abroad their livelihood depended upon the sea; therefore, so long as the sea was open to their shipping and their home base was secure they did not care to burden themselves with landed possessions. If the number of citizens became too large for the city—and the cities were all small—they did not try to expand inland, but rather sent out colonies overseas where their surplus population might develop new markets. In the interests of trade they asked for a quiet life; they would fight well in self-defence, but generally preferred to secure immunity by diplomatic means. If, as is probable, they took part in the Hyksos invasion of Egypt, that was only to reassert their independence against the imperialism of the Twelfth Dynasty Pharaohs; for the rest the Phoenicians show us the phenomenon, rare in ancient history, of a rich and an energetic people who insisted on liberty, quarrelled little amongst themselves and did not indulge in wars of aggression against their neighbours—though they might conduct slave-raids upon coasts where there was no chance of profit by trade, filling the role of pirate or merchant as the occasion arose.

CRETE

Urbanization in the islands of the Aegean started early. At Phylakapi in Melos the little town dates to the very beginning of the metal age, and from the elaborate structure of its outer walls one might conclude that self-defence was the chief motive that induced men to leave the open countryside and crowd together in strongholds; cities may have been the answer to piracy. In Crete a Neolithic town site has been found at Katsaba. At the beginning of the Middle Minoan I period Knossos had an enceinte wall of massive masonry and a lofty keep or tower dominating the northern entrance and the harbour gate—and in later days the northern approach to the palace itself (the approach, as Evans says, most liable to a piratical raid) was strongly fortified. It is not possible to trace the process of the city's growth, which was due to the vast wealth brought in by its overseas trade; but in the days of its greatest prosperity it can have had few rivals in the Middle East. The whole of the old walled town had been levelled to provide a site for the royal palace, a huge labyrinth of a building measuring about 120 metres in either direction and rising to a height of three or more storeys. Round it, and up to a distance of 400 metres from its walls, there were well-built houses, free-standing but set closely together, two storeys high, which clearly were the homes of the citizens of the upper class; beyond these again were the humbler dwellings of the poorer class, small and rubble-built, probably laid out on the block system that we find in such country towns of the period as Gournià and Palaikastro; while the 'aristocratic quarter' has a total superficies of about 1,125,000 square metres, the area of the whole town is very nearly twice as great. At first sight the general layout of Knossos appears not unlike that of some Sumerian city with its threefold division of Temenos, inner walled city and outer suburbs; but that superficial resemblance only emphasizes their real disparity. It is indeed true that in the Knossos palace there was room for a domestic shrine, or shrines, dedicated to the worship of the Snake Goddess, true too that the symbol of the double axe which is incised so freely upon its walls may have been meant to put the building under the protection of the god; but it is essentially a palace, planned to house the wealth and minister to the luxury of a human king and a pleasure-loving court; nothing could be less like the walled-in sanctum of an unapproachable god which formed the core of civic life in Mesopotamia.

ANATOLIA

If the walled cities of Crete were intended for defence against piracy, those of Asia Minor were built for protection against land enemies. The physical character of the country favours the subdivision of the population into relatively small communities each sequestered behind its barrier of mountain ranges; such was indeed the texture of society throughout history right up to the Turkish conquest (Map VI). By the beginning of our period the divergent cultural development of such isolated communities had already resulted in something akin to racial differentiation and perhaps even by that time immigration of completely alien peoples both from the Caucasus and from south-east Europe may have complicated matters further; each group under its own chief would feel the need to safeguard itself against its neighbours by concentration of its forces and the fortification of its dwellings.

A new factor came in with the exploitation of metal. Its great mineral wealth at once gave to various parts of Asia Minor an importance quite out of proportion to the cultural level of its inhabitants. Mining prospectors opened out new vistas of prosperity; but since the metal was of little value unless it had an outlet to a paying market, trade-routes became all-important. The producing areas had to export their products; the non-producers through whose territories the goods were obliged to pass could profit both by exchange and by imposts; in neither case could the full advantage be reaped unless there was an organized government to regulate business and a military power to enforce the government's policy. To a large extent therefore urbanization in Asia Minor was due to international trade, and the trade centre was the natural seat of government. As early as the twenty-fourth century BC, as we know from the Sargonid poem 'The King of Battles', Mesopotamian merchant colonies were established in the heart of

Asia Minor, and the excavations at Kultepe show that such a colony of foreign traders would be situated at the capital of the country concerned—but not in it; an open suburb immediately outside the city's walls, it guaranteed the concentration of trade but was completely under the control of the local ruler. Similarly, Troy owed its early foundation and its subsequent prosperity to the fact that it commanded the sea passage of the Dardanelles down which came the merchantmen bringing wool from south Russia and copper from the south shore of the Black Sea. Certainly the metal trade must have been responsible for the wealth of the chiefs of Alaca Höyük in the second half of the third millennium BC; not only the amount of gold and copper in their tombs but the remarkable technique of the craftsmen who made those vessels and ornaments is proof of this.

Naturally, as military conquests or political alliances, welding together what had been separate city states, created a new system, new capital cities arose to meet the changed conditions—an indirect result of the prosperity ultimately due to commerce. Thus the Hatti, gradually extending their power northwards, had two capitals in succession[12] before they finally settled upon Hattusas (Boğazköy). Again, in western Anatolia,

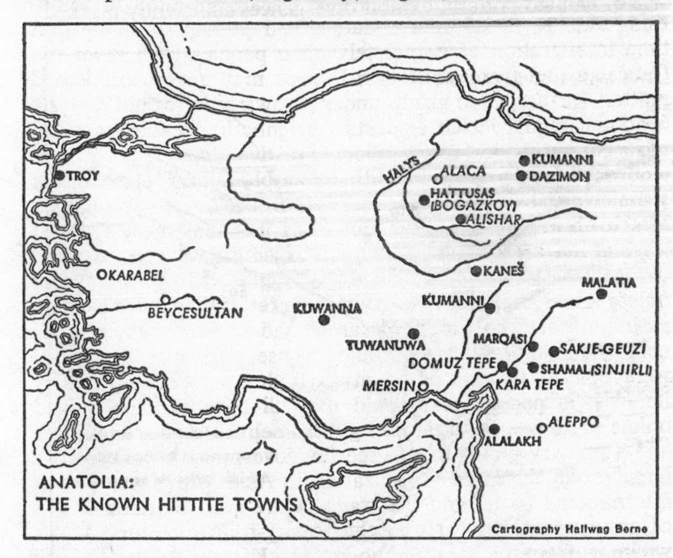

MAP VI

we find at Beycesultan a royal city (possibly the capital of the kingdom of Arzawa) in which, as early as 2000 BC,[18] the people were already familiar with the use of hieroglyphic writing and included at least an element of Indo-European stock. It would appear that in the first centuries of the second millennium the process of urbanization was far advanced in Asia Minor, and although it was never so thickly populated as was Syria, walled cities may have been numerous enough, and many of the city states mentioned in later Hittite records may have existed even then.

INDIA

There exists no literary tradition throwing light on the origin and growth of the great cities of north-west India. Archaeological exploration in the Indus valley and west of it in Baluchistan has brought to our knowledge the ruins of a large number of Early Bronze Age settlements (Map VII), some of which are of a size that warrants the description of them as towns and of a height that shows them to have resulted from a long period of growth. The remains, mostly in the form of painted pottery, exhibit divergences sufficiently marked

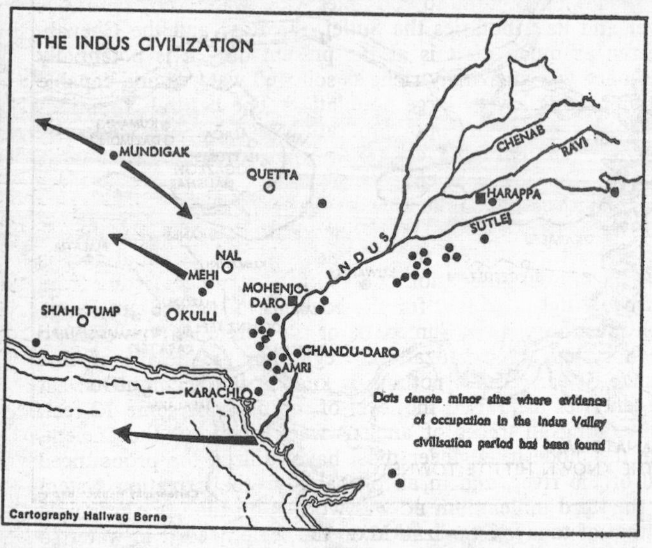

MAP VII

for the archaeologist to speak of different cultures; but the differences may well be due to the independent development of kindred communities isolated from each other by vast distances and by difficult country. Some at least of the towns were walled, but that is to be expected in a land infested by marauding mountaineers. For the most part they must have started as centres of agricultural districts, but in one or two instances trade considerations may have influenced the choice and character of the site; thus the so-called Kulli culture possessed at Mehi, in southern Baluchistan, what seems to have been a commercial harbour, and here there have been found decorated stone vases which prove a connection with Sumer in the Early Dynastic period of that country. Still earlier contact is suggested by the discoveries at Mundigak in southern Afghanistan; there, below the stratum in which the characteristic Kulli pottery occurs, there are massive mud-brick buildings whose walls are relieved with the half-column decoration topped by stepped merlons which is typical of Sumerian architecture (Pl. 1, b), and the pottery associated with the buildings is closely akin to if not identical with the 'Uruk' ware of Mesopotamia; this might well be a 'half-way house' for transcontinental trade.[14]

The valley of the Indus is a vast plain, an irregular triangle 950 miles long and up to 700 miles wide, watered by the Indus river and its tributaries the Sutlej, the Ravi and the Chenab. Barren as much of it is at the present day, it is potentially and once was amazingly rich, its soil well watered and capable of supporting a very large population. The natural conditions resemble those of Mesopotamia rather than of Egypt. The vast alluvial plain is faintly convex in profile and slopes towards the sea far more steeply than does the Euphrates delta (1:7,000, nearly double that of Egypt); the silt content of the river water (435:100,000) is less than that of the Euphrates but more than double that of the Nile; the essential fact is that the annual inundation occurs in the summer, lasting from May to August, so that for the purposes of agriculture irrigation must here, as in Sumer, be of the perennial type effected by a system of canalization. Regarding the details of that system in early times nothing is known; the accumulated silt of centuries has raised the level of the plain by some 12 feet, obliterating all traces of ancient waterways, but the ancient, like the modern, engineer must have utilized the pronounced fall of the river, and in all probability[15] the irrigation system of the third millennium BC was worked on the same principle as that of today. Canalization on the scale needed to water so great an area requires, as we have seen in the case of Sumer, a measure of centralization and co-operative effort which is beyond the scope of a village community, and we might, on the Mesopotamian analogy, expect to find the valley divided into city stages corresponding to irrigation units. There may be evidence for the early stages of such a social development in the fact that along the middle course of the Indus there is a chain of settlements, some of them (such as Kot Diji, 65 miles north of Hyderabad in Sind) of considerable size, representing for the most part the Amri-Nal culture, which is contemporary and sometimes coincident with the Kulli; but all of them, like the Kulli sites in general, either go out of occupation altogether or are overlaid by buildings of the Harappā type. After that, the uniform distribution of the Harappā culture seems to imply the political unification of the country—a unification parallel to that of Egypt under Menes; if the striking similarity in the planning of Harappā and Mohenjo-daro justifies us in regarding the two cities as twin capitals of the same ruling power, then their existence is fully explained by the difficulty of controlling from a single administrative centre the irrigation of an area so immense as that of the Indus valley.

The generally accepted term 'Indus Valley Civilization', resulting as it does from the accidents of discovery, must not be too literally stressed. The ruins of a very large city of the type have been found 75 miles south-east of Quetta, i.e. beyond the watershed that bounds the valley on the north. In the Nabada valley in Gujrat, and as far south as Cutch, town sites have been unearthed which share in the same civilization. Whether or not they were subject to the same government as the Indus cities we do not know; for a common culture need not mean a unified control. Certainly their existence proves that what we call the 'Indus valley' or the 'Harappā' civilization had a far wider extension than was at first supposed; but in the present state of our knowledge it is legitimate to assume that the centre of that civilization was in the fertile valley of the Indus and its tributaries.

The two main cities lie about 350 miles apart, Harappā on the banks of the river Ravi, Mohenjo-daro on the Indus. The archaeological evidence shows that their foundation marked a definite break with local tradition; it is a case of imposition, not of natural growth. Between the bottom of the massive brickwork of Harappā and the alluvial deposit that overlies the virgin soil there is only a thin 'occupation stratum' implying a village rather than a town, and the potsherds found in it are of the old Baluchistan ware, quite unlike that of Harappā itself. Even if it be held that the Harappā pottery might be really no more than a parallel development comparable to the variant wares of Amri-Nal, Kulli, Zhob and others found in different areas of Baluchistan and the Punjab, none the less it is certain that it did not develop at Harappā, any more than did the architecture and the metallurgy, which are without precedent in those other cultures. The entire civilization comes suddenly upon the scene already formed, already, in fact, so stereotyped that although the city was to pass through vicissitudes which must represent many centuries of time, yet in that time there was no change in its arts and crafts; the various superimposed strata afford no typological sequence whatsoever. Precisely the same evidence is forthcoming from Kot Diji, where the stratification was far more elaborate than at Harappā and gave a clearer picture. The eleven lower occupation-levels show a local 'Kot Diji' culture, apparently Neolithic, possessing certain affinities to the Amri culture; above these comes a layer of burnt material indicating the violent destruction of the settlement, and immediately above this a phase of the Harappā culture which seems to be earlier than that illustrated by Harappā itself and by Mohenjo-daro but is entirely distinct from anything beneath the burnt layer, which marks a break in cultural continuity. The excavator concludes that the Harappā people were responsible for the destruction of the Kot Diji town and 'came into the Indus valley with a fairly well-developed culture from somewhere, as no traces of the origin of that culture have been revealed by excavations at any of the sites of the Indus valley'. On this evidence we are justified in assuming that the builders of the cities were newcomers from some other region.

Harappā and Mohenjo-daro are unlike the other Middle Eastern cities with which we have had to deal in that they are purely artificial creations. Whether or not they were walled is still uncertain, though the citadels at least were strongly walled for defence (Fig. 16). Within the limits of the city (Fig. 17) we find systematic town planning on the grid principle, fairly wide main streets running quite straight and intercepting each other at right-angles; these form large blocks composed of a number of houses, often large, which may be approached by narrow alleys. The houses are built with a lavish use of burnt brick and are provided with bathrooms, rubbish-shoots and a common drainage system; they are eminently town houses, designed for the amenities of life and owned by people of considerable comfort and means. In each case there is on the west side of the city a citadel, raised on an artificial brick platform and enclosed by immensely strong fortifications; these strongholds dominate the surrounding country 'like the fortresses of mediaeval barons'. In the town proper there are

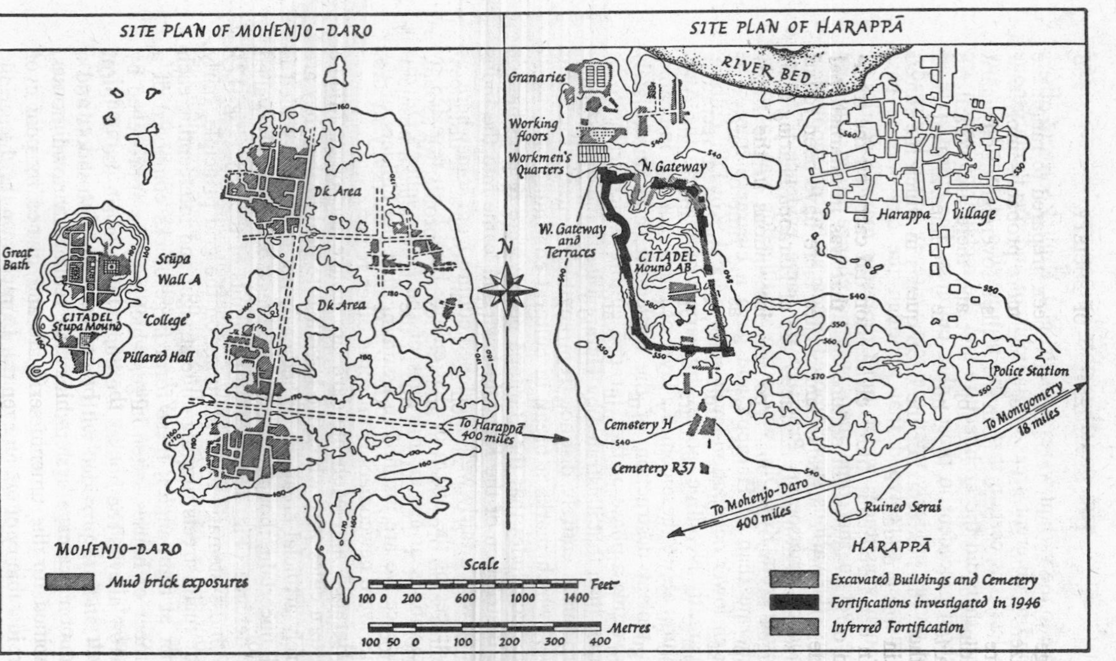

FIG. 16. *Mohenjo-daro and Harappā: the general plans compared (after Wheeler).*

huge granaries such as might have been prepared to ration the citizens in the event of a siege, but more probably imply that there was maintained within the walls a sovereign's bodyguard holding the populace in subjection; and there are workmen's quarters—rows of identical hovels like slave-lines, and attached to them the platforms for the hand-querns in which the stored grain was ground.

In one respect the Indus civilization did carry on the tradition of the older Kulli culture, and that was in international trade. On various Mesopotamian sites there have been found the square stamp seals characteristic of Harappā bearing both designs of the Harappā type and inscriptions in the Indus script; these begin at least as early as the time of Sargon of Akkad (twenty-fourth century BC), and the latest recorded hitherto was in a Kassite grave at Ur which must date after 1700 BC and more probably comes nearer to 1500. We shall be guilty of no anachronism if we conclude from this that from the twenty-fourth century onwards Harappā traders had their Indian agents domiciled in the cities of Mesopotamia; there is an exact analogy in the *karum* of Ganes in central Anatolia, where the Akkadian merchants lived, and at Ur, where Harappā seals are most common, there was a *karum* which may have served the same purpose.

International trade on such a scale and over such distances requires good organization and implies high profits; we should *a priori* expect therefore to find in the Indus valley a business aristocracy playing an important part in the economy of the state, and the character of the town houses fully supports that assumption. The close resemblance between the two cities of Harappā and Mohenjo-daro makes it look very much as if they were the twin capitals of a single government (that would be not unreasonable in a country of such extent) and rivalry between them seems scarcely compatible with the smooth functioning of international trade. The elaborate fortification of the citadels would hardly have been necessary to protect the cities against raiding-parties from the mountains of Baluchistan; more probably they were intended to overawe the countryside, the assumption being that the ruler and citizens were of an alien stock[16] which had reduced the indigenous inhabitants to the status of serfs; certainly the citizens did live apart in a luxury of which even the country towns of the period show no sign at all, and perhaps they could only maintain their privileges by force.

The character of the buildings inside the citadel of Mohenjo-daro, so far as they are known (those of Harappā have been

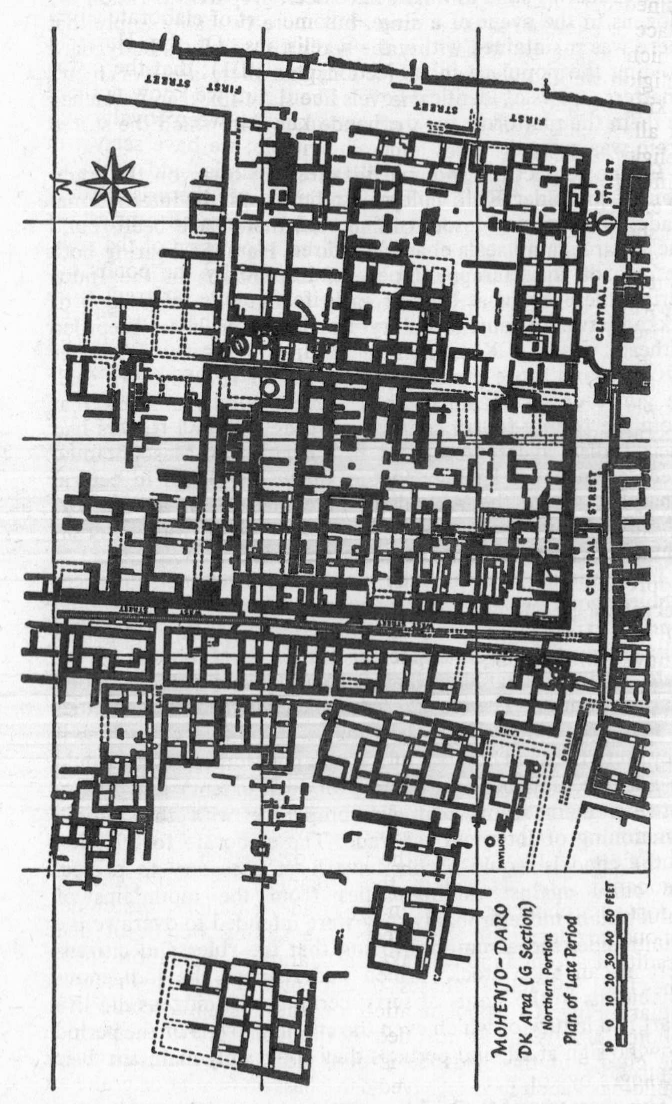

FIG. 17. *Mohenjo-daro: part of the town plan (after Mackay).*

ruined beyond recognition) suggests not so much a dwelling-place or a temple as the setting for some sort of elaborate ritual which might be either royal or religious. Of the Harappā religion we know very little (*v.* Chapter VIII); that there was a king we may safely assume, but about him we know nothing at all. A close connnection of some kind between royalty and religion is in early times almost inevitable; we have seen it in different forms in Egypt and in Mesopotamia, and probably it existed in the Indus valley also; but as yet there is nothing to show whether the ruler of Harappā was himself a priest, or a god, or simply a king under the direct protection of the gods. But under whatever pretext he held authority the conditions in which it was exercised were manifestly quite different from those of Mesopotamia or of Egypt. The city is here an artificial creation, not grown out of the soil, and the similar layout of the two capitals is evidence for an arbitrary and an absolute power; but the houses of the cities bespeak a wealthy aristocracy which must surely have been concerned with the business of government—a community of merchant princes such as surrounded the Doge of Venice—men of the same stock as their chief; and this close corporation ruled by force over a conquered populace, alien and enslaved. They ruled for at least seven hundred years and during that time made no appreciable advance of any sort. 'The dead hand of conservatism in design, rather than in technique, lies heavily on all the Harappā products. Complex technical processes were known, but the output suffered from standardization and an almost puritanical utilitarianism. Working within such narrow limits of traditional forms, fossilized over the centuries into a rigid, inescapable mental prison, the artist or craftsman could have found little outlet save in developing technical virtuosity. The pattern of Harappā civilization seems to have precluded great monuments such as temples, palaces, or tombs, wherein an outburst of artistic achievement could redound to the glory of the gods or the pride of a splendid spendthrift monarch. The secrecy of those blank brick walls, the unadorned architecture of even the citadel buildings, the monotonous regularity of the streets, the stifling weight of dead tradition all combine to make the Harappā civilization one of the least attractive phases of Oriental history."[17] Professor Stuart Piggott's condemnation of the Harappā civilization quoted here is indeed justified by the material evidence which he cites; but the evidence is one-sided, and while the brick buildings which have survived can boast no beauty or grandeur a different tale is told by some at least of the sadly few objects found in them. No critic confronted with such a masterpiece as the bronze dancing-girl from Mohenjo-daro (p. 540) could refuse to credit the people of the Indus valley with an artistic genius which, faintly reflected in the seal engravings and the painted pottery, finds its full expression in their sculpture.

If the origin of this state is unknown and its history almost a blank, there can be no doubt about its end. Towards 1500 BC —the date, based on Indian literary sources, is supported by the evidence of the seal in the Kassite grave at Ur—the Aryans coming by way of Afghanistan invaded north-west India and after hard fighting overthrew 'the walled cities'; in the *Rigveda* Indra is 'the fort destroyer', he 'rends forts as age consumes a garment', and 'in kindled fire he burnt up all their weapons'. The Harappā civilization was not indeed altogether sterile, as we shall see hereafter, but its material glories vanished completely.

The Aryan conquerors were a simple, not to say a barbarous people, pastoral nomads for the most part, some perhaps petty farmers, who had not even a word for 'brick' in their vocabulary; they could destroy, but they could not rebuild. Just as the Saxon pirates who settled in Britain shunned the Roman sites whose walls of massive stone seemed to their ignorance to be the work of devils, and when they in due course began to build did so under the influence not of Rome but of the contemporary architecture of the Continent, so it was with the Aryans. Harappā and Mohenjo-daro were left to moulder into shapeless mounds. True, in the topmost level are found shoddy huts built with re-used bricks above the ruins of the citadel, but the potsherds prove that such were inhabited not by the invaders but by a remnant of the old servile population who now squatted on the sites where their masters had lived. For more than a millennium after their arrival the history of the Aryans is shrouded in utter darkness;[18] when at last, late in the fourth century BC, the veil lifts a little to show us northern India under the Mauryan Dynasty possessed of a great urban civilization, those cities have nothing in common with the old Indus capitals. The burnt-brick-and-bitumen construction which was the most striking feature of Mohenjo-daro architecture is a long-forgotten art: in the earliest post-Harappā buildings of which we have any knowledge, those at Hastinapura, 80 miles north-east of Delhi, wood is the basic material, and the Mauryan palace at Pataliputra is also of timber. It would seem that when the Aryans began to build for themselves they made a fresh start; the monuments which they set up were certainly not inspired by any memories of Mohenjo-daro. At Hastinapura and at Pataliputra the remains are not sufficient to show the style of the buildings; but the earliest buildings in stone are obviously based upon timber originals, and when we look at such a structure as the north gateway of the Great Stupa at Sanchi it is difficult to avoid the feeling that the inspiration comes from the wooden architecture of China.[19]

CHINA

The astonishingly high Neolithic culture which we have seen spread over a large area of the Far East persisted, on the whole, long after the age of metal had succeeded that of stone in Mesopotamia and in Egypt, and when the change came it did not affect simultaneously all that area. How the change came about we have as yet no means of knowing, but at the earliest time for which material evidence is available, which is about the middle of the second millennium BC, it is complete; the Anyang graves prove that under the Shang Dynasty the technique of bronze casting had attained a perfection rarely equalled elsewhere, stone-carving and woodwork were fully developed and a system of writing had been evolved which was to endure, with relatively little change, until the present day.

This remarkable civilization, so far from being common to the whole of China, was confined to the northern provinces, its capital being in the rich loess plain on the north-west bank of the Huang Ho, some 200 miles south of Peiping. Protected on two sides by the river and on the west by a long mountain chain, the slopes of which provided heavy timber and wild animals for hunting whereas the level valley was ideal for the growing of grain and for pasturage, the region was admirably adapted to the development of a wealthy city state.

On the banks of the Huang Ho the Shang people built 'The Great City Shang', the capital city of an agricultural state. Through the flat loess plain the Yellow River winds in tortuous curves, its bed raised many feet above the general level of the earth, so that the tapping of its waters was easy enough and the difficulty lay rather in the need of drainage, which could only be accomplished by the digging of long canals. Every year, between July and September, the river comes down in spate, carrying with it a fantastic amount of silt—from 10 to 20 per cent of the total volume of flood water—and should it break its banks the results are disastrous indeed. Not only will the season's crops be lost, but the river is apt to change its course, finding a new bed at a lower level, and with that change the entire system of canalization is put out of action, and a fresh start must be made and new canals built to replace those now left high and dry. Chinese history is largely dominated by the struggle against the inundation floods; the struggle calls for highly co-ordinated effort and here, therefore, as in Sumer where the natural conditions were so similar, the centralized government of a city state is the necessary answer to the river's challenge. That the Neolithic barbarians whom the Shang people ousted when they took possession of the fertile province had failed to organize irrigation and flood-control is certain; they had lived from hand to mouth, profiting by a good season and starving when the river broke its banks and destroyed the harvest. The oldest examples of Chinese writing that we possess, the inscribed bones and tortoise-shells found in the Honan province, which belong to the Shang period, include numerous 'rain oracles' proving that in the second and third months of the year the Shang farmers were still anxiously enquiring about the prospects of the spring rainfall, i.e. irrigation had not yet gone so far as to make them independent of rain; on the other hand complex signs in the inscriptions such as 'flowing water—field' or 'water—rice' prove that irrigation was already practised. To expand the system and to maintain it required just that centralizing of government that the newcomers in fact introduced, and for this reason 'The Great City Shang' was built.

Presumably the Shang capital was a walled city, like that of Neolithic times which it replaced. The houses of the upper class, constructed of wood on raised platforms of beaten earth, were very different from the crude pit-dwellings of their predecessors, pit-dwellings which up to the end of the Shang period were still used by the lower classes, as well as by their nearest neighbours on the south-west, the Chou. On the long and rather narrow platform were set three parallel rows of posts supporting a gabled roof; the outer walls were merely screens, as in the modern Chinese house, which may have been of pounded earth (bricks had not been invented) or more simply of reed matting. The latter is the more probable in view of a (slightly later) text which says, 'in building a house, after all the toil of its walls, they have to plaster and thatch it', for in a riverine country (as in Mesopotamia) reed matting is the natural basis for mud plaster; but a description of the building of a royal palace (also written in a later period) does imply that in such a case the walls as well as the platform might be made of earth pounded between boards. Certainly this was the case with a building which may have been a royal palace attributed to the Chou period *c.* 1000 BC unearthed at a place called Abakan, on the river Verkhnaya Tunguska in the Khakass Autonomous Region. This had a very large central hall surrounded by smaller rooms and, on two sides, a further row of chambers, the hall a lofty building rising well above the surrounding rooms and these again higher than the outer chambers, so that there was a stepped roof-line; wooden columns supported the roof which was of terra-cotta tiles, some bearing Chinese inscriptions. Except for the tiles, this late structure (the earliest to give a complete plan known as yet) seems to perpetuate the style of the Shang structures and of those described in the Chou documents.

At Anyang the buildings excavated are all orientated to the north, and such uniformity may be taken to show that the city as a whole was laid out on a pre-arranged plan. No city walls were found, though their existence must be regarded as probable: traces of a wall have been found at the contemporary site Cheng-chou.

Regarding the form of government of the Shang people we have really no certain knowledge. The bone inscriptions help us very little, and the literary texts which purport to be contemporary are in fact of later date and, if not actual forgeries, are propaganda put out by the Chou rulers, tendentious at the best and in some cases deliberately misleading. There was a king of Shang, and the kingship was hereditary, the founder of the dynasty having been chosen by Heaven as the most worthy to bear rule. According to later tradition he was emperor of China, which assuredly was not the case. His dominions were strictly limited, wars with neighbours were of common occurrence and the constant fear of raids, to which the requests for omens bear witness, implies that the state was none too secure; but there is no doubt that conquest did extend his dominions over a number of alien tribes, for T'ang himself is said to have 'smitten the princes of Wei and Ku and dealt with the prince of K'un Wu', and Chou had to submit to a later king of his line. But the manner in which the kingdom was organized is doubtful. The Chous governed through a feudal system[20] and Chou writers represent the Shang system also as feudal—indeed, tradition says the same about ancient Hsia; but Creel and many other modern scholars reject both statements. They point out that in the early Chou period the titles of the feudal lords of varying rank had not been arranged in the graded hierarchy found in later times but are used rather indiscriminately, which they take to show that the feudal system 'had been created *de novo* out of the situation resulting from the Chou conquest'. The attribution of that system to the Shang régime would be part of a campaign of propaganda meant to legitimize the conquest; although the Chou writers admit that their rulers had once been vassals of the Shang house yet they give them the royal title, *wang,* which would seem to imply independent kingship; and the book *Shang Sung*, describing the Shang state, says,

> Heaven appointed the many rulers
> and established their capitals within the sphere of the labours of Yü,
> But for the business of every year they appeared before our king
> Saying 'Do not punish or reprove us;
> We have not been remiss with our husbandry',

from which it is clear that these 'many rulers' were not feudal lords enfeoffed by the sovereign but real kings, heaven-appointed as was the emperor himself, who had been forced by defeat in war to give tribute and make a yearly accounting to the conqueror.

On the other hand the situation after the Chou conquest—the wide extent of the dominions to be governed, the difficulty of communications and the undeveloped state of finance—was precisely the same as that before the conquest, and is likely to have been dealt with on the same lines, which the Chou writers claim to have been the case. Granted that in early Chou times the feudal titles were not exactly fixed, so that a man succeeding to his father's fief is called by a different title, it must be remembered that by the terms of European feudalism fiefs were not properly hereditary and might be renewed upon challenged conditions: 'The foundation of the feudal relationship proper was the fief, which was usually land. In return for the fief, the man became the vassal of his lord. The faithful performance of all the duties he had assumed in homage constituted the vassal's right and title to his fief.' Now in the quotation from the book *Shang Sung* cited above we seem to have just that annual renewal of the act of homage with its assurance of duties performed which mediaeval feudalism theoretically required, and the ruler's insistence on their husbandry is likely to be not a metaphor but a literal reference to their landed fiefs; one of the three main principles of feudalism was 'that every holder of land is a tenant and not an owner', and he would naturally have to give an account of his stewardship. At the same time, the description of the rulers as 'appointed by Heaven' does imply royalty, and it is quite certain that the chiefs of the vassal state of Chou were hereditary rulers who could claim the title of king. The anomaly can most reasonably be explained by assuming that T'ang, when he first achieved sovereignty, organized his domains on feudal lines, making grants of land to his followers; when later wars of aggression resulted in the acquisition of fresh territories then, if resistance had been unduly stubborn, the same policy would be enforced, but where a state surrendered with more or less good grace its native ruler would be confirmed in power as a vassal, on much the same terms as a Shang feudal lord but with a cloak of royalty which might help to reconcile his people to the Shang yoke. Such an inconsistency would present no more difficulty to the Chinese than it did to the mediaeval European, whose feudalism was also based on two disparate traditional practices. Of this it had been said, 'Feudalism in its most flourishing age was anything but systematic. Great diversity prevailed everywhere. But underlying all the confusion of fact and practice were certain fundamental principles and relationships which were everywhere alike. The chief of these are: the relation of vassal and lord; the principle that every holder of land is a tenant and not an owner; the principle that the tenure is one of honourable service.'

In so far as feudalism can be defined, the definition seems to apply to what we can learn about the Shang régime. It is certainly tempting to assume that the Chou disclaimer of any originality regarding the organization of government was an honest one, and that it was not those barbarians but the highly civilized Shang people who not only developed Chinese art and writing but also laid the foundations of the system whereby China was to be governed for nearly thirty centuries.

It is a tempting assumption,[21] but unproven; as has been said above, it is rejected by many scholars. If the question has been argued here at some length it is to show how dangerous it may be to deduce from purely archaeological material the details of state organization, social conditions and the like. Some at least of the attempts made in this direction appear to be unduly subjective. Thus the theory, confidently put forward, that in the Yin period family and clan relations predominated to the exclusion of territorial and administrative relations, i.e. central government, does not necessarily follow from the archaeological evidence—which indeed might be used to support the opposite conclusion. The organization of labour required for irrigation works seems hardly consistent with a clan system, and the king's anxious enquiries about the weather might imply that the government as such was directly concerned with the task; the encircling of cities with walls of stamped earth might be held to result from a central authority having the power to impose the *corvée*; and the wealth of some of the Anyang tombs might be thought incompatible with communal ownership. Actually Yin civilization had reached so high a level, undoubtedly after many generations of development, that a merely clan basis of society seems improbable; that primitive stage should have been outgrown long before.

What we can say with certainty is that there was a king, with vassal rulers under him; that there were rich people and poor people and, undoubtedly, slaves, if no others then at least the Ch'iang, foreign prisoners of war who were doomed to be sacrificed to the gods or the ancestors or at the obsequies of kings, but pending that doom would be made to labour for their captors. Society was organized on an urban basis, and while the bulk of the working class would be agriculturalists the differentiation of employment had gone very far, so that not only was the bronze-caster, for instance, a professional, but he might even devote himself to one particular branch of his craft, a whole workshop specializing in vessels of a certain type.

Surrounded as it was by backward peoples (the tribes to the east are regularly described as 'barbarians' and the Chou on the south-west had even in the fourteenth century BC scarcely advanced beyond the Neolithic stage) the Shang kingdom must have maintained its position largely in virtue of its superior armament; its wealth in metal made it formidable. The soldiers wore bronze helmets and perhaps bronze body-armour also; they carried bronze-headed 'dagger-axes' and powerful bows; together with the infantry there was a force of chariots, each bronze-fitted car drawn by two, or later by four, horses. The chariotry was the *corps d'élite* and the decisive weapon in warfare, so much so that the strength of a state was reckoned by the number of chariots it could put into the field—'a state of a hundred chariots' or 'of a thousand chariots'; and since the cost of a chariot and of its upkeep must have been considerable we may assume that service in the branch was part of the duties accepted by the great fief-holders, who would equip themselves at their own expense. As in the case of the Sumerians, so too the Shang kingdom was enabled by the possession of a well-organized military force not only to add to its territories but to spread the knowledge of its superior civilization. Thus the Chou, who after much fighting were reduced to vassalage (their rulers being left in power and intermarrying with the Shang royal family), remained as a nation barbarous enough, but the Chou aristocracy learned so far to appreciate the arts of Shang that when in the twelfth century BC they, in alliance with other tribes of western China, overthrew the Shang Dynasty, their mastery made surprisingly little difference to the country's culture. In the works of art of their time we can remark a certain loss of quality, which is but natural when the craftsmen's clients were not sufficiently educated to demand nothing but the best (though prior to the discovery of the Anyang tombs the Chou bronzes were considered by experts to be the finest ever made in China), but apart from this slight set-back the new régime carried on faithfully the traditions of the old. By the time the Shang Dynasty collapsed the foundations of Chinese civilization had been well and truly laid.

NOTES TO CHAPTER II

1. The railway line running by the ruins of Ur is 6 feet below the bottom of the bed of the Euphrates at Nasiriyeh, 10 miles away.
2. Professor I. M. Diakonoff points out that in 'civilized society those who are rich and powerful have opportunities for education; thus the intellectual ascendency of the upper class is the result of class differentiation inside the society. A system of government does not result simply from a sharper differentiation of professions but rather from the fact that no one would drudge in order to let another man have the privilege of intellectual life unless forced to do so. A system of government is indispensable to the ruling class.'
3. Compare the Jericho defences, where the house of Rahab the harlot was 'upon the town wall, and she dwelt upon the wall' (Joshua ii. 15).
4. Professor H. Frankfort was writing before the discovery of the Calah inscription, and he admitted that his arguments could not apply to Ur, of the extent of which he was unaware.
5. See pp. 577–78.
6. Professor John A. Wilson regards this point of view with some reserve. While generally true, it does not reflect the imperialist spirit of the Pharaohs of the New Empire, from the Eighteenth to the Twentieth Dynasties.
7. Professor I. M. Diakonoff observes that prior to the Third Dynasty the *ensis* did not necessarily hold their office from the kings. At the time of the Third Dynasty, the office was, however, no longer hereditary. The possibility exists that earlier conditions might have continued to prevail on the outskirts of the kingdom.
8. The nature of royal power may have evolved in Assyria over the centuries. According to Professor I. M. Diakonoff the Assyrian rulers were not autocratic before Samsi-Adad I, and were probably not autocratic after Samsi-Adad I until the times of Assur-Uballit I.
9. Professor W. Andrae prefers the appellation 'Hurri'.
10. The pre-Sargonid temple of Ishtar is strikingly like the Ishtar temple at Assur.
11. Professor I. M. Diakonoff suggests that the early settlers were fishing folk and that the sea-trade came later. He points out that the name Sidon means 'fishing place'.
12. Prior to Hattusas, the capital was Nesa, farther to the south in the region of the Salt Lake.
13. Professor E. Laroche points out that no hieroglyphic writing has been found at Beycesultan and that the date of 2000 BC must remain hypothetical.
14. This passage and that on pp. 94–95 refer to the same monument and both show some discrepancy in the opinion of Professor J. M. Casal who adds: 'As a matter of fact the pottery associated with the Palace displays affinities not with the "Uruk Ware" of Mesopotamia, but with the Second Style of Susa as well as with the Kulli

ceramic. This rectification, however, does not conflict with the concluding statement that Mundigak "might well be a 'half-way house' for transcontinental trade". This is precisely the conclusion I reached in the final report mentioned in note 49 of Part II, Chapter I based on evidence supplied by the numerous levels of the site throughout its long occupation.'

15. Professor Diakonoff insists on the conjectural nature of this hypothesis which remains open to controversy.
16. Professor I. M. Diakonoff and Professor G. F. Ilyin note that no conclusive proof exists that the ruling class was of foreign origin. The citadels may have been similar to the baronial castles of Germany in the Middle Ages. Furthermore, Professor Ilyin claims that the data which lead Sir Leonard Woolley to this conclusion are unclear. Sir Leonard Woolley, basing himself on the evidence, draws the attention (1) to the appearance of a new culture and (2) to the violent destruction of the old culture.
17. See Stuart Piggott, *Prehistoric India* (Penguin ed., 1950), pp. 200–1.
18. A scholar, on behalf of the National Commission of India, draws attention to excavations particularly at Hastinapura, which have thrown light on this period. See B. B. Lal, 'Excavations at Hastinapura and other Explorations in the Upper Ganga and Sutlej Basins, 1950–1952,' in *Ancient India,* Nos. 10 and 11 (1954–55), pp. 5–152.

    Sir Leonard Woolley, however, considers that these throw light on the archaeology, but not on the history; it is not even agreed whether the Painted Grey Ware represents the Aryans or not. (For fuller discussion, see *supra*, pp. 106–07, n. 37). A Ghosh in his official summary of the same article says, 'Only a fringe of the problem has been touched. The gulf of the Dark Age has been narrowed down but not filled.'
19. After thorough examination of the monuments in question, Sir Leonard Woolley maintained his point of view, in spite of a number of objections put forward by Professor Ilyin and others, noting that 'as regards Chinese connections, it is an impression, and there is no proof; but the impression is worth recording.'
20. Sir Leonard Woolley justified his use of this term in the following note:

    It has been pointed out to me that my use of the word 'feudalism' here and elsewhere in my history is likely to lead to misapprehension in that scholars of the Marxist school of thought employ it in a very different sense. In Marxist terminology 'feudalism' is a socio-economic structure of society which is characterized by the ruling (*feudal*) class living on the produce of peasants (and also artisans) personally dependent on members of the ruling class or on this class collectively (as, for instance, on monasteries, on the feudal state as a whole); the property of the ruling class in land being combined with tenure of land allotments by the peasants; the population being divided into hereditary estates with different civil and property rights.

    The above definition departs very widely from that which I give in my text. The latter agrees with that in Taswell-Langmead, *English Constitutional History* (5th edition, London, 1896)—'The two chief elements of feudalism are: (1) the personal relation of lord and vassal founded on contract and binding the parties to mutual fidelity, the one owing protection, the other service; (2) the holding of the usufruct (*dominum utile*) of land on the condition of rendering of military service, the ultimate property (*dominum directum*) remaining in the lord, the granter. Combined, these two elements constitut: feudalism; apart, neither is sufficient.'

It is true that the fiefs, originally tenable for life only, soon came to be hereditary, at least on the continent of Europe, where too with the possession of a fief was united the right of local judicature, and the practice of sub-infeudation gave to the great fief-owners a practically independent military and civil jurisdiction—an abuse which in England was forestalled by the *Gemot* of 1086, held on Salisbury Plain, when the Witan and the substantial landowners to the number of sixty thousand swore allegiance directly to the king as supreme feudal overlord; but, none the less, the essence of feudalism is that contained in the definition. For most readers my use of the term will seem understandable and justified; employed in the Marxist sense it certainly will not apply, but I trust that this explanation will prevent misunderstanding by a Marxist reader.

21. See Liu Tse, 'The Nature of the Western Chou Society,' in *Sun-Yat University Bulletin*, No. 1 (Canton, 1957), p. 195.

CHAPTER III

THE SOCIAL STRUCTURE

SPECIALIZATION OF OCCUPATIONS AND PROFESSIONS

In the last chapter an attempt was made to sketch the process of urbanization in the different countries whereof we have record, the development of village into town and of town into city. Side by side with that material growth, partly resulting from it and partly responsible for it, there comes a change in the manner of men's lives; what had been but an agglomeration of clans or families each more or less self-sufficing and morally and socially independent coalesces into an organized society wherein each citizen has his specialized role and must play his part as a member of a community, profiting by the co-operation of his fellows and bound with them by a common law.[1]

Primitive man, living in relative isolation and fending for himself, had necessarily been a Jack-of-all-trades. When he joined with others to make a village he discovered the need to collaborate and to compete with them, and it was to the general interest and his own that he should concentrate on the kind of work that he could do best. Specialization of this sort must have started very early and by degrees, but with the introduction of metal it became essential, for metal-working is a skilled job requiring a long apprenticeship, and it is an all-time job; indeed, as the growing population of the city assured a regular consumers' market for manufacture of all kinds, the various trades became ever more exclusive in their demands on the workers' time. It is true that agriculture remained the most important factor in the economy of the state, so much so that most, even of the city-dwellers, would have their own vegetable gardens or paddocks large enough to supply fodder for a few animals, but very often the care of the garden would be entrusted to hired labour or to a tenant who shared in its produce; the ordinary citizen was a craftsman, a smith, a potter, a carpenter, or shopkeeper, and, as the scope of business increased, a merchant. In most of the countries there was no standing army; war meant the raising of a citizen levy, and that would be only after the gathering of the harvest, in 'the season when kings go forth to war', so that in the early days at least soldiering was not a profession; but even then there was need of a *cadre* of regular officers, and the king would have his personal bodyguard about him, with the result that a military class did exist and was to become more important as imperialistic policies developed. In a theocratic state the priesthood was bound to figure largely. The head of each household would continue to conduct the services and the sacrifices of his domestic gods, but the ritual of state worship was the business of the government. The king might be himself the god, or he might represent the god, or he might be the High Priest, but in any of these functions he would necessarily be surrounded by a regular order of ministers, and where the distinction between religious and lay authority did not really exist but religion gave its sanction to the civil power, there the civil service, if not actually identical with the priesthood, was bound to be recruited mainly from the ranks of the clergy. With the introduction of the art of writing a new feature was added to the social aspect. It must be remembered that writing was a temple invention[2] and therefore first practised by the priests. It had to be taught, and the priests were perforce the teachers, but as the advantages of writing were realized others than professional priests would join the temple schools; a certain number of business men would acquire the new learning, but most of them, too busy to learn for themselves, would be ready to utilize the services of professional writers, and to meet their need there arose a regular class of scribes, public notaries and letter-writers, whose literary attainments would further recommend them for the minor posts of government.

It is clear that while such different occupations imply a vertical division of the citizens the categories so formed would not be all on the same social level; there was a horizontal division also. Officers of the army and the chief priests of the temples would by their functions be brought into closer relations with the king and so by reputation as well as by authority would rank above the common herd. The scribe, even if he were not in government employ, had the intellectual arrogance of the better-educated man and his contempt for the manual labourer. There is an amusing illustration of this in the *Teaching of Khety, Son of Duauf*, an Egyptian work perhaps dating as early as the Eleventh Dynasty but current in much later times, in which a father taking his son to school exhorts him to industry by passing in review all the other occupations and trades and showing how ill they compare with the blessings of the scribe's calling: 'I have never seen the smith as an ambassador, but I have seen the smith at his work at the mouth of his furnace, his fingers like the crocodile's, and he stank more than fishes' eggs. . . . The stonemason finds his work in every kind of hard stone. When he has finished his labours his arms are worn out, and he sleeps all doubled up until sunrise. His knees and his spine are broken. . . . The barber shaves from morning till night; he never sits down except to meals. He hurries from house to house looking for business. He wears out his arms to fill his stomach, like bees eating their own honey. . . . The farmer wears the same clothes for all times. His voice is as raucous as a crow's. His fingers are always busy, his arms are dried up by the wind. He takes his rest—when he does get any rest—in the mud. If he's in good health he shares good health with the beasts; if he is ill his bed is the bare earth in the middle of his beasts. Scarcely does he get home at night when off he has to start again.' Therefore, 'Apply your heart to learning. In truth there is nothing that can compare with it. If you have profited by a single day at school it is a gain for eternity.' As another and later text, the *Teaching of Amen-em-ope*, puts it, 'A scribe who is skilful in his business findeth himself worthy to be a courtier', which the Hebrew author of Proverbs in his admonitions to the young scholar paraphrases, 'Seest thou a man diligent in his business? he shall stand before kings'. (Prov. xxii. 29.)

This stratification of society obviously has its beginnings in the simplest form of communal life. As soon as there was any specialization of functions one type of work would claim superiority over another: the skilled craftsman not only looked down upon the mere labourer but because his skill could earn more in a shorter time did in fact enjoy more leisure and a better life. A tremendous impetus, however, was given to this social change by urbanization, which brought in the further distinction that the 'upper' classes were congregated in the towns whereas the bulk of the 'lower' classes, including all workers on the land, remained in the cultural outer darkness of rural existence;[8] at the same time it introduced the further cross-division between the brain worker and the manual worker. In any urban culture there will be found a ruling class—which may be very small—and under it a society comprising a middle class distinguished by profession, by technique or by wealth, and a lower or labouring class; but whether these *de facto* grades are confirmed by a differing political status is another matter; actually their character and standing will be found to vary from country to country and to depend upon local conditions and history.

Class Distinctions in Egypt

In Egypt, under the early dynasties, only two classes can be recognized, the government and the governed. Pharaoh as god was a being apart, incomparably superior to any mortal; but Pharaoh as ruler had to have associated with him officials to whom could be entrusted the executive functions of rule. The unification of the country had been effected by war; the old governors of the northern nomes, therefore, had been replaced by Pharaoh's nominees who, as his representatives in the provinces, kept their own almost independent courts and had their forces of armed retainers held at the disposition of the supreme ruler; these 'monarchs', together with the great functionaries of the royal court, the members of the royal family (for the sons of the Pharaoh took a prominent part in affairs) and perhaps also the officers of the royal bodyguard, 'the followers of His Majesty', formed the aristocracy of the Old Kingdom. Even as late as the Middle Kingdom the priesthood was still merely an incidental office held by a layman; the lower orders of officials, a few artists, highly skilled craftsmen and merchants might claim a superior status to that of the artisan or the agricultural labourer, but in reality all alike were indiscriminately Pharaoh's serfs.

This simple division of the nation into two main classes, the officials who administered Pharaoh's orders and the rest, mere cyphers, who obeyed them, held good only for the early phases of Egyptian history. The old nomarchs, the viceroys of Pharaoh in the various provinces of the kingdom, profiting by the tendency to make the office an hereditary one, established themselves as semi-independent rulers owing no more than a feudal allegiance to their sovereign and ready, if the opportunity offered itself, to rebel against him. In the civil wars that actually resulted their strength was largely exhausted, and after the expulsion of the Hyksos the Pharaoh Ahmose made a clean sweep of nearly all such as remained and confiscated their landed estates. The whole of Egypt thus became the personal property of the Pharaoh, and in place of the feudal lords the king's favourite nobles, his relatives and his partisans, administered the country in close dependence on the imperial officers who formed his cabinet. The continuous wars that had secured freedom from the Hyksos invaders and then were necessary to assure the frontiers in the south and in Syria had led to the formation of a standing army. Pharaoh was now not only a ruling god, he was also commander-in-chief, and his sons were generals in the forces. The rich booty that had been brought back from the Syrian cities encouraged the recruit and the chances of promotion open to the professional soldier and the prestige attaching to the newly introduced chariotry attracted the scions of the nobility who more or less monopolized this branch, providing their own equipment, and so adding greatly to the importance of the aristocracy. The army now becomes the dominant force and the chief motive power in the state, and its members could not but be recognized as belonging to a social rank superior to that of the mere labourer.

Side by side with the soldier there appeared another applicant for social distinction. The favour shown by the Pharaohs of the Middle Kingdom to the temples of the gods of Egypt was continued in the Eighteenth Dynasty, but now on a far greater scale. Of the wealth that poured into the country as a result of the sacking of foreign cities and the tribute paid by foreign kings, a large part was set aside as thankofferings to the gods who led the armies to victory, and in particular to Amon of Thebes. The administration of the temple revenues and the management of the temple estates demanded a staff whose numbers ever increased. The priesthood became a profession. The priests and officials attached to the local temples were now united in a single sacerdotal organization embracing the whole land with the High Priest of Amon of Thebes as its supreme head;[4] and the political power of that organization grew until it could in the end control and even supplant the divine Pharaoh himself.

A census official of the Eighteenth Dynasty divided the people of Egypt into 'soldiers, priests, royal serfs and all the craftsmen'. Naturally he omits from his classification those with whom he had no professional concern, namely, at the top of the scale, the royal family and court circle which formed the nobility, and, at the bottom, the slaves; he deals with what can be termed the middle and the lower classes of society, freemen and serfs. The character and the condition of the two classes need further examination.

Originally the Egyptian army had been a citizen force, a *levée en masse* called up by the Pharaoh for service as and when required. Since the vast bulk of the population were farmers, the call-up could be made only after harvest, for at any other season it would disorganize the entire economy of the country. After the establishment of the Eighteenth Dynasty Egypt's imperial commitments made a standing army essential, as we have already noted, but this, although it included large detachments of Nubian and Asiatic troops and (later) of mercenaries like the Sherden, had to be kept up to strength by regular recruitment in Egypt itself. The men thus enlisted were drawn from the freeman class, the so-called 'citizens of the army'; the census official's term 'soldiers' includes therefore all freemen other than priests because their liability to military service was indeed their qualification for freedom and had become the significant designation of their class. For very many of the 'citizens of the army' military service must have remained no more than a liability; they were never actually conscripted. There were small landowners whose civilian activities were of value to the state, some merchants (though the major lines of trade were run by the government), scribes, artists and petty functionaries of the crown; they could live their own lives undisturbed, and there was always the chance of promotion and royal favour; one such official can even boast of his humble origin: 'Ye shall talk of it, one to another, and the old men shall teach it to the youth. I was one whose family was poor and whose town was small, but the Lord of Two Lands recognized me; I was accounted great in his heart, the King in the splendour of his palace saw me. He exalted me more than the courtiers, introducing me among the princes of the palace.' Not all could rise so high, but at least there was scope for ambition here, as there was in the army and in the priesthood, and for all a comfortable manner of life. The growing prosperity of the middle class is reflected in the cemeteries. In the time of the Old Kingdom it had been the case that while the mastaba tombs of the court nobles, clustered round the pyramid prepared for Pharaoh, supplied them with the essentials for a happy life in the hereafter, the rest of the people had no such hope; their bodies were interred in nameless graves with, at most, some sustenance for the journey to that world in which their serfdom would be for eternity. To a certain extent that is true of the Middle Kingdom also, but a change was in progress and in the course of time became absolute.

During and after the Eighteenth Dynasty the middle class provided for themselves tombs and tomb-offerings and even tomb-chapels, things to which their forbears had never aspired; in the vast cemetery at Abydus about a quarter of the graves are those of priests; at el Amarna the nobles had their chambered tombs hewn in the hill-sides, but, apart from them, in the valley the gay little funerary chapels commemorate minor functionaries sprung from the lower ranks of society. It was no longer for the middle class a case of *nos numeri sumus*; the Egyptian freeman had risen to be an individual; he had a stake in the country, and if the future life was to perpetuate the conditions of the present it was a fair prospect than which he could ask nothing better. This bourgeois development is further illustrated by the houses of the living. In the Twelfth Dynasty town of Kahun there are the houses of the petty clerks and of the artisans, containing each from four to seven rooms, small, crowded and aligned in monotonous rows, and there are about a dozen great mansions of the nobility, each of about sixty rooms with large columned courts; and between these there is nothing, nothing to bridge the gulf between abject poverty and the extravagance of wealth. But in the Eighteenth Dynasty town of el Amarna we find far more variety. The royal palace and the mansions of the court nobility are on the scale of magnificence seen earlier at Kahun, but side by side with those, occupying, for example, a large part of the north suburb, we find the comfortable homes of the middle class. These houses are all detached, each standing in its own walled courtyard measuring as much as 70 yards by 50 yards (*c.* 65 metres by 41 metres) laid out as a garden with formal rows of shrubs and trees amongst which generally would be a tiny chapel for family worship. Each house contained a dozen or more rooms, including a columned central hall and one- or two-columned loggias opening on the garden; it was of a single storey but a staircase led up to the flat roof on which there might be a light loggia or sun-shelter; all this was for the use of the family and their guests, the kitchen and the servants' quarters being outside in the courtyard, to leeward of the main building. On a smaller scale and in a simpler form the dwelling of the bourgeois citizen reproduced that of the hereditary noble.

Along the narrow lanes behind these houses lie the 'slums'. Here the buildings are crowded together, ill built and irregularly planned, but by no means stereotyped; often the remains suffice to show that the poor owner was really making the best of the site and the means at his disposal, and the result has at least a certain individuality. Here lived the artisans and the lesser craftsmen and mechanics, men who were by law strictly forbidden to change their occupation and were not allowed to meddle in civic affairs. The most depressing evidence of their social standing is given by the walled village lying a mile or more to the east of the city of Akhetaton which was built for the labourers employed on excavating the rock tombs of the nobility; the monotonous rows of identical hovels laid out with mathematical precision look more like slave-lines than the homes of even the humblest citizens of imperial Egypt. Such 'artisans' ranked in the census list together with the agricultural labourer as forming the lowest order of society. Not all agriculturalists were included in this category; the 'small men', as they were called in Middle Kingdom times, small property-owning cultivators, were heavily taxed but at least their own masters; but the men who worked on the royal estates and on the temple lands or were employed by the holders of military fiefs were really serfs. They were not slaves, in that they could not be sold, and they had their own homes; but they were tied to the land and, if the land changed its ownership, passed automatically from the service of one master to that of the other, and they could be hired out for their master's profit; as citizens they had their legal rights, but they were always subject to the oppression of those of higher rank. They were exempt from military service, which would have raised them to a higher social status, for the simple reason that the fields had to be tilled; but when the Nile was in flood and also after the harvest had been gathered, in the agricultural 'dead seasons', they would be liable to the *corvée,* the strengthening of dykes, the cleaning and deepening of canals, and the porterage of stone for Pharaoh's huge building works. This predial serfdom therefore aimed at providing for the agricultural and religious requirements of the state, and normally it did so effectively and without over-great hardship. For a community to make use of some of its manpower for its own welfare is not even today considered necessarily to entail a form of slavery which reduces the individual to the status of a chattel.

Slavery in Egypt

These classes accounted for the whole Egyptian population of the Nile valley. In addition, there were slaves, but they were foreigners, prisoners-of-war, and from the point of view of Egyptian economy they count for curiously little. The number of slaves in private hands seems never to have been large; thus Ahmose, an army officer in the early days of the Eighteenth Dynasty, was given by Pharaoh four Hyksos prisoners —one man and three women—whom he had captured with his own hand, but the fact was sufficiently unusual for him to put it on record in his tomb. Owing to the unwarlike nature of the Egyptian peasant it has always been the custom to enrol foreign recruits and suitable prisoners-of-war in the Egyptian forces, firstly Sudanese—as is pictured in the wooden tomb-groups of the Twelfth Dynasty (Pl. 5, a)—but also Libyans and, when their turn came, Syrians;[5] only when the Syrian wars produced prisoners in greater numbers than the army required were they used for other purposes, and even then only within definite limits. Thutmose III brought back from his victorious campaigns captives destined to work as weavers, cooks, tailors, etc., in the palace and as agricultural labourers on the temple estates; these were lodged in *ergastula* and were therefore real slaves, but they were the slaves of the gods—of Amun-Rê and of the Pharaoh—who alone were the victors; they could not be, or were not, handed over to private persons. Amenhotep II and Amenhotep III each claim nearly a hundred thousand prisoners-of-war, as again does Ramses III, whose Syrian prisoners were set to till the temple estates and were kept in regular slave-lines. But very soon those 'slaves' were registered as tax-paying serfs; the Pharaoh distributed some of them amongst his courtiers, and they intermarried with their Egyptian fellow-servants; he employed great numbers of them on the building of his huge monuments, but later he enlisted them, branded with his name, in the ranks of the Egyptian army. As the growing power of the priesthood of Amun began to undermine the autocracy of the Pharaoh he found it expedient to surround his person with foreigners who owed allegiance to none but himself, and such guards and attendants, although slaves by origin, gained high office in the court and in the state. The fact is that whereas in most countries of the Middle East the institution of slavery has been a necessary condition of the development of civilization, Egypt, where all labour was at Pharaoh's service, was an exception to the general rule; historically and economically the constitution and the character of the country did not favour a large-scale development of the slave system. The Nile valley was thickly populated and the law ensured that there should be no shortage of labour for agriculture and for the essential trades, and the *corvée* system was so organized that the most elaborate public works could be carried through without detriment to the cultivation of the soil; the upper class, enriched by the favour of a divine king who owned the entire land and its immense wealth, had the leisure and the means to appreciate and to encourage the arts of civilized life. Egypt was in fact self-sufficient, and when by accidents of war slavery was introduced it was an excrescence upon the body politic.

Slavery in Mesopotamia and Anatolia

The case was very different in Mesopotamia and in Anatolia. There you had states not physically isolated as was Egypt but amongst neighbours with whom they might at any moment be involved in war. From the very beginning, therefore, any successful state was likely to have on its hands prisoners-of-war who would naturally be made to work for their conquerors. In theory, the enemies who have dared to attack or resist your state deserve death, and when you meet them in battle you kill them. If they surrender, and you decide to spare their lives, it is only because they can be more useful alive than dead;

they become your slaves, but if as slaves they cease to be useful you can kill them without compunction. That the Hittite law recognized this absolute right is clear from an exhortation in which the relation between master and slave is used to illustrate that between man and god: 'And if ever a servant vexes his master, either they kill him or they injure his nose, his eyes or his ears; or he [the master] calls him to account and also his wife, his sons, his brother, his sister, his relatives by marriage, and his family, whether it be a male servant or a female servant. . . . If then anyone vexes the feelings of a god, does the god punish him alone for it? Does he not punish his wife, his children, his descendants, his family, his slaves male and female, his cattle, his sheep and his harvest for it, and remove him utterly?' Also: 'If a servant is in any way at fault and confesses his fault before his master, then whatever his master wants to do with him he will do'—again the master is assumed to have unlimited right, including the power of life and death, to deal with the slave as he thinks fit; but the text goes on—'But because he has confessed his fault before his master, his master's spirit is soothed and the master will not call that servant to account'. The Hittite slave was a mere chattel which could be bought and sold, and his offences involved death for himself and all belonging to him; the writer of the exhortation insists on this as being an exact parallel to man's position when he sins against god, who will punish 'to the third and fourth generation'; but he insists equally that man can by confession obtain the mercy of god just as he himself forgives the trespasses of his slave. The implication is that the individual master's treatment of his slave would in practice be mitigated by common sense and by morality, but apart from that rather precarious safeguard it suggests no real alleviation of the slave's lot; it is therefore surprising to find that the Hittite code of law conferred upon the slave rights which are wholly inconsistent with what is normally termed slavery. By definition, a slave is a human chattel, the absolute property of his master, possessing no individual rights and enjoying no legal protection; the law is concerned with him only to the extent that it enforces his complete subjection to his owner. But in the Hittite economy this is not so. A slave could own property; he could marry, and, provided that he produced the necessary bridal gifts, could marry a freewoman; if he was assaulted and injured (presumably by someone other than his master) he could sue his opponent in the courts and receive money compensation (exactly half of what would have been paid to a freeman) and the money went to him, not to his master;[6] if he were the guilty party he was fined exactly half the amount imposed on a freeman for the same offence, except for one or two crimes for which the punishment was bodily mutilation. In the eyes of the law therefore the 'slave', so far from being a chattel, was a person, one whose life and bodily integrity and civil rights had to be protected; and if his value to the state was assessed at only half that of the free citizen his obligations to it were halved likewise.

A somewhat similar anomaly can be observed in Mesopotamia where again the slave is on the one hand no 'man' but a thing, shaven-headed and branded, whose father's name is never recorded because he is less than human, but on the other hand is a person enjoying rights of his own and a measure of protection from the state. But here the master does not even in theory possess the power of life and death over his slave; ownership was absolute as far as it went, but it had its limits. The Sumerian and the Babylonian law recognized and encouraged slavery as an institution, but the slaves formed part of the social state, a distinctly valuable part, and therefore could not be left entirely to the mercy of the individual citizen-owner; moreover, the status of the slave was accidentally and not necessarily permanent: so far from a man being a natural slave, the slave was potentially a freeman. The institution had to be enforced. For a slave to run away was, theoretically, a capital offence, though generally, if he were caught, his master would simply put him in shackles to prevent a second escape, or might even let him off punishment (we have instances of this in the tablets); and to connive at a slave's escape was a crime against the state which merited death; but the master could not kill his slave.

Slaves might be prisoners-of-war. In the early days of Sumer when most wars were fought between neighbouring cities, any captives taken were indeed citizens of a hostile state but they were of the same race as their captors; they were slaves only through misfortune, and at any time they might be ransomed; moreover, one could not but remember that at any time another war might reverse the positions of slave and master. Slaves might be purchased abroad and imported into Mesopotamia; but there is a remarkable proviso that should such a one, on reaching his new home, be recognized as a Babylonian then he must forthwith be given his freedom. But the slave might also be a free-born citizen. A bankrupt might himself be enslaved for debt or, as was more common, might sell his wife, his son or his daughter into slavery so as to acquire capital to pay off his debts, or might simply hand them over as payment to his creditor. If a son, or an adopted son, disowned his parents he could be cast out and enslaved; and we have cases where a man has been reduced to slavery because 'he kicked his mother' or 'struck his older brother'. The unfortunate who became slaves through debt could be ransomed at any time, and in any case their servitude was by law (though not necessarily in practice) only temporary—'Three years shall they work in the house of their buyer', says Hammurabi's Code, 'and in the fourth year he shall fix their liberty'; and in the meantime they were protected to the extent that should one die as the result of ill-treatment by his temporary master the latter's son was to be killed in retribution. In the case of real slaves, male or female, who had been temporarily transferred to another master in settlement of a debt, death from ill-treatment involved only a money fine payable to the original owner, and the master had the right to sell them for money if it suited his convenience to do so, and in the event of their being insubordinate could bore or cut off their ears. To this extent the slave is a mere chattel. On the other hand the Babylonian slave, at least in the first millennium BC and probably earlier than that, could, like the Hittite slave, own property and engage in business. According to Hammurabi's Code he could marry a freewoman, in which case his children would be free; but although, if he were assaulted and injured by a third party, his assailant was mulcted in a fine (one-half of what would have been paid for a freeman) yet the money went not to him but to his owner; similarly, were he sick, his owner had to pay the doctor (at a reduced rate) for medical attendance, but should the slave die under the treatment or suffer the loss of a member, then not he but his master was entitled to compensation from the unskilful practitioner. Obviously the Babylonian law attempts, at the expense of logic, to compromise between the rigorous definition of slavery which would make the slave merely an item of property and the recognition of him as a person entitled to the protection of the state. If we may trust the evidence of the tablets, the private owner found it more expedient—and perhaps more to his taste as a decent man—to be guided by the second view rather than to take full advantage of his theoretical rights, and the conditions of the slave's life were probably not nearly so miserable as some clauses of the law would lead us to suspect.

Slavery Amongst the Hebrews

That this mixed conception of slavery was more or less typical of the Middle East down to the close of the second millennium BC is confirmed by the Hebrew Code. This is based on Babylonian (or Sumerian) law but does on the whole go farther in its humanitarian modifications of the system. The master's absolute ownership of the slave is undisputed: if a man smite his servant with a rod and kill him outright he is to be punished (presumably because violence of the sort is anti-social), but if the victim only dies 'after a day or two, he shall not be punished: for he is his money'; i.e. the pecuniary loss is penalty enough. Similarly if a slave be gored by a neighbour's ox, known to be savage, the animal's owner has to pay compensation, but the money goes not to the injured slave but to his master. On the other hand if a master, punishing his slave, puts out his eye or causes him to lose a tooth, he has to set him free; any Hebrew slave acquired by purchase could be kept for six years only and 'in the seventh he shall go out free for nothing'. Slavery for debt was also, in the case of a Hebrew, made light and temporary: 'If thy brother be waxen poor and be sold unto thee, thou shalt not compel him to serve as a bond-servant, but as a hired servant and as a sojourner he shall be with thee, and shall serve thee unto the year of Jubilee', after which he and his family were free to depart. By the Mosaic Code real slavery was reserved for 'the heathen that are round about you; of them shall ye buy bondmen and bond-maids', and for such there was no redemption or chance of freedom: 'They shall be your bondmen for ever.' It was a religious rather than a racial or political sentiment that mitigated for a Hebrew the terms of servitude but maintained their strictest severity for the unbeliever.

Although some of the buildings at Harappā look very much like slave-lines it is impossible, in the absence of written records, to say whether slavery really did exist in the Indus valley civilization and, if so, what was its character; but for the Middle East it was, as we have seen, one of the basic features of society. The superstructure of society was formed of the free citizens. In the case of the Hebrews all these were of equal standing; there were 'elders' and 'heads of the congregation' who enjoyed a certain moral superiority and were the guardians of tradition, but legally there were no social distinctions 'seeing that all the congregation are holy, every one of them'; the accidents of riches or of poverty, except in so far as debt might reduce a man to temporary servitude, did not affect the status of the individual citizen.

Classes in Mesopotamia

In the Code of Hammurabi the distinction is constantly drawn between 'the gentleman', 'the poor man' and the slave. On the strength of this it might be imagined that Sumerian and Babylonian society, apart of course from the slaves, was divided into two categories according to their financial qualifications. For the purposes of the penal clauses of the Code this was indeed a convenient classification, and of course it is based upon fact, but it does not justify the deductions generally drawn from it. The terms used, *awlîum* or *amelu*, usually translated 'nobleman'[7] or 'patrician', and *mushkenu*, 'semi-free' or 'plebeian', suggest a ruling oligarchy lording it over the mass of the population, but such was certainly not the character of the Sumerian or Babylonian polity. The *mushkenu* formed a separate class; they were clearly distinguished from the slaves and in fact could themselves own slaves; they differed from the *amelu* in that the punishments inflicted on them for crimes of violence were less severe than those incurred by the *amelu* and, similarly, compensation paid to them for injuries done was only half of that due to the nobleman, though much more than that due to a slave; but most of the clauses of the Code are meant to apply equally to *amelu* and *mushkenu* and in some the equality is directly stated: 'If a slave of the palace or a slave of a poor man . . .'—the two are evidently on the same footing. On the other hand the *mushkenu* were not eligible for government office; it is probable that they could not own land in fee simple but only as tenants held land allotted to them by the government in return for certain services; and although they were liable to conscription they were seldom if ever allowed to carry arms, their duties being limited to those of camp-followers and of the army service corps. They were freemen, but they were held in subjection; they enjoyed most of the privileges of citizenship but were of less account than the gentry, and their loyalty to the state was not above suspicion. Probably they were descendants of old stocks which had been submerged by the successive invasions of Mesopotamia; they had not been enslaved, but they had never been admitted into full community with the later comers. Presumably they were small farmers, either on their own account or as hired hands, labourers, artisans and petty craftsmen, and just as their standing in the state was low so their numbers were not very great. Hammurabi's Code was here, as throughout, re-editing in an amended form the enactments of earlier Sumerian legislators, and in the old days strong measures may well have been required to repress a potentially dangerous element, but the danger would grow steadily less. Had the *mushkenu* been very numerous their exemption from carrying arms would have limited unduly the military forces at the disposal of the government, but they were a diminishing class and in later history they disappear altogether; some perhaps by success in business managed to rise in society, others on the contrary sank and were absorbed in the ranks of the slaves.

The term *amelu*, then, is a comprehensive one, applying to all free citizens; but it includes a variety of social grades.

As was to be expected with a constitution which was by origin purely theocratic and to a large extent maintained that character throughout Babylonian history, the king, who was god's representative on earth, and the priesthood which naturally came directly under the king, formed the dominant order. To them in time were added the scribes. At first the scribes must have been temple priests, but as education spread men trained in the temple schools could become scribes without taking orders; so honourable a profession was it that we have several instances of members of the royal family claiming the title of 'scribe' and scribes might hold the highest posts in the civil government; their position was indeed much like that of the clerks of mediaeval Europe. A second class was that of the hereditary nobility, the real 'patricians', who wore their hair long behind and were addressed in letters by the title *amelu* just as the German noble was entitled *Hochwohlgeboren*. They supplied the members of the Council of Elders of their native city or community and took a prominent place in the administration of justice both as judges and as assessors, and their decisions on points of fact were final; as courtiers they were in close attendance on the king and therefore, whether holding office or not, exercised a great influence upon the government; and they filled the higher ranks of the standing army in the Babylonian period just as earlier they had naturally assumed the command of the national levies.

Socially below these came the bulk of the free population. All of them were, in theory at least, liable to military service, and that liability was indeed the guarantee of their full citizenship; whether, or to what extent, they were actually called up in peace-time it is not possible to say, but the machinery certainly was kept in readiness. The recruiting officers both for the armed forces and for the transport and auxiliary contingents seem to have been on a permanent footing and had to perform their duties in person when summoned to the king's service; but in normal times they lived at home and cultivated their land. They were actually farmers. They were granted by the state fiefs which they were bound to cultivate and keep in good condition and which were inalienable;[8] the lands could not be sold or pledged, but on the other hand they could not be taxed or taken from the owner by the judgement of the courts or by the act of the governor of the province. The privileges which such a man enjoyed in respect of both his person and his properties (if he were captured in war and his liquid assets were insufficient to pay his ransom the debt became a charge on the local temple or, failing that, on the state) are quite inconsistent with a 'plebeian' status; but they were not the privileges of wealth—the 'gangers' were not rich men, as is clear from the clauses of the Code, and their fiefs were quite small; the distinction therefore between *amelu* and *mushkenu* is not that between rich and poor but between the full citizen and the 'half-free'. Owing to the secular rivalry of the Sumerian city states the army was, next to the cult of the city's god, the most important institution of society, and therefore the terms 'citizen' and 'soldier' were, as we have seen, virtually interchangeable. But the citizen-soldier was also, when not on active service, a farmer, an artist, a merchant, a manufacturer, a craftsman; all such then might be freemen of the state. Much of Hammurabi's Code is framed for the protection of this middle class, which was financially so vulnerable but from the legislative point of view ranked almost, though not quite, with the 'gentry'. The term *amelu,* which perhaps originally meant merely 'man', was arrogated to themselves by a ruling class whose members alone had value in their own eyes and formed 'the state' proper; it was therefore reserved to the narrow class of the nobility. But the content of the word widened as class distinctions became less clear-cut, and even in Hammurabi's day *amelu* must have been somewhat of an anachronism as implying noble birth, and in time it lost that special significance altogether and came to mean simply 'man'. The Sumerian and the Babylonian state, in spite of its autocratic monarch, its traditional nobility, and a priesthood in which was embodied the awe of the divine Power behind the throne, was none the less in some ways curiously democratic.

Classes Amongst the Hittites

The Hittite law distinguished sharply between freemen and slaves, but regarded all freemen as equal. There was no middle class, and distinctions of rank did not interfere with the parity of rights. It must be remembered that Hatti was a confederacy of various tribes some of which had been allies from the outset, some brought in originally under compulsion but accepted as fellow-members; they did not lose their identity in any way, retaining even their different languages or dialects, and that being so they were not likely to allow the prestige of their leading families to be overlooked. The 'Great Family' which formed the court of the king of Hattusas and shared amongst themselves the chief offices of state probably included what had been the royal houses of the old 'Hittite' tribes; if they were called the king's 'kinsmen' the term may well refer to the oath of blood-brotherhood which originally bound the tribes together, and this would explain the elective character of the kingship in the early days of the confederation. Naturally these great nobles ranked socially above the rest of the citizens, and together with their official underlings and with the fighting troops formed the *pankus* or Assembly which, again in the early days, might be called together as representing the entire community; but this, their sole political privilege, fell into abeyance as the kings ceased to summon the *pankus* and even socially the noble caste seems in time to have become less exclusive. Certainly it was to the advantage of the ruler to weaken a class which in the past had put forward rival claimants to the crown, and as his own power increased the legal equality of all free Hittite citizens put them more and more upon a common footing.

The fifteenth-century census lists found at Alalakh and the Mari letters are quite explicit on the subject of the social organization of the Hurri. Apart from slaves, who do not figure in the lists, which were drawn up for the purpose of levy for service and possibly for taxation, there were three well-defined classes. The lowest and the most numerous class was the *hupšu,* semi-free serfs who were subject to the *corvée* and to military service; the alternative name applied to them, *sabē namē,* probably means that they lived not in the towns but either on their outskirts or in the open country; they owned houses and small plots of land, but since they are often noted as 'having no ox (or cattle)' they might be men of very small substance. Above them came the *haniahu,* the middle class, which included tradesmen, gardeners, royal herdsmen and grooms, etc. The aristocracy, the *mariannu* class, was distinguished by the possession of a chariot (or wagon?), but since the rank was hereditary that material qualification might sometimes be no more than a polite theory, so that occasionally there is written after the man's name the note 'possesses no chariot'. The *mariannu* seem to have been the leading citizens in all walks of life, and the class was a small one—in Alalakh itself they numbered only thirty-four, and in the villages and small towns anything from one to thirteen; since, however, the head of one local levy had eighty charioteers under his command it must be supposed either that not all chariot-owners were of the *mariannu* class, or else that a rich member of the class might own a number of chariots. There are two or three references (*not* in census lists) to *mushkenu* impressed into military service, but such do not seem to have formed a social class; they may simply be 'poor men'.

THE ARMY

In the foregoing chapters constant reference has been made to the direct or indirect influence of the army upon the history of man's advance in civilization. In so far as the fighting forces of a country have protected its culture from destruction by hostile invaders or have by foreign conquest extended that culture into backward areas, their contribution has been obvious, and as an outstanding element in the social organization they cannot be disregarded. It must be remembered also that success in war and the resultant capture of prisoners was one of the chief sources of the slave-labour which for many early communities was essential to progress, and that the economic and administrative stability of governments has always been conditioned by the armed support at their command. While this is in no sense a military history, a brief sketch of military development and organization is needed to explain how, in different countries, the army came to play the part it did, affecting in varying degrees the lives of the people.

The origin of the army is, of course, the 'nation in arms', the *levée en masse* of the male members of the community for purposes of defence or attack. The Hebrew people did not pass beyond this primitive stage until the days of the Kingdom; every man was a fighting man at need, called up and commanded by the recognized head of his clan. The pre-Dynastic Egyptians had their territorial basis, each nome or district providing its own militia which marched under a nome standard and was presumably raised and commanded by the prince or great landowner who was the nome's governor. With the unification of Egypt the system was altered but little. The nomarch confirmed in office would, in the event of war, be summoned by the central government to produce his contingent; but it was a contingent of his own men, owing allegiance primarily to himself, and when in times of national disorganization the nomarch asserted his independence he could count upon his local troops to fight for him against his neighbours and the Pharaoh alike. But these local troops were not regular soldiers. Military service in Egypt was merely one form of the *corvée*. The peasant was called up now for digging irrigation canals, now for mining and building work, now for the army; and in each case when the work was finished he went back to his home labour. Such casual and intermittent compulsory service was neither meant nor expected to produce a regular army; the most it could do was to form a *cadre* of officers able to organize and discipline the raw levies supplied by the nomarchs; and these officers would be appointed by and responsible to the Pharaoh alone. It was an unsatisfactory system, for as long as the nomarchs retained their armed following the central government could not feel itself secure. The Middle Kingdom saw the final suppression of the old territorial nobility, and Pharaoh became the sole head of the Egyptian army.

It was under the Middle Kingdom rulers that aggressive warfare first in the Sudan and then in Syria changed the conditions of service. Troops were now required not to meet some sudden and short-lived emergency but to embark on foreign expeditions whose duration might well be prolonged, disregarding the regular 'season when kings go forth to war' which was the season after the safe harvesting of the crops. In these circumstances the old form of general conscription could not be enforced; the food-supplies of the nation would not be forthcoming unless the conscripted peasant were there to work the fields at the proper time. What was needed was a standing army, and for this trained officers were available; but the difficulty of raising sufficient troops without disrupting the country's economy remained. Morover, the Egyptian was by disposition no soldier, and the forces which had served well enough in domestic warfare against fellow Egyptians were not to be depended upon when it came to fighting Asiatics. The result was that the regular army was largely formed of foreign mercenaries. Even under the Twelfth Dynasty the royal bodyguard consisted of Sudanese regulars, and soon afterwards in the armies of Egypt that overran Syria the native Egyptians (professional soldiers by force of circumstances) were outnumbered by the Sudanese, Libyans, Shardanu and Syrians in the pay of the Pharaoh. The army, in fact, was not national but royal; the cost of it was defrayed by the ruler out of the enormous revenues of the crown, supplemented by the booty taken in war; it had very little to do with the people in general. The peasant might still, under the *corvée,* be called up for some para-military duty as camp-follower or whatnot, but to all intents and purposes he was quit of the army service which he detested and war—always waged far away on foreign soil—meant nothing to him.

In this, as in so many other respects, the course followed by Mesopotamia was radically different from that taken by Egypt. The beginnings were necessarily similar, the *levée en masse* of a village community threatened with attack; but as the delta came to be more sharply partitioned off into city states owing allegiance to different patron gods, land-hunger and, still more, jealousy regarding water supplies, led to endemic wars. Because it was the city's god who led the attack or marshalled the defence every pious citizen was bound to follow his standard, and the local *ensī* or king, who represented the god, naturally took command. The *ensī* was a permanent official, and the captaincy of the city's forces was one of his principal functions, and where those forces were so constantly engaged it was his duty to see that the citizen army[9] was adequate to its task; they might not be regular soldiers, but they had to be organized and trained for regular warfare.

On Eannatum's 'Stele of the Vultures' (Pl. 6, a) we can see how, by the early part of the third millennium BC, the Sumerians had evolved a military formation which has a definitely professional look, and on the 'Standard of Ur' that professional aspect is emphasized, and at the same time certain technical advances seem to have been made.

On the stele the best troops—the *corps d'élite*—are foot-soldiers uniformly equipped with bronze (or copper) helmets, big rectangular shields and long spears, who are drawn up in a six-deep phalanx; other troops, with helmets but no body-armour, wearing only the fleeced *kaunakes* kilt and carrying long lances, advance in double file; the ruler himself appears on foot at the head of the phalanx, wearing the fleece robe and carrying a short curved sword, and a second time he is represented at the head of the marching files, but this time he is mounted in a chariot and wields a long spear, while in a quiver in front of him there are light throwing-javelins. On the Standard (Pl. 5, b) there is again a phalanx, but it is differently equipped; the soldiers wear helmets and heavy cloaks (probably leather with metal studs) but have no shields, and instead of spears they carry short-axes. The light-armed skirmishers engaged with the enemy wear only helmet and kilt, or, at most, a light shawl, and their only weapon seems to be the club. The real innovation is the chariotry. The king still has his own royal chariot, but now there is a chariot corps; the cars, drawn each by four asses, carry two men, a driver and a fighter armed with battle-axe and a sheath of light javelins.

Such organization of the service into branches distinguished by their armament is the sophistication of military science attempting to forge a decisive weapon. But it is clear that everything is still experimental. The change in the character of the phalanx was an experiment. The ass-drawn chariot had long been known—since the Uruk period at least, for it is mentioned in the epic poem 'Enmerkar and the Lord of Aratta' which refers to the close of the fourth millennium BC; for Eannatum it is a royal distinction, on the Standard a divisional arm, and after that time it seems to have dropped out of use except, perhaps, for ceremonial purposes. Again, the bow was in common use in Sumer in the al'Ubaid period (as it was in Egypt, where archers formed part of the army throughout all history),[10] but it is only once figured on an early Sumerian monument and then as used against animals, not men; the arrows found in the grave of Mes-Kalam-dug at Ur—roughly contemporary with the Standard—were sporting arrows, not weapons of war; yet on the stele of Naram-Sin (Pl. 6, b) the king is shown holding a bow, implying that for the northern Akkadians at any rate it was an approved and honoured arm. The same stele suggests also that the kings of Akkad abandoned the phalanx drill and relied rather upon open fighting, tactics which would accord with the employment of archers.

The Sumerians had been, so far as we know, civilian soldiers, well-drilled and experienced volunteers in the service of the city's god. The Akkadian kings, however, conducting campaigns as far afield as Cappadocia and the Mediterranean coast, had need of a professional army; thus Sargon had a standing force of 5,400 men who 'ate daily before him'. Circumstances made the same demand here as in Egypt, but nothing could be more unlike the Egyptian army than that evolved by the Sumerian kings and perfected by Hammurabi.

The Babylonian army was based upon a system of conscription; lists of all those liable to military service were kept in the state registers. By no means all the population was liable. The *mushkenu,* as we have seen, were conscripted, but only as camp-followers, and even listed men might be excused if circumstances justified it, e.g. where two brothers were recruited one might be released if family affairs so required, a shepherd or a baker might, if indispensable, be returned to his civil occupation; but the appeal had to be approved by the king himself, and in some cases he would demand a substitute; on the other hand, it was a penal offence for a recruit to substitute another man for himself without the royal permission. No slaves and no foreigners were enrolled. So far as possible the men taken were the sons of old soldiers, and this hereditary calling meant the creation of a military caste and a corporate spirit which was invaluable. For the ordinary soldier was not kept permanently with the colours; unlike the personnel of the small standing army, 'the King's Troop', he could return to civil life in the intervals of service, rejoining the ranks when called up by the recruiting officer but rejoining a profession and a company already familiar to him. Discipline was necessarily strict, but the rank and file were protected against harsh or unfair treatment by the officers, and they seem to have been well fed and reasonably paid. Rations had to be supplied by the city governments for the troops in their area, and in addition special taxes were levied, apparently upon individual citizens, to provide pay; thus one Imlik-ilî states that he has paid five-sixths of a *mina* of silver for fifty soldiers, and this would appear to have been a compulsory payment rather than a voluntary subscription like the Greek 'liturgy'. But the main attraction to the military life was the gift of land. To every soldier the king gave a parcel of land on a feudal basis; it carried the duty to serve, but it was inalienable and (with the same liability) hereditary; during his absence in the field he could let the land or take a partner, but on his return, in not more than three years, he could reclaim it for himself, but he was bound to cultivate and crop his land; should he fail to do so for more than three years on end, and some other man tend the neglected property, then, and in this way only, did the freeholder lose possession—a very proper subordination of private ownership to the public good. Yet another privilege enjoyed by the Babylonian soldier was that if he were taken prisoner by the enemy and could not himself afford his ransom this should be paid by the temple of his home town or, failing that, by the king. He was indeed a favoured person; and, since both the favours and the command were vested solely in the king's person, his loyalty could be taken for granted, and in fact we hear of no such thing as a military revolt. That the Babylonian army degenerated as it did after the time of the First Dynasty of Babylon was in part due, it would seem, to the growing commercial wealth of the country which outbalanced the privileges of the military and made army service unpopular, so that a returned prisoner could say 'No more soldiering for me'; but in part also to the introduction of the horse-drawn war chariot, which revolutionized tactics and made the Babylonian army out of date.

The Hittites seem to have been the first of the Western Asiatic powers to make regular use of the horse. It had long been domesticated in central Asia, as at Anau. Horsed chariots were buried in the royal tombs of China in the fourteenth century BC. The chariot reached Anatolia (presumably through the Hurri acting as middlemen) not later than the close of the third millennium BC, and very soon formed the most important arm of the Hittite fighting force. The Kassites brought the horse into Mesopotamia, where a later Kassite king boasted that horses were 'as common as straw', and Syria took them over from the Hurri; if the Egyptians did not see them in Syria they were to learn of them when the Hyksos war-chariots broke into Egypt. Everywhere the horse was used for the war-chariot alone, not for ordinary draught purposes or for riding; but no country failed to recognize the value of the new weapon. Mesopotamia had long since discarded the old Sumerian ass-drawn chariot; the Egyptians had never used the ass for any draught purpose, for the excellent reason that their valley bottom, cut up by innumerable water-channels, was almost impracticable for wheeled traffic, and the natural method of transport was by water. The horsed chariot, therefore, was for the Near East a real innovation. It was a costly weapon and as such tended to emphasize social distinctions in the army. When, as was the case with the Hittites, the chariotry, like the infantry, were furnished by the cities of the empire, they took precedence over the mere footmen, whether those were fellow townsmen or the retainers of the great nobles, and yet more over the mercenaries such as the Sutu bowmen. Amongst the Hurri, chariot-owners formed the highest social class. When, as in Egypt, the charioteer provided his own equipment—which only the rich could afford to do—the development of the arm increased also the social position of the aristocracy in the state. In the latter half of the second millennium BC victory in war was held to depend upon the numerical strength of the chariotry engaged on either side, so that every effort was made to raise the largest force possible: if we can believe Egyptian accounts, the Hittite army at the battle of Carchemish consisted of 17,000 infantry and no less than 3,500 chariots. But it was a weapon whose real value was largely psychological, as is evidenced by the Hebrew dread of the 'chariots of iron' of the Philistines; it did indeed secure quickness of manœuvre, but more important was the terror which it inspired in the inexperienced foot-soldier. At the battle of Kadesh the infantry division of Rê, taken by surprise by the Hittite chariots, simply took to its heels, and the Amon division broke at the mere rumour of them; for a long time the struggle remained largely a chariotry battle in which the combatants seem seldom to have come to very close quarters, each side advancing and retreating alternately (the Hittite infantry was on the other side of the river); but as soon as the scattered Amon division rallied and marched up, and the Sutekh division appeared in the south, the Hittite chariots, unable to face unbroken infantry, simply withdrew across the river and abandoned the fight. It was not without reason that the Achaeans used their chariots to manœuvre and dismounted from them to fight; when the new weapon ceased to strike terror it ceased to be effective, and though the Assyrians were to use it still to good purpose, it gradually fell into disuse, becoming a parade weapon rather than an instrument of war.

LAW

It is, of course, obvious that no real community, however small and however primitive, can exist and hold together unless certain rules regarding the relations between members of the social unit are recognized as binding upon each and all. Such rules may originally have been imposed by the arbitrary will of the strongest member of the unit, or they may represent mutual concessions whereby the individual will submit itself to a régime tending to the common good; whatever their ultimate source, their observance is manifestly to the general interest, and therefore the free community as a whole will be prepared to defend and perpetuate them.[11] So essential are they to the very existence of society that, as custom crystallizes into precedent, they are apt to acquire an authority of their own which is independent of the views of the living members of the community; so far from the state being conceived as making the law, men tend to assume that it is the law that makes the state. But as life becomes more complicated under the conditions of an urban civilization, changes are bound to occur in the laws. As the government enlarges its scope and strengthens its authority it will include in its province much that in old days had been left to the jurisdiction of the village council or the *pater familias,* and it will insist on a uniform system to replace the varying customs of the once independent units; and it is also true that men living under the rule of law achieve in time a moral outlook different from that of the law's first authors, so that its tenets no longer satisfy them. A revision of the law, modifying the ancient precedents so as to bring them into harmony with the changed conditions of society, becomes desirable; but because it is dangerous to tamper with the law, any change is likely to be promulgated not by the state at large but by some individual whose undisputed authority ensures general obedience. The ancient 'codes' of which we have knowledge are almost all associated with the names of some such outstanding character—the Code of Hammurabi, the Code of Moses, the Code of Hattusilis or of Suppiluliuma, and so on.

Although it is possible to get an idea of legal practice from court records such as the Kerkuk tablets for the Mitanni country, or the 'Tomb Robbery' papyri for Twentieth Dynasty Egypt, the real nature of law can be understood only from the formal presentation of its tenets in the shape of a code. In view of the total lack of documentary evidence we can have no notion whatsoever about the laws of Harappā and of China under the Shang Dynasty. As regards Egypt, although Greek writers assure us that the Egyptians codified their laws, yet no fragment of any such code has come down to us—'indeed, we know remarkably little about Egyptian law in the concrete', observes Professor J. H. Breasted, 'and not very much concerning the spirit in which it was administered'.[12] In the case, however, of Sumer, Babylon, Assyria, Palestine and Hattusas enough of the old codes is preserved to illustrate the character and the development of the country's legal system.

As might be expected from the brief sketch of their origin suggested above, these 'codes' are not really codes at all in the modern sense of the word; they are not a codification of the laws of the land but partial redactions based on ancient practice or precedent. The law-giver is not attempting to produce a *corpus juris;* he is publishing a list of emendations of such clauses in older compilations as call for alteration or addition in the changed circumstances of his day, and clauses that need no emendation are not included in his list but are taken for granted. They are casuistical, not theoretical at all; Hammurabi, for instance, makes no apparent attempt to seek for legal principles; his purpose is to give instructions to the judge, and his clauses are not records of decisions commonly given but models for decisions to be given in the future. Hammurabi was bringing up to date a *corpus* of common law which had long before his time been 'codified' by Libit-Ishtar of Isin, by Ibi-Sin and by Ur-Nammu of Ur and by other and still earlier rulers of Sumer, as well as by his own ancestor, Sumu-la-ilum of Babylon. Legislating for a wide empire, he had to reconcile established Sumerian practice with the not necessarily concurrent views of his own Amorite stock and, in particular, he had to adapt the system to a society composed not of two classes, like the old Sumerian, but of three, a change which must surely be attributed to the traditions of the now predominant Semites. Similarly, too, in the Hittite Code the earlier version has to allow for different views regarding crime and punishment prevailing amongst different member-states of the Hittite confederacy, while the later versions attempt to rule out such anomalies and insist upon uniformity throughout the empire.

The clauses of the Code of Ur-Nammu, so far as can be gathered from the fragmentary text, can on the whole readily be recognized as prototypes of the similar but not identical laws of Hammurabi. The most significant difference is that the Ur-Nammu Code, in all probability, knows of two social classes only, the freeman and the slave, and does not take into account any social group corresponding to the *mushkenu* of Hammurabi's Code. In this respect it would appear that the Libit-Ishtar Code agrees with that of Ur-Nammu; generally speaking, however, it is very similar in structure and import to Hammurabi's, so much so that either Hammurabi copied Libit-Ishtar or both codes are derived from a common source. But in the later Babylonian Code there are often qualifying additions made to the Isin clauses; or even definite alterations; thus, whereas according to the Isin law the slave-born children of a free father have no part in the father's estate, the Babylonian law gives to the father the power to legalize such children by the simple declaration 'You are my children'.

It is remarkable that in Hammurabi's Code the principle of retaliation plays a larger part than it had done in the Codes of Libit-Ishtar and Ur-Nammu, and the death sentence is invoked more widely. This has been described as a case of 'archaism' on the part of the legislator; but it can equally well be explained as the result of a stronger and more centrally-organized government. In a primitive society the *lex talionis* answers to man's natural instincts; it is the individual who is injured and the individual attempts to do to the other as he has been done by. But because violent revenge, however justified, leads to fresh violence and is anti-social in its effects, the primitive community is anxious that peace should be made between the two parties, and this is best done on a 'financial' basis; the families interested in preventing a blood-feud meet together, if necessary under the presidency of their tribal chief, and assess the injury and arrange payment by the injurer. But with the growth of a centralized government what had been civil offences become crimes against the state, whose welfare is threatened by them. It is not for the private citizen or for the tribal gathering to deal with such crimes; the state must defend itself, and in proportion as the offence is more heinous the sanction must be more severe; retaliation takes the place of settlement. The fact that in most cases where Hammurabi introduces the death penalty it is for assaults on the upper class of citizen, i.e. on those who were of greater importance to the state, can be held to show that the increased severity of his code is a condition of social progress rather than an archaistic relapse.

The mere fact that these Asiatic legislators are concerned with the revision of older codes means that those codes were not looked upon as sacrosanct. It is true that all Sumerian law was nominally what Urukagina of Lagash claims his own code to be, the 'Word' of the city's god, but that is simply due to the fact that the Sumerian city state was theoretically a theocracy, and Urukagina, as the *ensī*, the human representative of the god, spoke in his name; similarly legal cases were heard in the temples with priests as judges, but that, too, was because the god owned the city and his ministers were the ministers of state. Urukagina's Code could be altered by any other ruler speaking in the name of the city's god. It is true, again, that Hammurabi headed his great edict with a carved relief showing him standing in reverence before the Sun-god who holds the measuring-rod and line, symbols of justice and straightforward dealing; the laws which the king promulgates are based upon the principles of divine justice, and in formulating them he has sought the inspiration of god. But the actual laws are not dictated by Shamash. Human law is but an approximation to the divine. The old code had been an honest attempt to legislate in accordance with the will of Heaven; but social conditions might change and also men's views of the will of Heaven might be broadened; a new version of the law might therefore be called for, but the revision would be based upon the divine justice no less than had the original. This is particularly clear in the case of the Hittite law; the whole tendency of the later version is towards the mitigation of punishment and the substitution of a fine for the corporal punishment of a less highly civilized era. On the other hand the Assyrian Code, which is based upon the Babylonian, is infinitely more severe; it faithfully reflects the brutal materialism of the Assyrian empire and the low moral standard of Assyria's gods with whose character the more humane enactments of Hammurabi were inconsistent; so that revision, in this case, meant revulsion.

A very different view of the law was held by the Egyptians and by the Hebrews. That an Egyptian Law Code existed long before the explicit mention of it by Greek authors is a reasonable assumption, but there is little material evidence to support it. In the time of the Eighteenth Dynasty we find an utterly obscure allusion to a clause in 'the Book of Memphis, being the Word of the Sovereign, the mercy of the Vizier', and in Rekhmirê's tomb, describing the induction of the vizier,[18] it is said 'and as for the office in which you judge, there is a spacious room in it full of [the records (?) of all (past)] judgements': there are what seem to be vague references to a code in the Middle Kingdom, and on such grounds it appears likely that something in the nature of a *corpus* of law went back to the early centuries of the third millennium BC. But while it might be too much to expect that a complete code should survive, what is remarkable is that at no period have we any evidence for a revision of the primitive law. Even Harmhab, who had to cope with the complete disorganization of society that resulted from the misgovernment of Akhenaton and his feeble successors, and who claimed that he had 'improved the laws of Egypt', really limited himself to a reform of the administration. Having acquainted himself with the corruption that was rampant everywhere 'he dictated to his personal scribe in his private chamber a series of highly-specialized laws to suit every case of which he had learned', but none of them altered or affected the old laws; they were all directed against the practice of extortion from the poor by fiscal and administrative officials; in other words, he made no change in the original code but merely added sanctions for breaches of it. Even the 'unprecedented' step whereby he relieved the salaries of local judges from income-tax charges so that they might have no excuse for illegally enriching themselves was but a treasury concession involving no change in the law as such. Judging from such evidence as we possess—negative evidence for the most part—it would certainly seem as if Egyptian law were throughout its history relatively static. Because Pharaoh was a god he could of course issue any order that he pleased and it would have no less authority than the traditional law; but if such *ad hoc* orders were made, as presumably they were, they were valid only for the time being, after which the old code resumed its vogue unchanged; there is no record of any official revision supplanting the original version of the law.

Something of the same kind is true of the Hebrews. Like Hammurabi, Moses[14] did not arbitrarily invent a code but drew up in codified form a list of traditional laws which were to be observed for the future. The traditions on which he relied were mixed. Some were peculiar to the patriarchal clan from which the Hebrews claimed descent, some were borrowed from the peoples with whom the patriarchs had been in contact—thus, the law concerning the bull that gores (Exod. xxi. 28) is taken directly from the Sumerian law which was to reappear as clause 251 in the Code of Hammurabi (compare also Deut. xxiv. 7 with Ham. § 14; Deut. xxi. 1–9 with Ham. § 23; Deut. xxiv. 1 with Ham. § 137)—and a few were original enactments prompted by experience. That all these should be set down in writing as a *corpus* of law was a course for which precedents abounded—both the Egyptian and the Mesopotamian Codes were familiar enough—but the circumstances of the Hebrews were altogether peculiar. They were a horde of nomads with no recognized government to execute the law. Moses (see p. 223, n. 14) himself was indeed a leader, but not a member of a ruling dynasty, and his ascendancy was purely moral and personal and afforded no guarantee that his enactments would be respected after his death; in that inchoate society the administration of the law had to be left very largely to the heads of families individually or to the same heads acting in conclave as a tribal council, and experience had shown how little reliance could be placed upon them. The only efficacious sanction for the Mosaic Code was the sanction of God. Accordingly, in that code purely religious clauses—the tenets of the Hebrew faith—are joined with the social and penal clauses selected from established law as being applicable to the manner of life of a nomadic community; and all of these alike are represented as commandments issued directly by Jehovah in person. This was a divine law. Later generations might—and did—add to it, claiming that they did so in the light of further revelation; but there could be no revision of the original code and no omission or modification of any of its clauses; the Word of the Lord was to endure for ever.

Amongst the ancient systems the Hebrew is unique in making religion the basis of law and thereby establishing a moral code. Actually its provisions, relatively few in number, vary widely in their ethical values, ranging from broad principles like the forbidding of murder to detailed regulations suited to the social organization of a primitive tribe or aimed at that tribe's perpetuation as such; it is even less systematized and less coherent than the Mesopotamian and Hittite 'Codes' and shows none of that progressive development which in them results from long juridical experience. But the social aspects of the Mosaic law as enunciated by its founder were so far in keeping with Hebrew conditions that they could easily be assimilated by the barbarous tribesmen, and with that acceptance went the recognition of the law's moral basis. If the historian desires to record the progress made by man in the course of the second millennium before Christ, in legal theory and practice, he will turn his attention to those more civilized lands wherein the ancient tradition of the courts was constantly adapted to social advance and the mutual relations of citizen and state were reconciled on the grounds of expediency and common sense; yet it remains true that the Hebrew Code was the first in which it is explicitly stated that law is something more than a compromise assuring the interests of the individual and of the government, that it depends not on historical precedent but upon ultimate morality. With the collapse of civilized states their traditional systems of law have for the most part vanished with them; few nations have suffered eclipse more complete than that of the Hebrews, but none the less 'the laws of the Lord, His statutes and His judgements' have survived unchanged up to the present day.

Whereas the Mosaic Code was put forward as a *corpus* of

law, a general guide to conduct, the Mesopotamian and Hittite Codes were, as has been said above, merely lists of emendations of older laws. Many of those laws, probably, had never been codified at all; they were traditional, and so far taken for granted that no reference to them was necessary. Hammurabi, for example, lays down no rule about murder, except when the killer's method was witchcraft, for which the penalty is death, or when a brigand murders and disappears, in which case 'the city and governor in whose land and district the brigandage took place shall pay one *mina* of silver' to the dead man's kin. The custom of the blood-feud whereby the murdered man's next-of-kin takes vengeance into his own hands was too well established to be subject to change, and so Hammurabi says nothing about it, though by legislating for manslaughter as opposed to deliberate killing he does confine the blood-feud within reasonable limits. In the same way the Hittite Codes deal only with exceptional cases of marriage and are altogether silent on such important subjects as adoption, inheritance and the laws of contract; they did not legislate on these matters because they were adequately regulated by the customary law of the people.

As a general rule the clauses of the law in any 'code' are put in the form of hypothetical cases followed by an appropriate ruling. Whether or not this quotes a precedent that has actually occurred in the courts of law, it is obviously an instruction to the judge trying such a case in the future. For the further convenience of the judge the clauses are roughly grouped according to their content, but the grouping does not seem to follow any logical classification of offences; even what we should call the fundamental distinction between criminal and civil law is here entirely disregarded. The underlying motive of all law was, evidently, to uphold the authority of the state and to preserve the social organism, for which latter purpose the family, as the ultimate unit of society, demanded special protection. Offences therefore can be classified as being against the gods, against the state, or against the individual; regulations are laid down for all family affairs such as marriage, adoption and inheritance, regarding which family quarrels might easily arise; in addition, conditions of trade, hire charges, wages and rates of interest are fixed by law so as to obviate disputes.

The economic clauses really explain the character of the code. That they were meant to be generally valid is unthinkable, for tariffs would necessarily vary according to supply and demand, and the ancient kingdoms did not dispose of a bureaucracy capable of enforcing an artificial uniformity on private business such as even under a modern government only begets a black market. Actually in Mesopotamia the terms of the business contracts of Hammurabi's time do not at all conform to the figures given in his Code.[15] It is quite clear that merchants were free to make their own arrangements, to fix their own rates for hire and to agree with their workmen as to the wages to be paid. But if there were no written agreement, or if the financial terms were in dispute and the case was brought into court, then the judge in assessing payments would base his finding on Hammurabi's edict. The purpose of the economic clauses is to secure uniformity and finality in the administration of justice, not in the transactions of the market-place; as instructions to the judge, they are on precisely the same footing as the social or penal clauses wherein a specific fine or punishment is prescribed for each offence.

The most serious offences were those against the state and against the gods, which according to ancient views are really one and the same; in Mesopotamia the gods of a theocratic state were in fact the government, and amongst the Hittites, though the various local gods were not literally the city's rulers, yet an offence against the god involved the whole city or state in the god's displeasure. In this matter tradition was so unmistakable that there was little need for new legislation, and in the codes that we possess very few clauses deal with such things, but always the punishment is severe. In Egypt a palace conspiracy against the divine Pharaoh was naturally punished with death; as is known from the records of the prosecution of the plotters against Ramses III, a special court would be commissioned for the trial, and, as a royal concession, the criminals would be allowed to commit suicide. In Hammurabi's Code the thief who steals from temple or palace, and the receiver of such stolen goods, are both condemned to death. According to Hittite law, rebellion against the king involved the death of the rebel's whole family; the theft of the bronze spear set up at the gate of the palace was a capital offence because the spear symbolized the authority of the king; the theft of a field consecrated to the gods originally required the death of the thief, but in a later and a milder age atonement could be made by the sacrifice of an animal in place of the man. The practice of black magic is also a penal crime; logically so, for not only is it an offence against the gods but also it circumvents state action and defeats the law—'rebellion is as the sin of witchcraft', and because the two fall into the same category witchcraft deserves death; so Moses, and so Hammurabi; only the more humane Hittite law substituted a fine for the death sentence, and then only in the case of a freeman.

In civil cases the punishments for offences against the person are based on the *lex talionis* which was the common tradition of all Middle Eastern peoples. Because this was regarded as a private matter, the individual repaying hurt for hurt or avenging a kinsman's death by the rules of the blood-feud, the older codes had nothing to say on the subject; only when a society recognized the need of putting a check on such violence was the *lex talionis* embodied in the law. The Mosaic Code explicitly confirms the tradition, 'an eye for an eye and a tooth for a tooth', and Hammurabi does the like where the victim is of the upper class, an *amelu,* but ordains money compensation where he is of the lower order, a *mushkenu,* or a slave, while the Hebrew Code grants liberty to a slave whose eye or tooth has been put out by his master's violence. In the case of homicide both codes maintain the old rule that vengeance for murder is the duty of the dead man's next-of-kin,[16] not of the state, and the avenger is guiltless in the sight of the law; but both distinguish between deliberate murder and accidental killing, as when two men quarrel and fight and one is killed but the other can swear that he had no intention of killing, and by the Hebrew law the slayer can take sanctuary and by the Babylonian he can escape with a money payment. It can fairly be argued that the motive of the legislator in retaining the principle of retribution was restrictive rather than permissive; the injured party could not inflict a greater injury than he had received, and though the judge, if the matter came before him, was bound to make 'the punishment fit the crime' yet there was no objection to the case being compounded out of court on more civilized lines. What is really important from the point of view of the development of man's conception of law is that, with the sole exception of murder, crimes of violence against the person are removed from the sphere of private vengeance and are brought within the competence of the state.

The Hittite Code, which is certainly in part derived from the Babylonian, is, in the form in which we have it, some centuries later in date than Hammurabi's and reflects a different national tradition and character; but it shows a marked ethical advance. Only in one case is private revenge allowed—where a husband surprises his adulterous wife with her paramour *in flagrante delicto* (in the very act) and kills them on the spot, he is guiltless in the eyes of the law; it is the *crime passionnel* that may well be self-excused; but, if he does not so act at once, the moment for vengeance is passed and he must needs have recourse to the law. Even the blood-feud is abolished, though a concession is still made to ancient custom; the state arrests and tries the murderer, but when sentence is to be pronounced upon him the victim's next-of-kin (the 'avenger' under the old régime) decides it: 'If he says "Let him die", he shall die; but if he says "Let him make restitution", he shall make restitution: the king shall have no say in it.' Throughout the Hittite Code 'retribution plays an inconspicuous part in comparison with the principle of restitution'. The only offences for which capital punishment is prescribed are defiance of the authority of the state, rape, and sexual intercourse with animals; and, in the case of a slave, defiance of his master's authority; and black magic; but even so the sentence of the court is not final but must be submitted to the king for his personal confirmation. This is in striking contrast to Hammurabi's Code, in which the death penalty is assigned for house-breaking, brigandage, rape, incest, causing abortion, faulty building that results in a fatal accident, black magic, kidnapping, the connivance at a slave's escape or the sheltering of a runaway slave, certain forms of theft and the receipt of stolen property. Bodily mutilation, which is not uncommon under the Babylonian system and becomes the normal punishment of the savage Assyrian Code, is confined by Hittite law to slaves, and then only for theft and arson; there is no use of the bastinado. Collective punishment is not inflicted except in the case of rebellion, already cited, and in cases of murder by a person or persons unknown when, if the crime occurs in the neighbourhood of a town or village, that community may be called upon to pay compensation. The law takes cognizance of intention, and of extenuating circumstances, as in its distinction between murder in cold blood, killing in the heat of a quarrel, and accidental homicide; thus, too, where a married woman has been raped 'in the mountains' her assailant is to be executed, but she is herself guiltless because it is presumed that only the loneliness of the spot prevented her cries for help from being heard; but if the assault took place in the woman's own house, where any outcry on her part would certainly have been overheard, she also must die as a consenting party. In this again there is an advance upon the ethical standard of the Babylonian Code; older Sumerian law, in defining the penalty for a blow dealt to a woman and causing abortion, did distinguish between the intentional blow and the accidental; but Hammurabi waives this distinction (paras. 208–14) and emphasizes only the social class of the sufferer.

For practically all offences committed by a freeman, whether crimes against the person or theft or damage to property, the Hittite law adopts the principle of restitution or compensation; retribution enters in only in so far as the offender may be required to pay several times the cost of the damage he has done.

Even so the tendency is to mitigate the penalties, e.g. (para. 63) 'If anyone steals a plough-ox, formerly they used to give fifteen oxen, but now he gives ten oxen'; and such mitigation might be due to the direct action of the king (para. 25): 'If a man puts filth into a pot or tank, formerly they paid six shekels of silver; he who put in filth paid three shekels of silver [to the owner?] and into the palace they used to take three shekels of silver. But now the king has remitted the share of the palace; the one who puts in the filth pays three shekels of silver only.'

There is no documentary evidence which would enable us to picture the legal principles and practices of the Far Eastern peoples. It would indeed be possible to argue back from later Chinese history to probable origins in the Shang or even in the Hsia periods, but such arguments would be subjective and of little value. Obviously the Shang people must have had a form of government and an apparatus of law such as is essential to any organized and urbanized community; but the oracle bones furnish no details regarding anything of the sort, and the sober historian can do no more than assert his belief that the Shang Dynasty, so far advanced in its material achievements, may well have anticipated much of the legal and moral system which he finds already established in China by the time when literature comes to his aid.

Confining ourselves therefore to the peoples of the Middle East, as being the only ones about whom we possess real knowledge, we find that in the course of the second millennium BC they had between them gone far towards evolving the conception of law which is that of the modern world. The steps forward were tentative and unco-ordinated; the actual provisions of their legal codes might still be primitive and even barbarous, according to the level to which civilization generally had attained; there could be retrogression as well as advance, that depending upon national character and the type of national government; no one people had grasped the theory of law as a whole, but more than one had contributed to that theory some essential element: that law has a moral basis and therefore a divine sanction; that it is the function of the state to assure by law the maintenance of order within the state, and fair play and straight dealing between its citizens; that the common interest must be reconciled with the rights of the individual; that the execution of justice is a matter for the state alone, not for the private citizen; and that in punishing crime the state will be actuated not by the spirit of revenge but by the need to make good the injury done by crime and so restore the balanced order of society. These are ideas which were alien to man in his savage state but at one moment or another were realized by the legislators of the second millennium.

LAW COURTS

The efficacy of the legal codes naturally depended upon the administration of the law, upon the machinery of the law courts and the manner of its working, and this was far from uniform in the various countries of the Middle East.

The Hebrews

In the case of the Hebrews the machinery of the law courts was non-existent. Down to the twelfth century—the limits of our enquiry in this volume—even the tribal system was scarcely operative; there was no central government and therefore no possibility of state control. The so-called 'Judges' were for the most part successful guerilla chiefs who, relying either upon their past achievements or upon a bodyguard of armed retainers, exercised a certain amount of control over a limited area and so might be called upon to maintain traditional rules of justice; but even where they might act as divinely favoured repertories of tribal custom they had little authority to enforce their decisions other than the brute force they could command. The task of keeping in existence the Mosaic Code of Law depended upon the heads of families; these might in cases of difficulty, where more than one family was involved, call in their neighbours to form a council of 'the elders of the congregation', but whether individually or collectively they were the sole executives 'every man did that which was right in his own eyes'. That in such circumstances the law was preserved in practice and in tradition was due to the fact that while it enshrined all that seemed essential in ancient family custom, it had been promulgated as the revealed Word of God, and only by apostatizing from his tribal faith could a man escape from the provisions of the Hebrew law.

Egypt

In Egypt, with its very different form of theocracy, all law emanated from and was subject to the will of the divine Pharaoh. There was no class of judges with exclusively legal duties; Pharaoh himself, with his two viziers, was in supreme control of the treasury and the judiciary alike, and therefore his officials of a lower grade represented him in both functions. In the time of the New Kingdom at least (and probably long before that, but information on the subject is sparse) the mayors or governors of the larger towns and the scribes and recorders of the smaller centres served as both the administrators and the judicial authorities of their districts. There were two 'Great Courts', one at Thebes and one at Heliopolis, presided over by the viziers of the South and the North respectively, and throughout the country there were local courts staffed by 'the great men of the town', the administrative officials of the district who were corporately empowered to try cases, and perhaps also by prominent residents co-opted by the officials; certainly the majority on the bench were priests. A man who lost his case in a local court had the right of appeal to the Great Court, and the final appeal was to Pharaoh himself as the ultimate source of law. In serious cases, as when the royal family was involved, Pharaoh might commission a special court, as was done by Pepı I in the Sixth Dynasty and by Ramses III in the Nineteenth, and might deny to the accused the right of appeal from such a court—'Ye shall go and examine them and cause those who should die to die by their own hand without my knowing it. And ye shall execute punishment upon the rest without my knowing it'; obviously Pharaoh here had prejudged the case and merely handed on to the royal commission the odium of passing judgement.[17]

All petitioners for civil redress had to submit their case in writing and, if possible, produce written documents in support of it; since all wills, contracts, tax payments, etc., were also recorded in writing and copies of them filed in the White House, the archive of the government treasury, it should have been easy, in most instances, to establish the truth; either side was free to produce witnesses who would give evidence under oath, and it would seem that all reasonable precautions were taken to secure the triumph of justice. Such certainly was the avowed aim of the government. Throughout Egyptian history justice is insisted upon. In such didactic writings as the Instructions of a king to his son Merikarê, the Instructions of Ptahhotep and the Instructions of King Amenemhet I, the advantage of just dealings are emphasized, and in the tomb inscriptions, especially those of the Middle Kingdom, the claim is constantly made that the dead man had honoured the rights of the poor; in the Eighteenth Dynasty the vizier Rekhmirê eloquently describes his own conception of the duties of his office—'Take heed that thou do all things according to what is in the law. Behold, men expect the doing of justice in the conduct of the Vizier. Behold the name given to the Vizier's chief scribe; Scribe of Justice is what he is called. As for the office in which thou givest audience there is a hall of judgement therein; and he who shall do justice before all men is the Vizier.'

Unfortunately, practice seems to have fallen far short of this lofty principle. Our knowledge of the actual working of the courts of law is based on very few documents, but all agree in painting a very sombre picture of juridical procedure. In criminal cases torture and mutilation were not only the punishment of the guilty (as in the Ramses III trial) but might be inflicted even on innocent witnesses as an incentive to truth-telling; thus in the Tomb Robbery trial before a special commission every witness was given a preliminary bastinado, whether he was suspected of complicity or not, and where he was suspected the treatment was worse: 'There was brought the scribe of the army, Ankhefenamun; he was examined by beating with the stick, the bastinado was given on his feet and on his hands; an oath was administered to him on pain of mutilation, not to speak falsehood. They said to him, "Tell the manner of your going to the places with your brother". He said, "Let a witness be brought to accuse me". He was again examined. He said, "I saw nothing." He was placed under arrest in order to be examined again.'

In civil cases, so far as we know, the evil lay not in the brutality of the court's methods but in its corruption. The Middle Kingdom story of 'the Eloquent Peasant' is simply that of a poor man who is robbed by an official and cannot get justice done; he appeals throughout to the high standard of impartial justice which one ought to expect from the Egyptian judiciary (actually the appeal is to Pharaoh, who has been apprised of the case but has ordered it to be dragged out so that he may have more of the man's amusing eloquence) and he never once attempts to prove his claim, which indeed has never been challenged, but is only concerned to persuade the steward presiding over the court to do his obvious duty. Thutmose III attempted to check the corruption of the local officials and of the inspectors sent out to investigate their corrupt dealings, but under the lax government of Akhenaton the bribery in the courts of law had become intolerable; so it was that when Harmhab set himself to 'improve the laws of Egypt' his task was not to reform the Code but to cleanse the administration of it. His edict ran, 'Now, as for any official or any priest concerning whom it shall be heard saying, "He sits to execute judgement among the council appointed for judgement and he commits a crime against justice therein", it shall be counted against him as a capital crime'. In spite of such severity it could happen that in the Harem Conspiracy trial of Ramses III's reign two of the judges appointed to the special commission let themselves be suborned by the accused. From the details of a civil action recorded in an inscription on the walls of the tomb of one Mes it is clear that Harmhab's reforms had had little effect. Mes was claiming an estate which had belonged to his family since the time of Aahmes I, the founder of the Eighteenth Dynasty, but as the result of a lawsuit had been seized from Mes's father, in the eighteenth year of Ramses II, by a certain Khay; Mes won his case on the grounds that not only were Khay's title-deeds forged but also there had been falsification of the land register at the time of the former trial. There is no doubt that corruption was so general as to nullify what may have been a just and a generous code of law; the ordinary Egyptian might well lose all hope of getting unbiased justice from the courts and in despair turn to the god Amon, 'the poor man's Vizier who does not accept the bribe of the guilty'.

Sumer and Babylon

In ancient Sumer the administration of justice was a prerogative of the priesthood.[18] It could indeed scarcely have been otherwise. When the city states were still largely independent and each was governed by a king (*lugal*) who was himself but the earthly representative of the city's patron god, or by a *patesi* (the term is variably read as *ishakku* or *ensī*) a 'prince-priest', the law courts, like everything else, were but a department of the divine government and would therefore naturally be directed by the god's servants; and further, since all land in theory, and a vast proportion of it in fact, belonged to the god, most economic questions would be of direct concern to him and would be regulated by his priests. The reforms introduced by Urukagina of Lagash show how easily the biased autocracy of the priesthood might be abused; but it is as representative of Ningirsu that the ruler introduces his reforms. When Sumer was unified under the powerful kings of the Third Dynasty of Ur the authority of the *ensī* inevitably declined, but they still kept the power of legal decision. The judges were still for the most part members of the priestly order, but it seems that they were no longer taken from that order at random but formed a specialized branch of it; the *mashkim* who under the Third Dynasty of Ur was present at all trials and was responsible for the judicial procedure most often belonged to the temple staff, and although men of this class were not, properly speaking, 'magistrates' they played the part of judge, arbitrator, notary, expert and jury. In accordance with tradition, cases were still heard in, or before the gate of, a temple and in the temple the judgements were filed; thus Bur-Sin, restoring at Ur the ancient gateway-shrine of the Ziggurat terrace, calls it 'the great collection of tablets' and 'the place of his judgements, the net which the enemy of Bur-Sin does not escape'. All kinds of civil cases, particularly those concerned with sales, came up before the *mashkim;* if he was incapable of deciding, professional judges (*di-Kud*) to the number of two or four were called in to assist him; an appeal from their decision might be made to the supreme court.

Even before the collapse of the Third Dynasty of Ur there had been introduced provincial courts of justice presided over by a civilian, the mayor of the town (*rabianu*) assisted by an assembly of notables (*shibuti*); we find Ibi-Sin of Ur addressing instructions to a court of the sort in the town of Bulum. Under the Semitic kings of Isin and Larsa the mayor became a more powerful person, and still more so under Hammurabi of Babylon. Hammurabi, who was not a god, as Shulgi of Ur had claimed to be, or even the representative of a god, was meticulously careful in religious matters but quite determined not to submit to priestly control, and it is in his reign that for the first time we see civil courts with secular judges in full power. Both the priestly and purely civil jurisdiction held good, but the ecclesiastical courts were being ousted and civilian judges were replacing the priests. From now onwards the regular court was that presided over by the local mayor with a bench of notables; whether they received any remuneration is not known, but they were reckoned as high officials entrusted with great responsibilities; if they revoked their decisions they were liable to be publicly deposed. At the trial both sides had to produce their 'tablets', the written deeds relating to the case; then the plaintiff and after him the defendant made their depositions; then the witnesses were sworn by the local god and by the king and gave their evidence, after which the judges gave their decision. Both parties to the case had the right of appeal to the upper court—'the Judges of Babylon'—and, if still dissatisfied, to the king himself. Instances of the royal interest in legal matters, appeals and re-trials, are common; sometimes it is clear that bribery was suspected or alleged; but although a certain amount of abuse of the system did indisputably occur (*v.* the Nuzu tablets) yet we find in Mesopotamia relatively little evidence of widespread corruption such as meets us in the literature of Egypt. But side by side with the manifest desire to do justice by a fair process of trial there is a shocking barbarity in the sentences prescribed by the law. The retention, in a few cases, of the ordeal by water is perhaps not unnatural considering that the courts were by origin religious courts; but freemen could be sold into slavery for debt, and for more serious offences the legal penalty might be mutilation or death by drowning, by burning or by impalement. The state avenges itself upon the individual by retribution of the most savage type.

The Hittites

The actual laws of the Hittite empire seem in their form and to some extent in their content to have been based upon Hammurabi's edict, as indeed might be expected in view of the great influence exerted by Babylon upon the Anatolian Hittites through the intermediation of the Hurri (see p. 58). Owing to the almost total lack of private documents (Anatolia has produced nothing like the vast collection of business tablets unearthed on Mesopotamian sites) we know very little about the Hittite tribunals and law courts, but it would appear that these were not very different from the Babylonian model. In every provincial centre there was a popular court formed of the mayor and the city elders (or aldermen), and it may have been held competent to deal with minor cases such as are settled in the police courts of the modern world; but if not in all cases at least in those of any importance the bench of local authorities was reinforced by an official representing the king, normally the military commander of the local garrison. It is clear that his judicial functions formed a large part of the duties of this officer (whom it is tempting to compare with the *mashkim* of the Babylonian court) and the detailed instructions issued to him show that his responsibility was by no means a light one. He was expected to co-operate with the local authority, 'Now the commander of the garrison, the mayor and the elders, shall administer justice fairly, and the people shall bring their cases'; but since a would-be plaintiff might be frightened of bringing an action before a bench of purely local dignitaries who might be prejudiced against him, the commander was to give public notice that he was prepared to conduct any trial: 'Into whatever city you return, summon forth all the people of the city. Whoever has a suit, decide it for him and satisfy him. If the slave of a man, or the maidservant of a man . . . has a suit, decide it for them and satisfy them.' He was to see that the law was administered in the right spirit: 'Do not make the better case the worse or the worse case the better. Do what is just'; and to assure this his decision as president of the bench of magistrates seems to have been final: 'the commander shall decide the case fairly and satisfy him'. The mayor and the elders would seem to have been primarily consultants and assessors, but for the verdict they could if necessary be overridden by the king's representative, whose sentence had the royal authority behind it: 'If anyone oppose his judgement his head shall be cut off.' None the less there was an opportunity of appeal to the king, and all cases involving the death penalty and those of sorcery and certain types of theft had either to be referred to the king or the sentence submitted to him for confirmation; should anyone venture to oppose the king's judgement it counted as an act of rebellion, one of the few crimes for which collective punishment was prescribed, and the man's whole family could be put to death.

Proceedings in the courts seem to have opened with a statement of the case for the prosecution followed by statements for the defence given under oath and supported where possible by written documents; the accused was then confronted by the witnesses for the prosecution and was cross-examined in the light of their several charges. All the statements and the evidence were taken down *verbatim* by the clerks of the court, and it is from texts of this sort that we learn what little we know regarding Hittite legal procedure; it is clear that the cross-examination was fairly conducted and that the accused was allowed complete freedom of speech. As Dr Gurney puts it, 'An outstanding feature of Hittite legal procedure is the immense trouble taken to ascertain the facts. We possess highly detailed minutes of courts of enquiry in cases of peculation and neglect of duty, which are unique in the literature of oriental peoples and have quite a modern ring. . . . The text shows a spirit of careful and unbiased investigation, which may perhaps be taken as typical of Hittite administration as a whole.'

Summary

From the brief sketch given above of those civilizations which are best known to us it should be possible to estimate the progress made during the Bronze Age in the conception and administration of law. Egypt shows us that static[19] spirit which in a greater or a lesser degree characterizes her whole culture, and even the suggestion of advance that some writers detect in the Middle Kingdom texts is stifled by the rank growth of corruption. In Sumer the theory of theocratic government together with the recognition of the family as the basis of the state did give rise to an ideal of 'justice' as a condition of social life, but the Sumerian priesthood who administered justice never advanced far beyond the primitive insistence on retribution, and this was to receive the wholehearted sanction of Babylonian law. Thus Libit-Ishtar of Isin seems to have substituted a money payment for the old death penalty in the case of certain offences such as the harbouring of runaway slaves; but Hammurabi, here as elsewhere, reasserts the severity of the retributive principle, and this later became the substance of the savage code of Assyria. In the theory of law a great step forward was taken by the Hebrews when they founded their code upon religion and morality; although the time had not yet come when the law could be put into practice by the machinery of an organized state, yet its 'statutes and judgements' were to remain valid for the later kingdom. In practice it would appear that the Hittites of Anatolia had evolved a system unique in the ancient world, progressively more and more conscious of individual rights and interest, and approaching in spirit the ideals of modern legislation. It is true that at the close of our period the Hittite state was to be swept utterly out of existence and its laws and customs to disappear from the land in which they had been developed; but even so their contribution to man's moral progress may not have been fruitless. Not only through the Syro-Hittite cities which were to perpetuate south of the Taurus range the civilization of Hattusas but also through the Achaean people with whom Hittites had long been in touch, there may have been handed down to after ages something of the liberal conception of law which we see in the 'Code of Suppiluliuma'.

The standards reached by the three principal nations whom we have considered differ so markedly that one is tempted to seek a reason for their disparity. It was not, of course, a question of race. The theory that a race as such should possess innate virtues and qualities superior to those of other races—the Greek theory of the φύσει δοῦλος, the 'national slave' on the one hand and that of the 'Nordic' *Übermensch* on the other—is by general admission absurd; the distinctive characteristics of a people result from the influence brought to bear upon them by the circumstances, the conditions of life, of their ancestors and of themselves. Egypt can be explained by the inertia of an agricultural people dominated by a divine Pharaoh and an unscrupulous priesthood.[20] The Sumerians, combining agriculture with an extensive trade, with manufacture and, in the early days, with a good deal of military service, developed a civic spirit which would demand justice and fair dealing for all; at the same time the theocratic basis of the city state, which made a social offence a sin against the city's god and set the seal of divine approval on retribution, was enough to prevent the humanizing of the primitive code. The Hittites, warriors establishing themselves by force in a strange land, would have to combine the fighter's individualism and love of independence with the disciplined solidarity required for the colony's defence and, as the different tribes bound themselves into an alliance, with mutual concessions to varying points of view; moreover, they were ruled neither by a god nor by an autocrat but by a monarch who, up to the time of Telepinus, i.e. throughout most of Hittite history, was an elected, not a hereditary ruler. When they absorbed, as they readily did, as much as seemed to them good of a higher civilization evolved by their neighbours, they still preserved that balance between the rights of the individual and his duties to the state which gives to their legal code something of the character of democratic law.

INTERNATIONAL LAW

In the history of the progress of civilization, not in any one country in particular but of mankind in general, emphasis must needs be laid on the contacts between the various peoples which fertilized man's imagination, spread new ideas and new techniques, and by the exchange of regional products enriched the resources of the ancient world. Such contacts could be warlike or peaceful. War in itself is, by reason of man's nature, a relatively simple matter, but the utilization of war for long-term profit demands organization and discipline; peaceful relations such as make possible trade between lands under different governments are far more difficult to establish and maintain and require something in the nature of international law.

In the second millennium BC, as in much later times, no ruler could admit that a declaration of war on his part was due to his private whim or personal ambition. War was a matter for the gods, and it was the god of his country that declared war on the god of the other. The king, in this as in all other cases, was but the mortal agent, the instrument of the divine will; his victories were the god's victories, and if he was defeated it was because, in the council of the gods, his own patron deity had consented to the general decision that 'kingship' should be transferred to the god of another city or country. The Egyptian Pharaoh, being himself a god, could not accept defeat, and any military reverse had to be represented as a triumph;[21] but, even for him, victory had to be attributed to the greater god of his worship, and the result of a successful campaign was to add new provinces not to his own possessions but to the empire of Amon-Rê. For the Sumerian there was no doubt as to the god's responsibility; when Lugal-zaggisi overcame King Urukagina and laid waste his city Lagash, the poet who bewails the destruction of the temples and the plundering of their treasuries exonerates Urukagina of all blame: 'of sin on his part there is none'; but no more does he blame the mortal enemy: 'but as for Lugal-zaggisi, *ensī* of Umma, may his goddess Nidaba bear this sin upon her head'. So, too, Hammurabi of Babylon says that 'encouraged by an oracle given by Anu and Enlil, who are advancing in front of his army', he defeated Rim-Sin of Larsa, and 'upon the command of Anu and Enlil' he destroyed the walls of Mari. To Zimri-Lim, the king of Mari, whom Hammurabi defeated on this occasion, there had come a warning from Adad, the god of the city Kallasu: 'Am I not Adad, who restored him to the throne of his father's house? I am the lord of the throne, of the territory and of the city, and what I have given I can take away.' War was indeed, like the ordeal by battle, the judgement of the gods; as Mursilis the Hittite said to the king of Arzawa, 'Now we will fight each other, and the Weather-god, my Lord, shall judge our judgement.' A victorious god might even carry off his victim into captivity, as when the statue of Marduk was taken from Babylon by Mursilis and imprisoned at Hana, or as when the Philistines laid the Ark of Jehovah before the cult image of Dagon; and the dominions of the vanquished deity passed into the hands of his conqueror.

A mere raid, like that of Mursilis against Babylon, would but enrich with booty the temple, and the palace, of the invading ruler. More often victory in war meant that he would impose his suzerainty upon the conquered; either he would set his own nominee upon the provincial throne or he would force the ex-enemy prince to sign a treaty acknowledging vassalage.

Vassalage

The position of a vassal prince was clearly defined by rule and precedent. He had to pay an annual tribute, sometimes bringing it in person to the court of his suzerain. All questions of foreign policy were reserved to his overlord. He was bound to assist the overlord with all his armed forces for any military operation, offensive or defensive. He was bound to hand over to his overlord any criminals or fugitives from justice who were native to the latter's territories. His own subjects had the right of appeal from the provincial courts to the supreme court of the overlord. In the event of disputes between vassals the overlord acted as mediator and arbiter; thus when two vassal princes quarrelled Zimri-Lim of Mari writes, 'Qarni-Lim and

Hammurabi of Kurda shall swear an oath by the life of the gods, and I will cause friendship to be established between them'; and again, when his vassal Arriwaz raided the principality of Asqur-Adad, he writes, 'Now Asqur-Adad is residing with me. You have raided his country. Everything that you took, gather it together and return it.'

No ruler or state would submit cheerfully to this subordination, and the suzerain was at pains to secure their loyalty either by force or by the gilding of their fetters. The method especially favoured by the Pharaohs in their Syrian empire was to set an Egyptian commissioner in the court of the vassal prince, backed, if necessary, by a resident garrison of Egyptian troops.[22] The overlord might flatter his vassal by giving to him in marriage a daughter of his house or at least a palace girl who could pass for his daughter; the Asqur-Adad mentioned above when submitting to Zimri-Lim ('seizing the hem of his garment') pleaded, 'Let him send his daughter and exercise kingship over Karanâ'; and in like fashion Solomon of Jerusalem was given a 'daughter' of Pharaoh for his wife. But in the end it was only the overwhelming strength of the suzerain that guaranteed the vassal's submission. Any obvious weakness in the central government, or the rise of any other power strong enough to menace that government, meant the break-up of the empire. The Tell el Amarna letters give a vivid picture of the gradual defection of Egypt's Syrian vassal states under the nerveless rule of Akhenaton. The death of Suppiluliuma, who had extended the Hittite empire to its widest limits and long held it grimly in check, coinciding as it did with a pestilence which was decimating the population of Hattusas, was the signal for a general revolt of the vassal princes as well as for the disaffection of the federal states. The rise of the Mitanni power was marked by the submission to their suzerainty of one small state after another, vassals of the Hittites or of Egypt, for whom loyalty to their far-off overlords was outweighed by the immediate threat of the formidable upstart. Changes, therefore, were apt to be kaleidoscopic, pieces regrouping themselves with every shift in the balance of power. 'Ten or fifteen kings will follow Hammurabi, King of Babylon, as many will follow Rim-Sin, King of Larsa, as many Ibâl-pî-el, King of Eshnunak, as many Amût-pi-el, King of Qatanum; twenty kings will follow Yarim-Lim, King of Yamkhad'; thus a military intelligence agent reported soon after 1780 BC. The news was really important, because a few years before the list would have been very different, and a few years later Rim-Sin was a dethroned fugitive, or dead, the dynasty of Yamkhad had fallen, and Qatanum had sunk to a position of vassalage.

Independent States

Relations between independent rulers (apart from wars of conquest) envisaged two principal objects, security and trade. Commercial prosperity required peaceful conditions, and peace could be secured only by mutual agreement. In an age in which the strong man was a law to himself it would have been the height of folly to trust to the mere forbearance of a powerful neighbour, to assume that either moral scruples or enlightened self-interest would force him to recognize the rights of others if those seemed to stand in the way of his immediate interests. There had to be a definite and a detailed bond, strengthened by sanctions which no one could lightly disregard. The independent states, therefore, when not at war with each other, were normally assured by a network of formal treaties of alliance.

In international as in private law a contract had to be set down in writing, and it had to be sworn to by the parties concerned in the presence of divine witnesses. In the case of a treaty of alliance preliminary negotiations were carried on by ambassadors exchanged between the two contracting powers; each party would have drawn up his own draft version of the text, and the duty of the ambassadors was to reconcile those in the final version; any important disagreement they would refer to their principals; thus Shamshi-Adad of Assyria receives from his envoy a copy of a proposed treaty with Eshnunna as drafted by the other side and at once objects: 'The matter which I removed from the tablet is still there. The men of Eshnunna are making difficulties.' In other cases the ambassadors were plenipotentiaries and arranged a satisfactory text between themselves, after which the date of ratification had to be fixed, a date not only convenient to both rulers but also approved by oracles as auspicious.

The ratification was a solemn function introduced by sacrifice. While the treaty was made out in the names of the kings who were to be bound by it, and was introduced by their full names and titles, no small part of its text consisted of a list of the gods and goddesses invoked as witnesses, the deities of each country separately described, followed by the curses which devolve upon the violator of the contract: 'He who shall not observe all these words written upon this silver tablet of the land of the Hatti and of the land of Egypt, may the thousand gods of the land of the Hatti and the thousand gods of the land of Egypt destroy his house, his country and his servants', and the corresponding blessings: 'but he who shall keep these words which are on the tablet of silver, whether he be Hittite or Egyptian, and shall not neglect them, may the thousand gods of the land of the Hatti and the thousand gods of the land of Egypt make him to be in good health and long life, as also his houses, his country and his servants'. It was an oath of the most solemn sort, so much so that the ceremony of signature was, by Babylonians and Syrians, called 'the touching of the throat', for when the sacrificial victim was killed, the king, in the presence of the gods and of the ambassador of the other contracting power, drew his hand across his throat, symbolizing his willingness to die in the same manner if he broke his word. The treaty tablets, once signed, were laid before the state gods of the two countries.

The most full and elaborate treaty of which the text is extant is that concluded between Ramses II and Hattusilis, from which come the sanctions quoted above, but others are generally of much the same pattern. The first clause would be a promise of perpetual friendship and 'brotherhood' between the contracting parties and an undertaking to observe territorial integrity. This would be followed by an alliance which might be purely defensive, each side promising to come to the other's help in the event of invasion by a third power or of rebellion by the subjects of the overlord; such were the terms of the Hattusilis-Ramses treaty: 'If some other enemy comes against Egypt and if Ramses, King of Egypt, thy brother, sends word to Hattusilis, King of the land of Hatti, his brother, "Come to my aid against him", forthwith Hattusilis, King of the land of Hatti, shall send his soldiers and his chariots and shall slay my enemy', with, of course, the reciprocal promise. The defensive alliance was indeed the more usual between independent rulers, but sometimes the offensive alliance which was obligatory where vassals were concerned ('He shall be the friend of my friend and the enemy of my enemy') was concluded also between equals; in special circumstances a neutrality clause was introduced, as when both parties agree to hold aloof from a quarrel between other states, intervention in which would mean their taking opposite sides.

Great importance was attached to the right of extradition. Not only criminals, but political offenders and fugitives of all sorts were to be handed back to the country of origin. In vassal treaties this was a unilateral obligation and did not apply to the suzerain, who might be interested in protecting even a pretender to the throne of a doubtfully loyal subject; a familiar example of this is the case of Jeroboam, who conspired against Solomon of Jerusalem, took sanctuary with Pharaoh, and was subsequently installed as king over Israel. Perhaps for that very reason treaties between equals insist strongly upon the mutual right and, at the same time, the contracting parties were most careful to be sure of their grounds before taking action; thus Aplakhanda of Carchemish when asked to return a palace girl who had been carried off by a raiding-party and was said to be in the hands of a man named Tappî-Il, replied to the ruler of Mari, 'Send word to me as to where she was seized, who seized her and who brought her here, the name of the girl and of the place where she was seized'. Always, in the Middle East, the fugitive has been able to find sanctuary by putting himself under the protection of anyone, even a total stranger, who is thereafter bound to defend him and cannot honourably hand him over even to lawful justice; it is, therefore, interesting to find that in the second millennium BC international law was able to override the traditions of individual morality. But that the contradiction was recognized and the strength of the moral claim not undervalued is shown by a remarkable compromise in the Hittite-Egyptian treaty; it comes at the end of the document as if added as an amendment to the normal extradition clauses: 'If a man flees from Egypt, or two or three, and they come to the great chief of the Hatti, the great chief of the Hatti shall seize them and have them handed back to Ramses, the great ruler of Egypt. But as regards the man who is handed back to Ramses, the great ruler of Egypt, his fault shall not be brought against him; his house, his womenfolk and his children shall not be destroyed, he shall not be killed nor maimed in his eyes, his ears, his mouth or his limbs, nor shall any charge be preferred against him.' This insistence on a personal amnesty for the surrendered fugitive, subordinating as it does political expediency to conscience, is perhaps without a parallel in the international relations of the ancient world.

Special rules are laid down for the arrest and return of runaway slaves. In this case it was not the government that was directly concerned, but the private citizen; accordingly, the slave's owner had to prove his case and pay a fixed reward to anyone who had caught the fugitive. Inter-territorial theft was dealt with in the same manner. Bandits raiding across the frontier were to be arrested by the authorities of the raided country, but 'You shall surely not detain them within your territory but must return them to my territory'; no ruler was prepared to surrender the right to try his own nationals.

A treaty of alliance was often strengthened by a dynastic marriage, and this would be the occasion for an exchange of gifts on a scale very much larger than would be called for in the case of a private marriage; thus for the betrothal of Ammitaku of Alalakh to the daughter of the prince of Apišal the expenditure amounted to seven hundred shekels of silver while for a private person the maximum would have been forty shekels. Between allies letters and gifts were exchanged regularly as a proof of friendship, but the transaction was of a businesslike sort, each side expecting to receive full value in return for what he had sent. The king of Babylon is perfectly frank on the point when, writing to Akhenaton of Egypt, he says, 'Your messengers have come three times and you have sent no fine present; and I, too, have sent no fine present to you. I have nothing valuable to send if you have nothing valuable to send'; and Iškhi-Adad of Qatanum who, at Išme-Dagan's request, had sent him two horses and received in return twenty *minas* of lead, writes complaining bitterly, 'Did you not receive from me without discussion and in its entirety? And you send me this miserable amount of lead!'

While special messengers bearing letters or gifts journeyed frequently to and fro between allied kings, there were also resident ambassadors through whose hands such things would pass. These were men of high rank who could be trusted to use their own discretion in most negotiations with the ruler to whom they were accredited; thus Ibâl-pî-el, ambassador of Zimri-Lim of Mari at the court of Babylon, boasts that, 'Whenever Hammurabi is turning over a matter in his heart he sends word to me and wherever I am I go to him. Whatever the matter that he is turning over in his heart he tells me of it.' The ambassador by frequent dispatches kept his master informed on all matters of interest, especially those of military importance; he dealt also with legal cases involving citizens of the two countries, and he arranged the exchange of royal gifts. There was thus a continual traffic of envoys between the courts; these travelled under the escort of a native of the area through which they passed (a method of assurance employed up to the present day in Arab lands, where the *rafîk* is a recognized institution), and the refusal by a ruler to provide such a safeguard was a breach of international courtesy and a deliberate insult to the other party. Commercial caravans would be glad to attach themselves to a royal mission, thereby profiting by its safe-conduct, and sometimes, at least, the envoys themselves carried merchandise for trade; thus the equipment of messengers going from Assyria to Telmun includes juniper seed and boxwood, which are not things likely to be needed on the road, and when Aplakhanda of Carchemish writes to Yasmah-Adad of Mari: 'This mission is mine. Let them not speak of the tax to my attendants', he is claiming exemption from customs dues on goods presumably intended for sale. Burnaburiash of Babylon claims a direct interest in a merchants' caravan carrying gold which had been plundered by brigands in Palestine, and he points out to Akhenaton, under whose feeble rule the outrage had occurred, that unless the criminals are arrested and executed trade between Babylonia and Egypt will come to an end; similarly Kadashman-Enlil of Babylon explains to Hattusilis that communications with the Hittite capital had been cut because the king of Assyria was refusing safe passage through his territory.

Obviously open war, political tension and the weakness of the central government in policing its provinces might close the roads to merchants and messengers alike; but for the most part common interest saw to it that commercial and political contacts should be maintained between the states. When it is remembered that, so far from there being any one supreme authority such as controlled the Middle East in Roman or in Islamic times, Egypt and Syria, Anatolia and Mesopotamia presented a mosaic of major and minor kingdoms with all their differences of culture and creed, their jealousies and ambitions, the tolerance that made possible international trade and international diplomacy is indeed surprising. There was, of course, no formulated international law, only recognized conventions, the origin of which must be sought in the internal laws of Babylonia. The Akkadian and Sumerian empires of the past had brought most of Syria and even parts of Anatolia under a common rule and a common law and had started a precedent which was to influence the Middle East long after those empires had fallen. The Akkadian language, written in the cuneiform script, was the diplomatic language employed even by the chancellery of Egypt; the regulations that governed Sumerian trade were adopted by independent kingdoms; actually we find in treaties of the second millennium BC expressions taken *verbatim* from those in a treaty of Naram-Sin of Akkad in the twenty-fourth century BC. On this measure of common ground there was built up a diplomatic apparatus which anticipates in many respects that of the modern world.

AUTHOR'S NOTE

(*to Note 1, p. 220*)

My Russian commentators, to whose help I am indebted, have urged that my readers should be acquainted with the different views existent among modern scholars on the important question of the process of development of mankind and, especially, with the point of view of Marxist philosophy, which directly opposes the theory that 'human history is no more than a kaleidoscopic change of whimsical patterns with no inner consistency and no principle in their development'.

'According to our view,' they say, 'the first stage in the history of humanity is primitive communal, or pre-class, society, characterized by communal property in land and mostly also in other means of production, by the organization of the population in clans, tribes and other communities mostly based on a real or supposed blood affinity, by the absence of a constant division of labour between artisans and land cultivators within the community and by the absence of a state apparatus, the chiefs of the clans being only the more experienced and revered of the tillers, hunters or whatever the members of the community may be, and the authority of the chiefs being based on the necessity of voluntary community discipline.

'The next stage in the history of mankind is represented by the early "urban civilization"; it is characterized by the growth of private property, by the division of society into classes, by the creation of the state which enables a part of the population to live on the produce of the other part, i.e. it is characterized by the exploitation of one individual by another. The exploiters tend to make the most of the labour of the exploited; and thus the complete proprietorship of the slaveholder over the workman who is turned into a slave becomes now the optimal form of exploitation enabling the owner to acquire not only all the surplus product of the slave but also part of the product necessary to the latter's maintenance. Other types of exploitation exist side by side with slave-owning. We usually term this stage of history "slave-holding society". A great part or even the majority of the population remain in this period personally free and retain their organization in the form of different, more or less self-ruling communities—rural or urban. City life and writing are characteristic of this period. Communal property in land is no longer the general rule.

'With the development of technical knowledge, with the improvement of tools and means of production, the slave is no longer the optimal type of the exploited worker; a new type of worker with more interest in the effectiveness of his work, and with more initiative, is needed; on the other hand, the formerly free land cultivator becomes now dependent on the big owners of landed property, and thus the third, "feudal" stage of society commences.

'The historical facts depicted in this book are in accord with the historical process as outlined above. Our outline gives, of course, only the general trend of historical development, which presupposes different local varieties following from the specific conditions of time and place. But, according to our view, only such a conception of the historical process allows of a correct interpretation of the facts. If the author could group the facts according to a system which follows from the successive development of primitive communal and slaveholding structures of society, the facts would also be more easily grasped by the reader.'

Since the whole purpose of this book is to trace man's progress it obviously does not regard history as a 'kaleidoscopic change of whimsical patterns'; but none the less do I find it impossible to fit the stages of progress in general to the Procrustean bed of what my Marxist friends term 'the law of social development'. In my view 'the different local varieties following from the specific conditions of times and place' rule out any such conformity. Were the historical facts grouped according to a theory of the successive development of primitive communal and slave-holding structures of society those facts might be more easily grasped, but the history would be misrepresented. Slavery was, of course, a usual feature of ancient society, but in the different societies the importance of the part played by it varied very greatly; thus, in Egypt, civilization attained its zenith in the Sixth Dynasty, but not until the Eighteenth Dynasty did the institution become a considerable element of Egyptian society; there is no evidence to show that the civilization of the city states of Tyre and Sidon was based on slave ownership. Again, the 'law of social development' whereby a 'feudal' stage results from slavery with the development of technical knowledge cannot be of universal application, if only because not all ancient civilizations passed through the feudal stage. The Marxist view seems to me to lay upon slavery a quite unwarranted emphasis. That there was, in the early urban civilization, exploitation of one individual by another can reasonably be said, as it can of every other phase of human existence; but that is an accidental, not an essential feature. When it is urged that in that period 'the richer proprietors, the professional rulers, the priests, the merchants, concentrating in the towns which were mostly transformed into walled cities, could now by virtue of their greater opportunities create a governing apparatus to enforce and keep up the conditions which enabled them to live on the surplus production of the entire population', this is an *ex parte* judgement. The governing apparatus did indeed aim at maintaining and perpetuating the existence of the state, and the governing class did not itself produce food with its own hands; but for an organized society the function of the governing class was, and was generally recognized to be, as essential as that of the farm labourer, and the smooth running of the state and its defence against external enemies was in the interest of all classes alike.

In this chapter the subject of slavery is discussed at some length and in considerable detail. That at some times and in some countries society was based on the slave system is made clear; but I have purposely avoided the use of the term 'slave-holding society' because I wished to avoid that term's implications: the detailed discussion will perhaps justify me, but it was written objectively and not in support of any theory.

Professor I. M. Diakonoff, having read the above discussion, asked for the following rejoinder to be added:

'Sir Leonard Woolley seems to have misunderstood me when arguing that "not all ancient civilizations passed through the feudal stage". In my opinion *no* ancient civilization had reached the feudal stage (in the Marxist sense of the word "feudal" as quoted by Sir Leonard above). Defence against external enemies was necessary in pre-urban (or pre-class) society also, but the pre-class tribes were not ruled by a state. A class division was no doubt necessary for the progress of society in ancient times, but nevertheless, in those times as well as in all others, no one would drudge in order to ensure a safe and prosperous life for the governing class, unless forced to do so, be the governing class ever so important for the progress of civilization. The state is necessary for the "smooth running" of class-society, not because it defends society against external enemies.'

NOTES TO CHAPTER III

1. cf. Author's note at end of chapter, pp. 217–20.
2. In face of objections raised on this point Sir Leonard Woolley recognized that writing originated for book-keeping, primarily for the accounts at temple stores. It was therefore a temple invention, but certainly did not originate as a religious function.
3. The history of the English word 'boor' and the Latin word *paganus* shows how generally true this was.
4. In reality the High Priest of Amon did not administer the Egyptian clergy as a whole. There was a 'Director of Priests of all the Gods of Upper and Lower Egypt' who was an actual minister of worship rather than sovereign pontiff of Egyptian religion [cf. G. Lefebvre, *Histoire des grands prêtres d'Amon de Karnak* (Paris, 1925), p. 78; and E. Drioton, *Journal des Savants* (1930), p. 321]. Moreover, the priests of other gods such as Rê at Heliopolis, Ptah at Memphis and Thot at Hermopolis also had their own political aims and pretensions, and even, on occasion, their own triumphs. See H. Kees, *Das Priestertum im aegyptischen Staat vom Neuen Reich bis zur Spätzeit* (Leiden-Köln, 1953).
5. As Professor John A. Wilson points out the Semneh dispatches of

the Middle Kingdom show that the Sudanese (Madjoi) came to the Egyptian frontier post to *enlist* in the Egyptian army. The Brooklyn Papyrus edited by W. C. Hayes, *A Papyrus of the Late Middle Kingdom in the Brooklyn Museum* (Brooklyn, 1955), shows that in the Late Middle Kingdom Asiatic slaves were used as weavers, brewers, and other household slaves. W. C. Hayes believes that they were not captives, but acquired through a slave-traffic.

6. This statement has been challenged by Professor I. M. Diakonoff who says:

'This is not so; cf. clauses 11 and 12 of the Hittite laws: "if anyone breaks the arm or leg of a freeman, he must give him 20 half-shekels of silver . . . if anyone breaks the arm or leg of a slave or a slave-girl, he must give 10 half-shekels of silver"—obviously to his master.'

This is a gloss for which Sir Leonard Woolley can see no justification—the text of the law says nothing about the master; the only thing emphasized is the different rate of compensation.

Professor Diakonoff goes on to say, 'The cause of the slave being fined for his offence only half of the amount imposed on a freeman for a similar offence is also obviously the fact that the fine would in most cases be paid by the master. The lawgiver could not think it fair to punish the master for the crime of his slave in the same way as he would be punished for his own crime.'

An equally obvious interpretation is that because the slave was a much less valuable member of the society than the freeman, injury to him was assessed at only half the price of that of the freeman; because he had at most very limited means, the half-fine imposed upon him for an offence would be as severe a punishment as the whole fine imposed on the freeman; but that the fine was imposed on the slave, not on his master, is surely shown by the fact of bodily mutilation being the punishment for certain heinous crimes—it was the guilty slave, not his master, who was mutilated, and the same principle of law would hold good in the case of a money fine.

Sir Leonard Woolley's contention that the civil rights of the slave were protected by the law is challenged on the grounds that 'Clause 1 of the Hittite law runs: "If anyone kills a man or a woman in a brawl he must bury him and give four 'heads,' men or women. . . ." Thus,' it is urged, 'the freeman, if he was rich enough, could pay for his offence with his slaves and went free himself. If he was poor, the "heads" probably included his wife and children or himself. How can we say in view of this that the civil rights of the slave were protected?'

For Sir Leonard Woolley, however, the 'giving of a head' does not mean, as these commentators imply, that the victims were killed; this indeed would be against the whole spirit of Hittite law, which would not condone the exaction of four lives for one; the four people were handed over as slaves to the kin of the murdered man, i.e. retribution was combined with compensation. And the law does discriminate between slaves and freemen. Those handed over would certainly be slaves already, if the offender was a rich man (in which case he was mulcted of the value of four slaves); and if he were a poor man he would pay with his own liberty and that of his family; to the law, that was a matter of indifference.

Considering the rejoinder of Sir Leonard Woolley, Professor I. M. Diakonoff added: 'There seems to be a misunderstanding. What I stressed was the fact that, in the case of the freeman, the culprit had to pay *him*, while in the case of a slave the pronoun *him* is not used—obviously because, as in other slave-holding countries, the fine was paid to the master. A slave might be mutilated for a crime, but that does not prove that he had money of his own, which did not belong to his master.'

The above gloss could not, of course, be examined by Sir Leonard Woolley, and it is printed here at the request of Professor A. A. Zvorikine, Member of the Bureau of the International Commission for a History of the Scientific and Cultural Development of Mankind.

7. In the second millennium it is *awîlum; amelu* is a later form. In the view of Professor I. M. Diakonoff, he was not a nobleman (or a member of the gentry), but a freeman enjoying full citizen's rights.
8. Professor I. M. Diakonoff does not think it was only the recruiting officers who were on a permanent footing and were granted what the author calls 'fiefs' by the state; in his view it applies in general to the permanent part of the army, which was the nucleus of the armed forces.
9. In the view of Professor I. M. Diakonoff, the armed forces of the *ensīs* consisted of temple personnel, not of citizens.
10. The defences of Buhen, the frontier fortress at the First Cataract (opposite Halfa) illustrate the extent to which the Egyptian commanders of the Twelfth Dynasty relied upon archery.

The wall proper, some 31 feet thick and at least 33 feet high, had in front of it a flat berm and then a rock-cut ditch about 19 feet deep beyond which was a curtain wall set back from the lip of the counterscarp. Along the top of the scarp ran a brick wall leaving

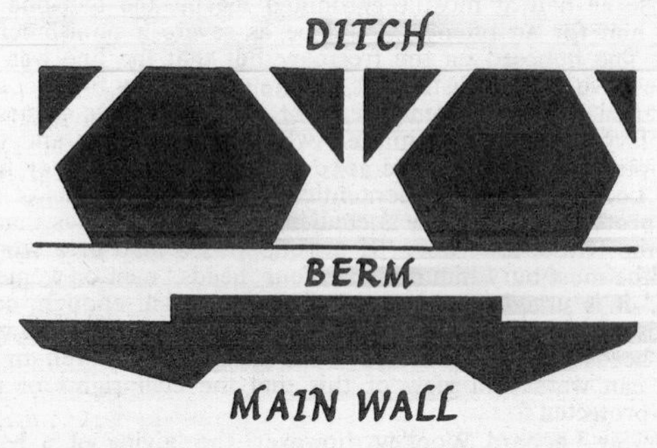

a manœuvring passage between it and the wall proper; from it rounded bastions at intervals projected into the ditch; these bastions had a double range and the wall-stretches between them a single range of embrasures each having three divergent loop-holes intended to give the widest possible field of fire; in the bastions the embrasures arranged in a double line were for kneeling and standing archers respectively, who could pour in a flanking fire on any enemy who had broken through the counterscarp wall and climbed down into the ditch; the whole defence was organized for the use of bowmen. It is worth noting, however, that Buhen was stormed and destroyed after the time of the Twelfth Dynasty; see W. B. Emery in *Illustrated London News* (June 21, 1958), pp. 1048–51, Fig. 12, and (September 12, 1959), pp. 232–3, 249–51; *Kush*, VII (Khartoum, 1959), pp. 7–14, Fig. 6, phot. Pl. 9, 2 plans.

11. Professor I. M. Diakonoff does not think it admissible to say that

the Hittite laws or even the laws of Hammurabi serve the interest of the poor and the slaves; the laws of a state always serve the interest of a ruling class.

12. *Cambridge Ancient History*, II, p. 210.
13. The vizier's instructions are known not as official documents proper, but as private inscriptions engraved on several Eighteenth Dynasty tombs, including that of the celebrated Rekhmirê. These bear witness to an earlier tradition, since they derive from some unknown original of the Middle Empire (in all probability dating from the Thirteenth Dynasty, but referring to Twelfth Dynasty affairs); see W. Helck, *Zur Verwaltung des Mittleren und Neuen Reichs* (1958), pp. 2, n. 1, 29–43.
14. Sir Leonard Woolley was, of course, well aware that many scholars have refused to accept Moses as an historical personage, but did not consider it useful to enter here into so vexed a question. The earliest Hebrew laws must have been enunciated by someone, and whether that someone was Moses or 'another person bearing the same name' matters very little. Sir Leonard Woolley uses the name for convenience, and with reference only to those clauses of the Hebrew law which by the common consent of scholars go back to an early stage in the history of the Hebrew people. This excludes the innumerable enactments which were added in later times, after the settlement in Palestine, but were piously fathered upon Moses so as to give them the authority of the first lawgiver. See also p. 515, n. 40.
15. The charge-fixing clauses have caused much difficulty to commentators. The explanation often given that they are 'maximal tariffs' disregards the fact that the charges recorded in business tablets are nearly always considerably higher; moreover, in the numerous known cases the judges never refer to the laws and often give judgements at variance with them. That the law fixes the rates to be paid by the palace and the temples (as distinct from individuals) seems also to be inconsistent with the evidence of the tablets. Dr W. F. Leemans is in general agreement with the explanation given in the text by Sir Leonard Woolley: 'When immovable property was sold the price was paid on the spot; disputes about the price could not arise afterwards. But when a workman or cattle were hired, or a ship handed over for repair, no document had to be drawn up; often, no price would be fixed in advance trusting that the right price would be paid. . . . In these instances the prices fixed by the king may have been valid, and if a case came before the judges they had to apply them. But, as the prices were fixed by law, there was no use in going to law, and this may explain why no records of lawsuits on this subject are known to us.' In short, the code guarantees a minimal rate for the labourer or hirer not protected by a formal contract.
16. Professor I. M. Diakonoff does not think that murder was avenged in Babylonia by the family of the victim; in his view, the reason for the absence of laws against simple theft and murder in the laws of Hammurabi is that Hammurabi's laws were innovations; in cases that needed no innovations the customary law of the communities probably remained in force.
17. As Professor J. A. Wilson points out, scholars differ in opinion as to the circumstances of the meeting of the court summoned to pass judgement on the 'Harem' conspiracy. A reconstitution of this legal case has been possible thanks to three papyri: the legal papyrus of Turin and the Lee and Rollin papyri, both originally forming part of the same papyrus. Many think that the conspiracy succeeded, and it is out of the realm of the dead, and through the agency of his son,

that Ramses III commissioned the court; in that case his disavowal of knowledge and responsibility is understandable as coming from the realm of the blessed. A number of scholars, on the other hand [see A. De Buck, *Journal of Egyptian Archaeology*, Vol. XXIII (1937), pp. 152 sq.], are of the opinion that Ramses III survived for a short period after the discovery of the plot and was still alive when the inquiry opened; in which case his disavowal of knowledge is more perplexing.

18. Professor I. M. Diakonoff cannot agree with what Sir Leonard says on the administration of justice in Sumer. He doubts whether the *lugal* was an earthly representative of the city's patron god and thinks he was the representative of the community *before* the patron god.

19. Professor J. Leclant points out that while its conception of the world may have been static, Egyptian civilization itself was far from stagnant; see H. Frankfort, *The Birth of Civilization in the Near East* (London, 1951), p. 99. The ancient Egyptians had no sense of progress; they were not orientated towards promises concerning the future. On the contrary, Egypt, springing from the heart of the Neolithic Age and destined, in a series of sudden leaps and bounds, to realize outstanding achievements, remained faithful to the memory of these early successes, seeking never to fall short of the accomplished pattern of its early days, rejoicing in the mirage of a Golden Age, an Age of Gods and Ancestors.

20. The Egyptian priests should not all be judged with the same severity. Autobiographical texts by more than one priest show high ethical principles: witness the famous maxims in the tomb of Petosiris, the good priest of Thot at Hermopolis, published by G. Lefebvre. Even if this homage paid to values of the highest order failed to correspond to the actual life of the priest, it constitutes none the less an ideal worthy of our admiration; see E. Otto, *Die biographischen Inschriften der aegyptischen Spätzeit* (Leiden, 1954). A number of fine texts engraved in the temples of Egypt specify priestly duties and bear witness to their ideals; see M. Alliot, *Le culte d'Horus à Edfou au temps des Ptolémées*, I (1949), pp. 181–95.

21. Professor J. Leclant points out that the Pharaoh, in his dual functions as possessor and servant of Maat (Truth/Justice) was responsible for the order of the world, in a sense not far removed from what was to be, at a much later period, the doctrine of the Stoics. Thus the Pharaoh, as the demiurge who had overcome primeval chaos, must of necessity always emerge victorious. In the Egyptian conception of the cosmos, all its elements being linked by a series of interrelationships, the sovereign is responsible, generally speaking, for success in every domain: it is he who inevitably triumphs over his enemies, who must also, by his intervention with the gods, ensure abundance and economic prosperity for his country. In such a scheme of things, constantly professed, there can obviously be no place for failure of any kind. Thus there is no vainglory, no systematic falsification in the constant affirmation of victory circling the walls of the Egyptian temples, but rather a figurative representation of a systematic theme translating an overall conception of the universe.

22. Children of vassal princes were often brought up at the Egyptian court, where they served as a kind of hostage and grew up acquiring Egyptian habits.

CHAPTER IV

TECHNIQUES, ARTS AND CRAFTS

THE MAJOR TECHNIQUES

Agriculture

AGRICULTURE in the great river valleys necessarily took on a complexion very different from that of the upland farming which had been the rule for the greater part at least of the Neolithic Age. The farmer was now independent of the rainfall of the winter season; the river provided all the water that his crops required. We have seen (Chapter II) that in Egypt water was employed for basin irrigation, which was gradually —but very early—introduced to supplement the natural action of the annual flooding of the Nile, whereas in Mesopotamia, owing to the different date of the flooding of the Euphrates and to the different contour of the valley, the method adopted had to be that of canalization from the river, i.e. perennial irrigation, the flood-water being used only occasionally to fill reservoirs which could be tapped later in the year. But that was not the only change. In the first place, there was now permanence of occupation.[1] In the old days man had cleared by fire a patch of wooded land and from the soil thus enriched had raised his crops, and when the soil was exhausted he had simply moved on and repeated the operation elsewhere; but in the valley the soil was renewed every year by the silt-laden waters that spread over it, and the same ground could be tilled generation after generation and lose none of its fertility. Because the farmer was now practically *adscriptus glebae* it was worth his while to plan for the future instead of merely exploiting the land for his immediate profit; an elaborate canal system built up by co-operative effort would not have been possible without security of tenure. Moreover, the scale of things was vastly greater; instead of the little forest clearing there was spread out the wide expanse of flat and fertile soil which needed only to be worked to produce all that man could ask; mere area demanded improved methods of tilling the soil.

The primitive fashion of sowing, dropping the seed into holes dibbled in the ground with a pointed stick, had given place to hand-furrowing, and this continued for a very long time; the settlements of the al'Ubaid people, the first immigrants into the Euphrates valley, are marked by the vast numbers of heavy flint hoes which litter the site. Such stone tools were crudely effective, especially in the light silt of the riverine countries, but their use meant slow work, limiting the area that could be cultivated—and in southern Mesopotamia at least they had to be imported, which added to the cost of farming. The wooden plough, involving first male labour and thereafter that of oxen too, brought about the change from plot cultivation to field tillage; at what date it was introduced cannot be determined, for of the implements themselves all traces have disappeared and the first mention of them in writing or the first representation of them in art gives us at best but a *terminus ante quem*; but in Mesopotamia and in Egypt the ox-drawn plough (Fig. 18) was in use by 3000 BC (and perhaps long before that) and in India almost as early, by the time of the development of the Harappā culture. There is no means of telling which country is to be credited with the invention; but that matters little; communications were far more rapid in the ancient world than one is liable to suppose, and the knowledge of anything so eminently practical as the plough would be passed from one country to another very quickly provided that local conditions were suited to its use. Naturally people in a lower stage of culture, such as those of central

FIG. 18. *Egyptian agriculture (Ola Kingdom): ploughing, breaking sods, and sowing by hand (after Breasted).*

Europe, would have less need to adopt a mechanical device intended for large-scale production; but even so, the plough is figured on rock carvings in far-off Sweden as early as the middle of the second millennium BC, a thousand years before it is known to have been in use in China.

Given the plough, man was able to till a much greater area;

the bigger harvest that resulted called for an improvement in the method of reaping. In the upland clearings the thin crop had been gathered by hand—as indeed is still done in the Middle East when the sowing has been on poor land and the growth is sparse; but on the rich irrigated silt mere hand-work could never cope with the harvest. Man therefore invented the sickle. In Egypt the reaper used an adaptation of a tool whose history went back to Natufian times; flint flakes were mounted in a straight wooden bar and this made a fairly effective cutting implement. In Mesopotamia the same principle was employed but the handle might be of baked clay and it was curved in the fashion of the modern sickle. But a curious alternative was also in common use; on the sites of village settlements of the al'Ubaid period there are always found numerous terra-cotta sickles with a sharp cutting-edge; the clay is fired so hard as to be not infrequently vitrified. Admittedly clay seems a most unpromising material out of which to manufacture a cutting-tool, but the drawback was overcome by the ingenious idea of over-firing (examples have been found of two or three sickles fused together by the actual melting of the clay in the furnace) and the thin and rather jagged blade-edge would certainly cut straw; such sickles are brittle and would easily break, which may account for the vast quantities found, almost every one of them broken. None the less, the clay sickle was a makeshift. No example has been recorded later in date than the al'Ubaid period, and it is fairly safe to conclude that the Uruk people, free users of metal, brought the copper (or bronze?) sickle with them into Sumer or else produced on the spot copper sickles imitated from the clay originals. At a time when metal was rare and expensive metal tools would never be thrown away; when too worn for use they would be melted down and re-cast; consequently it is not surprising that the earliest metal sickle recorded from Mesopotamia dates only from the Early Dynastic time; but the merely negative evidence justifies us in saying that they were introduced not later than 3000 BC.

The wheat which was first cultivated was einkorn, the one-kernelled type, which originated in the Near East and gradually spread over Europe and north Africa. But it was ousted from popular favour even in prehistoric times by the two- or six-rowed barley and by the husked two-kernelled emmer wheat which originated apparently in the Zagros region and soon reached Mesopotamia and then Egypt, where at the end of the prehistoric period it seems to have constituted about one-fifth of the crops grown, the two-rowed barley being 23 per cent and the six-rowed barley 57 per cent of the crop. In the Middle

East emmer gradually gave way to its superior derivatives, the naked wheats, but it had a greater vogue in prehistoric Europe. The naked wheats of the emmer group, particularly durum, are most typical of Egypt and together with barley and millet were the staple crop throughout the whole of the Bronze Age; they were the wheats of Palestine and Syria and of Mesopotamia during the al'Ubaid period, but not later. At Lachish, in about 3000 BC, emmer and einkorn form 80 per cent of the grain found, the remainder being for the most part hulled barley, and club wheat (*Triticum compactum*), with a certain admixture of darnel. At Lachish, as on all sites throughout the Middle East, the lentil is very common; in Egypt it is found in pre-Dynastic tombs. The wheats of the spelt group, which appear to have had a northern origin, were those used in early times in the Indus valley. This is shown by a basketful of grain found at Mohenjo-daro; it is of the species *Triticum sphaerococcum,* but 'the grains show a remarkably wide range in size and shape, as if they had been derived from several strains', possibly a form of *T. compactum* combined with *T. sphaerococcum.* The mixture seems to indicate that in 2000 BC the process of hybridization was not fully complete though a certain standard has been reached, justifying the general definition as *sphaerococcum;* moreover, the specimens found at Harappā are of this type. They are found also in early levels at Anau (near Ashkhabad in Transcaspia) and in the Jamdat Nasr period are introduced into Mesopotamia, where they quickly drive the wheats of the emmer group off the field and become the prevalent Mesopotamian type; but they never got into Egypt, because the emmer group is more suited to Mediterranean conditions and so was able to hold its own there.

In China wheat was introduced only late; on the other hand, barley is mentioned as such in the bone inscriptions from Anyang. The main food of the Chinese was, however, millet; this has been found on Neolithic sites and it is constantly mentioned on the bone inscriptions, which may further differentiate between two varieties, the spiked and the panicular. The same sources give the character for 'rice'. Although Anyang lies somewhat north of the best rice-growing country, imprints of the cultivated grain have been found on Neolithic pottery from Yang-shao on the south borders of the Anyang territory, so that the Shang people may have raised rice-crops of their own rather than have it imported from the south; but even so rice, as compared with millet, must assuredly have been for them a luxury food.

The development and local standardization of particular types of cereals are, of course, in part dictated by varying conditions of soil and climate, but none the less do they bear witness to conscious experiment and to the intelligent observation of natural data; even if cross-breeding started accidentally, the ancient farmers of the Middle East were quick to take advantage of the accident. People who were capable of planning and carrying out the vast canalization schemes of Sumer, people who had been able to establish the solar calendar for the benefit of the First Dynasty Egyptian agriculturalist (see p. 419–20) were fully qualified to select the grains which best suited their country's soil and climate and even to improve artificially the varieties provided by nature.

In the case of Mesopotamia we have literary evidence for the early development of varying grain types. In the myth of Lahar and Ashnan it is said that prior to the creation of man

> the *shesh*-grain of thirty days did not exist,
> the *shesh*-grain of forty days did not exist,
> the small grains, the grain of the mountain, the grain of the pure living creatures, did not exist

which means that at the time when the legend took its form the slow- and quick-maturing grains were already distinguished, as well as those suited to different altitudes. A proverb of the third millennium speaks of the early barley and the late barley, and the myth of the Wooing of Inanna describes

> The farmer who makes plants grow abundantly,
> The farmer who makes grain grow abundantly

and specifies the wheat, the beans and the lentils. But the progress of agriculture in general is best shown by the (unpublished) 'Farmer's Almanac', dated to about 1700 BC, by which time it was already a classic[2] supposed to embody the instructions originally given by the god Ninurta. 'In days of yore a farmer gave instructions to his son: When you are about to cultivate your field, take care to open the irrigation works [so that] their water does not rise too high in the field. When you have emptied it of water, watch the field's wet ground that it stays even; let no wandering ox trample it. Chase the prowlers, and have it treated as settled land. Clear it with ten narrow axes [weighing no more than] ⅔ lb. each. Its stubble [?] should be torn up by hand and tied in bundles; its narrow holes shall be gone over with a drag; and the four sides of the field shall be fenced about.' In the summer, when there was no work to be done in the sun-baked fields, the farmer was to make his household and hired help prepare in advance all the necessary tools, implements, baskets and containers: 'The yoke-bar should be made fast, your new whip should be fastened with nails, and the handle to which your old whip was fastened should be mended by the workers' children.' He must see to it that he

FIG. 19. *Mesopotamian plough with seeder: from a Kassite seal-impression found at Nippur (after Kramer).*

has an extra ox for the plough. Before beginning to plough, he should have the ground broken up twice by the mattock and once by the hoe; where necessary the hammer must be used to pulverize the clods. He was counselled to stand over his labourers and see to it that they did not shirk their work.

The work of ploughing and seeding was carried on simultaneously by means of a seeder—that is, a plough with an attachment that carried the seed from a container through a narrow funnel to the furrow, a type illustrated on a Kassite seal-impression found at Nippur (Fig. 19).

The farmer was instructed to plough eight furrows to each strip of approximately 20 feet; he was to see to it that the seed was placed at an even depth—'Keep an eye on the man who puts in the barley seed that he make the seed fall two fingers [apart] uniformly', and if the seed failed to penetrate the earth properly, he must change the share—'the tongue of the plough'. Ploughing must not be always in the same direction: 'Where you have ploughed straight furrows, plough diagonal furrows; where you have ploughed diagonal furrows, plough straight furrows.' Following the sowing, the furrows had to be cleared of clods, so that the sprouting of the barley would not be impeded. 'On the day when the seed breaks through the ground' the farmer should say a prayer to Ninkilim, the goddess of field-mice and vermin, lest these harm the growing grain; he should also scare away the birds. When the barley had grown sufficiently to fill the narrow bottoms of the furrows, he was to water it; and when it was dense enough to cover the field like 'the mat in the middle of a boat' he was to water it a second time. A third time he was to water the 'royal' grain. Should he then notice a reddening of the wet grain, it was the dread *samana*-disease that was endangering the crop. If the crop showed improvement he was to water it a fourth time, and thus get an extra yield of 10 per cent.

When the time came for harvesting, the farmer was not to wait until the barley went under its own weight, but was to cut it, 'in the day of its strength'. Three men worked as a team on the standing grain, a reaper, a binder and another whose duties are not clear.

The threshing, which followed immediately upon the harvesting, was done by means of a sledge drawn back and forth over the heaped-up grain stalks[8] for a period of five days. The barley was then 'opened' with an 'opener' which was drawn by oxen. By this time, however, the grain had become unclean through contact with the ground; therefore, after an appropriate prayer, it was winnowed with long-handled winnowing-fans and thus freed of dirt and dust as well as the chaff.

From these elaborate 'instructions' it is clear that in Mesopotamia the technique of practical agriculture as carried on in the Middle East had been perfected by about the end of the third millennium BC, and all the available evidence goes to show that in Egypt, with its different conditions, development was almost, if not quite, as early.

Somewhat similar progress was made with stock-breeding. With the introduction of the ox-drawn plough, cattle had become more valuable, but it was not in the ploughing season alone that the large-scale farmer could make use of them. In Sumer they were employed as draught animals probably as early as the beginning of the Uruk period: at Ur and at Kish there have been found the heavy solid-wheeled wagons drawn by them, and although these actual examples date from the Early Dynastic period yet clay wheels from model carts go back much earlier. The bringing-in of the harvested crops and the carrying of the grain from the farm to the city required that manpower should be supplemented by 'mechanical' transport. For the winnowing of the corn the Egyptian farmer usually clung to the primitive method of threshing with a one-piece flail (the jointed flail dates from the Iron Age) but in Palestine, Syria and Mesopotamia (and sometimes in Egypt also), an alternative to the flail was the treading-out of the corn by oxen. In those countries, too, other than Egypt, vast numbers of flint chips polished by use which are found upon early sites probably imply the use of threshing-sledges such as are employed at the present day—the corn is spread on the threshing-floor and an ox drags round and round over it a heavy wooden sledge whose under-side is studded with flint flakes, thus breaking up the ears and at the same time cutting the straw into short lengths fit for fodder. If the ox was to be a beast of labour, careful breeding (as well as good food) was needed to produce a strong type; that developed in Sumer, as can be learned both from representations in art and from skeletal remains, was a long-horned breed of about the size of modern European domestic cattle and generally resembling the Chartley bull. Because in the enervating climate of southern Mesopotamia the type was bound to deteriorate, fresh stock had to be imported for breeding purposes, and the Sumerian farmer was fully alive to this necessity; thus, in the temple-farm at Drehem there was kept a stud bull imported from the highlands of Elam. The zebu was known in the Diyala region.

In the same way with sheep; the traditional garment of the early Sumerian was the *kaunakes,* a kilt of sheepskin worn with the fleece outside, and the heavy wool represented in the drawings and statuettes implies long and careful domestication. It is not necessary to assume that the thirty-one different variations of the sign *UDU* in early texts correspond to different breeds (see Chapter VI), indeed it is far more likely that the type was fairly uniform throughout Sumer, but the valley sheep were certainly far superior to those of the nomad *sutu* in the Syrian desert; that much at least is witnessed by the *kaunakes.*

In Egypt the sheep seems to have been almost unknown in early times and its place was taken by the goat. The ram which is the symbol of the god Khnum may possibly represent an indigenous species which died out early in the Dynastic period, or again it may have been taken over from a non-Egyptian source and imply that the god himself was of foreign origin. That the Egyptians knew of the existence of the sheep would appear certain inasmuch as the flocks of the Semitic nomads of Sinai could scarcely have escaped their notice, but for some reason or another it was not admitted into the Nile valley until well in the Dynastic Age, after which time two breeds are represented. Even the Hebrews have put it on record that 'shepherds were an abomination to the Egyptians'.

The other domestic mammals of the Middle East were the dog, the ass, the goat and the pig, and of birds the goose and the duck.

The case of the camel is peculiar.[4] The true camel, the two-humped species (*Camelus bactrianus*), is a native of central Asia, ranging from Iran to the Gobi desert. Camel bones have been found at Shah Tepe in domestic levels dating to 3000 BC and at Anau in the beginning of the Copper Age, while remains found in a prehistoric settlement in the Kiev area would imply that it was domesticated in the steppe zone at least as early as 2000 BC. Presumably it was used quite early by the nomads of south-east Russia, for there are many Aryan names, like that of Zoroaster himself, which end in '-ushtra', 'camel', i.e. 'owner of camels', and it may have played an important part as one of the links between the Middle and the Far East. A single bone of a camel (but the species is doubtful) was found in the excavations at Mohenjo-daro. The single-humped dromedary (*Camelus dromedarius*) is the southern species. Fossil remains of it have been found in Egypt, and its existence in later times is amply proved. From the pre-Dynastic period we have an ivory tablet found near Gurnah showing a man riding a camel, and a terra-cotta figurine from Ma'adi. A rope made of camel's hair found in the Fayum is dated to the Third Dynasty. A camel's skull, also from the Fayum, is attributed to the Middle Kingdom, as are some rock drawings in the Wadi Hammamat. There are four or five representations of camels of New Kingdom date. This evidence, much of it coming from outside the Nile valley proper, is not sufficient to prove local domestication of the camel, but does make it clear that the animal was known to the Egyptians; probably it was used and kept by neighbours, the desert dwellers whom the Egyptians hated. Biblical references to the camel (Genesis xxiv and xxxvii) fully harmonize with this. We are indeed obliged to conclude that in Arabia at any rate the camel was domesticated at an early date, its employment anticipating and leading up to the highly-organized commercial traffic on which was based the prosperity of the Minyean kingdom of the fourteenth century BC. The silence of the texts, both Egyptian and Babylonian —and even in late times when camels are known to have been in use they are seldom mentioned in contracts or letters—may be due to the fact that the Sutu-Beduins had a monopoly of the carrying trade across the desert and, as was the case in recent times, rarely brought their animals inside the towns, so that little notice was taken of them by the writers.

The horse first appears in the Middle East early in the second millennium. It was brought into regular use in Mesopotamia by the Kassites[5] in the seventeenth century BC and reached Egypt in about the time of the Hyksos possibly through their agency;[6] it was brought into India by the Aryan invaders perhaps two centuries later.[7] For a long time its use, both in Egypt and in Mesopotamia, was confined to the drawing of military chariots; the Mitanni might ride on horseback, i.e. on stallions, but in the eyes of the native Mesopotamian that was an unseemly habit.

India apparently had no asses, but had the water buffalo,

the short-horned cattle of Mesopotamian type, a long-horned urus type, and the great humped zebu; that these were domesticated is shown by the fact that on the seals they are usually represented standing before a manger or an offering table; sometimes they are garlanded, implying that the bull was sacred then as now. The elephant also had been domesticated and is pictured wearing a collar. Whether or not the sheep was kept in the Indus valley is doubtful; the goat, on the other hand, is well attested by seals and by clay figurines.

By the time of the Shang Dynasty the Chinese had domesticated cattle (most of the oracles are inscribed on cattle bones), the horse (skeletons of horses are found in the Anyang graves with the war chariots), sheep and dogs. The elephant and the rhinoceros were kept, certainly in the pleasure-parks of the rulers, and probably elephants were used in war and for some kinds of work. China at a very early period had domesticated the hen, which slowly moved westwards, was acclimatized in Elam and was introduced into Egypt in the Eighteenth Dynasty, when the Pharaoh boasts of having received (from Elam?) 'birds that give birth every day'. There is a drawing of a cock on an ostrakon of that period.

In all countries of the ancient world where agriculture achieved any notable advance men were quick to supplement the natural resources of their own lands by importing new foodstuffs from foreign parts. It is quite characteristic that Sargon of Akkad should bring back with him from a successful raid into central Anatolia specimens of vines, figs and roses for acclimatization in Mesopotamia; and although the Egyptian queen Hatshepsut was perhaps influenced more by religious than by economic motives in importing myrrh trees from Punt to be planted in front of her Deir at Bahri temple others before her had introduced into the Nile valley plants more generally useful. Perhaps the most interesting case of acclimatization is that of the grape-vine. A native of Anatolia, and probably of the Syrian ranges of Amanus and Lebanon, it spread early over the Near East—discoveries made at Lachish show that at the beginning of the Bronze Age, *c.* 3000 BC, grapes were dried and eaten as raisins as well as being used for wine-making. The vine spread early into Europe, but eastwards it made slow progress, being grown fairly early in Persia, but not beyond. It probably came into Afghanistan, and so into India, in the wake of Alexander's armies, and it did not reach China until the year 128 BC when the Chinese general, Chan K'ien, found it in Bactria and was led by his appreciation of the wine drunk in Ferghana to send grape-seeds home for the emperor to grow. At what date the vine was brought into Mesopotamia we cannot say, but even in the south it was grown as early as the time of Urukagina, who mentions the royal wine cellars (*Saki,* 57, i. 5, 2–4), so that Sargon was merely collecting new varieties, not introducing something hitherto unknown —and the same is true of the fig, which also was mentioned in texts of Urukagina.

It is now certain that the grape was known in Minoan Crete, and grape-seeds have been found on Mycenaean sites such as Orchomenos, Tiryns and Mycenae in the Middle Helladic (Late Bronze) Age, so that the Homeric picture of vine cultivation in Ithaca, with varying species that ripened at different times (*Od.* xxiv, 340) need not be thought exaggerated. The Dionysis legends make it clear that the Greeks owed their knowledge of the grape, and of the making of wine, to Anatolia; the channel whereby that knowledge came to them is not yet certain, but it may well have been the Achaeans, established on the Asiatic mainland in the neighbourhood of Miletus, who passed it on to their kinsmen on the islands and in Greece proper.

The wild Oleaster or Olea from which the various species of olives are derived seems to have been indigenous in Syria and Palestine, this being the spineless variety, while a type with spines seems to have originated in Crete. The cultivation of the olive tree and the extraction of olive oil began in Palestine (Lachish) before 3000 BC, and in Crete at least as early as the middle of the third millennium BC; the huge *pithoi,* storage jars for oil, found in the magazines of the Knossos palace prove that the wealth of the Cretan kings early in the second millennium BC was in part based on the export of olive oil. In Syria it must have been exploited at an early date and after 1500 BC, when the use of olive oil became common in Egypt, Syria must have been the main source of supply. It never spread into Mesopotamia, where the climate was unfavourable, and its place was taken by the sesame, but it gradually established itself throughout the Mediterranean lands. Its progress, however, was slow. Homer knew of it, but as a luxury reserved for the rich and not produced in Greece; it was probably only after 1200 BC that the tree was acclimatized on the Greek mainland, and only in the course of the first millennium did it reach Italy and France.

In the course of the Bronze Age the agricultural economy of the ancient world assumed the form which it was to retain with very little change until mediaeval if not until modern times. By 1200 BC the peoples of the different countries had selected and developed the types of cereal that best suited local conditions, and since a large proportion of the grain was grown in artificially irrigated soil they were reasonably assured of a harvest, independently of the vagaries of weather; the methods and the tools used by the farmer would be used for another millennium at least, the only change being that iron would soon take the place of bronze. All the domestic animals of the present day were already in man's service, though the role of the horse was still but a small one, limited to the war chariot. Of tree fruits the fig, apple, pomegranate, peach and mulberry were all cultivated; dates were the most important product of southern Mesopotamia, where many varieties were grown, and were cultivated in Syria and Egypt and as far eastwards as India, where date-stones have been found in the ruins of Mohenjo-daro. The market-gardeners produced a considerable variety of vegetables; Ur-Nammu of Ur (*c.* 2100 BC) claims that as a result of building a temple to Nannar 'he saved the vegetables in the garden plot'; onions were specially favoured, as were leeks, cucumbers and melons of many sorts.

Apart from foodstuffs the main crop grown in Egypt was flax; since the Egyptians never wore woollen garments and linen was the only cloth in general use, flax-growing had to be on a large scale and as an industry must have rivalled in importance the growing of grain. In Mesopotamia, where wool was generally preferred for clothing, the flax industry was at best a secondary interest and a good deal of the linen that was used may have been imported from Elam, where it had been manufactured from a very early date. That flax was grown in India also is probable, but no evidence of it survives; in view, however, of the unlikelihood of such a material being preserved in the Indian soil the negative argument cannot be stressed. On the other hand, traces of woven cotton fabric have been found at Mohenjo-daro, proving that the cotton plant was cultivated in India as early as 2000 BC at least. Judging by the large number of spindle-whorls too small and light for the spinning of wool which are found on the Indus valley sites cotton cloth must indeed have been in common use locally; that it was manufactured for export also is proved by the fact of a fragment of cotton fabric bearing a seal-impression of the Harappā type being found in Iraq. Cotton-growing, on the other hand, did not spread from India either to the west or to the east until very much later times. In China linen was used from an early date, for fibres of some sort of hemp have been found at Anyang. Silk also seems to have been known to the Shang people; the character for 'silk' has been identified (with some hesitation) on bone inscriptions, but actual silk fibres have been discovered in the Anyang tombs. This does not, of course, prove the cultivation of the silkworm in Shang times, but as early Chou graves have produced jade carvings of silk-worms, and as Chou literature not only mentions silk very frequently but even describes the gathering of young mulberry-leaves for the feeding of the silkworms, it is reasonable to suppose that artificial silk-production goes back to the immediately preceding period and that it should be reckoned amongst the agricultural activities of the Shang people.

Architecture

The settled life of the agriculturalist demanded from the outset some form of shelter for his household. As in the course of time and with the increase of wealth the primitive hamlet developed into the town and the town into the city, social distinctions would generally lead to more ambitious building for the well-to-do individual citizen, but always the central government, which was a condition of civic existence, would symbolize its authority, whether secular or religious, by palaces or temples distinguished in scale and splendour from the houses of ordinary men. In all countries alike the same progress can be discerned, and in all alike it is the patronage of the rich and powerful that gives to the builder's craft the stimulus which engenders the art of architecture; but in each country the particular character which architecture takes on is largely decided by the materials available to the builder.

This truth is clearly brought out by Vitruvius in his *History of Architecture* when he describes man's earliest efforts in house construction: 'Some of them', he writes, 'began to make roofs of leaves, others to dig out caves under the hills; some, imitating the nests and constructions of the swallows, made places into which they might go, out of mud and twigs. Finding then other shelters and inventing new things by their power of thought, they built in time better dwellings. . . . At the beginning they put up rough spars, interwove them with twigs and finished the walls with mud.' The Roman author rightly insists upon materials and methods of construction rather than upon the shapes or styles of building; man did not invent an architectural form and then look about for the material best suited to the concrete realization of his new idea; he began by making what use he could of such material as nature offered him, and very soon found that the form was imposed upon him.

The failure to realize the extent to which material determines form has given rise to a good deal of discussion amongst historians as to whether the circular or rectangular building comes first in point of time. Certainly the evidence available suggests the priority of the circular construction, but it must be remembered that the evidence is conditioned by the possibilities of survival. Probably the oldest houses yet discovered are those in the Lower Neolithic strata at Jericho; they are dry-stone buildings roughly circular in plan, and it is only in the higher levels that rectangular huts of stone rubble occur. Similarly at Hassuna in northern Iraq, where there was a settlement of the period when agriculture was just beginning to replace the food-gathering existence of the nomad hunter, round huts were the first to be erected, these again being of stone rubble. On many prehistoric sites where, in default of stone, men made for themselves shallow dugouts with sides of heaped earth and roofs of boughs, the dugouts are round, as in prehistoric China.

The primitive dwellers in caves and rock shelters could easily —and did—learn how to pile up stones into a screen to narrow an entrance or to divide the space; how early they could profit by that experience is shown at Jericho, where the massive rubble walls built by Neolithic man go back, apparently, to the seventh millennium BC. The technique of placing one stone upon another came easily to them, and in the case of a town wall very little planning was wanted—they knew what they had to enclose, and the wall-line would take its direction almost automatically. The case of the house was quite different. When, with a changed manner of life, the cave became inconvenient as being too far from the cultivated land, and people moved down to the foothills and the valleys, their experience in heaping up stone screens still stood them in good stead—where there was no natural cave they could build one. But here something in the nature of a plan was necessary. The old cave had been a place inside which they had lived, and it was that—the inside, not the outside—which they wanted to reproduce, for there had never been an 'outside' to the cave. Consequently the stone hut was built from the inside; you stand in the middle and arrange the stones all round you; and the result is, automatically, a circular building. Similarly with a dugout; you take your stand where you want your hut to be and you dig, throwing the earth outwards, and the earth forms a circle with you as the centre; you cannot help it. In countries therefore in which stone is the obvious material for building, e.g. in northern parts of Mesopotamia and Syria, in Anatolia and in the Greek islands, we should expect the round house to be the earlier type; only when men have become relatively sophisticated and want bigger rooms do they perhaps learn that a roof of straight beams is more easily laid across parallel walls. But the case was very different in the great river valleys which give birth to the world's oldest civilizations; in them stone was hard to come by and the different materials that men perforce employed imposed upon them a different type of architecture. Those materials were less enduring than stone, so that direct evidence of the buildings can seldom be adduced, and owing to the late formation of the riverine lands the settlements in them are not likely to date back to so early a date as that of the Jericho houses; but none the less are we justified in defining the character of the buildings and in asserting that they were indigenous to those lands and the first to be set up by the inhabitants of them. For the history of the beginnings of architecture the Mesopotamian record is by far the most detailed, and an account of it will serve as a background for the study of developments in more or less similar conditions in the other valley centres.

In the Euphrates delta all that nature supplies is mud, reeds and palm-trees. In that country, therefore, the simplest and the most obvious thing to build is the reed hut; that is true of the present time and was equally true at the time of man's first arrival here; the reed-stem and the woven reed-leaf mat were the first materials used for house-building.

The method of construction is this. First you plant upright in the ground two fascines or bundles of tall reeds (single stems would not be strong enough to resist the wind) and then you lash to them cross-bars made of smaller bundles so as to form a framework, to which you fasten reed matting to complete the wall; it is a simple enough process, and immediately the influence of material upon style becomes manifest. The fascines forming the horizontal bars are straight and rigid; automatically therefore the matting wall is a straight wall. It can, of course, be prolonged indefinitely by the addition of fresh uprights, but these must be planted in line with the first two; to enclose a space—which is the whole purpose of house-building—the last upright has to be taken as a corner-post for an angular return, the result being that the ground-plan is rectangular. In practice, the two long sides of the building are set up simultaneously, two rows of fascines being planted parallel one to another, the fascines in the two being equally spaced so as to correspond exactly; the upright bundles are thinner at the top and therefore pliant; opposite members can be bent inwards and lashed together across the middle and you have the framework of a tunnel-like room which can be covered in matting, vaulted roof and all. The process is best illustrated by modern examples, the reed buildings of the Marsh Arabs of southern Iraq; Pl. 7, a, shows the start of such a building, with the upright fascines inclined outward so as to resist the strain of the inward bend that makes the roof, while Pl. 7, b, shows the completed structure, in this case a guest house, a large building which is certainly not without architectural merit. This is precisely the type of building represented on a stone relief of the fourth millennium BC now in the British Museum (Pl. 8, a) and again upon a frieze of about 2700 BC from Ur. Sumerian legends state that reed huts were used before the Flood, and at Ur there were found underneath the silt deposit left by the Flood fragments of thick slabs of clay bearing on one side the impression of reed-stems, which were bits of the mud plaster of a reed hut. For that is the second phase. The matting walls are not proof against draught, and the obvious remedy is to plaster them with the ubiquitous mud; walls and roof alike can be plastered, and as every now and then a fresh coat will be desirable, the mud-work in course of time becomes very thick. Supposing that such a house catches fire, which may easily happen (the pre-Flood plaster found at Ur came from a hut which had been thus accidentally burned), the hardened mud will still be left standing upright, enough at any rate to suggest to some observant individual the novel idea that reeds are perhaps after all not essential, but that a house could be built with mud only. One way of doing so is to use *terre pisée*. This was the regular method in China in the Shang period and for long after, but to hammer the earth really firm requires a caisson of wooden planks which for the Chinese were ready to hand but in southern Mesopotamia were hard to come by, so that examples of it, although they do occur in Sumer, are rare. Another method is to pile up basketfuls of stiff kneaded clay. For rough work such as building a garden wall it serves well enough and is indeed still in use in Iraq; but it is clumsy at best, and when the wall is more than shoulder high the weight of the basket-load makes further building difficult; so some ingenious builder conceived the idea of conveniently small lumps held together by mud mortar.

Brickwork. At first these would be mere lumps pressed together by hand, as in the Neolithic levels at Jericho, but later they were moulded in an open wooden frame, instead of the old round-bottomed baskets—and the frame, being of wood, was necessarily rectangular, and rectangular lumps were vastly easier to lay—and at once the practice of brick-making spread far and wide. In Sumer moulded bricks, both crude and kiln-fired, were used side by side with reed-hut building even in the pre-Flood period (al'Ubaid I) and the examples found underneath the Flood deposit are probably the oldest yet known to us, but whether or not they were a local invention it is impossible to say. In Egypt bricks seem to have been introduced towards the end of the pre-Dynastic period, when they replace the wattle-work smeared with mud which was normal in pre-Dynastic times; brick-making therefore begins later there than in Sumer and may well be due to a borrowing of ideas. In the farther east, the ruins of Mohenjo-daro and Harappā show us an architecture uniformly carried out in brick—crude bricks for terrace foundations and perhaps for the upper parts of walls of private houses, burnt bricks, often set in bitumen mortar, for most walls—but are far too late in date to throw any light upon origins. Some of the pot-stone decorated vessels found in Mesopotamia but made in Mehi represent the façades of buildings in which brickwork is used side by side with matting applied to a timber frame (Pl. 8, b); the combination of the two materials suggests a transition in building methods and on those grounds it is perhaps legitimate to assume that Baluchistan learnt the art of moulding bricks not long before the beginnings of the early Dynastic period in Sumer (to which the vases in question belong) and probably learned it from the Sumerians—an assumption which is but reasonable in view of the trade relations between the two countries and, in particular, of the Sumerian character of the buildings at Mundigak. The Chinese, on the other hand, clung to their traditional *terre pisée* and never used bricks at all.

But whether the Sumerians invented the new medium or adopted it, they applied it to an art whose main lines had already been decided. In the matter of wall construction, the primitive builders of the reed hut had laced their matting on the inside of the framework just as do the modern Marsh Arabs (Pl. 7, b). When, then, they laid on their mud plaster the upright fascines produced the effect of half-columns dividing the wall-face into panels. This had a distinct decorative value, and would be most noticeable in the case of larger buildings in which the uprights would be more numerous, heavier, and therefore standing out in more prominent relief, and probably closer together so as to obtain solidity in a higher construction; this is well illustrated by the modern 'guest house' on Pl. 7, b. The temples of the early al'Ubaid people must have looked very much like that 'guest house', and, because religious traditions are binding, the builders in brick copied their old models faithfully. The rounded half-columns might be kept, as we see at Erech, or, since the bricks were rectangular, might more easily be translated into square buttresses but for a religious building the panelled wall was essential, and the convention held good down to the last days of Babylon. Actually it was confined to temples; originally because there was no point in imitating the few and flimsy uprights of the private individual's house and later because it had become so closely associated with temples that its lay use would have implied impiety—man arrogating to himself the peculiar features of the house of God; but the house of God must for all time be as it was in the beginning.

The reed hut had other lessons to teach the architect. Where it was small and square the tops of all four corner uprights could be bent inwards and tied together, and the result had been a dome. That could be reproduced. One of the royal tombs at Ur, *c.* 2700 BC, has a dome of limestone rubble set in mud mortar constructed over a timber centering; on the Ziggurat terrace at Ur, King Ur-Nammu (*c.* 2150 BC) built a cistern surmounted by a brick dome, and the dome seems to be implied by the constructional features of some of his as well as of later buildings such as the Dublal-makh shrine at Ur in the Larsa and Kassite periods. The tunnel-like reed hut, mud-plastered all over, inevitably suggested the arch and the vault. In Sumer the true arch appears early; one may suspect that it started by laying bricks over the arched matting, in which case the bricklayers cannot have failed to notice the principle of radial jointing which the bricks would automatically follow; naturally arches built above-ground can very seldom survive, but there is evidence enough to prove that the form was employed by Mesopotamian architects to the end of Babylonian history. Thus, the doorway of one of the royal tombs as Ur is capped with an arch of burnt bricks; to the same Early Dynastic period belong a mud-brick arch in a drain at Nippur and another at Tellô; mud-brick arches occur in tombs of the Third Dynasty and Larsa periods; a fallen arch of burnt brick was found in a doorway of a Larsa private house, and a fifteenth-century arch of burnt bricks set in bitumen was found in the Ur shrine Dublal-makh as reconstructed by the Kassite ruler Kurigalzu (Pl. 9, a). In Egypt the arch (in mud-brick) first occurs in the Third Dynasty but is never common and was never used as an architectural feature; where used at all it is masked, generally by a flat lintel. Similarly the barrel vault, used in most of the Ur royal tomb chambers, can safely be attributed to temples of both the Larsa and the Kassite periods, and is the normal roofing of mud-brick tomb chambers from the time of the Third Dynasty down to early in the Kassite period, after which burial customs changed and tomb chambers went out of fashion. These vaults were built without the support of centering, the brick rings being laid at an angle, leant against the end wall, so that each successive ring was supported by resting on its predecessor, as shown in the diagrammatic sketch (Fig. 20); the bricks used were not voussoir-shaped but normal rectangular bricks and the voussoir

FIG. 20. *Method of ring vaulting construction.*

effect was produced simply by putting extra mud, mortar, or sometimes mortar mixed with potsherds, at the upper end of the joint. Although the outward form of the vault was derived from the reed hut, the method of construction was by no means obvious; the slanting of the rings and the raising and strengthening of the end wall against which they lean are altogether in the brick techniques and imply a real knowledge of stresses and ingenuity in meeting them.

When, therefore, we find an identical technique in Egypt at a later date, we are probably justified in considering this to be a case of borrowed art. The earliest surviving Egyptian example is of the Twelfth Dynasty, in the workmen's dwellings at Kahun; at no time was it common, and its first use in a major monument seems to have been in the Nineteenth Dynasty Ramesseum; certainly not until then did it seriously affect Egyptian architecture, whereas the layout of a good many Mesopotamian temples seems to have been dictated by the intention of the architect to employ the vault and by the limitations of his skill. A barrel vault with sloped rings can be built very easily across a small span, e.g. over a tomb chamber not more than a metre and a half wide, but as the span increases so does the difficulty of construction. To some extent the difficulty is met, or lessened, by the use of voussoirs, and such have been found, e.g. at Ur, though never *in situ*; at Alalakh, in northern Syria, long narrow chambers, up to 2.50 metres wide, probably magazines, in the royal palace of the twenty-fourth century BC, were vaulted with well-shaped voussoir bricks, and Alalakh must certainly have learned from Sumer, seeing that the kingdom had business relations with Mesopotamia and that the true vault is not a feature of the native architecture of Syria. But where the span to be covered by the vault was at all large the Sumerian builder, perhaps mistrusting his powers, preferred the corbelled vault set up over a wooden centering. Such was the case with the stone rubble chambers of the royal tombs, where the span is 2.20 metres, and with the 3.60 metres-wide chambers, built with burnt bricks and bitumen, of the mausoleum of the Third Dynasty kings of Ur; in later times corbelling is freely used for the small mud-brick tombs of private citizens of Babylonia, and here again size is the determining factor. Mud-brick is indeed the worst possible material for corbel vaulting owing to its low tensile quality; burnt bricks if set in a really binding mortar such as bitumen serve the purpose much better, but because of their small size require careful laying to assure an adequate counterpoise. Stone is the only satisfactory material, and where stone is normally used for building there is no need to suppose that the technique of corbelling is necessarily borrowed; even if no timber centering be employed to give support during construction; yet it is so natural to bring the walls together by making each course overlap slightly the line of the course below that there was no need of a foreign teacher to show how it should be done: and a very little experience, perhaps dearly bought, would instil the lesson that there must be a counterpoise. The corbel vaulting of the Grand Gallery in the Great Pyramid at Gizeh has a projection for each course of three inches (0.075 metres) only, an exaggerated precaution that seems to imply an experiment on original lines; similarly the stone corbel-roofed tomb chambers of Ugarit (fourteenth century BC) (Fig. 23) and the beehive *tholoi* of the Mycenaeans need not owe anything to Sumer, and for the origin of the corbelled stone tombs of Spain we need look no farther east than Crete.

The early Sumerian builder in brick derived his knowledge of principles from the reed hut of his predecessors, but could not always apply them directly. The reed building with its arched-over roof might be quite large, and clients demanded something not less impressive in the new material. It was easy to plan a great hall and to set up its walls in brick, but since you were not dealing with pliant reed-bundles and the span was too great for vaulting (even supposing that the mud-brick walls would have stood the outward thrust of a brick vault), something else had to be done. All that was needed was a modified use of the old materials. Light poplar poles—the poplar grew freely in the Euphrates valley—were laid as rafters from wall to wall, and over them reeds laid at right-angles; on the reeds mats were spread and on the matting earth and a top coating of mud; the flat roof of the ancient and of the modern

Middle East is the natural outcome of building in brick. Such a roof, flat or slightly sloped for drainage, is most effective, cool in the summer and in the rainy season reasonably waterproof; but it does need a fresh coat of mud after the winter, and the original thickness (which should be about 65 millimetres) is soon multiplied; mud is heavy and the load upon the roof-poles becomes too great and therefore, if the span be at all considerable, the roof will require support, which means a column or columns.

Until quite recently it had been assumed that the column was unknown in ancient Mesopotamia, so much so that when an American excavator announced his discovery at Nippur of a columned hall dated to the fifteenth century BC he was held up to ridicule on the grounds that columns were only introduced into the country by the Greeks. It was an absurd assumption, because where nature supplies the palm-tree man can hardly help adapting it to use as a column; true, no column had been found, but that was because actual palm-logs had been employed and these had of course decayed and left no trace of themselves. Now there have been found at Erech huge columns, 2.5 metres in diameter, built of specially moulded radial mud-bricks and overlaid with elaborate mosaic; they date from somewhere about 3000 BC. Similar but rather smaller brick columns recur two or three centuries later at Kish, and at much the same time the king of Alalakh, following the fashion set by his Mesopotamian business clients, built similar columns for the façade of his palace. The little temple at al'Ubaid, built by A-anni-pad-da about 2700 BC, had columns of real palm-logs either sheathed with copper or covered with a polychrome mosaic reproducing the scales of the palm-trunk. The brick column was used by Ur-Nammu (*c.* 2100 BC) in one of his temples at Ur, and a later example (by Warad-Sin, *c.* 1800 BC) is of moulded bricks which reproduce the scale-pattern of the palm-trunk in relief. The column then was a perfectly familiar feature of Mesopotamian architecture, and its origin was no less familiar.

In Egypt, because from the Third Dynasty onwards the columns that adorned temples and palaces were of stone, the evidence for their use exists in uncounted quantities, and because they are translations into stone of originals in other materials they illustrate perfectly the art of periods for which no direct evidence survives.

There are two standard types of Egyptian column (Fig. 21); one imitates the palm-trunk, the other a bundle of papyrus reeds tied together at the top and bottom. The palm column has a capital either of palm fronds or in the form of a flower-calyx, rather like an inverted bell. The papyrus column at its first appearance (in the pyramid-temple of King Zoser of the Third Dynasty, Pl. 9, b) has a severely rigid shaft and no true capital but what may represent mud-plaster applied over the upper tie. But this is a unique case, and normally the reed bundle is realistically rendered, showing the ties and the swelling above the lower tie due to the reeds bending under the pressure of the roof; the shaft therefore is naturalistic, but the flowering heads of the reeds, pressed outwards by the roof's weight, could not well be rendered in stone and are ingeniously conventionalized into an opening lotus-bud. There are variations of detail, of course; in the great Luxor temple the straight shafts are reeded for two-thirds of their height and plain for the top third; at Tell el Amarna, again in the Eighteenth Dynasty, the reed column is given a palm-frond capital; but, with the single exception of the ugly Hathor-head capitals which were never much in favour until Ptolemaic times, the Egyptian column as a whole preserves the memory of the palm-trunk or the papyrus-bundle of the prehistoric age.

By the middle of the second millennium therefore the architects of the two countries which led the way in Middle East civilization had evolved all the basic features of architecture as it is known today. In every case the evolution starts with the forms which were imposed upon primitive man by the materials at his disposition and is conditioned by the character of those materials; the genius of the builder showed itself not in the invention of forms but in the use of new materials and his combination of their peculiar characteristics with his inherited tradition.

Materials and Techniques. In Egypt, although the flat floor of the valley is built up of water-borne silt, the desert on either side supplies stone in plenty. In Middle Egypt the cliffs are of limestone, farther south sandstone takes its place, and in the district of the First Cataract—at Wadi Halfa—the rock formation through which the Nile bursts its way is of granite. The Egyptian builder, therefore, was able to use stone for his craft and to select the sort most suited to his purpose.

It is curious that in the earliest known case of stone being used at all—the floor of the tomb of the First Dynasty king Udy-mu, at Abydos—the material is not the local limestone but granite brought down-stream from Aswân; possibly it reflects the nostalgia of the southern conqueror! The work is rough, the blocks only slightly squared, and as a mere pavement it cannot be termed a building. In the Second Dynasty 'the first tentative use of stone in actual building was made'.

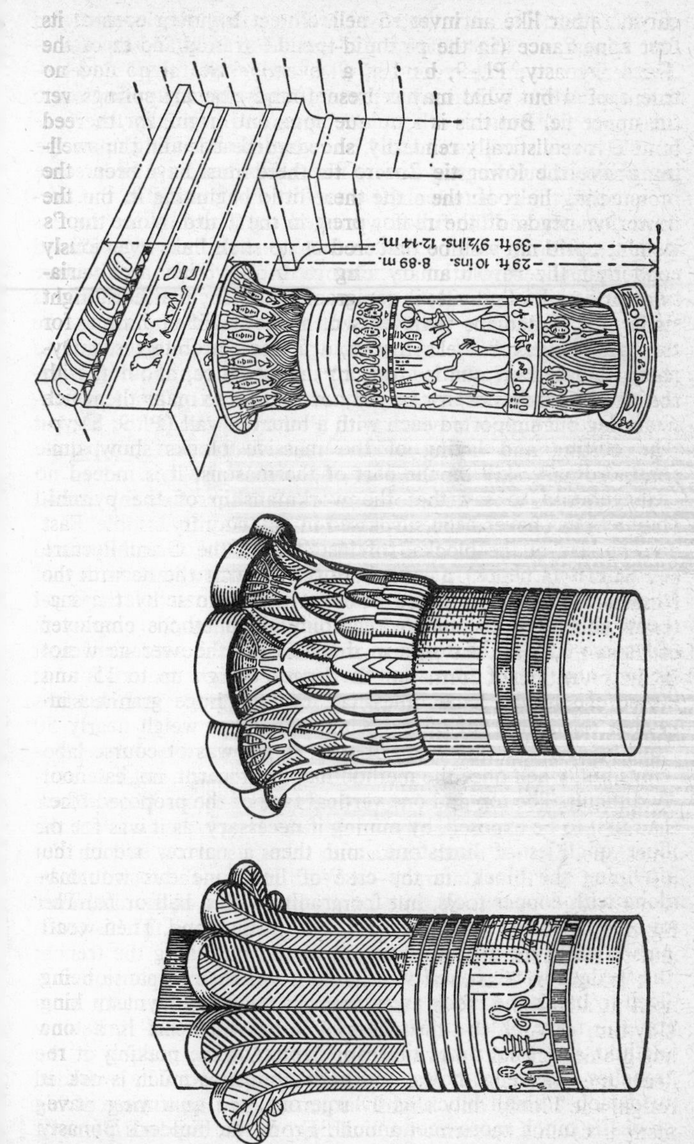

FIG. 21. *Types of Egyptian columns (after Fletcher).*

In the Third Dynasty the royal architect Imhotep constructed for King Zoser at Saqqâra the Stepped Pyramid and the amazing series of temples round it, all of stone. So far no development of stone building has been found; the art springs into existence full-blown without any apparent origin, for the Second Dynasty work can hardly be regarded as leading up to the magnificent buildings of Zoser. Yet there must have been some connecting links between the poor little beginning in the Second Dynasty and the full flowering in the Third. None the less is it tempting to assume that in fact no such links ever existed and that the revolutionary change in Egyptian architecture was due to the individual genius of Imhotep; that certainly is what the Egyptians believed when they deified him as the supreme inventor. It is true that Zoser's architect seems to have had certain qualms, due to inexperience, about the stability of his columns, for he did not venture to make them free-standing but supported each with a buttress wall (Pl. 9, b); but the cutting and laying of the massive blocks show quite extraordinary skill on the part of the masons; it is indeed no exaggeration to say that the workmanship of the pyramid builders has never been surpassed in any country.

The size of the blocks, for instance, in the Great Pyramid of Khufu (Cheops) at Gizeh, together with the accuracy of their jointing, constitutes a problem which no scholar has yet been able fully to answer regarding the methods employed. Of some 2,300,000 stones in the building the average weight is two and a half tons, but the largest weigh up to 15 tons; these are of the local limestone, but the huge granite slabs which form the roof of the King's Chamber weigh nearly 50 tons apiece. The quarrying of such stones was of course laborious but, when once the method had been learnt, not essentially difficult. The top and one vertical face of the proposed block had first to be exposed, by mining if necessary, as it was for the finer qualities of limestone, and then a narrow trench cut outlining the block; in the case of limestone this would be done with copper tools, but for granite with a ball or hammer of some such material as diorite, held in the hand. Then wooden wedges were driven into wedge-holes cut along the trench; the wedges were soaked with water, and their expansion sufficed to break the block away from its bed, leaving clean faces for the start of the next blocks. Obviously this is a slow method, but what takes time and labour is the making of the trenches and wedge-holes, and since almost as much is needed to detach a small block as a large one, the quarrying of big stones is much more economical. From the builder's point of view also large blocks were preferable, if not essential; temples and pyramids were constructed on the dry-stone principle (in the pyramids a very small quantity of mortar was used in the horizontal courses, but only as a lubricant, not as an adhesive) and they simply could not have been built with small stones and no binding mortar; only big blocks would by their sheer weight assure solidity. On all counts therefore large stones were desirable. Nor was the difficulty of transport so great as might be supposed. Quarry-men and builders were skilled craftsmen, limited in number, but of unskilled labour there was no lack, especially during the three months of the inundation period when agriculture was at a standstill, and the hundred thousand men said by Herodotus to have been employed on the Great Pyramid could easily have been forthcoming. The blocks were dragged from the quarries on sleds, and the sled could carry one large block as easily as ten small ones. Water was poured in front of the sled runners, and on the surface of greasy mud the going was not too difficult, and the team of haulers, working under the foreman's lash, need never be short-handed; a Twelfth Dynasty tomb relief pictures the transport of a colossal statue (Fig. 22) which probably weighed about 60 tons, mounted on a sled pulled by gangs totaling 172 men. To raise the stones into position on the ever-rising building was also a manual task. They were not lifted, for the Egyptians did not use the pulley, nor are there any lewis-holes[8] in the blocks, though these commonly have bosses which show that levers were employed to manœuvre them. Against the stonework of the monument under construction there was built a solid ramp of crude brick (which was heightened with each course that was laid on the building proper) and up this ramp the blocks were hauled or rolled. After the building was completed the ramp would normally be removed, but, as it happens, one such did until recently survive against the (unfinished) First Pylon of the temple of Karnak, and remains of others have been found against the pyramid of Meidum and that of Amenemhet I at Lisht. With a ramp, the difficulty was not great. Given a reasonable slope, an experienced foreman unembarrassed by machinery can, with twenty men, two stout poles, crowbars and a really strong rope raise a three-ton block in a very short time. Much more remarkable than the transport was the accurate dressing of the stones. The heights were standardized so that the top of each course presented an absolutely level surface as a bedding for the next course; but the vertical joints were often not at right-angles, i.e. either the front edge was not at right-angles to the base, or the side face of the block was not at right-angles to the frontage-line; it would seem as if the stones had to be as-

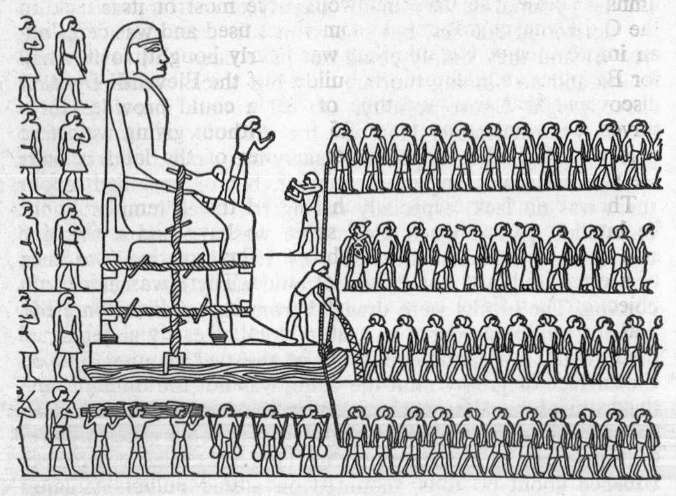

FIG. 22. *The transport of an Egyptian colossus (after Edwards).*

sembled either at ground level or (in the case of a pyramid) on the flat top of the construction for the final trimming that would secure a perfect joint before they could be laid in the course. In any case, the finishing and polishing of the outer face of the stones was done after they were in position.

All the stone-built tombs and temples of Egypt can be described as megalithic. That they were constructed after this fashion is not merely due to the economy effected by the use of large stones. According to the Egyptian belief, a man's survival after death was in large measure dependent upon the preservation of his earthly body in the tomb, and therefore upon the permanence of the tomb itself; a man built his mastaba or pyramid during his lifetime and naturally planned something that might well last for ever; the more massive the tomb the better his hope of immortality. Temples, also, as being the houses of the eternal gods, ought to last for all eternity. The principle was so firmly impressed upon the Egyptian architect that temple roofs as well as temple walls had to be of stone, and even the fine timber imported from Lebanon might not be used for the purpose; in the early periods this was a serious handicap because limestone, the ordinary building material, was, owing to its fissile nature, useless for architraves of more than about 9-foot span; for a small building that did not matter, but a large temple with massive stone columns so closely set together would lose most of its effect. In the Old Dynasty granite was sometimes used and was certainly an improvement, but one that was dearly bought; fortunately for Egyptian architecture the builders of the Eleventh Dynasty discovered that the sandstone of Silsila could provide architraves that would span up to 25 feet without giving way, and it is with this that all the great temples of the later periods are roofed.[9]

The religious principle which insisted that a temple should be built of stone throughout[10] seems to have had a negative side also. There is not in the whole of Egypt a single instance of a dwelling-house being built of stone. There was indeed no objection to a lintel or a door-frame being of limestone, but that sort of thing was not constructional; the actual fabric of the house had to be of mud-brick only. And this applied to all classes. Pharaoh was, of course, a god, and the building destined to be the setting for his essentially god-like functions was properly more a temple than a house, so that the great 'palace' of Merreptah at Memphis or that of Akhenaton at Tell el Amarna could be stone-built (though the Memphis building has columns and doorway pylons of stone but mud-brick walls), but in those official buildings there were no residential quarters; the dwelling-house even of the Pharaoh was of mud-brick alone. Perhaps for a mortal to be housed in like manner to the immortal gods would have been an example of *hubris,* 'that reckless and defiant insolence which formed the matter of ancient tragedy and is at war with the harmonies of human life'; but whatever the reason the stone house was taboo. It is curious to find an echo of this in Sumer. There, owing to the lack of stone in southern Mesopotamia, all buildings were of brick. But the foundations of one of the earliest temples at Erech were of limestone brought laboriously from at least 60 miles away; at Eridu, the oldest of Sumerian cities, the wall enclosing the Ziggurat terrace was of stone rubble, and that may date from the al'Ubaid period; at al'Ubaid the foundations of the First Dynasty temple platform and the stairs leading up to it were of stone. At Ur the wall of the Ziggurat terrace, built in the time of the First Dynasty of Ur, had on its outer face four or five courses of heavy limestone boulders —and the interesting point about this was that the stonework was not there to give strength to the wall, was, in fact, not constructional at all, but was a mere skin applied to a core of mud-brick already *in situ*; it was a pious fraud, and one can only deduce that there was a tradition requiring the use of stone for the construction of the house of God, that normally burnt brick was considered an adequate substitute but that sometimes a more scrupulous builder conformed to tradition or compromised with it. Again, the burial-chambers of the Early Dynastic royal tombs at Ur were generally built entirely of stone or, at any rate, had some stone in their construction, whereas nothing of the sort is ever found in any lay building above ground. In Egypt then, where stone was available, it had to be employed for tombs and temples but was eschewed for private houses, while in Sumer, where there was no stone, it was none the less theoretically the proper material for tombs and temples, but for private houses no one would think of using it. The practice common to the two countries must be explained by a religious scruple also common to both.

In the other stone-using countries there was no such taboo. In Anatolia and in north Syria any building of importance would have heavy stone foundations which, carried up rather above the level of the house floor, served as a dry-course; in time this purely utilitarian function became secondary in that at floor level the rubble foundations gave place to ashlar blocks, usually of large size, about 3 feet square, which added much to the dignity of the monument. Later again the decorative character of the blocks was increased by their surfaces being carved in relief, so that by the thirteenth century BC there was fully developed the characteristic Hittite style of architecture in which the base of the wall is adorned with orthostats of limestone or basalt (the two materials sometimes used alternately) covered with reliefs or with hieroglyphic inscriptions picked out with colour. Such orthostats were originally constructional, as has been explained, but as their ornamental value outbalanced their functional purpose the solid block tended to reduce its proportions to those of a facing-slab; in the hands of the Assyrian imitators of the Hittite fashion the great reliefs carved in 'Mosul alabaster' which enriched the palaces of Nineveh and Calah were but a panelling quite irrelevant to the wall structure.

As a general rule this massive stonework of the northern builders was confined to a single course;[11] above that the wall was of half-timbered construction, the framework of stout beams filled in with stone rubble or with mud-brick according to the character of the countryside; thus on a north Syrian site such as Alalakh, in a plain formed of river silt, mud-brick was the natural material (Pl. 8, c), whereas in Crete, where stone is plentiful and soil is precious, rubble is invariably used. Incidentally, the palace of Knossos, whose style and construction alike are derived from the Asiatic mainland, is, owing to its state of preservation, by far the best illustration of the full development of the architecture of the northern school.

On most of the mainland sites the buildings are too ruinous to give evidence as to style, but what little survives generally points to an Anatolian origin. On the other hand it may fairly be argued that both the Minoans and their successors the Mycenaeans may have borrowed the principles of architecture but in execution improved upon their models. 'Cyclopean' masonry is common to Anatolia and to Greece, but the finely-fitted polygonal masonry of, e.g., Mycenae surpasses in quality anything that an Asian site can show; the vaulted galleries in the walls of Tiryns might have been matched by those of Boğazköy, and their crude strength is admirably suited to works of military defence, but, so far as we know, it was left to the Mycenaean builder to use the corbelled stone vault with the refinement that we see in the tombs of Ugarit (Fig. 23), while the *tholos* tombs of Mycenae (even if it be held that they are in the line of descent from the domed shrines of Arpachiyah in the Upper Zab valley) have no parallel at all in Asia. It is curious that the palaces of Knossos and Phaetos boast no stone carving such as that of the doorway of the 'treasury of Atreus' at Mycenae, where the decoration of shafts and entablature is far too sophisticated to be experimental; both in the constructional technique and in the ornamentation of the underground *tholoi* the Mycenaeans had evolved something for which Crete afforded no precedent.

The true arch was unknown to the northern architect, but the false arch and the corbelled arch were employed for monumental works, while for smaller openings the flat lintel was normal, as indeed is to be expected wherever heavy timber enters freely into the construction. Columns were a regular feature; they were always of wood, usually resting on (not let into) circular stone cushion bases, and the shafts, both in Crete and on the mainland, were tapered, the diameter at the top being greater than that at the base (Pl. 9, c). Anatolia had by a very early date developed the *megaron* type of house, whose main feature is the great hall with its roof supported by four columns grouped round a central fireplace. Late Bronze Age examples of the *megaron* occur at Beycesultan, but at Kultepe one has been found going back as far as the twenty-second century BC and one in the first level of Troy is two centuries older still; it is clear that the prototype of the Homeric house is derived from Asia Minor. In some cases, too, the Asiatic *megaron* was entered from a deep columned porch which would seem to be the origin of the temple *in antis* of the classical Greek world. It may be that a modification of the traditional *megaron*, adapting the living-room to ceremonial and official purposes, produced the 'Hall of Audience' in which a long room is divided into two equal parts by columns set between shallow buttresses or pilasters projecting from the side walls and supporting a wooden architrave; this is characteristic of north Syrian palace architecture, and again is found at Knossos.

In striking contrast to the normal buildings of Egypt, the northern house or palace was of several storeys and, in a palace at least, the principal rooms were not at ground-level but formed the *piano nobile* on the first floor, often built over a series of magazines containing the palace stores. Consequently stairs were essential, and in the more important buildings a

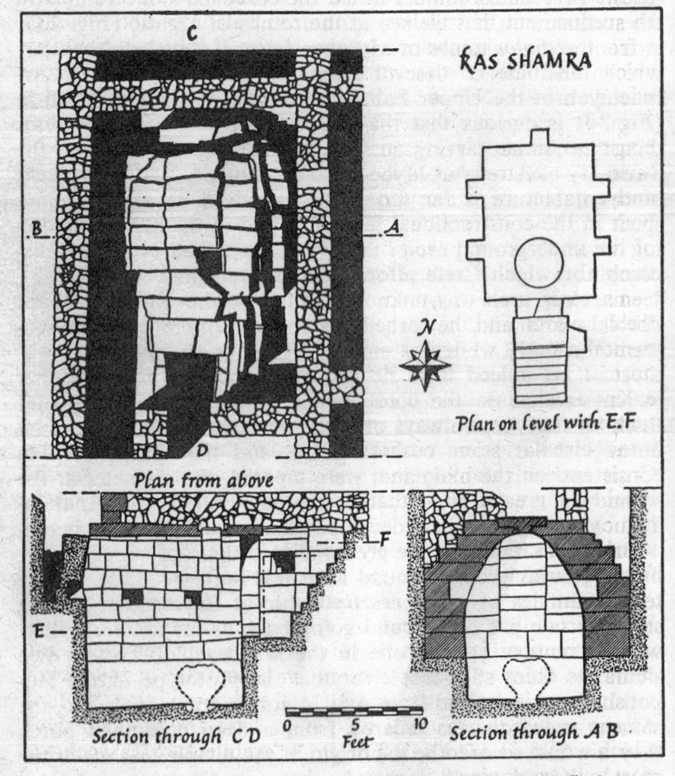

FIG. 23. *Ugarit: stone vaulted tomb (after Schaeffer).*

monumental staircase was a prominent feature; the most striking example of this is given by the Palace of Minos, in which the Grand Staircase, built of stone and wood with its ascending flight of columns, is a masterpiece of ancient architecture. Thanks to the plentiful supply of heavy timber and of stone both soft and hard, the Minoan architect was able to evolve a style wholly unlike anything to be found in the countries to the east and the south, approaching more nearly to the architecture of later Europe. In this he was helped by the climate. In Crete and in Asia Minor the heat and glare of the sun are less oppressive; consequently, while the Mesopotamian house was enclosed by high blank walls, the Cretan house or palace required windows and its façade was relieved by a system of fenestration which could be used for artistic effect, and (since the summer sun is still hot) columned balconies and awnings in front of the windows might give to the elevation a lightness which the massive stonework of Egypt could not rival; the little house-façades in coloured faience found at Knossos (Fig 24) illustrate a type of domestic architecture unlike anything we should have expected to encounter in the ancient world. The reconstructed drawing of a section of the frontage of the Palace of Minos in Fig. 25 shows in what a modern spirit the Cretan architect dealt with the problem of achieving variety with a purely rectilinear building method and of combining dignity with grace. That this was a conscious effort seems to be proved by the wall thicknesses. Walls of stone rubble set in mud mortar, even though they have a timber framework and are strengthened by a facing of cement plaster, must be reasonably thick if they are to rise to any height; but at Knossos the great majority of the walls are less than 3 feet thick and very few indeed measure more than 4½ feet; it was because the builders recognized this as being the minimum consistent with stability that the domestic quarters above the second floor were constructed not in stone but in mud-brick, a much lighter material.

Brick was far more freely used in some of the mainland buildings which belong to the same northern school of architecture but the different material did not seriously affect the style; certainly the palaces of Alalakh, modest though they were in comparison with those of the Minoan sea-kings, are similar to them in conception and in execution; in the use of polished stone orthostats, or half-timber construction, of lime cement and of the columns with stone base and wooden shaft they are indeed identical. For brick architecture as such we must look to Mesopotamia.

FIG. 24. *Cretan faience house plaques (after a photograph by Josephine Powell).*

Brickwork—Mesopotamia. Because in the river valley timber was scarce and stone non-existent all buildings, from the al'Ubaid period onwards, were built of brick.

At a very early date kiln-dried brick was introduced. Burnt bricks were used at first only for important buildings and then mostly in the foundations, but they might be carried up in the façade to a height of 3 to 4 feet above ground-level (thus obtaining much the same effect as was given by the stone orthostats of the northern school of architecture) and as the country grew richer they were more lavishly employed. It was quite a normal thing for a king of the Third Dynasty of Ur to pull down a mud-brick temple built by his forebears and to rebuild it entirely in burnt brick; and at about the same time bitumen imported from the pits at Hit on the upper Euphrates might be substituted for the mud mortar regularly employed in earlier days; it had the great advantage of being a better adhesive and also waterproof. Bitumen, owing to its cost, was used only in temples and other buildings erected by the government, but building with burnt bricks laid in mud mortar became so general that under the Larsa kings (*c.* 2020–*c.* 1790 BC) the outer walls of private houses at Ur were of burnt brickwork at least to the level of the upper floor if not to their full height, and even the inner walls, in the case of the richer houses, up to 3 feet or more; the upper parts of the walls were of mud-brick. In and after the Kassite period burnt brickwork is rare—probably because in the nearer parts of the desert the camel-thorn which was the normal fuel for the brick-kilns had been exhausted and the cost of bringing in supplies from farther afield was prohibitive—and even the temples built by Assyrian and Neo-Babylonian rulers are generally of mud-brick throughout.

Brick construction does not lend itself to decoration. Mention has already been made of Warad-Sin's bricks moulded in relief to form a palm-trunk column (p. 245) and another Larsa king, Sin-Idinnam, seems to have relieved the monotony of a temple façade with crescents in moulded brick. In the fourteenth century BC the Kassite king Kurigalzu attempted a much more ambitious scheme: the whole front of one of his temples at Erech (and apparently of one at Ur also) was adorned with life-size figures of deities in the half-round built of bricks specially moulded. Inspired, probably, by the Osirid figures of an Egyptian temple, it was aesthetically an unfortunate experiment and was seldom repeated—indeed, the only

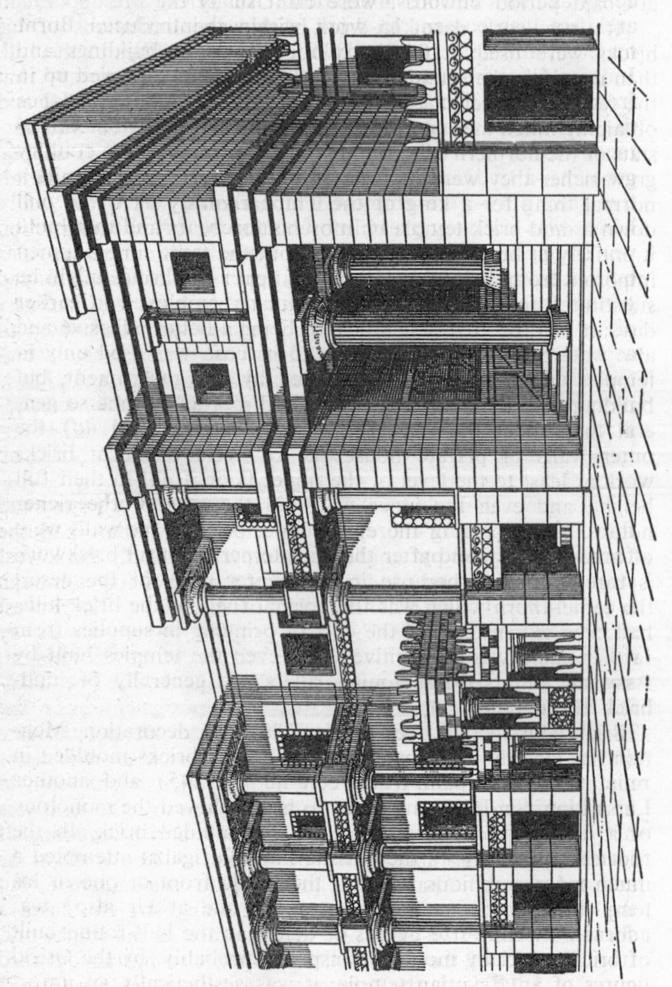

FIG. 25. *Knossos, Palace of Minos, reconstruction (after Evans).*

other instance of it known is in a building at Susa set up by Kutur Nakhunti in the twelfth century BC, so that it may count as but a curious aberration. Usually the Mesopotamian architect was content to work within the limitations of his material, and he certainly exploited its possibilities to the full. Judging from what remains of the buildings we can say that from the Third Dynasty of Ur onwards the arch, the vault and the dome were in common use; in the treatment of wall surfaces closely-set half-columns divided by vertical T-shaped grooves—a tradition derived, as we have seen, from the primitive reed hut—were employed, apparently, where the wall's height was not very great; more often the brick construction was emphasized by substituting for the half-column rectangular buttresses, usually with a double salient and a central T-shaped groove (see Fig. 26); the object was to break up the blankness of the wall into panels whose proportions were calculated to accentuate the height of the building. That the Sumerian architect knew something about optics and deliberately aimed at a particular visual effect is clearly demonstrated by a well-preserved building such as the Ziggurat of Ur, set up by Ur-Nammu, first king of the Third Dynasty of Ur, in about 2100 BC (Fig 27).

This great structure, which was in fact nothing more than the base supporting the shrine of the god Nannar, had the form of a stepped pyramid three storeys high; only the lowest stage is today in good condition, but of the upper stages enough is left to certify the reconstruction of the whole. The lowest stage measures 200 feet by 150 feet; its walls, relieved by shallow non-functional buttresses which accentuate their height, are built with a pronounced batter, their converging lines leading the eye upwards and inwards so as to fix attention on the shrine. The architect realized that the towering superstructure (which was essential to the religious purpose of his building) might so impress the spectator that its weight might seem to him too much for the 60-foot-high base, constructed as it was not of massive stones but of small bricks; and he set himself to counteract this appearance of weakness. The method he adopted was remarkable. The ground-plan is a rectangle, but the sides of the rectangle, instead of being straight, have a slight outward curve of 1:125, and the face of the brickwork, from the foot of the wall to the parapet, also has an outward curve of 1:100; it is the principle of entasis which the Greeks were to re-invent in the fifth century BC, but here it is used by the Sumerians of the twenty-second century and that with such delicacy as to produce a real optical illusion, precisely as in the Parthenon; the curves are not noticeable as such, but

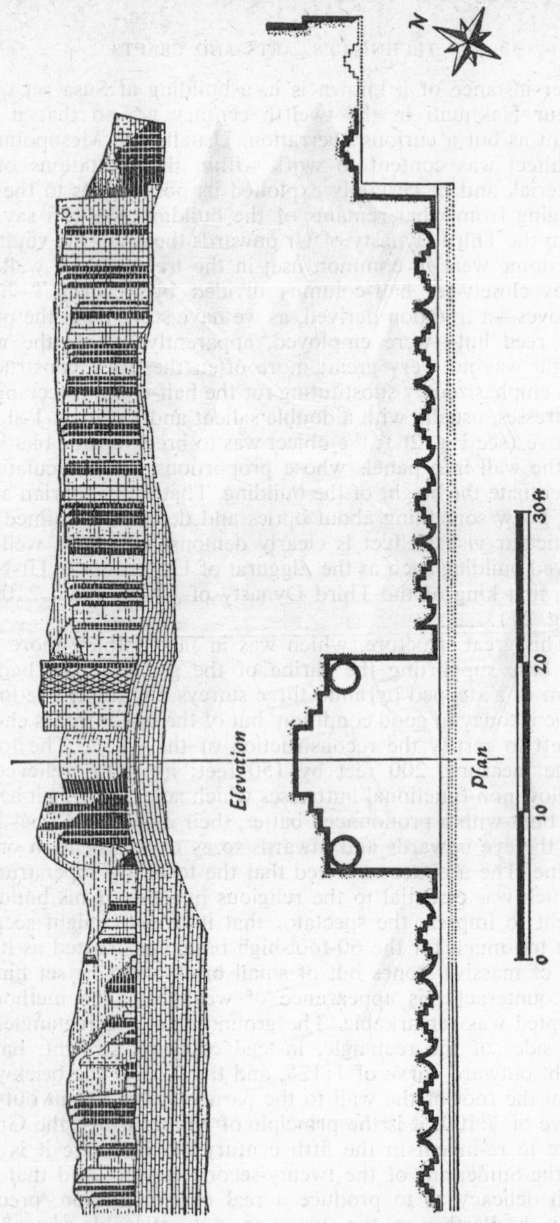

FIG. 26. *T-shaped grooves in half-column walls.*

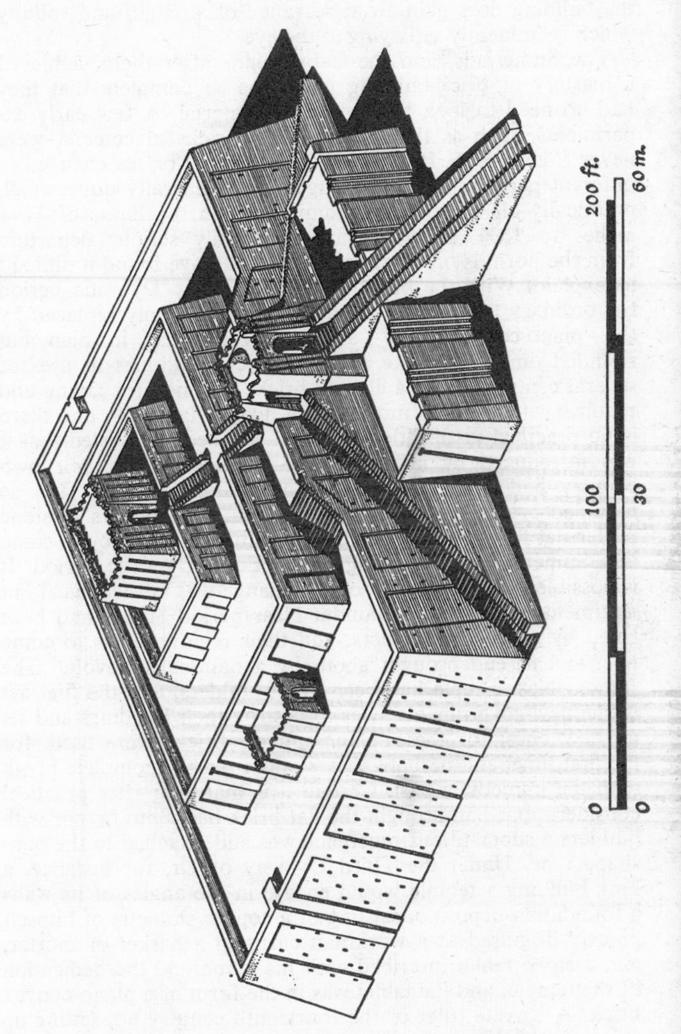

FIG. 27. *Ur-Nammu's Ziggurat; reconstruction.*

the building does gain an appearance of strength and solidity which is eminently satisfying to the eye.

The Sumerians, and the Babylonians after them, achieved a mastery of brick-building technique so complete that they had no need to look for any other material. A few early experiments, such as that of moulding bricks in cement, were never followed up. It is true that the size of bricks changed in different periods, but the changes were generally quite small, practically all the varieties coming within the limits of 11¾ inches to 13¾ inches square. The only serious departure from the norm is one that archaeologists have found it difficult to explain. With the beginning of the Early Dynastic period the ordinary flat brick is suddenly and uniformly replaced by the 'plano-convex' type—a brick rectangular in plan but rounded on the top like a bun—which continues in use for several centuries. It is a clumsy brick, unhandy for laying and requiring much more mortar than does a flat brick, and there is no practical justification for it. It has been suggested that it was introduced by newcomers to Sumer who in their own country had been accustomed to building in stone and so moulded bricks in the form of pebbles; but builders in stone prefer flat flakes to rounded pebbles, and no new peoples came into Sumer at the beginning of the Early Dynastic period. It is possible that the reason for the change was not technical but sentimental. During the Jamdat Nasr period Sumer had been ruled by foreign interlopers, and their régime seems to come to a violent end brought about by a nationalist revolt.[12] The Jamdat Nasr people had been great builders, and the first act of the new governments[13] was to destroy their buildings and set up new ones; for these 'plano-convex' bricks were used, for the first time, and perhaps they symbolized the complete break with the immediate past. Certain it is that long after practical considerations had brought the flat brick back into favour with builders a superstitious reverence was still attached to the bun-shape type. Under the Third Dynasty of Ur, for instance, a king building a temple would encase in the angles of its walls a foundation-deposit consisting of a copper statuette of himself piously disguised as a workman carrying a basket of mortar, and a stone tablet inscribed with his name and the dedication of the temple; and the tablet was in the form of a plano-convex brick. A Kassite ruler of the fourteenth century BC, setting up a new altar, hid in its core miniature clay models of plano-convex bricks. In Assyrian times, and in the days of Nebuchadnezzar of Babylon, down to the sixth century BC, when it was the custom to bury under the floor of a building painted clay figures of the Seven Spirits that would ward off evil from the house, each figure was placed in a little sentry-box made of ancient plano-convex bricks which must have been dug up out of the Early Dynastic ruins deep underground. Just because Mesopotamian brick construction was of so high an order a technical aberration such as the introduction of the plano-convex brick calls for expanation; that its origin was a sentimental one seems less unlikely when we find the sentiment persisting throughout two millennia.[14]

Owing to the nature of the Indus valley the people of the Harappā culture were necessarily builders in brick. On two or three outlying sites beyond the valley's edge advantage has been taken of the local stone and walls are constructed with roughly-squared blocks; but the twin capitals, Harappā and Mohenjo-daro, are built entirely of brick. For kiln-fuel the Sumerians had to rely upon the light camel-thorn of the western desert, but a large part of ancient Sind must have been covered with thin jungle, and, as a result, kiln-fired bricks are used in the Harappā cities far more freely than in Sumer; crude brick was used for the cores of city walls and platforms and, perhaps, for the upper storeys of the poorer houses, but the bulk of the existing ruins are of burnt brick throughout. The bricks are for the most part of a standard size (11 by 5½ by 2½ inches), well fired; the laying is good, with proper attention to bonding, and there is a considerable use of bitumen mortar. In view of this it seems natural to see a connection between the cultures of Harappā and Sumer, and such is indeed not unlikely, but if the Indus valley was indebted to that of the Euphrates for its architectural techniques the loan was but a partial one. In the development of architectural forms Harappā got no farther than the corbelled arch; this is used for small spans only, such as house doors (not more than 3½ feet), drains and ventilation openings; roofs were flat, resting on wooden rafters, and the true arch, the vault and the dome never occur. The Harappā people were skilful bricklayers, and that is perhaps the best that can be said of them; their aims were purely utilitarian and their architecture remained dully functional. In this branch of culture at least the achievements of the Indus valley were to exercise no influence at all upon historic India. The mere technique of kiln-fired brick may possibly have been handed down—though all connecting links are missing, and the possibility of re-invention cannot be ruled out; but of their house designs and of their town-planning nothing survived, and neither the timber constructions of Asoka's time (with their apparently Chinese connections) (see

p. 159), nor the imaginative splendour of Dravidian stonework bear any relation to 'the blank brick walls and unadorned architecture' of Mohenjo-daro.

Metallurgy

Archaeologists, and historians following their example, have found it convenient to draw a dividing line in the course of man's advance towards urban civilizations between the Stone Age—the subject of the first part of this volume—and the Bronze Age with which we are now dealing. The distinction is a real one, but the vast gulf that separates the cultural status of Neolithic man from that of the developed Bronze Age was due not only to the use of metal as such but to the many other arts and activities, such as sculpture and carpentry, which accompanied and were encouraged by metallurgical knowledge, so that the expression 'Bronze Age' is in fact but a label denoting something far more complex than the words imply. Also, the line of demarcation is not easy to draw. This was recognized when scholars proposed to divide the early metal-using phase into a Copper Age followed by a Bronze Age; but although that would seem to be a natural order yet insistence on it leads to an inextricable confusion, for not only is it generally impossible to say when the one metal supplants the other, but in some instances the 'natural' order has actually been reversed in practice. An alternative suggestion was to intercalate between the Neolithic and the Bronze Ages a 'Chalcolithic' Age, defined as that in which metal (i.e. copper) was indeed known but, being extremely rare, was used only for small objects, ornaments, pins, etc., whereas tools and implements were still made of stone. This term can be employed with advantage, but it requires more accurate definition. It will then be seen that there is here no intercalation; the Chalcolithic Age, in spite of the fact that metal is used, is but a late phase of the Neolithic and has nothing in common with the Bronze Age, because the basis of distinction is not the existence of metal but man's knowledge of metallurgy.

Far back in the Neolithic Age, man had been accustomed to seek the raw materials for his handicrafts—flint, obsidian, chert, etc.—both by collecting the stones exposed on hill-sides or in stream-beds and by the more laborious but more remunerative process of mining. Apart from such utilitarian stones he would pick out some that appealed to him simply by their colour and could be used as ornaments; quartz and malachite, turquoise and lapis lazuli could be pierced to form beads and pendants, and because of their rarity and beauty might soon have attributed to them magic qualities which enhanced their value and made them objects of inter-tribal trade. The most attractive of the 'coloured stones' was gold, and this was readily found. For either gold occurs as nuggets of native material or else gold-bearing minerals enclose small but recognizable particles of comparatively pure metal; no smelting therefore was required, only, at most, the crushing of the gold-bearing ore and the separation of the gold particles from the enclosing rock; but in early days it was the alluvial nugget that drew man's attention. But when he proceeded to deal with the nugget as he dealt with other stones, trying to chip it to shape, he discovered that it was malleable; by simply hammering it he could make it take what form he chose. Sometimes, in some parts of the world, there would come to notice stones of a pleasing greenish-black or purplish-green colour which, when scratched or rubbed, showed underneath a tint not unlike that of gold, and these too proved to be malleable; with these man, instead of flaking and polishing his tool, could by hammering produce much the same result as regards shape but with a colour and a gloss superior to that of most of his worked stones. In the course of time accident showed him that the malleability of his native copper was increased by heating, and his implements began to assume forms more peculiar to metal instead of merely reproducing the traditional stone types. Up to this point man had contented himself with using on metal the processes which he had for ages past used on stone, bone or fibre; now, with the annealing of his native copper, he was making the first advance in what was to become metallurgical technique; but at that point he stopped. There was as yet no such thing as metal production. Man made use of the pure metal, gold or copper, that nature set ready to his hand, but he had not the least idea of what it was or of how a larger supply of it could be obtained; he was still in the Stone Age. The phase is illustrated in relatively recent times by the American Indian burial-mounds in the Mississippi plain. In this area there is found 'float' copper carried by the ice masses of the glacial epoch from the rich strata of Lake Superior (where the ferrous sandstone contains nuggets and lumps of practically pure native copper ranging in weight from a few pounds up to many tons) down as far south as the river mouth and deposited there amongst the detritus of the rocks. The Indians used this to make ornaments and implements, the latter mostly related to stone types, and such occur freely in the grave mounds. Not a single example has been either smelted or alloyed or cast; every one is hammered from the float copper. The Indians knew about the malleability of native copper and employed that alternate hammering and heating which we call annealing; for the rest, they cut and trimmed the metal with stone tools and smoothed or polished it by abrasion with stone; in short, it was to them only a peculiar kind of stone. Even the highly developed civilizations of the Maya, the Aztecs and the Mexicans, for all their astonishing goldsmith's technique, were entirely ignorant of metallurgy. Copper axes from Mexico and Ecuador seem to be of natural metal, hammered and annealed, and it is doubtful whether the Aztecs employed even native copper before the time of the Spanish conquest; until that date the New World was still in the Neolithic Age.

If we turn back to the Old World we shall find plenty of evidence for a similar Chalcolithic phase during which natural copper was used more or less freely according to the extent to which in the different countries it was available in surface deposits or was obtainable by trade. The total amount in use cannot have been great, so that it was definitely a luxury product, and it did not in any way oust stone as a working material. For very many purposes stone was indeed preferable to the soft metal, and the constant annealing required to keep a copper axe sharp involved more labour than the knapping of a fresh flint—but for such small objects as pins and bodkins it was invaluable, and copper ornaments were only less attractive than those of gold. Therefore the copper-producing lands found a ready market for their wares in the river valleys which had given birth to the great civilizations based on agriculture; Egypt and Mesopotamia gladly exchanged their surplus grain for the nuggets found by the barbarians of the hill countries, and although their technique in dealing with the metal was still that of the Stone Age yet they could, by their experience, so far appreciate its potentialities that they were ready, when the time came, to take advantage to the full of the discovery of metallurgy, the discovery which Professor Childe has described as the most dramatic leap in the history of mankind. For it was with copper that early man learnt to experiment in the use of metal, it was with copper that he discovered the miraculous transformation by fire of certain brightly coloured stones into a fusible metal which before he had regarded as malleable only, and the very method of its production taught him for the first time the real 'art and mystery' of the smith's trade. Not only could he now multiply indefinitely the output of copper but, with the enthusiasm of a creator, he could attack other types of coloured stone, produce other metals, mix ores or metals to obtain yet more useful alloys, and change the face of the earth by applying his metals to art and industry.

It is not possible to say precisely where the smelting of copper ore first began nor which people were responsible for its discovery. Obviously the discovery was made on the spot, somewhere where the ore was ready to hand, for no one would have bothered to export the crude stone in bulk before the possibility of extracting metal from it had been recognized. Again, it can have been made only by a people who disposed of the means for securing the heat required to smelt the ore. The old and often-repeated theory that the fusible quality of copper was found out through the accident of a copper tool being dropped into the camp fire and melting is a mistaken one; the temperature of a wood fire will hardly rise above 600–700° C., whereas copper does not melt at anything below 1,085° C., so that no such 'accident' could occur. The reduction of the oxides and carbonates of copper (the sulphides were not used until the middle of the second millennium) requires a heat of 700–800° C., again too much for the open camp-fire, and even the charcoal-burning pot-bowl or 'hole-in-the-ground' furnace will not give the necessary high temperature unless aided by the blowpipe or bellows, neither of which had been invented at so early a date. Experiments have shown that the only primitive furnace yielding the temperature requisite for the reduction of copper ore was the pottery kiln, but even so it would have to be a kiln of the type used by people making a really hard-fired pottery very different from the lightly-baked wares of most Neolithic societies. It has been suggested that the actual discovery was made by the accidental reduction in such a kiln of the blue copper frit or glaze which was certainly used by potters at a very early date; that may be, though the evidence we possess is not enough to prove the case; but in any event it would appear that the potter's kiln is the origin of the smelter's furnace.

Copper ore is so widely spread (see Map VIII) that the mere occurrence of the metal constitutes by itself no argument for deciding the whereabouts of the first experiments in metallurgy. The archaeological evidence is more reliable, but it has to be remembered that the regular scrapping and re-casting of old tools at a time when copper was still an expensive luxury forces us to base our judgement upon what may be a very unrepresentative survival, and again the relative chronology of the different cultures is only approximately fixed.

The copper deposits in the desert east of the Nile valley were not worked by the Egyptians until the Twelfth Dynasty. The rich mines of Sinai were not exploited until the time of the early dynasties, e.g. by Sekhemkhet of the Third Dynasty,[15] which was indeed but natural, seeing that only a strong cen-

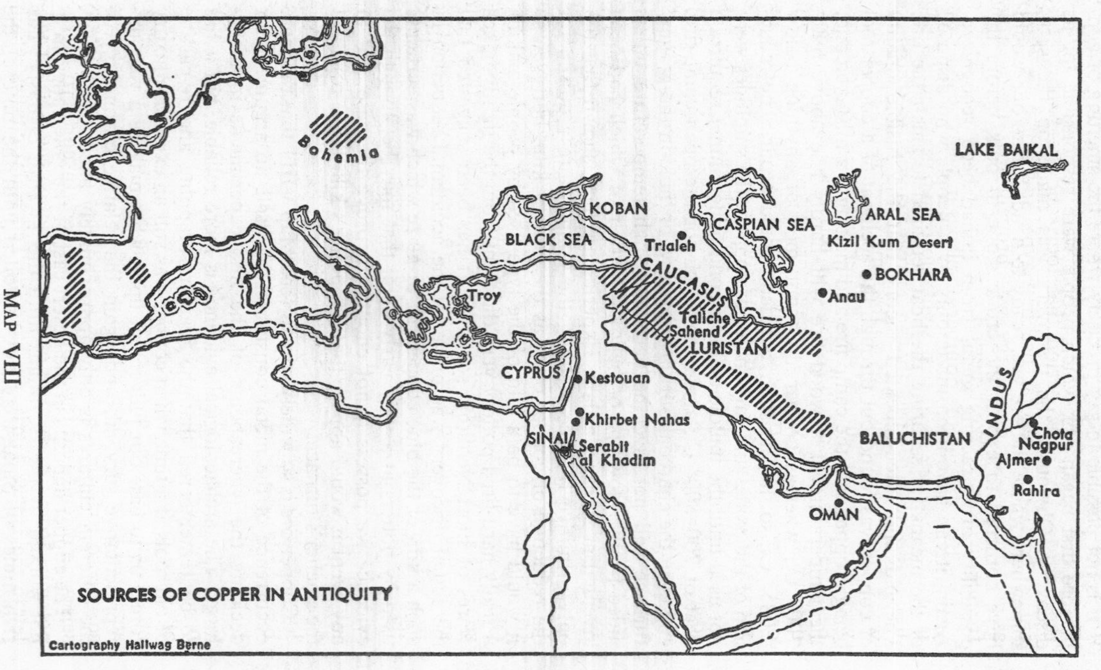
Bohemia
LAKE BAIKAL
KOBAN
BLACK SEA
Trialeh
CASPIAN SEA
ARAL SEA
Kizil Kum Desert
BOKHARA
Anau
CAUCASUS
Troy
Taliche
Sahend
LURISTAN
CYPRUS
Kestouan
Khirbet Nahas
SINAI
Serabit
al Khadim
BALUCHISTAN
INDUS
Chota
Nagpur
Ajmer
Rahira
OMAN
SOURCES OF COPPER IN ANTIQUITY
Cartography Hallwag Berne

MAP VIII

tralized government could have organized so elaborate an expedition and provided for its defence. Actually it is only in the Late pre-Dynastic period that tools and weapons of cast copper came into regular use in Egypt, and it can be safely assumed that true metallurgy was brought into the country from Asia in the Gerzean period.

If we turn to Asia the number of places in which copper ore is to be found seems at first sight more embarrassing than illuminative, and it is true that in a great many of them the ore was worked at least as early as the time for which we first have written evidence; but for the earlier periods, for the actual beginnings of the industry, we must rely upon archaeological data. In the last fifty years excavations have been carried out on a large number of Near Eastern sites whose stratified remains take us back well into the fourth millennium BC; the gradual development of metallurgical technique can be followed reasonably closely, and the progressive diffusion of metal types does at least suggest the direction taken by the spread of knowledge and therefore its ultimate source. It would seem quite certain that that source lies somewhere in the great mountain chain that stretches from eastern Anatolia through Armenia and Transcaucasia to the Caspian Sea and is continued through Khorassan and Bokhara; this, as can be seen from Map VIII, contains the richest mineral deposits of the Old World, and, incidentally, its well-wooded mountain-sides supplied all the fuel that the smelter could ask. Practically all authorities are agreed that this northern region saw the start of true metal-working, but while some are inclined to locate it to the east of the Caspian Sea on the strength of the evidence given by such sites as Anau, the great number favour the western end of the range where exploitation certainly did begin early and was active throughout all historic times. Perhaps the strongest argument is that to which reference has already been made, the development of kilns able to generate the degree of heat required for the smelting of ore and the melting of copper. The Chalcolithic pottery of the eastern regions does not imply the use of such a kiln. On the other hand we have the al'Ubaid culture in Mesopotamia, which is Chalcolithic at its outset but produces copper castings in its later phases, characterized by a hard-fired pottery made in kilns whose heat was so intense (and incidentally so ill regulated) that the clay vessels were often fused together and vitrified. In northern Mesopotamia, from Carchemish eastwards through the Khabur valley to the Upper Tigris, we have the Tell Halaf culture which in time overlaps with al'Ubaid but may have begun somewhat earlier, also producing its fine painted pottery hard-fired in properly regulated beehive-shaped kilns of mud-brick; and to the later stages of this culture are attributed weapons of cast copper as against the hammered 'natural' copper instruments of its early stages. When we find that settlements of the Tell Halaf culture occur in the neighbourhood of Lake Van, in the heart of the copper-producing area, we are justified in concluding that the advance which these people did make from the Chalcolithic stage to the Bronze Age proper was due to their own invention rather than to any borrowing from hypothetical pioneers in Khorassan. Our necessarily vague chronology of the different sites does not warrant the assertion that the cast copper artifacts of Anau antedate those of Tell Halaf, and the Tell Halaf people had the ore ready to their hand and possessed the means for smelting it; the balance of probability therefore is in favour of metallurgy starting in eastern Anatolia.

When once the discovery had been made that the coloured stones could be transformed into precious metal the knowledge of it spread quickly. But the world had not reached the stage at which the publication of a scientific formula would automatically result in the general adaptation of a new technique; the miracle was still miraculous and the process by which it was performed was a complex one. Because it dealt not with nuggets of natural metal (the obvious supplies of which must by now have been well-nigh exhausted) but with ore which could be treated in bulk, mere collection had to be replaced by professional mining, and the miner's job was a full-time one. Pottery-making had long been a specialized profession; now, when the ex-potter was using his kiln for the more difficult and elaborate process of smelting and refining metal, he was yet more exclusively engrossed in 'the art and mystery' of his trade. Again, the smelter produced the actual copper in the form of ingots, but that took up all his time; the working-up of that copper into useful shapes involved a further subdivision of labour, and the smith came into his own; casting, hammering and annealing were an art in themselves. Here then were three occupations, all requiring special knowledge and technical experience, producing in common a commodity that commanded a ready sale everywhere and fetched high prices. Obviously the craftsmen would keep their profitable secret to themselves for as long as they could; so far from publishing their formulae they would exaggerate the miraculous character of their art. They could, and did, export their finished goods far afield, but that meant paying middlemen's profits, and transport was difficult; local production and direct sales meant the highest gain. From the original centre, therefore, mining prospectors set out in search of new supplies of ore in places where their exported goods had already secured a market, and with the miners went the smelters and the smiths; the wide dispersion of particular types of tools and weapons which field archaeology has established is in some cases due to international trade but very often means the arrival of one of these bands of itinerant metallurgists bringing with them the fashions they had evolved at home.

Map VIII illustrates the dispersion. Eastwards the line of advance inevitably followed the oriferous deposits of the mountain chain to Khorassan and Bokhara; from there the spread was in two directions, southwards into Baluchistan, whose mines very likely supplied copper and bronze to the people of the Indus valley, and north-eastwards by way of Bamian and the Kizil Kum desert; it must have been the extension of this line that brought metal to the knowledge of the ancestors of the Shang tribe of the Yellow River. In northern Persia the mines in the Tiyari mountains are certainly early (they are mentioned in Babylonian records) and to the east of those Mount Sahend and the Kara Dagh, producing easily-reducible carbonates, may well have been the source of the metal worked by the smiths of Luristan. Mesopotamia throughout nearly the whole of its history drew all its copper supplies from the north, though in the Early Dynastic period the Sumerian smiths profited by the finer ores from Oman on the Persian Gulf, apparently the Magan and Melukhkha of early texts. We have no knowledge of any exploitation in very early times of the relatively small deposits in Syria which were to be worked later (the bronze industry of Tyre and Sidon is thought to have made use of local supplies, and there are very rich veins in the coastal range south of Alexandretta) but here again import from Anatolia was easy. But at a very early stage prospectors from Asia Minor sailed across to Cyprus and there started an industry so important that the names of the island and of the metal became synonymous and the ancient Greeks attributed the discovery of copper to the Cypriot king Kinyras; from Cyprus the art of metallurgy passed on to Crete.

The westward advance was slower. This was the natural result of the very different levels of culture attained by man in different parts of the world. Countries like Mesopotamia and Egypt already in the Chalcolithic phase were ripe to derive full benefit from the free use of metal and—what is equally important—were able to pay the price of it; but at the end of the fourth millennium BC the barbarous tribes of Europe offered but a poor market to the metal-merchant. In Anatolia the early diffusion of copper-working was patchy, in spite of the proximity of the mines; there were pockets of relatively high culture as in the Halys basin and on the western sea-coast, and here local schools had been formed before the middle of the third millennium BC; but the mountain tribes could boast no more than casual imports of foreign-made copper tools and weapons. Through Troy (Troy II) and up the Danube valley merchants carried the new art into Europe a little before 2000 BC, into the valley lands of the Elbe and the Saale, and started the central European metallurgical industry; we find at the outset types which go back to Sumerian originals, but thereafter development was upon independent lines and new methods were evolved for dealing with the specific ores of central Europe.

This was indeed the normal course of events. The itinerant craftsmen could not keep their secrets for ever; they could hardly avoid employing local labour, and their apprentices, in the more civilized centres at least, were quick to learn the trade. By 3000 BC or very little after, Sumer, Egypt and Cyprus had their individual schools of metallurgy; Egypt started to exploit the mines of Sinai, the early Pharaohs thus securing the sources of supply and obtaining a monopoly of the metal trade of their country, while Sumer imported from Oman. The latter fact was of great import because the Oman copper ores contain both nickel and tin, so that the smelted metal is a natural bronze, objects from the royal cemetery at Ur showing as much as 14 per cent of tin and anything up to 2 per cent of nickel; since bronze is far more easy to cast than is copper the Sumerian metallurgist enjoyed a great advantage over the users of pure copper, such as the Egyptians, and produced finished goods which were technically far superior to anything made elsewhere. This early Sumerian bronze was accidental, not an artificial alloy; the existence of tin as a separate metal seems not to have been realized. On the other hand it is probable that the Sumerian smelters did discover, by experiment, that the best results were obtained by mixing in definite proportions what they supposed to be two varieties of copper ore; at any rate, we find that the tin content is much higher in an axe or dagger than in a toilet-pin; and it is possible that by the end of the Early Dynastic period, which saw the smith's technique developed to a pitch never excelled in later Mesopotamian history, they had recognized the difference between the copper ore and the cassiterite and even identified the latter with the 'stream tin' discovered in alluvial gold-working. But with the conquests of Sargon of Akkad, which put an end to the Early Dynastic period, bronze disappears and vastly inferior hammered axes of unalloyed copper replace the splendid bronze castings of the royal cemetery. Perhaps the Oman veins were exhausted; more probably political reasons cut the conqueror off from the country's old source of supply, and all ore had to be imported from the north, to which Sargon as a northerner would naturally turn: in the epic poem *The King of Battles* he is represented as leading his armies into the heart of eastern Anatolia to uphold the rights of Semitic merchants settled there, and these can have been none other than the middlemen of the copper trade. But the demand was now for bronze, and prospectors, metallurgists and traders struck out west in search of supplies, whether of tin or of cassiterite or simply of such mixed ores as Oman had yielded formerly; the mixed ores were duly discovered in Bohemia, and gradually an overland trade in them (or perhaps in tin only) was established between Bohemia and the Near East via the bridge-head at Troy. Rare though the alloy must still have been, the bronze castings from Alaca Höyük show that it was available in central Anatolia, and could be exported so far afield as Egypt, where bronze objects first appear sporadically in the time of the Middle Kingdom.

Later, about 1600 BC, two important discoveries were made. In the first place the metallurgists learnt how to smelt the sulphidic ores—a much more complicated process than had sufficed for the oxides and carbonates—and thereby put vastly greater stores of copper at the smiths' disposal, and in the second place they succeeded in reducing cassiterite separately, obtaining tin-metal which could be mixed with copper to form bronze; and now the tin content could be regulated so as to make different alloys suited to different purposes. The amount of tin required could not be got from the alluvial deposits of western Asia, which had never been considerable and must by now have been virtually exhausted, so again the prospectors set out, this time by sea as well as by land. Granted that our chronology is still vague, it is at least probable that the people of the El Argar culture had already begun to exploit the tin deposits of north-eastern Spain and had made independently the discovery of the technique of bronze alloy; in any case, whether because of information received or by mere good luck, it was here that the Aegean sailing-vessels put in and the prospectors, having found what they sought, opened up the Spanish tin-trade which was to supply the Middle East throughout the Bronze Age.

But long before this date the primitive metallurgists, miners and smelters, had in their search for copper come upon other ores which by similar methods could be made to produce other metals. One of these was gold. In the early days all the gold used by goldsmiths had been alluvial. The rich treasures from the royal cemetery at Ur are all of alluvial metal, often with a high percentage of silver, and since the petty kings of Ur are not likely to have been more wealthy than others the total supplies available must have been very large. There is no means of identifying the source, and one can only suppose that a great many river valleys contained auriferous detritus which was so thoroughly worked in antiquity that no trace of metal can be found today. Assyrian texts vaguely refer to the highlands of Asia Minor, and we know of deposits in the Choruk basin near Artvin in Lazistan which may have supplied the famous Chalybes; other references to the Khabur area and to 'Chachu', possibly in the Kharput neighbourhood, suggest that the whole of the Anti-Taurus range, seamed as it is with torrent-beds, may have kept the gold-prospector busy with 'the dust of its mountains'. Even today the gravel bed of one of the rivers in the Amanus mountains near Antioch contains a fair amount of gold dust, but most, like the famous Pactolus 'rich in gold', were exhausted in the Bronze Age, and the same is probably true of the north Persian rivers. As the local supplies gave out more and more gold had to be imported for the needs of the great Mesopotamian rulers; one important source may have been the west coast of Arabia where the Nabataeans and the Debae controlled fairly rich alluvial deposits, and the southwest, the modern Yemen, which may have been the Ophir of the ancient world; caravans thence could pass by way of Nejd, itself a gold-producing area, and Kuwait into Babylonia. Gold may have come from India also, by way of overland trade and perhaps by sea as well, brought not directly but by cabotage; the bill-of-lading of a ship discharging at Ur in the reign of Sumu-ilum of Larsa (*c.* 1925 BC) mentions gold and precious woods and ivory, and for the latter two India is as likely a source as the east African coast.

But by far the richest gold deposits of the Middle East were in Egypt, extending almost the entire length of the eastern desert; there there can be seen more than a hundred ancient mines, and the valleys in the schists are full of alluvial workings. By the time reef-mining had supplemented the output of the pan-washer, and the crucible could be used to refine the metal separated from the quartz by the hand-quern, the Pharaohs of Egypt, who held the monopoly of the mines, had virtually a corner in gold-production. The opening-up of the First Cataract for boat traffic by Mernere, the advance by Sesostris I to the Third Cataract, and the fortification of the Second Cataract by Sesostris III were all steps aimed at the safeguarding of the southern or Nubian goldfields. Gold was indeed essential to the fabric of the Egyptian empire. The astonishing treasure found in the tomb of Tutankhamen, an ephemeral ruler in a time of national decadence, witnesses to the vast hoards of precious metal stored in 'The Double Goldhouse' of the royal treasury; and all was at the absolute disposal of the Pharaoh. With the 'Gold of Praise' and the 'Gold of Valour' he rewarded the services and assured the loyalty of his officers of state, and with gold he hired the mercenaries who formed the hard core of the Egyptian army. The foreign policy of Egypt was backed by gold. If Pharaoh raided Syria, towns captured by him would of course be systematically plundered and thereafter made to pay tribute, and in the early days of conquest south Syria provided him with a considerable amount of gold brought up, presumably, from western Arabia; but where his conquests stopped and frontiers had to be protected against powerful neighbours it was the treasury, not the war office, that gave protection. The Kassite rulers of Babylon, the kings of Assyria, of Mitanni and of the Hittites were constantly demanding gold and yet more gold from the inexhaustible coffers of the Pharaoh. If Amenhotep III sent twenty talents to Assurnadin-akhi of Assyria, the latter's son saw in this good reason to demand another twenty from Amenhotep IV, and at once the Kassite king Burnaburiash II, as overlord of Assyria, claimed as much again; Dushratta of Mitanni writes: 'Let my brother send gold in very great quantity, without measure, and let him send more gold to me than to my father. For in my brother's land gold is as common as the dust.'

Silver makes its appearance quite early. In Egypt it is found, together with lead, in the Middle pre-Dynastic periods; in Crete in the Early Minoan; in Troy I it occurs with lead and in Troy II is common and the silver is exceptionally pure; in Mesopotamia silver is already known in the al'Ubaid period, and in the Jamdat Nasr period lead is in very common use.

It is almost certain that Asia Minor was the first and for a very long time the principal source of both metals. Almost certain too is it that while some of the early silver is really electrum, mixed with varying percentages of gold and copper, and may be regarded as a by-product of gold-working, by far the greater part was extracted from lead. The mountains of eastern Anatolia contain immense deposits of galena; this is the easiest of the lead ores to work and the Anatolian galena is particularly rich in silver, some of the lodes in Karahissar yielding as much as 600 ounces of silver to the ton of lead (1.84 per cent). Primitive metallurgists who had mastered the secret of dealing with copper ore and were ready to experiment with other 'coloured stones' that might bring them profit would almost inevitably try their hand with galena, whose bright metallic appearance and high specific gravity could not fail to excite their curiosity; the separation of the silver from the lead is the natural result of the smelting process, and it would not be long before the workers noticed that they were getting two metals instead of one.

Of the two metals, lead was not of any great use to early man. It had none of the qualities required for weapons or tools, and although it was sometimes employed for making small ornaments the effect could not be called decorative. In Mesopotamia it enjoyed a brief vogue in the Jamdat Nasr period, the graves of that age very commonly containing leaden bowls or tumblers, but none of later date has been found; we get some sheet lead in one of the royal cemetery graves, late in the Early Dynastic period, and it was used for solder in a First Dynasty of Ur relief from al'Ubaid; the Cappadocian tablets (*c.* 1950 BC) describe the export from Ganes in eastern Anatolia of two qualities of lead, 'pure' and 'loose' lead, in considerable quantities, the price of it being one-quarter that of silver, and the metal seems to have been very plentiful in early Assyria; but, so far as we can tell, its contribution to culture throughout the Bronze Age was very small. Early Hittite bronzes sometimes contain lead which seems to have been added deliberately and the Egyptians occasionally used it instead of tin for bronze castings of a ceremonial or votive character, i.e. those which were not to serve any practical purpose, and in and after the Eighteenth Dynasty manufactured lead glaze; but there is much to be said for the theory that lead was valued more as the source of silver than for its own sake.

For silver was prized from the outset for its beauty and its brilliance. Pliny says that, compared with gold, silver 'is brighter and more sun-like', but because of its white colour its general association is with the moon; in Mesopotamia it is the metal of Sin, the Moon-god, in Egypt the bones of the Sun-god Rê are fashioned of silver; for charms and amulets therefore it was held to be most efficacious. Because Egypt had no silver of her own (the galena ores of the eastern desert are rich in lead but valueless for silver production) and had to import all her supplies from the north, silver was prone to be more costly in Egypt than gold; as late as the Hyksos period it was worth twice as much, and although in the New Kingdom the conquest of Syria brought vast quantities as loot or tribute the gold-silver ratio was still only 5:3. In lands nearer to the sources of supply the relative values were very different: in Akkad, in the region of Sargon, gold was eight times the price of silver, at Ur, under the Third Dynasty, ten times and in the reign of Bur-Sin seven times only (perhaps there was a shortage of supply due to troubles in Armenia) but for a long time after that the gold-silver ratio of 1:10 seems to have remained fairly constant. It would appear that Egypt's advantage in possessing the richest goldfields of the Old World was to some extent set off by the price she had to pay for the silver which she coveted. The beautiful examples which we possess of Egyptian silverwork dating from the Middle Kingdom prove that the goldsmiths of the Nile valley could do full justice to the imported metal—in later times, as the Tell el Amarna letters prove, they were exporting manufactured silver goods to Cyprus; but it was in Asia that the best use was made of silver, if only because there the craftsmen had better opportunities to learn and to exploit its qualities. The amount in circulation must have been very great. It should be remembered that in the damp and salty soil of Mesopotamia silver tends to be resolved into soluble chlorides, and an incalculable proportion of the silver objects buried there have in this way disappeared completely; but at Ur in the tomb of Queen Shub-ad alone there were forty-eight vessels of silver and in the tomb of A-bar-gi the silver objects registered numbered ninety. In the humbler graves both of the Early Dynastic Age and of the Sargonid silver rings, pins, ear-rings, etc., were of common occurrence; Sargon indeed led his victorious armies to 'the mountains of silver', thereby securing free access to the mines. The metal was so valued that already by the time of Manishtusu, king of Kish (*c.* 2400 BC) it was a recognized standard of exchange, one *mina* of silver being equivalent to 60 *gur* of grain. Under the Third Dynasty of Ur sums of silver are lent at various rates of interest and silver objects such as rings and vessels are regularly paid in to the palace as revenue. It is likely that in the case of silver, as of gold, certain standard types of ornament, rings, ear-rings, etc., were also standardized in respect of the purity of the metal and therefore could be accepted as currency; thus Abraham when buying the cave of Machpelah weighs out 400 shekels of silver, 'current money with the merchant', and Jacob buys a field at Padan-Aram for 'an hundred pieces of money', just as the betrothal-money for Rebekah was 'a golden ear-ring of half a shekel weight and two bracelets of ten shekels' weight of gold'. Refined silver as distinct from crude silver is mentioned in the Cappadocian texts of *c.* 2000 BC and in Troy II there were found six ingots of very pure metal each weighing exactly 40 shekels of the heavy *mina;* obviously these are media for exchange; it has even been suggested that small silver plaques marked with the sign

H for the larger and I for the half-type, found at Knossos and at Enkomi in Crete and dated to the Late Minoan period, were actually coins. Silver was useful only for ornamental purposes and for such purposes was (except in Egypt) but a cheaper substitute for gold. Its use involved no new technique but only that already developed by craftsmen working in the more precious metal (it is worth noting that in the grave of Queen Shub-ad at Ur there were one gold fluted tumbler and more than twenty silver tumblers of identical form, two oval gold bowls and three of the same type in silver); in view of this we may perhaps say that the most important contribution to the progress of civilization made by silver lay in its employment as an exchange medium, and so in its encouragement of international trade. The mere accidents of survival and discovery do not enable us to say to what extent—if at all—stamped ingots like those from Troy II continued in circulation; the next example, a bar weighing exactly one *mina,* found at Zinjirli, dates to the close of the eighth century BC, at which time it seems to have been usual for various cities to stamp silver as a guarantee of refinement. If the logical step of issuing a regular coinage was not taken earlier it was probably due to the fact that there was no central government strong enough for its guarantee to be internationally recognized, and in the meantime the stamped ingot served the purposes of the trader well enough.[16]

Just as it has been insisted that the Bronze Age begins with the smelting of ores and does not include the Chalcolithic Age in which natural copper was worked more or less on the stone technique, so too the Iron Age begins with the production of hardened iron—'steel'—the only form in which the metal was superior to bronze and so would naturally replace it. The point of departure is not the first use of iron as such, but the metallurgical discovery which made iron really useful.

The earliest iron objects of which the authenticity is undisputed are made of meteoric iron treated, as were other native metals, by hammering, and possessing therefore no metallurgical interest; such are the pre-Dynastic beads from el Gerzeh in Egypt, a Sixth Dynasty lump from Abydos found by Petrie with a hoard of copper objects, a thin blade set as an amulet which is perhaps of Old Kingdom date; from Byblos we have iron set in the bezel of a gold ring found in a royal grave; from Mesopotamia, remains of an iron object from a grave of the Jamdat Nasr period at al'Ubaid. Meteoric iron is widely spread over the earth's surface and a meteor was always likely to attract attention, so that the utilization of the natural metal is not surprising; but the smelting of it required a degree of heat far beyond the capacity of any primitive furnace, and the technique of working meteoric iron remained that of the Stone Age. On the other hand the recognition of the celestial origin of the meteor caused men to ascribe to the metal mysterious and occult qualities; this religious awe persisted long after iron was in general use—indeed, it survives until the present day in many popular superstitions—and strengthened that belief in uncanny powers which in so many lands had made of the smiths a people apart, social outcasts perhaps, but to be feared.

It is possible that the production of man-made iron began, in Egypt,[17] as a by-product of the refining of gold, for the gold gravels of Nubia have an iron content of over 65 per cent, and when this sand was washed for gold about half of the residue left in the pan would be magnetite; and since the Egyptians melted the gold in crucibles in a reducing atmosphere, the crucible at the end of the operation would contain liquid gold at the bottom, rich iron slag at the top, and in the middle a layer of pasty iron ready for forging. The iron amulets and model tools found in the tomb of Tutankhamen and other examples of iron jewellery may have been made of such local metal; but the total amount produced by the gold industry would have been extremely small; it was valuable because it was rare, but because it was only soft iron and would obviously be far less serviceable than bronze for tools or weapons there was small inducement to exploit its discovery on a large scale.

The evidence of archaeology, of folk-lore and of religion is conclusive on the point of iron being a late metal. The fact that iron-working not only implies a knowledge of the techniques used in dealing with other metals but also requires special techniques of its own (and special tools as well) confirms its late appearance but is in addition a strong argument for its diffusion from a single centre. It has been argued that that centre was in eastern Europe, in the Hallstatt region, the richest of all in spathic iron, which is the ore best adapted to the experimental methods of the early metallurgist, whence the knowledge spread southwards into Asia Minor. But the theory is not supported by the archaeological evidence and most authorities are agreed in accepting the classical tradition according to which iron-working, as we have learnt to understand it, i.e. the 'steeling' of man-made iron, originated somewhere in the Hittite realm of eastern Asia Minor, probably in the Armenian district, and so, by land and by sea, made its way westwards and northwards into Europe.

The smelting of the Anatolian ores certainly began at a fairly early date, for examples of man-made iron appear in the first half of the third millennium BC not only in Asia Minor itself, at Alaca Höyük, but in northern Mesopotamia, at Tell Chagar Bazar, at Tell Asmar and at Mari. The latter were of course imports, as were later examples found at Ur, at Ras Shamra in northern Syria and at Gezer and Tell Mutesellim and Beth-Pelet in Palestine, these ranging in date from 2100 to about 1350 BC. All the metal thus exported was soft iron, produced directly from iron ores in a bloomery. The spongy mass resulting from the smelting was re-heated and hammered into compact blocks which could be sold to the smiths; it was malleable when heated white-hot, but it was not fusible, so that, whereas the craftsman could cast bronze into any form he pleased, iron could be shaped only by the laborious process of continued heating and hammering. But a wrought-iron tool thus fashioned will not keep its cutting-edge for long; it requires constant annealing, quenching and hammering, so that its maintenance cost in terms of labour and of skill is much greater than that of bronze; it could not, therefore, rival bronze in the world's market. Thus we may expect to find, and we do find, iron objects dated far back in the Bronze Age, but the Iron Age could not begin until man had invented the 'steeling' of iron.

It is impossible to say precisely when or where or how that invention was made. The earliest literary mentions of iron are in a letter from Mari mentioning an iron bracelet which came as a gift from the king of Carchemish (implying that the metal was a rare luxury) and in an Alalakh tablet in which King Ammitaku claims that he has captured from those who opposed him booty including four hundred weapons of iron. As Ammitaku reigned somewhere around 1750 BC the date is unexpectedly early, at least if we are to assume that the 'weapons' were necessarily of steel and not of soft iron; it is, however, possible that the 'weapons' were sacred symbols in the form of daggers and were not intended for use in war.

The invention of the 'steeling' process is most likely to have been made in the Caucasian area where the crude metal was produced; this would agree with the classical tradition regarding the Chalybes as the original workers in steel, and it is certainly supported by the fact that for two centuries and more after 15 BC the Hittites controlled the steel trade and were the only people from whom the Pharaohs of Egypt could obtain a niggardly ration of the precious metal. The Hittite monopoly applied to the eastern Mediterranean, and it may be that knowledge of the new technique spread very quickly in other directions, into central Europe (the earliest iron finds in northern Europe, at Seeland and Bornholm, are ascribed by some authorities to the fourteenth century BC) and possibly via the

Balkans to Noricum; but even in Europe the Iron Age proper cannot be dated much earlier than 1200 BC. In northern India the Rigvedic hymns seem to make it clear that steel was known at the time when the hymns were composed; iron, *ayas,*[18] is described as both malleable and ductile, tough and strong; it must have been introduced before—but not necessarily long before—1000 BC, but it took another five hundred years to popularize it in the Dravidic south.

In China iron, as a precious metal, may have been used for jewellery and ornaments as early as the close of the Shang Dynasty.[19] It had come into ordinary use by the Chankuo period, and iron farm-implements have been found belonging to the time of the Warring States (fourth–third centuries BC) from which fact it can be deduced that the metal was then common and had been introduced very much earlier; but in any case the Chinese Bronze Age continued until long after 1200 BC.

The discovery of the secret of steel-making must have been due to accident, and, as the literature of a much later age proves, its manufacture remained purely empirical. It was not necessary to understand the metallurgical processes involved; experience showed that in certain conditions iron acquired new and valuable properties, and all that was required was to observe those conditions and to reproduce them. The primitive smith when forging a bar of wrought iron had to re-heat it often, and if he achieved this heating by embedding his bar in the heart of a charcoal fire and maintained the temperature by using a blast insufficiently strong to penetrate the heart of the hearth the outer surface of the bar would become carburized to a depth depending on the length of the treatment; he would find that his tool had a steel case-hardening which added enormously to its efficiency. Repeated experiments would show him just what it was that had produced the unexpected result, and he would in future re-create the conditions of his first success, not putting a theory into practice but simply modifying his working routine. Most of the ancient iron weapons and tools, therefore, exhibit this cementation or carburization of wrought iron, but the carbon content varies throughout the mass of the object, the purified bloom being partially and unevenly steeled; the process had been applied to the outer surface and the cutting-edge only, the core remaining relatively unaffected.

An alternative method of carburizing iron—the 'poling' system—must also have been discovered by accident. The primitive smelter, using some form of basin bloomery-furnace, might try to expedite the separation of the bloom from the slag by stirring the fused mass with a wooden pole; if his attempt was prolonged the end of the pole, charred by the molten metal in which it was immersed, would carburize it sufficiently to bring about a noticeable improvement in the metal's quality. In the course of time the workman would trace this improvement back to its source and would utilize the accident and improve on it by deliberately mixing freshly-cut wood with the ore and so producing steel. This 'poling' method is the prototype of the 'green withy smelting' which was used by the pre-Roman Celtic ironworkers in the Weald of Kent.

That the method of making steel should have been discovered nearly three hundred years before the superior metal was produced in such quantities as to oust bronze in the manufacture of tools and weapons is not surprising. The technique had been developed by a relatively small professional group of craftsmen whose interest it was to keep the secret to themselves. In doing this they were helped by the fact that the centres of production where they worked were far removed from the markets in which their goods were sold and lay for the most part in areas difficult of access; moreover, they were themselves a people apart, isolated by the superstitions that attached themselves to the mysterious alchemy whereby stones were transmuted into the hard white metal that daunted even the elemental spirits. Amongst all ancient peoples[20] we find smith-gods. Vulcan and Hephaestus, Brahma and Agni and Indra, Ea and Girru, Loki and Wieland, and the early smiths share something of their superhuman character, as do the Telchines and the Dactyloi of Greek tradition; it would be dangerous for ordinary mortals to pry into their mysteries. As has been said, the smelter's methods were empirical, and he needed a vast amount of experience before he could learn so to regulate his practice as to be sure of producing steel in any considerable bulk or with uniform success; in the meantime it paid him better to restrict his output and to maintain a high price-level. When a thirteenth-century Hittite ruler writes, 'There is no good iron in my "sealed house" at Kizzuwadna. It is a bad time to make iron, but I have written ordering them to make good iron. So far they have not finished it. When they finish it I will send it to thee', he is not necessarily making false excuses. 'Steeling' was still a chancy, hit-or-miss operation, and the Hittite rulers, who were the regular exporting agents, could not be sure of a punctual delivery. It is, of course, possible that for security reasons the armaments trade with foreign countries was strictly limited and that the Iron Age was well advanced in Anatolia some time before it started in other Asiatic lands. Otherwise we must assume that the manufacture of steel made very rapid progress in the second half of the thirteenth century; for the Peoples of the Sea who flocked down into Syria and Palestine just before 1194 BC were armed with the new metal, and the Philistines from their first appearance were using iron not only for weapons of war but also for agricultural tools.

The Techniques of Metal-Working

If we bear in mind the slow development of the Neolithic Age, when the *floruit* of a particular type of flint instrument has to be reckoned in centuries if not in millennia, we may well be astonished at the speed with which man mastered the

FIG 28A. *The blowpipe in use, detail from relief on the tomb of Ti at Saqqarah.*

FIG. 28B. *Metal-workers' shop, Old Kingdom (after Breasted).*

art of metal-working. During the relatively short Chalcolithic stage there is still the hesitancy of slow-witted savages trying to apply their traditional ideas and techniques to an alien material, but from the moment the discovery of ore-smelting was made new skills and inventions crowd one upon another with the exuberance of a world in its springtime.

The work of the smelter is difficult and that of the smith impossible without a forced draught for the kiln and the hearth. To raise the temperature of the glowing charcoal a fan or a blowpipe would both be effective, but the latter had the great advantage of directing the blast air on the precise point required, and for that reason it was indispensable for fine work such as that of the goldsmith. Illustrations of the blowpipe in use (Fig. 28A and B) in Egypt are in Old Kingdom reliefs and a blowpipe is perhaps the origin of a sign in a Susa text of the Uruk period (Legrain, DP. Vol. XVI, p. 31), but we may be sure that its use goes back to the first days of metal-working, just as it persists up to the present time. For large-scale work the blowpipe is scarcely adequate, and at an early date it was supplemented by the bellows. The oldest form, the skin-bellows, seems to have been evolved in the Near East (or perhaps in central Asia); the goatskin bag with its nozzle fitted into one leg and a slit which could be opened and closed for letting in the air seems to have been introduced in the third millennium BC (at Tello in southern Sumer nozzles found near a furnace dated to about 2100 BC) and remained the standard type for a long while; the bellows of Hephaestus' forge as described by Homer (*Iliad* xviii, 468) were of this sort, and so probably were those of the Tegean forge described by the Pythian oracle (Herodotus i, 67). In Egypt a more elaborate form came into use by the Eighteenth Dynasty and is represented in, for example, the tomb of Rekhmirê (Fig. 29); this is the dish-bellows with solid chambers probably of earthenware and a skin moved by strings; in southern or eastern Asia, man invented yet another form, the pump-bellows, with a piston moving inside a wooden or a bamboo cylinder; an intermediate type, the dish- or drum-bellows with a loose diaphragm fitted over a solid chamber, worked either by hand or by strings or sets of sticks, was developed apparently in India and later spread thence into Africa where it is still in use. Blast-air was necessary if the metal now available was to be of any service, and human ingenuity was quick to answer the challenge; even if we grant that the simple skin bag was the earliest form of bellows and inspired the rest, yet the local variants, each meant to be an improvement on the original, testify to the quickening effect of the metal age on man's imagination.

To some extent, the craftsman was content to carry on his new trade of metal-working with old-fashioned tools, the reason being that he found them adequate. Throughout the greater part of the Bronze Age the hammers used by the smith were of stone and without handles; such are represented in Egyptian reliefs, and goldsmiths' hammers of polished haematite have been found at Ur; these differ very much in size and shape,

FIG. 29. *Leather workers, cabinet makers, and pottery makers, tomb of Rekhmirê (after Cottrell).*

each adapted to a different purpose, just as the skilled worker of today will have as many as twenty hammers to be used as occasion demands. But almost the first things to be made of metal were tools; the wood-worker asked for knives and saws, the metal-worker required chisels, and everywhere chisels are found in the lowest Bronze Age strata; with his stone hammers and his bronze cutting instruments, with an anvil and, generally, with bronze tweezers for gripping the hot metal on which he was to work, the smith was equipped for his task.

The vast hoard of metal objects from the royal cemetery at Ur—the earliest that gives us a general conspectus of the metal-worker's achievements—shows that by the first quarter of the third millennium BC the Sumerian craftsman could do very nearly all that can be done by the modern goldsmith and could do it almost if not quite as well. One tool, the modern snarling-iron, he did not know; lacking steel, he could not engrave bronze, though he did sometimes engrave gold; he had not learned the spinning of metal bowls—the earliest example of that technique seems to be an Egyptian bowl of the Eighteenth Dynasty; he could not weld copper or bronze or gold because he could not get the right temperature (the earliest welded joint known is on an iron head-rest from the tomb of Tutankhamen, *c.* 1350 BC, but Anatolia must have discovered the technique earlier than that) and, except in the case of gold leaf, he could not manage cold pressure-welding because he could not get sufficient pressure per square inch. But in the field of pure craftsmanship, in sinking or raising sheet metal into bowl or vase form, in repoussé work, in chasing, in inlay, he had nothing to learn (Pl. 10). He was familiar with the use of stamps and dies; he would cast gold or bronze not in the open one-piece moulds of the early days but in closed moulds of two or more pieces—this for solid casting, or, to save metal, by the *cire perdue* process, the most sophisticated of techniques. The joining together of metal plates by means of copper rivets, a process illustrated by handled bowls from the royal cemetery and later on by statues of cattle from a temple at al'Ubaid of the time of the First Dynasty of Ur, *c.* 2600 BC (Pl. 11, a) and in Egypt by the life-size statue of the Sixth Dynasty Pharaoh Pepi I, is a fairly obvious utilization of the malleable quality of the metal; but more commonly joints were made by soldering. Solder may be defined as 'a metal or alloy whose melting-point is lower than that of the metal or alloy to be soldered, which may be run in between the parts to be joined to fasten them together'. The use of solder, therefore, implies not indeed any abstract chemical knowledge but at least a recognition, gained from experience, of the fact that certain alloys will melt at lower temperatures than others and can be used for brazing. But only experiments continued over a long time could turn the observed fact to practical advantage. It is true that with a copper-tin alloy the melting-point is lowered in almost direct ratio with the percentage of tin; but though gold alloyed with 18 per cent of copper melts at a heat of 878° C. instead of 1,063° C., yet with any further increase of the copper content the melting-point rises; and the same is the case with a silver-copper alloy where the melting-point is lowest when the copper percentage is 28 and rises sharply thereafter. Judging by the actual objects that have come down to us, the Sumerian metal-worker of 2700 BC could undertake a soldering job—i.e. hard-soldering—with complete confidence; it was no longer a case of hit or miss: he knew from experience precisely what alloy would give the desired result and could be used without damage to the object to be soldered. The most surprising evidence for this is given by a few gold objects from the royal cemetery decorated either with open filigree work of fine wire (cut, not drawn) soldered on to solid back-plates or with 'granulation', minute beads or grains of gold arranged to form patterns; the difficulty of this is that the flux when heated tends to displace the grains and the solder clogs the fine texture of the grain- or wire-work. The secret of the technique employed by the Sumerians, by the Egyptians of the Twelfth Dynasty and afterwards by the Etruscans was lost, and recovered only in the 30's; it is delightfully simple. The gold background is painted with a mixture of fish glue, a copper salt such as copper hydrate [$Cu(OH)^2$] and a little water, and the beads or filigree are arranged while the glue is wet, any plain parts of the background being cleaned up before firing. When heated, the copper salt turns to copper oxide and the glue is carbonized; the carbon combines with the oxygen in the copper oxide and goes off as carbon dioxide, leaving the finely divided metallic copper in the join; so delicate is the process that the grains are in no way 'flooded' by the solder. Again one must beware of attributing to the early goldsmith a chemical knowledge which was certainly far beyond his ken, but careful observation and controlled experiment (the first elements of science!) were needed to give birth to the empirical knowledge which was the 'mystery' of his trade. The same ingenuity in profiting by experience is shown by the treatment of electrum. The gold used by the Sumerian smith varied much in quality, ranging for the most part between 14 and 22 carat, i.e. with a gold content of from 58 per cent to 91 per cent and silver from 40 per cent to 7.7 per cent and a maximum of 2.3 per cent copper; this is precisely what one would expect of native alluvial gold, though a few examples in which the silver outweighs the gold may be of artificial alloy. Where the silver content was such as to affect the colour (as in the case of a spear-head, gold 30.3 per cent, silver 59.37 per cent) the Sumerian adopted the same trick as did the makers of 'pinchbeck' gold in Victorian England; the finished object was soaked in brine, which would dissolve the silver from the immediate surface, leaving a spongy gold which was then burnished (perhaps with some acid; the Victorians used strong ale) and made a casing of pure metal, the core remaining virtually white.

That metallurgical technique should have developed to this extent in the comparatively short period of time between the beginning of the Bronze Age and 2700 BC bears witness to the extraordinary impetus given to civilization by the discovery of metal. Throughout the rest of the Bronze Age the metal-worker did little more than exploit the methods invented by the date of the royal cemetery. There is no evidence to show in what particular region those inventions were made, nor indeed does that greatly matter, for any new technique was likely to spread fairly rapidly; even if travelling smiths did not start manufacture in the areas which they visited, the mere export of finished objects would soon be followed by their imitation. The parallel development in Mesopotamia and in Egypt, the two countries best documented for our study, makes this evident. Thus, in the royal cemetery, the cheaper beads are made of gold foil laid over bitumen; the more difficult operation of true plating, gold leaf on copper, is common in the Sargonid Age; and it appears in Egypt at about the same time. A few objects from the cemetery illustrate in simple form the inlay of gold in bronze, a tradition carried on in Mesopotamia by the splendid silver and electrum vase of Entemena found at Tello; this art was practised in Egypt, but it reached its zenith in the amazing polychrome dagger-blades from Mycenae which prove that Homer's description of the bronze shield of Achilles with its golden vines trained over silver poles, the grape-clusters of niello, the tin fence and the ditch of blue-black steel did no more than justice to the Achaean craftsmen in metal. Similarly the rather tentative experiments of the Sumerians in cloisonné work were to culminate not in anything produced in Mesopotamia but in the pectorals of the Twelfth Dynasty (Pl. 11, b) jewellery hoard found at Dahshur in Egypt. The manual skill of the Egyptian craftsmen in the Early Dynastic period was such that they could perfectly well have copied and in time have improved upon imported models of inlay or cloisonné work, or might have invented the process for themselves; but some of the metal techniques could not have been acquired in that way but must have been learnt from personal instruction. If bronzes from Mohenjo-daro were cast by the *cire perdue* process the fact can only be explained as a result of direct contact between the Euphrates and the Indus valleys in the time of Sargon of Akkad; just as there were Indian business men in Sumer so Sumerian smiths can have travelled eastwards and instructed the local craftsmen in the secrets of their trade. The *cire perdue* process, as well as that of casting bronze in sectional moulds, was known to the Shang tribe when the Shang state was an oasis of civilization in the middle of a barbarous China. The Chinese metal-worker was indeed a complete master of his material. The mere size of some of the great bronze vessels (Pl. 2, c) cast by him was such as to challenge the technical powers of the metallurgist of any age, and while the delicate relief that covers the surface shows the most sensitive appreciation of the qualities of his material the details of high relief, often produced into the round, are a triumph of developed technique. He was not an artist only, but an all-round workman. No deposits of usable ore are known to exist anywhere in that region, and the finding at Anyang of pieces of malachite, slag mixed with charcoal and pottery vessels apparently used in refining suggests that some at any rate of the copper used was produced locally, but as the cast vessels are made of an alloy containing as much as 17 per cent of tin it would further appear that the Shang people mixed the ores or the metals deliberately for the production of bronze. It is, of course, possible that while a certain amount of local smelting of copper was practised yet more was imported and that the bronze at any rate came to Anyang ready-made; certainly the knowledge of how to work it must have been derived from the west. The remarkable thing is that the Shang bronzes are, as castings, technically superior to those made in China at any subsequent period of its history, which surely implies a long apprenticeship in the art; the forms in which the vessels are cast are typically Chinese and can in some cases at least be traced back to those of the earthenware vessels of Neolithic or Chalcolithic north-eastern China, and they are decorated with motifs which had their roots deep in the life and thought of the Chinese people. Artistically then, the Shang bronzes are wholly independent of any western traditions; if the technique was originally borrowed, as we are driven to suppose, that had happened so early that by the time of the Shang Dynasty the craftsmen had evolved a style essentially their own and essentially Chinese.

The general lines of the northward and westward expansion of metallurgy have been traced already (see Map VIII). At the outset the technique was borrowed and fashions were set by imported models, but in a shorter or a longer time local schools arose to satisfy the demands of local tastes and habits. The objects from the Alaca Höyük tombs, dating from a little before 2000 BC, illustrate this mixed parentage; technically they must be classed as provincial, falling far short of the perfection achieved by the Sumerian goldsmiths and bronze-casters, but typologically they owe nothing to Sumer. The treasure of Maikop in the Kuban province also derives its technique from the Sumerian, but the art is related rather to the Anatolian, though with a difference which makes it truly individual. Of the later development of the Anatolian school very little is known; a powerful bronze statuette from Bogazköy, so far resembling the stone relief of the warrior in the King's Gate of the city that we can describe it as definitely Hittite and probably of the fourteenth century BC, is so closely related to various bronzes found in northern Syria that we must assume a common Hittite-Hurri school of metal-casters; but from which of the two elements the inspiration came it is not possible to say.

The country in which metallurgy originated was not likely to be that of its higher development; the latter must needs depend not upon the local possession of the raw material but upon the cultural level of the country's inhabitants. The comparatively barbarous peoples of the Caucasus were fully occupied with the mining and the smelting of the metal; they made easy money by its export, and while they could themselves make the simple tools that their manner of life required, anything more elaborate could be purchased from their clients. The civilized peoples such as the Sumerians had more sophisticated needs, more imagination and more leisure to perfect their technique; in manufacture therefore the producing centres lag behind.

At Trialeti in the tableland of the Lesser Caucasus, east of Tiflis, Russian scientists have in recent years excavated a number of rich barrow tombs of the Late Bronze Age as well as a number of smaller and earlier tumuli which illustrate a remarkable local school of metallurgy. Some of the objects found here link up with those of the Kuban graves and of the Maikop treasure north of the Caucasus, and on the other hand they show connection with the contents of graves in the Talyche cemeteries of Azerbaijan, on either side of the Russo-Persian frontier on the west coast of the Caspian Sea, and also with many of the heterogeneous bronzes that have come from the plundered graveyards of Persian Luristan. This school, or, it would perhaps be better to say, this chain of kindred schools, can be traced back to a reasonably early date, the Middle Bronze Age here seeming to start about 2200 BC; but in each case the dates can be determined only by analogy with Sumerian types. The fact is that all of them are largely derivative, later in point of time than the Sumerian and, in point of style, dependent upon Sumer. That original motifs and forms are introduced cannot be denied—such are to be expected where the craftsmen come from a different stock with different surroundings, and they are of great value as documents for the history of local cultures. But so far as can be told at present the east-Caucasian schools were in the end sterile; they played no part in the history of invention and they exercised no influence upon the art of later times. Kuban, it is true, may rank as a precursor of 'Scythian' art, but Luristan remains little more than a curiosity.

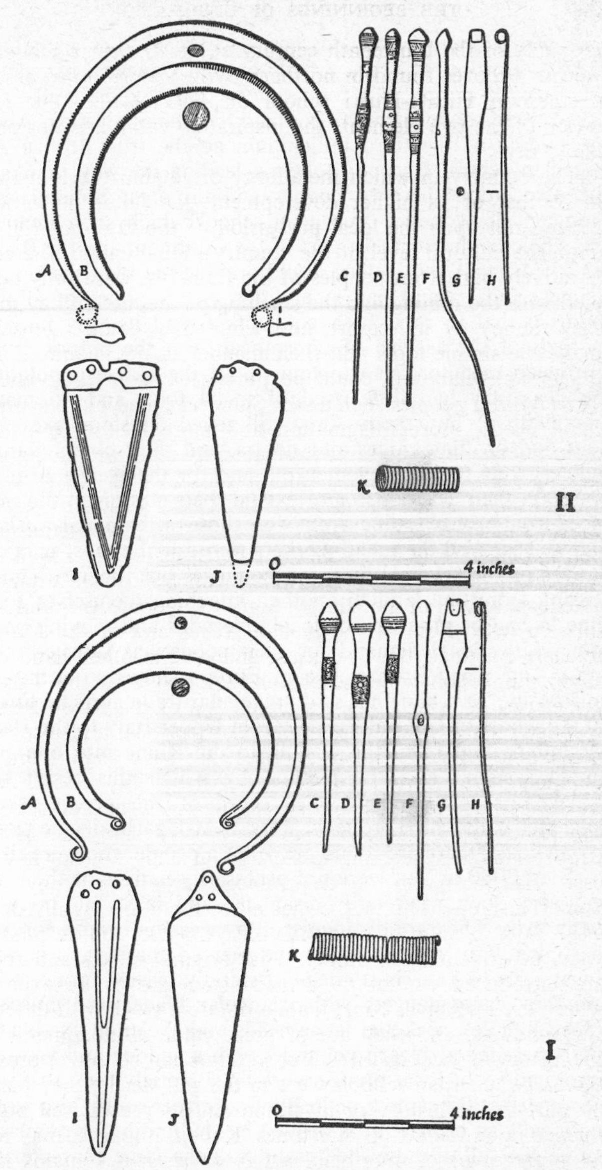

FIG. 30. *Torques and weapons. I. Syria, II. Alsace. A and B: torques; C-H: pins; I and J: aaggers; K: coiled rings (after Schaeffer).*

It was from Anatolia, as we have seen, that metallurgy reached Europe, to some extent through Caucasia by way of the Russian steppes but for the most part by the well-established trade-route through Troy and the Danube valley. About the middle of the third millennium BC the true Bronze Age began in central Europe, Bohemia leading the way thanks to the association there of copper and tin ores; Bohemia and Hungary developed a European school which soon included the whole of the northern part of the Continent and the British Isles; Cornwall and Ireland could provide the requisite tin and copper, and Ireland had in addition rich supplies of alluvial gold, so that in time Irish goldwork found its way into the markets of the eastern Mediterranean. But the output of the European metallurgists was limited. Of the sparse population, the peasantry had little need of metal tools and no means wherewith to buy them—they still relied on stone axes and hoes and on flint knives and sickles, and their chiefs wanted only trinkets for their womenfolk and for themselves arms to maintain their positions or to extend their authority; the only specialized bronze tools current were those of the metal-workers themselves. And the metal-workers were for the most part not natives of the several European countries but itinerant smiths passing from one land to another, attaching themselves for a time to one or other of the local chieftains and moving on as soon as the local demand for their goods was satisfied; that is why the early Bronze Age in Europe shows so striking a uniformity. As Childe has said, 'A regular trade in metal linked up the whole of Central Europe from Upper Italy to the Hartz Mountains and from the Vistula to the Rhine into one economic system'; and the method by which this result was achieved is explained by the record of the people whom Schaeffer calls 'the Torque-wearers'.[21] At Ugarit, on the north Syrian coast, there are found graves of a people who were there in about 2000 BC but were not necessarily natives of the place and very soon afterwards disappear and leave no trace of themselves. They are distinguished by wearing bronze torques, long pins with bulbous heads and pierced shafts, and curious rings, perhaps hair-rings, made of spirally twisted bronze wire, and they carry daggers with triangular blades and crescent-tipped handles, socketed lance-heads and eyeletted axe-blades; their presence at Ugarit coincides with a sudden and vigorous development of local bronze-working. Precisely the same people appear at the same time in Byblos, farther south, also working locally in bronze, as is proved by the finding of numerous votive jars full of unfinished castings of the same characteristic ornaments and weapons; it is quite possible that the offerings were made by metallurgists exploiting the deposits of stanniferous copper ore in the nearby mountains of Kesrouan. At Byblos, as at Ugarit, the evidence suggests that whoever these people were their stay in the place was transitory. Now exactly the same torques and pins, coiled rings and daggers are commonly found in Bohemia and Hungary; graves containing identical objects occur in Bavaria, Württemberg, Baden, Switzerland and Alsace (Fig. 30); the wandering gypsy-like smiths went everywhere, and everywhere they made and sold things of standard patterns even though they might combine that with more original work as a concession to local taste.

Towards the close of the second millennium BC local taste had prevailed and Europe of the Late Bronze Age was producing fine and individual work; but it still lagged far behind the Near East both in artistry and in technique; its promise was more important than its performance, and it needed the stimulus of the Iron Age for the north and west to make its full contribution to progress.

CRAFTS AND INDUSTRIES

Mesopotamia

Specialization in industry began very early and almost inevitably. Certain trades, as we have seen in the case of miners and metal-smelters, were in their nature whole-time jobs, leaving a man no leisure for anything else. There were others in which a man could expect to sell his products, i.e. to make a living by them, only if he acquired a greater skill than most people possessed, and to do that with the elementary tools available he was obliged to devote himself entirely to the one task. In both cases, especially in the latter, the skilled worker had to protect himself against undue competition; it must not be too easy for others to learn what he had learnt, to profit by his hardly won experience and by over-production to bring down the value of what he made; the number of craftsmen must be kept within reasonable limits and the secrets of the trade jealously guarded. The natural result of this jealousy was the organization of craft guilds.

In Mesopotamia the craft guild was not a social organization independent of government control; it was recognized and utilized by the government. The guild-master, the 'Chief of the Joiners' or 'Chief of the Weavers', did indeed look after the guild's interest—he was, for instance, responsible for the recruiting of new members; but he also furnished the government with lists of the membership, he received orders from the government regarding the amount of the guild's produce that was required for the state's use, and arranged for the distribution of labour accordingly; and where the produce was liable to excise duty he had to see that the taxes were paid. The fact of the guild's having an official representative was obviously an advantage to both the guild and the government, and made their relations easier. Each trade occupied its own quarter of the city, as has ever been the custom in the Near East, and the practice of it descended from father to son, though outsiders, including slaves, might be admitted to apprenticeship; the term of apprenticeship for the weaver was five years, for the stone-mason four years, for the fuller two and a half years, while the baker could learn his profession in no more than fifteen months; during that period his master had to initiate the pupil in all the 'art and mystery' of the profession.

The phrase 'art and mystery' was indeed not lightly used. According to Sumerian tradition all the arts had been introduced by the divine creature Oannes 'since whose time no new inventions have been made'. Every craft was inspired by and under the protection of a god. This was most obviously true of the metallurgist whose work was a daily repeated miracle; with the help of the Fire god he conjured the metal out of its ore, softened it and shaped it as he pleased; about all that he did there was something super-human, and therefore he was a person to be feared and respected. In early days in Sumer he seems to have enjoyed a form of priesthood. Gudea of Lagash (*c.* 2200 BC) describes how 'he built the temple with precious metal; he caused the craftsmen in precious metal to dwell therein. He built the sanctuary with fine stone; he caused the stone-masons to dwell therein'—clearly these are professionals who were called in and had to be lodged on the site; but 'he built the temple with copper and lead; he brought the smiths, the priests of Nin-tu-kalam-ma, before her'; the smiths are more than professional craftsmen, they are priests, and their work requires the presence of the goddess their patron. This is perhaps an exceptional case, and certainly in later times smiths do not rank as priests; but in none of the crafts was the god very far away. Just as medicine was half magic, so in the instructions for performing what we should call a straightforward technical operation we find that some ritual act is interpolated, or some verbal charm has to be repeated, to ensure the success of an experiment whose result long experience has made familiar but which is none the less miraculous; the reason for its working is beyond man's understanding and depends upon the good will of the god.

The crafts were largely hereditary and the knowledge of

them was confined to the initiate. That is why Uta-napishtim, the Sumerian Noah, takes with him into the ark all manner of handiworkers; their traditional skill must not be lost to the world. To divulge secrets divine in origin, except within the closed circle of the guild, would be impious, and clearly to the guild's detriment; the master was obliged under pain of a heavy fine to give full instruction to an authorized apprentice, but some of that instruction would be given, as surviving technological texts show, in a craft-jargon unintelligible to the outside world. The best illustration of this is given by a text in the British Museum (120960) which further proves the success with which a trade secret, and therefore a trade monopoly, could be preserved. One Liballit-Marduk of Babylon, in the seventeenth century BC, writes down for the benefit of his guild or his family a recipe for the glazing of earthenware—the glazing of frit and steatite had long been known but nobody had yet succeeded in making glaze adhere to pottery; he writes it in a cryptogram so elaborate that it might pass for a charm to allay the pangs of childbirth. The recipe was not published in clear until the beginning of the seventh century BC. For a thousand years the output was so small that archaeologists believed the invention must have been made about 800 BC; in that century a few examples were made for royal use and thereafter glazed ware becomes relatively common. The discovery at Alalakh of stray specimens dated to the fourteenth, sixteenth and seventeenth centuries proved that the old recipe had indeed been used and also that a monopoly in the process had endured for a millennium. The reality of guild discipline in Mesopotamia cannot be questioned.

Because secrets were so jealously guarded certain kinds of work could be done only by certain individuals, who therefore might move about, following the opportunities of business. Thus Gudea for his temple brought in skilled labour from Elam and Susa, just as Solomon for his temple in Jerusalem brought in Phoenician masons. When Amenhotep III of Egypt, and his son Akhenaton after him, wanted painted floors for their palaces these could not be supplied locally; Egyptian painting on tomb or temple walls had always been *tempera* painting *a secco,* water-colours on dry plaster, and such would never have stood up to the wear of feet on a pavement; what was needed was true fresco (Pl. 15), and for that the Pharaoh had to import decorators from Crete: in quite poor houses at Tell el Amarna there are found the Mycenaean vases which the Cretan workmen brought with them from home. Crete itself had learnt the art of fresco from Asia, and Asiatic architects helped to plan and build and Asiatic artists adorned the Palace of Minos; in the time of Ramses II the Great King of the Hittites for the same purpose persuaded a leading architect of Egypt, Parimakhu,[22] to come to Hattusas; good artists and skilled craftsmen were always in demand, and Nebuchadnezzar was following very ancient precedents when he carried off 'all the craftsmen and smiths' from Jerusalem. While the hereditary nature of the crafts made for conservatism, the son, or the apprentice, following the precepts of the older generation, the itinerant specialist on the other hand introduced new ideas and new processes (he would recruit local assistants who in time would learn his methods) and by internationalizing knowledge did much to advance the progress of the arts in general, even though that progress was in a uniform direction, ruled by historic precedent.

Egypt

In Egypt the craftsman was not his own master, nor did he normally enjoy the esteem accorded to his Mesopotamian *confrère;* that which raised the Egyptian above the common ruck was government office, and in comparison with the educated man, the civil servant, all who worked with their hands, builder or smith, stone-mason or baker, were as contemptible as they were unfortunate. There is virtually no literary evidence regarding the organization or the activities of so subordinate a class; the best source available is the sculpture in the great tombs of the Old and Middle Kingdom.

The craftsmen, like the agricultural labourers, were serfs; later there were slaves similarly engaged. The reliefs in the tombs of the landed nobility in the Old Kingdom and of the nomarchs in the Middle Kingdom show, side by side with scenes of agricultural life, the ploughing of the field and the droving of cattle, the hunting and the fishing, pictures of craftsmen of all sorts. Not only are there domestic scenes such as might be expected in a great house—the baking of bread and the preparation of food, the spinning of thread and the weaving of cloth, but we find too the goldsmiths and the copper-smiths, the potters and the boat-builders, the makers of stone vases, the carpenters and the wood-carvers. The estates of the Egyptian noblemen were self-supporting and everything that they required was made at home; they lived in luxury, they built houses, they loved fine raiment and costly jewellery, and their establishments therefore included skilled craftsmen of every sort. There must have been, of course, workers plying similar trades in the towns, but they would be of small account. In ancient Egypt the gulf between the rich and the poor was immense, and the poor had simple needs and very little with which to satisfy them; the fine stuffs and the beautiful gold work made by the nobleman's retainers would find no purchasers in the town bazaar, and the independent craftsman would be one with no more skill than sufficed for making the crude products, tools or trinkets, that the peasant wanted and could afford. All good work was done in the houses and to the orders of the wealthy patrons.

Under the New Kingdom, when the feudal nobles had been eliminated and the great estates had reverted to the Pharaoh, it was he who employed all the best of the craftsmen. The Pharaohs of the Eighteenth Dynasty were indefatigable builders, directly or through the Amon priesthood, and now a whole imperial court had to be maintained in befitting splendour, the courtiers had to be rewarded with splendid robes and collars of worked gold, a standing army had to be equipped, and a whole reign was not too long for the preparing of the treasures which should accompany Pharaoh's body to his tomb. No skilled man would lack employment in those days. When Akhenaton was feverishly building his new capital there were not enough experienced carvers to cut the inscriptions that covered the walls of his temples, and mere journeymen had to be supplied with plaster of Paris casts of the texts which they had mechanically to reproduce.

Though nothing could alter the fact that the craftsmen, like all other workers, were serfs, not freemen, yet the direct service of Pharaoh did give opportunities for advancement. In the royal workshops, regularly inspected by the vizier, exceptional skill was likely to be noticed and rewarded, and the personal interest of the ruler in his grandiose constructions would signal out for his favour any individual whose genius served to build or adorn them. The earliest architect known to us by name is Imhotep, who worked for Zoser of the Third Dynasty and became a legend in Egypt. Under the New Empire we have Senmut, renowned as the architect of the beautiful Deir el Bahri temple (though this is in fact a plagiarism, an adaptation of the Eleventh Dynasty temple of Mentuhotep on a neighbouring site) and one of the most influential officers at Queen Hatshepsut's court; we have Ineni and Thutiy, workers in metal to the same queen, Amenhotep son of Hapu, Amenhotep III's architect who introduced the peripteral cella-temple, Bek, sculptor to Akhenaton, and others. Always, under an autocratic monarchy, an individual here and there may by his special gifts rise to fame and power; that happened with craftsmen in Egypt[23] and it did not happen, so far as we know, in Mesopotamia; but in all other respects the Asiatic was the better off. In Egypt the trades were hereditary, by law as well as by custom, but because the workers were not free no guilds could really protect them; tied to the service of Pharaoh, they could not travel in search of a fresh clientèle; fed and clothed and housed by him, they could not better themselves socially or economically; as the field labourer was *adscriptus glebae*, so the artisan was chained to his bench, to all intents and purposes a slave.

'The Urban Revolution', writes Dr R. J. Forbes,[24] 'brought in the basic crafts of modern technology. The later classical world had very little to add to these early achievements.' It is indeed true that an amazing advance was made in the course of the Bronze Age. It is not within the scope of this book to attempt a history of technology as such, but the technical exploits of early man must be noted and the level of his achievement put on record.

Pottery

The first really mechanical device, ushering in a new age, was the potter's wheel. It first appears in Mesopotamia, introduced into that country by the northerners who in the second half of the fourth millennium BC started what archaeologists know as the Uruk period.[25] The painted wares of the al'Ubaid period had all been hand-made; the monochrome Uruk pottery is turned on the wheel, and in the lowest level representing their culture an actual specimen of the potter's wheel has been found, a pivoted disk of baked clay about 3 feet in diameter and 5 inches thick, heavy enough to revolve of its own momentum after being swung by means of a wooden handle set close to its rim. From that time onwards all Mesopotamian pottery is wheel-made. In Egypt the wheel did not come into use until much later, and even in the Fifth Dynasty tomb reliefs show the potte. still employing the 'slow' wheel, which is turned by hand and revolves only at the hand's speed: in the Middle Kingdom the true wheel had been generally adopted. Machinery enabled the craftsman to produce vessels with a wider range of shape, and far more quickly; but it did not help towards artistic improvement, and since as wealth increased vessels of stone and of metal replaced those of earthenware in the houses of such as could afford them, the potter had less inducement to make things of oeauty, and the quality of his pots tended to deteriorate. Both in Egypt and in Mesopotamia pottery, though skilfully made, is for the most part strictly utilitarian and of small artistic merit, comparing very unfavourably with the wares of the Chalcolithic period. The same cannot quite be said of the Indus valley. The Harappā pottery, all of it wheel-made, is for the most part plain, mass-produced and purely utilitarian, but side by side with such we find elaborately painted vessels, usually in red and black but sometimes polychrome, whose decoration may have been ultimately derived from the earlier Kulli ware but in the developed form in which it occurs at Harappā and Mohenjo-daro is peculiar to the Indus valley culture. The designs on these pots are admirable and the actual painting is done with much skill and accuracy; the pains taken show that the makers were consulting the tastes of fastidious clients prepared to pay high prices for luxury goods. In the case of anything like pottery it is demand that creates supply, and only an appreciative public will induce the potter to make vessels of artistic quality; in Egypt and in Babylonia that appreciation was lacking, and the pottery in consequence is poor; on the other hand Crete, where social conditions were different, produced the finest wares of the ancient world.

Shortly before 2000 BC the potter's wheel was introduced into Crete, presumably from north Syria or from Asia Minor, and the potters of the succeeding age—the Middle Minoan period—made use of the machine not for crude mass-production but for the refinement of their traditional wares. It is remarkable that very many of their shapes are borrowed from metal vessels, which shows that the richer Cretans were accustomed to using tableware of gold, silver or bronze, and from the later examples known to us either by survival or from the pictures in Egyptian tombs we might suppose that such treasures would inevitably drive earthenware off the market. But the Cretan potter was prepared to meet the competition of the goldsmith. He learnt how to make an egg-shell-thin pottery, lighter to the hand than anything in metal, and as against the uniform glitter of the silver cup he painted his clay with gay polychrome designs which could not fail to appeal to so colour-loving a people as that of Crete; alike on the little tumblers and on the great store-jars of the 'Palace period' there are decorative patterns or stylized naturalistic scenes painted by craftsmen who had a real sense of artistry (Pl. 12). Since the painted pottery is found freely in the palace itself, where if anywhere vases of precious metal would have been used, it is clear that the former was in high repute. It was made for home consumption, but exported specimens have been found at Abydos and at Kahun in Egypt and at Ugarit on the Syrian coast; a hundred and fifty years after the 'Palace style' had ceased to be made a north Syrian potter must have seen an imported example of this delicate ware, preserved perhaps in a temple treasury, and reproduced the old Minoan design upon his own 'Atchana' vases.

Down to the end of the second millennium BC the European potter produced nothing worthy of note. The conditions of life throughout the continent were not such as to encourage or even allow the making of fine earthernware. The wheel remained unknown. The older painted wares of the Tripolye and Dimini schools had died out. The unpainted pottery of Bohemia and Hungary, spreading gradually westwards, that of the Apennine and Terramara cultures of Italy, the beakers and the food-vessels of western Europe and the British Isles, are invaluable for the evidence which they give concerning the movements of peoples and the dissemination of cultures; but they do little to illustrate the development of the potter's art in human history, they embody no original inventions affecting technique and can claim very slight aesthetic value.[26] On the other hand, the little that is known about Chinese pottery of the Shang period gives to it a real importance. Some of it is hand-made, some turned on the wheel, so that probably the wheel had only recently been introduced; it is kiln-fired, but the kilns seem to have been of a rudimentary type since the heat was evidently ill-regulated. Most of the vases were of a grey clay firing to red and many of them have simple impressed or incised decoration. A minority are of white China clay (kaolin) supposed to have been brought from an area some 17 miles north of Anyang, Tz'ŭ Chou, which under the Sung Dynasty was a famous centre of the porcelain industry; these white vases, decorated with designs carved in the wet clay, were made for ceremonial purposes, and fine examples of them are buried in the Shang royal tombs. A certain number of pots, made of a brownish clay and decorated with wavy parallel lines, have part of their surface covered with a grey glaze. The first point of interest regards the shapes of the vessels. H. G. Creel[27] states, 'Almost every form that we find in Shang and later Chinese bronze ceremonial vessels is found in the Shang pottery'. It is therefore to the credit of these early craftsmen that they standardized the types of ceremonial vases which were to persist throughout Chinese history; granted that some were not invented by them but inherited from the Neolithic past, none the less their contribution to Chinese art was a memorable one. The second point is that by the use of kaolin clay and by the application of glaze they seem to have laid the foundations of all the ceramic art of after times.

Glass

From a very early date the Egyptian potter had, as a sideline to his ordinary business, practised the making of vessels in glazed frit. Glaze had been known at the beginning of the Dynastic Age and was applied to small objects cut out of steatite or moulded in frit (or siliceous paste) and soon vases were made in the same way; the technique spread quickly, and beads of glazed frit occur fairly freely in Sumer in the Early Dynastic period. The glaze was, of course, glass, and about a dozen objects (nearly all small beads) made of real glass can be assigned to relatively early times—in Egypt to the Eleventh and Twelfth Dynasties and in Mesopotamia to about 2100 BC —and on the whole it seems that Mesopotamia may here have been the first in the field, especially as an example of glass from Eridu is a fair-sized lump, unshaped, a piece of the manufacturer's raw material.[28] But shortly before 1600 BC the discovery was made that slender rods of coloured glass, half-melted, could be twisted round a core into the form of a bottle, then re-heated so that the rods should coalesce, and then polished; during the second stage the soft surface could be 'combed' so as to produce waves in the rods, thus variegating the pattern at the craftsman's pleasure; the result was a little polychrome vase, lustrous and semi-translucent, unlike anything else known and certain to command a high price. The earliest examples of such come from Syria, to which country the invention may be credited, but by the beginning of the Eighteenth Dynasty the Egyptians had taken it over and were making vases finer in quality than the Syrians had ever made (Pl. 11, c). The same technique was used for manufacturing beads, large balls with polychrome inlay in the form of 'eyes' or rosettes; these gaily attractive ornaments, easily portable and not too fragile, were ideal objects of trade with the peoples of less civilized or of barbarous lands, and they were exported widely, westwards to Italy and across the European continent, to come to light again in graves in Britain, while the eastern trade took them to China and to Indonesia—'eye-beads' from Loyang (the Chou capital) are proved by spectrographic analysis to be identical with others from Qau in Egypt. The Chinese imitated such imported beads with great success—so much so that the polychrome beads made in south China are only to be distinguished from the foreign examples by their marked barium content, whereas the Egyptian and Syrian glass contains no trace of barium, and also by the presence of lead, which in the west is not found in glass until shortly before the Christian era. The facts seem to show that lead glass—'flint glass' as it is often called—was a Chinese invention; it is an invention that has had far-reaching results in glass manufacture, but it was due to experiments prompted by the beads of silica-soda-lime glass coming from the Middle East.

Stone Vases

It has already been said that the potter's craft was liable to suffer through the competition of stone vases.[29] Throughout the Middle East and as far away as Mehi (in what is now Baluchistan) stone vessels of all sorts were regularly manufactured (Pl. 8, b), and sometimes in great quantities, and in China the fact of the earliest porcelain being admittedly an imitation of jade suggests that the same was true in that country also.

In Egypt it was in the later pre-Dynastic and Early Dynastic periods that the art of making stone vases reached its zenith; the craftsmen used not only the softer stones such as steatite and alabaster (aragonite) but also the more refractory types, breccia, syenite, diorite, porphyry and obsidian, fashioning out of these materials huge bowls, as much as 2 feet in diameter, with a dignity of form and a precision of workmanship that are truly admirable. It was the export of such early Egyptian vessels to Knossos that roused the Cretan craftsmen to competition, and by the end of the Early Minoan period they were making exquisite little vases in stones of many colours; since such are found not only on the Palace site but, as at Mochlos, in the graves of ordinary citizens, we may conclude that they were in general demand and that the output was on a considerable scale.

In Mesopotamia too the craft was at its best in early times. In the Uruk period and afterwards in the period of Jamdat Nasr, i.e. in the second half of the fourth millennium BC and therefore rather before the vogue started in Egypt, the stone-cutters were making the most elaborate vases, sometimes covered with designs carved in relief, sometimes inlaid with varicoloured stone, sometimes composite, made of two or more stones of different colours joined together. In the Jamdat Nasr period stone vases had become so common that in the graves they often outnumber those of clay. Most are plain bowls of white limestone of a purely utilitarian type, but for larger vessels other materials are used and there the artistic sensibility of the makers is evident, the strong and severe outlines of a diorite vase contrasting with the delicate cutting of one in alabaster, worked down to an almost paper thinness so as to do justice to the translucent quality of the stone. In the Early Dynastic period which followed, the popularity of the stone vase as such is clearly on the wane; simple little limestone bowls are still fairly common and a vessel of translucent green calcite or of lapis lazuli would obviously be prized for its rarity, but elaborately carved vases or those of materials such as diorite seem from this time onwards to have been intended for dedication in temples rather than for ordinary use. So too in Egypt, the great hard-stone vessels went out of fashion and, during and after the Middle Kingdom, stone vases, common though they are, are nearly always small in size and in material limited to alabaster and steatite; they were 'toilet vases', intended to contain scented oils and unguents such as could not be kept in porous clay pots, or the eye-paint kohl, which had to be protected against damp. Utilitarian in purpose they certainly were, but the traditional shapes which had been dictated by that purpose (they would be termed 'functional' today) were excellent and deserved to be perpetuated; it is only when we see the technically fine but artistically monstrous alabasters from the tomb of Tutankhamen that the utter degeneration of the stone-cutter's craft in Egypt becomes manifest.[30]

Because Egypt is a land rich in stone of all sorts the stone-vase industry there was a natural growth; but its development in Mesopotamia is remarkable, seeing that no fit stone is to be found in the Euphrates valley and all the material had to be imported. That there was a trade in finished goods is certain, for decorated soft-stone pots of the Kulli culture are found on Mesopotamian sites in the Jamdat Nasr and Early Dynastic periods, imported from southern Baluchistan, but these are

FIG. 31. *Egyptian workmen drilling out stone vases (after Breasted).*

comparatively rare; the vast bulk of the vases were fashioned on the spot from imported material. The Egyptian stone vases were hollowed out by means of tubular drills either worked by a bow or, in the case of larger pots, weighted and turned by hand, a technique illustrated by tomb reliefs (Fig. 31). The same process was employed in Mesopotamia, but side by side with it there was used an alternative technique which seems to have been a local invention; on sites of Jamdat Nasr date there are found drill-heads of hard stone, rather less than half a sphere, with slots at the sides to take the pincer-ends of the drill shaft, which exactly fit the standard-size diorite bowls found on the same sites; there can therefore be no doubt as to the existence of a local industry. It is curious that whereas the shapes of the early Mesopotamian stone vases are original, showing no relation to those of Egypt, yet in the Early Dynastic period the commonest shapes of 'alabaster' vessels are identical with those from the Nile valley and would pass for imports but for the fact that they are made not from Egyptian aragonite but from the stalagmitic calcite found in the southern part of the Persian Gulf. Either the Sumerians obtained by trade Egyptian vases which they so admired that they proceeded to look for and to import a stone that would allow of their imitation—which seems hardly likely—or the vases were made by people of the Gulf who had ready access to the stone and traded their products to Mesopotamia and possibly to Egypt also, in both cases setting an example for imitation.

The importation of foreign stone for vase-making is well illustrated in the case of obsidian. The material was particularly esteemed for its beauty and perhaps also because of the difficulty of working it. The principal sources were Melos, which supplied a grey stone, and eastern Anatolia, which furnished a dark grey and a black variety. The Egyptians used the black variety, making small, rather heavy pots which depended for their charm on the polished glass-like surface; in Mesopotamia both the black and the light grey types were employed and the stone (especially the light-coloured stone) was ground down to the thinness of blown glass, thus taking full advantage of its translucence, a process which must have involved an immense cost in time and labour. Attached to a royal building of the eighteenth century BC at Alalakh there was found a vase-maker's shop containing the raw material, obsidian imported from eastern Anatolia. It came in the form of rectangular blocks measuring *c.* 12 by 8 by 8 inches (0.30 by 0.20 by 0.20 metres)—some may have been larger—which were very carefully squared and ground, an unnecessary refinement, seeing that they were intended for cutting up, but perhaps an excuse for raising the price. The vases were shaped by chipping, the old flint-knapper's technique, the interiors were bored out with tubular drills, and the rough surface was then ground down and finally polished with haematite as an abrasive. When then at Alalakh we find alabaster vases identical in shape with those from Egypt and from Mesopotamia already mentioned, it does not necessarily mean that we have to do with objects imported ready-made from the one country or the other; it is equally probable that such are the work of local craftsmen using imported raw material and copying foreign models which experience had proved to be popular; already by the eighteenth century BC international contacts had gone far towards uniting the countries of the Middle East in an artistic commonwealth.

Ivory

More tangible evidence of the sharing of artistic styles is afforded by the ivory trade. From pre-Dynastic times this exquisite material had been a favourite with the Egyptians and always it was one of the luxury goods in greatest demand. Ivory was carved into statuettes such as the portrait figure of Khufu, Pharaoh of the Fourth Dynasty, or that on Tutankhamen's head-rest, into spoons and toilet-boxes, fan and mirror handles, amulets and gaming pieces in the form of lions or jackals, and it was used for the decoration of furniture, whether as simple bands and checker patterns or carved and enriched with paint or with gold and coloured stones and faience as we see it in caskets and thrones from Tutankhamen's tomb. The raw material came from the south, of course; ivory from central Africa was brought up overland to Libya and so to Egypt, and it was also one of the staples of the Sudan trade; thus in the Sixth Dynasty Sebni, governor of Elephantine, returning from an expedition to the Sudan, sends on in advance a large ivory tusk as evidence for Pharaoh of his success and boasts that he has one of five feet. In the Eighteenth Dynasty Queen Hatshepsut boasts that she has obtained seven hundred tusks from Libya. The main source of ivory supply was accessible to Egypt alone;[31] the rival civilization of Sumer used for similar purposes the big conch-shells of the Persian Gulf, an admirable substitute so far as small objects were concerned but very limited as regards size—the largest shell plaque found in the royal cemetery at Ur measures only two-and-a-half inches either way (0.06 metre square). It might have been expected, therefore, that the Egyptian craftsmen, skilled as they were, would have kept a monopoly of the material; but in the latter part of our period (and yet more so in the first millennium) it was the ivory workers of the Phoenician coast towns whose reputation stood highest and whose goods travelled far along the trade routes of the Middle East. The Phoenicians had little artistic imagination and for that reason, or because their market was better suited so, the designs of their ivories are generally copied from Egyptian originals; it would appear that they were under-cutting the Egyptian industry by unfair imitation. This might have been the case had the Egyptians been freemen; as it was, they were Pharaoh's serfs and presumably the whole of their output was not more than sufficed for the requirements of the court; Pharaoh was not interested in retail trade with foreign parts and any surplus raw material would be sold readily enough to foreign factories. The Phoenicians then were licensed to receive ivory, and their imitations were what their clients wanted.

The ivories of Alalakh carry the matter farther (Pl. 16). Apart from the Sudan the only source of ivory in the Middle East was Niya, a tract of scrub jungle on the middle Euphrates, where there were still herds of elephants more or less artificially preserved by the Syrians and enthusiastically hunted by such Egyptian Pharaohs as pushed their conquests so far north—Thutmose III claims to have hunted 120. The more powerful of the Alalakh kings extended their dominions to include the elephant reserve and thereby secured the monopoly of the local ivory; actual tusks were found in the magazines of the palace of Yarim-Lim. Some of the ivory may have been sold as raw material to Syrians or Phoenicians (no evidence is forthcoming on the point), but certainly much of it was worked by local craftsmen, and the examples found show a remarkable variety of styles. Toilet-boxes in the form of ducks or adorned with the head of the goddess Hathor are indistinguishable from their Egyptian prototypes, but there is no reason for thinking that they are imports from Egypt; some reproduce faithfully a design found at Carchemish, presumably Hittite; one would on stylistic grounds pass as Hurrite, several have Cretan designs and might well have come from Knossos; yet all alike were made in this one centre in north Syria. The fact is that the interchange of ideas had gone so far that a skilled craftsman was sufficiently familiar with the arts of his neighbours to be able to manufacture for each market the type of goods that would appeal to the people there; admittedly the Syrian might be attracted by a Cretan-style object, but he would in that case want something that looked genuinely Cretan, and the ivory-worker therefore had to be well versed in the characteristics of each school of art. At Ugarit there has been found a magnificent ivory, a relief of the goddess who is 'Our Lady of

Beasts' (Pl. 17); it is Cretan in conception, but there is no means of deciding where it was actually made. The countries of the Middle East had their different art traditions, clearly defined, but the skilled craftsman of the fifteenth century working for export was apt to disregard frontiers.

Carpentry

Only in the dry climate of Egypt, in its hermetically sealed rock-cut tombs, does woodwork have a chance to survive the centuries; elsewhere it has almost perished; for actual specimens of the woodworker's craft we must therefore look to Egypt, and from the similarity of tools and from illustrations in other media assume that technique and fashions in other lands followed on much the same lines.

The Egyptian carpenter was handicapped by the lack of good native timber; the Nile valley supplied sycamore, fig, tamarisk, willow and acacia, but none of these is satisfactory material; most of his wood had to be imported, and from Africa and from the Lebanon he obtained cedar and cypress, ebony, juniper, fir, yew and oak. The small size of the native trees and the cost of imported timber were a challenge to the carpenter's ingenuity, and from a very early date he developed a remarkable skill in joinery;[32] as early as the Third Dynasty he was making coffins with halved, mitred and concealed mitre joints; a royal barge of the Twelfth Dynasty is built entirely of small pieces of wood set longitudinally in a sort of patchwork; he had learnt the use of thin veneers and could even make plywood—a six-ply of different sorts of timber. He had practically every tool used by the modern carpenter (except for the plane and the spoke-shave), and set squares and levels to control his work; many of these can be seen in use in a model of a workshop (Pl. 18) found in an Eleventh Dynasty tomb at Deir el Bahri showing a gang of carpenters at work together.

Partly because of the scarcity of wood having a pleasing grain, more, perhaps, because of Oriental taste, the Egyptian furniture-maker was apt to regard his woodwork as a frame or a background rather than something that could stand on its own merits; thus in the tomb of Tutankhamen there is wooden furniture in plenty, but in almost every piece the wood itself scarcely shows; it is painted, or it is masked with inlay, or it is entirely covered with gesso and gold foil. All-gilt chairs and beds would naturally not be found in every house—even in the royal tomb of Yuya some of the woodwork of the bed is exposed—but painted and inlaid furniture must have been very common. It has to be remembered that the Egyptian house was sparsely furnished; there were beds, tables, chairs, stools and chests or caskets, but very little else, so that the scope of the cabinet-maker was strictly limited. On the other hand, the well-to-do client would want to make the best effect possible with the few things that he required, and would prefer something coloured. Ruling out of consideration here the magnificent wooden reliefs and statues (such as the Old Kingdom panel of Hesire [Pl. 19, a]—but even this was originally painted—or the statue called 'the Sheikh el Beled'), because those were made by artists, not by craftsmen, we may say that the Egyptian woodworker, for all his manual skill, depended largely for the fine finish of his work on men of a different trade, on the ivory-carver, the goldsmith and the painter.

The same fashions must have prevailed over most of the Middle East. In Mesopotamia and in Syria the same carpenter's tools were in use, and there is no reason to suppose that the carpenters were less skilled than those of Egypt. The Syrians had much better wood ready to their hand and the Mesopotamians could easily get oak and walnut from the northern lands of the Upper Tigris, and they may therefore have been less inclined to mask their handiwork; certainly for the Early Dynastic period the royal cemetery at Ur gives us one example of wood inlaid with wood of a different sort and one of a wooden panel carved in relief and not disguised by any overcoat; Queen Shub-ad's big chest had only a single band of mosaic inlay, but whether the rest of the wood was exposed or was painted it was impossible to say. But already inlay was freely employed to embellish furniture, as in the case of the queen's sledge chariot, and, as with the gaming-board, the entire surface might be covered with encrustation in shell and coloured stone. In the fourteenth-century palace at Alalakh a mass of little squares and triangles and slips of ivory and narrow gold beading showed that the furniture had been encrusted very much in the fashion of the Damascus tables of today, and we can be sure that the 'ivory' bed of Hazael, king of Syria, found at Arslan Tash, represents a very ancient tradition. In China, in the Shang period, the walls of the wooden chambers of the Anyang tombs are sometimes painted (or enamelled) but sometimes very finely carved in relief; in some cases the wood is inlaid with carved pieces of boar's-tusk ivory. What is true of the tombs was presumably true of the houses of the living also; but though we know that wood entered largely into their construction nothing remains to show its character; all that can be said, in the dearth of further evidence, is that art of the late Chinese woodworkers seems to have its roots in the craftsmanship of Shang.

Textiles

As with woodwork so in the case of textiles Egypt is the only country in which so perishable a material has survived in quantities sufficient to illustrate the history of manufacture and the precise nature of the goods manufactured. It is from that point of view unfortunate that throughout the Bronze Age the range of Egyptian weaving was peculiarly limited. There is evidence enough to show that elsewhere techniques were employed and effects produced which were not paralleled in the Nile valley; long before the Bronze Age ended the weaver's art was fully developed and, in one country or another, centres of production were supplying their own or neighbouring peoples with fabrics of the most varied sorts.

Any attempt to trace these varieties to a single source would be misguided. Such a thing as the method of smelting copper, an operation difficult in itself and requiring a combination of circumstances which cannot occur often, is not likely to have been invented independently by different people, and we are justified in looking for a single place of origin. But weaving is essentially a simple and natural process. The interlacing of rushes or of grass is a child's amusement, and the savage employs it for his primitive needs; the advantage of using a finer fibre is obvious and the spinning of such, or of the wool and hairs of animals, was the common property of man in the Stone Age. And so simple is the actual weaving that it requires no machinery whatsoever. At the present day a village woman of north Syria with a few hanks of coloured wool and one stick driven into the ground will make an elaborate belt for a young man to wear; the belt, with its set pattern of design, its open-work and its tassels, is identical with those worn by the Hittite captains on a stone relief from Carchemish of the eighth century BC which must have been made in the same way; with a modern loom the rate of production would of course be speeded up indefinitely, but the machinery for the setting-up would be really intricate.

The development of the loom from the primitive business of hand-weaving was largely due to the desire to save labour. A number of warp pegs driven into the ground would take the place of the single stick carrying all the warps; then the warps are tied to a warp beam which itself may be secured by pegs; and each step forward prompted a further step. At a very early date we find in use the mat-loom, with which the process is really that of mat-making, the horizontal ground-loom, the vertical two-beamed loom and the warp-weighted loom, as well as small hand-frames; their dispersion shows clearly enough that these were not evolved one out of another but were invented independently. The horizontal loom is most characteristic of Egypt, the vertical two-beamed loom of the Levant and the warp-weighted loom of Europe; but by the time of the Eighteenth Dynasty at least Egypt was using both vertical and horizontal looms and Syria and Mesopotamia were doing the same. Ideas were exchanged and models were imitated, but that is not necessarily the explanation of the facts. The Syrian used both types of vertical loom, and it cannot be supposed that he borrowed the warp-weighted type from Europe; somebody in the east invented it, and it continued in use because for making certain sorts of cloth it had the advantage over the beamed loom of allowing more play to the warp threads. Europe did not borrow the warp-weighted loom from the Levant since, in the first place, all the evidence is in favour of its having been indigenous and, in the second, when closer association with the Levant introduced to them the two-beamed loom the European weavers quickly changed over from the one type to the other. India and China were equally independent in their invention.

In all these looms the weaving was at first done with the fingers. Later on the shed-rod was brought in to separate the alternate warp threads, then the rod-heddle to lift the alternate threads while the shed-rod gives passage to the weft, then the comb for pressing the weft tightly, then, for more complicated work, the heddles were multiplied; these were labour-saving devices which were of the greatest benefit to the weaver, but they were only new methods of producing what had already been produced without them; thus the draw-loom harness, used very early in China, was not introduced into Egypt until late in the first millennium BC, but long before that small all-over diaper patterns had been laboriously worked by hand.

To some extent the character of the loom was influenced by the nature of the thread used, which differed in different countries, and again local taste or prejudice decided the class of goods in local demand and therefore of the machinery used for their production.

Egypt was pre-eminently a flax-growing country, so would naturally make linen cloth;[33] the Egyptians also had a ritualistic prejudice against wool, as something essentially unclean, and although a little wool was woven for rugs, etc., that was a very minor industry. Linen is difficult to dye, and although a few experiments in this direction were made in early times (an example with blue warp stripes was found in the pyramid of Unas, Fifth Dynasty) they were soon abandoned; for personal wear the Egyptian preferred white, and the weavers accordingly concentrated their efforts on the production of white goods. In early times, naturally, it was the plain weave that they used, and this was indeed standardized until about 2500 BC; but after that date they manufactured a very wide range of linen cloth.

Linen fibre is very fine and very strong; when spun it makes a thread which is not only tough but also smooth, so that on a cloth loom the warp threads can be set up so closely as to touch each other and yet suffer no damage by friction when the weft is beaten in among them; when the warp is so closely set the number of wefts has to be reduced, the traditional Egyptian ratio being two or three wefts to four warps. In such 'plain' weaving it is the warp that bends to enclose the weft, and the latter remains relatively straight. Weaving of this sort is best done on a horizontal loom, with the warp not too tightly stretched, and with each shot the weft is taken across the entire width of the fabric. By varying the size and quality of the yarn an extraordinary variety of cloth can be made with what is really the same weave. Egypt became famous for the fineness of its tissues, the weavers making the stuff for those diaphanous garments which are so often represented in Egyptian paintings and reliefs; a striped effect was obtained by using a thick soft warp with an almost invisible weft, a spotted effect by 'snarls' in over-spun yarn on a muslin-like ground; from 2100 BC onwards the looped technique worked with rods was introduced, sometimes with an all-over effect like a Turkish towel, sometimes dispersedly, in uniformly spaced spots, and selvage fringes were produced in the same way. Down to the Eighteenth Dynasty white linen materials made on the principle of the plain weave in its many varieties formed the entire output of the Egyptian weavers, and so long as that was the case the horizontal loom met all their requirements. In the Eighteenth Dynasty the vertical loom also came into use.

Wool and the Vertical Loom

In Syria and Mesopotamia flax was grown relatively little and the natural material for the making of cloth was wool.

The wool fibre is fairly long and well adapted to spinning, but its surface is scaly, instead of being smooth as is that of the flax fibre, and instead of being straight it is crimped; the spun thread is loose in texture, is apt to stretch and is rough to the degree that threads in close contact catch on each other; consequently in weaving the warp threads have to be widely spaced, and, to prevent sagging, have to be kept under constant tension. Since tense warps could not bend round the weft, as in linen weaving, the weft had to be slack enough to bend round the warp; because the warps were spaced, more weft threads could be used, and the weft had to be beaten tightly together so much so that the warp did not show at all; this is the tapestry weave in its simplest form. For these technical reasons Syria and Mesopotamia preferred the vertical loom; it secured the warp tension more effectively and it facilitated the beating of the weft.

With the vertical loom (on which the alternate warp threads are pulled forward instead of being lifted) the shuttle does not easily pass between the warps, and if a single shot of weft were run through from selvage to selvage the slack necessary for its bending round the warp would not be evenly distributed; therefore only a few warps are opened at a time, and the resulting small section of weft is beaten in before the run is completed, and the weft can be turned back in the course of the row, so that adjacent patches can be worked in different colours. Wool takes colours more readily than does any other material, and from the outset the peoples of Syria showed their preference for gay clothing. In Egyptian wall-paintings Asiatics are always distinguished by their decorated garments, the 'cloak of many colours' woven for the young Joseph; such may be simple stripes, like the 'Seven Kings' of the modern Aleppo looms, or patterned goods for the making of which the tapestry loom was indispensable. Seeing that no actual fabrics are preserved it is mainly upon the Egyptian paintings that we must rely for information regarding the types of stuff manufactured in Syria, but literary sources leave no doubt as to the renown gained by the Syrian weavers throughout the Near East. Not only cloth for garments was produced; curtains, i.e., *killims* woven in the Gobelins technique and bearing patterns some of which survive to the present day, were in great demand, and the carved marble thresholds and floors of later Assyrian palaces merely reproduce the hand-woven carpets which for many centuries past must have been made in the factories and by the tent-dwellers of Mesopotamia and Iran (Pl. 14). In the late Middle Kingdom and in the Eighteenth Dynasty Syrian weavers were brought into Egypt, and from the time of Thutmose IV (1405 BC) the tombs in the Valley of the Kings furnish us with a series of splendid pattern-weavers in which the design is Egyptian but the technique Asiatic, while the material is still the linen traditional in Egypt. Presumably the Egyptian prejudice against wool still held good, but the use of linen in its stead, though it enforced a more limited range of colours, did have the advantage that its finer threads made possible a design more intricate than could have been produced in wool; thus the girdle of Ramses III (*c.* 1170 BC) gives a surface count of 173 by 77 threads to the square inch, and to get the pattern four or five threads are required for every one shown on the face. The very elaborate bands with figure subjects which adorn the dresses of kings and courtiers on Assyrian bas-reliefs would have been of Asiatic make, whether in wool or linen, and like the similar bands on one of the tunics from Tutankhamen's tomb may have been of embroidery worked by hand on a frame, but could have been made on a tapestry loom, though anything up to ten heddles would have been needed. The fact is that by the end of the second millennium BC the Middle East was producing both in plain weave and in tapestry most known types of fabric and those of a quality not easily surpassed.

For early Indian textiles we have virtually no material and absolutely no literary evidence. At Mohenjo-daro a few minute specimens of cloth have been found adhering to metal, enough to prove that the thread is of cotton, as indeed was to be expected, since cotton is indigenous to India. One example rather larger than the rest showed three weft threads to each warp thread, from which it would appear that the fabric was tapestry-woven on a vertical loom, but no more than that can be said. In the classical period India was exporting cloth and yarn made of wild silk (*Tusseh*) to the Middle East, and examples of it have been found at Palmyra, but for its manufacture at an early date there is no evidence. Real silk got from *Bombyx mori* was a Chinese monopoly until well on in the present era. Its early history remains unknown, the oldest actual examples found being tiny fragments preserved on bronzes of the Yin period, *c.* 1000 BC, which show patterns of twill damask; but Chinese technique was, at the time when comparisons first became possible, more highly developed than that of the western world; in the Han period the looms themselves were better and the satin and damask weavers were definitely superior. The silk thread, long, fine and smooth and as readily dyed as wool, offered a challenge to Chinese ingenuity; and the people whose craftsmen, in the Shang period, could produce by the *cire perdue* process the finest bronzes ever made in China, are likely to have responded successfully to the challenge.

In the art of weaving no other countries of the Old World could compete with those whose industry has been described above. In central Asia and in the Russian steppes the nomad breeders of sheep and goats used the wool—particularly the sheep's wool—for making felt, as they have made it up to the present day, and did not spin it into thread for the manufacture of cloth. In so far as they were brought into contact with their more civilized neighbours they did in time pick up some knowledge of textiles, but for the most part they were content to import ready-made goods; the craft of carpet-knotting they did take over, for the machinery required for that is of the simplest, and carpets are useful as tent furniture; but weaving proper was introduced late and was never highly developed.

Europe learnt the use of the vertical loom from Syria at a quite early date. Whereas in Syria both the two-beamed and the warp-weighted loom were in use simultaneously, Europe preferred the latter type, and it seems to have been the only one employed even in lands where culture was most advanced; right across the continent, from Greece to Norway, the finding of great quantities of loom weights on Bronze Age sites proved the ubiquity of the machine. Because the standards of life were so much lower in these countries than in Egypt or Mesopotamia there was no call for the fine qualities of stuff made there; because too on the warp-weighted loom the cloth is woven from the top downwards and the weft cannot be driven home so tightly, the tendency is for the cloth to be loose in texture and relatively coarse. The earliest examples come from the Swiss lake villages and date to the middle of the third millennium BC; they are of linen. Some of these are in twined work like basketry and can scarcely be called textiles, but others are definitely woven on a warp-weighted loom; a few have weft stripes, and there is one specimen, dated to about 2000 BC, of Soumak weave in which there are alternate rows of plain weave and weave with the weft wrapped with the fingers round the warp threads.

The next examples—and there are plenty of them—are those, well preserved by the action of peat, found in Scandinavian graves of the twelfth century BC; they are woollen stuffs, plain weaves with a maximum count of 13 warp and 10 weft threads to the square inch and therefore very coarse in comparison with contemporary Egyptian fabrics in which the count may be as high as 150 by 60. Some of the garments have patches of embroidery. It would seem that the Europeans of the Bronze Age experimented with and mastered a number of weaving techniques, but they did not originate them; the weavers borrowed the principles of their craft from Asia and, because their simple-minded clients were none too exigent, they aimed at no more than a modest quality of production; moreover, whereas in the eastern markets demand was such that weaving became a professional industry, in Europe it long remained a domestic task limited to the needs of the house, non-competitive and therefore conservative in the character of its output.

In the eastern countries also weaving had started as a purely domestic duty carried out by the women of the family, and right down into the Iron Age the housewife continued to be the 'spinster' and the weaver of household stuffs. In the great houses of the Egyptian nobles the womenfolk would be so employed, as we can see on the tomb reliefs in the wooden models of the Twelfth Dynasty, and in this as in other respects such a house would be largely self-sufficing; thus in the older Egyptian texts the terms 'weaver' and 'maid-servant' are synonymous, and it is only occasionally that their special task is distinguished by the title 'servants of the goddess Neith', the patroness of the art. In Middle Kingdom texts male weavers begin to be mentioned, and even 'weavers' shops', from which it is clear that weaving was becoming a commercial industry. Later we hear of 'chiefs of weavers', and the actual operatives are sometimes described as 'foreigners' or, more explicitly, 'Syrians', but nothing is said as to the way in which the industry was organized. Since Pharaoh himself owned the greater part of the flax-growing areas of Egypt and his harvest was so important that it was placed under the control of a high officer of the court, it may well be that Pharaoh held a monopoly of cloth-making, as of so many other trades—a monopoly, that is, of cloth made for trade and export, which would not interfere with the domestic industry practiced in the noble houses[34] and in the cottages of the serfs alike; certainly the employment of Syrians would be consistent with royal ownership.

In the other Middle East countries also weaving was at the beginning the women's task but tended to pass into the hands of men when finer makes required greater skill and when public demand so raised prices as to make the business worth a man's while. Thus with the Hebrews of the Exodus the elaborate hangings of the tabernacle, 'embroidered in blue and in purple, in scarlet and in fine linen, the work of the weaver, of those that devise cunning work' were made by Aholiab son of Ahisamuch and the 'wise-hearted men' taught by him; but ordinary weaving was done by the women, as when Hannah made yearly 'a little coat' for her son.

The Factory

For the Mesopotamians, dependent as they were upon foreign trade, and with woven fabrics of all sorts the chief items of export, cloth-making was too important economically to remain a domestic industry; men took part in it early, and it was carefully organized. The profession was hereditary. All professional weavers, wherever they worked, were members of a guild headed by a guild-master; he carried through all negotiations with the government officials, supplied them with lists of the members and arranged the payment of taxes due upon the goods produced. Most weavers worked not independently but in factories.[35] Work was highly specialized; the spinners, the dyers and the fullers belonged to separate guilds, but even within the weavers' guild there was specialization—we hear of linen-weavers, wool-weavers, weavers of coloured goods. Some of the factories were private concerns run by wealthy merchants; there may have been royal factories, for King Gimil-Sin, of the Third Dynasty of Ur, seems to have owned the workshops in which 'the garments of Gimil-Sin' were made; many belonged to the temples and manufactured goods not only for use in the service of the god but for the export trade also. The archaeological evidence for this is limited to a single case (one service room in the great Nin-gal temple at Ur had contained a loom—judging from the fact that there was a weaver's pit in the floor it would seem to have been a treadle loom) but numerous tablets throw light upon the subject. The weavers employed in the temple factories were both male and female; very often they were slaves (and in that case might be detailed for quite different work, such as helping to clear out irrigation-channels) but others were free citizens, and judging from the receipts issued by the temple authorities some of these may have worked at home, taking the thread from the temple stores and bringing back the finished cloth. Detailed account-tablets list the individual workers, the amount of wool received by each, the quantity, weight and quality of the cloth made, and the payment in kind (which in the case of slaves would be merely rations) over periods of a month or of six months; note is taken of deaths, of absences or of substitutes employed in place of a sick employee (Ur Texts, III, 1554); an item such as 'payments for the sick, for the days of absence (when unclean), and sundry expenditures of female workers for one month' has a curiously modern ring. Not less businesslike was the stocktaking, as, for instance, in the cloth-stores of Nannar, the Moon god, in his temple at Ur; the lists are immensely long (Ur Texts, III, 1504) and most detailed, giving measurements, weights and qualities and noting issues, generally against receipt—'Gift of wool to the royal musicians at the great smithy; receipt of Mašaga'.

Very similar employment ledgers and stock lists deal with other trades carried on in the Third Dynasty temples; we have those of the sculptor's shop, the goldsmith's shop, the lapidary's shop, the carpenter's shop, the smithy, the fuller and tanner's shop, the tailor-cutter's shop and the caulker's shop (Ur Texts, III, 1498), summing up the business done in them for the twelve months of the eleventh year of King Ibi-Sin. It is clear that the great bulk of goods intended for the market were manufactured under factory conditions and that under the Third Dynasty of Ur the temple workshops were the main producers; but that there were plenty of private concerns cannot be doubted, and constant references in the temple records to the hire of outside labour—including skilled labour—imply that there were also independent craftsmen working on their own.

After 2000 BC conditions seem to be modified. Individual workshop-owners play a larger part and civilian associations take over a good deal of what had been temple trade. The temples and the royal estate were still manufacturing centres but were now working for the market much more than formerly, and they now had to meet far more competition; the business documents of the Larsa and Kassite periods come for the most part from the archives of civilian merchant families. The change of ownership must have had the result of increasing the power of the trade guilds and, incidentally, of raising the status of the craftsman; in the temple workshops the majority of the workers were slaves; in the privately run factories the majority would be freemen though slave-labour also was used,[36] and even when a slave was apprenticed to learn the trade his rights were properly safeguarded and he might even look forward to entering into partnership with his master at the end of his term of apprenticeship.

NOTES TO CHAPTER IV

1. Professor F. Schachermeyr points out that the great river valleys were not the only sites of permanent occupation as attested by the discoveries at Jarmo and Jericho. See L. Braidwood, *Digging beyond the Tigris* (New York, 1953), and K. Kenyon, *Digging up Jericho* (New York, 1957). For the controversy surrounding the dating and relative age of the sites of Jarmo and Jericho, see *Antiquity*, XXX (1956), and XXXI (1957).
2. S. N. Kramer, *From the Tablets of Sumer*, p. 61. The quotations are for the most part *verbatim*.
3. See p. 520.
4. On the difficult problems concerning the domestication and utilization of the camel see, among others, R. Walz in *Zeitschrift der Deutschen Morgenländischen Gesellschaft*, 101 (1951), pp. 29–51, and IVème Congrès International des Sciences Anthropologiques et Ethnologiques, Vienne, 1952, *Actes* (publ. 1956), pp. 190–204; W. M. Misekell, in *Southwestern Journal of Anthropology*, XI (Albuquerque, 1955), pp. 236–42. On the camel in Egypt see also the bibliography in Institut Français d'Archéologie Orientale, *Bulletin*, XLIX, n. 2 (Cairo, 1950).
5. Professor F. Schachermeyr stresses also the role of the Hurrians and the Mitanni to both of whom the use of the chariot was known.

There is evidence that horses were imported from Armenia at an even earlier date. See F. Hancar, *Das Pferd in prähistorischer und früher historischer Zeit* (Wien, 1956), pp. 550 sq.

6. Cf. *supra,* pp. 104–05, n. 25.
7. Some authorities have maintained 'that the Indus valley people knew the horse at about 2500 BC at the latest'. See R. C. Majumdar, ed., *The History and Culture of the Indian People:* I, *The Vedic Age* (London, 1951), p. 194.
8. Lewis-holes are slots cut in the stone so as to provide a grip to pincers or other tools used in moving the block.
9. Professor J. Leclant observes that Egyptian colonnades, particularly during the later period, were covered with wooden roofs [see *Les Cahiers Techniques de l'Art* (Strasbourg, 1957), p. 37, n. 71]. Wooden beams of considerable dimensions may have been employed, since, as early as the Old Empire, during the Fourth Dynasty, the boat found near the Cheops pyramid comprised enormous planks of wood up to 23 metres in length; see H. Ricke, *Orientalische Literaturzeitung* (1959), col. 22, and *infra,* pp. 319–20, n. 32.
10. Professor J. Leclant draws attention to the fact that the Egyptian temples also included considerable areas of brickwork; all the surrounding walls were, for instance, in brick. Nor should it be forgotten that this far less resistant material has not always survived the passage of millennia, nor has sufficient attention always been paid to it by excavators who were almost always primarily in search of stone and who experienced the utmost difficulty in extracting the bricks which were mixed with the accumulations of silt in which they lay. On the difficulty of the excavation of sun-dried brick in Egypt, see *Orientalia,* Vol I (1950), p. 362, and Figs. 2–5.
11. An exception to this is the city wall of Hattusas where there remain at least five courses of heavy masonry; but the blocks are roughly cut to shape but not dressed as ashlar. There are late exceptions, as one at Carchemish.
12. Professor I. M. Diakonoff doubts whether nationalist sentiment played any role here.
13. Professor I. M. Diakonoff maintains that it is impossible to speak of government before the end of the urban revolution.
14. Professor I. M. Diakonoff considers that the attribution of sentimental origins to plano-convex bricks lacks conclusive evidence.
15. The discoveries of Sakaria Goneim at Saqqarah have led to the abandonment of the idea that the Sinai relief is First Dynasty Semer-Khet. It is rather a Third Dynasty Semer-Khet relief. cf. *Orientalia,* XXIII (1954), p. 304; J. Cerny, *The Inscriptions of Sinai,* II (1955), p. 53.
16. It is worth remarking that when a state silver coinage was introduced in Asia in the eighth century BC the Syrian merchants commonly surcharged the coins with their private stamps as a guarantee of the purity of the metal.
17. On iron metallurgy in Egypt, the Sudan and Africa, see Jean Leclant, Colloque International. Le fer à travers les âges, *Actes* (Nancy, 1955); Memoire No. 16, *Annales d'Histoire* (Nancy, 1956), pp. 83–91.
18. Doubts have been expressed as to the exact nature of the *ayas.* See R. C. Majumdar, ed. *The History and Culture of the Indian People, I, The Vedic Age* (London, 1951), p. 397.
19. Professor Shigeki Kaizuka and his colleagues point to the discovery of an example of iron edge put on bronze weapons which appears to date from the latter part of the Shang dynasty.

20. To the ancient Egyptians, the God Ptah was the patron of the goldsmith craftsmen, connected with dwarfing and certain forms of physical deformation. See P. Montet, 'Ptah-patèque et les orfèvres', in *Revue Archéologique,* 6ème série, XL (1952), pp. 1–11.
21. See C. F. A. Schaeffer, *Ugaritica,* II (Paris, 1950), pp. 56–115. If the facts are beyond dispute, Schaeffer's theory seems hypothetical to Professor F. Schachermeyr.
22. Parimachu (or rather Pareamakhu, which is the transcription of the ancient Egyptian Paraemhab, or Paraemhat) seems in fact to have been a doctor. (E. Weidner, *KUB,* III, No. 67); see E. Laroche, *Revue Hittite et Asiatique,* XV, 60 (1957), p. 87, No. 174, 3, and the bibliography contained in Jean Leclant, *Bibliotheca Orientalis,* XV (1958), p. 232, n. 44.
23. A case in point is that of the architect Nekhebu in the Sixth Dynasty. He says, 'His Majesty found me a common builder, and His Majesty appointed me to the offices of Inspector of Builders and Superintendent of a Guild. And His Majesty placed me as King's Architect and Builder, then Royal Architect and Builder under the King's supervision. And His Majesty appointed me Sole Companion, King's Architect, and Builder in the Two Houses.'
    In fact, Nekhebu's elder brother held all these offices and Nekhebu had worked under his brother continuously, so that a certain amount of nepotism may be suspected; and Nekhebu was never a 'common builder' for he was an educated youth apprenticed to his brother 'to do the writing'. His rise, however, was none the less spectacular.
24. See Dr R. J. Forbes, *Studies in Ancient Technology* (Leiden, 1955), p. 123.
25. As a scholar on behalf of the National Commission for Israel points out, the potter's wheel appeared almost contemporaneously in Mesopotamia and Palestine, some time in the second half of the fourth millennium BC. Clear traces of the wheel can be observed on Chalcolithic vessels from Ghassul beyond the Jordan.
26. In the opinion of Professor D. J. Mulvaney, students of prehistoric art might dispute Sir Leonard's remark regarding the slight aesthetic value of the Beaker pottery.
27. See H. G. Creel, *The Birth of China* (London, 1936), p. 105.
28. The subject is carefully treated by H. C. Beek, 'Glass before 1500 BC', in *Ancient Egypt and the East* (London, June 1934).
29. Professor F. Schachermeyr points out that in the very earliest periods, before pottery had been invented, there was a very important stone-bowl culture in Cyprus, Syria, and Palestine (Jericho, Abu Gosh) as well as Mesopotamia. Later on, stone bowls were brought from Tell Halaf to Anatolia, Soskie and the Danubian basin.
30. The reference is to alabaster lamps and unguent jars; the lids oı the Canopic jars were carved by sculptors, not by vase-makers, and the difference is striking.
31. There were, however, elephants ın north-western Syria. See pp. 305, 544 (n. 15); also R. O. Barnett, *Journal of Hellenist Studies,* 68 (1948), pp. 6–7.
32. Professor J. Leclant draws attention to the great cedarwood boats of the Fourth Dynasty, the elements of which were discovered in 1954 in perfect order in something resembling a dry dock to the south of the Cheops pyramid at Giza. These 43 metres long, and as high as 7 metres at the stern and 5 metres at the prow. The longest pieces serving as the framework of the hull are 23 metre-planks, 50 centimetres thick and 75 centimetres high, each weigh-

ing 2 tons. The monoxylic oars were 9 metres long. Thus excellent raw materials were available to the Egyptian carpenters. Particular attention should be given to the method of mounting the craft, almost entirely without the aid of any metal element (only three copper nails were found for the whole boat).

The planks were pierced with holes making it possible to thread cords binding one plank to another. These cords were passed inside the boat and, except in rare instances, were not visible from the exterior. Thus the boat was constructed of planks literally 'sewn' together. In the water the wood swelled, while the cords tightened, thus ensuring perfect junction of the elements, and making the boat waterproof, so that it was unnecessary to caulk the hull.

33. 'The priests wear only a linen garment and shoes made of papyrus; it is forbidden for them to adopt other clothes' (Herodotus, II, 37); 'the priests do not introduce woollen garments into the sanctuary, nor are they buried in them; the religious law forbids this' (Herodotus, II, 81). Similar taboos are set forth in the Gnomon of the Idiologue (71, 75–76) and various Greek papyri.
34. H. E. Winlock, *Models of Daily Life in Ancient Egypt* (Cambridge, Mass., 1955).
35. Professor I. M. Diakonoff would have preferred the word 'workshop' rather than 'factory'; for him the latter term is more usual in connection with machinery and hired labour.

    But for Sir Leonard Woolley a single craftsman has his 'workshop'; what is discussed here is a big shop with numerous work people employed by a single owner who is not himself a craftsman. Places of this sort did have machinery—for weaving, for instance—and much labour, even if it was slave-labour and not hired labour.
36. The text of this paragraph is based partly on the comments of Professor I. M. Diakonoff.

[B.M.

14 *Assyrian reproduction in stone of a woven rug. London, British Museum*

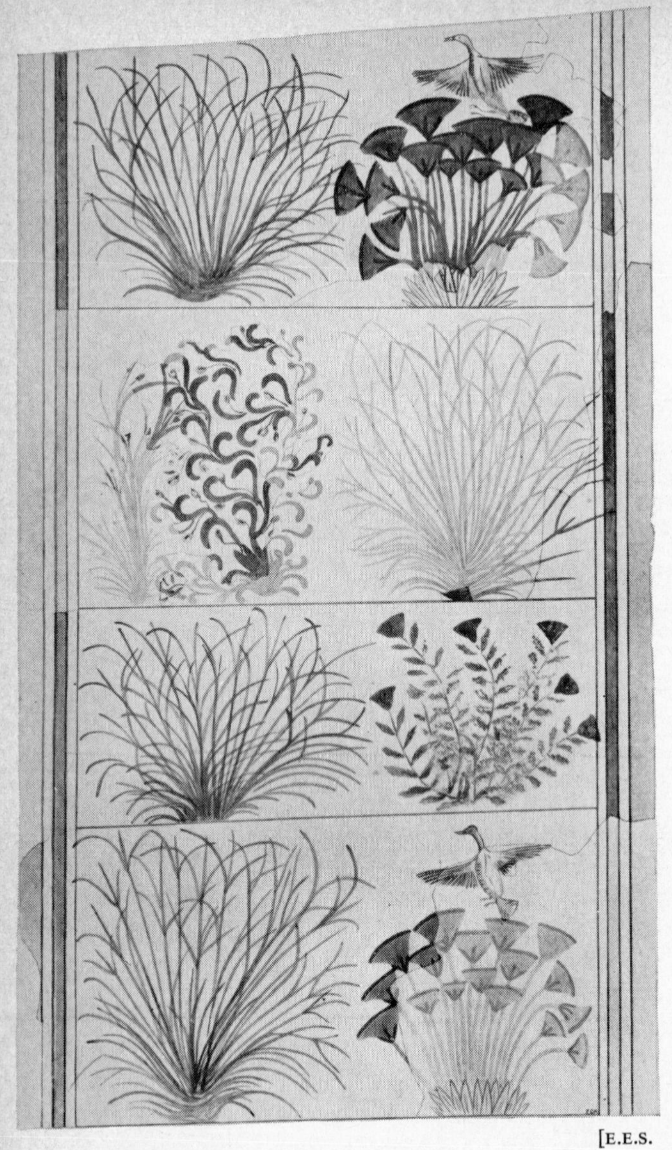

[E.E.S.

15 *Tell el-Amarna: floor frescoes*

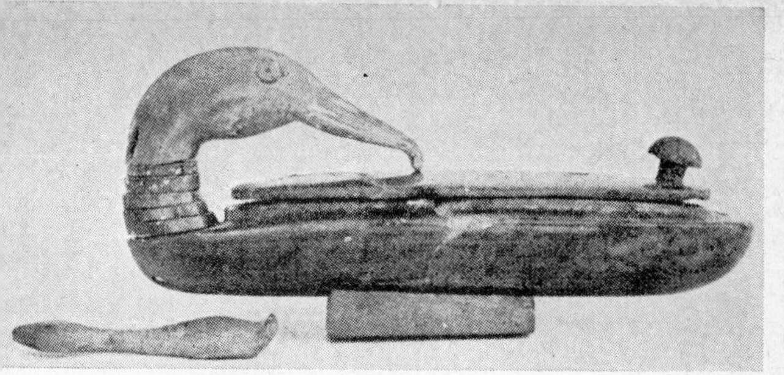

[Antakia

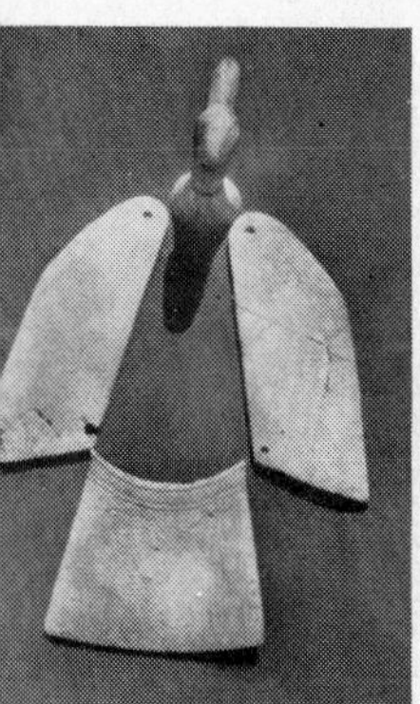

[Antakia

[B.M.

[B.M.

[B.M.

16 *Alalakh: ivory work*

[Schaeffer

17 *Ugarit (Ras Shamra): 'Our Lady of the Beasts'*

[photo Egyptian Expedition, M.M.A.

18

Egyptian carpenters at work. New York, Metropolitan Museum of Art

(a)

[D.A.E.

(b)

[D.A.E.

19

(a) *The palette of Narmer*
(b) *Wooden relief of Hesire*

[H.M.

20 *The Phaestos Disk. Museum of Candia, Crete*

(a)

[B.M.

21

(a) *Proto-Dynastic ivory statuette of a king. London, British Museum*

(b) *The Lion palette. London, British Museum*

(b)

[B.M.

(a)

[D.A.E.

(b)

[M.E.

22 *Egyptian Sculpture I*

(a) *Statue of Khafra*

(b) *Statue of Ramses II. Turin, Museo Egizio*

(c) *Prostrate figure of Ramses II*

(c)

[D.A.E.

(a)

[*photo Chuzeville*

(b) [C.G.F.

23 *Egyptian Sculpture II*
(a) *Bust of Akhenaton. Paris, Louvre*
(b) *Twelfth Dynasty head*
(c) *Head of Thutmose III*

(c)

[D.A.E.

(a) [Jean Leclant

24 (a) *Akhenaton kissing Queen Nefertiti, relief from the tomb of Mahu, Tell el Amarna*

(b) *Karnak: relief of Seti I*

(b) [D.A.E.

(a) [M.M.A.

25 (a) *Thebes: Tomb of Neferhotep, mourners on boat*
(b) *Akhenaton's daughters. Oxford, Ashmolean Museum*

(b)

(a) [D.A.E.

26 (a) *Egyptian tomb painting: the dead 'watches' life*
(b) *Tutankhamen's painted casket*

(b) [D.A.E.

[photo Chuzeville

27

Mari: The King's investiture, wall painting. Paris, Louvre

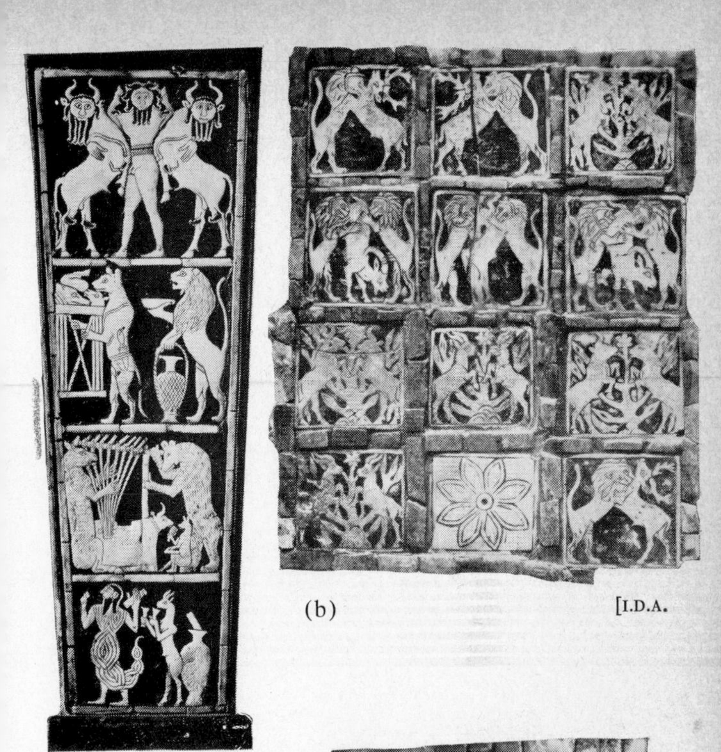

(a) [Penn

(b) [I.D.A.

(c) [B.M.

28 *Ur shell plaques*

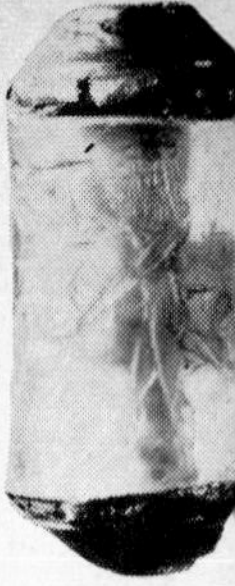

[I.D.A.

[Penn

[B.M.

29

Sumer: Early Dynastic and Sargonid impressions from cylinder seals, c. *2500 B.C.*

[Penn.

CHAPTER V

THE ECONOMIC STRUCTURE

TRADE

TRADE, in the simple form of barter, is as old as man. Man's wants have never been limited to what he could produce for himself; and if he could not by force seize that which he coveted then he was prepared to acquire it by exchange. Should he happen to possess something that other people desired he might be able to live on the proceeds of barter; when local demand was satisfied he would look for clients farther afield, and where the objects to be bartered were small and easily portable his market might extend very far. Thus in the Chalcolithic Age, we find in the house ruins of the early al'Ubaid period at Ur beads made of amazonite which must have been imported from the Nilghiri hills of southern India; presumably they had not come directly but had been passed from hand to hand, but even so they illustrate in a surprising fashion the ramifications of international exchange. Such early contacts, casual as they may be, are noteworthy as explaining the interaction of local cultures, but they are no more than the background of trade proper; the sporadic and unorganized adventures of the individual pedlar led up to but scarcely form part of the history of commerce.

As we have seen (Chapter IV, Metallurgy), it was the introduction of metal and the development of metallurgical science that more than anything else made trade essential. The smith had no time for anything outside his own profession, and he was manufacturing things which other people could not make but everybody needed; exchange therefore was a mutual necessity. But the smith's raw material was seldom to be found close at hand; he had to rely upon large-scale imports, which again had to be paid for, and that meant organization of a far-reaching sort; the retail trade with his neighbours at home was easy enough, but the importation of ore or crude metal from abroad was a business with which he could not cope himself.

In different countries the problem was approached in different ways. On the one hand we have, in Egypt, where 'Egypt' and 'Pharaoh' were identified, a system which corresponds to what in the modern world would be called the nationalization of industry. On the other hand, in Mesopotamia, by what we may term a capitalist system,[1] the individual merchant acts on his own initiative but within the limits of the law and subject to the taxation imposed by the state in the general interest. And, lastly, in certain communities such as the Phoenician coast towns, it would seem that the merchants (of whom the ruler would be one) controlled the state in the interests of trade. These differences were not due to ideologies deliberately formulated: man had not then acquired so philosophical an outlook; they resulted mainly from their economic character and resources; but they were very real, and it is interesting to observe the success or failure—and the reasons for the success or failure—of commerce organized on principles so fundamentally opposed.

Egypt

In Egyptian texts, down to the end of the second millennium BC, there is nowhere any mention of merchants. This silence does not mean, as some authorities have assumed, that commerce was non-existent, but it does imply that private merchants, even though they existed and might become wealthy, yet enjoyed no such social rank as would enable them to build rich tombs for themselves and thereby leave a memorial that could endure to our time. We have no knowledge of any Egyptian laws regulating trade, and this again tends to show that the private trader played no very important part in the land's economy. The fact was that all commerce was in the hands of Pharaoh, and the divine Pharaoh was, of course, a law unto himself.

As regards internal trade, it must be remembered that in theory at least the whole land of Egypt was the personal property of Pharaoh. It is true that the feudal nobility installed by him after the conquest of the delta by the rulers of the First Dynasty did in time encroach upon the royal authority and attempt to make themselves independent, but the establishment of the Eighteenth Dynasty saw the elimination of those hereditary peers and the confiscation of their landed property, which all passed again to the crown. It is true too that the great temples acquired by royal gift enormous territories, the revenues from which provided for the maintenance of the priesthood and the observance of the ritual service of the gods; but those possessions did result from royal gift, and the gift could be revoked, as when Akhenaton closed down the

Amon temple at Thebes and seized its property. The time was yet to come when the priests would prove more powerful than the king, and in the meantime the Pharaohs of the Empire could fairly look upon Egypt as their personal estate. The entire produce of the land therefore was Pharaoh's. An army of administrators supervised the rural economy of the Nile valley, regulated the canal system and collected the proportion of the harvest that the tenant farmers owed as taxes to their overlord; there was little opening here for the private speculator, and although, obviously, a man might sell his superfluous grain to a townsman, or to the local baker, this was all small-scale dealing in which the state was not called to interfere. All major operations could be carried out only by the controllers of the royal granaries. Again, Pharaoh enjoyed an absolute monopoly of the stone quarries, of gold and copper mining, and of major building operations.

It was clearly to the country's advantage that the exploitation of the rich gold-fields in the eastern desert should be reserved to the state and not left to the mercy of private speculators intent on making fortunes for themselves; gold had very early become a weapon far too powerful for the ruler to allow of its source passing into the hands of possible rivals, and the embargo upon gold mining was justified both upon public grounds and as a dynastic safeguard.

With copper the case was somewhat different. The mines of Sinai lay far off, in a desolate country where the maintenance of mine-workers required elaborate organization for food and transport and where troops were needed to ward off raids by the wild nomads; the accounts that have come down to us of the expeditions to Sinai show that nothing short of the royal authority could have undertaken what were in fact military campaigns on a large scale. Pharaoh's monopoly of copper mining was natural and indeed inevitable in the circumstances.

The monopoly of stone quarrying and that of building construction are complementary. Only the Pharaoh built temples.[2] He was also obliged to construct his own tomb—pyramid or rock-hewn chambered shaft—with its mortuary chapel, etc.; and he would reward the faithful service of his officers by the bestowal of a tomb such as the *mastabas* that surround the pyramids of Gizeh or the (unfinished) carved and painted rock tombs in the hills behind Tell el Amarna.[3] No other stone buildings were erected in Egypt (Chapter IV, Architecture), and therefore no other than Pharaoh had need of building stone; but his own works were normally on so vast a scale that no private contractor could have undertaken them, even if it had been morally possible for Pharaoh to delegate to another the most essential of his royal duties.

The well-being of Egypt depended upon the goodwill of the gods, whom therefore it was important to propitiate, so that the building and the upkeep of their temples was an essential function of the government, that is, of the Pharaoh. It was also bound up with the personality of the divine Pharaoh, and the country could not afford his extinction, which would result from the corruption of his mortal body and from the neglect of the ceremonies which assured his continued life in the after-world. The building of the colossal tombs of the Egyptian kings was as much an act of faith as was the building of the great cathedrals of mediaeval Europe, and its object was not simply to minister to the vainglory of the ruler but to take out, as it were, an insurance policy for the country. Therefore from the moment of his accession to the throne Pharaoh was busy with the preparation of his tomb, and this had to be done by direct labour. There was no question of letting out the work to contractors; the vast numbers of labourers required were called up by the *corvée* system put into force at the time of year when agricultural work was slack, and they were in Pharaoh's own service, organized on military lines (the larger gangs were called *aperu,* a military term) and supplied with rations from the royal stores. Quarrying, transport and building were all under Pharaoh's sole control, but matters did not end there. Tombs and temples alike required sculptors and goldsmiths and skilled craftsmen of all sorts, and they too were in Pharaoh's service, as is made clear by, for example, the reliefs and inscriptions in the tomb of Rekhmirê, who was responsible for their inspection. Theoretically the craftsmen were free men; but the ablest of them were engaged by the king at a wage for life, and their sons after them; undoubtedly there were also free craftsmen working privately, sometimes in the employment of a great noble, sometimes entirely on their own, finding their clients in the local market; but such would scarcely be the masters of their craft.

With the state, in the person of the Pharaoh, exercising such complete control over the natural resources and over the labour forces of the country, there was clearly very little scope left for 'big business' by the private merchants. Their place was taken by an elaborate civil service acting with the authority and for the benefit of the crown. Of course there was always plenty of petty retail trade in the village market-square and in the town bazaar, though most of the things sold there, grain or oil, animals or manufactured goods, had to pay taxes to the government. But even in the field of direct trade the merchant's opportunities were very limited; as early as the Third Dynasty we hear of a 'director of all the King's flax'[4] and we may be sure that in all commodities the main stocks were either owned or controlled by the Pharaoh.

But if the internal trade of Egypt was to so large an extent a royal monopoly, the same was yet more true of foreign commerce.

Egypt, as organized by the Pharaohs, was to an unusual degree self-sufficing. The ordinary citizen could be housed, clothed and fed, could furnish himself with the tools of his trade, with the raw material required by his craft and with the ornaments desired by his wife, entirely from the resources of the kingdom; a bountiful nature supplied all the necessities of life. Egypt's foreign trade was a trade in luxuries, so far as the individual was concerned, but some at least of those luxuries were really needed for the land's well-being. The temples could not be built without heavy timbers of hardwood such as did not grow in the Nile valley, and the temple ritual demanded the use of incense which, too, the valley did not produce. Oil—'the remedy of the body'—was needed both for medicinal and for magico-religious purposes; myrrh, cassia and resin were used for mummification; silver was not found in Egypt and was therefore precious as well as beautiful, so that silver offerings would be peculiarly acceptable to the gods. Obviously it was Pharaoh's duty to arrange for the import of things serving such religious purposes and obviously it was to his interest to keep it in his own hands; foreign trade therefore became a royal monopoly.

The only profitable commercial lines were two, northwards to the Syrian coast and southwards to the semi-fabulous Land of Punt; for the first, sea traffic was essential; for Punt, goods could be carried overland by way of the Sudan, or, better, could go by ship from a port on the Red Sea.

Byblos was at the start the outlet for Syrian trade. Egypt's connection with Byblos goes back to very early days, before the Two Kingdoms of the Nile valley had been unified and before Semitic incomers had founded the cities of Sidon and Tyre. From the temples of Byblos there have been recovered Egyptian polished stone axes, flint knives, beads and palettes dating to the pre-Dynastic age;[5] then comes an alabaster vase fragment bearing the name of Khasekhamui of the Second Dynasty and later others with the names of Cheops, Mykerinus, Unas, and, for the Sixth Dynasty, Teti and the two Pepis; clearly no private merchant could have brought royal treasures of the sort. Actually the Third Dynasty Pharaoh Sneferu mentions the return of a fleet of forty vessels bringing pine logs, some destined for the roofing of the royal palace and some for naval construction; Egypt was therefore already building sea-going ships of imported Syrian timber, probably on the Syrian model, but judging from the reliefs in the funerary temple of Sahuré (Fifth Dynasty), by methods which were inherited from the old boat-builders of the Nile. In the same reliefs we see that the ships carried their complement of regular troops, a further proof that the vessels of the Byblos line (they were called *'kebent'*, Keben = Byblos) were royal property. That a great deal of the merchandise from Byblos, and later from Tyre and Sidon, was carried in Syrian bottoms to some Egyptian port designated for their use (as Naukratis was for the Greeks of after times) may be taken for granted; we see this in the case of Wenamon who, although an envoy, the High Priest of Amon in the days of Ramses XI, travelled in a Syrian ship to Byblos, and what was true of the late period must have been true of the early. The regular cabotage traffic was conducted by the shipmasters of the Levant coastal towns and only when some special project called for extraordinary supplies did a whole squadron of the Pharaoh's *kebent* cargo ships go out to sea; their successful return from such a mission was an event worthy to be recorded in the royal annals. But we never hear of privately owned Egyptian vessels taking part in the Levant trade.

The strict control of sea-borne traffic must have been a matter of mutual agreement, but it is not easy to determine exactly what was the relation between Pharaoh and the merchant princes of the Syrian coast. With Byblos the connection was very close. On a sculptured relief dedicated in a local temple Pepi actually calls himself 'Lord of Byblos', but the phrase may imply not so much suzerainty as seniority in a partnership. Similarly, when Pepi I's officer, Uni, leads an expedition by sea and lands on the coast below Mount Carmel to punish a rebellious tribe, the Pharaoh may merely have been striking at the base of the Beduin who had been raiding the far-off Egyptian frontier, or he may have been called in by his Syrian business ally to police the latter's hinterland. In any case, commercial relations depended upon goodwill, and where one of the parties was the Pharaoh of Egypt that goodwill was bound to have its political aspect. The various objects bearing the names of early Pharaohs found at Byblos were presumably the honorific presents bestowed upon a friend less important than the giver but none the less independent; but the danger was that the senior partner might aim at undivided control. The big portrait statues of Twelfth Dynasty kings unearthed at Ugarit were set up there not as signs of friendship but as evidence of Egyptian domination over yet another outlet for Asiatic trade; commerce was, as often, the forerunner of imperialism. The other danger involved in the royal monopoly was that international trade was made dependent upon the political and military strength of a single individual or dynasty. The story of the luckless Wenamon is familiar, but that example (coming after the end of the period dealt with in this volume) had its precedents in earlier times of Egyptian weakness; when the Sixth Dynasty collapsed the Levant trade collapsed with it: 'Now that the ships go no more to Byblos how shall we replace for our mummies the "*ash*" wood of which one used to make coffins for the priests and whose resin served to embalm the nobles?'

Trade with the south—with the ill-defined Land of Punt, at the south end of the Red Sea, which perhaps embraced the Yemen as well as Somaliland—was easily reserved against private enterprise but, outside the Egyptian frontier, was not subject to Pharaoh's political control. The principal imports were precious woods, ivory, myrrh and frankincense, gold and panther skins and ostrich feathers. Much of this could come overland or by way of the Nile to the southern boundaries of Egypt, brought there by Sudanese merchants or more simply by wandering tribesmen, casually, often in small consignments passed, it may be, from hand to hand (hence the ambiguity of the name 'Punt') and carried north because rumour said that high prices could be got in Egypt. Traffic of this sort goes back to pre-Dynastic times, when frontiers were ill defined, but with the unification of Egypt steps were soon taken to safeguard the southern boundary against Sudanese raiders and, at the same time, to take advantage of the commercial possibilities of the land. The obvious centre of control was the cataract region where the barren desert closes in on the rocky ravine of the Nile, forcing all traffic to take one and the same route; incidentally, it was from this ravine that Pharaoh could quarry the granite which was so prized for temple building. Khasekhamui first, and after him Sneferu, invaded the Sudan and established his frontier;[6] its maintenance was entrusted to the nomarchs of Elephantine the head of whose family bore, in the reign of Mernere, the title 'Keeper of the Door of the South', while other officials of his staff were entitled 'Caravan-conductor, who brings the products of the countries to his Lord'. Elephantine in fact became the customs house and collecting centre for overland trade with the south. Not content with the irregular arrival of merchandise dribbling up through the Sudan, Pharaoh now began to send expeditions southwards from Elephantine. These were military raids intended to maintain Egyptian prestige, to loot, and to buy. Harkhuf, the Lord of Elephantine, conducted three such expeditions under Mernere and a fourth under Pepi II; on his third journey he brought back three hundred donkey-loads of 'incense, ebony, oil (?), grain, panther skins, ivory, boomerangs and all manner of good things', and on his fourth journey he secured a pigmy, reckoned by the royal court to be the chief treasure of all. Under the Sixth Dynasty a new fortress and customs-house was built at Kerma, at the head of the Third Cataract, which might act as an advanced trading-post to which the Sudanese could bring their goods in exchange for the jewellery and the knives, the strong scents and the rolls of white or dyed cloth which then, as in the nineteenth century AD, found a ready market in Africa.

But these royal expeditions were expensive and dangerous (we hear of more than one being cut up by the savage tribes whom they encountered) and not likely to be always profitable; moreover, the difficulties of transport meant that the heavier and bulkier goods could be obtained only in very small quantities. The alternative was to make use of the sea route, but that was an adventure which, so far as we know, could be risked only occasionally and when demands were more than usually urgent. The first Punt mission recorded in Egyptian annals was organized by Sahuré of the Fifth Dynasty (there may have been earlier expeditions about which we know nothing) and it must have taxed even the royal resources. The barges that brought copper across from the Sinai mines were too small for the present purposes and probably not seaworthy; ships, therefore, sea-going vessels of the *kebent* type, had to be built on the Red Sea coast, and all the timber for these, the carpenters and the sailors, together with all their rations and equipment, had to be transported from Koptos to the improvised dockyards. When the ships were ready the soldiers had to come too, for there was no knowing what reception the squadron would get in the strange lands for which it was heading. In order to benefit by the monsoon winds the ships had to sail in June and start back about the beginning of October, and even so the last 350 miles would have to be covered with the oar in face of the north wind; January or February might see them safely home—granted, that is, that the pilots knew enough about the weather conditions and that the people of Punt could be induced to come to terms quickly. Sahuré's expedition was a success and encouraged his descendants; he brought back 80,000 measures of myrrh, 6,000(?) weight of electrum and 2,600 planks of ebony. Isesi, a later Pharaoh of the Fifth Dynasty, sent a mission which managed to procure him a pigmy. Under the Sixth Dynasty more expeditions were made, and by the time of the Middle Kingdom matters may perhaps have been made easier by the digging of a canal connecting the Nile with the Red Sea so that ships of the Mediterranean fleet could be transferred to the African trade route. In the Eleventh Dynasty the Pharaoh Mentuhotep III not only sent ships to Punt but also built road-stations and dug wells along the Koptos track. Under Sesostris II of the Twelfth Dynasty expeditions had become more or less normal affairs; but the most famous of all was that sent by Queen Hatshepsut in the Eighteenth Dynasty which brought back thirty-one living myrrh trees to decorate the façade of her temple at Deir el Bahri. That expedition was apparently the first which had gone from Egypt to Punt since Hyksos times; 'Why have ye come hither to this land which the people of Egypt know not?' cried the astonished Puntites; 'Did ye descend upon the roads of heaven, or did ye sail upon the waters, upon the sea of God's-Land?' The long gap in a profitable traffic shows again how, with a government monopoly in foreign trade, the collapse of the government means the complete severance of commercial ties; there were no merchants in Egypt to carry on Pharaoh's business for him.

Mesopotamia

In Mesopotamia the development of the high civilization of the Sumerians and their successors depended entirely upon foreign trade. The amazingly fertile soil of the river valley gave them an agricultural surplus, which was the essential medium of exchange, and the leisure which could make possible specialization in the arts and crafts as well as the appreciation of the amenities of life; but their country produced no good timber, no good stone, no gold, silver or copper; all the raw materials for the arts and crafts had to be imported in return either for agricultural produce or for manufactured goods. Some of the raw materials had to be brought from very far away, and the carriage of bulky goods such as grain over great distances was both difficult and expensive, so that it was better to make payment in something more portable and of greater value in proportion to its size and weight; the need was best met by manufactured goods, but those had to be of a quality that would find them a ready market abroad. If you wanted a good life you had to import, and to import successfully you had to develop taste and technique in industry; local conditions enforced civilization upon Sumer. Thus it is hardly a paradox to say that the Sumerians were, in their day, the world's best metal-workers because they had no metal of their own. The credit for the discovery of the principles of metallurgy must go to the peoples of eastern Anatolia, living in the Lake Van–Caucasus area; but because those people found that they could get easy money by the export of their copper they had no incentive to carry the art of metal-working beyond its purely utilitarian stage; as metal-workers they were almost immediately outclassed by their Mesopotamian clients, and it was only after the second millennium BC that they developed a school of their own—and the Urartu school even then is largely derivative. The Sumerians were driven into trade, and the trade took them far afield; they were driven into manufacture, and what they made for export had to sell on its merits; the Sumerian city states were based on agriculture, corresponding roughly to the canalization areas of the river valley, but the Sumerian cities flourished as centres of business and industry.

According to Sumerian belief the patron god of the city state was the absolute owner of the state territories. Parts of the divine estate would be retained and were farmed directly by the god's priests, with serfs as labourers, but the vast proportion was let to individuals; the latter had of course to pay their rent to the temple, in grain or cattle or farm produce, but with what was left to them they could do as they pleased, and their freedom to sell inevitably gave birth to a professional class of wholesale merchants. The temple priests also engaged in trade; the enormous stocks accumulated in the god's store-chambers were more than sufficient for the needs of the temple and the surplus could be sold, providing funds for the maintenance and adornment of the shrine; and since in the theocratic state of early times the god and the government were synonymous we find the state competing in the market on equal terms with the private merchant. The interesting feature of the Sumerian economy is just this. Because trade was the life-blood of the community the government was bound to supervise and regulate the activities of the trader; it was obliged to ensure fair dealing between buyer and seller, because fraud destroys credit, and to protect the merchant, because his business is to the state's advantage; but, as if recognizing that individual initiative is more likely to succeed in commerce than is a bureaucracy undisturbed by competition, it made no attempt whatsoever to replace the private trader by the state. Throughout Mesopotamian history the merchant had, within the limits of the law, a free hand to carry on his business, and it is worth noting how far more effective his purely commercial activities were than those of a government department with its political background. Thus Pharaoh of Egypt might solicit a Hittite ruler, over whom he had no control, for a consignment of iron, and receive a more or less polite refusal, or when his military powers ceased to command respect, might find his demand for cedarwood contemptuously rejected by a petty prince of Byblos; but the Mesopotamian merchant could carry on trade with central Anatolia—a land into which a Mesopotamian army had only once ventured—or with an Indian state distant beyond surmise. Moreover, with this capitalist system, the breakdown of the political state did not involve the collapse of trade. Ur, as the capital city of Mesopotamia under the kings of the Third Dynasty of Ur, must then have reached the height of its prosperity; it was sacked and laid waste by the Elamites, but under the Larsa Dynasty which the Elamites installed, the city, reduced politically to the grade of a provincial centre, carried on its manufactures and its foreign trade much as before and seems still to have ranked as the commercial capital.

The Code of Hammurabi has preserved for us some at least of the laws regulating both internal and foreign trade. Because it was a strict rule that the details of every commercial transaction should be recorded in writing, and many thousands of such documents survive, much can be learnt about the operation of the laws and the general activities of the merchants; in addition there are various texts which incidentally throw light upon trade questions, while archaeological discoveries have contributed not a little to our knowledge. Out of the vast amount of specialized detail it is possible to obtain a fair picture of the general principles and methods of commerce, both internal and external, for the whole period with which we are here concerned.

Retail trading in the home market had of course begun with simple barter. But at a very early date such transactions, though they retained the outward form of barter, goods of one sort being exchanged for goods of another sort, were in fact sales; the objects were not merely balanced one against another but were separately valued by reference to a common standard, and those values had to be brought to a common total; thus A sells to B a house worth six talents for three rolls of cloth, value four talents, and ten sheep, value two talents. The original medium of exchange, natural in a land pre-eminently agricultural, had been grain—just as the original unit of weight was a barleycorn. With the introduction of metal a second medium was added, copper, the ratio between them being fixed, so that in a written assessment of price both media would be mentioned, or either. Later, as wealth increased, silver and gold came in as standards; gold (in the form of rings) came very seldom into actual use, but silver, weighed in the balance and duly tested for quality (though it might be guaranteed by a stamp such as 'the seal of Babylon') was normal currency; thus in Hammurabi's Code agricultural wages and hiring rates are reckoned in grain, but those of the townsman in silver, while at the same time the concession is made that if a debtor has not money (i.e. silver) or corn to pay but has goods, 'he shall give to his merchant according to what he has brought, and the merchant shall not object'.

In the same way, loans were reckoned either in grain or in silver—never in terms of any other commodity. Because of the prime importance of agriculture and of the productivity of the soil in lower Mesopotamia, where a thirty- or forty-fold return was but a normal crop, interest on loans was high; under the Third Dynasty of Ur the rate was 33⅓ per cent, and this was confirmed by Hammurabi's Code so far as grain was concerned, but for silver the rate was only 20 per cent, and in the Larsa period grain too came down to the same figure. The fact was that it was impossible to fix any rate by law. In the case of a dispute brought before the courts the law would be invoked and the legal rate of interest would be imposed; but in commercial ventures the rate charged by the lender would obviously be in proportion to the risks involved and every such transaction would be decided on its merits; thus, under the Third Dynasty, we find an instance of the interest on a silver loan reaching 25 per cent, and very often it falls well below 20 per cent. It was to the state's advantage that money should be easy, and the palace and the temple (i.e. the state) would prevent an exaggerated rate of interest being exacted by private moneylenders by granting loans at 12 per cent or less; thus at Sippar, in Babylonian times, the god Shamash was lending barley at 20 per cent and silver at 6¼ per cent. Further to protect the borrower against overcharge, Hammurabi enacted that the contract should be drawn up before a government official, failing which the lender forfeited his rights to the capital, and an attempt to exact interest in excess of the legal maximum nullified the agreement and the creditor lost his title to the debt.

The solicitude of the state towards the borrower only reflects the importance of trade to the community at large. Foreign trade required heavy financial backing, and it was essential that the merchants should be suitably financed. Moreover, to be successful, trade must be honestly conducted, and therefore commercial dishonesty of any kind, or anything that opened the door to fraud in business, was severely punished. Every transaction in real estate, loans and, in certain conditions, sales had to be in writing, with the names of the parties recorded;

without that, no claim by a professed lender or seller was valid. To buy, or to receive on deposit, a man's property from his son or his slave (i.e. from other than the responsible owner) without a written bond duly witnessed, involved the death penalty. The use of false weights or measures annulled any claim made by the creditor, and the prudent merchant therefore employed weights engraved with the guarantee of the state department. The creditor on his side could require a pledge as security for his loan, and this might mean that the debtor, if he had no land or house to his credit, might hand over his wife or his children as slaves; by Hammurabi's Code such bondage could be for three years only, but in later times no limit was put to its duration so long as the debt was unredeemed.

Straight dealing in the town bazaars could be ensured by a competent police force, and petty fraud, easily defined, was a matter for the local courts; the strenuous legislation to which our sources bear witness was drawn up in the interests of foreign trade. It was in the sphere of international commerce that the Sumerian and later the Babylonian people displayed an initiative and a genius for organization which was to affect profoundly the history of man.

The goods which the Mesopotamian merchants sought had to be obtained from sources lying outside their own borders and often not even in neighbouring countries but in dominions distant by two or three removes from their own. In these circumstances a travelling merchant could not be protected by the armed forces of his own government but had to rely upon the goodwill of the government of the land through which he passed, which could be earned only by, on the one hand, the payment of customs and transit dues and, on the other, the extension to the subjects of that government of similar free-conduct rights in his own land. Generally the states of the Middle East were too well aware of the benefits they derived from the passage of merchandise to interfere with the caravans; war might, of course, cut communications and there was always risk from outlaws and robber bands, but the governments as such normally encouraged trade. Their attitude is illustrated by a late incident. A Babylonian caravan carrying a consignment of gold while passing through Canaan had been attacked and plundered by brigands; King Burnaburiash of Babylon writes to the Canaanite ruler demanding that the brigands be executed and the gold returned, otherwise 'trade between us shall stop!'; evidently he could think of no threat likely to be more efficacious. Foreign merchants were indeed welcome. When Sargon of Akkad boasted that the ships of Meluhha, of Makkan and of Telmun were lying alongside the wharves of his capital his pleasure was in the arrival of trading missions from the south of the Persian Gulf; and when Ur-Nammu of Ur claims that he had 'brought back the ships of Magan' (apparently by clearing the silted-up canals) he had indeed re-opened the trade-routes, but for the use of the foreigners, not of his own sailors.

Whether by sea or by land, a traveller could pass through the countries of the ancient world with tolerable safety. However, a single journey—and this was especially true of land travel with all its difficulties of transport—would not make a merchant's fortune; for that he had to have regular traffic and regular contacts. Since he could not expect to find just the goods he sought ready to hand in the course of a brief visit unannounced beforehand, he needed an organization on the spot which could order commodities in advance, act as a collecting centre, make introductions and arrange payments. Some kind of local agency was indispensable. Gudea, *patesi* (or *ensī* = prince) of Lagash in about 2200 BC, describes all the stocks of building material which he imported from many lands for his temple of the god Nin-gir-su—timber from the cedar-forests and from Magan and Meluhha, porphyry, also from Meluhha, marble from the 'marble mountains', copper from Kimash, gold and silver and lead, asphalt and bitumen from Madga, the ships laden as corn-ships are laden when they bring in the harvest from the fields. The *ensī* may claim in self-glorification that 'Gudea the High Priest of Nin-gir-su made his way into the cedar-mountains which no man had penetrated before him', but that can be no more than a figure of speech; undoubtedly he sent his own envoys rather than employing middlemen, but to fulfil so large an order he must have used the ordinary trade channels; we may even assume (thus interpreting Gudea's phrase) that a resident agent had arranged in advance for the exploitation of a stretch of virgin forest to meet his requirements.

The character of these trading outposts differed according to the conditions of the various countries.

In central Syria, in the second half of the third millennium BC, we find at Qatna, on the middle Orontes, what is really a Mesopotamian town; it was built round a temple of Nin-Egal, a goddess particularly in favour at Ur, and associated with its King Adad-nirari (an Akkadian name) there is a high official whose title, *šakkanaku,* is in that age exclusively Babylonian. Syria was not a great power but parcelled out into petty states (in the four cuneiform texts found at Qatna more than half a dozen 'kings' are mentioned) no one of which would be able to guarantee the safety of a foreign trade agency against the jealousy or the rapacity of the others; here then the best solution was to have a purely Mesopotamian colony ranking as a kingdom on a par with its neighbours but secured against them by the military power of the home government.

In the extreme north of Syria, where the Orontes turns westward to break through the Amanus range and reach the Mediterranean by way of Antioch, the little royal city of Alalakh commanded the approach to the famous 'Mountain of Cedars' and the road across the Aleppo plateau to the eastern-most bend of the Euphrates—the road along which the cedar logs would be hauled for embarkation or to be floated downstream to Babylon and Sumer. That the timber merchants had their representatives here is likely, to say the least of it, but the two or three Mesopotamian cylinder seals found in the excavation of the early levels do not amount to proof, though the fact of a royal palace being designed on Mesopotamian lines supports the likelihood. Sargon of Akkad effectually did away with middlemen's profits by seizing the country and so getting the sources of supply into his own hands, and his grandson also made himself master of the Cedar Mountain. For the later periods the tablets found, coming as they do from the royal archives, tell us nothing about private trade, but in the early part of the eighteenth century BC there is mention of two hundred measures of wool coming from the controller of Idma or Arazik, on the Euphrates; woollen cloth was one of the regular articles of Mesopotamian export, and here again the Babylonian title of *šakkanaku* is applied to an official in charge of stores containing cloth.

Kultepe

Much more illuminating is the case of Ganeš. An epic poem, 'The King of Battles', describes how Sargon of Akkad led his army across unknown mountain passes into the heart of Anatolia to champion the cause of a colony of Akkadian merchants whose rights were being flouted by the local ruler. This, if not the actual settlement whose ruins, on the site now called Kultepe, have been excavated by the Turkish Historical Society with outstanding success, must have been of the same character. Outside the eastern rampart of the walled native town of Ganeš there stretched a built-up area of rather more than a kilometre's length which was for the exclusive use of the merchants of Assur. Clearly they were not allowed to live inside the town but were isolated and kept at arm's length—probably as much by their own wish as by the prejudice of the Anatolians; the *Karum*, as their quarter was called, might be compared with the 'factory' established by the old East

India Company outside Calcutta, or, again, with the town of Naukratis which the Egyptian government assigned to the Greek traders of the seventh century BC. The date of the foundation of this colony is not yet known, but it flourished throughout the time of the Third Dynasty of Ur and until the nineteenth century BC. It was a closely-knit organization, self-governing and independent; but because it was much too far from Mesopotamia to get any military assistance thence (Sargon's expedition was a unique exception to the general rule), it had to rely for its existence upon the tact of the merchants in their dealings with the rulers of Ganeš and upon the indisputable profit that their activities brought to the country. Their main business was the export of copper and as the tablets found in their archives prove they had by their strict application to the business brought their commercial technique, and also the legal practices arising from their profession, to a stage even more advanced than that of their colleagues at home.

Kultepe is not the only Anatolian site where a Mesopotamian trading outpost has been discovered; there was one at Bogazköy, and there were probably others conforming more or less to the same pattern. For the pattern has its analogies elsewhere. At Ur itself there was a *karum* lying outside the walls of the city, and as appears from one of the phrases used, administratively distinct from it; merchants were members of the *karum,* they settled their accounts there, they could keep their business assets there and if they managed their assets from there they did so as members of the merchants' guild. It was not a residential area as the Ganeš *karum* was forced by local conditions to be, but more like what the Royal Exchange was for eighteenth-century London, and a member of it was supposed to act 'like a gentleman'—*mâr awēlim*—that is, to observe certain ethical and social standards of conduct; all agreements were made and contracts lodged in the local temple of Shamash the Sun god (we have already seen Shamash acting as banker in the city of Sippar), so that the religious sanction re-enforced the moral code.

The texts made it clear that the *karum* was pre-eminently the changing-house for external, i.e. inter-city or international trade. Accordingly we may assume that there the Ur merchant met the representatives of the merchants of India. The archaeological evidence for the Indian trade takes it back to Early Dynastic times; from the royal cemetery at Ur come beads of artificially bleached cornelian identical with examples from Mohenjo-daro, there was a golden monkey on a pin in the grave of Mes-kalam-dug, and carved stone vases from Mehi (of the 'Kulli' culture, see p. 151–52) are not uncommon in that period. By the twenty-fourth century BC we begin to find on Sumerian sites, and more especially at Ur, engraved and inscribed seals of the Indus valley type which must have belonged to Indian residents, agents of business houses at Harappā or Mohenjo-daro engaged in the import and export trade between the two countries. The connection held good throughout the Third Dynasty of Ur and into the Larsa period, and perhaps the early Kassite, when it ends abruptly, probably with the downfall of the Indus valley cities. Judging from the number of seals (Ur alone has produced a dozen, which in view of the accidents of survival and discovery must represent a great many more) the Indian colony was fairly large and trade therefore must have been on a considerable scale. There is no written evidence to explain the nature of the merchandise involved or the traffic arrangements employed, but considering the difficulty and the cost of overland transport it is likely that most goods were brought by sea to Telmun.

Telmun

Towards the close of the second millennium Telmun, the modern Bahrein island, developed into one of the most important trading stations of the Middle East. Itself producing nothing more important than vegetables (Telmun onions were famous) it served as an entrepôt for goods from all the lands oversea. We have seen (p. 333–34) that in earlier times the ships of Makkan, i.e. of Oman on the Persian Gulf, and of Meluhha, a country which for the Mesopotamian was almost fabulous but may have been the east coast of Africa, discharged their cargoes directly upon the wharves of the riverine cities. Business documents from Ur show that as late as the reign of Ibbî-Sin, last king of the Third Dynasty of Ur, an Ur merchant would ship his goods and travel himself directly to Makkan, though whether the vessel belonged to Ur or to Makkan is not stated. But in the Larsa period Telmun enjoys a monopoly of the Gulf traffic; everything was discharged there and transshipped for its final destination. It was perhaps the development of the Indian trade that so benefited Telmun. The big deep-draughted dhows that in the monsoon season undertook the long voyage from the Persian Gulf to Karachi or Ceylon were quite unfit for the navigation of the rivers and canals of Mesopotamia, whereas the Mesopotamian river craft had always been accustomed to the cabotage of the Gulf ports; transshipment was therefore a necessity, and Telmun offered a convenient anchorage. But for the Ur merchants it would be a great saving of time and expense if a single port and a single agency could deal with the whole cargo of the ship; moreover, since most goods were sent not on order but as a speculation in the hopes of sale, a single market dealing with commodities of all kinds was to everyone's advantage; consequently the direct voyages to Makkan ceased and all trade was concentrated at Telmun.

Ur, with easy access to the sea by canal and river (*v.* Ur-Nammu's inscription cited above, p. 334), was in a favourable position to profit by this trade. The ship-masters of Ur were formed into a guild, the *alik Telmun,* which seems to have had a monopoly of the traffic, the master acting as both captain and supercargo, doing most of the buying and selling himself, though he might agree to take with him individuals speculating on their own account. They were indeed more merchants than sailors if we may judge from their insistence on the dangers of the voyage, from the prayers and offerings made by their families on their behalf and from the ex-votos which they and their crews dedicated on their safe return. On the outgoing trip they would carry cash, i.e. silver, rolls or garments of woollen cloth, scented oils, etc., and they would bring back raw copper—the standard commodity of the Telmun trade; a tablet mentions as much as 13,200 lb. of copper in a single cargo—ivory, hard woods such as ebony, stone beads, lapis lazuli, gold, eye-paint and pearls (?). With so wide a range of goods a skilful buyer could make a handsome profit.

The history of the Gulf traffic is not without interest. Under the Third Dynasty of Ur the Makkan ships were financed out of temple funds and the merchant-adventurer paid tithe to the temple of Nannar; moreover, the title used for him is that of a palace functionary, and when Ur-Nammu revived the Makkan trade he did so for Nannar his god. It is clear that the government was at this time directly engaged in the business, either in competition with the private capitalist or possibly as holding a monopoly. In the Larsa period, on the other hand, the trade has passed entirely into the hands of the private merchants and 'the palace' contents itself with imposing considerable customs dues on the imported copper and in addition the importer pays a tithe on all goods to the temple of Ningal; his old official title has now given place to that of *alik Telmun,* and his sphere of operations does not extend beyond Bahrein island. The concentration of trade in Bahrein saw the fullest development of its commerce; even in Mari, far distant on the middle Euphrates, the palace archives show contacts with the island—messengers arrive from Telmun and the king of Mari dispatches caravans thither; presumably the last stages of the journey would be by the ships of the *alik*

Telmun of Ur. But it also meant the gradual restriction of the mercantile horizon as direct contacts with the more remote sources of supply ceased. Then events in the Far East, probably the overthrow of the Indus valley cities by the invading Aryans and possibly some political upheaval in the south which affected Ceylon, put an end to the trade with those parts. The advantages of a general market no longer attracted to Telmun the copper of Makkan and the precious woods of Meluhha; the port dwindled, and letters written from Nippur in the fourteenth century show the island rather as a supplier of certain kinds of dates than as a commercial emporium; it had reverted to its original status, with dates instead of onions as its main agricultural asset.

The travelling trader could be the agent employed by the home merchant—this seems to have been the more common practice for overland business in the early period—or he could be in partnership with him, which was the normal rule in the later trade with Telmun. The clauses in the Code of Hammurabi which regulated the relation between principal and agent, in so far as they survive (many of them are lost), aim generally at securing honest dealing in transactions in which fraud on either side was only too easy. A written document had to define the exact duties of the employee and the value of the money or goods entrusted to him, and he had to keep account of all his operations and note all profits realized. On his return he had to repay the whole capital to his employer, obtaining a receipt for it, and from the profits he took the percentage due to him by the original agreement. If through his own negligence or incapacity profits were unsatisfactory he had to return twice the capital. Obviously the merchant expected to make a profit of not less than 100 per cent on the money he risked; but if the agent could prove that losses were due 'to the hand of god or of the king's enemies' he was absolved from all liability. If the commercial traveller could not produce receipts covering his expenditure he had no claim to reimbursement. In the case of dispute between the two parties then, in the absence of written proof, the case was heard before witnesses in the temple—presumably the temple of Shamash in which the contract would have been drawn up; if the traveller was found to be in default he had to pay three times the sum owed, if the financier, six times; from the severity of the penalties one can estimate the remunerative character of the business.

Tablets of the Larsa period found at Ur, many of them actual contracts, throw much light upon the working of the overseas trade. The simplest course was for the *tamkarum*, the capitalist, to advance the necessary funds to the merchant-adventurer at a fixed rate of interest without running any risk himself; thus, 'A and B have borrowed from X 2 *mina* of silver and 5 *gur* of oil and 30 garments as capital for a partnership for an expedition to Telmun to buy copper. After the safe termination of the voyage X will not recognize any commercial losses incurred by A and B; they have agreed to satisfy X with 4 *mina* of copper for each shekel of silver as a just [price?].' But because profits might be very high the capitalist might try to improve his position; thus we find a certain Zubabum lending 11 shekels of silver, without interest, to a group of five partners one of whom is himself; on a fixed date the entire capital is to be repaid to him by any one, or all, of his four associates while he, as full partner, shares equally with them the profits of the enterprise. Similarly the travelling merchant was anxious to spread the risk of the voyage. Before starting on it he might sell for cash 'a share in the sea expedition', thus effecting a form of maritime insurance; usually he would insert in the contract a proviso that the cash advanced by his *tamkarum* partner was due for repayment only on the safe return of the ship; sometimes the advance is specified as 'a favour', i.e. an advance made on the credit of the borrower without any pledge or security being deposited with the lender, in which case the loss of ship and cargo would fall entirely on the financier. Another safeguard for the *alik Telmun* was to spread his investments; thus one and the same man on three occasions appears as captain and supercargo borrowing the cash to finance his voyages and on twelve occasions advances money himself to finance the voyage of others.

A ship setting out for an overseas market could be laden with any kind of saleable goods, but for the commercial traveller journeying by land with only donkeys for transport bulky and heavy merchandise was to be avoided as far as possible.[7] He could take silver, but that being itself an import, its use abroad would not prove of advantage to the exporter, though it might be in some areas the best medium for purchases; its intrinsic value too made it a risky thing to carry. The difficulty was solved by what might be called letters of credit, a system facilitated by the existence of established agents on the trade-routes. The traveller, starting with a consignment of grain, might sell it in some town on his road, receiving a signed tablet with the value expressed in copper possibly, or in silver, with which he could buy there or elsewhere something to the same value which he could sell at a profit farther along on his journey. Again he might realize his promissory note not necessarily in the form of the actual goods mentioned therein, or even in actual goods at all, but in the form of another note guaranteeing the delivery of some commodity for which there was a demand farther north. A clever salesman could effect several operations, and make a profit on each, in the course of a single journey. Since there was no coined money he was not troubled with difficulties of foreign exchange at the various frontiers; his tablets, payable on demand by the agents to whom he was accredited, were the ancient equivalent of a paper currency based on commodity values, and made possible a commerce extending far beyond the boundaries of his own country.

Phoenicia

We have not the evidence to show how far such a system was worked in other lands than Mesopotamia. The presence of Indians in Ur suggests something of the sort, but there are no documents to supplement the witness of the seals, and for China in the Shang period even archaeological evidence fails us. As for the cities of the Syrian coast, they undoubtedly lived by and for trade. Down to 1200 BC most of their business was done in Egypt, to which they sent timber from the Lebanon forests, olive oil, cloth dyed with the famous *murux* purple, and gums; their skilled craftsmen, who were not gifted with imagination but would readily copy or adapt the designs of their Egyptian clients or of their Asiatic neighbours, manufactured in the precious metals and more especially in ivory luxury objects which commanded high prices and were eagerly sought after, as references in Homer show.

The Phoenician ships did not yet venture across the open sea; theirs was a cabotage trade along the Syrian coast and no farther out than Cyprus, itself in sight from the mainland, but the ramifications of their commerce penetrated far. Excavation on a Phoenician site brings to light a remarkable medley of weights: side by side with the Phoenician shekel of 224 grammes, itself possibly a corruption of the 258-grammes Babylonian shekel, we find the true Babylonian shekel and the Egyptian *sep* and *deben* weights, as well as units of other systems not yet identified; it is clear that the merchants of Tyre and Sidon were dealing with a mixed clientèle which included citizens of all the principal countries around them. This international trade was a very important factor in the progress of man's civilization in that it resulted in an interchange of inventions and ideas between peoples who otherwise might never have been brought into contact; the Phoenicians and the Cretans, also a commercial people whose sea-going ships had a wider range, acted as the middlemen of a cultural exchange so general in its scope and so fertilizing in its spirit that in the thirteenth century BC we can speak of an 'Eastern Mediterranean' civilization. The effects were indeed profound, but of the machinery by which they were realized we know very little. Texts from Ugarit show that the various states were in accord to protect the interests of their travelling merchants, but no documents survive to explain the organization of the Phoenician market or the accountancy system employed by the Phoenician financiers. This silence is the more curious in view of the fact that commerce was the sole reason for the existence of these maritime states; everybody there was engaged in trade. The story of Wenamon shows us the prince of Byblos as a glorified huckster; Hiram of Tyre has his own merchant fleet and is eager to undertake building contracts for his neighbours; and so it had been from the beginning. We may, if we so wish, assume that the Mesopotamian *karum* had its counterpart in the Syrian coast towns, but so far as real evidence goes the methods of the Phoenician and Cretan dealers might have been the most primitive methods of barter.

Europe

Those primitive methods were still, at the close of our period, characteristic of trade in the European continent. By the middle of the third millennium BC Baltic amber was already finding its way to Troy and to Knossos, and in the course of the second millennium the metal-workers of Hungary and Bohemia were marketing their goods westwards across Europe and into Britain; the fact of the trade's existence and its influence upon the development of western culture are of prime importance, but the manner of it was that of a world still savage. Wandering gangs of smiths would extend the knowledge of metallurgy, bronze weapons would pass from hand to hand, exchanged for foodstuffs or skins, for Whitby jet or for Irish gold; but for the history of organized commerce such traffic tells us nothing more than can be learned from any barbarous country. The needs of a civilized and a sophisticated world require for their satisfaction a trade system at once standardized and flexible, based on ultimate values but operating largely through credit; only in Mesopotamia can we observe the elaboration of such a system, and there it was developed to a state which anticipates modern business.

COMMUNICATION AND TRANSPORT

Land Transport

Land transport in the ancient world was difficult and costly. Man could and did travel freely and for great distances, but what he could take with him was strictly limited to that which he could himself carry or could load on a pack animal, and the porterage of heavy or bulky goods would therefore be reduced to the minimum.

It is true that the wheeled vehicle was introduced to Mesopotamia at an early date; clay models of such, children's toys or votive objects occur in the Jamdat Nasr and perhaps in the Uruk period, i.e. in the latter half of the fourth millennium; the earliest actual examples and the most detailed illustrations come in the Early Dynastic period, about 2700 BC. But this did not solve the problem of transport. In the first place, the vehicles themselves were unsuitable. The war chariot, which if it was to be effective at all had to be fast-moving, was made as light as possible, but the four clumsy wheels, of solid wood built up in sections and fixed to the axle-tree, were a serious handicap; although only two men were carried in the car it none the less required four asses—or onagers—to draw it. The other type, wagon rather than chariot, had to be drawn by two oxen; since two such wagons were found in a king's grave it would seem that they were used for ceremonial purposes, not for the carrying of merchandise. Obviously the ox-carts could have been employed for draught also, slow as they were, for short hauls but for short hauls only; for a long trek across country they would have been useless. For the second and decisive objection to wheeled traffic was the absence of roads. In the Euphrates valley itself the heavy carts could move about, making use of the canal banks as highways; but even there they could with difficulty risk going on the softer soil of the watered fields (it was not without reason that Queen Shub-ad's pleasure-car had sled runners instead of wheels) and for a long journey through wooded or mountainous country they were manifestly impossible. Even when, early in the second millennium, the horse was introduced into Mesopotamia and then by way of Syria into Egypt, the transport problem was not affected. For the armies of the Middle East it meant a revolutionary change, and the military power of a state depended largely on the chariotry it could put into the field; but since the right way of harnessing a draught horse had not been discovered the use of the horse for transport was hopelessly uneconomical; and, again, the lack of roads ruled out long-distance wheeled traffic of any sort.

In Egypt and in Mesopotamia therefore the transport of goods overland relied entirely upon the pack ass. In Egypt the lords of Elephantine, who were responsible for the Sudan trade, had the title of 'caravan-conductor' and one of them, Harkhuf, returning from the third expedition on which the Pharaoh Mernere had sent him, had three hundred laden asses in his train. In Mesopotamia asses were indispensable even for inter-city trade if that meant going up-stream, and for journeys abroad they were always in demand; 'As for the asses that you need', writes one merchant to another, 'come and buy the asses. Come and buy them before they go off again'; and in the days of Sargon of Akkad a pack ass cost upwards of thirty shekels of silver, about twenty times the price of a sheep. In early days the temples and the rulers of the city states kept large herds of asses, one of the uses of which would be to bring in the produce of the temple or royal estates and the tithes due from tenants. Similarly in Egypt all local transport from field to town was done by pack asses driven along the high canal banks; in the wall-reliefs of the tombs of the nobility they appear as a necessary part of his possessions.

To the transport animals employed by the ancient peoples of the Middle East one would naturally expect to add the camel—or rather, the dromedary, the single-humped species of southern Asia, in later times so characteristic of those countries as to be an apt symbol of them. But in fact the subject is strangely difficult. The question of the domestication of the camel is discussed elsewhere (*v.* pp. 232–33), and here we are concerned only with its use, but the evidence is far from satisfactory.

In Mesopotamia the dromedary is represented by a fourteenth-century terra-cotta head from 'Aqar Qûf and by Kassite clay figures from Warka; and it must have been known earlier because it has a Sumerian name, 'Ass of the Sea', a name implying that it came from the extreme south, i.e. from Arabia; but references to it in literature are very few and far between. Only in the reign of Tiglathpileser I, 1098-1068 BC, do the sculptures show that the Assyrian army had camel transport; a single limestone relief from Carchemish figuring an archer on a riding-camel (apparently a dromedary) may possibly belong to the second millennium BC but is more generally attributed to the ninth or eighth century. The Egyptians certainly knew about the camel. but it is equally clear that they did not keep camels or use them for transport, and Egyptian literature has nothing to say about them.

On the other hand there are numerous references to camels in the early books of the Old Testament. Abraham is said to possess camels, Jacob has camels, both when living at Haran and later in Palestine, and Joseph is sold by his brethren to 'Ishmaelites coming from Gilead with their camels bearing spicery and balm and myrrh, going to carry it down to Egypt'; also, the Hebrews are forbidden to eat the camel's flesh. Because the Old Testament story contrasts so markedly in this respect with the silence of Egyptian and Mesopotamian literature, and also because, with seeming inconsistency, it says nothing about camels being used either by Joseph's brethren when they came down into Egypt or by the Hebrews at the exodus, it has been suggested that we have to deal here with anachronistic interpolations by a late editor of the books. There is no ground for this suggestion. Historians are agreed that the rise to wealth and power of the *mukarribs* of Saba, and of the Minyean kingdom of Arabia, was wholly due to camel-breeding and to the transport of myrrh, spices, etc., to Syria and Egypt; the Minyean success was due not to the sudden introduction of the camel but to the organization of a business which the Beduin clans had exercised in a desultory fashion for a very long time past. The trade of the ancient Middle East becomes largely unintelligible unless we admit the part in it played by the Beduin of the Arabian and Syrian deserts and their dromedaries. As nomads they were subject to no man and were the enemies of town-dwellers. Nobody but themselves could venture across the desert tracks, so they had the monopoly of the carrying-trade, but they did not mix with the people at either end. Just as the modern Anayzeh camel-drover prefers not to enter a town but to load or unload his beasts in a market outside it, and if he must needs go in will wrap his head-cloth across his face to keep out the townsman's stench, so, probably, the ancient 'Ishmaelite' stopped at the borders of Egypt and there handed his goods over to the Egyptian consignee; he would not wish to go farther, and the Egyptian, who hated and feared the desert people, would scarcely have admitted him. If, as is likely, the Egyptian regarded the camel as unclean, that would explain why Joseph's brethren, seeking food from Egypt, brought only asses with them; certainly they would keep no camels in Goschen, on Egyptian territory, and the Hebrews may have got their prejudice against the camel from the Egyptians. Both the Egyptians and the Mesopotamians knew of the camel, but they knew of it only from a distance—it is hard to imagine one of the hated Sutû leading a train of loaded camels through the narrow lanes of Ur—and they had no need to mention it. None the less, the myrrh and spices of Arabia Felix and the foreign goods which the dhows brought from Africa or Ceylon to the harbours of the Hadhramaut and the Persian Gulf were carried up into Syria or across Sinai by camel caravans centuries before the rise of the Minyean kingdom proved how important that traffic was.

Water Transport

Land transport was difficult and costly; water transport was infinitely more economical; wherever then it was possible goods were carried by water.

The Sumerians and the Babylonians had the advantage that two great rivers ran through the entire length of their country, affording a double waterway which tapped the whole eastern half of Anatolia and the northern part of Syria. Down the Tigris would come timber, copper, obsidian; bitumen came from Hit on the middle Euphrates, cedar-wood from the Amanus mountains, dragged overland by oxen or by men along the easy road from Alalakh via Aleppo to the river where it runs nearest to the Mediterranean; from Biridjik would come the na-lû-a stone which Gudea imported for the building of his temple, and marble from the anti-Taurus. For this traffic three forms of craft were used, all of which still ply upon the same waters. The first was a real boat with keel and ribs overlaid with heavy planks, with blunt bows and square stern, its lines kept as straight as might be so that the need of bending the planks might be reduced to the minimum; it had a lateen sail and heavy paddle-like sweeps. The boats were built in the north country where timber was available; anything up to 30 feet in length (9 metres) and broad in the beam, they could carry a heavy and a bulky cargo downstream. Once down in the south, they could be used for local traffic on the rivers and canals, their big sails enabling them to make good headway against the river current; but they could not get farther north than the rapids below Hit, and therefore could not be used for the export trade to places beyond the Mesopotamian border. If they were not wanted for local needs they were broken up and the planks and baulks were sold; the modern version, the *belem*, is used in precisely the same way.

The other two types of river craft were, properly speaking, not boats at all. One of them was a circular leather coracle, the bitumen-coated *guffa* of today, which Herodotus described as being, after the city of Babylon itself, the most extraordinary thing in all the land; the other was the *kelek*, the ancient *kalakku*, a raft of timbers lashed together and buoyed up by inflated skins, capable of carrying a heavy cargo. The vessels came downstream easily enough, carried by the current with but little need of oars, paddles or poles except for keeping course amid-stream; but against the current they could make no headway at all, and for the boatmen therefore it was a one-way traffic. When the *guffa* reached its destination and its cargo had been discharged the leather covering was stripped from the wicker frame and put on donkey-back, to return by land to the north and to be reused for another voyage down-stream; similarly the *kelek* was dismantled, the logs sold as timber, and the skins carried north again. This meant that whereas the Mesopotamian importer did not have to worry unduly about the size or weight of his imports—King Samsu-iluna of Babylon (1749–1712 BC) boasts of having shipped from the mountains of the west a block of hard stone of more than 35 feet (11 metres) in length, and a piece of marble of 80 talents' weight—the goods which he sent in payment had to be of a sort that pack asses could carry. It was fortunate that the Mesopotamians were skilled weavers whose cloths were held in high repute everywhere, for cloth can be baled in convenient loads; but when one considers the character of the export trade in ancient times it is well to remember to what extent it was conditioned by the possibilities of transport as well as by the taste of clients.

The Egyptians, for their inland traffic, had the Nile. In this they were even better off than were the Mesopotamians, for the great river is navigable in both directions. Going down-stream a boat is carried by the current and bare-masted can make reasonable progress; going upstream the sails are hoisted and the north wind that blows steadily almost throughout the year ensures good headway. Only in the Korosko bend where the river runs from north to south and both wind and current are contrary is the vessel travelling upstream unable to advance except by the laborious help of the tow-rope, and only when the wind shifts to the south, as it does sometimes in winter in the neighbourhood of the Mediterranean and in springtime when the *khamsîn* blows, is the rest of the upstream passage at all difficult; in normal times the boatman could not ask for conditions more favourable to his craft.

The first Nile boats were modelled on the papyrus floats of the prehistoric age. Those had been mere bundles of papyrus stems, lashed together with the ends up-curved to make a pointed stem and a higher stern, the whole thing solid and therefore supported on the water by the buoyancy of the dry reeds only, not by any hollow in the hull. Such would carry but little freight, and the Egyptian therefore set himself to make a real boat, preserving the outward form of the old float but making it hollow inside; for this he required timber, and at once the difficulty arose that the Nile valley produced no better trees than acacia and sycamore whose hard and knotty growth affords at the very most a baulk of 6 foot (2 metres) length. The problem was solved by a method of boat-building unknown in any other part of the world.

The Nile boat had no keel and no ribs. The acacia baulks, a foot or more thick, were laid one upon another, like bricks, as Herodotus says, and fastened together with wooden bolts, the ends overlapping so as to dovetail together, the base line from prow to stern making a uniform curve, the cross-section more or less semicircular below and rising to the vertical above the water-line. The hull, built up in this piecemeal fashion, was caulked with tow and papyrus; it was not decked, or quarter-decked, but had thwarts for oarsmen; these in early days used paddles, sitting and facing forwards, but later on swivelled oars were introduced; paddles, one or more, served as rudders, and a single mast took the small rectangular yard-sail.

For river transport a vessel so constructed fulfilled its purpose admirably, but it was ill adapted for voyages oversea. From the representations of sea-going ships we can see that the Nile boat design was modified to meet the different conditions. The deck from fore to aft is now flatter and the overhang of bow and stern is very much reduced with the intent that the ship should cut through the waves rather than be lifted and ride over them. The ship-builders had learnt, probably by sad experience, that longitudinal dovetailing of their hull baulks was a poor substitute for a solid keel; riding over a wave and suspended amidships with bow and stern above water the ship simply broke its back. Accordingly the sea-going vessels represented in the pyramid reliefs of Sahurê are undergirt fore and aft with heavy cables. A cable network carried along the whole length of the hull a little below the bulwarks binds it together, while high inboard a huge twisted rope, resting on forked crutches graduated in height which give it a curve complementary to that of the base of the hull, runs the whole ship's length, its ends securely fixed to prow and stern, to counteract their tendency to drop and cause the vessel to break amidships. The type of sail is also changed; the two-legged composite mast still used by Sahurê soon gave place to a single mast set amidships, and a very long spar hoisted to mast-head supported a single sail, an enormously wide stretch of canvas, its lower edge laced to a boom almost as long as the ship, which could be trimmed to the wind.

It was in ships of this sort that the Egyptian sailors ventured on the voyage to Punt and on the Mediterranean coastal trips to Byblos and the Phoenician ports; but it is hard to believe that they were indeed seaworthy. The fact that Sneferu, in the Third Dynasty, imported from the Lebanon pine logs for ship-building shows that the Egyptians themselves had little confidence in their own patchwork vessels held together with rope; the name of Sneferu's ships, *kebent*,[8] may imply that their design was taken from the ships of Byblos, and Amenemhet, the Twelfth Dynasty Pharaoh, had twenty ships of cedar-wood; but foreign wood was expensive and only occasionally did Pharaoh feel the need for keeled ships. The river Nile was at all times crowded with craft, all built on the old lines; but foreign trade was in the hands of Pharaoh and all sea-going ships were his, and the fact was that he had little use for them. This is very clear in the case of Punt. The Punt merchandise was highly prized, and maritime trade with Punt depended entirely upon Egyptian shipping, for the Puntites had no fleet of their own; yet expeditions thither were few and far between; the Twelfth Dynasty popular tale of the marvellous adventures of a mariner shipwrecked in those waters means not that they were familiar but, on the contrary, that they were well-nigh outside human experience; when Queen Hatshepsut sent her famous mission there hers was the first Egyptian squadron to anchor off the coast of Punt for about four hundred years.

For the eastern Mediterranean trade Pharaoh must have relied very largely upon Syrian shipping lines. Phoenician merchantmen could always be hired, and when a strong Pharaoh like Thutmose III controlled south Syria as a province of his empire he could regard the Syrian ships as his own. When Ramses III had to meet the naval forces of the 'Peoples of the Sea', the ships which he manned with the Egyptian archers who eventually won the day were probably not Egyptian ships at all but those which had fled from Syrian harbours before the threat of the invaders and joined Pharaoh in the defence of their homes. The Egyptian merchant fleet had never played an important part in the Mediterranean;[9] after the reign of Ramses III nothing whatsoever is heard of it.

Throughout the Bronze Age the carrying trade of the Mediterranean was shared by the Syrian coast towns and by Crete. The Phoenicians of that time were not adventurous seamen. Undoubtedly they were good boat-builders and made full use of the fine timber so ready to their hand in the Lebanon forests but, keen business men, they sought nothing more than a market for their goods and finding that in Egypt they felt no call to travel farther afield. Theirs was a cabotage trade; hugging the shore and never losing sight of land, they carried their cargoes of oil and cedar-wood, silver, copper, spices and purple dye to the mouth of the Nile and came back with linen stuffs, ivory, jewellery and trinkets which their clever craftsmen could imitate for the benefit of Syrian clients in the inland towns; their maritime horizon was limited to Pelusium in the south and in the north to Cyprus, whose eastern mountains could be seen from the slopes of the Amanus, and the Cilician plain. As the link between the various civilizations of the lands bordering on the eastern Mediterranean the Phoenicians influenced the growth of each and furthered their progress; undoubtedly their own great contribution to civilization, the invention of an alphabetic script, was prompted by the polyglot nature of their business; but the colonial expansion of Phoenicia and the exploitation of the western Mediterranean was not to come until the dawn of the Iron Age.

A more adventurous and equally important part was played by the merchant fleet of Crete. The beaked vessels, driven by both oars and sails, single-masted in the early days but sometimes in the Late Minoan period having two masts, square-sailed and with high-railed bulwarks, were ocean-goers; they were built for long voyages and the Cretan mariners had no fear of the open sea. There is no literary record to give us the details of Cretan trade, but something of its extent can be gathered from the widespread discoveries of Cretan goods.

Mention has already been made of Minoan pottery found at Ugarit on the Syrian coast and in Egypt (p. 83). Exports to Egypt must have been frequent; Middle Minoan vases are found there in the Twelfth Dynasty; in the Eighteenth Dynasty come Late Minoan I vases, one example occurring as far south as Anibeh in Nubia, while on the walls of tombs there are represented the splendid vases and bull-head rhytons characteristic of Minoan art, professedly tribute brought to Pharaoh by his Cretan vassals. An alabaster vase-lid inscribed with the name of the Hyksos Pharaoh Khyan, found in the palace at Knossos, might be a gift rather than an object obtained in the way of trade, and the same is true of a diorite statue of User, but definite proof of commercial relations is given by the Minoan weights, for many of those bearing numbers correspond exactly with the Egyptian gold units, and the parallel can only mean a common market.

Ships that could face the voyage of 300 and more miles to the mouth of the Nile would have had no difficulty in making the coast of Cyrenaica, only 180 miles away. If, as seems fairly certain, one of the signs in the Cretan hieroglyphic script represents the silphium plant, the export of which was a main source of revenue for Cyrene in the sixth century BC (as is clear from the vivid pictures on the Arkesilaos vase in the Bibliothèque Nationale), then Knossos was trading with the north African coast, and the use of the silphium plant for a hieroglyph witnesses to the importance of the trade. Such a close relation between Crete and Cyrene would explain how it was that in 1220 BC Meryey, king of Libya, could engage mercenaries from the sea peoples of the Aegean to assist him in his invasion of Egypt.

More important however were the relations between Crete and Greece. The classical Greeks, down to the time of Thucydides, preserved the tradition of Minoan sea power, as indeed they well might. The archaeological evidence of the innumerable objects of Cretan art found in Rhodes and Melos, and, on the Greek mainland, at Tiryns and Mycenae, at Pylos and Thebes, and Orchomenos, proves that the influence of the Minoans extended across the Aegean and was firmly established on the peninsula; whether or not this amounted to actual conquest of mainland bases matters comparatively little; the important and indisputable fact is that the Cretan commercial fleet opened up south-eastern Europe to the art and civilization of the Middle East. The rulers of Knossos were not the only ones whose wealth was amassed by international trade; but whereas the Egyptian ships were scarcely seaworthy and the Phoenicians were content to hug the coast, the Cretans built for themselves stout sailing-craft for long sea voyages; and their merchant-adventurers, the pioneers of the old civilization, laid, as we now begin to see, the foundations of classical Greece. When, after 1460 BC, the Mycenaeans dominated Crete, they carried on the maritime traditions of the island and, because the centre of their power lay farther west, on the Greek mainland, extended their sea-borne commerce even more widely over the Mediterranean, to Sicily, Marseilles and the Spanish coast.

There was one other sea passage which has to be taken into consideration when we study the commerce of the ancient world, but it is one concerning which our knowledge is very small; literature has nothing to tell us about ocean-borne trade between the Middle and the Far East.

The river craft of Mesopotamia have been described above, and it is manifest that such were not adequate for voyages over sea. There have also been described the guilds of the merchant-mariners of Ur who had the monopoly of foreign trade, but their very name, the *alik Telmun*, shows that they went no farther than Bahrein. Mention has been made (p. 337) of 'the deep-draughted dhows that in the monsoon season undertook the long voyage from the Persian Gulf to Karachi or Ceylon', but in fact nothing is known about them. When Sargon of Akkad speaks of the ships of Meluhha, of Makkar and of Telmun he is speaking of foreign ships, not of Mesopotamian ships that visited those ports—indeed the Mesopotamians seem never to have known where Meluhha was. After Bahrein was established as the port of transshipment we hear no more of any foreign vessels, for the simple reason that they no longer visited Mesopotamian waters; but the goods that came to Bahrein were still carried by them. From very early times there must have been the precursors of the modern Arab dhow engaged in the same business as that of the dhow within living memory; based on south Arabian harbours whose names are not recorded, taking advantage of those monsoon winds the secret of which westerners were not to learn until Roman times, they must have plied their long-distance traffic, the tenuous link between India and Ceylon on the one hand and the Middle Eastern markets on the other. History is silent about them, but those Arab sailors, as for want of a more distinctive name we may call them, were a considerable factor in the history of man's progress.

PRODUCTION AND TAXATION

Egypt

In Egypt and in Mesopotamia alike civilization was based ultimately upon agriculture and the country drew its wealth from the fertility of its soil. Consequently the primary source of government revenues was bound to be the agricultural produce of the land, and in each country the collection of such revenues was simplified by the character of the constitution.

In Egypt the divine Pharaoh was from the outset the Lord of the land and in time, with the suppression of the old feudal nobility, could claim to be its actual owner. In Mesopotamia the entire territory of a city state was the personal property of the city's god, and the ruler, king or *ensī,* as representative of the god—although in the administration he was assisted by the city council—was the real proprietor of that territory. In both countries therefore the government, vested in the person of the ruler, was in theory entitled to the whole produce of the fields; either he could exercise that right literally, taking everything to himself subject only to the costs of production, or he could work the land indirectly, letting the cultivators make what profit they could for themselves, while he received from them a fixed percentage of the harvest.

It would appear that the Egyptian Pharaohs of the Old

Kingdom exploited the country directly for their own benefit. But with the organization of Egypt into districts or nomes the former system was modified. The nomarch, belonging to an old noble family, possessed certain lands of his own, the 'paternal estate', entailed in the family; he had also the 'count's estate', a fief conveyed to him by Pharaoh as the prerogative of his office, which reverted to the crown on his death; an unspecified part of the nome remained crown property, and a royal commissioner, together with 'overseers of the crown possessions' was attached to the nomarch's suite to take charge of the royal herds, etc.; but all the revenues from the nome were collected by the nomarch and passed by him to the treasury of the central government: 'I carried all their dues to the king's house; there were no arrears against me in any office of his.'

The dangerous semi-autonomy of the nomarchs led to their suppression and the transfer of their task to fiscal officials appointed by the crown and directly responsible to it. But side by side with this growing centralization there developed a divided ownership. Pharaoh owned Egypt in his capacity as a god, and it was seemly that his brother deities should have their share in it; Pharaoh therefore endowed the temples with estates of their own, by the alienation of crown lands, and these might enjoy certain tax exemptions. An ambitious priesthood did everything to encourage so pious a policy, with the result that before the end of the second millennium BC one fifth of the whole country had come to belong to the temples, Amon of Thebes being the chief landowner after Pharaoh himself. Of the remaining four-fifths the greater part was worked by the king's serfs under the supervision of officials appointed by him. To relatives, or to favourite courtiers, Pharaoh might grant fiefs of land which were permanent and indivisible, held upon fixed terms, and to other meritorious persons he might grant tenant-holdings which were divisible; holdings of either sort could be transferred by will or by sale very much in the manner of a modern leasehold, the liabilities on them being unaffected by the change of ownership. The tenants might in addition hold other crown property such as cattle, asses, etc., for whose use again they paid an annual assessment recorded in the tax registers kept in the White House, the central office of the treasury. All taxes were paid in kind and stored in the royal magazines; it is illuminating to find that all the goods thus brought in, grain, cattle, wine, linen, are invoiced indiscriminately as 'labour'; in other words, they are put on precisely the same basis as the *corvée* whereby Pharaoh's serfs, the people of Egypt, were called up to build a pyramid or to clean out a canal. The people and what the people produce are equally the property of their divine ruler.

The Egyptian records do not state the proportion of the harvest that actually came to the royal granaries after the necessary deductions for the livelihood of the serfs; Hebrew tradition, recounting the story of Joseph, puts it at 20 per cent, and this may be true; but the amount paid in probably had but little relation to that collected. Corruption on the part of the tax collectors was endemic and, at times when the central administration was weak, assumed vast proportions; the reforms of Harmhab in the Eighteenth Dynasty were almost entirely concerned with correcting the abuses of the financial bureaucracy, against which the peasants were helpless. Extortion by the fiscal authorities and by the soldiery was almost a matter of course, and Harmhab put his finger on the root of the evil when he remitted the taxes imposed on the officials themselves. For while the agricultural tax was the main source of state revenue a secondary but still very important source was the tax upon government offices. This may theoretically have been but the natural extension of the agricultural tax; thus, if the mayor of El Kab had to make a yearly payment to the treasury of 5,600 grains of gold and 4,200 grains of silver, and his assistant 4,200 grains of silver, a necklace of gold beads, two oxen and two chests of linen, it is fair to assume that this represented the proceeds of *octroi* and market taxes collected from the townsmen. But because the amount due to the central government was fixed and did not fluctuate with the amount of business done, it means that the mayor was really in the position of a tax farmer obliged to pay in a certain sum but free to extract from the taxpayer as much more as he possibly could, so as to defray any official charges upon himself and to supplement his official salary, if any.

The number of these fiscal officers was very great and the value of the goods sent in annually by them to the White House must have been enormous—unfortunately no full account of the Egyptian revenue survives—but it must be remembered that only a small proportion of the total revenue was derived from what can properly be termed taxation; by far the greater part was no more than the return on the invested capital of the Pharaoh. The peasant who cursed the exactions of a corrupt collector would never have dreamed of disputing the justice of his statutory dues, because that payment was in his own and everybody's interest; Pharaoh was Egypt, and the well-being of Pharaoh and that of the nation were synonymous. Absolute autocracy had so simplified the economy of Egypt that the viziers in charge of the treasury had no need to invent new methods of raising money; the whole wealth of the country flowed into the exchequer automatically. For the Egyptian individually the pattern of life was assured; he was left enough to live upon, no fresh demands would come to make things more difficult, and in the event of a bad harvest—the only possible disaster—he could hope to receive state assistance.[10] Viewed from the purely financial standpoint the Egyptian system was primitive in the extreme; the theory upon which it was based—the divinity of Pharaoh—is one inconceivable in the modern world. It is therefore interesting to find that, granted the identity of Pharaoh with the nation and the state, the practical application of the theory can be described in terms which seem to bring it strangely in touch with a Marxist philosophy founded on principles so wholly different. The nationalization of land, in part made possible by the liquidation of the old land-owning nobility, and the exploitation of much of it by a system of collective farms; the state monopoly of all production, mines, etc.; the state control of manufacture and of craft guilds; the state monopoly of foreign trade; the religiously held conviction that while it was the state's duty and interest to secure the well-being of the individual citizens, yet those individuals, Pharaoh's serfs, existed only for the state; all this, which has so curiously modern a ring, affords the strongest possible contrast to the financial principles of the other ancient state whose economy we can examine in detail.

Mesopotamia

In early days the entire territory of a Sumerian city state was the property of the city's patron god. It would seem that in practice this was modified to the extent that certain areas were the communal property of the citizens (who, as the followers of the god, ought to have their share in his possessions) with no further liability than that of paying tithes to the temple. The greater part however remained in the hands of the god and might be let on lease to private individuals or let on condition of services to the temple personnel, or might be worked directly by the temple; the *ensī* (*patesi*), the human ruler who acted as 'tenant farmer' of the god, was the obvious person to manage the god's estates, directly or indirectly,[11] and to all intents and purposes therefore he was himself the lord of the land. Inevitably this led to abuses. Urukagina, the reformist *ensī* of Lagash, describes how his predecessors had appropriated the temple lands for their own use—the oxen of the gods were employed for the irrigation of the lands of the *ensī* and 'the best fields of the gods formed the *ensī*'s kitchen-gardens and cucumber fields';[12] the ruler had himself to set the example of reform and 'in the house and field of the *ensī* he installed Nin-Girsu, their master; in the house and field of the harim he installed the goddess Bau, their mistress; in the house and in the field of the children he installed Dunshagga, their master'. For a brief moment, and in the city state of Lagash, the theocratic basis of the Sumerian economy was re-affirmed.

Throughout all Mesopotamian history the various local gods remained land-holders on a large scale; many of the temple estates were worked directly by slave- or serf-labour under the direction of priests, but in this case the head of the state, *ensi* or king, was the chief administrator, combining in one office the management of the divine and the royal domains. But always there was the tendency to substitute private ownership for that of the community or of the god, and the process becomes more marked as Sumerian tradition is gradually submerged beneath practices imported by foreign conquerors. In the time of Manishtusu of Kish—who was a Babylonian Semite—we find the king purchasing three very large estates,[18] presumably communal land, ousting the 1,564 labourers who had been employed on them in order to install there his own nephew and other men of noble family. The old habit of making grants of land, either to assure loyalty or to reward service, became more common; thus, in Hammurabi's time, the officers responsible for recruiting for the army and the police received small-holdings which were inalienable, transmitted only in the male line and on the condition that the original obligations were fulfilled (or an *ilku* tax paid in lieu of personal service) but, on the other hand, were tax free. Contract tablets show that in the second millennium land was more freely bought and sold than in the past; it would certainly appear that to a large extent the original state-ownership had been waived in favour of a tax upon its value. Under the Kassite kings of Babylon the practice was extended, and the familiar *kudurru* or boundary stones bear witness to this; they contain copies of the actual title deeds (which were on clay tablets) and define the areas of the estate, and the text ends with curses upon anyone who interferes with the owner's rights, which are further placed under the protection of various deities whose emblems are sculptured upon the stone. The insistence in such monuments on the divine protection of private property in land suggests that the growth of a rich landed class was unpopular with the community in general, and that not only because it went against tradition but also because it tended to lower the status of the small-holder, and also to impoverish the exchequer; too many tax-free grants had been made in the past, and the Kassite kings were particularly generous in their remission of dues; thus Melí-Shipak, in the thirteenth century, confers large estates upon his son and frees them of all taxes and tithes and excuses all the labourers employed upon them from the *corvée*. Under the powerful rulers of the earlier periods, down to the First Dynasty, the temple lands paid taxes—thus Hammurabi has the temple managers and the cattle-masters of the Shamash temple brought to Babylon for the checking of their accounts—but the Kassite king Agum-kakrime granted immunity from all taxes to the estates of the gods Marduk and Szarpânâtu and gave to the priests tax-free houses and gardens, and his successors went even farther and supplied the temples with sesame, butter, wool, etc., out of the civil revenues.

Since the produce of the temple lands was very largely absorbed by the requirements of the god's service immunity from taxation may not have involved so serious a loss to the state as might at first sight appear; but the fact remained that those vast estates, the estates of the king and of some of his nobles, and a great many smaller holdings in private hands contributed little or nothing to the state treasury. Moreover, it would seem that after the fall of the First Dynasty of Babylon some of the cities also managed to obtain exemption from the royal taxes, which again would have been a serious loss of revenue. To meet the expenses of the government therefore the Mesopotamian state had to rely far more than did the Egyptian upon sources of revenue other than the tax upon land and produce.

The cost of public works was to a large extent defrayed by the *corvée* system of forced labour, which was in fact a tax upon the individual. The slaves on the big estates and the freemen small-holders were alike liable to be called up for such tasks as the digging and cleaning of canals, road-making, etc.; generally these were local needs and the district authorities would enrol local labour, but sometimes the work was of national rather than provincial importance and the net would be cast more widely, as when Hammurabi says of himself, 'by the call-up of the people of his country he has built the foundations of the city walls of Sippar'; or auxiliary gangs might be sent from a distance: to quote Hammurabi again, 'I am now sending you herewith 360 porters; 180 porters shall be on the Larsa building, 180 porters shall be on the Raxaba building; they will help'. The peasant would receive a properly signed and dated summons such as 'Task: brick-carrying for one day'; he could protest, and the provincial governor would hear his case; and he could obtain exemption by means of a money payment; the fact that he could do so shows that labour under the *corvée* was regarded as a tax paid in kind.

All agricultural taxes were paid in kind. Since they were not fixed but reckoned on a percentage basis they could only be assessed when the year's produce was ready to hand, for grain, after the harvest was gathered, for sheep, after the lambing season, for wool, after the shearing; and whatever the tax collector took had to be sent in to the government depots. Delays were frequent, and the exchequer did not endure them patiently—'Why have you not yet sent to Babylon the 30 lambs as your tax? Are you not ashamed of such behaviour? I am now sending you a post; as soon as you have had sight of my letter send the 30 lambs as your tax to Babylon. If you do not bring them, you will have to pay one shekel of silver for each lamb.' A very careful account was kept of all incomings and they were turned to advantage as soon as possible; the animals might be sent to join the state herds; other perishable goods were sold or lent to merchants at regular rates of interest, or were handed over to government factories for manufacture. Theoretically the annual tax was 10 per cent of the produce, but the grower would seldom escape so easily. The collection was made by tax farmers who were not professional civil servants—even the superintendent-general of taxes was not properly speaking a government official—and extortion was easy whether for their own enrichment or to gain favour with the authorities; it is clear from the tablets that the actual payments might amount to a fifth or even to a half of the yield of the land; presumably the poor suffered most.

To supplement the inadequate returns from the land there were the taxes on town goods, manufacture and trade. Here again collection was in the hands of tax farmers, but payments were for the most part in gold, and an elaborate registration of all taxpayers enabled the treasury to forecast the budget with a certain amount of accuracy and also lessened the opportunities for corruption; thus we hear of a case where two citizens had defaulted and the tax farmer had been unable to collect the amounts due from them, but none the less he had to make the full return to the exchequer; it is clear that the total had been estimated beforehand in great detail. This was made possible by the census. A register of births was kept, so that a poll-tax could easily be applied; but for taxation in general the lists dealt with property as well as with persons. The best preserved of such lists are those of the fifteenth century BC from Alalakh—not therefore actually Mesopotamian, but modelled on Babylonian originals—recording the inhabitants of villages subject to the city; their names are given and they are distinguished (as in Babylonia) into three classes. First come the peasants, semi-serfs, subject to the *corvée* and to military service, owners of small plots of land or vineyard, of whom it is often remarked 'has no cattle'; the next in order are the middle class, amongst whom we find tradesmen, gardeners, herdsmen and grooms; last come the gentry, distinguished by the possession of chariots (though of a few it is said 'possesses no chariot'), 'knights', if the chariots are really military, or, if otherwise, 'carriage folk'. Other lists enumerate the houses in each village, qualified by the social position of the occupant, to which in the case of a craftsman his trade may be added; we may suspect therefore a graduated house-tax.

The elaborate inventories of raw materials and manufactured goods which are common in Third Dynasty and later periods in Mesopotamia are in many cases the accountancy tablets of the temple stores and workshops, but others seem to refer to factories outside the temples and to be certified stocktaking lists used as a basis for taxation. Import duties were levied on goods from abroad and *octroi* duties on the country produce brought into the towns; the guilds, together with the *karum*, the Chamber of Commerce, had to furnish information regarding their business and the profits accruing from it.

NOTES ON CHAPTER V

1. Objections to the use of this term have been raised by Professor I. M. Diakonoff on the grounds that 'The economic system of Mesopotamia, based as it was on slavery, cannot be termed a capitalist system, because the latter is based on hired labour'.
   The English definition of capitalism is 'The possession by individuals of capital or funds used in production'.
   The objection of Professor Diakonoff unduly exaggerates the part played by slavery in the Mesopotamian economy (as has been shown above) and the laws of Hammurabi and in particular the business tablets of the Old Babylonian period from Ur (*Ur Texts*, Vol. V) both show that the merchants not only used their own and borrowed capital but also hired labour. Sir Leonard Woolley has kept the term 'capitalist' in the text because to the English-speaking reader it conveys precisely the meaning that he intended; it is quite possible that some other term will prove preferable in translation.
2. An exception, as Professor John A. Wilson points out, was the funeral temple at Thebes built by Amenhotep, son of Hapou, the famous architect and great favourite of Amenophis III; see C. Robichon and A. Varille, 'Le temple du scribe royal Amenhotep fils de Hapou', *Fouilles de l'Institut Français du Caire,* XI (1936).
3. The question of the construction of private tombs in Egypt deserves further exploration.
4. Lepsius, *Denkmaeler,* Vol. III, 229.
5. A scholar on behalf of the National Commission of Israel points

out that these pre-dynastic objects were found below the floor of the temples; their association with the temples is, therefore, not certain.

6. As Professor J. Leclant observes, Egyptian attempts to penetrate southwards remained very fragmentary under the Old Kingdom and there cannot be said to have been any systematic policy of colonization. The Egyptians did, however, reach Nubia as early as the First Dynasty: according to a discovery made by Dr A. J. Arkell, we should read the name of King Djer on a graffito at Jebel Cheikh Soliman near the Second Cataract. The sign *stg* on the tablet of his predecessor King Hor-Aha may equally well indicate Nubia or what was later to become the first name of Egypt, north of the First Cataract. This is also true of the Hieraconpolis fragment showing King Khasekhamui slaughtering a prisoner. No contemporary document of King Djoser mentions an expedition to the south during his reign: the famous 'Stele of the Famine' represents only a decree of Ptolemy V Epiphanes, which, in 187 BC, mentions in pictorial form the return of the southern provinces to the crown. From the time of Sneferu (Early Fourth Dynasty) on the contrary, relations between Egypt and the south become more active: warlike raids, the exploitation of diorite quarries, and commercial expeditions along the desert lanes steering clear of the obstacles encountered in the valley. Doubtless under the Fourth Dynasty, if we accept the evidence of the Qar inscription, the role of Pepi I was of considerable importance. The frontier of Egypt remains, however, at the First Cataract. No 'march', no territorial exploitation was systematically organized south of Egypt. The deepest sallies of the Egyptians did not bring them into contact with the Negroes; their contacts were with the Hamites. The Sudan at this time enjoyed a mediocre culture, the so-called Group B culture, lasting from the Thinite period until the end of the Old Kingdom.
7. Much could of course be floated *down* the rivers, as Herodotus remarked in the case of timber; but anything going north had to be carried on pack animals.
8. Professor John A. Wilson points out that Sneferu's boats are not always called *kebent;* this name is attested only under the Sixth Dynasty [cf. K. Sethe, *Zeitschrift für Aegyptische Sprache,* 45 1908–09), p. 8].
9. The importance of the Egyptian merchant marine seems somewhat underestimated by the author; see T. Säve-Söderbergh, 'The Navy of the Eighteenth Egyptian Dynasty', Uppsala Universitets *Arsskrift* (1946), 6.
10. Under the Eleventh Dynasty, the treasurer was authorized by the king to relieve the needy. Similarly, under the New Empire, the royal granaries were used to succour the poor [W. Helck, *Zur Verwaltung des Mittleren und Neuen Reichs* (1958), p. 79 and n. 6].
11. According to Professor I. M. Diakonoff, in Jamdat Nasr times it was managed by the elders; in Fara times it was managed by the priests; towards the end of the Ur-Nanshe Dynasty the *ensī* becomes 'lord of the land' as lessor of temple land.
12. This reading has been suggested by Professor I. M. Diakonoff.
13. Professor I. M. Diakonoff is of the opinion that this was by no means exclusively a foreign practice. The Sumerian ruler of Lagash, Enkhegal—the earliest ruler known by name—already purchased land.

CHAPTER VI

LANGUAGES AND WRITING SYSTEMS: EDUCATION

LANGUAGES AND WRITING SYSTEMS

THE art of writing seems to arise naturally and almost inevitably from the condition of urbanization and also to be essential to its maintenance. In no part of the world has civilization at any time advanced to any considerable height or achieved any permanence unless by the aid of writing; but just as civilization generally implies the development of city life so writing has never been introduced in any other than an urban society.

To justify so categorical a statement it is necessary to define exactly what is meant by writing; for it is evident that in primitive communities signs, symbols and pictures have been employed to which the term writing can loosely be applied. It is true that such are the material out of which writing may be evolved, but in themselves they are not writing. The quite illiterate nomad Arab of the Egyptian desert by hammering with a flint will inscribe on a convenient rock-face the *wasm,* the emblem of his tribe—the same as he brands on his camels —to show the future passers-by that a man of that tribe has been there; or he may draw, for instance, a circle with a vertical stroke above it representing the *dilu,* the leather bucket hanging from its rope, to show that he has dug there and found water, and someone else can do the like. Here a sign conveys a definite message (provided that you know the convention) but it is not really writing because it can only be used for that one message inherent in itself; you cannot add other signs to qualify or expand the message; it is an isolated sign, not one element in a system. Some of the North American Indian tribes painted or embroidered on their buffalo-skin robes elaborate pictorial records sometimes biographical, sometimes calendary, sometimes historical; the earliest known of these is the famous cloak of Pocahontas now in the Ashmolean Museum. Most of those surviving are of late date, generally of the nineteenth century, and show clearly the influence of European art; but none of them could be described as written records for the simple reason that in themselves they have no coherence and no logical significance; they are illustrations to a story and it is only if you know the story that you can make sense of the illustrations. 'Records' such as these are not to be brought into line with any kind of written record; with far more truth they can be compared with, for example, the long series of mediaeval carvings in the Chapter House of Salisbury Cathedral which illustrate the book of Genesis; an admirable and striking commentary to an exposition of the Old Testament delivered by a cleric to the illiterate English country-folk of the fourteenth century, they would be a complete puzzle for anyone not familiar with the Old Testament story; unintelligible individually and having no relation one to another, they would tell him nothing.

It is hardly too much to say that 'picture-writing' is a contradiction in terms; but that pictures form the basis of any writing system is indisputable. The North American Indian and the Beduin stopped short at the first stage because that was all that their manner of life required and all that their social background could evoke; the former relied upon the tribal story-teller for his history and had no need to write it, though he might enjoy hearing it to the accompaniment of a 'picture strip'; the latter was concerned at most to record a single fact for the information of others leading a life as simple and direct as his own.

So far as we know, the Sumerians were the first people to evolve a proper system of writing, and we are fortunate in that we can in their case follow the process of evolution more closely than is possible with any other people.

As soon as men came to live together in groups larger than the family groups or clans of the Neolithic period and as industry tended to be specialized, the question of personal property grew more complicated. In the old days of the family or clan the head of such a group, by the conventional rules of patriarchal life, was the sole owner of everything belonging to the group; the use of a thing might be exclusive to one or another member of the community, but regarding its ultimate ownership there could be no doubt at all. But when various groups were associated in the new unit of the town, then there could be confusion, and the claim to ownership could be called into question.[1] Something was needed to certify the right to property. Consequently we find, at the very beginning of the metal age, i.e. at the very outset of urbanized society, the engraved personal seal. The stopper of the store-jar, the knot in the cord that tied up the bundle of spare garments, was smeared with clay bearing the impression of a seal that bore the recognizable mark of the proprietor—his *wasm*. The mark bore no relation to its meaning; it might be pictorial—the drawing of a dog or a cow, in which case one may suspect but cannot prove either a nickname or some sort of play upon words—or a decorative design, or more simply, an arrangement of straight lines; what mattered was that it should be individual, that it should be unmistakably the mark of so-and-so and of no one else. Each owner of property therefore required a seal. But since in the Sumerian city state the city's god was the chief, if not the sole, lord of the land and of all its fruits, the god's temple wherein the produce of his estates was stored stood in the greatest need of all to have some distinctive mark if the god's property was to be duly safeguarded against peculation. What, then, was the mark to be? The owner was in the first place a god, a member of the hierarchy of heaven; in the second place he was an individual god bearing a special name and possessing special attributes; in the third place he was the god of the city state which, as such, was identified with him; it was in the last capacity that he owned the goods stored in the city's magazines. To brand his goods as simply the property of 'a god', as divine property, scarcely answered the case, and the goods were his in virtue not of his personality but of his rights of lordship. Consequently on seal-impressions of the pre-literary period which come, certainly, from temple stores, we find conventionalized pictorial symbols which can be recognized as the prototypes of those signs which in later times stood for the names of cities. The door of a building, or a tower, represents the temple which, since the god is king, is the real heart of the city; cap this with the rising sun and you have Larsa, *UD.UNU.KI*, 'the abode of the Sun'; with the evening star, and you have Uruk; with a snake, Der; the recognized symbol of the god makes the meaning of the pictogram obvious to anyone, and it was quite easy to draw.

But while the private citizen might be content with the simple mark that identified as his the household supplies stored for his use, the god's establishment was on a vastly bigger scale and required much more orderly supervision; to do their work properly the priests in charge of such wealth had to keep accounts. So it was in the temples and in the service of the god that writing began. Again, the initial stages were easy enough. You had to keep tally of the cattle and the sheep, the jars of butter and the measures of grain; a picture of a sheep, of a cow's head, of an ear of corn or of a fish followed by one or more impressed dots or circles gave you precisely the information that was needed—sheep, so many, cattle, so many, corn, so many (standard measures, not ears). That is, in fact, the character of the earliest clay tablets found in Mesopotamia, at Erech and Jamdat Nasr;[2] they are the economic records indispensable for the business of the temples. This is a stage at which man can arrive without any undue exercise of the imagination; we see just the same thing on tablets from Minoan Crete (though there, at a much later date, the system of enumeration is more elaborate) where the contents of the palace stores are listed, so many adzes, so many chariots, so many measures of saffron. Quite a number of people have got so far and then have stopped—at least they have stopped so far as their own initiative was concerned, and if they have subsequently gone on to writing properly so-called, it was because they borrowed the idea of it from others, from the Sumerians.[3]

For it must be emphasized that these temple accounts are records, not writing. The early pictograms denote things, but that is all; they cannot make statements, and they cannot convey thought. As long as the pictogram means what it says writing is impossible, for you cannot make a picture of action or time or quality or thought, or of anything but a thing;[4] you cannot put down anything that makes sense. Pictorial representation ends and true writing begins at the moment when an indubitable linguistic element first comes in, and that can only happen when signs have acquired a phonetic value. The gap which divides the pictogram from the hieroglyph and ultimately from the phonetic sign is so great that for most peoples it has proved impassable. It is to the credit of the Sumerians that they were able to bridge that gap, and as soon as they had done so their neighbours were quick to adopt not necessarily the Sumerian system, but the Sumerian idea, and there arose a number of scripts which differed completely in form from the Sumerian but were indebted to it for the basic conception that a written sign might represent not a thing but a sound.

All the archaeological evidence available seems to prove that true writing was first developed in southern Mesopotamia, and in view of the incalculable importance of the invention for human progress everywhere we are entitled to ask the further question, *why* was that invention made by the Sumerians rather than by any other ancient people? The answer seems to be that it was owing to the peculiar character of the Sumerian language.

The theory has been propounded that the idea of making the picture signs represent sounds instead of the objects pictured was first suggested by the existence in both the Sumerian and the Egyptian languages of 'homonyms', that is, of words having the same sound but different meanings. If we accept the theory, then we must admit that the art of writing could have been invented independently in both countries and that the apparent priority of Sumer may have been merely the result of accident or again may rest simply upon the incomplete character of the archaeological evidence at our disposal. Obviously that is a possibility that we must take into consideration.

The earliest known example quoted as illustrating this method of extending the range of pictorial signs comes on tablets found at Jamdat Nasr, a site on the Tigris, a little north of Babylon, and dated about 3300 BC. In them occurs the personal name En-lil-ti, which in Sumerian means 'Enlil [the god] causes to live'. The word-sign *TI* is the picture of an arrow, but in the spoken language the sound *ti* is a homonym, meaning both 'arrow' and 'life'; the latter would be difficult to represent pictorially and therefore, according to this theory, the scribe uses the arrow sign, which could be drawn, to mean 'life'. Similarly in Egypt we find the familiar sign representing a scarab beetle (hpr) transferred to the homonym hpr meaning 'to exist'. Now as an observation this is indisputable, and it can fairly be claimed that homonyms did at one stage help in the development of script; but the theory that they suggested the transition from the pictorial to the syllabic sign reverses the historical process, because the play upon words, *ti,* arrow, and *ti,* life, holds good only for the sounds of speech; not until the sign had come to represent a sound instead of a thing could the fact of the sound having more than one meaning affect the value of the sign.

There are homonyms in modern languages, but even when they are represented by the same signs, i.e. when their spelling as well as their pronunciation is identical, the play upon words does not suggest itself so readily as the 'homonym theory' requires; the appropriate meaning is generally so well defined by its context that no other meaning presents itself to the mind. Thus, if an English journalist or broadcasting announcer reporting a cricket match were to remark that 'Mr Blank carried his bat after a valuable innings', no reader or listener would ever think of the successful player as nursing a specimen of *Vespertilionidae*. But for the Sumerian that latent ambiguity simply did not exist. The modern language, starting from the sound of the spoken word and using an alphabetic system to express sounds, can make the same group of letters stand for totally different things if their names happen to be pronounced alike; but the Sumerian was working in precisely the opposite direction; he began with actual material things, not with sounds at all. It is true that in his spoken language the sound *ti* meant 'arrow' and also meant 'life', though even in the spoken language the correct meaning would be so defined by the context that the alternative was no more likely to be evoked in the hearer's mind than in the case of the English word 'bat'. But when the scribe drew upon his tablet the word-sign *ti* in the form of an arrow that sign did not mean the sound '*ti*'—it meant neither more nor less than the material arrow which he had been at pains to represent; and between that and 'life' there was no connection whatsoever. The essential thing for the development of writing is that the written sign loses its purely representational character and comes to signify a sound, and the homonym could not effect that momentous change. That being so, the mere existence of homonyms in the Egyptian language has no bearing on the problem of how and where writing was invented, and, accepting the archaeological evidence, as practically all authorities agree in doing, we have still to ask, 'Why did the Sumerians evolve their syllabary before the Egyptians learnt to write?'

Sumerian was unique amongst the languages of the ancient Middle East in being agglutinative;[5] it belonged in this respect to the same group as Chinese (though Chinese is from an analytical point of view generally classified as 'isolating') and Turkman and the later related languages, Finnish and Hungarian. Most of the root words are monosyllabic, consisting of one, or two, vocalized consonants; such would be the words invented by primitive man as the names of the things he encountered in his everyday life—incidentally, the names of things of which you could draw pictures; there are a number of dissyllabic and a very few trisyllabic words, but these may be of later formation. The Sumerian language was, by the time when we first encounter it, already so developed that the process of its growth cannot be traced; but although that growth had in many respects followed different lines, yet parallels with the similar language of China are numerous enough to justify us in making a general comparison; and since Chinese has up to the present time perpetuated many of the linguistic methods of the primitive age we may adduce it for the explanation of early Sumerian practice. Using then the analogy of China we can say that an agglutinative language, in order to express more complicated or novel meanings, selects the simple words which together suggest the required meaning and strings them together without any change or inflection; thus, the Chinese trisyllabic word for 'magnet' is merely the three monosyllabic words 'pull—iron—stone' juxtaposed. In a compound word of this sort each syllable is a separate word which retains just so much of its original meaning as is needed to complete that of the compound; but the meaning of the compound, i.e. that of the word-syllables in combination, is something new—not just a collection of the things named but something that results from the association of the ideas of those things. And because by the word as spoken an idea is conveyed which is related only indirectly to the various things named by the several elements composing it, one tends to pronounce the compound without thinking much about the specific meaning of its individual parts; thus, even in English, one can speak of a politician as 'a tub-thumping wire-puller' without for one instant thinking of him as thumping a tub or pulling on a wire; we are describing characteristics that have nothing to do with wires or tubs, although the metaphor was ultimately derived from such. The complete word conveys a new idea. The literal meaning of its parts becomes subordinate to their sound; it persists to the extent that it subserves the sense of the compound word, but it is not stressed beyond that; in proportion as the compound word becomes familiar in use, the elements of it lose their character as names of things and become syllables. Now if in speech you string together the names of things to make a new word, and if you have been accustomed to drawing pictograms that represent those things, then it requires no great effort of the imagination to see that by stringing together the pictograms you automatically represent the new word. The grouped signs, representing things, simply reproduce the grouped words which are the names of those things, but because they are similarly grouped the effect of their association is similar; the pictographic sign becomes syllabic because the spoken word has done so already. The drawing of a fish still means 'a fish' when used by itself, but as an element in a compound word its representational value tends to disappear in favour of the name-sound; it becomes the syllable *FISH*. When that happens the gulf between non-writing and writing has been bridged.

In the case of an agglutinative language a syllabic script results almost inevitably from the character of its root words, and because it accords with the genius of the language there is little motive for changing it; the Chinese syllabary persists to the present day, and the Sumerian was modified only by peoples of a different type of speech, for which it was ill adapted. As against an alphabetic script, the main drawback of a syllabary for general use is that it uses a vastly greater number of signs and so makes greater demands upon the powers of learning and of memory. The number of signs in the Sumerian syllabary was, in point of fact, systematically reduced. In the early tablets from Erech (and those early tablets are mostly lists of offerings in the temple accounts, so that it is not surprising that the sign for 'sheep' should occur frequently) there are no fewer than thirty-one variations of the sign *UDU* (sheep), corresponding in part, no doubt, to the many kinds and conditions of sheep used for ritual or other purposes in the temples. But in the next main level only three signs for sheep remain, and in the top stratum only two. Here, then, is a deliberate rejection of an almost unrestricted tendency to differentiation. At one stage of the Uruk (Erech) period (Uruk IVb, *c.* 3500 BC) two thousand signs were in use; tablets found at the site of Fara of a date perhaps three hundred to four hundred years later indicate that their number had dwindled to about eight hundred. By *c.* 2900 BC another two hundred signs used in the Fara texts have disappeared.[6]

One may suspect that some of the variants for 'sheep' in the early tablets were due not so much to the variety of the animals as to the divergent efforts of different scribes to represent a sheep; but the deliberate policy of reducing the number of signs is evident. It may well be that advantage was taken of the existence of homonyms in the Sumerian language to effect further economies. If two things had names that sounded alike in speech and one of them was easy to draw and the other difficult, the fact that the sign for one of them, having already been used as a syllable in a compound word (just as the spoken word was), had acquired a phonetic value would suggest its use for the other word also. Thus in Sumerian the word *TI* means both 'arrow' and 'life'; you can make a recognizable drawing of an arrow, but 'life' you cannot draw; but as soon as your drawing of an arrow has ceased to be limited to its representational use and has come to mean the sound *TI*, then it can perfectly well mean 'life' too. Again, when once it is realized that a sign can represent a sound instead of having its meaning limited to a particular object the scribe is no longer tied down to the drawing of material things; he can invent a sign and arbitrarily assign it to a particular sonant value. Thus in the case, let us say, of an adjective, a simple monosyllable which could not be 'spelled out' by a combination of syllabic signs, a conventional sign having no pictorial basis could be adopted, or, again, the picture of an object might be transferred to the quality inherent in the object; the drawing of something essentially big might be made to mean 'big' without any reference to the thing itself or to the sound of its name, the emphasis being solely on its size. It is certainly the case that in the Sumerian syllabary adjectives such as 'great' and 'good' have signs peculiar to themselves which are not pictures of anything definable; the explanation given above is theoretical, based on analogy only, but it is not improbable.

One cannot define the stage at which the written sign was recognized as being phonetic and syllabic, and no longer necessarily pictorial and having only a specific and material connotation; the process must have been gradual and use may well have anticipated theory. But it is possible that the development of the Sumerian cursive script itself helped in some degree to effect that change in the value of the characters, or, at any rate, helped towards the recognition of the change. As with the use of the stylus on clay the sign became formalized, the original drawing first assuming a rectilinear form and finally resolving itself into a diagram composed of wedge-shaped impressions which bore no recognizable resemblance to the thing which the drawing represented, that thing would be lost sight of and the sign would be identified not with it but with the sound of its name; what had been 'a fish' would become *FISH*.

But while *FISH* used by itself as an ideogram would still mean 'fish' (not because the sign any longer looked like a fish but because the name of the thing was pronounced like that) it might also, owing to the existence of homonyms, mean something quite different.[7] This difficulty can be avoided by the use of an alphabet because words pronounced in the same way can be spelt in different ways, as, for example, in English we write 'mays', 'maze' and 'maize'; but with a syllabary that cannot be done. Consequently very many Sumerian signs were polyphones, capable of being read with two or more totally different meanings. In English, of course, there is the same difficulty, when 'bat' may mean either an implement for a game or an animal, and the reader must judge from the context which is intended. The Sumerian had another system. In the first place, he used determinatives—the ambiguous word might be introduced, in the written document, by a sign which was not meant to be pronounced but gave the necessary clue for the pronunciation of the word, or, at any rate, for its meaning. Thus the sign for 'plough' might have as a prefix the sign for 'wood' or that for 'man'; the determinative informed the reader whether he was to read the word as 'plough' or as 'ploughman'; the system is virtually that of the Chinese[8] where signs or 'radicals' indicating 'money', 'water', 'foot', 'food', etc., are added to a phonetic sign such as *chien* to indicate 'the *chien* associated with money', i.e. 'mean', 'cheap'; 'the *chien* associated with foot', i.e. 'to tread'; 'the *chien* associated with water', i.e. 'to splash'; 'the *chien* associated with food', i.e. 'a parting gift of food', etc. Again, to avoid ambiguity two simple words are attached together, each of which may have several meanings but of those several only one is common to both words, so that the duplication of that one idea leaves no doubt as to the sense. Thus, modern Chinese has over a hundred different words all pronounced *i,* one of them being 'meaning' or 'thought'; used by itself it would be hopelessly ambiguous; another word, *ssu,* having the meanings 'servant', 'private', 'meaning', 'thought', 'control', etc., is almost equally confusing; the Chinese therefore puts the two together—*i—ssu,* and the only signification common to the two, i.e. 'meaning' or 'thought', is inevitably the right one. In much the same way with the Sumerian polyphone signs a word may be formed with two or three of these, each of which may have two or three values; but in the Sumerian language only certain sound-combinations are possible, and so most of the apparently alternative readings of the compound word would be instinctively rejected by the reader and he would without hesitation pronounce the word correctly. For the modern scholar, groping towards an understanding of the language, this is a stumbling-block, and he may long hesitate as to whether the Third Dynasty king should be called Dun-gi or Shul-gi; but for the Sumerian it was plain sailing. In the second place the Sumerian, having identified his signs with syllables, could employ them as phonetic complements and by so doing change the value of the sign to which they were attached. The stem-word *DU,* which was originally a drawing of, and meant, a human foot, was obviously one which should be combined with other words to render such abstract concepts as 'walking', 'standing', etc., and that regardless of the pronunciation of the words for such concepts; thus, *gin* meaning 'to go' and *gin-na* 'going', greater clarity could be got by combining the 'foot' sign with *gin* and 'going' would be written *DU-na;* but the reader, being warned by the *na* suffix, would recognize *DU* as being a mute determinative introducing '*gin*' and would pronounce the word as '*gin-na*'. To most people this may seem an uncalled-for complication, but since it is paralleled by the synonym-compounds of Chinese we must conclude that it arises naturally from the idiosyncrasies of an agglutinative language.

In the early part of the third millennium BC the Sumerian system of writing consisted of a syllabary containing some five hundred to six hundred signs. Most of these still served as ideograms, fulfilling exactly the part played by the original pictures. However necessary syllabic signs might be, the need for them was limited, because in the agglutinative language of the Sumerians the words, mostly monosyllabic, were inflected not by any internal change but by the addition of prefixed or suffixed syllables, and comparatively few signs with syllabic values were enough to fulfil this purpose and to represent phonetically such awkward words as could not be represented pictorially. When, however, the Babylonians took over the Sumerian script they were obliged to develop further the syllabic system because their inflective language could be expressed only by the help of phonetic signs; an ideogram could indeed be used by itself as a sort of shorthand character, uninflected, but otherwise they were compelled to spell out each word syllable by syllable. The basis of the Sumerian system of writing had been word-values, that of the Akkadian was syllable-values.

This mixed use increased the complication of the script. In the course of time every sign became a polyphone, representing completely different sounds, so that the employment of ideographic signs as determinatives was essential; where the polyphones were used syllabically their pronunciations would be decided, as we have seen, by the values of the other signs with which they were associated in each case. Again, many sounds could be represented by totally different signs. Thus, *DU* could be represented in twenty-three different ways, i.e. by twenty-three different pictures of things whose names happened to be similar; DU_1 is a human foot, DU_6 is a hill or mound, DU_7 'to gore', is a butting ox, DU_{11} 'to speak', is a man's head with the mouth specially marked, DU_{12} 'to play a stringed instrument' apparently figures a plectrum, and so on; as pictograms such are unequivocal, but when they become phonetic syllables all having, necessarily, similar values, they tend to be used indiscriminately for one and the same sound. But those sounds are always syllabic. None of the signs represents a single consonant; all are at least biliterate, consisting of at least one consonant plus a vowel, and many have two or sometimes even three consonants, and for that reason they were not likely to lead up to an alphabetical system. Involved and clumsy as this method of writing must appear to people accustomed to an alphabet, it suited the peculiar genius of the Sumerian language and so far accommodated itself to the Akkadian that apart from the development of the actual script it remained radically unchanged from its first invention to the close of the Late Babylonian period, 2,500 years later. Even the script altered but little, and the original modification was due entirely to the medium employed, not to any will to improvement. The first sketches executed with a sharp point on clay were inevitably simplified and conventionalized; because on damp clay it is easier to impress marks than to draw them, the triangular-ended stylus replaced the point, and the design was modified automatically. In the case of inscriptions cut in stone the rectilinear signs which first developed from the old pictures persisted longer; for the stone-cutter they were very easy to do, and the stone-cutter is a leisured and therefore a conservative craftsman. The ordinary scribe, writing as he always did upon a clay tablet and overburdened with accounts, wanted something in the nature of shorthand; a deft handling of the stylus produced the wedge-shaped impression and the signs—their pictorial origin completely lost in the formalized script—could be written quickly and almost mechanically. After that there was no need for further change; even for inscriptions on stone the cuneiform script soon became the norm, and so far as the writing of Sumerian was concerned finality had been reached.

If the genesis of the art of writing can be traced back to the peculiarity of the Sumerian language its stereotyping must be attributed to the character of the people and therefore to the use that they made of the art. It had been developed in the temples by the scribes who needed a convenient instrument for the keeping of the elaborate accounts of the revenues of the god, and in a society which was essentially industrial and commercial the main function of writing was the furtherance of business. From the ruins of the Mesopotamian cities a great bulk of 'literary' material has been recovered, and it can be roughly classified into three categories, business documents, royal inscriptions and religious texts; but it is to the first category that the vast majority of the tablets belong.

The business tablets, which include contracts, letters, deeds of sale, etc., as well as mere inventories, answer to purely practical ends; not only was the script fully qualified to deal with matters of the sort but the scribe had no inducement to improve upon or to beautify its character; it was a utilitarian instrument with which aesthetics had nothing to do. It might have been thought that royal inscriptions would call for something more decorative or more monumental than the shopkeeper's shorthand; but in Sumer such was not the case. It was very seldom that a written text formed the major part of a royal monument; for a public largely illiterate a picture was more impressive than any writing, and on Eannatum's 'Stele of the Vultures' (Pl. 6, a) or on a limestone plaque of Ur-Nina (the name is also read as Ur-Nanshe) the sculptured figures made the direct appeal and the written text added for the benefit of the few is relegated to the background. But the bulk of the royal inscriptions were not intended even for the literate few; they were meant for the eyes of the god. The king's statue stood in the temple to represent the king as perpetually a worshipper in the god's presence, and the inscription (generally recounting the ruler's pious services) was a perpetual reminder of his deserts; it was not at all an advertisement to the public, and in fact only a few priests would ever see it. But most of the royal inscriptions—Gudea's long-winded cylinders, the clay cones of Ur-Nammu, Rim-Sin or Kudur-Mabug—were never seen by anyone; they were immured in the brickwork of the temples built by the kings and were meant for no eyes but those of the god. Clearly such texts had to be well written, good examples of the calligraphy of the time, but they were in the nature of private records and did not call for monumental treatment; they had no effect on the script in normal use.

Documents of our third category are almost without exception of relatively late date. So far as one can tell from the tablets that have been preserved, the priests of early times were (as is indeed natural with members of an exclusive guild) content with oral tradition. It is possible that a few hymns and liturgies were committed to writing in early days, as is perhaps suggested even by some of the Uruk tablets, but for the most part they were learned by heart. It was only when the Semitic north had gained the ascendancy, and Sumerian as a spoken language was dying out, that the Sumerian priests set themselves to perpetuate in writing the religious literature of the old civilization and what they could of its history; for the former, memory had obviously served them very well, but as regards historical detail the confusion in the King Lists shows how little had hitherto been written. This belated salving of the ancient formulae was a purely practical measure, providing no motive for the modification of the old script; on the contrary, just because it was conservative in spirit it would be the more inclined to cling faithfully to the old conventions. So it was that having elaborated a system adequate to their needs and suited to their language, the Sumerians, using the system for utilitarian ends such as had prompted its invention, felt no need to modify or diversify the form of their writing any more than to tamper with its syllabic character.

At the time when writing began Sumer was by no means an isolated country but was itself expanding widely and also was in touch through trade with neighbours on the east and on the west. Just because the invention was a utilitarian one adopted for commercial and economic purposes it was bound to come to the notice of and to appeal to the foreign countries which had trade relations with Sumer and had themselves reached a stage of culture at which writing would serve a useful purpose.

It was not likely that such people should simply take over the Sumerian syllabary, which would have been ill-adapted to their different languages, but they could, and did, learn that a picture, representing a thing, could on the new recognized principle of phonetization stand for the sound of the thing's name.

Accordingly, it is in the Jamdat Nasr period, at the time when the phonetization of the Sumerian pictographic script was in progress, that the Proto-Elamite writing makes its appearance in Iran. Since the documents in this script are relatively few in number and are still illegible, little can be said about it; but the tablets are clearly of a commercial or economic and not of a literary type; the characters, which are semi-pictographic, are not taken over from the Sumerian, so that to that extent the system was original. But the two countries were too closely in touch for a distinctive writing to have much chance of survival. Already in the pre-Sargonid Age Elamite rulers were using the Sumerian script and even the Sumerian language, and after the Sargonid conquest of Elam the local script seems to have fallen altogether into abeyance. It was indeed resuscitated in the twelfth and thirteenth centuries BC as part of a nationalistic revival, but soon vanished again as a result of the conquest of the country by Babylon. From the point of view of man's cultural progress the chief interest of the Proto-Elamite syllabary lies in the fact that it supplies definite evidence of the dispersion of the ideas originating in Sumer and illustrates the readiness with which, at this stage of history, countries would take advantage of their neighbour's inventions.

Because Elam was an immediate neighbour of the Sumerians and from the earliest times connected with them by cultural and political ties (the latter are best illustrated by the legend of Enmerkar and the Lord of Aratta, recording events of the Uruk period) such cultural exchanges are natural enough; but Sumerian trade extended much farther afield, so that even in the case of remote countries the possibility of indirect Sumerian influence has to be borne in mind.

The earliest examples of the Indus valley script that have yet been found date to about the twenty-fourth century BC. At that time the system appears to be fully developed, the characters are uniformly stylized, and there is nothing to throw light upon their genesis. But in the twenty-fourth century BC the Harappā people were in direct contact with Mesopotamia, as is proved by the finding of numerous seals of the Harappā type on Mesopotamian sites, and the contacts would seem to go back to a far greater antiquity; that India owed its art of writing to the Sumerians cannot be proved, but it is highly probable. Just as, at a much later time, the Aryans of northern India were to find inspiration for the development of their own Brahmi script in the Aramaic writing evolved by the peoples of the Syrian coast, now the traders of the Indus valley must have turned to their own uses the invention which traffic with Mesopotamia brought to their notice. What was borrowed, here as in the case of Egypt, was not the form but the idea of writing.

Granted that there may be resemblances between some of the characters in the different scripts, such did not constitute a valid argument; the characters being originally pictograms would have represented the ordinary things of life, which would be more or less the same everywhere, and the drawings of those things done by the scribes of different countries would bear a certain family likeness; but the sound values of the similar signs would be determined by the names of the things in different languages and would be therefore entirely unrelated one to another. Since the Harappā texts at present known are all very short inscriptions on personal seals, probably giving the names of individuals, and since we know nothing about the language in which they are written it is impossible to establish any definite connection between them and any other script, but the existence of the texts is of the greatest interest as witnessing to the probability of the eastward spread of the invention of writing.

The dependence of the Chinese script upon the Sumerian has been urged by some scholars and by others rejected altogether. In view of the basically similar character of the two languages[9] all the arguments that have been adduced to prove that of the peoples of the Middle East the Sumerians alone could have invented a syllabic script would apply equally to the Chinese; it is therefore impossible to deny, *a priori*, the independence of the Chinese invention, but, because no documents exist which illustrate, as do the Warka and Jamdat Nasr tablets in the case of Sumer, the successive stages in the development of Chinese writing, it is equally impossible to assert it. The supporters of Chinese independence have relied chiefly on the argument that the date of the earliest known Chinese inscriptions is too recent to allow of any connections with Sumer, for the idea of a syllabic script based on pictographic characters could have been borrowed only at a time when the pictorial nature of the signs in the parent script was still recognizable. It is true that the bone and tortoise-shell texts from Honan are not earlier than the Shang-Yin Dynasty (*c.* 1766–1122 BC), but it is also true that the script on them is well developed and executed with much elegance and technical skill, implying considerable previous experience in writing; moreover, it is thought that a historical document of which a copy is preserved in the Confucian classics ('Yao's Calendar', included in the Canon of Documents, Shu Ching) can on astronomical grounds be dated to the twenty-fourth century BC,[10] in which case it would seem to prove that already at that time the Chinese were skilled astronomers and had formed the habit of recording memorable events in writing. If that be so, the time gap becomes almost negligible; and while we may admit that two peoples of similar speech might independently effect the transition from the purely pictographic to the syllabic script, that they should have done so at more or less the same time does involve an unlikely coincidence. On the whole it is more probable that the Chinese, like the people of Harappā, derived from Sumer the principle of writing.

Chinese being fundamentally a monosyllabic language[11] the characters of its script, originally of course pictographic, are necessarily syllabic; and that a syllabic script is the most fitting vehicle for such a language is proved by the fact that in China it has never been abandoned; the pronunciation of the words has, in the lapse of many centuries, changed beyond recognition, but the written characters have retained their form, subject only to calligraphic modifications—the purely formal character of today can always be traced back to its pictorial origin.

If it be the case that the Chinese did not independently invent the art of writing but borrowed the idea of it from Mesopotamia, then they must have done so in the relatively early days when the characters of the Mesopotamian script were still so unconventionalized as to be recognizable pictures of things; only at that stage would they suggest to a foreign people the possibility of using similar pictures for their own language. There is nothing in Chinese writing that resembles in any way the perfected cuneiform script, and the modification undergone by the pictograms followed a very different course. The Sumerian invented writing for the purposes of accountancy and developed it for the use of the temple and the warehouse. He was a practically minded man with few literary interests; even the hymns used in the temple services, which had to be preserved exactly in their traditional form and therefore were best entrusted to writing, were not written down until the end of the third millennium but before that time in business of every sort the witness of the written tablet was preferable to the spoken word; he required, and developed, a script which could be written quickly, was as uniform as possible and was unambiguous; the more mechanical it was, the better. For the Chinese, on the contrary, writing was, from the outset, inseparable from literature; it was the implement for the composition and perpetuation of works of art, and therefore it partook of the nature of a work of art. Because he used a brush and silk (or bamboo) instead of a stylus and a clay tablet the Chinese scribe was bound to conventionalize his script otherwise than did the Sumerian, but his mental attitude rather than his medium decided the lines along which Chinese script was to develop. Calligraphy was on a par with painting. In the course of centuries the characters of the script have been radically transformed, but always with an eye to the aesthetic effect, and their functional value has remained unaltered. That this should be so results naturally from the character of the Chinese language. The languages of most civilized peoples show a more or less marked tendency to simplification, e.g. by dropping of moods and persons from the paradigm of verbs, the substitution of particles for inflected case-forms of nouns and the elimination of gender from adjectives; the process is a gradual one and very far from uniform in different countries. In China it appears to have been precociously rapid, for the relative absence of grammar from the Chinese language is a mark not of primitive simplicity but of development carried to its logical extreme. In the earliest texts there survive inflective case-forms for the personal pronouns, but such have long since disappeared and the Chinese 'sentence' resolves itself into a collocation of monosyllabic words whose relation to the sentence and to one another is expressed not by any marks in the words themselves but, in the first place, by a fixed word-order and, in the second place, by the addition of words the original concrete sense of which is so far faded that they can be used for formal purposes somewhat like the auxiliaries of modern Indo-European languages. Where all stem words are monosyllabic and are never elaborated into disyllables by derivative affixes or varied by inflection, and where abstract ideas are expressed in speech by compound words of which each syllable is a separate and recognizable stem word, there a writing system composed exclusively of originally pictorial syllabic signs meets all the requirements of language and calls for no revolutionary change. No such change has affected the Chinese script in the course of millennia; probably none would have affected the cuneiform of Mesopotamia had its use been confined to the Sumerian inventors of it; it was only when that script was adopted by peoples speaking languages of an entirely different type that difficulties of expression arose which led first to the modification and finally to the extinction of the Sumerian syllabary.

Before we deal with those adaptations of cuneiform which marked the later phases in the history of Mesopotamia and its neighbours we should examine that other great system of writing which characterizes the civilization of the Nile valley.

It is not possible to trace the development of writing in Egypt with the same detail as in Sumer, following up each successive phase in the advance from primitive picture-making to the full elaboration of the syllabic script; the simple but sufficient reason for this is that the Egyptians took over the principle of writing ready-made from the Sumerians[12] and so were able to achieve in a very short space of time and with the minimum of experiment results which the inventors of the principle had evolved slowly and painfully.

Had they been left to themselves the Egyptians could hardly have evolved any such syllabic system of writing as they actually employed. Their language was not, like the Sumerian, agglutinative, so that compound and abstract words were not built up by the simple collocation of one-syllabled words retaining in combination their original form; the great majority of their verbal roots contained either two or three consonants, and from the latter at least 'syllables' could be got only by a process of analysis wholly foreign to the primitive mind. The transition from the meaning denoted by a pictorial sign to the sound of its spoken name, which is the essential step in the development of writing, is not really in keeping with the character of the language and would not have suggested itself to the Egyptian mind unless prompted by a foreign example proving its feasibility.

By a fortunate coincidence the monuments which illustrate the beginnings of Egyptian writing also leave us in no doubt regarding the source of the scribes' inspiration. The magnificent votive palettes carved in slate which were found at Hierakonpolis must be assigned to the later pre-dynastic period and to the earliest years of the First Dynasty and are therefore contemporary with the latter part of the Jamdat Nasr period in Sumer, the period which saw the birth—or at least the early growth—of writing in that country. The carvings on these royal palettes prove more manifestly than any other Egyptian works of art the strong cultural influence which at this time Sumer exercised at any rate upon the upper class of society in the Nile valley; and where the motives and the style of stone carving could be passed on from one country to the other it was inevitable that Pharaoh's court should learn also of the Sumerian invention of writing and should be quick to adopt it. It is not to be supposed that the inscriptions on the slate palettes are actually the earliest ever written by Egyptian scribes, but they do come so early in the course of hieroglyphic history that they combine in themselves most of the stages of that history.

On the palette of Narmer (Pl. 19, a) the greater part of the field is taken up by a dramatic picture of the king gripping a vanquished enemy by the hair and about to brain him with a mace, while others of the enemy are in flight beneath his feet. This, of course, is simply a picture which anybody could understand; the towering Pharaoh with his royal crown is unmistakable, and equally obvious are the naked enemies with their outlandish beards. But the group in the top right-hand corner of the palette is very different. Here a hawk, familiar as the symbol of the god Horus, is perched upon a cluster of six papyrus stems and with a (human) hand grasps a cord which is passed through the nose of a severed bearded man's head projecting from the oblong whence rise the papyrus stems. The Horus hawk and the bearded foreigner are self-explanatory; they are quite definitely pictures, and it required no stretch of the imagination to understand the further point, that the hawk has taken the man prisoner. But the other signs are not merely pictorial, they are hieroglyphics. The oval is an ideogram—a word-sign—meaning *ta,* 'country', which reappears in early texts; the papyrus growing out of it is the symbol of the delta, of which it is the characteristic plant, and the combination of the group with the man's head gives it a syntactical value; while finally a wavy line joining the head to the arm of the king completes what is as good a sentence as was possible for the scribes of the beginning of the First Dynasty, though not yet a true sentence seeing that it is intermediate between pictorial representation and linguistic expression. It is intended to read, 'Horus brings to Pharaoh the foreign captives from the land of Lower Egypt'. It is further possible that in this early period the papyrus might be used as the lotus was regularly used afterwards for '1,000', as on the Kha'sekhem statues from Hierakonpolis, in which case we should read 'six thousand foreign captives'.

But at the top of the palette there is carved another group of signs; enclosed within the square frame which throughout history was to be the cartouche of the Horus name of a Pharaoh are the two signs (a fish and a chisel?) which, as giving the king's name, must clearly be not pictorial but phonetic—possibly their small size hints at their being recognized as such.

On this single monument, therefore, there appear simultaneously three stages in the development of writing, but, it should be remarked, not the final stage. The palette inscriptions are still no more than logography, the words uninflected and simply strung together, so that the grammatical construction of the 'sentence' is suggested only by the visual effect made by the signs and their arrangement. But the phonetization of the signs gives them almost automatically a syllabic value, and with that the next step, that of writing down a word by its sound regardless of the original meaning of the signs, is not difficult. The period of transition did indeed produce documents whose interpretation is very doubtful, but in a short time, probably to be measured by three or four generations, the Egyptian scribes had perfected a system which in principle remained unchanged to the end of the history of Egyptian writing.

In the fully developed script there are three classes of signs: ideograms where the meaning of the original pictograph is retained, phonetic signs and determinatives. To this extent the system reproduces that of Sumer, and the Sumerian script had just reached this stage when the Egyptian started. But although there are some striking similarities between the two scripts the differences are equally marked, e.g. the Sumerian generally placed its generic determinatives before the more specific sign whereas the Egyptian placed them after; and again in Sumerian the determinative is not essential, not even usual, whereas in Egyptian it is a necessary and very important element of the system. One must indeed emphasize the fact that the scribes who developed the Egyptian script did not copy the Sumerian system; they took over from it the main idea, that a written sign could have a phonetic value, and also the threefold distinction of signs; but for the rest they were guided by the character of their own language.

The definition commonly given of the Egyptian phonetic signs as being syllabic and therefore on the same footing as the phonetic signs in Sumerian is not strictly correct. Of the Egyptian signs about two dozen contain one (initial) consonant and about eighty contain two consonants; they are necessarily vocalized, but they are not really syllabic because (1) there is no stability in the accompanying vowel sounds, (2) there may be no vowel between the two consonants, one of them being in one syllable and the second in another syllable, and (3) the uni-consonantal signs often had a purely alphabetic function. Thus, , transliterated *mn,* might stand for *man, men, mon, mun, mana, menu, etc.,* indefinitely; it can be divided as in *em-naf;* and in the latter word we see used as a phonetic complement of and possessed of a purely alphabetic character. Obviously the script as a whole cannot be called alphabetic, since the vast majority of the signs are biconsonantal and since too there are no signs for vowels; but neither is it properly syllabic, and the fact is of the utmost importance, because although the Egyptians themselves preserved to the end the mixed character of the script elaborated by their earliest scribes it was their alphabetic use of certain signs that led to the development in other hands of a real alphabet.

As regards the history of that script, it is characteristic of Egypt that the Hierakonpolis palettes which illustrate the early stages of hieroglyphic writing should be royal monuments. The Sumerians had evolved the principle of writing as an instrument of accountancy; the Egyptians adopted the principle for different purposes.[13] They needed to keep a trustworthy calendar so that they could have advance notice of the annual Nile flood, and they needed to give permanent form to those magic spells which ensured a good harvest and the not less necessary spells which secured a man's passage to the next world, such spells as we have in the Pyramid Texts. Further, writing was calculated to enhance (as in the case of the slate palettes) the glorification of kings. The inscriptions with which a Pharaoh would overlay the walls of a temple were not hidden away where only a god could see them; they were meant to impress the world at large. Consequently they should be decorative and, since most people were illiterate, more or less pictorial; even those who could not read them would be more struck by rows of pictures—many of them identifiable—than by meaningless signs. The purpose of the hieroglyphic script was largely monumental, and for that reason its elaborate pictorial signs preserved their character throughout, so that between the writing of the First Dynasty and that of Ptolomaic times the difference is really very small. But the hieroglyphic script was clearly ill suited to practical uses, and something more cursive was required to supplement it; accordingly the hieratic script—really a sort of shorthand—was introduced and displaced the hieroglyphic for everyday purposes. This script appears fully developed as early as the fourth Pharaoh of the First Dynasty (incidentally the fact that it came into use almost simultaneously with the more representational script from which it was derived gives strong support to the view that the principle of writing was borrowed ready-made from abroad); it was written with a brush or with a reed pen, primarily on papyrus, often on potsherds or flat slivers of limestone, and the materials employed would naturally conduce to a cursive rendering of the characters. In the early periods few people outside the priestly orders would have been literate, and the main use of writing was for religious purposes, e.g. for incantations, magical formulae and such funereal texts as the extracts from the Book of the Dead; but in the course of time the art was more widely diffused and its subject-matter was vastly extended. About the eighth century BC a still more rapid form of writing—the demotic—was introduced; but in neither cursive script was there any basic modification of the structure of Egyptian writing as it was first formulated in the hieroglyphic.

That the system endured for so long with relatively so little change might be taken to mean that it was peculiarly suited to the genius of the Egyptian language. Actually it was an extremely clumsy and difficult medium. So far from its being simplified as time went on, the need to clarify expression and to avoid ambiguities of meaning led to an even greater complication, more and more signs being inserted as determinatives or phonetic complements; only the astonishingly static character of Egyptian culture in general and the conservative influence of religion would seem to account for the retention of an instrument so unhandy. But its retention was of real importance for the history of writing in general. It was not to be expected that any other nation should adopt in its entirety so difficult a system, and in fact none did; but because it preserved the primitive pictographic form out of which writing proper had been developed the Egyptian hieroglyphic script was able to suggest to peoples of a different speech the way in which they could fashion a script of their own, as the formalized cuneiform of Mesopotamia could never have done; the Cretan and the Hittite hieroglyphic scripts were directly inspired by Egypt,[14] not by Sumer.

In western Asia the genesis of writing had been due to temple business; its further history was to be decided very largely by politics. At the very beginning of the literate age war and trade together resulted in a remarkable extension of the Sumerian civilization. Not only did their immediate neighbours to the north fall under the domination of the Sumerians, but with the establishment of such outlying city states as Mari on the middle Euphrates and, later, Harran in the north and Qatna in the centre of Syria the cultural influence of the Mesopotamian people was able to take root far afield. Their culture was indeed so obviously superior to anything that surrounding peoples could boast that the latter were prepared and eager to make it their own; great leaders such as Sargon of Akkad and afterwards Hammurabi of Babylon, Semitic though they were by race, were so thoroughly imbued with the civilized traditions of the south that their accession to power affected that civilization curiously little. In Hammurabi's time the Sumerians were dying out as a people, and even the old language was being rapidly supplanted by the Semitic speech of Babylon; but the Babylonians were content to take over the Sumerian script—incidentally the vehicle for those religious beliefs and practices which also they had readily assimilated—and to adapt it with the minimum of change to the needs of their own language; it was not particularly well suited to the Babylonian and Assyrian dialects, but these two Semitic peoples never showed any great literary originality and that fact, together with their veneration for what was almost a sacred formula, induced them to disregard its inconvenience. The Sumerian language, increasingly ill-understood, survived only in the ritual of the temple services, but the Sumerian script in the hands of the Semitic conquerors had a use more widespread than ever.

It is probably true to say that the Akkadian cuneiform system was, at the time, the best and most accurate vehicle for conveying thought in writing, and long continued to be so; its disadvantage was that the number of signs used was great, that an intricate system of ideographs and syllabic signs had to be grasped, and that the phonetic value of individual signs had to be gathered from their context. When this had been understood, the literate Assyrian or Babylonian had at his disposal a very subtle instrument for the expression of his thought—but it needed many years of study for him to become literate; and for anyone using a different language the difficulty was greater. When the Phoenicians invented their alphabetic script its main advantage was that its signs could so easily be committed to memory and were unambiguous, so that a man could become literate in a matter of weeks.

Under the influence of cultural proximity and trade the Hurri had already adopted the Babylonian cuneiform system, but for the most part were content to write in it in the Akkadian dialect for which it was the recognized vehicle; as far to the west as Alalakh all business was transacted in documents which might just as well have originated in some city of the lower Euphrates. Thanks to the establishment of trading colonies Mesopotamia had from very early times exercised the main cultural influence over eastern Syria, and when that was interrupted by the invasions of the Pharaohs of the Twelfth Dynasty the Mesopotamian sovereigns had to make good the balance both by wars of conquest and by diplomatic intrigue; contact therefore was close, and communications were kept open by regular correspondence. It was in this way that the Babylonian language written in the cuneiform script became the recognized diplomatic language of the Middle East. Even the Pharaoh of

Egypt had to correspond with his satellites, the princes of Syria, not in Egyptian hieroglyphic but in cuneiform, and the foreign chancellery of Hattusas had to observe the same custom. The Hittites, indeed, having learnt the Babylonian system originally through the Hurri, who acted as middlemen between the two countries, made cuneiform the normal script even for their own archives. It was not at all a convenient medium for an Indo-European language such as the Nesite dialect of Hattusas and had to be modified accordingly; the Hittites retained all the characteristic elements of the Akkadian, the ideograms, the syllabic signs, the determinatives and the phonetic complements; but they cut down the number of the syllabic signs to about 130, and they incorporated in their text not only Akkadian ideograms (which would be read as Hittite words having the same meaning) but also Akkadian spelt-out words or phrases which were reproduced in their original spelling but were meant to be pronounced as the equivalent in Hittite; for example, the two signs *id-din,* Akkadian for 'he gave', might be used to denote the Hittite *pesta,* 'he gave'. The decipherment of the Hittite tablets found at Bogazköy was made relatively easy for the modern scholar by the presence of so many 'allograms', Akkadian quotations, as it were, scattered throughout the Hittite text.

From north Syria, then, through Damascus and up into Anatolia the cuneiform script was current in the second millennium BC.

It was this wide expansion that gave rise to new invention. A number of peoples were forced to recognize the utility of writing,[15] but the system, or rather the systems, in vogue were ill-adapted to the requirements of their respective languages and might be considered to have the further disadvantage of implying subjection to a foreign and perhaps hostile civilization. The Hittite monarch, like the Pharaoh, might not object to the use of Akkadian in his government offices, but it was at least invidious that royal monuments set up for the edification of his subjects and the celebration of his majesty should be inscribed in characters of a very utilitarian appearance, unintelligible to the public at large but bearing only too clear witness to the cultural superiority of his Assyrian rival. The Pharaonic monuments gave just the effect desired, but the Egyptian hieroglyphic system was impossibly difficult—the attempts of Egyptian scribes to transliterate foreign proper names showed how difficult; but at least its pictorial signs suggested, as the conventionalized cuneiform could not do, the right way to approach the problem. Accordingly, the Hittites invented a hieroglyphic system of their own; the idea seems to have been borrowed but the signs were in no case copied from the Egyptian—the whole point was that they should be purely Hittite. The system itself was based upon the already familiar structure of the cuneiform; of rather more than two hundred signs fifty-six are phonetic, i.e. syllabic, and the rest are ideograms; the syllables begin with a consonant and end in a vowel, but whereas the consonantal value is fixed, the vowel sound is variable; certain syntactical devices are introduced, diacritical marks, for the proper rendering of the grammatical construction of a sentence. There were two forms of the script simultaneously in use, the full hieroglyphic sculptured on stone in relief and a more cursive type which was incised on monuments of less importance and was occasionally used for fugitive writings on potsherds, etc.; the former admirably fulfilled its function as a decorative element on the walls of palace or temple. Apart from its content, which does not concern us here, the chief interest of the Hittite script lies in the fact that it illustrates the impetus that was given by the spread of the practice of writing and the recognition of its usefulness to the imagination of peoples for whose languages the existing scripts were inept. The Hittite hieroglyphic system fell out of use at the end of the seventh century BC, when the last of the Syro-Hittite kingdoms was destroyed, and was replaced by Aramaic or Phoenician; to the later history of writing it contributed nothing, but that it should even have arisen was an indication of progress.

Very similar was the case of Crete. There, soon after 2,000 BC, there appear pictographic signs which in the first half of the second millennium combine into a definite system of writing ('Hieroglyphic B') and between 1900 and 1700 BC comes a cursive form, 'Linear A', to be followed in the fifteenth century by 'Linear B'. That the three scripts represent three stages in the development of a single system seems to be shown by the fact that nearly a third of the phonetic signs of Linear B are directly derived from the hieroglyphys; but this does not warrant the assumption that the language is in all cases the same. It is now generally accepted that the language of Linear B is an early form of Greek, spoken by the Mycenaeans who perhaps as early as 1460 BC occupied Knossos and eventually overthrew the Minoan kingdom; they adopted the Minoan script for their own purposes, but whether the language for which that script had been invented was also related to Greek cannot as yet be decided.

Most if not all of the tablets hitherto discovered are inventories of stores kept in the palace, or accounts; they are not therefore particularly informative. The signs include numerous ideograms, which are introduced by names, words or sentences written phonetically; there are about eighty-five different phonetic signs which are without question syllabic. Nearly all of them are composed of a single consonant allied to a vowel, and the vowel is not variable but is as important as the consonant in so much as different signs denote the different vocalization of each consonant, and there are also separate signs for the simple vowels; since inflections show the gender, case and number of nouns and adjectives and the person, number and tense of verbs the system is more fully elaborated than would seem to be necessary for the mere keeping of accounts; it was quite adequate for literary purposes and may have been so employed. One need not hesitate to assert that the Cretans borrowed from the older civilization of the Asiatic mainland the principle of a syllabary; the Mycenaeans could not go altogether beyond that principle, but they did simplify and improve upon it so as to make it a better vehicle for their own language than anything that had been devised in Asia. Their invention was short-lived in the sense that after 1200 BC the Mycenaean world ceased to exist, and the script disappeared together with their own arts; but the Linear B writing presaged the achievements of the later Greek stock.

Closely connected with the Minoan, at least in the form of its signs, is a Bronze Age script used in Cyprus. About one hundred inscriptions are known, all incised on clay vessels or ostraka, and they give sixty-three different signs together with signs for numbers. The script, originally devised for a non-Greek language, was later adapted by the Cypriotes for the writing of Greek, for which it was ill-suited. The characters are syllabic, each consisting of a consonant followed by a vowel. The use of the script seems to have been confined to the island, and although continued into Classical times did not in any way influence the development of writing in general.

Most remarkable both for its character and for its implications is the object of baked clay known as the Phaestos Disk (Pl. 20). Found by the Italian excavators of Phaestos in conditions which proved it to be contemporary with Minoan writing of the class Linear A, it has nothing to do with that writing, nor has it necessarily anything to do with Crete; a certain resemblance has been remarked between the script on the disk and that on some ex-votos found in the Arkalochori cave in central Crete, but even if the analogy holds good it can be urged that ex-votos may be dedicated by foreign visitors to a shrine as well as by local worshippers. Sir Arthur Evans[16] has adduced evidence showing that its most likely place of origin is in south-western Anatolia, but up to the present nothing in any way resembling it has been found there.

Each face of the flat disk is marked by means of an incised line with a spiral along which runs the text of the inscription, starting at the outer edge and finishing at the centre; vertical incised lines divide the signs into word-groups. There are 242 signs, giving forty-five different characters, all of a very detailed pictorial sort, so much so that men and women and even different racial types of men are distinguished, and these are not incised but stamped by means of separate punches pressed into the soft clay; the disk is, in fact, printed with movable type.

Nobody would go to the trouble of making a complete fount of type for the sake of printing a single document; such is necessary only for production on a considerable scale. Although the Phaestos Disk, in its exotic surroundings, remains a unique document, we can only assume that it is one of a large class awaiting discovery in the country of its origin. Moreover, the text of the inscription is clearly continuous and contains no number signs: presumably, therefore, it does not deal with lists and accounts, as do the Minoan tablets, but is rather of a literary nature.

While the number of the signs, and their grouping, makes it certain that they form a syllabary either of the Aegean or of the Hittite type, no attempt at the decipherment of an isolated document is possible and the content of the inscription must remain an enigma. But at least we may be sure that any survey of Middle East writing made now is incomplete in that it must omit one area wherein a hieroglyphic script was freely employed for literary ends.

A number of documents, in many cases too isolated, too short or too fragmentary to be very informative, prove that about the middle of the second millennium BC various peoples on the Asiatic mainland were attempting to work out new forms of writing. The authors of such attempts were for the most part western Semites who, in contact with either Egypt or Mesopotamia or with both, were familiar with the scripts of those countries but realized their unsuitability for the conditions of western Semitic life. The main part was played by the Phoenician inhabitants of the Syrian coast towns whose commercial activities supplied them with both the need and the opportunity for invention of the sort. A travelling merchant would find it greatly to his advantage if he could keep his own business records instead of having to employ an expensive scribe, and if at the same time he could avoid the clumsy roundabout transliteration which so distorted his Phoenician language that it was difficult to make sense of the written words. He and his fellows had regularly employed the cuneiform script, and the characters were easy to form; it was their syllabic value that was the trouble. But he knew that in Egypt some of the hieroglyphic signs representing uniconsonantal syllables were used in a shortened form—the vowel sound was dropped and only the single consonant retained; and if that could be done with the hieroglyphic why should it not be done with the cuneiform also?

At Ugarit there have been unearthed numerous clay tablets inscribed with a peculiar kind of cuneiform writing in which the cumbrous Babylonian system is reduced to its simplest form. There are only thirty signs, so that the script is properly speaking alphabetic; twenty-seven of them are taken over from the Babylonian, being originally normal syllabic signs consisting of an initial consonant plus an indeterminate vowel, but here used purely as consonants, while three represent vowel sounds only, *'a, 'i* and *'u,* and a special sign marks the division of words. The script, which was used both for the Semitic and for the Hurrian language, seems to have enjoyed a certain vogue, for examples of very similar writing have been found in Palestine, at both Beth Shemesh and at Mount Tabor, and it is indeed surprising that it should not have been more generally adopted; but whether because its career was cut short at an early stage by the destruction of Ugarit at the hands of the Peoples of the Sea, or for some other reason, it disappeared and left no further trace upon the history of writing.

Much more important from the point of view of later history are the Proto-Sinaitic inscriptions. The first ten of these were found by Sir Flinders Petrie, at Serabit al Khadim in central Sinai, and later expeditions discovered twenty-six more. All the texts are short and ill-written, apparently the work of Semites who, in the early part of the fifteenth century BC, were employed by the Egyptians in the Sinaitic mines; most are rock inscriptions, but a few are upon stone figures of a votive character. Professor Sir Alan Gardiner, who with Professor Peet published the original ten texts, was struck by the oxhead sign (*aleph*') with which one of them begins and recalled the old contention of Gesenius that the prototypes of the Phoenician letters must have had the shapes indicated by the Hebrew (and Greek) letter-names; having established first the high antiquity of those letter-names he could then attribute due importance to the fact that such of the Proto-Sinaitic signs as were clearly pictorial represent objects whose names occur as the names of letters in the Hebrew and Greek alphabets. On applying the principle to a group of four letters which recurred no less than six times in the inscriptions he found that it read *Ba'alat*, the Semitic equivalent of Hathor, the Egyptian goddess of Serabit al Khadim where the inscriptions were found. Gardiner's identification of the word *Ba'alat* has been generally accepted, but the acceptance of his conclusion necessarily involves acceptance of the premises on which it was based, i.e. that the Proto-Sinaitic script is alphabetic in character, and that its letters, or at any rate some of its letters, are identical in name and function with those of the Hebrew alphabet.

The number of different signs yielded by the thirty-six known Proto-Sinaitic texts is about thirty, which is an almost decisive argument for their being alphabetic and not syllabic, a syllabic system requiring a very much greater number. The individual signs are mainly, if not entirely, pictographic and are close copies of Egyptian hieroglyphs, as indeed might have been expected from a people familiar with Egyptian monuments. But the selection they made is quite arbitrary; those signs were chosen which were easy to draw and easy to recognize, but their sonant values did not follow the Egyptian but were taken from the Semitic names of the objects represented; e.g. the picture of a mouth, in Egyptian *r*, from *ri* meaning 'a mouth', is, in the Semitic, *p*, from *puw*. The Serabit al Khadim texts are so short and so illegible that attempts to translate them are not entirely in agreement. They are certainly Semitic and in all probability northern Semitic, i.e. Canaanite. According to their date, which again is still a matter of dispute (Gardiner assigns them to the eighteenth century, whereas Albright, in agreement with Flinders Petrie, puts them to the fifteenth century and places the Lachish, Shechem and Gezer inscriptions between 1700 and 1550 BC), they represent the first, or at least a very early essay made by a Semitic people to evolve a writing system of their own, and as forerunners of the developed Phoenician system they reveal the origin of the modern alphabet.

In Palestine and in Syria there have been found a few isolated inscriptions, generally short *graffiti* on vases, some of which resemble the Proto-Sinaitic script while others, although differing from that script, illustrate efforts in the same direction.

From Tell el Hesi and from Gezer come very short texts resembling the Proto-Sinaitic, and from Lachish a series which both in development and in date (the latest seem to be of the late thirteenth century BC) come closer to the Phoenician and help to bridge the gap between the Proto-Sinaitic and the Phoenician scripts; another example of somewhat earlier date comes from Shechem and shows the advance of the Sinai script northwards in the direction of Philistia. Taken together these sporadic discoveries illustrate the gradual reduction of pictorial to non-pictorial letters, the latter bearing an even closer resemblance to the Phoenician.

At Byblos there have been found numerous inscriptions in a linear script (not yet decipherable) belonging to the fourteenth century or later; their connection with the Lachish inscriptions and still more with the Proto-Sinaitic inscriptions is not apparent, but we can probably regard these and other isolated monuments[17] as representing ephemeral stages in the evolution of the final script—a progress not necessarily consistent but diversified by local and more or less independent attempts to forge an adequate system. Conventionalized alphabetic signs are engraved upon bronze javelin-heads found at el Khadr near Bethlehem and attributed to the early years of the eleventh century; but the full realization of the attempts to evolve a true alphabet is best seen in a group of inscriptions found at Byblos and dated to the tenth century; two from the tomb of King Ahiram, *c.* 975 BC,[18] one on a building erected by King Yehimilk, and two, of Kings Abibaal and Elibaal, which being inscribed on statues of Shishak (*c.* 945–924 BC) and Osorkon I (*c.* 924–895 BC) respectively can be considered as well dated. The main Ahiram inscription is the long text on the coffin itself, but the script must have been evolved very much earlier than the date of Ahiram's death, for on the wall of the *dromos* leading down to the tomb chamber there is a *graffito* carelessly written by someone who evidently was not a professional scribe, so that knowledge of the script must have been already common property. From this script, with its twenty-two signs all purely linear in form, were to be descended not only the later forms of Semitic writing but also the Greek and all modern alphabets.

The linear signs of the tenth-century Phoenician script had in most if not in all cases a pictorial origin, their forms being taken over from Egypt via the Sinaitic; where no resemblance to any Egyptian sign can be recognized we may allow for the possibility of an original creation without invalidating in any way the general rule that the system was borrowed from Egypt. What the authors of the new script did was to jettison all ideograms and all phonetic signs connoting more than one consonant, concentrate on the twenty-four 'simple' signs of the Egyptian system and use those as the basis for their own. As has been stated above, the Egyptians themselves did on occasion employ these signs as alphabetical, although they never felt it necessary to advance from the syllabic to the alphabetical principle of writing; it is symptomatic that they used the signs alphabetically for the purpose of transliterating foreign names which did not lend themselves to a syllabic rendering.[19] What was true of foreign names was equally true of a foreign language as a whole; the Phoenicians recognized this (as is evident also from the form taken by the Ugarit texts in alphabetic cuneiform) and they therefore eliminated the vowel component and reduced the connotation of the sign to a single letter. Although a few scholars have maintained that the Phoenician script preserved the syllabic character of the Egyptian model it can safely be asserted that it already resembled the later Semitic scripts in being alphabetic. A very strong argument in favour of this view is given by the letter-names, which seem to date back to the first invention of the system; they are the names of letters, not of syllables, and therefore imply an alphabetic system. Experience had shown that a syllabary, however adequate it might be for an agglutinative language, was ill-adapted to a language in which the inflections of a given root word are rendered not by the addition of suffixes, etc., but by internal variation of the vowels, as is the regular practice in the Semitic tongues (e.g. *ktb,* derivatives *katab,* to write, *aktib,* I write, *kâtib*, a writer, *kitab*, a book, *maktab,* an office, etc.) and occasionally in the Indo-European (e.g. sing, sang, sung, song). To express those changes by means of a syllabary would have meant a different sign for each combination of the same consonant with the different vowels, an immense multiplication of signs, whereas on the alphabetic system little more than thirty signs suffice. The difficulty had already been solved by the inventor of the Ugaritic cuneiform alphabet, who introduced special signs for the vowels, but the authors of the Phoenician script seem not to have known of this, or, if they knew of it, they disregarded it; their alphabet was consonantal only; vowels were simply omitted, the reader being trusted to know from the context what vowels had to be supplied. In that it left so much to the imagination, the script might also be called a kind of shorthand, but it is true that in Semitic speech the part played by the vowels is complementary whereas that of the consonants is decisive; the chances, therefore, of misreading are not so serious as might be supposed. For the Semite a purely consonantal alphabet agreed so well with the genius of his language that the Phoenician example was followed in the derivative scripts and still persists in Arabic and Hebrew; even when the advantage of expressing the vowels was impressed upon him the diacritical marks were the only concession he would make to modernity, and no new signs were added to his alphabet. But when in due course the Greeks, in whose Indo-

European language the vowels played a much more prominent part (especially for terminal inflection) took over the Phoenician alphabet in its entirety they were able to complete it with special signs for the short and long vowels just because it had now become possible to spell a word; sounds had been analysed into their component parts and vowel and consonant were upon an equal footing. In the Phoenician alphabet there were signs representing 'weak consonants' not employed in the Greek language; they had occasionally been used in the *plene* writing of some of the Semitic systems, introduced about the ninth century BC, as more or less pure vowels, and the Greeks may have been aware of this; in any case, instead of inventing new signs they adopted those and gave them a purely vowel content; thereby they regularized as an essential feature of writing a device which seems to have been unknown earlier and only sporadically used in later Semitic texts.

In speaking of the Greek alphabet we are, of course, anticipating events. The position about the year 1200 BC was this. The old cuneiform script was still flourishing in Mesopotamia, used by Babylonians and Assyrians alike. Farther north it was adopted by the scribes of Urartu, in the district of Lake Van; it was the normal script of the Mitanni and Hurri people, extending from the Assyrian border westwards to the Mediterranean; in Anatolia it was freely employed for purposes other than monumental, but there for royal inscriptions the Hittite hieroglyphs were preferred; and it was still the diplomatic script for the foreign chancelleries of Syria. The Egyptian systems, hieroglyphic and hieratic, were the only ones in use in the Nile valley but did not extend beyond it—Phoenician craftsmen might use hieroglyphs as ornamental motives but reduced them to a meaningless muddle. On the Syrian coast the Phoenician script was in process of being established, ousting altogether such inchoate essays as had made their brief appearance in Sinai, in Lachish and elsewhere; if in Ugarit, the northernmost of the Phoenician cities, the local cuneiform alphabetic script persisted side by side with the syllabic cuneiform, both alike were doomed to speedy extinction by the act of war. Cyprus had its own syllabary which was to survive into classical Greek times, and in Crete flourished the Linear B script whose use extended to the Mycenaean strongholds of mainland Greece, Mycenae, Pylos and others. Apart from western Anatolia and the Ionian coast, as to which we know nothing, it can be said that throughout the whole of the eastern Mediterranean world the art of writing was familiar and in most of the countries was no longer the prerogative of an exclusive priestly caste but had become in popular hands the necessary vehicle for business and private affairs of all sorts; even in conservative Egypt crude *graffiti* show that education of a kind was not confined to one class. How widespread was the itch for writing is shown by the fact that at a later period two forms of syllabic script are found in use in Spain, the Tartesian in the south-west, the Iberian in the south-eastern and eastern parts of the peninsula; these must surely have had their beginnings in the early centuries which saw so many experiments in the eastern Mediterranean, experiments from which the Spaniards could not hold aloof.

For farther Asia the material at our disposal does not permit us to follow the course of the development of writing with such detail as is possible in the Mediterranean area. As regards India the complete blank in our knowledge may perhaps not unfairly reflect a blank period in history. So far as our evidence goes, the Harappā script disappeared and left no direct descendants; the fierce Aryan warriors who overthrew the Harappā civilization[20] are not likely to have been writers, and although the Kshatriyas, their knightly caste, were also spiritual leaders of the people and produced poets and philosophers, their works are more likely to have been transmitted orally than in writing; the Aryan epics must have been so transmitted for many centuries. It is only in the later Vedic period that a more settled form of civilization led to the founding of great cities in which literary studies were pursued; but there survive no written documents of that age, and when at last writing is in evidence the script bears no relation whatsoever to that of Harappā. On the other hand, it is gradually being recognized that the Indus valley culture, which at first seemed to be a disconnected episode in Indian history, isolated from anything before or after it, did in fact in some respects link up with later ages; 'Capta, ferum victorem cepit'. Future archaeological discoveries may yet show that, even if the form of the Harappā script perished, yet its tradition influenced the development of Sanskrit writing.

EDUCATION

The use of a syllabic script, which involves a sign-list at least ten times as long as an alphabet and also allows of differing phonetic values for identical signs, adds greatly to the difficulty of writing. Alike therefore in Egypt and in Sumer the would-be scribe specialized at an early age and had to serve a long apprenticeship in his profession. For a priest attached to a temple writing was an essential accomplishment; all priests therefore would learn to write. Seeing how much advantage could be drawn from the scribe's ability it is easy to believe that the learned would not willingly share the 'art and mystery' of their profession with too many possible rivals. The state service demanded more writers than there were temple priests, and the illiterate public required notaries to assist them in certain matters, so that a class of scribes came into being side by side with the regular priesthood; but it would seem that in Egypt the priests did retain a monopoly of education and that schools were normally attached to temples.[21] Scholars are generally agreed that the Egyptians who could read and write formed a very small minority of the population. They must have been recruited from the well-to-do classes, for the poor could not have afforded the cost of the long years of schooling, especially if, as appears to have been the case, the schools were boarding schools, so that the pupil's living expenses were added to the teacher's fees. Parents who could meet those charges were eager enough to have their sons educated, because education was the key to the Civil Service, and the poem already quoted (see p. 169–70) on the superiority of the scribe to any manual worker shows how enviable were the rewards of scholarship. On Egyptian organization and on the educational methods employed there is no information at all for the early period; from the mass of material dating from the New Kingdom and later we are at liberty to argue back—assuming that the system changed but little in the course of time—and in that case shall conclude that school life in Egypt during the Old and Middle Kingdoms was much the same as that in Mesopotamia in the same period. But while that assumption is probably justifiable there is no need to elaborate it in the case of Egypt by further deduction from later ages, because for Mesopotamia we are fully documented and can cite contemporary evidence for every detail of the description.

The literate element of the Sumerian and Old Babylonian population was proportionately larger than in Egypt. There were 'junior' and 'high' scribes, scribes of the temple and 'royal' scribes of the palace, scribes who served as leading officials in the government and scribes who specialized in particular categories of administrative work, schoolmasters and notaries public, the latter being the more in demand because of the immense importance of foreign and domestic trade and because the law required documentary evidence in any civil action that came before the courts. It may well be that apart from all these professional writers, who numbered many thousands, the business man also might acquire at least a smattering of literary education for his own purposes; in any case it is clear that there must have been numerous scribal schools.

The 'tablet-house' could be attached to a temple, in the early as in the later periods; a school established in the Nin-gal temple at Ur under the charge of Bel-shalti-Nannar, daughter of Nabonidus (555–539 BC) had a predecessor in the same building as early as the fourteenth century BC. At Mari in the royal palace (*c.* 1800 BC) two rooms containing rows of brick benches might be schoolrooms but, since no school tablets were found in them, are more likely to have served as an official *scriptorium* for the palace scribes; the best example of a school is one in a private house of the Larsa period (*c.* 1780 BC) at Ur.

No. 1 Broad Street was a moderately sized house of normal type built round three sides of a courtyard; it could indeed be described as a small house because the disproportionately large area devoted to the domestic chapel left only half the site for the living-rooms. According to the original plan (see Fig. 32, A) the front door, at the Carfax corner of Broad Street, opened on the usual entrance lobby (1) from which one passed by a doorway in the east wall into the courtyard (2); facing one was the guest room (4) with its little closet (3) at the end; on the south side was the staircase (5) leading to the rooms on the upper floor, with the lavatory beneath it, and on the west side a doorway to the servants' room (6) which gave access to a passage (7–9) running along two sides of the chapel (8). But at a later time the entire plan was modified (see Fig. 32, B). A new doorway from the street was cut through the courtyard wall; the doorways from the court into rooms 1, 6 and the lavatory were walled up, and new doorways were made from room 1 to room 6 and from the latter into the lavatory; consequently the courtyard and the guest room now formed a self-contained unit cut off from the rest of the ground-floor rooms. Judging from tablets referring to temple affairs which were found in the passage (7) Igmil-Sin, the owner of the house, was a priest (which might account also for the unusually large chapel) but it was very obvious that his alterations in the building were intended to adapt it to the purposes of a school. In the courtyard and rooms 3 and 4 there were found nearly two thousand tablets including some hundreds of the round bun-shaped type of 'school exercise' tablets used for 'fair copies', etc. It was a small school—it could scarcely have accommodated more than two dozen boys —but presumably it was typical of the schools of the time, and certainly it was not just an elementary school but one catering for pupils of all ages. The bun-shaped tablets, bearing on one face the teacher's fair copy and on the other the pupil's attempt to reproduce it, start with single syllabic signs, then have lists of words beginning with the same syllable, and go on to proper sentences and extracts from the classics. Of the other tablets many were religious texts which were probably used for dictation or for learning by heart; there were numerous mathematical tablets—multiplication tables, rules for extracting square and cube roots, etc., problems in practical geometry, e.g. land surveying or the calculation of the amount of earth to be moved, given the measurements of an excavation, and there were also what one must call *belles lettres,* amongst them a favourite classic describing school life. Such, then, was the material setting of the educational system, a setting of the simplest sort; the scene in the Broad Street school, with the boys seated or squatting in rows in the courtyard and guest room, waiting for the headmaster to come downstairs from his private quarters while the ushers or pupil-teachers supervised the preparation of the morning lesson, is precisely that described in a (later) cuneiform text:

> Into the meeting of master, the courtyard of the tablet-house
> Come, my son. You shall sit before my feet.
> Now I am going to talk to you; open your ears.

Only boys attended the schools. Women scribes existed, and examples of their work have come down to us, but how they received their education we do not know; girl students are never mentioned in the literature of the schools. The boys were for the most part of the upper classes of society; of some five hundred scribes of the early part of the second millennium BC who have put on record the names and professions of their fathers, most are the sons of governors, 'city fathers', ambassadors, temple administrators, military officers, sea captains, tax officials, priests, managers, supervisors, foremen, scribes, archivists and accountants. On the other hand, cases are known in which a charitable person who had adopted an outcast baby—'rescued him from the jaws of a dog'—crowned his benefaction by sending the child to school to 'learn the scribal art': this may have been a rare exception, but at least it means that education was not confined exclusively to a favoured caste.

The school staff consisted of the headmaster, the 'school father' as he was called, and technical assistants—'the scribe of mathematics' or 'of mensuration', 'the man in charge of drawing', 'the man in charge of Sumerian', the 'overseer' or 'man in charge of the school regulations', 'the man in charge of the whip', but for the younger boys at any rate a great deal of the teaching was done by the 'big brother', a senior pupil

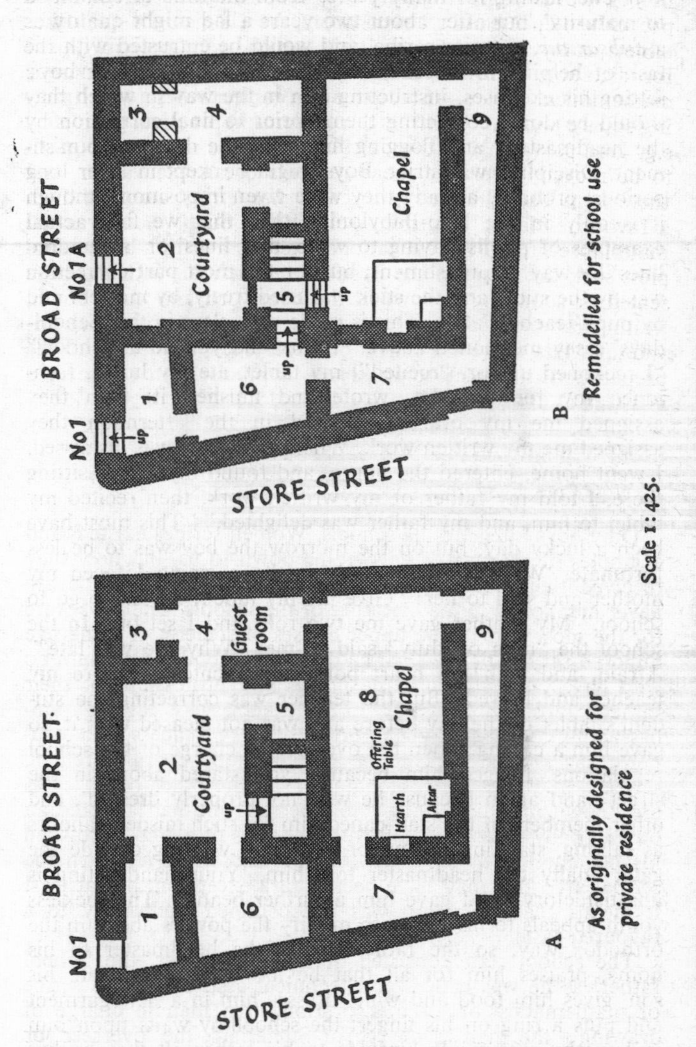

FIG. 32. *Ground plan of the school at No. 1, Broad Street, Ur.*

acting as usher or pupil-teacher. The full school course was a long one, lasting for many years, 'from the time of childhood to maturity', but after about two years a lad might qualify as a *dubsar tur*, a junior scribe, and would be entrusted with the task of helping in the education of one of the smaller boys, setting his exercises, instructing him in the way in which they should be done, correcting them (prior to final correction by the headmaster) and flogging him when he deserved punishment. Discipline was strict. Boys might be 'kept in' over long periods; probably already they were given impositions, though it is only in the Neo-Babylonian time that we find actual examples of pupils having to write 'fifty lines' or 'a hundred lines' by way of punishment; but for the most part correction was by the stick, and the stick was used freely, by masters and by pupil-teachers alike. This is made very clear in the 'School-days' essay mentioned above. ' "What did you do at school?" "I reckoned up [or, "recited"] my tablet, ate my lunch, fashioned my [new] tablet, wrote and finished it; then they assigned me my oral work, and in the afternoon they assigned me my written work. When the school was dismissed, I went home, entered the house, and found my father sitting there. I told my father of my written work, then recited my tablet to him, and my father was delighted." ' This must have been a lucky day, but on the morrow the boy was to be less fortunate. 'When I awoke early in the morning I faced my mother and said to her: "Give me my lunch; I want to go to school." My mother gave me two rolls and I set out. In the school the "man on duty" said to me: "Why are you late?" Afraid, and with my heart pounding, I entered before my teacher and bowed.' But the teacher was correcting the student's tablet of the day before and was not pleased with it, so gave him a caning. Then the overseer 'in charge of the school regulations' flogged him because 'you stared about in the street', and again because he was 'not properly dressed', and other members of the staff caned him for such misdemeanours as talking, standing up out of turn, and walking outside the gate; finally the headmaster told him, 'Your handwriting is unsatisfactory', and gave him a further beating. The luckless youth appeals to his father to mollify the powers above in the orthodox way, so the father invites the headmaster to his home, praises him for all that he has done to educate his son, gives him food and wine, dresses him in a new garment and puts a ring on his finger; the schoolboy waits upon him and in the meanwhile 'unfolds to his father all that he has learnt of the art of tablet-writing', and the gratified teacher reacts with enthusiasm: 'Of your brothers may you be their leader, of your friends may you be their chief, may you rank the highest of the schoolboys. You have carried out well the school's activities, you have become a man of learning.' The schoolboy, claiming now the proud title of 'Sumerian', becomes in his turn a pupil-teacher and realizes that a backward pupil is a trial to his patience:

> But you are a young dunce, a braggart;
> You cannot shape a tablet, the clay you cannot mould.
> You cannot write your own name, the clay is not suited to your hand.
> Clever fool, stop, stop your ears. You cannot be like me—I am a Sumerian.

Also, he discovers that discipline is not easy to maintain, and the scene ends with a riot which is stilled only by the appearance of the headmaster with his stick.

The picture is, of course, satirical to the point of caricature. Admittedly, in the private schools at any rate, the headmaster had to make his living by means of the tuition fees collected from the students and may have been glad enough to receive something in addition; admittedly methods of instruction were primitive and sometimes brutal; yet the Mesopotamian schools did provide a sound education and did uphold the general respect for learning as such. The old Sumerian school, probably an appendage of the temple, which aimed at no more than a course of vocational training, had in time become secularized and, with an ever-widening curriculum answering to the needs of a more complex society, had developed into a real centre of learning. 'Within its walls', says Professor Kramer, [22] 'flourished the scholar-scientist, the man who studied whatever theological, botanical, zoological, mineralogical, geographical, mathematical, grammatical and linguistic knowledge was current in his day, and who in some cases added to this knowledge.'

NOTES TO CHAPTER VI

1. In the opinion of Professor I. M. Diakonoff, patriarchal life develops late, sometimes nearly contemporaneously with the urbanization of society; the rights of ownership of the 'patriarch' are not diminished in early urban society. In the early Sumer, it is an individual family or clan that sells and buys land through its 'chosen men' (*lu-sa-pad*) and a part of the price is paid over to the members of the family. Later, in Old Babylonian as in Middle Assyrian times, it is the head of the family alone who sells the property and receives the price.
2. The whole process of development can be followed in the light of

tablets found on various sites. The lowest stratum at Erech, Uruk IV, produced tablets the text of which consists entirely of pictured objects and numbers; these should be dated as approximately 3500 BC. Texts from Jamdat Nasr (*c.* 3500 BC) are generally similar but for the first time use signs with determinative values; the same is the case with tablets from Uruk III. Tablets from Ur dated as about 3250 BC show a few signs sparingly used as syllables to indicate the case of nouns and verbal inflexions; this is the beginning of true writing. The process is carried on by tablets from Fara, wherein signs representing syllables are used not only for inflexions but also for the phonetic spelling of difficult words, a stage reached by about 3200 BC, while in Uruk I, *c.* 2900 BC, signs are employed as syllables for the phonetic complement and for plural ending and the signs generally are strongly conventionalized. As Driver says, archaeologically the sequence is clear.

3. Professor Ralph Turner notes that on this and the following pages the author champions the idea of the Sumerian origin of writing. He holds that the *idea* of writing was only invented once and was taken over from Sumer by other peoples. Scholars are not, of course, all agreed on this hypothesis. See also pp. 70 and 104, n. 20.
4. Dr D. C. Baramki points out that there is a transition between pictograph and hieroglyph. It is true that one cannot convey action or thought in a pictograph, yet one can convey action in a non-phonetic ideogram. Some Uruk reliefs did convey action. This action cannot be read but nevertheless conveys a message and a thought.
5. Professor A. Caquot points out that Sumerian is not the only agglutinative ancient eastern language. Hurrite and Urartaean were also agglutinative. It is, however, true that less and less importance is now being attached to purely 'typological' classifications.
6. According to Professor I. M. Diakonoff, Assyriologists usually propose later dates for the Uruk IV and Fara periods than Sir Leonard Woolley and many other archaeologists.
7. Dr William C. Sturtevant considers that there is no reason why a syllabary cannot distinguish homonyms, just as an alphabet does, by representing the same sound by more than one symbol—although in so doing, each becomes less 'phonetic' and more 'ideographic'. Sir Leonard Woolley recognizes that this is quite true in theory; but in fact the sound *FISH* is represented by the same syllabic sign, whatever its meaning.
8. The following passage on the Chinese writing system has been suggested by Professor Shigeki Kaizuka.
9. For Sir Leonard Woolley's view, see p. 366 sq.
10. Professor Shigeki Kaizuka *et al.* draw attention to the fact that the dating of 'Yao's Calendar' is much disputed; whether there was writing at this period is doubtful.
11. Dr W. C. Sturtevant points out that many of the greatest specialists do not consider Chinese originally a monosyllabic language; see Otto Jespersen, *Language: Its Nature, Development and Origin* (London, repr. 1949), p. 367 sq.; H. A. Gleason, *An Introduction to Descriptive Linguistics* (New York, 1955), pp. 305–6, and others.
12. See p. 104, n. 20, and above, n. 3. Professor I. M. Diakonoff and other specialists point out that the first texts from Egypt seem to date from the last quarter of the fourth millennium BC as do those from Sumer.
13. Professor J. Leclant points out that in Egypt writing is contem-

poraneous with the creation of the single state, and with the systematic organization of irrigation. Writing was, in effect, originally an instrument for the communication of orders, rather than for a registration of ideas. It is absolutely essential for organization and command.

14. The most recent research disagrees with this position; the point of view presented by Sir Leonard Woolley farther on (p. 385) doubtless corresponds more closely to the facts. See E. Laroche, *Les Hiéroglyphes Hittites,* Part I. *L'Écriture* (Paris, 1960), p. 255: 'There are undoubtedly analogies such as are inevitable between two pictographic systems, thus both in Egyptian and in Hittite a weapon-bearing arm is linked to the idea of "strength". Certain special signs (such as the cross of life and the winged sun) have been borrowed. But the idea of any large-scale copying of Egyptian hieroglyphs by the Hittites must be abandoned.'
15. According to Professor I. M. Diakonoff, the knowledge of the utility of writing is not in itself a sufficient reason for borrowing the practice of writing: the people in question must also have reached a certain level of economic development; the ancient Germans knew of the idea of writing for centuries and even had developed a kind of alphabet of their own (the Runes), but did not apply their writing system to anything better than magical uses until they had reached the stage of class society. Sir Leonard Woolley and Professor Ralph Turner do not consider there is any essential connection between a *class society* and *writing*. There is a connection between writing and the possession of an economic surplus. All writing had its origin in economic uses, but there is no *direct* connection between writing and class. However, writing intensified differences; for instance, literate versus illiterate classes and literate versus preliterate peoples.

    Professor Diakonoff, having read the above commentary, requested that an additional explanation of his position be given:

    'This critique of my position is due to a misunderstanding. I never maintained that there was a direct connection between a class society and writing; but a class society develops *when* there is an economic surplus. What I call "class society" Sir Leonard Woolley calls "urban civilization", and the use of writing is included in the definition of "urban civilization".'
16. *Palace of Minos,* I, pp. 654 sq.
17. Such as the Wadi Ganah text which Hooks wrongly describes as Proto-Sinaitic.
18. Professor I. M. Diakonoff and Dr D. C. Baramki both emphasize that the dates of King Ahiram are still controversial, certain scholars dating him considerably earlier.
19. Professor John A. Wilson observes that the Egyptians did in fact have about two dozen signs which were monoconsonantal and which, therefore, we call 'alphabetic'. However, their use was not as rare as held by the author; a common use is given on p. 380 (the wavy line *n*). These signs were chiefly used for normal Egyptian writing. Foreign names from the Eighteenth to the Twentieth Dynasty were presented in a formalized way in which the essential element was an old biconsonantal sign rather than a monoconsonantal sign.
20. For detailed discussion of this viewpoint cf. p. 107, n. 38.
21. Professor J. Leclant observes that education took the form of lessons given by masters particularly well qualified by their age, their experience and their patience. Certain celebrated teachers of the Old Empire are known to us: there were princes, viziers, high

officials, such as architects and sometimes priests. Under the New Empire, besides high officials in the army or the administration, we find also simple scribes in no way connected with the priesthood (cf. H. Bruner, *Altaegyptische Erziehung* (Wiesbaden, 1957). Whatever their grade or function in society, the best school for officials was at the feet of their own father or of some influential relative who could provide them with an education. W. Helck, *Zur Verwaltung des Mittleren und Neuen Reichs* (1958), pp. 435 and 541.

22. S. N. Kramer, *From the Tablets of Sumer*, p. 4.

CHAPTER VII

THE SCIENCES

GENERAL INTRODUCTION

IN that wide field which we call the arts and sciences the area covered by early man was limited; he was more interested in evolving and improving the things which were suited to his conditions of life than in inventing such things as would radically change those conditions. But within those limits he did achieve a technical and artistic success comparable to that of man in recent times. The public of today is often astonished, and disconcerted, by the material evidence which shows that the ancient craftsman was in skill and technique the near rival if not the equal of the more sophisticated craftsman of the twentieth century AD; on the other hand the student is prone to insist upon the fact that all this knowledge and technique were purely empirical and lacked altogether that scientific background which is the guarantee of modern production. The astonished admirer is only too apt to falsify history by accrediting to ancient man some esoteric science or illumination of which the secret has been lost; the student is right in his judgement provided that he does not let his criticism of method blind him to the merits of performance.

The ancient craftsman did depend entirely upon empirical methods. He experimented, blindly for the most part, but with infinite patience; and in so far as he did experiment and observe his results he was fulfilling the first requirement of science. But when he had once hit upon the way of doing what he wanted to do, he was satisfied. Modern man summarizes his successful series of experiments in a scientific formula which, by explaining how the process works, rationalizes the problem and is conveniently understood by his fellow-workers. Ancient man merely laid down the rule of what you should do (i.e. of what he had done) in order to repeat his initial success; it was as simple and as practical as a recipe in a cookery-book. Thus the rules for making glazed earthenware, codified by a master potter at Nineveh in the seventeenth century BC, can be followed by the modern potter[1] and produce precisely the desired effect. But whereas the modern potter explains the process by the use of chemical formulae, the Nineveh inventor was content to know not how the process worked but how he was to work the process. He was of course aware that there was something behind his recipe, but it was not his business to enquire into it: all these changes and transformations were, in their way, miracles. You did certain things in the right order (and probably said the right words as you did them, or even offered the right sacrifice) and the miracle happened; which obviously was the work of the gods. The modern man, assuming that because his chemical formula defines the *how* it also explains the *why*, looks no farther than the formula and does not think of the god as a necessary postulate; in scientific terms he has correlated the 'recipe' with the observed processes of natural law; and mere empirical success has little value for him until it has been thus rationalized. For the craftsman of the second millennium BC the universe was not rational, because the gods who ran it were moved more by whims and passions than by reason; so he was satisfied if he could obtain the knowledge, or the ritual, which made miracles possible. In the two cases the practical result might be much the same, but the approach was very different.

In Chapter IV there has been described the process whereby the ancient goldsmith made that granulated work the secret of which was lost until a few years ago, and it was there pointed out that whereas the principle involved is that if a copper salt and a glue be heated together the former turns to copper oxide and the latter to carbon, and that the carbon, combining with the oxygen in the copper oxide, goes off as volatile carbon dioxide, leaving metallic copper, that principle was entirely unknown to the old craftsman, who understood only the practical technique. In most fields technical knowledge anticipated theory, and this is particularly true in the chemical field. Metallurgy, in which wonderful results were obtained, yet remained a mystery to the workers. The mere fact that metal could be got from stone, as by a transmutation of matter, was inexplicable except as a divine miracle; but it encouraged experiments of all sorts. Men found out how to refine metals and to alloy them, so that for gold alone Akkadian has sixteen different names mostly denoting different colours; the tablets give us recipes for synthetic copper and synthetic silver, and that alone is enough to prove the ingenuity of the experimenters and their chemical ignorance. They were, of course, mistaken in thinking that they could manufacture synthetic metals, but the mistake was a natural one, seeing that there was so much that they could do and that they had no means of deciding what was and what was not possible of achievement. Thus, the Egyptians coloured gold surfaces by dipping the metal in a solution of iron salts and then heating it, and dyed stone with iron vitriol. The Sumerians made, or perhaps imported from the Indus valley, cornelian beads etched with elaborate patterns in white—the cornelian was coated with a layer of carbonate of soda and heated until it was bleached white; then the parts which were not intended to be white were stopped out with a cement containing oxide of iron and the colour was restored by re-heating. Lapis lazuli was highly treasured both in Egypt and in Mesopotamia for jewellery and small objects, but since it could be obtained only from the mines of Badakshan it was a costly luxury and in both countries a synthetic substitute was very popular; the recipe for this was to mix together in powder form silica, malachite, calcium carbonate and natron and to heat the mixture for twenty-four hours at a temperature of between 800° and 900° C. Clearly, a formula so elaborate could have been arrived at by people ignorant of chemistry only as the result of prolonged experiment, and in the course of that they would learn incidentally a great deal about the properties of various substances, all of which knowledge might be turned to practical uses. This unco-ordinated invention can be illustrated by the somewhat curious fact that neither the Egyptians nor the Mesopotamians succeeded in making soap, in spite of the importance which both attached to personal cleanliness and in spite of the fact that the detergents in use were very numerous; boiled oil and alkali was the commonest recipe, but in addition we find references to fuller's earth, natron, potash, soda, resin and salt, together with palm-oil and castor-oil, and lyes from the ashes of beech-wood, rue and other plants; the cleansing properties of all these had been duly noted, but not until late in the first millennium was real soap made from them.

The ancients experimented, studied and observed, and in a rather elementary way they classified their knowledge. To the root word which was the name of the *genus* the Sumerian language adds various suffixes denoting characteristics peculiar to the species or individual; and although these generally deal with outward appearances yet some imply actual tests, as when a species of stone is distinguished as being liable to effervesce if treated with acid, or when the reactions to heat are described. They did in time amass a vast lore concerning the properties —including the chemical properties—of a wide range of natural substances; but all these items of empirical knowledge, instead of being treated collectively as a body of data from which scientific conclusions might be drawn, were treasured in isolation, each one a new fact related not so much to the accompanying facts as to the ultimate divine order. If this knowledge had to be classified and a term invented for each new 'species' discovered or invented, it was to satisfy not science but superstition: to know the name of the thing gave one power over the thing and so helped one to obtain mastery over nature. Of course there was speculation, but it was along such lines as these, and the secrets of the metallurgist were in time taken over by the alchemists and astrologers as the material for magic.

MATHEMATICS, INCLUDING GEOMETRY

Egypt

Man's advance in knowledge throughout the Bronze Age was seldom uniform, in spite of the interrelations between different countries to which reference has constantly been made, and this is specially true of mathematics. We cannot treat of the Middle East as a whole; rather is it necessary to emphasize from the outset the absolute contrast presented by the two leading civilizations. The Babylonians possessed a scientific knowledge of algebra, geometry and arithmetic. The Egyptians, on the contrary, had in these subjects no real science at all.[2]

So categorical a denial may seem inconsistent with known performances which we certainly cannot afford to underestimate if our account of man's progress is to accord with historic facts. The Egyptians, early in the Dynastic period, drew up a calendar which is at the base of that in use today, they designed and built their pyramids with no appreciable error of measurement or calculation, they could estimate areas and bulks accurately, and they had squared the circle with a closer approximation to the truth than was reached by any other people until Greek times; these achievements, stressed by many writers, make it not altogether surprising that ancient Egypt has been popularly credited with an esoteric knowledge of science unrivalled in later ages. The facts are indisputable, but the conclusion drawn from them is fantastically wrong.

The Egyptian had mathematics as the basis of geometry, and for him the basis of mathematics was simple addition. He never, so far as we know, formulated general principles; he did not study the subject for its own sake but merely wanted certain working rules which would enable him to deal with practical problems in daily life, and so long as the method evolved met his immediate needs he was content, and the method remained in use without any thought on his part that it might be improved or simplified. The documentary evidence from which we derive our knowledge of early Egyptian mathematics—one leather roll and five papyri, a mere six in all—date from the Twelfth Dynasty (*c.* 2000 BC) or from the immediately following Hyksos period; the stage at which we then find them may quite possibly have been reached (as some authorities believe to have been the case) as early as the Pyramid age (*c.* 2700 BC) but whenever it was, having reached that stage they seem to have simply stagnated; certainly Egyptian multiplication on the additive principle maintained itself unchanged right up to the Hellenistic period. The point is that the system could be made to work, and for purely utilitarian ends that was sufficient. The Rhind papyrus (our principal source) does indeed in its exordium profess to teach 'complete and thorough study of all things, insight into all that exists, knowledge of all secrets', but really it deals only with numbers and the calculation of fractions for the solution of practical problems, those of the administrator, the tax official and the architect; only a few purely theoretical problems are set, to provide exercises on the calculation of fractions.

The Egyptians had a decimal system of numeration. There were separate signs for unity and for each power of 10 up to a million; there was no zero sign, and as there were no separate signs for numbers between 1 and 10, or for multiples of 10, signs were repeated up to the requisite number of times and merely had to be placed in a row (from right to left) to give the complete number. Thus:

𓏤 = 1 therefore 𓏤𓏤𓏤 = 3 𓏤𓏤𓏤𓏤𓏤 = 5

𓎆 = 10 therefore 𓎆𓎆 = 20 𓎆𓎆𓎆𓎆 = 40

𓍢 = 100 therefore 𓍢𓍢 = 200 etc.

and the number of 142 is written 𓏤𓏤𓎆𓎆𓎆𓎆𓍢, 257 is written 𓏤𓏤𓏤𓏤𓏤𓏤𓏤𓎆𓎆𓎆𓎆𓎆𓍢𓍢; it is a clumsy form of numeration, but an easy one.

The entire system, as has been said above, was based on addition. Given the numeration, the process was a simple one, for all that one has to do is to count the numbers of units, tens, hundreds, etc., and enter them accordingly; thus for the two numbers 142 and 257 the sum total is written

||||||||| ∩∩∩∩∩∩∩∩∩ 999

the addition of the parts yields the sum of the whole.

A special case of addition, and the most straightforward, is duplication, when the number is simply added to itself. This was, for the Egyptian, the basis of all more advanced calculations.

Multiplication by any number larger than 2 is done, according to the teaching of the Rhind Papyrus, by doubling the given number the requisite number of times and then adding the results; thus, to multiply 12 by 12 the following steps are taken:—

| (1) ||∩ = 12
|| (2) ||||∩∩ = 24
|||| (4) ||||||||∩∩∩∩ = 48
|||||||| (8) ||||||∩∩∩∩∩∩∩∩∩ = 96

and since 4 + 8 = 12, four times 12 and eight times 12 are to be added together; accordingly in the papyrus those numbers 4 and 8 are marked with a tick and the corresponding quotients 48 and 96 are added to make 144, which is written, together with the hieroglyphic *dmd* (a sealed scroll), as the final result ||||∩∩∩∩9 (scroll).

Where a number was to be multiplied by 10 no such calculations were involved because it was only necessary to substitute 'ten' signs for units, 'hundred' signs for 'tens' and so on. Another of our main sources, the Kahun mathematical papyrus, shows how advantage can be taken of this decimal factor to shorten the multiplication process; one can multiply by 10 and also (by means of halving that result) by 5. Thus the sum 16 × 16 can be worked out, by the same additive method as when the multiplication was by 2, as follows:—

| (1) ||||||∩ = 16
∩ (10) ∩∩∩∩∩∩9 = 160
||||| (5) ∩∩∩∩∩∩∩∩ = 80

and since 1 + 10 + 5 = 16, we have the total

||||||∩∩∩∩∩99, 256 (scroll)

Division is simply the inverse of multiplication; it is identical in principle and looks identical when written down. In the Rhind Papyrus the formula leaves no doubt as to the view taken by the Egyptians of the process of division: it runs 'Add, beginning with 80, until you get 1,120', i.e. 'divide 1,120 by 80', which is done in the following way:

I	(1)	∩∩∩∩ ∩∩∩∩	= 80
∩	(10)	99999999	= 800
II	(2)	∩∩∩9 ∩∩∩	= 160
IIII	(4)	∩∩999	= 320

Since the number 1,120 is given by the sum of the multiplication results of 10 and 4, these added together give 14 as the answer to the division sum.

For the practical purposes which the Egyptian mathematician had in view, e.g. the distribution of rations amongst workmen or the calculation of volumes, fractions would often have to be used. Now the Egyptian had no notation for expressing mixed fractions with numerator and denominator as employed today. He recognized the few 'natural' fractions, $\frac{1}{2}$, $\frac{1}{3}$, $\frac{2}{3}$, $\frac{1}{4}$ and $\frac{3}{4}$, for which he had specific names, and by a quite early date he had extended the list to include all unit fractions, i.e. those having 1 as the numerator, but anything more complicated than that he could not express. Mixed fractions had to be broken down into a series of unit fractions which together made the desired total—i.e. he obtained his result by the same additive method as lay at the root of all his mathematics, so that our fraction $\frac{7}{12}$ would be resolved into $\frac{1}{3} + \frac{1}{4}$, or $\frac{1}{2} + \frac{1}{12}$.

The simplest calculation is with 'natural' fractions having the same denominator, examples of which are given in the mathematical leather roll BM 10250, dated to about 1700 BC:

$$\frac{1}{6} + \frac{1}{6} = \frac{1}{3}$$
$$\frac{1}{6} + \frac{1}{6} + \frac{1}{6} = \frac{1}{2}$$
$$\frac{1}{3} + \frac{1}{3} = \frac{2}{3} \text{ (using our notation)}$$

deduced from which we find further relations applied in the Rhind Papyrus:

(1) $\frac{1}{3} + \frac{1}{6} = \frac{1}{2}$
(2) $\frac{1}{2} + \frac{1}{3} + \frac{1}{6} = 1$

(3) by adding $\frac{1}{6}$ to each of the members of (1) above, we obtain the important formula:
$\frac{2}{3} = \frac{1}{2} + \frac{1}{6}$
and by again adding $\frac{1}{6}$ to both sides and then writing the result from right to left, we get:

(4) $\frac{1}{2} + \frac{1}{3} = \frac{2}{3} + \frac{1}{6}$
and by adding $\frac{1}{6}$ to both sides of (2) above, we get:

(5) $\frac{2}{3} + \frac{1}{2} = 1 + \frac{1}{6}$

These rules are not stated explicitly in the Rhind Papyrus but are taken for granted, since every Egyptian computer was expected to know them by heart; they supply all that he needed to know about calculations with halves, thirds and sixths; thus, if he wanted to work out $\frac{2}{3}$ of a unit fraction such as $\frac{1}{11}$, he took formula (3) above and obtained $\frac{1}{22} + \frac{1}{66}$. Moreover, by dividing the figures in these formulae by 2, 3, 4, etc., he could get further relations between fractions; these, being more difficult to remember, might be given in tables of reference such as are found in the leather roll:

$$\frac{1}{9} + \frac{1}{18} = \frac{1}{6}$$
$$\frac{1}{12} + \frac{1}{24} = \frac{1}{8}$$
$$\frac{1}{15} + \frac{1}{30} = \frac{1}{10} \text{ etc.}$$

On the principle of the five formulae above, the Egyptian was able to deal with all fractions whose denominator was divisible by 2 or by 3; with fractions of other types a typical method was that of *regula falsi*, i.e. an assumption, followed by such alteration as was needed to give a correct result. Thus, to take an example from the Rhind Papyrus, the problem is 'What number added to its seventh part gives nineteen?'; the number most easily divisible into seven parts is 7, so we take that and add the seventh part, yielding 8. Now we have to 'operate with 8 so as to obtain 19'. Doubling 8, we get 16, which is 3 short; so we take one-half of 8 and do that again and again, thus:

1	8
2	16
$\frac{1}{2}$	4
$\frac{1}{4}$	2
$\frac{1}{8}$	1

and since $16 + 2 + 1 = 19$, the result is 2, $\frac{1}{4}$, $\frac{1}{8}$ ($2\frac{3}{8}$ in our notation) which multiplied by 7 gives the answer $16\frac{5}{8}$.

Another and more scientific method of duplicating fractions whose denominators contain the numbers 5 and 7 was contained in the rule 'To calculate $^2/_n$ (*n* being the denominator in question) divide 2 by *n*'. To us, accustomed to our own notation, this seems tautologous; to the Egyptian it was not, because the problem of duplicating ⅕ is totally different from his accustomed additive problem which he stated in the words 'Calculate with 5 until you obtain 2'. To duplicate $^1/_n$ by dividing 2 by *n* was a new idea. It was worked by means of the ½ and the ⅔ sequences; the question is asked, 'What part is 2 of 5?'; the answer is, one-third of 5 is 1 + ⅔, a fifteenth of 5 is ⅓, and since these two (1 + ⅔ + ⅓) add up to 2, the result of the division is ⅓ + $\frac{1}{15}$. 'What part is 2 of 7?' A quarter of 7 is 1 + ½ + ¼, a twenty-eighth of 7 is ¼, and since these two (1¾ + ¼) add up to 2, the result of the division is ¼ + $\frac{1}{28}$. Because these divisions are too complicated to be memorized easily, they were embodied in tables of reference; these are straightforward up to the divisor 29, but from 31 onwards are worked on a different system which introduces auxiliary figures (distinguished on the tables by the use of red ink!) corresponding in our notation to the numerators of fractions reduced to a common denominator. The rule would seem to be, 'When a somewhat complicated sum of fractions has to be compared with another such sum, or has to be complemented to 1, then the smallest of the fractions is taken as a new unit and the other fractions are expressed in terms of it'. Beyond this, Egyptian computation technique could not go; but, clumsy though the system of auxiliaries may be, yet by its means every division, no matter how complicated, could be carried out.

It will be seen that Egyptian mathematics (ultimately multiplication) is essentially a written operation; there were no principles which could be applied generally, and every problem had to be worked out individually, nor could any algebraic formula be adapted to the system of notation. By dint of considerable ingenuity and of infinite patience the Egyptian was able to meet all his practical needs by the use of a means childishly imperfect; the sources available to us suggest nothing in the nature of advanced science, and we may well believe that in that respect he was incurious as well as ignorant.

His geometry is a case in point. He could, for instance, if given the height of a pyramid and the measurement of its base, calculate its inclination; thus, the height being 250 cubits and the base 360 cubits, he calculates, half of 360 is 180; $\frac{180}{250}$ equals ½ + ⅕ + $\frac{1}{50}$ of a cubit; a cubit being 7 hands, multiply by 7 and the inclination, i.e. the number of hands by which the inclined plane departs from the vertical in a rise of one cubit is 5$\frac{1}{25}$ hands. The area of a triangle or a rectangle he could determine correctly by multiplying height by base, the base, in the case of a triangle, being first halved 'in order to make the triangle square'. His approximation for the square of the circle, $\pi = 3.1605$ . . (See pp. 420, 425, 441), was remarkably correct; it was obtained by squaring $\frac{8}{9}$ of the diameter, and the formula may be thought to suggest (though this must remain a mere suggestion) that it resulted from laborious experiment with squares and right-angled triangles adjusted to a circle. This empirical method, however, cannot explain how the Egyptian was able to calculate correctly the volume of the frustrum of a square-based pyramid, given the height and the measurements of lower and upper base, the formula for which operation is found in a Moscow papyrus; the problem, unique in Egyptian mathematics as known to us, can scarcely have been solved on the purely arithmetical base elsewhere invariable, and may indicate a borrowing from Babylonian algebra.[3]

Mesopotamia

In contradistinction to the Egyptians, the Babylonians approached mathematics by way not of arithmetic but of algebra. Their predecessors, the Sumerians, who were admirable arithmeticians, had invented a sexagesimal notation for whole numbers and for fractions which enabled them to calculate with fractions as easily as with integers. The system is simple. Numbers under 60 are written in the ordinary decimal notation; the vertical cuneiform wedge = 1, and is repeated for all numbers up to 9, after which the double wedge [4] stands for 10 and is repeated up to 50, but with 60 we start counting anew, with 60 represented by , the value of each symbol being determined by its position in the group of symbols which together give the number. This is, of course, precisely the same as the system in use today, the only difference in the notation as a whole being that (*a*) the Sumerian is a sexagesimal instead of a decimal system, and (*b*) it contains no cypher (later on, a special sign was used for the empty place between the digits, but not until the Greek period was the zero sign used also at the end of a number) so that there can be an ambiguity as to the value to be assigned to the integers. The positional notation was an enormous advantage. Whereas a Roman, for instance, would normally work out his multiplication sums by the help of an abacus, the Babylonian had a series of multiplication tables to assist his memory and to save trouble[5] in working out sums. With the same tables he could as easily multiply sexagesimal fractions as if they were whole numbers, just as we today deal with decimal fractions as if they were whole numbers and after multiplying put the decimal point in the proper place. If to those accustomed to a decimal system the sexagesimal appears over-complicated, that is really due more to habit than to any inherent difficulty of the latter; actually for fractions the sexagesimal denominator was of the greatest advantage, and is still retained for time fractions—minutes and seconds—and for the divisions of the circle. The fundamental principle of the positional notation is that 1 and 60 are represented by the same symbol, though for 60, the 'big unit', the symbol may be drawn rather larger than when it stands for 1; by a natural process of simplification, since 1 squared = 1, the 'big unit' squared (3,600) could also be represented by 1. This square, called the *šár*, originally terminated the system, but later the 'big *šár*', or 60 cubed, was added as the final unit.

The origin of the system is still in dispute, but most authorities agree in attributing it to metrology. Certainly the weights are consistently sexagesimal—180 grains make a shekel, 60 shekels make a *mina*, 60 *mina* make a talent, and as in each case the larger unit is sixty times the smaller, so, conversely, the smaller is 1/60th of the larger, and it is noteworthy that in the sexagesimal system 1/60 is known as the 'small unit'. But however it arose, the important fact is that the Sumerian notation and the Sumerian arithmetical technique made possible the highly developed algebra evolved by the Babylonians. Not only was the Babylonian scribe in the time of Hammurabi perfectly familiar with square and cube roots (we have tables of exact square and cube roots, and tables giving the approximate computation of square roots) but he knew also how to solve linear and quadratic equations involving two or more unknowns. He would normally have by him, for the convenience of ready reckoning, multiplication tables and tables of inverses $(1/x)$ and also of squares and cubes; the tables were arranged in a practical manner so that all operations, whether with integers or with fractions, could be carried out by a single reference and without further thought. If a division left a remainder, or if it was desired to find the square root of a number which was not a perfect square, then an approximation was used, repeated adjustments reducing the error to a minimum.

The algebraical texts, most of which date from the early part of the second millennium BC, do not give general formulae such as we should expect to find in a modern work; they set problems, but since these are solved by the same methods of calculation it is evident that the formulae existed although they are not set out in abstract terms. Again, because the problems are individual, the Babylonian does not use purely algebraic symbols like our x and y; but as the signs which he does use for length, breadth, area, content, etc., are not declined they serve precisely the same purpose as our more formal x and y and the Babylonian equation can be expressed in our notation without doing any violence to the original; thus, the problem:

I have multiplied length and width, thus obtaining the area. Then I added to the area the excess of the length over the width; 3·3 (i.e. the result was 183). Moreover, I have added length and width; 27. Required, length, width and area.

can be expressed in our terms:

$$\begin{aligned} xy + x - y &= 183 \\ x + y &= 27 \end{aligned}$$

The method employed for the solution is given in a series of steps which in our notation are as follows:

First, a new variable, y', is introduced in place of the actual width y, thus $y' = y + 2$, i.e. $y = y' - 2$. Then, by adding the two original equations, we get

$$\begin{aligned} xy' &= 183 + 27 = 210 \\ x + y' &= \ \ 27 + 2 = \ \ 29 \end{aligned}$$

and the solution of this simplified form is got by a fixed recipe which appears constantly in other texts and may be described thus:

$$xy' = P;\ x + y' = a$$

the solution of which is:

$$\begin{aligned} x &= \tfrac{1}{2}a + w \\ y &= \tfrac{1}{2}a - w \\ w &= \sqrt{(\tfrac{1}{2}a)^2 - P} \end{aligned}$$

this last formula not being directly stated but implicit in all examples given of this method of calculation.

The problems set may involve systems of equations with three or more unknowns, cubic equations and mixed cubics, sometimes of a sort difficult even for the modern mathematician. The Babylonian did not have to work out all these for himself, but by reference to the tables of roots; the problems are school exercises intended to teach the scholar the use to which his tables should be put. How the underlying formulae were obtained we cannot be sure; possibly they were worked out by the use of diagrams, after the fashion of Euclid, and it is certain that a square of a number was regarded as the area of a square; but on the other hand a diagrammatic basis is often ruled out altogether, as in the problem quoted above, in which the area, xy, and the linear measurement $x - y$ are simply added together, which is a geometrical absurdity. For the Babylonian these were all pure numbers, and the mental process by which the problem was approached was algebraic. The problem may be definitely geometric, but the scribe merely had to know—and he did know—the area of a triangle and the area of a trapezoid, and the rest was done by algebra. An example cited by Professor Neugebauer (MKT I, p. 130) solves a difficult geometrical problem without any reference to a diagram: the area of a trapezoid is divided into two equal parts by a line x which is parallel to the bases a and b of the trapezoid; find the length of x. The formula used is $x^2 = \frac{1}{2}(a^2 + b^2)$, a purely algebraic solution in abstract form, without numbers.

If, for the area of a circle and for the length of its perimeter, the Babylonian, taking $3d$ as the circumference and $3r^2$ as the area, where $d =$ the diameter and $r =$ the radius, arrived only at an approximation not so close to the truth as the Egyptian, the fact is really beside the point;[6] we may perhaps surmise that it resulted from his trying to solve the problem by abstract calculation which proved to be beyond his powers, while the Egyptian used the empirical method with a success measured by his patience and perseverance. The truth remains that in arithmetic and algebra he not only far surpassed the Egyptian pragmatically, but further had worked out those scientific exercises of geometry which for the Egyptian were a closed book; thus, the Babylonian knew the 'theorem of Pythagoras' about the square of the hypotenuse of a right-angled triangle being equal to the sum of the squares of the other two sides, and again, by discovering a method of finding right-angled triangles whose sides are expressed in integers he anticipated by fifteen hundred years Pythagoras and his Greek followers.

THE CALENDAR

Any people whose economy is based on agriculture must needs observe the seasons, and since the farmer must plan ahead he requires something in the nature of a calendar which will give him due warning of the year's changes. Again, religion demands that certain festivals should be celebrated at fixed times; these are seasonal, generally related to agricultural happenings, and they too have to be planned in advance, and that with more accuracy than is called for by field work, for here it is a matter of special days and not merely of seasons.

The drawing up of a formal calendar involves more prolonged and concentrated observation than the farmer himself can afford, and demands a record best kept in writing, which is beyond the farmer's powers; it is a task which would naturally be allotted to the leisured and the educated, i.e. to the priests or priestly scribes.

Mesopotamia

In Mesopotamia most of the land belonged to the temples. The procession of the seasons was regulated by the gods, and the agricultural operations proper to each, and the fruits of them, all fell within the provinces of the various deities, so that from the farming as well as from the ritual point of view the priests were intimately concerned. At a very early date, therefore, an official calendar devised by the priests was issued and came into general use. It was a practical working system, based on a somewhat muddled compromise between two conflicting principles.

We have already, in Chapter II, remarked on the unpredictable character of the annual floods in southern Mesopotamia, on which the whole of agriculture depended; its very uncertainty made a calendar essential, but afforded no help towards the drawing up of one; something more stable had to be found. The most obvious regularly recurrent time-measuring phenomena were the changes of the moon, and the important place in the Mesopotamian pantheon accorded to the Moon god Nannar is in accord with this. The Babylonian calendar, therefore, was based upon the lunar months, consisting of 29 or 30 days each, the change not coming in any regular order but determined by observation of the new moon —observation, of course, by some duly authorized person who would make his report to the government. Experience over a very short period sufficed to show that the number of longer and shorter months was about the same, and also that at the end of 12 lunar months one had returned to much the same season (reckoned by crops, etc.) as one had started from, so 12 was taken as the number of months required for a year. In early Sumer the names given to the months varied greatly in the different city states; they were generally called after the religious festivals celebrated in the course of each, and the cities, with their different patron gods, would not keep the same feast-days; only in Hammurabi's reign was uniformity imposed and the names assigned to them which are still used n the Jewish calendar. The four phases of the moon led to a livision of the month into four seven-day weeks with one, or two, feast-days ('Month days') added at the end to make up the full tally; this was the official calendar which because it was ruled by the moon best suited religious requirements. But the uncertainty regarding the extra feast-days was an unwelcome complication for the business man; consequently, in order to regularize such matters as the calculation of interest and the dates of payments another parallel system was introduced whereby the fundamental unit, the mean month, was divided into six weeks of five lunar days each. This system was regularly used by the merchant colony of Kanesh, Anatolia, and seems to have been employed at the same early date (2000 BC) in Sumer also; these 'lunar days' under the name 'tithis' survive up to the present day in Indian calendars. The origin of the five-day week is not known, but since the day was divided into 12 'double hours' the week of 60 'double hours' may have been an artificial invention basing itself on the hexagesimal unit. The day began at nightfall.

Thus far, then, the lunar principle was strictly observed by the calendar-makers. But Shamash the Sun god 'rules the ways of Heaven and of Earth' and therefore the Babylonian year was a solar year. It started in the spring. We do not know what event was taken to fix the year's beginning; it may have been the barley-harvest, it may have been the equinox. The most primitive of people would learn that in winter the days were shorter and the nights longer than in summer, whereas the Babylonian 'lunar day' was uniform throughout, and more curious observation would discover that twice in the year the periods of light and darkness in that day were exactly equal, and again that this balance recurred with absolute regularity. Some such fixed point was necessary for estimating the length of the solar year, and because gradually increasing daylight seems to give promise of new life the spring equinox might well commend itself as the natural beginning of the year. However that may be, the calendar-makers started their year in the spring and determined its length as approximately 12 months and 11 days, making roughly a total of 365 days; this was what Shamash had ordained and they accepted it.

The fact that the solar year was hopelessly inconsistent with the months ordained by Nannar had to be accepted also; this was Heaven's doing, and man must just make the best of it. The 12 months of 29 or 30 days each was the closest approximation possible, but as their total gave only 354 days the discrepancy was very serious in practice; thus, for instance, in the course of little more than a generation, the spring festival at which the god's marriage was the guarantee of earth's fertility would have been celebrated progressively through the entire cycle of the seasons. The remedy was to insert an intercalary month whenever necessary, so as to restore harmony between the two systems and the two deities; but since the divinely instituted order of the months could not be disturbed, by a pious fraud an existing month was simply doubled in length without any change of name. At a later period this leap month was inserted every second or third year, and later still—after 500 BC—there was a regular intercalation of seven months in nineteen years;[7] but in the early times with which we are concerned there was no fixed interval and only when nature and the calendar were impossibly at variance was the truth checked by the stars and the government took the requisite steps; thus Hammurabi, writing in the month Ulûlu, issues his instructions, 'This year has a deficiency. The coming month shall therefore be entered as "second Ulûlu".'

In its later form, when the intercalation of the leap months was regularized, the Babylonian calendar as a working compromise between two inconsistent principles was quite effective and must have served the needs of everyday life as well as could be desired; already, in about 1100 BC, the Assyrian Astrolabe B associates the working rules of agriculture with the names of the months and with the constellations rising about that time of year. But in earlier times although the official calendar would meet the requirements of temple ritual and of government or commercial business, yet with its irregular intercalation it was nothing like so reliable as the first visibility of the fixed stars for the farmer's purpose.

The Lack of an Era

The modern calendar is normally headed with the date of the year, i.e. its number in a series reckoned from a fixed point taken as the start of an era, Christian, Moslem, Jewish, etc. The Babylonians, before Alexander's conquest, had no such system, and to the lack of it is due our uncertainty regarding the historical chronology of Babylonia; we are provided with no framework for the building up of history. Each year was named after an event which took place in the course of it; the name, therefore, would normally be given only during the year or after its end; it generally referred to a military exploit or to a religious celebration as the local ruler and his priestly advisers might decide; occasionally the same name might be given to two years, and in Early Dynastic times different city states might give different names to the same year; not until the reign of Ur-Nammu of Ur (2120 BC) did the central power enforce a uniform nomenclature. Presumably a record was kept of the year-names in their due order, but if so no copy of it survives; the modern scholar may be able, largely from external evidence, to arrange the sequence of these undated years, but that in part only. It was only in the Kassite period that the Babylonian scribe revived and formally adopted the simple system which had been used by some of the *ensīs* of Lagash in the third millennium BC of dating by the regnal years of the ruler for the time being—these he correlated with the official year-name, 'Year 5; the year in which Anshan was laid waste', 'Year 8; the year in which he brought into the Sun god's temple a great statue of copper.' But on the accession of a new ruler the count of the years started again at 1, and there is therefore no real continuity. The effect upon chronology of the lack of any system of consecutive dating is illustrated by the fact that the last of the kings of Babylon, Nabonidus, himself an enthusiast for ancient history and having at his disposal all the documentary evidence that there was, could yet state that 'Naram-Sin, the son of Sargon' of Akkad, reigned 3200 years before his own time,[8] i.e. in 3753 BC, an error of some fourteen hundred years, and even for Hammurabi of Babylon the date which he gives[9] is far from correct. The extraordinary confusion of the early Sumerian king-lists is due to the same cause. When, in the Isin period, the scribes set themselves to draw up an outline of their country's history the chance collection of undated and unrelated documents of which they could avail themselves defied analysis. There was nothing to show whether events were contemporary or consecutive, there was no fixed point by which dates could be reckoned, no way of estimating the length of periods, and if they chose to introduce the *šár*, the period of 3,600 years, the square of the 'big unit' which was the basis of their sexagesimal system of arithmetic, that was a literary convention which had nothing to do with history. The lack of any sequence-dating of the years would not have been noticed by the makers of the calendar nor did it concern them; they were not constructing a historical skeleton; their aim was to meet the interests of the priest, the farmer and the economist by framing an instrument which might regulate the essential activities of those professions month by month and day by day within the limits of the year, and men asked of a calendar no more than that.

Egypt

In Egypt, as in Mesopotamia, the farmers and the priests, and later on the business men also, required a timetable to regulate their activities, and a calendar therefore was formulated at a very early date; the Pyramid Texts appear to show that it was in full working order before 2400 BC, and it continued in use until the Roman period.

The Egyptians had the advantage that the rise of the Nile, with its promise of renewed life after earth had been parched into sterility by the heat of summer, recurs with astonishing punctuality; for an agricultural people it was the greatest seasonal event of all, and a natural start from which time could be reckoned. No very prolonged observation was needed to establish the fact that the average length of the period between inundation and inundation was 365 days. This, then, was taken as the year, a Nilotic year which had nothing to do with astronomy. It began with the river's rise about what in the Julian Calendar is July 19th and the first of the three seasons into which the year was divided was named 'the Inundation Season'; the name indicates that the calendar was introduced at a time when the beginning of this 'season' did really coincide with the rise of the flood-water.

The three seasons of the year consisted of four months each, and each month consisted of 30 days. It is quite clear that the months did not determine the year's length; that had been fixed before, and independently by observation of the Nile's rise, and the months had to be accommodated to the year. Originally they were lunar months, and the actual length of a lunar month is 29.53 days. That the Egyptians knew this is proved by the fact that in a papyrus from Illahûn the entrances of the *phyle*-priests upon their duties are set down for alternate periods of 29 and 30 days, which can only mean that their monthly service depended upon lunar reckonings; their count of 30 days to every month was therefore quite unrealistic, and it is difficult to suppose that it was other than a purely numerical adjustment, 30 being the maximum flat rate for 12 months in a 365-day year. Because the total for the standardized months was only 360 days, there were added to it five 'epagonal' days which were celebrated as the birthday festivals of the five principal deities and were *dies non* for business purposes—they were in the year but not of it, and were quite deliberately disregarded, as in the explicit statement[10] 'Behold, a temple-day is the 1/360th part of a year'. By this somewhat naïve convention of important but non-existing days the numerically schematized division into months and the discordant facts of nature were brought into harmony in one and the same civil calendar.

The possibility that there existed, side by side with the civil calendar, a second calendar which was purely lunar in character and origin is a matter on which Egyptologists are in disagreement.[11] The Illahûn papyrus quoted above indisputably proves that the monthly service of the priests depended upon lunar considerations, but the papyrus dates these varying lunar intervals by means of the civil calendar; there are calendaric tables, such as the Ebers Calendar, in which lunar dates are reduced to civil dates, and similar double-dating occurs in several documents. These facts are taken as evidence of a lunar calendar used simultaneously with the Nilotic Calendar; but it must be admitted that in the Ebers Calendar the months are not of alternating length as lunar months should be and as they are in the Illahûn papyrus, and there is nowhere any suggestion of the intercalary month which a lunar calendar should contain. It is the case that various temple festivals were fixed by reference to the moon, and consequently the occasions of them would in different years fall upon different dates in the civil (non-lunar) calendar, so that the priests would require tables of cross-reference. That such tables existed is evident, but their existence does not necessarily imply that there was a regular lunar calendar in use. In England today the Church of England Prayer Book gives elaborate tables for the finding of Easter in any year, and those are based upon the lunar reckoning of the Jewish (and ultimately the Babylonian) system; but it would be absurd to conclude from this that England normally uses two calendars. In Egypt the tables of cross-reference were made essential by the shortcomings of the civil calendar.

It would be too much to expect of those observers who at the dawn of history recorded each summer the rise of the Nile waters and counted the days that elapsed between the floodings, that they should have been more meticulously accurate than their practical purpose required. In any case, a year had to consist of a definite number of whole days, and they arrived at the right number, so that the Egyptian year had 365 days just as do the years of today. The later Egyptians realized that 365¼ was nearer the truth (which is that the solar year has 365.2422 days), but the early Egyptians certainly did not, and therefore the need—and the possibility—of inserting as we do an intercalary day once in every four years never occurred to the authors of the calendar. Their calendar, therefore, was progressively inaccurate. In Mesopotamia, as we have seen, the discrepancy between the calendar and the seasons became so quickly obvious that steps to correct it were soon taken; but in Egypt it would be long before the discrepancy was noticed at all. Regular as the Nile's rise is, it does not necessarily begin on exactly the same day every year, and if the calendrical New Year's Day were even as much as a week out by reference to the flood the farmer would not be seriously upset; but with every year the error became more palpable, and although it took over 1,460 years for New Year's Day to box the compass of the seasons yet long before that happened the calendar had become topsy-turvy and its 'Inundation Season' a ludicrous misnomer.

The Egyptians of the time in which the calendar was formulated could not possibly have foreseen this, but as the calendar, by almost imperceptible degrees, got more and more out of relation to the march of the seasons, they could not fail to recognize the fact. But at a very early date they remarked that the heliacal rising of Sirius (which they called Sothis) took place just before the Nile flood was due[12] and they associated the two portents—an ivory tablet from a First Dynasty tomb at Abydos hails Sirius as 'Bringer of the New Year and the Inundation'. Sirius was even more dependable than the Nile, and in due course, therefore, was adopted as the proper check upon the calendar.

This is the origin of the 'Sothic cycle' of 1,460 years which has played so large a part in the chronological speculations put forward by Egyptologists.[13]

The Greek mathematician Theon of Alexandria records that a 'Sothic cycle' started in the year 139 AD (i.e. in that year the rising of Sirius coincided with the first day of the calendar year), and remarks that before that it had been 'the epoch of Menophres', i.e. of Ramses I; since Ramses I was on the throne in 1321 BC, which would be the first year of a 1,460-year cycle ending in 139 AD, the evidence would seem to fit perfectly. The two preceding cycles will then have begun in 2781 and 4241 BC respectively. Whether the calendar was introduced in the neighbourhood of the one or the other of these dates is still a matter of dispute.

It should be emphasized that the Sothic cycle results not from the heliacal rising of Sirius but from the imperfection of the Egyptian civil calendar. That imperfection would be noticed only one or two centuries after the calendar had come into use, by which time any record of its beginning would possibly have been lost. Moreover, to discover the cycle of 1,460 Sirius years, systematic observation and recording of the date of risings of Sirius during many years would be necessary. It is even possible that the cycle was not discovered before Greco-Roman times. Whereas some writers have not hesitated to assume that the Egyptian year was from the outset a solar (or, more correctly, a sidereal) year based on observation of the rising of Sirius and have even gone so far as to postulate a 'Sothic Calendar' existing from the beginning side by side with the civil calendar in general use, it is quite certain that no such calendar did or could exist. In the whole of Egyptian literature there is no reference to a Sothic cycle earlier than that of Theon cited above, and, as Neugebauer has pointed out, the Sothic cycle has nothing whatsoever to do with ancient Egyptian chronology. The 365-day year was not a solar or a sidereal but a Nilotic year; the rising of Sirius, an important event from the religious point of view and one which coincided in theory at least with the start of the official calendar, was used as a check upon its vagaries. Thus when a scribe notes that in the seventh year of the reign of Sesostris III Sirius rose on the sixteenth day of the eighth month (Pharmuthi) he presumably does so because it happened to be of interest to record at what season of the year an event occurred, and the calendar date by itself would have been uninformative on that point. Apparently this was the reason why in the Ebers Calendar calendral dates are referred to the Sothic rising, for certain medical prescriptions were dependent upon the seasons, and consequently the practitioner needed guidance if he was to carry out properly the instructions given in his pharmacopoeia.

It might be asked why, if the Egyptian recognized quite early that his calendar was at fault and also learnt in time that this was due to the inexact estimate of the year's total length, he did not take steps to correct the anomaly. In the first place, the Egyptians were a religious people and may well have been prevented by religious conservatism from tampering with an order immensely ancient and manifestly originated by the gods. Secondly, the practical inconvenience involved was not so great as it appears to the precise judgement of the modern scholar. For the bulk of the population of the Nile valley what mattered was the inundation. There the calendar did not help, but the priests who observed the rising of Sirius would give advance notice of the flood, and a more immediate warning came from the office of the vizier, to whom reports were sent by the watchers of the Nilometers in the extreme south. With that, the farmer's year began, and thenceforward his activities were directed by the familiar routine of the seasons; the official calendar was something that concerned the palace, the temple and the law court, but the farmer did not need it to teach him his business. The priest, on the other hand, had to meet the problem of the religious festivals. Each calendar month was distinguished by a temple festival occurring in the course of it (the month-names and the festival names are often identical), and since the months shifted in relation to the seasons of the year[14] the times of the festivals shifted also. But certain festivals, including some of those that gave their names to the months, were really seasonal, and therefore the difficulty arose that a feast definitely associated with, for instance, the rebirth of life in springtime, might by the calendar be assigned to the dead days of mid-summer. The problem was solved, simply and easily, by duplication. The Egyptians distinguished between 'festivals of the times', those celebrated on the dates given by the calendar, and 'festivals of the heavens', which were irrespective of the calendar and were fixed by seasonal or astronomical events; the two might not be identical, and for the priesthood this multiplication of feast-days would be not without its advantages. When, as early as the Fourth Dynasty, we hear of two New Year's Days, one called 'The First of the Year' and the other 'The Opening of the Year', there is here no confusion nor yet reason for surprise. The 'First of the Year' was the calendral New Year's Day as laid down by the law; separated from it by a varying time-gap was the rise of the Nile (and of Sirius) which for the agriculturalist was the opening of his working year, ordained for him by the facts of nature.

China

Until quite recently it was not possible to make any definite assertions regarding the calendar of the Shang Dynasty. But now the position has been changed greatly. The study of the material from the site and tombs of Anyang, in particular of the 'Oracle Bones' which number over 100,000, but also of the inscribed bronze vessels and of *graffiti,* has thrown entirely new light upon the problem. Because a date may be essential to the required prognostication, the oracles are often dated accurately by months and years, a fact which obviously proves the existence of a calendar. The details of the dates, the terms used, and the references to lunar eclipses and to the solstice further make it evident that the calendar of the Shang period —or, at any rate, of the late Shang period after the capital had been moved to Yin (Anyang)—was closely connected with Chinese calendars of subsequent times. In the Han period we are given a list of the 'Six Calendars' which includes the 'Hsia Calendar', the 'Yin Calendar' and the 'Chou Calendar', and although the complete description of these is lost yet references to them in other works suffice to prove that all alike have the same basic principle as the *Ssu-fen* or 'Quarter-day Calendar' of the Eastern Han Dynasty regarding which more will be said hereafter; what matters for the moment is that the 'Six Calendars', described by scholars of the West Han period, include three which are expressly attributed to earlier dynasties, two of them falling within the ages wherewith this volume deals.

According to Professor Tung Tso-pin[15] (whose views are not accepted by all scholars) the Shang Dynasty used the Ssu-fen Calendar, which he describes as follows: It was a mixed lunar-solar calendar. The day started with sunrise. The months were lunar and started not after the first appearance of the new moon, as was the case in Mesopotamia, but after the previous night, when there is no moon at all; this more scientific definition of course implies careful observation of the phenomena. The month consisted of either 29 or 30 days; there is reason to think that the exact length of a lunar month had been worked out at 29.5305106 days, approximately the same figure as the modern calculation of 29.530585 days.

The year consisted of 365 days. Its true length had been worked out at 365.25 days, which again is a remarkable approximation to the truth. Twelve months went to the year, the necessary number of days being completed by the use of intercalary months. The year started in the spring, but the First Month was not the same for all calendars.

The last point is of importance as bearing on the date of the inception of the Chinese calendar. The 'Question of the Three Primes', i.e. the question whether the first month of the year should be identified as the month *tzu,* the month *ch'ou,* or the month *yin,* was raised by the Han Dynasty writers, who agreed that there were three such different systems and attributed them to the practice of the Chou, the Shang and the Hsia Dynasties respectively. This tradition has been discredited by modern historians; but the oracle bones prove conclusively that in the Shang period the year did start with the month *ch'ou:* for the Chou period a number of calendral notices survive, but in them there is no case of a 'Prime' month which does not contain the winter solstice, which is the typical feature of a *tzu* month: the obvious deduction is that tradition was right in its third attribution also, and that assumption is supported by the definite statement of the Tso Chuan, a commentary on the early Chou 'Spring and Autumn Annals'. That there was a Hsia Calendar would therefore seem to be a not unreasonable assumption.

According to the oracle bones the intercalary month was, in early times, placed at the end of the year as 'the thirteenth moon'; this is mentioned, for instance, on an inscription (now in the British Museum) which records a lunar eclipse in the twenty-ninth year of the reign of Wu-ting, November 23, 1311 BC. Soon after this, by the reforms introduced by the Shang ruler Tsu-chia (1273–1241 BC), the intercalation was made immediately after any moon whenever the difference between the solar year and the lunar year was seen to amount to a substantial number of days. Thus, for example, in the tenth year of Ti-hsin (1165 BC) an intercalary month of 29 days was inserted at the end of the ninth month and was entitled 'the ninth'. This intercalation was not merely a make-shift expedient arbitrarily adopted to correct an obvious error; it was, on the contrary, the application of a principle which had been worked out on the basis of scientific observation as set forth in the Ssu-fen Calendar of the East Han Dynasty. The purpose of that 'Quarter-day Calendar' was to reconcile the solar year of 365¼ days with the 'common' year of 365 days; the solution found was to insert seven intercalary months in each period of nineteen years. The Chinese calendrist, therefore, recognized time-units longer than a year, namely the *chang* or 'chapter' of 19 years or 235 moons, and the *fu* or 'cycle' of 76 years or 940 moons or 27,759 days. At a later date longer units, the *chi* and the *yuan,* were introduced, but they were purely theoretical, invented to conform to the sexagesimal system, and do not concern us here; and until quite lately it was reasonable to maintain that the *chang* and the *fu* also could not be earlier than the Han period, so that any supposed connection between the Ssu-fen figures and the Six Calendars of Han tradition must be an anachronism, the Han writers having attributed their own knowledge to their remote ancestors. But an inscribed tortoise-shell found at Anyang in 1936, dated to the reign of Wen-wu-ting (1222–1210 BC), proves the case. A piece of farm land was to be let for 548 days (the text says 547, but since the day of divinition was not reckoned in the total at the time when this oracle was written, we should read 548) starting at the winter solstice and ending at the summer solstice of the following year, i.e. for exactly one-and-a-half years. If the 'years' in question were 'common' years of 365 days the figure of 548 is as much as half a day out; but if they were solar years, put by the Ssu-fen at 365¼ days, then the year-and-a-half (365.25 plus 182.625 = 547.875) is in practical agreement with the 548 of the text. This, as Professor Tung insists, cannot be mere coincidence, and in itself[16] amounts to proof that the Yin Calendar, i.e. that in use when P'an Keng moved the capital of Shang to Yin (Anyang) in 1384 BC, was based upon the Ssu-fen figures, which again could only have been arrived at after prolonged observation and study. The conclusion, then, is that the Ssu-fen Calendar, having as its basic feature the *chang* unit of 19 years or 235 moons (228 lunar months of 29–30 days plus 7 intercalary months) anticipates by more than a thousand years the famous Metonic Cycle, the solution to the same problem of reconciling the lunar and the solar years, which was promulgated in Mesopotamia in the Hellenistic period. The longer *chang* unit of 76 years (4 *changs*), the reason for which would seem to be that it was a period sufficiently long to allow for accurate observations to be made of the effect of the 19-yearly intercalations,[17] corresponds to the 'Period of Calippus' of the Hellenistic scholars. While we are not justified in denying absolutely to the Greek and Babylonian astronomers the credit of an independent origin for the Metonic Cycle, we are none the less bound to admit that by the second millennium BC the Chinese calendar had been framed with a scientific accuracy which neither Babylon nor Egypt could rival.

It is perhaps strange that, having achieved such precision with the Ssu-fen system as Professor Tung claims for it, the Chinese should, in later ages, have persisted in calendral reform. Some of those efforts were but theoretical exercises, but the result was that throughout most of their history they recognized two quite separate official calendars, one for the peasant, which followed the seasons, and one for the scribe, which was a pure—perhaps pedantic—number-system.[18] But the duplication seems to have been due not to ignorance or incompetence but to reasons of political or social convenience: in later time the rise of a new dynasty regularly involved a re-casting of the calendar.[19] Indeed, in the case of China, as in that of Egypt, we have to remember that the social utility of a calendar is its primary *raison d'être,* and its scientific accuracy is, for most people, a secondary consideration; inconsistencies, however glaring in theory, are accepted with equanimity by a public habituated to them.

In the Western world of today only the extreme purist would object to the ninth, tenth, eleventh and twelfth months of the year being named the seventh, eighth, ninth and tenth, September, October, November and December. The irregular length of February is the cause of jesting, not of worry. Few complain because the dates of the two chief religious festivals, together with the civil holidays attached to them, are not fixed; that Christmas falls every year on a different day of the week because the number of days in the year is not divisible by seven, and that Easter may shift its date by as much as a calendar month because it is based on a lunar reckoning entirely alien to the calendar. So conservative is man in this respect that calendral reform in England was opposed by rioters shouting 'Give us back our eleven days', and in Greece and in Russia (until 1918) was blocked by the religious objections of the

Orthodox Church. The Egyptian calendar, which fixed absolutely the duration of the month and of the year, was far better calculated to serve administrative purposes (from the government's point of view its real object) than was the Babylonian calendar with its irregular intercalations and months of different lengths, and for the same reason it was preferred to any other by later astronomers such as Ptolemy.

ASTRONOMY

In the discussion of the calendars it has been pointed out that astronomical observations helped the calendar-makers in their task; particularly in the case of Egypt we have seen that the heliacal rising of Sirius was adopted as a check on the civil calendar. Conversely, the need of a calendar, in Egypt and elsewhere, encouraged observation; and a motive equally practical in the eyes of ancient man was supplied by the religious awe with which he looked upon the heavens above him. That being so, it is incumbent upon us to enquire into man's achievement in astronomical science during the period which ends with the close of the second millennium BC.

The enquiry is the more necessary because popular opinion has mistakenly ascribed to the Mesopotamians and still more to the Egyptians a profound understanding of astronomical phenomena. It is indeed a fact that various buildings in Egypt and elsewhere were oriented on heavenly bodies; and to people for whom those bodies have no particular significance this seems to be a mysterious fact implying scientific knowledge of a very abstruse sort. It really implies nothing of the kind; it is simply the result of careful observation of what could not safely be disregarded. Mere observation of the heavenly bodies, if carefully maintained, will suffice to show that their relative positions change and repeat themselves in a definite space of time, and such movements can be related to the agricultural seasons or may themselves determine the times for religious celebrations. The sun, the moon and the planets were gods who, as such, directly influenced man's fate. Civil life depended upon the regular succession of days and months and years, all of which are fixed by the course of the sun and the moon, and similarly the gods moving about in the upper spheres bring peace or war upon earth, destruction or prosperity; their movements, therefore, must be watched and, if possible, interpreted in the light of experience or analogy. Consequently from a very early time such phenomena were observed and recorded, but that is not the same as saying that astronomy begins early;

men's interest in the celestial bodies was calendral on the one side and astrological on the other. Professor Neugebauer has defined the matter succinctly and authoritatively: 'Astronomy does not originate with the recognition of irregular configurations of stars or the invention of celestial or astral deities. Scientific astronomy does not begin until an attempt is made to predict, however crudely, astronomical phenomena such as the phases of the moon.' That attempt came later. The lunar month, i.e. the time required for the moon to pass through all its phases, is so obvious a unit that it can be determined by the most primitive people on the strength of watching for no more than a single year, but this gives an approximation only which in Egypt, all through the Bronze Age, was checked by actual observation of the waxing and waning moon; only in the course of the first millennium BC did Babylonian astronomers succeed in *predicting* the lengths of the lunar months and it was only from Babylon that the Egyptians subsequently acquired such knowledge.

The advance from observation to prediction was really made impossible for the Egyptian by the elementary character of his mathematical system, which could not cope with the elaborate calculations demanded by astronomy. It would appear that having once obtained, by very simple observation, the agricultural and ritual data necessary to an ordered life, he had no urge to pursue the matter further. Thus we find in the Egyptian texts no reference at all to lunar eclipses;[20] such must presumably have appeared to the Egyptian as isolated events due to some supernatural cause and therefore incalculable and having nothing to do with the regular course of things. From China we have, in one Anyang bone inscription, a very early record of an eclipse which took place 'on the fifteenth day of the twelfth moon of the twenty-ninth year of King Wu-Ting', i.e. on November 23, 1311 BC,[21] which shows an interest, and possibly a knowledge, antedating anything of the sort in Egypt. The inscription by itself is insufficient to prove that the interest went beyond the recording of a striking phenomenon, and the fact that the record figures in an oracle text may well raise doubts as to its scientific value. But in the Chou records we are told that in the thirty-eighth year of the reign of the Shang 'emperor' Ti-hsin (1137 BC) the Chou ruler Chou-wen-wang ordered a sacrifice to be offered because 'the eclipse happened not on the right day': it occurred on the sixteenth day of the month, according to the calendar, instead of on the fifteenth. This, if the construction put upon it be correct, surely implies that as early as the twelfth century BC Chinese astronomers were able to calculate the lunar eclipse in advance, and that with such confidence that an error of twenty-four hours was enough to alarm the authorities. The Anyang inscription may possibly imply similar knowledge two centuries earlier.

On the other hand the Mesopotamian omen texts, which go back as early as the First Dynasty of Babylon, *c.* 1800 BC, base many auguries upon lunar eclipses, according to the day and the month of their occurrence, and this must mean that such phenomena were duly remarked and recorded, but the only explanation of the eclipse was that the Moon god was being attacked by evil demons, an explanation which for long precluded any attempt at prediction. The Late Babylonian astronomical tablets give tables for the prediction of lunar eclipses—purely mathematical computations not involving any general hypothesis concerning the mechanism whereby eclipses were brought about—but they date from about the third century BC and although they must be the product of much previous observation and study they afford no reason to believe that systematic operations started before the eighth century BC.

The Babylonians, possessing a mathematical basis for astronomical calculations much superior to that of the Egyptians, made far greater progress in the astronomical field and started at quite an early date to amass a *corpus* of information which would ultimately supply the material for science. The earliest computations were concerned with (*a*) the duration of day and night in the different seasons, (*b*) the rising and setting of the moon, and (*c*) the appearance and disappearance of Venus. From the time of the Third Dynasty of Ur (*c.* 2100 BC) onwards the omen texts, which combine astrological forecasts with astronomical observations, prove the careful attention paid to astral phenomena.[22] Thus the sixty-third tablet of the great astrological series 'Enuma, Anu, Enlil' which was put into shape between 1400 and 900 BC, contains a list of the heliacal risings and settings of Venus during twenty-one years of the reign of Ammizaduga; the observations must have been made at the time, i.e. in the late seventeenth or early sixteenth century BC. But what we have here is simply observation which was carefully conducted over a considerable period; it does not involve any scientific theory.

Further evidence that interest in the stars began in early times can be got from the (late) star-lists. In the Epic of Creation, which unquestionably goes back in all essentials at least to the beginning of the second millennium BC,[23] it is said, 'Marduk fixed three stars' (or 'constellations') 'for each month of the year'. Now in other texts there are lists of the thirty-six stars described as 'the Stars of Ea, the Stars of Anu, the Stars of Enlil', twelve of each, corresponding to the twelve months of the year, so that there are indeed three stars for each month. Again, there are lists of 'Stars of Elam, Akkad, and Amurru', one star for each country and each month, and the three stars for every month given in these lists are identical with the 'Stars of Ea, Anu and Enlil' for the same month. The territorial divisions agree with the political conditions of Old Babylonian times, and it would appear that in drawing up the threefold lists for the use of the unified realm the scribes incorporated local lists of pre-First Dynasty date.

But while it may be assumed that even before the collapse of ancient Sumer the different areas of Mesopotamia had already classified the calendar stars which in each of them served as timekeepers for priest and farmer,[24] none the less we do find that not until the latter part of the second millennium were there developed the more speculative views which are forthcoming in the Assyrian astrolabes from which the star-lists are taken. A much later list, the MUL Apin list, gives the thirty-six heliacally rising stars together with the date differences of the brightness of them; the actual text is of the seventh century BC, but Professor van der Waerden has calculated that the observations on which the list was based must have been made between 1300 and 900 BC, i.e. in the latter part of the second millennium; 'the differences between text and calculations were so small', he says, 'that we are bound to conclude that the observations were made with considerable care, probably over a period of several years', and this degree of accuracy surely suggests a genuinely scientific curiosity. 'The results show that not only was the period 1400–900 BC the classical period of omen astrology, but that there were scientific astronomers at work as well, making careful observations of the annual rising and the daily rising, setting and culmination of fixed stars. Still, our knowledge concerning this period is rather limited. We know for certain only the following facts: (*a*) the composition of the great omen series, "Enuma, Anu, Enlil"; (*b*) the accurate observation of the heliacal rising of stars; (*c*) the observation of daily rising, setting and culmination; (*d*) the composition of the astrolabes before 1100 BC. Moreover, we can ascribe to this period with a certain degree of probability (*e*) a very primitive representation of Venus phenomena by arithmetic series and constant differences between successive phenomena; (*f*) the computation of daylight and night by means of rising and falling arithmetic series, starting from the crude extreme ratio 2:1; (*g*) the computation of the rising and setting of the moon by means of rising and falling arithmetic series (this is found in the fourteenth tablet of the great omen series, but may go back to our period); (*h*) speculations on the distances of fixed stars. This last, based on a much-discussed tablet from Nippur which is certainly earlier than the eleventh century BC (the "Hilprecht tablet") is really only a mathematical problem-text of a normal type except that star-distances are used instead of the more usual weights or money-amounts; it represents the pre-scientific stage of Babylonian astronomical speculation, not the beginning of scientific astronomy; but at least it shows that the Babylonians had already recognized that the stars were at varying distances from the earth (not fixed to a uniform empyrean as primitive belief would have it) and that those distances might conceivably be measurable.'

The evidence that we possess justifies us in saying that by 1200 BC in Babylonia the foundations of real astronomical research, as that is defined by Professor Neugebauer, had been well and truly laid. Further it appears likely, though it cannot be definitely affirmed, that already the first tentative steps had been taken in the direction of scientific thinking over the data which careful observation had amassed, and that certain rather crude and elementary results had been achieved which in the course of the following millennium would be developed into the astronomical science inherited by the Greeks.

SURGERY AND MEDICINE

The peoples of the Bronze Age, like their descendants in the Middle Ages and like not a few persons at the present time, considered that aches, pains and diseases were caused by the gods, or by evil spirits, and might even be due to 'possession', the demon having entered into and taken physical possession of the sick man's body. Medicine therefore went hand in hand with religion, or with magic, and although drugs were to be used yet their efficacy might consist rather in their unpleasantness to the possessing demon than in any directly beneficial action on the body. In most ancient techniques prayer and sacrifice played their part, but with medicine they were most intricately concerned, because here the doctor might be called upon not merely to placate a god but to defeat a malignant power. Where, on the other hand, the trouble was due to human agency or to palpable accident, as in the case of wounds incurred in battle or of broken limbs, there was less need of exorcism or charms, and though the patient might profit by prayer the operating surgeon relied upon his own skill and professional traditions.

Surgery

In Mesopotamia there is not much evidence to show what progress had been made in surgery by the end of the second millennium BC. The Code of Hammurabi, which dates from about 1780 BC, but may be re-casting clauses taken from some much older code, fixes the fees to be paid 'if a doctor has treated a gentleman' (or a poor man, or a slave) 'for a severe wound, with a bronze lancet, and has cured the man; or has opened an abscess of the eye with the bronze lancet and has cured the eye' and again, 'if a doctor has cured the shattered limb or the diseased bowel'. From this it may be gathered that surgical operations of a fairly serious character were regularly performed in Sumer and Akkad; but as the code goes on to say that if, in the first case quoted above, 'the doctor caused the gentleman to die' or 'caused the loss of the gentleman's eye, one shall cut off his hands', it would appear that in a really difficult case the patient's chances of a cure were not very good. The purpose of the law was not simply (as might be supposed) to ensure a high level of practical skill by penalizing the quack or the careless; rather was it to preserve the reputation of the profession. Surgery and medicine were divine functions—in Mesopotamia they were exercised by the goddess Bau—and where deity was involved there must be no failures; if such did unfortunately occur they must be attributed to the fault of the human agent, and the divine omnipotence must not be called in question. Hammurabi's condign sanction would naturally stop any surgeon from operating except in cases where he was confident of success; and it is therefore in harmony with the Babylonian medical rule, which we find several times repeated, that a physician must not prescribe for a patient who was certainly going to die, nor for any disease which, like leprosy, was considered incurable. But because so severe a punishment for failure would discourage any idea of experiment it would undoubtedly block the road of scientific progress, and it is therefore not surprising that up to the end the Babylonian's knowledge of anatomy appears to have been very slight.

In this respect he was surpassed by the Egyptian, who had the advantage that the elaborate process of embalmment which religion demanded gave him every opportunity of studying the human body. The fact that over a hundred anatomical terms occur in the texts is proof that the Egyptians had learnt to distinguish a great many organs and organic structures which their Mesopotamian contemporaries failed to recognize, and for the gross anatomy of the body their terminology is fairly accurate. On the other hand, the nerves, muscles, arteries and veins are all denoted by one and the same word; these they had entirely failed to understand, regarding them all as parts of a single system forming a network over the whole of the body; when we find that there is no verbal distinction between the blood-vessels communicating with the heart and the leg-muscles that have to be treated in cases of rheumatism we must realize how curiously limited was the Egyptian knowledge. The preparation of bodies for embalmment had taught them that the brain is enclosed in a membrane and that its surface is patterned with convolutions, and experience with accidents had shown them that injury to the brain may cause a loss of control over various parts of the body; yet to the brain they attached very little importance. For them the most important organ was the heart, so much so, indeed, that in the process of mummification it was not removed together with the rest of the viscera but was carefully left in its place in the thorax: 'The beginning of the science of the physician', says the Ebers papyrus, 'is to know the movement of the heart and to know the heart; there are vessels attached to it for every member of the body', as can be seen from the sympathy of the pulse in various parts of the body with the beating of the heart itself. But the description in the same papyrus of the functions of the 'vessels' as the vehicles not of blood but of air, water, mucus, semen and other secretions betrays complete ignorance of the working of the living body.

The sections of the Egyptian medical papyri that deal with such purely surgical matters as wounds in the head and thorax, fractures, boils and cysts, affections of the stomach and gynaecological troubles are very much more scientific in their approach than are those concerned with medicine, and it is obvious that familiarity with the body had given to the surgeon a confidence which the doctor could not share. The texts have, for each case, formulae arranged in regular order—a title, the symptoms to be observed by examination, the diagnosis, the opinion as to whether a cure was possible or not, and finally, if a cure were thought possible, the treatment required. Further evidence of methodical surgery is afforded by the character of the papyri generally: thus the Kahûn Papyrus, which dates from the Twelfth or Thirteenth Dynasty but is derived from an older original, deals only with gynaecological troubles; the Chester-Beatty Papyrus (of Nineteenth Dynasty date) only with affections of the anus and rectum; the Edwin Smith Papyrus almost entirely with wounds and fractures, and each long section of it is concerned with a specific organ or region. Whereas, then, we have no literary sources from Mesopotamia to inform us of the methods of surgery in that country, Egypt provides a quite remarkable wealth of such, and the mere fact that the knowledge acquired by experience and experiment was thus systematically put on record would seem to imply a standard of practice greatly superior to the cautious empiricism of the Babylonian surgeons which could not be rationalized into a code. None the less must we be careful not to over-estimate Egyptian surgical science. Not only do the texts show that the functions of the living body were fundamentally misunderstood, but accompanying or interspersed with the surgical formulae there are in the texts the medico-magical recipes and incantations which bring us back to the primitive beliefs in the curse, the evil eye and possession by devils.

Medicine

It is curious that the earliest Sumerian medical text, a tablet dating from the latter part of the third millennium BC, is altogether free from mystical and irrational elements. On the other hand, a hymn to the goddess Ninisinna, or Bau, of about 1750 BC, calls her 'the great doctor of the black-headed [Sumerian] people' who had charge of the divine laws set up before the creation of the world for the art of healing; it attributes the diseases to demons, and the cures consist primarily of incantations. In Sumer and in Egypt alike, the art of the physician was inseparable from the 'oral rite' and the 'manual rite' of the magician.

The Pharmacopoeia

In the Sumerian language the same word, *šammu,* means both 'vegetable' and 'medicine'. Of the medicinal compounds for which the recipes are given the vegetable ingredients are by far the most numerous; thus, out of some 550 species mentioned 250 are vegetable, 120 are mineral and the animal or unidentified substances total 180; but what really matters is not so much the number of plant ingredients used as the frequency of their occurrence in the recipes, and out of 5,880 occurrences no less than 4,600 are of vegetable origin. To these must be added a few substances in common use which are vehicles for drugs rather than drugs in themselves—alcohols of various sorts made from grapes, beer, fats, oils, wax, honey and milk.

Apart from actual recipes there are Assyrian tablets which list the plants supposed to possess medicinal properties, as well as purely botanical lists which are much fuller and include the plants of no use to the doctor. The differences between the lists show that the drugs were not selected at random; Campbell Thompson indeed insists that the more they are studied the more obvious becomes genuine knowledge possessed by the doctors and chemists of Nineveh, which knowledge was, of course, the result of many generations of experience. Thus, for narcotics they used opium (made from three varieties of poppy), hemp, belladonna, mandragore and water-hemlock—the last a very poisonous drug; for stomach troubles camomile is recommended, as also is rue; mustard in water is an emetic, the seeds swallowed whole act as a laxative, and it makes a good poultice; hellebore was so important both for external and for internal use and as a fumigant that there is even a poem about it; rose-water, sometimes imported from Iran but also manufactured in the temples of Babylonia, was an expensive drug with many uses, almost a panacea. These and the like are the 'simples' that have been used by different peoples at all times; experience had proved their efficiency in certain cases, and many of them still find a place in the pharmacopoeia of the modern herbalist. But one's confidence in the acquired knowledge of the ancient physician is shaken by the heterogeneous properties which he attributes to one and the same drug; thus *imhur-pani* (probably the marigold, *calendula officinalis*), is recommended in the form of an unguent for scorpion-stings, toothache, as a head-wash and for the ears and eyes; in the form of a drink, for jaundice, snake-bite, dyspnoea, stomach troubles, venereal disease and possession by a ghost. This last prescription shows how closely the old pharmacopoeia comes to magic, and how little it is based upon any real scientific knowledge; rather is it true that where experience has proved the curative value of some herb for a particular ailment, this was regarded, by a people totally ignorant of physiology, as a magical virtue inherent in the plant which must therefore be generally efficacious. Nor is such virtue necessarily inherent in the nature of the plants themselves; as likely as not they may owe their power, at least in part, to magical conditions, to the place of their growth or to the time of their gathering; thus for certain diseases the roots of the thorn-bush specified in the recipe must have come from above a grave, while for others it must have been dug up before sunrise—'slips of yew Sliver'd in the moon's eclipse'. The animal elements remind us even more closely of the concoctions of Shakespeare's witches—swine's head, tongue of mouse, hair of dog, hair of fox, fat of a black snake, milk of a white cow, eye and blood of a hen; all of them are clearly more magical than medicinal; and just as the mediaeval doctor held that 'Gold in Physick is a cordial', so his Babylonian predecessor mixed in his drugs not only verdigris but powdered copper, haematite and lapis lazuli, crushed terra-cotta and dust collected from the ruins of some deserted house or temple. The various ingredients had to be carefully prepared. Some plants were pressed to extract the sap; more often they were dried and powdered in mortars and then mixed and decocted in water or in fat, the process being repeated several times if necessary. The proportions of the different substances are seldom specified in the recipes but are left to the judgement of the working chemist.

A doctor was well advised to administer his drugs at night-time, or just before sunrise. The drugs might take the form of ointments for external application, often in combination with massage, or of pills or potions to be taken through the mouth; but it might suffice to powder the drug and sprinkle it over the ailing part or to wrap it in a piece of goatskin and lay it over the place (possibly a poultice is here meant) while for fever a mixture of the proper herbs might be burnt over a fire of thorns and the sick man's head fumigated therewith. We are assured that the mere 'smell' of pulverized copper (presumably inhaled through the nostrils) will relieve all the pains of child-birth, and that the laying of a spangle of red gold in a man's hand will cure him of jaundice. But side by side with this sympathetic magic there is a great deal of common sense. 'For feverish headache, half a measure of mustard pounded and filtered and kneaded with rose-water, to be smeared over the patient's head and secured with a bandage; the bandage to remain undisturbed for three days'; such a prescription is typical of the lore of the 'wise woman' of all times. The Mesopotamian doctor fully recognized the importance of the free action of the bowels, and was quite prepared to administer an oil enema, and for digestive troubles he had various methods of inducing vomiting; he realized that by such means the pain of internal diseases could be lessened, and he would follow up the more drastic treatment with a milk cure or an ordered diet. But he lacked any more thoroughgoing knowledge of the real nature of disease. For one and the same malady a dozen or more different prescriptions are recommended, and in the event of one failing the physician is told to try another and yet another, the choice having apparently no relation to cause and effect; there is here nothing that can be termed science, only an unco-ordinated empiricism based on experience of a very superficial kind.

Exactly the same is true of Egypt. The medical papyri will

list a number of remedies and either leave the choice to the physician or instruct him to try one after another. The remedies themselves were of the same type as the Mesopotamian, with vegetable ingredients predominating, but the mineral ingredients were here more varied and of greater real curative value; the Egyptian chemist used nitron (a natural mixture of sodium carbonate and sodium bicarbonate), several alkalis, salts, alum, etc., and his prescriptions may well have been more efficacious than those dispensed by his Babylonian contemporary. None the less, magic played an even more prominent role in Egyptian than in Mesopotamian medicine. In the papyri the recipes for drugs are regularly interspersed with the magical spells which were supposed to make the drugs more effective. These spells are what has been called the 'oral rite', and they are usually followed by instructions as to the performance of the 'manual rite'; the magical formulae had to be recited with appropriate gestures over some object, a clay or wooden image, a string of beads, an amulet, a knotted cord or a stone, and the charm thus charged with power would be attached to the patient's body; or, again, the drugs themselves might be so charged and given to the patient to swallow; in the latter case they might contain particularly noxious ingredients calculated to drive the possessing demon out of the man's body in sheer disgust. If the Sumerians employed the same words (*azu* and *iazu*) for physician, seer and scribe, showing thereby how closely associated were the functions of the three professions, the Egyptians went still farther towards identifying the arts of medicine and of magic.

The Commonwealth of Medicine

Just as the papyri may deal specifically with different categories of disease so, too, there tended to be a certain amount of specialization in the medical profession. Hammurabi's Code makes mention of veterinary surgeons, and in both countries, Egypt and Mesopotamia, we hear of doctors specializing in particular complaints and sometimes acquiring a great reputation in that branch, a reputation not necessarily confined to their own land. More perhaps than any other art was medicine in the ancient world internationalized.[25] A famous Egyptian doctor might travel far afield to treat an important patient. Thus Parimachu[26] the Egyptian was summoned to Asia Minor to the sickbed of the king of Tarkhuntash. Ramses II, according to a late story, sent his court physician to Hattusas to cure Bentzesh, the sister-in-law of the Hittite king Hattusilis—it is interesting to note that, when the doctor failed to drive out the demon that possessed her, Pharaoh was constrained to send the holy image of the god Khonsu, by whose aid the cure was duly effected. The same Hattusilis, negotiating for a treaty with Kadashman-Enlil II of Babylon, was at pains to explain away the embarrassing fact that a Babylonian physician visiting the Hittite country had been forcibly detained there. Personal visits of the sort were really not uncommon, but what more than anything proves the universality of medicine is the fact that medical books circulated freely from one country to another; Hittite copies of Babylonian medical tablets have been unearthed at Bogazköy, and it is evident that the pharmacopoeia and the prescriptions based upon it were in some measure the common property of doctors throughout the Middle East. It is this internationalization of medicine, and the great reputation won by Mesopotamian physicians, that account for the adoption by European peoples (through Greek and later through Arabic) of numerous Mesopotamian plant-names, while, on the other hand, the tablets definitely explain certain plant-names as being foreign and the herbs consequently imported, as, for instance, *ricinus* from Elam and *cardamom* from Anatolia. But while the evidence shows that in the art of healing there was throughout the Middle East a certain amount of free trade in medical service and in medical knowledge, it must still be remembered that by common consent the actual drug was held to be less potent than the magic rites with which it was administered. The successful physician was he who best knew both sides of his profession, and it was because of this duality that there was a limit to the international character of medicine. The gods of the different countries were not the same, and a charm that worked satisfactorily in Babylon might fall upon deaf ears in Memphis; in the incident of Khonsu related above, Pharaoh's court physician failed by his Egyptian spells to exorcise the Hittite devil and could succeed only when the gods he knew were present to help him.

NOTES TO CHAPTER VII

1. *Iraq,* III, p. 87, and X, p. 26.
2. Professor A. P. Yushkevich contends that in both Ancient Egypt and Babylonia mathematics was primarily of an empirical inductive nature; the elements of separate proofs (geometrical and arithmetical transformations) were more developed in Babylonia, where algebra was widely applied.
3. Sir Leonard Woolley's point of view is here open to controversy. While B. L. Van der Waerden, *Science Awakening* (Gröningen, 1954), pp. 34 ff., is of the same opinion as Sir Leonard, the contrary view is expressed by O. Neugebauer, *The Exact Sciences in Antiquity* (2nd ed., Providence, R. I., 1957). Professor A. A. Vaiman con-

siders that there is no proof of Egyptian borrowing from the Babylonians on this point: indeed it is, in his opinion, possible to assume with equal justice that the Egyptians had their own method of deducing the rule (based on the rule for computing the volume of a pyramid from its base and height).

4. Made by impressing the corner of the stylus in the clay, and representing the ☾ of the earlier pictographic texts.
5. Each table contained one 'top number' (of 1, 2, or 3 sexagesimal places) multiplied by 2, 3, . . . up to 19, and thereafter by 20, 30, 40 and 50. The 'top numbers' were numbers like 12 or 16, 40 or 44, containing only factors 2 and 3 and 5, in addition to these the 'irregular' top number 7. In order to multiply, e.g. 18 by 29, one had to split 29 into 20 + 9 and use the table of multiples of 18, adding together the two figures given.
6. Professor A. A. Vaiman draws attention to the discoveries made at Susa in 1936 which throw light on our knowledge of Babylonian geometry. It appears that the Babylonians had a better approximation for the area of circle and the length of its perimeter which corresponds to the approximation $\pi = 3\frac{1}{8}$. See O. Neugebauer, *The Exact Sciences in Antiquity* (2nd ed., Providence, R. I., 1957), p. 47.
7. The Jewish calendar is based upon this 19-year cycle.
8. VAB. IV. Nabonidus, No. 1, pp. 226, 57–8.
9. VAB. IV, Nabonidus, No. 3, pp. 238, 21.
10. Siut I, 285.
11. Concerning the question so much debated among Egyptologists as to whether there existed, side by side with the civil calendar, a lunar calendar, Sir Leonard Woolley, in response to a suggestion by Professor B. L. Van der Waerden, summarized as follows the opinion of Professor R. A. Parker, author of the latest work on this subject [*The Calendars of Ancient Egypt* (Chicago, 1950)], which is in contradiction to his own view.

    Certainly all authorities agree that lunar months were in use in the temples. The days of the lunar months had names of their own, e.g. the second day was called 'new crescent day', the fifth day, 'day of offerings on the altar', the thirtieth day, 'day of going-forth of Min'. Parker gives good reasons for his opinion that the lunar month began on the morning when the old moon sickle could no longer be seen.

    The differences of opinion between authorities mainly concern the question whether these lunar months may be said to have constituted a calendar, i.e. whether sequences of twelve or thirteen lunar months were considered to form a year. Parker's opinion is that such a lunar year did exist, and that its beginning was connected with the rising of Sothis (Sirius) in such a way that the feast of the rising of Sothis always fell into the last month of the lunar year.

    Other authorities maintain that there also existed, besides the civil and the lunar calendar, a fixed Sothis year beginning with the rising of Sothis. In favour of this opinion texts may be quoted such as the following inscription in the temple of Denderah: 'years are reckoned from her [i.e. Sothis's] shining-forth'. However, these texts may also refer to the beginning of the lunar year which follows the rising of Sothis.
12. Sir Leonard Woolley notes that an observation of this sort does not imply any astronomical knowledge: for a primitive people the temporary disappearance and reappearance of prominent stars is a phenomenon as obvious as it is presumably important. The South

African Bushmen, for example, note the heliacal rising of Sirius and Canopus and use their later movements as an index of the passage of winter; and in many parts the rising and setting of the Pleiades is taken as a check-point for agricultural activities.

13. This, the generally accepted figure, is in fact only an approximation; the solar year being really less than the assumed 365.25 days, the Egyptian year would lose one day not in every four years but in 4.126 years; the cycle therefore would be 1,506 years. Most scholars now agree that the beginning of the calendar was reckoned from approximately 2776 BC rather than from an earlier cycle starting about 4231 BC. The following paragraph should be read with this proviso in mind.
14. It seems possible that at some time—before the reign of Amenhotep III of the Eighteenth Dynasty—there was a change in the order of the months; but, if so, the innovation was theological rather than calendral. It does not in any case affect the matter under discussion.
15. Tung Tso-pin, 'The Chinese and the World's Ancient Calendars' in *A Symposium on the World Calendar*, ed. by the Chinese Association for the United Nations (Taipeh, 1951), pp. 3–22.
16. Professor Tung produces other arguments in support of this conclusion, but that quoted here is the most striking.
17. The very slight error in the Ssu-fen calculation of the lunar month would result in one day too many in about 307 years; the error in the calculation of the length of the solar year would mean one day too many in about 107 years. In the latter case the discrepancy would be obvious at the end of the *Fu* cycle of 76 years. The saying of the Han astronomers about the need to revise the calendar every three hundred years is clearly aimed at the lunar month. It further implies that the Ssu-fen calendar (apart from which the saying is meaningless) had actually been under observation for many centuries before the Han date.
18. There is no evidence associating the genesis of the Chinese calendar with the period treated in this volume.
19. Professor Shigeki Kaizuka *et al.* observe that when a new dynasty received the Mandate of Heaven and became the ruler of the empire, it was believed that certain steps should be taken which would symbolize the fact that it was a new reign, independent of the preceding dynasty. One of these was calendar reform. This is the reason why in early times the succeeding dynasties rotated the month on which the year began, the 'prime' month. For this reason some sort of calendar reform was almost a 'must' for a new dynasty.
20. Professor J. Leclant, however, suggests references to a passage of the inscription on the Bubastis Gate at Karnak concerning the year 15 of Takelot II, i.e. *c.* 820 BC [R. A. Caminos, *The Chronicle of Prince Osorkon* (Rome, 1958), pp. 58 sq.]: 'the sky swallowed not the moon'—the interpretation of which has led to a very considerable flow of ink.
21. It should be noted that the date is not accepted by all scholars.
22. The character of the 'omen texts' can be illustrated here by two examples; one, dated to the time of the First Dynasty of Babylon, reads, 'If the sky was dark [on the first day] the year will be bad. If the sky was clear when the new moon appeared the year will be happy.' A more elaborate text, taken from the Ammizaduga tablets, reads, 'If on Sabatu 15th Venus disappeared in the west, remaining three days from the sky, and on Sabatu 18th appeared

in the east, catastrophes of kings; Adad will bring rains, Ea subterranean waters; king will send greetings to king.'

23. The prominence of Marduk at once suggests the First Babylonian period.
24. The importance of astral phenomena for the agriculturist has been noted above, in the section dealing with the calendar. So Hesiod, 'When the Pleiades [the daughters of Atlas] rise, it is time for harvest and time for sowing when they go down again.'
25. In contrast to the journeyings of Egyptian doctors, we may note that about 1372 BC Tushratta, king of Mitanni, sent to Amenhotep III of Egypt a healing statue of Ishtar of Nineveh, with the reminder that the goddess had already visited the banks of the Nile in the time of his father.
26. For Parimachu, cf. *supra*, p. 319, note 22.

CHAPTER VIII

RELIGIOUS BELIEFS AND PRACTICES

To a very large extent the development of religious ideas amongst the primitive groups of mankind was conditioned by the social organization of each group. In Chapter II of this volume an attempt has been made to trace the growth of those organizations and to define the varying principles that underlay them; thus Egypt with its centralized government exercising a unified control over the entire valley of the Lower Nile was contrasted with Mesopotamia, where individual city states flourished in independence and preserved their identity even when forced to submit to the political suzerainty of a stronger neighbour, and, as against both these, we have seen, in countries where agriculture was impossible and nothing invited urbanization, the conditions of the Stone Age perpetuated by the families and petty clans of desert-haunting nomads. To surroundings so different the same religious beliefs were ill-adapted; local creeds were bound to take their colour from local circumstances, and the Egyptian, the Sumerian and the Beduin Sutu could not be expected to think alike.

SUMER

The Sumerian religion is not, strictly speaking, autochthonous. The earliest inhabitants of the delta were immigrants and they brought with them a system of belief already formulated. This is quite obvious from the fact that all the city states acknowledged the same pantheon; each had its own patron deity, locally supreme, but that god or goddess had a recognized place—and not necessarily the highest place—in the great Council of the Gods who were the gods of Sumer. That is something which could not have been brought into being if the local cults had originated independently, for neither alliances nor civil wars between the cities could ever have resulted in a common creed and in a harmonious hierarchy of heaven; the fundamental conformity in matters of religion of the distinct and often hostile states goes back to beliefs shared by all the settlers long before the cities were built and the states developed.

Of the ideas held in that prehistoric age there is, of course, no contemporary record. We can infer them only indirectly, from the customs and the traditions of a much later time; but religion, though far from static, does tend to be conservative at least in its outward forms; mythological tales are shown by their very character to go back to primitive ages, and popular superstition as exemplified in such things as magic will preserve the crude beliefs of early man long after they have been banished from the orthodox creed.

In common with other men in a like stage of development the first settlers in southern Mesopotamia moved and had their being in a world which was very much alive. The phenomena about them were not inanimate; in or behind each of them there was a personality no less real than man's and to be comprehended only in terms of the personality of man. This did not mean that everything was a god; it did mean that in and through everything god was to be apprehended. A reed growing in the marshes was, of course, just a reed; you could use it in the building of your house, the shepherd could cut from it a pipe to make music to his flock, the scribe could trim its stem into the pen of the ready writer; but all these powers together, which made a reed what it was, were combined in the personality of the Reed goddess. It was Nidaba who produced the reeds (did they not sprout from her shoulders?) and taught the herdsmen his tunes and inspired the scribe; 'she was one with every reed in the sense that she permeated it as an animating and characterizing agent; but she did not lose her identity in that of the concrete phenomenon and was not limited by any or even all existing reeds'. When, in the Flood legend, the god Ea wants to warn Uta-Napishtim of the coming disaster but is afraid to betray the secrets of the gods to a mere man, he whispers the news to the house-wall, saying 'Reed-hut, Reed-hut, listen', and so salves his conscience, because after all the reeds partake of the nature of god. So, in magic spells, such things as salt and grain—and not the natural grain alone but the flour of man's grinding and the bread of man's making—are not merely inanimate substances; each of them has, or at least represents, a personality which is independent of man and may be beneficial to him or harmful as it pleases. Clearly these personalities are not all on the same plane; if measured by their power to help or to hurt, some of them must be infinitely greater than others.

Accordingly, man's worship must needs recognize a hierarchy of the gods. But the Sumerian gods are not symbols invented to explain and illustrate a rationalized theory of the cosmos. The Sumerian did not evolve the gods from his inner consciousness, he encountered them; they revealed themselves to him in and through the phenomena of the physical world, and his conception of them is proportioned by the degree to which they affected him in that revelation.

Living in the flat Mesopotamian valley a man cannot fail to be impressed and at times overwhelmed by the vast expanse of encircling sky, to realize his own insignificance in the face of its unbridgeable remoteness—'Godhead awesome as the far-away heavens', said the Sumerian; and the Power that he saw there was one of serene majesty:

> Around the ancient track march'd, rank on rank,
> The army of unalterable law.

and so in Anu, Lord of Heaven, was to be found the source of all law and order.

But human experience shows only too clearly that law and order, if they are to be effective, require the backing of force. Under the vault of the sky blows the storm-wind, and the force and the violence of it is Enlil, who executes the will of Anu and guarantees order against chaos; but Enlil has in himself the horrible wildness of the storm also, so that he who upholds the universe may turn his powers to its destruction; the thunder is his voice, his weapon the lightning:

> O father Enlil, whose eyes are glaring wildly
> How long till they will be at peace again? . . .
> O mighty one who with thy fingers has sealed thine ears, how long?
> O father Enlil, even now they perish!

None the less is Enlil, the Air god, the great benefactor of mankind who establishes plenty and prosperity in the land and teaches man the use of the pick-axe and the plough.

And, naturally, the third great Power is the earth. Not the world, with its barren deserts and inhospitable mountains, but the kindly earth that yields grass for the cattle and grain for the food of man, in whose green fields the ewes and goats bear their young and the cows give milk, so that man prospers and is fruitful in his turn. This is Mother Earth, the inexhaustible and mysterious source of all life, who as Nin-tu, 'the lady who gives birth', or Nin-makh, 'the exalted queen' or, as she is called later, Nin-khursag[1] takes her place together with Anu and Enlil in the Council of the Gods.

Man at one moment looks on the ploughed field and sees in it the promise of life and the manifestation of 'the Mother of all children'; and again he sees it scorched by the sun and the crops withered for lack of moisture, to be recovered only if water be brought to refresh the soil. So, from the beginning, there was another Earth god, En-ki, 'Lord of the earth', the male element who fertilizes the passive womb of Nin-tu with the life-giving waters from river and spring and well. But as time went on the god's sphere was more exactly defined; as Enlil's minister he was more particularly the Water god, lord of the streams and canals that run through the fields, but also of the mysterious waters that are below the earth, those on which indeed the earth is upheld, which are discovered in springs and wells; and because running water is devious in its ways, as if with a will and an intelligence of its own, and because the underground waters are profound, dark and brooding, En-ki is the god of wisdom and of creative thought, and he is the god of magic whose powers are shown in the incantations of the priests which purify the unclean and drive away evil spirits. Connected with the earth again was Nergal, once a Sun god, but embodying the evil power of the sun's rays which smite with fever and death, who with Eresh-ki-gal, his spouse, ruled over the infernal regions deep down below the earth. Obviously the sun itself was a god, Utu (the Shamash of the Semites), though he ranked after Nannar, the moon; the planet Venus was Ininna, Ishtar. In and behind everything that man saw or conceived he could recognize a god.

Now just as the fruitful land of Mesopotamia where man lived so decent and orderly a life had only risen from the primeval marsh by the curbing of the turbulent waters of the flood, so too must it have been in heaven. Everything had begun with the dark and formless waste of waters which the Babylonians called Ti'amat, and from that chaos, born of its ruling goddess, had emerged beings from whom were descended the gods, and these had at last subdued chaos and introduced order and rule. But in an earthly state order and rule can be assured only by a formal government, and since all things begin with the gods and earthly phenomena are but a manifestation of the divine it follows that the universe must be directed by just such a government, namely by an Assembly of the Gods. There are many texts describing how that assembly was conducted. The gods met together—i.e. those whose superior powers gave them, as it were, full rights of citizenship; Anu presided and his son Enlil stood at his side, and one or other of the two introduced the matter at issue and it was then debated, sometimes heatedly and at length, by any gods who cared to speak, but the voices of 'the seven gods who determine destinies' had the greatest weight. The vote had to be unanimous, and, when all the gods had assented, saying 'Let it be', Anu and Enlil announced the decision as 'the verdict, the word of the assembly of the gods, the command of Anu and Enlil'. The proceedings scarcely warrant the description of the meeting as 'primitive democracy' which some writers have applied to it, for although the opinions of all the gods present are asked and can be freely expressed yet it is clear that the necessary 'unanimity' is in the end imposed by the moral authority of Anu, who is no mere chairman but 'the King of the Anunnaki'. At the same time the earthly parallel to this divine assembly is not, one imagines, the royal council chamber of a fully fledged city state but rather that of the days when first the early townships became kingdoms.

It was during the long ages that elapsed between the first immigration of the al'Ubaid people and the dawn of real history that Mesopotamian religion developed its peculiar character.

The first settlement must have been by families, or by small groups so far related by blood that they could count as a family clan, and under a patriarchal social system the head of the family was its absolute master; he was also its religious leader. As the community grew in size and the need for cooperation for such works as the digging of canals brought outside or distantly related families into what had been a closed circle, the head of the chief family would retain and extend his authority even though he might collect about him the heads of minor families as consultants or as delegates. The change was gradual and unpremeditated and its process seemed to involve no radically new ideas—the new town was only the old village 'writ large'; but when with time the social organization had crystallized, when precedent leading down to precedent had turned custom into law, when in fact the city state was an accomplished fact, then men's beliefs had to accommodate themselves to changed conditions. The city state was a phenomenon, recognizable as such, and, like all phenomena, it must be divine in that it was the outward manifestation of a particular deity; behind the city state, animating and characterizing it, there must be a god; but it was only the form of his manifestation that was novel; the god himself was no new arrival but one of the familiar hierarchy of gods, and regarding his identity there could be no doubt whatsoever.

When at a later date Sumerian theologians attempted to find a religious basis for the organization of the state as it existed in their time they pictured a divine pantheon functioning as an assembly with a king at its head. It was by the decision of that synod that man had been created, and he was created for one purpose only, to supply the gods with food, drink and shelter, so that they might have full leisure for their divine activities:

> The Anunnaki eat, but remain unsated,
> The Anunnaki drink, but remain unsated;
> For the sake of the good things in their pure sheepfolds
> Man was given breath.

To ensure the success of this plan the gods established lands and cities, appointed one or other of the pantheon as the divine ruler of each, and he in turn selected his human representative who was the king of the city state. The Sumerians were dealing with the facts as they knew them, but the territorial claims of the various gods, which they attributed to an arbitrary division of the earth by the divine assembly, must be capable of a historical explanation.

Each of the original families or clans had been under the special protection of one or other of the gods chosen out of the common pantheon, the *paterfamilias* being the minister of his cult. If the family grew in numbers and authority that was due to the god's favour; the greater the material advance the more certain was it that the god identified himself with the clan's fortunes; the more essential became the service due to him and the more significant the relation between the *paterfamilias,* who now ranked as head of the state, and the patron deity. It was not by any conscious process of reasoning and not by any revelation but by the inevitable logic of development that the Sumerian came to recognize the theocratic nature of his city state.

The god had taken up his abode amongst his worshippers. Whatever they had done had been done by and through him, whatever they had acquired had been of his getting and was his property. Now, as things had evolved, the city was his capital and all the state territories were his domains; the city's human head owed his position to being in a peculiarly close relation to the god and the authority that he in fact exercised could be his only as it was delegated to him by the god; he was the steward of the city's real lord. This was no legal fiction but a plain statement of fact. The whole country was literally the god's property;[2] the fields might be farmed directly by the ministers attached to the temple which was 'the House of the God' or they might be let to tenants, but they were inalienably his; any attempt to expropriate them, even on behalf of the king, was an act of impiety which a reformer such as

Urukagina was obliged to make good; even where fields had been granted in fee simple to the heads of patriarchal families these were the god's beneficiaries, and we find the ruler buying in such fields so as to re-incorporate them in the state property. The entire economy of the state was directed to the proper maintenance of the god's temple and its ritual, and, although the king might delegate some of his religious duties (as Entemena seems to have appointed Dudu to be chief priest of Ningirsu at Lagash), yet the principal sacrifices of the year were conducted by the king in person, his chief function being that he was the administrator of the landed possessions of the god.

From the beginning of the proto-literate period, when first we have written documents whereby we can test what hitherto have been deductions, we find that the theocratic city state is an accomplished fact. Each state is the domain of a particular god; Nippur belongs to Enlil, Ur to Nannar, Lagash to Ninurta, Uruk to Anu, and each of these gods is, within the limits of his domain, an absolute monarch.[8] Now had each god represented a different theological system the position would have been simple in that each state would have been a distinct unit having nothing in common with its neighbours; but in fact all the gods alike were members of one and the same pantheon acknowledged by all the states. The citizen of Ur, while he hailed Nannar as his divine king, fully recognized the divinity of the other gods and maintained in his own city temples for their worship; the difficulty was to reconcile the supreme overlordship of Nannar at Ur with his position in the traditional hierarchy of the gods. That difficulty was successfully overcome by the characteristically Sumerian expedient of relating the divine with the human, the supernatural with the physical world.

Heaven is organized on the lines of a state. At the head of it is Anu, to whose authority the other gods voluntarily adapt themselves, and he assigns to each his task and sphere. The great gods associated with him form the Council of Gods, over which Anu presides; there the destinies of the universe are discussed and decided by the assent of the seven leading members of the Council and the execution of the decrees is entrusted to Enlil or some such other god as is deemed fittest for the task. And as on earth so in heaven the delegation of power can, in times of crisis, involve radical changes. When Ti'amat threatened to destroy the gods, Anshar, who was then the supreme god, bade his son Anu meet her in battle, but Anu failed and 'all the Anunnaki ranged in assembly sat speechless with their lips covered'; at last Anshar proposed the young Marduk as champion, and Marduk accepted the mission, but on his own terms, that he should be given the kingship of the gods. A meeting was summoned at Nippur and, after a banquet at which the gods drank deeply and forgot their cares, they conferred upon Marduk the insignia of royalty; he slew Ti'amat, and thereafter ruled as the chief of the gods, 'King of the Anunnaki'.

Now this story is a re-casting of an older one according to which it was Enlil who played the part of champion and was therefore hailed as king of the gods; the original version has been edited to correspond to historical fact. The Sumerian knew perfectly well that on earth each god actually lived in his own territorial domain and was absolute master therein; he ruled by divine right and it was Enlil himself who had defined their respective kingdoms: 'according to the sure word of Enlil, King of the Lands, Father of the Gods, have Ningirsu and Sara [the god of Umma] marked out the frontier between them'.[4] Should trouble arise, a quarrel, for instance, about water-rights on a doubtful boundary line, a war between two states meant that each god was maintaining what he believed to be a just claim, and whichever side won could obviously invoke the decisive judgement of Enlil. But should the king of a city state embark upon a war of conquest and subject other states to his imperial rule, how could that accord with the divine rights of the patron gods of those states? The case had actually arisen. Babylon, the city state of Marduk, hitherto not a very prominent deity, had successfully made war upon its neighbours and the Babylonian king—not even a Sumerian, but a Semite—claimed the title of king of Sumer and Akkad; but if the other city states were to admit that claim the *de facto* position had to be legalized in accordance with Sumerian beliefs. The answer to the problem was the logical one given by the remodelled myth; what happened on earth was but the phenomenon corresponding to what had happened in heaven, where the High Assembly of the Gods had decided to entrust to another of their number, namely Marduk, the insignia of supreme authority. But that supremacy did not invalidate the divine rights of the other gods within their allotted spheres. When, in an earlier day, Ur-Nammu of Ur had conquered Babylon he was indeed extending thereby the overlordship of Nannar, his own city god (Ur-Nammu even calls him 'King of the Anunnaki'), but he could not interfere with Marduk's absolute rule over Babylonian territory; what really happened was that he took the place of the Babylonian prince as priest and administrator of the landed possessions of Marduk (i.e. the temple revenues now passed through his hands), and it was as that god's viceregent that he rebuilt the huge Ziggurat at Babylon. Only a foreign invasion could upset an order of things which every Sumerian recognized as part of the cosmic scheme; the Elamites might destroy the temples of Ur and carry off the statue of Nannar; infidel Hittites might lay Babylon waste and take Marduk away as prisoner to Khanî; but a Sumerian conqueror, even though he might destroy a temple in the heat of battle, yet would afterwards be at pains to rebuild it in the god's honour. The unification of the empire under a Sumerian dynasty brought no change to the cults of the subject cities except that the new dynasty took over the maintenance of the cult from the former prince; nothing could dispossess the god himself of the territory which Enlil had assigned to him.

The strictly limited sphere of his earthly kingdom had no bearing on the divine powers and attributes of the deity. Nannar was king of Ur and his royal prerogatives stopped short at the frontiers; but as Moon god he was equally reverenced throughout all Sumer and had temples dedicated to him in other cities, just as at Ur there were temples of other gods than him; he was one of the great gods universally recognized. But at Ur he was at home; there was a marked difference between his temple there and those of other gods. Many writers have emphasized the fact that in the Sumerian language (as also in Akkadian) the word for 'temple' is *E*, 'house', implying that according to Sumerian beliefs the god actually lived in the building precisely as the human citizen lived in his house, and this is undoubtedly true—the temple was in a literal and not only in a metaphorical sense 'the House of God'. But it is a mistake to stress overmuch the linguistic argument and to assert that the difference between a 'temple' and a 'house' is determined not at all by the character of the building but only by its ownership, and that the functions of the two are identical because the same word may be used for both.

The types of building are, in fact, very different. The god was to live in his house just as did the man; but because the functions of a god are not the same as those of the private citizen, and the houses must answer to the respective functions of the occupants, the plans of the houses cannot be the same. The only lay building that resembles a temple is the royal palace; there we find an obvious likeness, but it does not support the linguistic argument. The city's ruler is not merely, *quâ* ruler, housed better than his subjects; he is the representative of the god and must vicariously perform the god's functions and therefore require a similar setting. So his palace is unlike a private house and approximates to the god's temple.

Actually the temples differ one from another according to the particular function that they had to serve; thus at Ur the E-nun-mah, being the god's harem (it was dedicated to Nannar and Nin-gal together), is wholly unlike the normal building with its forecourt, inner court and sanctuary which constituted the reception hall of the deity; and according to Herodotus the shrine that surmounted the Ziggurat of Babylon was a single bed-chamber. For most purposes the reception-hall type of building best met the case, and this is the pattern of all or nearly all the temples to other gods; here they receive their worshippers and the offerings of the faithful can be duly placed before them. The city god himself would also have such a temple, though with the growing wealth and elaboration of his kingdom there would be added to the nucleus of the shrine all manner of subsidiary buildings, vast magazines for storage, kitchens, scribes' quarters, administrative offices and working rooms for weavers or metal-workers or other craftsmen. But whereas the temples of the gods in general might be built anywhere—thus at Ur the temple of En-ki is on the southern rampart looking across the plain to his own city of Eridu, and that of Dim-tab-ba is on the highest of the mounds made by the ruins of the prehistoric town—the city god has a place apart. The simple expression 'the House of God' which in contrast to such a word as *templum* seems to reduce the temple to the dimensions of a human dwelling, is corrected for us by the fact that the 'house' is set in a *temenos,* a whole quarter of the city set apart for its divine ruler. This 'Sacred Area' was cut off from the lay town by massive walls with monumental gateways; its ground level was artificially raised so that it formed a high terrace dominating its surroundings; there would be a number of separate buildings within the walled area, but all were dedicated to the service of the patron god of the state.

It happens that the Temenos of Ur has been more thoroughly excavated than that of any other site and a description of it can therefore be more fully detailed; but what is true of Ur would be generally true of any Sumerian state capital.

In the time of the Third Dynasty of Ur (*c.* 2100 BC) the Temenos was a rectangle measuring about 270 by 220 yards, oriented with its corners to the points of the compass. Towards the west corner rose the Ziggurat, set on a higher terrace surrounded by a double wall of defence and entered through a monumental gateway, 'Dubal-makh', at its eastern angle (see the plan, Fig. 27). The Ziggurat tower faced NE and had an open space in front of its triple stairway (*v.* Chapter IV, p. 259) though it is possible that part of this was, as in later times, occupied by twin shrines flanking the central stairs; between the NW side of the Ziggurat and the terrace wall was the lower shrine of Nannar, consisting for the most part of the kitchens in which the god's food was prepared, though whether it was actually offered to him here or in the Holy of Holies at the summit of the great tower we do not know. In front of the Ziggurat terrace, occupying the north corner of the Temenos, was the great courtyard of Nannar to which were brought all the rents and tithes, payable in kind; round the court were the magazines in which the goods were stored, and the offices wherein the record of them was duly kept. To the southeast of the courtyard lay E-nun-makh, a temple dedicated to the Moon god and his wife Nin-gal, twin sanctuaries hidden away in a complex of service chambers. South-east of the Ziggurat terrace was the Gig-par-ku, Nin-gal's own temple, built like a fortress, with the sanctuary at its NW end and the living quarters of the priestesses in its SE half. Whatever building there was in the eastern corner of the Temenos has disappeared; there remains only Dubal-makh, the gateway to the Ziggurat terrace, which was itself a shrine and the Court of Law, where 'the judge sat in the gate to give judgement'. King Ur-Nammu, as the human representative of the god, had his palace built on a lower terrace set against the SE side of the Temenos proper.

The entire complex of the Ur Temenos was named E-gish-shir-gal, the first component being the word '*E*' or 'house', and the inner terrace on which stood the Ziggurat was named E-temen-ni-gur; in neither case does the building bear any relation to the 'house' of the private citizen; rather does the similarity of names emphasize the difference between man's dwelling and 'the House of God'.

Something of the sort must have been true from the beginning, for the Ziggurat of the Third Dynasty of Ur is but an elaboration of the simpler platform-tower of the earliest times and represents the tradition of the first settlers in the Euphrates valley who from their upland home brought the belief that the gods lived on the mountain-tops and required 'High Places' for their worship. But by the time of the Third Dynasty of Ur, towards the close of the third millennium BC, the ever-growing formalism of the state religion had accentuated beyond measure the gulf that separated the divine ruler from his human subjects.

It is tempting to compare the position of Nannar at Ur (and the same would hold good for the patron deities of other city states) with that of the sultan of Turkey in the ultimate decadence of the Caliphate. Nannar was the absolute autocrat of the state which he embodied. The land itself and its material wealth were at his sole disposition and were held only on sufferance by individuals; the mortal king was no more than his vizier exercising a delegated authority; his priesthood formed a court headed by ministers who presided over the various functions of the state, ministers of war and agriculture, of commerce and justice, and their subordinates filled the minor posts of government so that the whole conduct of everyday life was permeated by the influence of organized religion; but the god who was the mainspring of all the city's activities remained in the seclusion of his *temenos,* unapproachable by his lay subjects whose acts of homage could be performed only vicariously through the medium of the priests, unseen except on rare occasions such as the spring festival when he went in solemn procession to the outlying shrine where was consummated the sacred marriage that ensured the fertility of the earth. The citizen of Ur could not but be conscious of his supreme overlord. He had only to lift up his eyes to find his horizon dominated by the towering mass of the Ziggurat. The schoolmaster of his youth had been a priest of Nannar; his doctor and oracle-manager was a priest; his garden-ground outside the city was temple property; to the temple he had to pay rent and tithes, and his social standing obliged him to make voluntary gifts for the sacrifices on feast-days innumerable; if he went to law, it was probably a priest who would hear the case, and even in business matters the factories and the wholesale warehouses with which he had to deal were as likely as not to be dependencies of the house of the god. None the less, the barrier remained insuperable, and it extended also into the moral sphere. Just as the god's image was secluded in the temple sanctuary and could be approached only indirectly through the intermediary priesthood, so the god himself could not be approached even in thought by a mere mortal. On the personal seals of the citizens of Ur at the time of the Third Dynasty the commonest subject represented is the adoration of Nannar. The Moon god is seated on his throne and his worshipper, the seal's owner, comes before him; but an invariable feature of the design is a third figure, that of the worshipper's personal god (see below p. 457) who introduces him into the divine presence and acts as mediator and intercessor between him and a power too great for him. The picture summarizes very faithfully the relation of man to the major gods.

What was true for the chief god, the divine king of the city, was in its degree true of the other great gods also. They were fellow members with him of the same hierarchy and their divinity was not lessened by the fact that in his realm they did not share his territorial rights. The Temenos at Ur was the special property of Nannar and of Nin-gal his wife, and although there were within the Temenos shrines and side chapels dedicated to numerous other deities, those were the minor gods who formed as it were the court of Nannar; thus in the Nin-gal temple there were chapels dedicated to no less than nine gods who, as members of the goddess' retinue, had their allotted places in her 'house'. But with the great gods it was different; they had 'houses' of their own outside the Temenos walls, temples built by kings and maintained out of the state revenues. Thus, Ur-Nammu builds at Ur temples for Anu and Enlil, for Nin-sun, Nin-ezen, and En-ki; we have records of the building or repairing of the temples of Inanna, Nirgal, Nana, Shamash, Ninni, Ilabrat, Ninsianna, Tammuz, Belit-ekallim and Adad; in the interest of the state all the great powers had to be propitiated with sacrifices and offerings, their houses adorned and the ritual of their service duly ordered by their own priests. Ultimately it was the citizens that paid for all this, but the cost of the temples was a premium on a policy of national assurance and the individual citizen had no say in the matter; it was the business of the government. If, as well might be, an individual wished to win the favour of one of the 'great gods' for some special reason, he could, of course, make his own contribution to the temple—an offering to the treasury, a victim for sacrifice; but he had no personal access to the deity; just as in his prayers he needed the mediation of his personal god so it was only through the priest that he could vicariously approach the altar.

The aloofness of the gods from common life was the logical outcome of the gods' royal status. As the city state grew in size and in complexity the differentiation between government and governed became more and more clearly marked, and the human head of the state tended to withdraw into the narrow court circle which traditionally hems in the Oriental monarch.[5] In the temple the same tendency was emphasized by the more formal ceremony owed to a god; certainly in the periods of the Third Dynasty of Ur and of Larsa, for which documentary evidence is most available, contact between the citizen and the city god had been reduced to a minimum.

But the mere fact that Nannar and his consort Nin-gal remained almost from year's end to year's end in the seclusion of the Temenos, and that a jealous priesthood barred men's access to the 'great gods', did not mean that the religious element was at all lacking in the life of the individual Sumerian. Rather, the contrary is true. The gods of Sumer were innumerable; the recorded names of deities run into thousands, and although some, or even many, may stand for different aspects of one god rather than for distinct beings, yet there must have been a vast number more whose names do not happen to occur in documents extant today. Seeing that behind every phenomenon in the physical world there was an immanent deity it was indeed impossible to set a limit to the host of heaven, and in whatever man did some god or other was concerned. It is in this way, apparently, that we must explain the chapels of the minor deities found in the residential quarters at Ur. In the relatively small area excavated there occurred amongst the houses four buildings of a religious character. They were quite small, simple and none too regularly planned—in two cases at least part of a private house had been sacrificed to make room for the chapel—but the layout, with forecourt and sanctuary, was modelled on that of a normal temple. Tablets found in them showed that they had been founded by private citizens at their own cost and were maintained largely by voluntary contributions, though there might be some small endowment which assured the attendance of a regular priest on certain days. Only in one case was the dedication ascertained, and there the shrine's owner was Par-sag, an insignificant goddess whose only known function was the safeguarding of travellers in the desert; her help might be invaluable on occasions, but such occasions would arise intermittently if at all and would concern individuals, not the state. Judging from the actual discoveries made, it would appear that in the city as a whole there were very numerous little shrines in honour of the lesser 'departmentalized' gods and goddesses, set up by the piety of individual citizens and serving the casual needs of ordinary laymen. There is no mention of anything of the sort in the religious literature of the time, and we have to rely upon archaeological evidence alone; but if that be rightly interpreted we cannot but realize that formal religion—or superstition—played a larger part in the life of the Sumerian than the exclusive ritual of temple liturgy would suggest. The city and the city's god being identical, a man's duty to that god was virtually done when he had paid the dues and taxes that enabled the machinery of state to run smoothly. On the other hand there were in everyday life all manner of risks and chances, incalculable events whose outcome lay in the hands of the gods, and to propitiate the right god in each case was what any prudent man would do. And it was a personal matter. These minor deities were approachable; their humble chapels faced upon the public street, and the doors stood open so that anyone could go in and lay his offering upon the altar and look the god's statue in the face; and since he would not go in unless he felt a real need, his petitions were likely to be more or less sincere.

But there was another aspect of Sumerian religion which was yet more personal and intimate.

From the earliest times the people had had some kind of belief in a future life. In the al'Ubaid period men put in the graves of their dead not only the vessels of food and drink that they might require in another world but also clay figures of what may be the goddess of that world, as if to commend the newcomer to Eresh-ki-gal, 'Queen of the great earth'. Tomb-offerings continue in the Jamdat Nasr period, and for the Dynastic Age we have the astonishingly rich burials of the 'royal cemetery' at Ur. It would be unwise to draw general conclusions from the 'royal tombs', because in their case there was a ritual entirely different from that of the ordinary interment, and because kings and queens, being god's representatives on earth and themselves semi-divine, may well have been thought not to share the common lot of mankind—they did not die, but moved on to another and a better world. A like immortality must have been extended to the followers whose bodies were found in the royal tombs:

> His beloved concubine,
> his musician, his beloved entertainer,
> his beloved chief valet . . .
> his beloved household, the palace attendants,
> his beloved caretaker, . . .
> whoever lay with him in that place. . . .[6]

for these had no burial furniture of their own; they were not dying in the ordinary sense, nor were they merely sacrificial victims, but as faithful servants they accompanied their lord and master. It was a custom, and a creed, which persisted into the period of the Third Dynasty of Ur when the divine Shulgi shared his mausoleum with the members of his court whose service had won for them the privilege of passing with him to heaven. For the limited number thus associated with the divine the surrender of mortal life need have had no terrors, but that was certainly not true of others. The picture given in the mythological and religious texts is of a next world which exists indeed, but as a place of gloom and horror, 'the land of no return':

> Ghosts like bats flutter their wings there;
> On the gates and the gateposts the dust lies undisturbed,

and it is hard to say which are the more miserable, those who enter the abode of shades or those who, not having received proper burial, are shut out from it and must haunt the living world in impotent malevolence. Perhaps it was partly to placate the departed that the food and drink offerings were placed with the body; but surely the more luxurious furniture found in the richer graves, stone vessels, objects of gold and silver and even gaming-boards and instruments of music, suggest a belief in another world not wholly unlike this; and whether it was fear or hope that prompted the offerings they do at least imply that death was not regarded as the final end.

Such a belief was shared, so far as we can tell, by most races in the ancient world, and there was nothing peculiar in the Sumerian custom of making provision for the dead. But about 2000 BC, during or at the end of the time of the Third Dynasty of Ur, a revolutionary change took place in the ritual of burial. Up to now the dead had been laid to rest in regular cemeteries which might be within the city walls[7] but were special areas reserved for the purpose; but with the establishment of the Larsa Dynasty we find a new rule universally observed—the dead are buried in the houses of the living. At the rear of the house, i.e. as far as possible from the part into which strangers would be admitted, there was a long narrow court roofed for half its length; under the pavement of the open half was the brick-built family vault (it might contain a dozen bodies) and the roofed half was a chapel dedicated to the worship of the family god. At the same time there is a change in the ritual of burial; after the door of the vault had been sealed up a platter and a clay water-jug might be set against its brickwork, but that was all, and inside the vault, even when the household was obviously wealthy, there were no offerings whatsoever. The intention is quite clear. The dead man continued to inhabit his familiar home; he was still a member of the family, and took part in the family prayers conducted by the head of the household; he required no special tomb furniture because everything in the house was still at his disposal; when the omen texts speak as they do of apparitions of dead members of the family haunting the house this is only the unpleasant aspect (which due piety could avert) of what otherwise was a previous link between past and present generations. The domestic chapels bear witness to a changed view regarding life after death, and also to an aspect in the religion of the Sumerian that was much more intimate and personal than could be the state ceremonial in the temples of the great gods or his occasional recourse to the minor deities of the wayside shrines who might further such projects as came within their peculiar provinces—more intimate than anything known before. From quite early times, apparently, an individual had been wont to place himself under the protection of some lesser member of the pantheon who ranked as his 'personal deity', safeguarded his interests and interceded for him with the major powers;[8] but it was not an arbitrarily-chosen personal god that was worshipped in the domestic chapel of the private house. Just as a great god was immanent in the city state, so the family, which was the ultimate social unit, more real and more vivid than the state itself, a phenomenon greater than the sum of the individuals composing it in that they might die but it persisted, was the manifestation of a deity; that deity, whose high priest was the head of the house, had no distinctive name, and needed none, because he *was* the family and could not be distinguished from it; he was not called in to help, as an outsider might be called in, because he was inseparable from the household. The concept does not necessarily imply any high spiritual ideals, for the main function of the family god was presumably to assure the family's material well-being, but at least it did bring man into closer touch with the divine. Probably for most citizens personal religion consisted in the family ritual and in regular consultation of those omens and magic rites the knowledge of which was the most valuable asset of the regular priesthood.

The Sumerian gods were not moral beings. The myths that are preserved, such as those of Enlil and Ninlil, are quite astonishingly gross; lust, cruelty and outrageous violence are characteristic of most of the major deities, and since man was made merely for their service the only 'virtue' that in their eyes a man could possess was the blind obedience of a slave. But just as in the Assembly of the Gods there had to be order and discipline, the acceptance of authority, so as the city state developed society demanded the civic virtues of law-abiding obedience, loyalty, honesty and truth. Such were primarily social duties, but because the state was in the most literal sense a theocracy the ultimate sanction for them was divine, and so in the end the proper rewards of virtue, namely health and long life, honoured standing in the community, many sons and wealth, were given by god.

EGYPT

In the Nile valley, as in Mesopotamia, early man recognized a personality behind every phenomenon; every external object, just because it was external and therefore not under his control, was a manifestation of some power independent of himself but to be understood only in terms of his own personality. In so far as the conditions of his life were peculiar to Egypt his beliefs were bound to take on a local colour, to emphasize certain aspects of the apparent universe in a manner which would differentiate his beliefs from those of men in other lands and, though starting with a common stock, develop an Egyptian religion quite distinct from that of Sumer.[9]

The dominating feature of existence in Egypt was the sun. In that virtually rainless land it crosses the heaven unclouded from sunrise to sunset 'and nothing is hid from the heat thereof'; the Egyptian, who hated cold and darkness (at night 'the earth is in darkness as it were dead') recognized in it the source of life, and accordingly the personification of the sun's power was for him the supreme god and the creator of all things. None the less, the sun was only one god amongst very many, and even his supremacy seems to have been due, at least in part, to a syncretic process whereby variant local beliefs were brought into a specious harmony.

In the beginning there was the waste of waters which is Nun. But because in Egypt the annual flood is that which makes life possible, the act of creation did not result from the wars of bestial powers such as Mesopotamian legends describe, but was an orderly and peaceful process. Just as when the Nile flood begins to ebb there may come to sight a rounded bank of fertile mud rich in its promise of green growth, so from the waters of chaos there rose the primeval 'hillock of appearance' which was the nucleus of the earth. It was made by the creator god; it could even be the god himself; in any case it was the spot chosen by him for his earthly temple. To the modern mind the difficulty is that there were many such mounds, each alike regarded as authentically original—the sites of temples at Heliopolis and Hermonthis, at Thebes and Philae and elsewhere; probably in the course of time every Egyptian temple claimed to occupy the world's primordial hillock; and those temples were in different places and were the homes of different gods. To the Egyptian this presented no difficulty at all; the conception of the creation-hillock was essential, its location in space did not matter; indeed, because it was a universal truth, all the stories could be simultaneously true. If in the very early days, when Egypt was split up into more or less independent nomes, districts each acknowledging allegiance to a different chief god, the act of creation was attributed to varying deities, that too mattered little; when the country had been united under a dynasty for whom Rê was the supreme deity those religious anomalies could be smoothed away by the simple expedient of tacking the name Rê on to that of the local god. In this way the required uniformity was secured, and yet the eternal verities held good.

Actually there are no documents informing us directly of what religious beliefs prevailed in pre-Dynastic times; the pyramid texts are our earliest authorities, and although much of their content must be derived from old tradition yet the form in which it is presented is that of a more sophisticated age. According to them Atum the Sun god, self-created and alone on his primeval hillock, creates Shu, god of the air, and Tefnut, goddess of moisture; these give birth to Geb, the Earth god, and Nut, the goddess of the sky, and they in their turn produce Osiris and Isis, Seth and Nephthys; and later other gods came into being.

This is an orderly account, but it achieves order only by disregarding all inconsistencies; there were different stories as to how Atum created Shu and Tefnut, by spitting out one and sputtering out the other, or by making them out of his own semen; in one tale Shu is the natural father of earth and sky, in another they had been one and he tore them violently apart; according to one legend, preserved by Plutarch, Isis and Osiris were not Egyptian deities at all but were brought in from Byblos[10] where they were known as Ishtar and Tammuz and had nothing to do with Geb and Nut; and again there were 'gods' before Atum the creator emerged from chaos and 'began to rule that which he had made'. Perhaps the most striking instance of the way in which the Egyptian accepted what seem to us contradictions is the magnifying of Ptah. When the country was consolidated by the Pharaohs of the First Dynasty and Memphis was selected by them as capital of the Two Kingdoms the difficulty arose that Memphis had never before been an important town and its local god, Ptah, was of minor rank, whereas obviously he should, as god of the royal city, enjoy pre-eminence. Accordingly, while the old story of creation was retained, it was now explained that Ptah was 'the heart and the tongue' of Atum; it was he that conceived Atum's thoughts, and it was he that, by giving utterance to those thoughts, brought them into existence as phenomena; more than that, it was Ptah who first conceived the idea of Atum and by naming him created the creator. By Ptah, by his thought and speech, were all things made that were made—the gods, the earth with its provinces and its towns allotted to the several gods, all human arts and crafts and all moral issues; 'thus it was discovered and understood that his power is greater than that of the other gods'. Nothing of the old order is explicitly rejected, but it is made to assimilate a new element which is in fact contradictory; and Egyptian theology was prepared to accept both versions without question.

In very much the same way, when Heliopolis became the capital city, Rê the Sun god, whose seat was at Heliopolis, is identified as Rê-Atum, both sun and creator; at a much later date, when Thebes was the royal city of the empire, Amon-Rê acquires such overwhelming importance that other gods find it expedient to bolster up their dignity by assimilation to him, and we hear of Khnum-Rê, Sobek-Rê, Montu-Rê and Rê-Harakhte; there is no loss of identity, but by the use of the name Rê the local deity obtains for himself the virtue which is in Rê just as a magician uses a man's name to gain control over him.

The pyramid texts, dating from the Fifth and Sixth Dynasties, on which we have to rely for our knowledge of Egyptian religion in the early times, show that already in the Old Kingdom the principal part in it was taken by sun-worship, and next in importance is the cult of Osiris and the deities associated with him. But it must be remembered that these texts are purely funerary in purpose, intended for the use of the dead Pharaoh in leaving this world and in entering and dwelling in the next; they do not, therefore, cover the whole field of belief, and they do not necessarily reflect the beliefs of ordinary men. The parts dealing with funerary ritual and tomb-offerings, of course, apply only to the funerals of kings and have no general significance. But the great bulk of the texts is a jumbled conglomerate of extracts from myths and legends, charms and prayers, some of them certainly of great antiquity, going back in substance to pre-Dynastic times, and from these it is possible to gain some idea of the character of the earliest religion.

The substratum of that religion was certainly a totemistic system.[11] The 'standards' of the nomes or provinces of ancient Egypt represent the actual totems which were revered in and gave their names to the different nomes when the Nile valley was parcelled out into some forty independent little principalities; each of those had its local god (the 'town god' of later times) who probably was by origin no more than the non-human thing—beast, bird, plant or whatnot—from which the leading clan fancied itself to be descended. This much is certainly true, but to assert, as some have done, that 'sun-worship, and indeed the whole cosmic system of which it is typical, was secondary in Egypt, imposing itself upon a substratum of totemism', is to exaggerate grossly. The totem was a clan affair, owing its territorial significance to the territorial ascendancy of the clan affiliated to it, and it was in no way inconsistent with other beliefs. The early Egyptian, as has been said above, recognized the personality behind every phenomenon, and the belief that he was himself descended from an ibis did not prevent him from seeing god in the sun or in the moon; what he did tend to do in the course of time was to identify his totem with one or other of the gods, so that the falcon becomes Horus, a solar deity, and the Moon god Thoth takes on the form of an ibis. Just as the political unification of Egypt left the nomes in existence as administrative units, so a sufficient uniformity of religion could be brought about without any brutal deletion of the primitive totem-cults or any forced imposition of sun-worship; the sun-worship was already there, and if the new creed and the old were in any way inconsistent or contradictory nobody could object to that; they were both true.

A change was indeed inevitable, because totemism as such is suited only to primitive conditions in which the clan is the largest social unit. As society becomes more complex and its horizon widens, the theory of common descent from a non-human ancestor loses grip and the greater gods, recognized by one's neighbours equally with oneself, come into their own; the totem is either identified with one of those gods or relegated to the sphere of mere heraldry. The change must have been going on throughout the pre-Dynastic period and when the first Pharaoh insisted upon the pre-eminence of Rê—which he would naturally do seeing that his totem, the falcon, had become Horus and he himself was 'the Horus'—he did nothing to shock his subjects; it would be more true to say that he merely confirmed what was already the popular belief.

Egyptian religion was still, at that time, in a very fluid state. The pyramid texts show that there was a very rich—and terribly confused—mythology, some of the characters of which were to become the gods of Egypt while others were to remain merely mythological, possessing neither temple nor form of worship. There were temples, certainly, but there was no order of priesthood; the local nobleman (i.e. the head-man of the clan) acted as priest on the necessary occasions and was assisted by a body of laymen who took it in turn to serve in the temple for a stated period. Sometimes the god might be represented by the old totem now identified with him—the hawk, the crocodile, the jackal or the cow—but this was no more than a symbol; animal-worship as such was unknown and the cult marks the late decadence of Egyptian history.[12] But there is really nothing to show quite how the early Egyptian imagined his gods. It is a curious fact that in the vast mass of pre-Dynastic and proto-Dynastic material recovered by archaeology there is, apart from the nome standards, scarcely an object that can confidently be said to illustrate religion. There are no figures of deities, practically no scenes of mythology or of ritual[13] such as we find in Mesopotamia in the Jamdat Nasr period; the available evidence suggests that the formal service of the gods played a very small part in the life of the ordinary inhabitant of the Nile valley, whatever beliefs he may have held privately. If this was indeed so, it was perhaps but the natural result of the circumstances of his daily life. He knew that the sun would shine almost every day from a clear sky; he could confidently depend upon the annual flooding of the Nile just at the time when seed was due to be sown, and he could count upon the rich soil to give him an ample harvest; it was quite clear to him that kindly gods had made everything on earth for man's enjoyment, and therefore as long as he was upon earth he need not trouble himself very much about the gods; their goodwill could be taken for granted. On the other hand, the evidence amply proves how great a part was played by his belief in a future life.

'The two central features of the Egyptian scene were the triumphant daily rebirth of the sun and the triumphant annual rebirth of the river. Out of these miracles the Egyptians drew their assurance that Egypt was the centre of the universe and their assurance that renewed life may always be victorious over death.' From the earliest times men had been accustomed to place in the graves of their dead the things that they had used and enjoyed in this world and would equally require in the next. About the existence of that world there was no doubt whatsoever. In the early days, as is clear from the pyramid texts, the abode of eternal blessedness was in the northern section of the heavens where the circumpolar stars swing round the North Star and never disappear below the horizon but are those that 'know no destruction'. Later, as sun-worship became more dominant, the Elysian Fields were shifted to that underworld through which the sun passed at night to be reborn in the east; it was the sun that gave promise of life renewed, and for man to share in that he must follow the sun's course; so Dat, lying between the waters of Nun whereon the earth floats and the counter-heaven which is the term of space, becomes the realm of the immortal dead.

The inconsistencies and contradictions which the Egyptian mind accepted with such equanimity make it difficult to discover quite what was his conception of the future life, and here the pyramid texts are apt to be misleading. In them the Osiris cult is only less important than that of the sun; but that is because the pyramids were the tombs of kings and the king was himself a god and Osiris was himself a dead king or at least a personification of dead kingship. In the texts the king and the god are identified, so that the dead Pharaoh is named 'the Osiris King' and receives his funeral rites from the hands of his son Horus, incarnate, for the occasion, in the person of the living Pharaoh who succeeds him. That is correct and natural for Pharaoh, but the tombs even of nobles of the Old Kingdom show no such predisposition for the Osiris cult, and the ordinary Egyptian did not associate Osiris with himself; *he* was not joining the Assembly of the Gods but was beginning a new life very similar to that which was ended.

That the Egyptian of the Old Kingdom believed firmly in a future life is certain, but it is extremely difficult to say quite what the belief was. He recognized, of course, the fact of physical death, but he was unable to conceive of any form of existence other than that of physical life;[14] the difference, therefore, between the living and the dead was one of degree rather than of kind. The dead lived, but in a less real manner. They required food and drink, just as they had done in this world, and a prudent man would do all that he could to assure that provision was regularly made for his soul's sustenance; but since it was patently true that the dead could not and did not eat or drink, it was the spirit of the offering rather than its substance that mattered, and a loaf of painted wood was as satisfactory as a wheaten loaf, the wine-jars and the trayful of meats carved in relief on the walls of the tomb chamber were as sustaining as actual meat and wine, and had the advantage of being incorruptible. The dead man was actually alive in his tomb. That was the reason for the care taken to preserve the body from decay or destruction, and, because decay was only too probable (for proper mummification was not practised in this early period) a portrait-statue was immured in the chapel of the *mastaba* tomb which in case of need could act as the body's substitute. For the body was indispensable. Every man at his birth received a *ka,* which co-existed with him throughout his life and after death; the word might be translated 'vital force', or 'character' or 'individuality' (so ill-defined are the Egyptian conceptions);[15] but in any case the *ka* plus the body is the man, and if body and *ka* are separated the man ceases to exist. Another aspect of or element in the man's individuality is represented by the *ba,* which generally assumes the form of a human-headed bird who grasps the symbol of life and, by holding this to the nostrils of the dead, assures his continued existence as an *akh,* a 'glorious one' still functioning as in life, the *akh* also, like the *ka* and the *ba,* being not something separate from the man but himself as conditioned by the future life, the man *sub specie eternitatis.*

The Egyptian was not given to reflective thought and was

not in the least worried by the fact that his ideas concerning the phenomena of reality were hopelessly incompatible. He could not but recognize the fact of physical death, but because he hated it he refused to admit it; the dead was not dead, he was alive. A curious illustration of his belief in the literal truth of the dogma is afforded by some of the Second Dynasty *mastaba* tombs at Sakkarah in which there are lavatories provided for the occupant; it was impossible for him to conceive of any form of existence other than that of normal human life, and since that meant the life of the body, the body was essential to immortality. It was not the case that the body perishes and the *ka,* or the *ba*, survives, nor yet that the body must be preserved or a portrait figure be substituted for it in order that the disembodied spirit may enter into it should it choose to revisit the tomb. The body and the *ka* are inseparable, and it is the man himself who in the tomb continues his physical existence and, leaving the tomb-chamber, can pass through the false door into the offering-chamber of the *mastaba* to take part in the mortuary banquet.

An outstanding feature of the elaborate tombs of the Old Kingdom nobility is the carving upon their chapel walls. Always the principal figure is that of the tomb's owner, dominating by his greater stature the entire scheme of decoration. In front of him rows of reliefs represent the characteristic scenes of Egyptian life; labourers plough the fields and harvest the crops; tally-clerks keep check of the sacks of grain stored in the granaries; the herdsmen drive the cattle from the pasture; there are scenes of duck-hunting in the Nile marshes and of fishing in its waters; servants prepare the meals of the household and make ready the banquet; there are workshops of the goldsmith and the maker of stone vases, the ship-builder's yard and the open-air market; before the eyes of the dead man are pictured all the familiar activities of the world as he knew it.

These pictures are not in any sense a memorial of the wealth and luxury that the man had enjoyed in his lifetime. It has been supposed that they represent scenes in the next world, characteristically conceived as being a replica of this, and that their presence in the tomb would, by sympathetic magic, ensure for the dead man the enjoyment of just such things as he had most enjoyed in life—there, too, he would be the lord of broad acres, owning the cattle so realistically figured on the tomb walls, feasting and hunting just as the reliefs showed him doing. Such a belief does seem to have been developed in the later phases of Egyptian history when men were obsessed to a far greater extent with the thought of another world; and the germs of it may well have been present, even in the time of the early dynasties, in the muddled minds of the Egyptians. But the original purpose of the pictures was different.[16] They are not abstract symbols; they are realistic excerpts from ordinary life, objective, light-hearted and full of bustling activity; but the owner of the tomb plays no part in them; schematized and hieratic, he looks on at all that is done, from the outside; as the inscriptions say, 'he watches'.[17] He is not dead. Living in the tomb he looks on at life as he has known it, seeing through the pictures the living world in which —one hates to admit the fact, but one cannot escape it—he no longer can play a direct part. The early Egyptian was not very deeply interested in another world to which man may go after death; the whole of his elaborate funerary ritual aimed at securing the continuation of life in this world subject only to those somewhat different conditions which the fact of death imposed.

Such a creed is the creed of a prosperous and a happy people who enjoyed life so whole-heartedly that they could not endure the thought of losing it. Our evidence for it is necessarily one-sided; it comes from the tombs of the rich nobility who could afford an elaborate ritual, and we cannot be sure as to how far their belief was shared by the poor, for whom costly burial was impossible; presumably they got as much happiness as they could out of life and vaguely hoped for the best thereafter. But a creed based on prosperity is peculiarly vulnerable. When the Old Kingdom collapsed, when, as the sage Ipuwer said in his *Admonitions*: 'The desert has spread throughout the land; a foreign tribe from abroad has come into Egypt; blood is everywhere. Gates, columns and walls are consumed by fire. No craftsmen work. Men are few, women are lacking, and no children are conceived. All is ruin'; when, too, men saw that the old precautions against death had proved futile, that the tomb-chapels of the nobles were falling to decay and even the pyramids of the Pharaohs were plundered, then religious belief could scarcely fail to be affected by the changes in the world.

The immediate effect of the disastrous fall of the Old Kingdom was a wave of utter pessimism so overwhelming that one of the literary documents of the period, the 'Dialogue of the Man-weary-of-life with his Soul', actually ends with a panegyric on death; a constant phrase on the grave stelae of the previous age had run, 'O ye who love life and hate death'; now we read, 'Death is before me today like the longing of a man to see his home when he has spent many years in captivity'. There could scarcely be a more striking reversal of values than this, but it is not purely negative; it does at least imply that, if life be miserable, death may be the beginning of something better—'Death is before me today like the convalescence of a sick man, like going forth after an illness'. The Egyptian, as we have seen, had always cheerfully assumed that the gods were on the whole kindly beings; if now the whole fabric of society which summed up his ideal of happiness had broken down that was, of course, the act of the gods; but were the gods to blame, or had there been something wrong with society? A sense of moral unworthiness as the cause of misfortune begins to show itself.

This was not a revolutionary change in Egyptian thought but it was a revelation of Old Kingdom ideas, new in the emphasis which it laid on ethics. An Old Kingdom writer could hardly have said, 'More acceptable is the character of a man just of heart than the ox of the evil-doer'; still less could he have put into the mouth of Rê as the god of creation this quite remarkable statement of his purpose for man:

> I made the four winds that every man might breathe thereof like his fellow in his time.
> I made the great flood waters that the poor man might have rights in them like the great man.
> I made every man like his fellow. I did not command that they might do evil, but their hearts violated what I had said.
> I made that their hearts should cease from forgetting the West, in order that divine offerings might be made to the gods of the provinces.

Here is a definite assertion of human rights. In theory, that is, in accordance with the divine plan, opportunity should be equal for all; men were created equal, and the social inequalities of the world are the result of man's violating the will of the Creator. But that perversion is limited to this world. Rê calls upon all men to fix their thoughts upon 'the West', the realm of the blessed dead, where the divine purpose holds good and there is no distinction between rich and poor, between Pharaoh and the peasant. The Pharaoh of the Old Kingdom was a god and on his death entered as by right the heaven of the gods; now every Egyptian can enjoy eternity on the same terms, every Egyptian when he dies becomes Osiris.

There was an old legend according to which Horus at one time had been hailed by his uncle Seth before the tribunal of Rê; he stood his trial and was acquitted as being 'true of voice' or 'justified'. Similarly the dead man now identified with Osiris had to be judged by Rê and the tribunal of the gods before he could enter into the state of blessedness; and this trial was conducted on ethical lines, that which was evil in the man's life being weighed in 'the balance of Rê' against that which was good. In theory at least morality and religion are here made interdependent: 'As for the court who judge sinners, mark thee that they will not be lenient on that day of judging miserable men, in the hours of performing their function. Wretched is he who is accused as one conscious of sin. Put not thy faith in length of years, for they behold a lifetime as an hour. A man survives after death. His deeds are laid beside him for treasure. Eternal is the existence yonder. He who has made light of it is a fool. But he who has reached it without wrong-doing shall exist yonder like a god, stepping forward boldly like the lords of eternity.' Such are the instructions given to his son by a Pharaoh of Egypt, probably of the Tenth Dynasty, and on the strength of such we can assert that in the troubled days between the Sixth and the Twelfth Dynasties religion reached a moral height which it had not attained before. Of the Egyptian pantheon two gods were now predominant, the ancient Sun god Rê who had made all men equal and cared equally for all, and Osiris, 'justified' by *ma'at*, by uprightness, righteousness and truth; and salvation was open to all men who followed virtue, so that they became as gods. But the royal instructions cited above are in their character unique amongst the documents of the period; the lesson had not yet been generally assimilated and the coffin texts as a whole fail to recognize any close connection between religion and morals, and, although the good seed had been sown, the young growth was doomed to be choked by 'the care of this world and the deceitfulness of riches'.

With the establishment of the Twelfth Dynasty and the accession to the throne of Amenemhet I, described by a contemporary writer in terms of almost Messianic prophecy, prosperity returned to the Nile valley. Internal peace was assured, civil order was maintained, abundant wealth poured into the country; life was again worth living, and a good life was all that a man could ask. The Egyptian had always loved life and had done his best to defy death; now, with the extension of the Osiris cult, death lost much of its old terrors, since every man could become a god, and since he could not conceive of another world except in terms of this, he would continue to enjoy in the hereafter all the good things with which he had surrounded himself here. Guaranteed immortality had given increased value to the individual; he could claim rights for himself, but he was obliged also to recognize obligations to others; the Middle Kingdom saw a greater degree of social consciousness than the Old Kingdom had known, and in the tomb texts much emphasis is laid on *ma'at*, the dead man's righteous dealing with his fellow-men, the virtue that would weigh heaviest in the 'balance of Rê' at the last judgement. Unfortunately virtue is not always consistent with the acquisition of material prosperity; the latter could not be forgone, but the last judgement could not be disregarded. The practically-minded Egyptian solved the dilemma by the use of magic, against which the gods themselves are powerless. A set form of words, accompanied by a set ritual of action, can, if properly used, exercise compelling force. Already in the old pyramid texts the dead king had been instructed in the use of certain utterances whereby he could propitiate the malevolent beings of the other world; now the general public shared the privileges of the ancient kings. However much evil a man had done in his lifetime he could face the judgement of the gods with equanimity provided that he knew the right thing to say and the right way of saying it; in case he should forget, the formula was written on the inside of his coffin and was a sure passport to the realms of the blessed dead. 'If a man says this section', the text states explicitly, 'he shall enter into the West after he has gone up. But as for anyone who does not know this section, he shall not enter in.' No good deeds will atone for ignorance. Later, under the Eighteenth Dynasty, the whole thing was stereotyped, and the apposite portions of the Book of the Dead were placed as a matter of routine in the coffin so that every awkward question put by Osiris (who by that time was regarded as the Judge) was countered automatically and the trial of the soul was reduced to a farce. Obviously this meant the complete divorce of morality from religion. A prudent man would observe the rules of social justice and right dealing just so far as was expedient and would disregard them when he could do so safely and to his own advantage; he had no need to take the divine sanction seriously.

Of the two cults now predominant that of Osiris affected most the individual citizen, involving as it did constant forethought and a great expenditure of money on the preparation of his funeral rites; but since he was himself to be Osiris all this expenditure was purely self-regarding; its motive was not ethical but the safeguarding of his own future enjoyment. At the same time the institution at Abydos of festivals at which the Osiris myths were presented in the form of 'passion plays', to which the public was admitted and even participated in them, gave to the cult something in the nature of a popular religion. But ecclesiastical religion played a very small part in the average Egyptian's life; sun-worship, the most ancient and from now on the most important cult in Egypt, was the concern not of the individual[18] but of the state.

In the old days the shrines of the local gods had been very humble affairs and the priests attached to them had enjoyed but small authority. Only in the time of the Twelfth Dynasty did the temples grow in actual size, and in the numbers of their attendant personnel, and in landed property, thanks chiefly to the munificent gifts made to them by the successful Pharaohs; during the same period and through the same means the Sun god was able to eclipse all the other deities of Egypt. The Pharaohs of the Twelfth Dynasty were natives of Thebes, and the local god of Thebes was Amon, one of the forms of Rê.[19] The divine Pharaoh, claiming to be the actual son of the Sun god, naturally gave precedence to his father; Amenemhet I at once began to build a new and more pretentious temple of Amon at Thebes, Sesostris I enlarged it and also built a new temple of Rê at Heliopolis; each ruler in turn prided himself on adding to the majesty of the god who was the ancestor and patron of his house, and in order to share in the royal favour the old local gods found it expedient to identify themselves with the sun, so that the Crocodile god Sobek became Sobek-Rê. By the time when the Twelfth Dynasty ended, the Sun god's position was so firmly established that his cult could survive even the disastrous phase of civil wars and foreign conquest that followed. Fortunately Thebes itself, although forced to pay tribute, did not fall directly into the hands of the Hyksos invaders who 'overthrew that which had been made, while they ruled without Rê', and it was a Theban king who ultimately expelled the barbarians from the Nile valley and pursued them into Syria; the triumph of Egyptian nationalism and the founding of the Egyptian empire were the triumph of Amon-Rê.

Rê had always been the chief god of the Nile valley. Now Pharaoh, son of Amon-Rê, had extended his own and his father's dominions far beyond the confines of Egypt, and the realm of the Sun god included Palestine and Syria right up to the banks of the Euphrates. Each fresh victory had meant further glorification of Amon-Rê, the enlarging of an old temple or the building of a new; each newly gained province sent its yearly tribute to the god's already overflowing treasury, and his priests, trained in the College of Priests at Thebes, forming now a professional caste, acquired ever more political and economic power. In the anarchy that had followed on the fall of the Middle Kingdom the old nobility had disappeared; the higher ranks of the government service were no longer filled by the members of a privileged and more or less hereditary class but were appointed by the king at his pleasure; and since the priesthood enjoyed a better education than the layman and was *ex officio* in closer communion with the god of the empire, priests were the most obvious candidates for appointment. A close corporation of the sort, holding many of the great offices of state, immensely rich, owning vast landed properties which were steadily increased by the custom of assigning lands to the priesthood for the upkeep of funerary rites in perpetuity (it is calculated that at one time the Temple lands amounted to not less than one-fifth of the whole area of Egypt) and therefore having direct control of a vast personnel, a corporation, finally, backed by the divine sanction, was invested with such power that it might easily threaten the independence of Pharaoh himself. This actually came about under the Twentieth Dynasty, when the nominal ruler of Egypt was no more than a puppet in the hands of the priesthood, but the danger was apparent long before that.

Under Amenhotep III a high priest of Amon had been the chief treasurer[20] of the kingdom, and another had been Grand Vizier; towards the end of his reign, however, the king appointed a new Grand Vizier, Ramose, who was not a priest; and he also introduced a change of worship, both actions probably being aimed at undermining the power of the Theban priesthood. In that imperial age, when Pharaoh's dominions seemed to have no limits in space, the Egyptian had tangibly before him a world-concept which naturally led on to the idea of a world-god. That that god was the sun no one could doubt, but was it the old Rê of Heliopolis, or Amon-Rê of Thebes, or any one of the many local gods who by now had hyphenated their names with that of Rê and claimed his prerogatives as their own? Amenhotep[21] may have thought of by-passing these sectarian pretensions when he built a chapel at Heliopolis in honour of Aton, which was an ancient name for the actual sun, added to his own name the adjective 'dawning like Aton', and even approved of Aton being described as 'the sole god', very much as, more than two hundred years before, the Semitic Pharaoh of the Hyksos, Apopi III, took Sutekh for his Lord and 'served no other god in all the land but him'.

Amenhotep IV* followed in his father's steps but quickly outdistanced him. Aton-worship was to be the state religion. Aton was identified with the old Rê to the extent that he was the sun, and his High Priest (the Pharaoh himself) used the same title, 'the Great Seer', as was used by the High Priest of Rê at Heliopolis. But Aton was not merely the sun; his name, the word Aton, was employed instead of the old word (*neter*)

* Usually referred to by the name of Akhenaton as explained below.

to mean 'god', and Aton himself was the vital heat which, coming primarily from the sun, is the source of all life and it was through the rays of the sun that he was active. This was symbolized, for purposes of representation, by depicting the sun as a disk from which there radiated downwards divergent beams, each ending in a human hand; the power issuing from its celestial source finds at the end a human contact. The merit of the symbol was that everyone could easily grasp its meaning; the old Egyptian symbols for the sun, the falcon or the pyramid, were familiar to Egyptians but conveyed nothing to those Asiatic subjects of the empire who now had to be considered no less than the natives of the Nile valley; the god of the empire had to be recognized by all alike.

At the beginning of his reign the young Pharaoh, for all his enthusiasm, seems to have observed a certain moderation; the worship of all the old gods of Egypt was tolerated, although now vast sums of money that had formerly gone into the treasury of Amon-Rê were diverted into that of Aton. The Theban priesthood, however, were furious, not only because of the loss of revenue but also because of their exclusion from the high offices of state, for those were distributed at the king's pleasure and it was only too clear that his favours were reserved to adherents of the upstart faith; and either in overconfidence or in desperation they attempted to oppose the heresy. But Amenhotep IV was not only a religious fanatic. Little more than a boy in years, he was an absolute monarch strengthened by the enormous prestige of his house and the material resources amassed by his father, and by character and training he was a self-centred egoist; the mere idea of opposition to his will drove him into frenzy. By a royal order all the old gods of Egypt were proscribed; the priesthoods were dispossessed, the temple services were forbidden, and the names of the gods were erased from reliefs and sacred monuments. Even the word 'gods' where it appeared in an inscription was often hacked out, and the mortuary chapels, the tombs and the statues of the king's ancestors were violated without mercy, and because his father's name was compounded with that of Amon even that name had to be obliterated from the walls of the great buildings wherewith he had enriched Thebes. Thebes, as the headquarters of Amon, was in any case hateful[22] and now, with all the monuments which he had defiled forming a standing reproach of his impiety, Pharaoh decided upon a complete break with the past. He changed his own name to Akhenaton, and set up a new capital of the empire, Akhetaton, on a virgin site on the Nile bank nearly three hundred miles below Thebes; so urgent were Pharaoh's orders that already in the sixth year of his reign the mushroom city was an accomplished fact, his gay palaces and pleasure-pavilions in full use, and in a huge temple the 'Great Seer' could lead the services in honour of Aton, the sole god.

Pharaoh's devotion to Aton was, unquestionably, enthusiastic and exclusive, and the famous hymns supposed to have been composed by him illustrate that devotion in its highest aspect, in language astonishingly like that of the Hebrew Psalm civ. In their insistence on the goodness and loving-kindness of the Creator the Aton hymns carry much farther that conception of deity which was first apparent in the religious literature of the Middle Kingdom, and they show a tendency to monotheism much more clearly marked than was the case in, for instance, the hymn of Amon-Rê of a hundred years earlier; there Amon-Rê 'the righteous one' is hailed as chief of all the gods, unique amongst the gods, father of the gods and creator of all things; but in Akhenaton's hymn Aton is 'the sole god, whose powers no other possesseth, beside whom there is no other'. This indeed looks like pure monotheism, but it must be remembered that in the earlier days of the revolution the cult of the other gods of Egypt was permitted and the intolerance of the later stages was due as much to pique as to conviction—just as there was but one Pharaoh ruling the empire so Pharaoh's god must be the sole god of all his subjects.

But in any case Aton did not stand alone; Akhenaton was himself a god, as his forefathers had been, and that from the beginning of time—'Since thou didst establish the earth', he says in his Aton hymn, 'thou has raised up [mankind] for thy son who came forth from thy limbs, the King, living in truth'. His vizier Nekht calls his master 'the god who makes man, the god who formed all men'. That parade of domesticity which is repeated time and again in the reliefs and paintings of the royal city is not meant to bring the Pharaoh down to the level of ordinary man; rather, so much is he a god that the most intimate scenes of his life acquire divinity and can worthily replace the representations of other gods and the ritual of their worship which had adorned the temples of an unregenerate age.

Akhenaton's creed was monolatrous rather than monotheistic. Moreover, however elevated in its expression and poetical in its sentiment, it contains only a sensuous beauty and is wholly unethical; 'the king', says Professor Breasted, 'has not perceptibly risen from the beneficence to the righteousness in the character of God, nor to His demand for this in the character of men'. Even the Pharaoh's constant emphasis on *ma'at* does not bear witness to any moral advance. The usual translation of the word as 'truth' is misleading. In the sense of 'justice' it was equally prominent in the Middle Kingdom, when daily the ritual was observed of the king presenting to the god the symbol of the goddess Ma'at; to Akhenaton it may have had the further meaning of 'realism'—that whatever *was* was right and proper, always with the proviso that whatever *was* derived ultimately from the king himself; no other could know the divine Aton 'save thy son Akhenaton; thou hast made him wise in thy designs and in thy might'. In the field of art *ma'at* became an exaggerated realism, and the sculptor (whom his Majesty himself taught) was obliged, in the interests of 'truth', to abandon all the traditions of court propriety and faithfully portray the king's ungainly and malformed person; but there was no humility involved in this—rather the reverse; the king *was* deformed, and therefore deformity was right and proper, so much so that an ambitious courtier would in a portrait of himself suggest that he, too, suffered from—or could boast—a like deformity. The phrase 'living in truth' invariably attached to the king's name carried very little moral significance.

The 'teaching of Pharaoh' had but small positive effect on his subjects. It was, of course, accepted with blatant enthusiasm by the courtiers who were bribed to conformity by the gifts of high office and gold in abundance—'Hang gold at his neck before and behind, and gold on his legs; because of his hearing the teaching of Pharaoh concerning every saying in these beautiful seats which Pharaoh has made in the sanctuary in the Aton-temple in Akhetaton'. The ordinary citizen of the new capital conformed because his livelihood was involved, but the local craftsmen continued to mould and the local people to wear glazed amulets in the form of Bes and Taurt, Hathor and Osiris; and even before the city was deserted one Ptah-may, 'praised one of the Aton', could set up in his funerary chapel a stele with prayers to the goddesses Isis and Shed and an inscription in honour of Amon 'the good ruler eternally, lord of Heaven, who made the whole earth'. A second Amon inscription from Tell el Amarna shows that Ptah-may was not alone in his divided allegiance, and outside the boundaries of Akhetaton the effect of the revolution on the Egyptians must have been almost entirely negative. They saw the old temples defaced and closed, the state priesthood disestablished and an interdict laid upon the public services of the gods, but there was no one to teach them anything about the new religion which a royal edict had brought into being; in itself the idea of a 'sole god' did not appeal to them, for they were accustomed to, and liked, gods in plenty; they were therefore driven back more than ever to the minor cults and superstitions which had always meant more to the humbler classes of Egyptian society than did the formalized worship of the state.[23]

With the disappearance of Akhenaton the whole of his religious movement disappeared also; the capital was moved back to Thebes, the cult of Amon-Rê was revived with greater splendour than before, and the very name of Aton was banished from the language of orthodoxy. But it would be wrong to say that it had had no effect upon religion. Sir Alan Gardiner insists on 'the ever-growing tendency to monotheism manifest in all Egyptian writings' of post-Akhenaton times, but such a tendency, important as it must be held,[24] was confined to the small body of thoughtful and more or less philosophic writers; only in a few Theban votive or memorial stelae does there appear any evidence suggesting that the Aton worship may have lastingly influenced the traditional beliefs of ordinary people. That in these few texts there is sentiment of a high order cannot be denied. 'Beware of Amon', runs one of them. 'Repeat his name to son and to daughter, to great and to small. . . . Tell of him to the fishes in the stream and to the birds of the air. . . . Thou art Amon, the lord of him who is silent, coming at the call of the poor. I called to thee when I was in trouble, and thou didst come and didst save me; thou didst give breath to the poor and didst rescue me who was in bondage. . . . I made for him praises to his name because of the greatness of his might. I cried, "Lord of the poor" before him in the presence of the whole land for Nebamon when he lay sick and about to die, being in the power of Amon because of his sin. . . . While the servant was wont to sin yet was the Lord wont to be gracious. The Lord of Thebes spends not a whole day in wrath. His anger lasts but a moment and there is nought remaining.'[25]

If such a prayer as this can indeed be derived from the Aton worship it has gone very far beyond anything that Akhenaton taught, and it has gone very far beyond the somewhat vague belief held in the time of the Middle Kingdom that future happiness must in some degree depend upon present virtue. But it was the prayer of a minority neither influential nor permanent,[26] and we shall look in vain for this conception of a moral and a merciful god in the orthodox religion of Nineteenth Dynasty Egypt. There the development was to absolute sacerdotalism; by a judicious use of the oracles which they controlled the priests of Amon were in time able to control the whole policy of Egypt and finally to transfer to their own order the temporal power of Pharaoh. For the populace, the cult of Osiris more than held its own, but this, too, was a matter of magic—the mechanical assurance of the dead against the dangers of the passage to eternity—and had no ethical or spiritual value. Under all the pomp and splendour of liturgical and funerary ritual there was but a dull and lifeless formalism. The exuberant individualism of the Old Kingdom had given place to man's passive submission to the established order of things in this world, and if he could hope at all for better things in the next, they were to be won not by individual merit but by the priestly spells which could bind, or cheat, even the jealous gods.

THE HURRIANS AND THE HITTITES

The reasons for treating these two peoples under a common heading have been given in Chapter I and are well summarized by Dr Speiser: 'The relations between the Hurrians and the Hittites prove to be unusually intimate, a fact which is abundantly reflected in virtually every phase of the Hittite civilization. Indeed, we are justified in speaking of a Hurro-Hittite symbiosis which for closeness and effect is second only to that blend of Sumerian and Akkadian elements which constitutes the composite culture of Mesopotamia.'[27] This is generally true, and not least so in the sphere of religion.

Of the indigenous religion of the Hurro-Hittite area little is known.[28] From Tell Asmar, the easternmost border of the Hurri land, from Anatolia and, outside Asia, from the Cycladic islands and from Crete, there come the curious 'violin-shaped' idols of the earliest Bronze Age which can only be taken to be symbols of a mother-goddess, the goddess of fertility. Representations of snakes, almost equally widespread and culminating in the sophisticated snake-goddesses of Knossos, may imply a cult of the nether gods. The enigmatic metal 'standards' of Alaca Höyük—sometimes accompanied by figures of bulls or stags—may mean sun-worship, and the animals certainly reappear in later times as the attributes of individual gods, the bull being the regular companion of Teshub, the Lord of the Storm, and the stag that of a god who is apparently the protector of wild animals and therefore the hunter's god. That elements of the primitive religion should survive in after ages, taken over by the Hurrite and Hittite invaders, is but natural, and unquestionably both peoples were peculiarly ready to adopt the gods with whom they were brought in contact. The eastern Hurrites, living amongst or in the neighbourhood of the far more civilized Sumerians and Akkadians, assimilated their own god, Teshub, with the Mesopotamian deity Addu, adopted the god Zababa, and took over wholesale the mythological legends of Sumer; the western branch, mingling with the less advanced Syrians, were content to accept the local West Semitic deities as their own gods masquerading under other names and so could adapt themselves to local practice. But the Hittites were even more acquisitive. By the time of the New Empire, when documentary evidence is for the first time available, we find that the Hurrian goddess Hebat (the consort of Teshub) and the Mesopotamian Ishtar were both reckoned amongst the 'gods of the palace' of Suppiluliumas; the personal seals of Muwatallis, Suppiluliumas's grandson, mention two forms of Teshub, and Teshub and Hebat of Aleppo are described as gods 'of Hatti', as also are some of the Babylonian deities; even in the great rock-sanctuary of Yazilikaya, adjoining the Hittite capital, the hieroglyphic inscriptions give Hurrian names to the gods and goddesses worshipped there.

Of course these foreign deities were superimposed upon a native Hattic religion. The chief place in it was held by the Sun goddess of Arinna—but since she has two attributes, as dissimilar as the dove and the lioness, she would seem to be already a synthesis of two or more deities. The Sun goddess is the spouse of the Storm god or Weather god, a deity whose powers and direct influence upon man's life could not but be recognized by peoples whose homes were in the mountain areas of Asia Minor. The Weather god is undoubtedly a synthesis, including in his identity a number of what were once independent gods, for every important Hittite city had a Storm god of its own, called after the city's name; in time all these are either merged in the person of the national Storm god or combine to form a Storm god who is at the same time a Sun god and ranks as the son of the Sun goddess of Arinna and her Storm-god husband. Judging from the evidence of Alaca Höyük we may class as indigenous the Stag god who is protector of wild life; such also may be Telepinus, the god of vegetation who, like Adonis, disappears from the earth and has to be sought and brought back in order that life may go on; such too Kubaba, the Mother goddess, whose cult was carried by the Hittites as far afield as their armies could at any time advance so that whereas in the east she had a temple on the acropolis of Carchemish, in the west her statue looks down from Mount Sipylus upon the Gulf of Smyrna. The Hittite scribes speak of 'the thousand gods of the land of Hatti'; of course many of these were really local variants of the same god who preserved their identity—and their importance—as being the patron deities of their several cities; thus there were

Storm gods innumerable, but they could scarcely be differentiated, except by the names of their city temples, from the Storm god of Hattusas who is called 'King of Heaven, Lord of the land of Hatti' and represents the nation just as Amon represented Egypt. At the same time the official attempts at syncretizing the gods did not always take into account genuine differences of function, with the result that the same god may be a Storm god in one place and a god of agriculture or of war in another, the different attributes of divinity merging insensibly one into another. The pantheon was strangely eclectic and confused, but it resulted from and reflected the composition of the Hittite people, which was not a race apart but a confederacy of tribes, speaking different dialects and different languages, some of them undoubtedly Anatolian by origin, others Indo-European immigrants coming probably by way of the Caucasus. About 1500 BC a further complication was added when the Aryan kingdom of Mitanni established itself in the Hurri country and the Aryan gods Indra, Mithras (Mitra), Varuna and the Nasatya joined the Hurro-Hittite pantheon; of these, Mithras long survived in the Middle East and was destined to play an important part in the religious developments of the early Christian era.[29]

The rich archives of the Hittite empire found at Bogazköy give much detailed information regarding the cult. The gods, of course, had their temples and their attendant priests, maintained by a levy raised not from the individual citizens but from the king, the palace revenues and the municipal governments. For the daily sustenance of the god the provision was simple—bread, wine and beer; the god's portion was strictly reserved to himself, but the rest was eaten by the priests inside the temple. Any Hittite citizen could demand to be fed at the god's expense, and he would be admitted to the temple and given food and drink; but only if what was provided for the day exceeded the requirements of the priests might they take anything away for the benefit of their families. The rules applying to the priests were strict, especially as regards physical and ritual cleanliness, and punishments for the breach of rules were severe, including the death penalty for various offences; but the priesthood as such does not seem to have exercised any undue authority in the state; they lived at home, not in the temple precincts, and married and had families like the ordinary citizen; only a few of the upper order, who participated in the great festivals, enjoyed a certain precedence.

The chief priest was the king. The Hittite ruler was not a god, as was the Egyptian Pharaoh, nor yet the mortal agent and representative of the god, appointed by him,[30] as was the king of a Sumerian city state. The Hittite monarchy was elective; a prince was designated by his father as his successor but only became king after he had been approved by the competent assembly consisting of the royal family, the nobles and the warriors. The king personifies the nation. Because the gods are the masters of the universe and men are but their servants whose whole well-being depends upon the goodwill of the gods, the service of the gods is the first duty of the nation and, since the nation is embodied in the king, the king's prime function is to assure that goodwill and so to secure the prosperity of all his subjects. In theory, therefore, all sacrifices were performed by the king. In practice, of course, this duty had to be to a large extent delegated to officers appointed by him, but there were certain festivals so important that the king had to celebrate them in person, and even the conduct of a military campaign could not excuse him from taking the chief part in, for instance, the festival of the Great Goddess of Arinna; the extent to which the normal functions of royalty were in Hatti overshadowed by the duties of priesthood is made clear by the fact that on Hittite monuments the king is almost without exception represented as wearing his sacerdotal garments and performing some religious rite.

The deities worshipped with so much state ceremony were at once formidable and kindly. 'Thou, Sun goddess of Arinna, thou art a benevolent goddess; man, O Sun goddess of Arinna, is dear to thee, thou dost grant him pardon; thou art the light of heaven and of earth, thou art the father and the mother of all lands.' But they were severe, visting the sins of the father upon the children: 'If any man offend the spirit of a god, will the god for that sin punish him alone? Will he not punish that man's wife, his children and his descendants, his household, his slaves male and female, his flocks and his herds, his harvest? Will he not completely destroy him? For your own sakes therefore fear greatly the word of god.' The divine wrath is caused by man's sin; therefore man must make humble confession of his sins; 'if a slave commits a fault and he confesses his wrongdoing to his master, the master does to him what he will, but because he has admitted his fault to his master the spirit of his master is calmed and the master does not punish his slave'. So should the gods act towards the sinner who confesses his trespasses; the prayer of penitence, therefore, if it is to be effective, should begin with a humble confession; the king himself, speaking in the name of all his people, will say, 'Thus is it, this and that have we done'. Naturally, the suppliant will plead excuses; the offence may be of old standing, 'I was a child then and know nothing of it'; but the fact remains, there has been sin, 'our fathers have sinned', and there must be confession and due amends in order that man may be restored in the favour of the gods. In striking contrast to the religion of Mesopotamia, that of the Hurri and the Hittites had a very definite ethical content, so much so that the moral virtues were personified and deified; there was a god of sincerity, a god of righteous dealing and a god of justice. Nor was this a mere form; for such a quality as sincerity the Hittites showed a genuine regard. No Babylonian monarch would have begun his autobiography as King Idri-mi of Alalakh did, with the frank admission that he had spent the first seven years of his reign in exile, nor is there any eastern parallel to the *apologia* of Hattusilis III of Hatti; there the Great King, victor in many wars, who could conclude a treaty on equal terms with the Pharaoh of Egypt, recognizes that there have been incidents in his life which might be interpreted as showing disloyalty and ill faith, and he attempts to justify himself by giving what purports to be a simple and straightforward account of the facts; that such a man should feel justification of himself to be necessary is a striking tribute to Hittite ethics.

In his *apologia* Hattusilis describes how he received instructions from Ishtar, the goddess of Samuha, in dreams. Dreams were one of the regular channels through which man might enter into relations with the gods and, to obtain such, incubation was practised; thus, when King Mursilis wanted to learn the cause of the plague that was devastating the land he ordered all the priests to sleep in a holy place and prayed that one of the gods should manifest the truth through their dreams. Whether or not there was an answer depended, of course, on the god's goodwill; there were other channels whereby a response of some sort could always be secured, by sacrificial omens, by the flight of birds, and by the casting of lots. The first method, the examination of the liver of the sheep or other victim of sacrifice and the interpretation of the marks thereon had been learned from the Mesopotamians, as is evident from the fact that in the Hittite texts dealing with the subject the technical terms are taken over from the Akkadian; at Alalakh there was found a clay model of a liver mapped out diagrammatically to show the significance of its markings which closely resembles examples from Babylonia; a similar liver in bronze found at Piacenza in Italy witnesses to the cultural influence of the Hittites on the Etruscans. Auspication, the obtaining of omens from the flight and action of birds, was essentially a Hurro-Hittite custom. King Idri-mi in exile consulted the birds as well as the sheep's intestines before he could shape the policy of his return. Mursilis II had sent his general Nuanna to repel an invasion of the armies of Hajasa, and the general writes to say that his senior officers demand omens of success before risking a battle—'Will not the matter be determined by the birds and the entrails?' The king, who was far away, at Carchemish, kept there by threats of a possible Assyrian attack, answered, 'I have demanded for thee the oracles by the birds and by the entrails, and the matter has been determined for thee by the birds and by the entrails. Forward! The Storm god, my Lord, has already delivered this enemy of Hajasa into thy hands, and thou shalt smite him.'

More often these omens were consulted not to foretell the future but to determine the source from which had come any evil that afflicted the consultant, so that he might know how to deal with it. If the source were an evil spirit, then magical rites were called for; but if he was afflicted by god, then he must confess and must make atonement. The distinction may seem fine-drawn, but it is a real distinction based upon Hittite theological belief. The gods are good and therefore cannot be the source of evil; if evil shows itself, it must be due either to malicious and evil spirits or to man's offences against the gods, for such automatically involve the punishment which the justice of the gods is bound to enforce. There can be no propitiation of the evil spirits; they can and must be overcome by charms and spells. If, however, divination proves that man is ultimately to blame ('We are sinners. Mankind is evil', declares Mursilis II, and 'Mankind is evil', repeats his successor Muwattalis) then by prayer and sacrifice the gods may be persuaded to temper justice with mercy. Sacrifice was essential, because the purpose of sacrifice was not merely to give to the gods the food they needed; before sacrificing, the man must purify himself; he can lay upon the victim his own guilt and so acquit himself by its death; the blood of the victim forms a special libation poured out before the god (not smeared upon the person of the suppliant as in Phoenician ritual) and creates a bond of mystical union between god and man; and the sacrificial banquet which followed brought god and man into still closer communion.

Such a conception ruled out altogether the human sacrifices which were demanded by the religion of the Semites of Syria. It is true that this has been disputed, chiefly on the strength of one 'ritual of purification', but the text really implies nothing of the sort. The ritual states that if troops have been defeated by the enemy 'they cut in halves a man, a goat, a puppy and a little pig; they place half on this side and half on that side, and in front they make a gate of . . . wood and stretch a [?] over it, and in front of the gate they light fires on this side and on that, and the troops walk right through, and when they come to the river they sprinkle water over them'. There is no reference here to any god or to any normal ritual of sacrifice. The troops have been beaten, and the punishment for cowardice should be death or, at least, decimation; instead, one man is chosen as scapegoat for the disgraced army and is killed, as are three animals, two of which, be it noticed, are unclean and not fit offerings for the gods. With the halves of the victims, and with wood and fire, there is built a 'gate-way', a sort of Caudine Forks, through which the troops must march, and by that act of self-degradation, followed by purification in running water, they are purged of the stigma of defeat. This is no case of 'human sacrifice';[31] it is a ritual for restoring military discipline at a minimum cost; everything that we are told about the very human character of the Hittite gods shows that a feast on human flesh would have been most distasteful to them.

Sacrifice was the proper accompaniment of prayer, whether prayer was for forgiveness or to secure blessings; the servant must by such means win the favour of his divine masters. What the Hittite sought to obtain from the gods was their protection in general, against all the misfortunes that assail mankind, and, in particular, good health, long life, and prosperity for himself and his descendants, all material blessings. In the many prayers that have come down to us there is no mention of anything to do with life beyond the grave. In so far as the custom prevailed of placing objects with the ashes of the dead it would seem that the Hittites entertained some ideas regarding a future existence. The practice of cremation is not inconsistent with such, although it rules out the cruder tenets which informed the funerary rites of the Egyptians, and it is difficult to assume that the Hittites rejected altogether any belief in life's continuance when we see dolls and toy soldiers arranged around a child's cinerary urn. But the silence of the texts may well imply that the belief played a very small part in formal religion.

Just as the Hurri and the Hittites adopted and syncretized the gods of various lands and various tribes, so too they borrowed freely the mythological stories current amongst those with whom they came in contact. The Babylonian legends of the Creation and of the Flood were taken over and given a certain amount of local colour. In the Telepınus myth we have a nature-story which, like the Babylonian Ishtar legend and the Syrian Adonis legend, recounts the desolation that overwhelms the earth when the green growth of springtime is killed by the summer heats; it may be derived from the Mesopotamian original (in which case it has been very radically remodelled) or it may be an independent version of an almost universal allegory; in the Hittite tale Telepinus is not killed but from some personal whim chooses to disappear from earth, with the result that all life dries up and withers, and the gods themselves are hard put to it to find food. The Sun god sends an eagle to search for Telepinus in the valleys, the mountains and the depths of the sea; but the eagle fails; the Storm god himself goes in search and looks in the temple of Telepinus, but he is not there. The eagle is sent out a second time but returns, saying, 'I find him not'. Finally the mother of the gods sends out a bee, saying, 'Go, search for Telepinus; if you find him, sting him in the hands and the feet and get him to appear; take of your wax and clean his wounds, make him pure and sound, and bring him to me'. The Storm god is doubtful of success, but the mother of the gods replies, 'Leave the bee alone; she will go and find him', and the missing god is safely brought back. Obviously the detail of the myth is purely Anatolian. The Kumarpi myths are definitely Hurrite by origin; the myth of the serpent Illujanka, which has for its hero the Storm god of Nerik, is presumably, therefore, Anatolian.

The myths with their primitive savagery seem to have little in common with the developed religion as presented by the texts of the fourteenth and thirteenth centuries BC; they belong to an old tradition and may originally have been associated with one or other of the local cults which later were combined into a single and more or less harmonious system. But even under that system the local variants preserved something of their independent character, and an outstanding instance is that of the Storm god whose special attribute was the double axe; it was perhaps his cult that was adopted by the Cretans of Knossos, and it survived till far later times as that of Zeus Labrandeus. The influence of the Hurro-Hittites upon Greek religion is indeed remarkable. The classical Greeks themselves were aware that the cult of Dionysos came to them from Asia; now we find that the Hesiodic theogony is in part derived from Anatolian sources. Some of this borrowing may have been due to trade connections; thus, the legend of Zeus and Typhon is based upon that of Kumarpi and was probably brought to Greece by Greek merchants who lived at the trade-port at the mouth of the Orontes, under the shadow of that Mount Kasios which, according to Greek and Hurri versions alike, was the scene of the divine battle. Some stories and beliefs may have come through the 'Achaeans' of western Asia Minor. But in many cases, whatever the channel may have been, the source is beyond doubt. When we consider further the *haruspices* of Etruria and of Rome, and remember that the Flood story of the Hebrew Genesis is definitely coloured by the Hurri version (actually the longest extant account of the Gilgamesh epic is represented in the Hurri translation)[32] we shall realize that for the study of ancient religion that of the Hurri and the Hittites has a quite peculiar importance.

SYRIA

The peoples who at the beginning of the third millennium inhabited what we may call Syria, forebears of those described in the Old Testament as Moabites, Edomites, Canaanites, Phoenicians and the rest, were all of Semitic stock and shared what were essentially the same religious beliefs;[33] but the very different conditions of life of the different peoples inevitably introduced variations in the local cults which almost obscure the underlying unity. It was not to be expected that the nomads of the eastern deserts should be moved by the same ideas as were natural for the dwellers in the fertile coastland, nor would the southern tribes have those political contacts which in the north added such a god as Hadad to the native pantheon. The Phoenicians, according to their own tradition (and it is presumably correct), were immigrants whose original home had been far to the east, somewhere on the Persian Gulf, and the faith that they brought with them was in all likelihood the relatively simple one which in much later times persisted in the east. It happens that we are far better documented on the subject of the Phoenician religion than on that of any of the other peoples of these regions (except the Hebrews), and we can see how profoundly their religion had been modified by environment towards the middle of the second millennium BC.

The soil of the coastal strip is naturally fertile. The high mountain range which cuts it off from the interior attracts a rainfall which can be considerable but is capricious and may sometimes fail almost entirely, and there is no water supply that could be utilized for artificial irrigation. The growing crops may be injured by the hot breath of the *khamsîn* wind blowing from the southern desert, or annihilated by that other desert plague, the swarms of locusts. The transition from the rainy season of winter to the parched and torrid summer is abrupt. The rivers are too few and too small to have much importance, but abundant springs break out all along the foot of the mountain range and even in the sea. A people so situated was bound to emphasize the cult of the agrarian gods—the gods of the soil, of water, of vegetation, those who represented the contrasting powers of summer and winter; moreover, a settled people made wealthy by trade and long accustomed to city life was bound to formalize its religious practice with an elaboration unknown to the desert dweller.

The original head of the pantheon, Elyon, 'the Most High God', from whom and his consort, the Earth goddess, were descended all the other gods, seems to have been in the course of time supplanted by his son Bel, a solar deity who is king of heaven, the author of creation and the supreme judge.[34] Ba'al, afterwards identified with Hadad, the northern god of the storm, was primarily the lord of the mountains whose home was in the Lebanon range and on Carmel; his son, Aliyan Ba'al, a god of the nether world, was lord of the springs and wells and of the mountain torrents which come from the mountains, and, because there are fresh-water springs in the sea, lord of the ocean also. The Semitic god of vegetation, the inventor of barley and of the plough, was Dagan, whose worship can be traced from Ashdod in Philistia northwards to Mari, where he was 'the King of the land', into Assyria where Shamshi-Adad I, contemporary of Hammurabi, proclaims himself as 'he who reveres the god Dagan', and southwards again into Sumer where the kings of Isin bear the names Idin-Dagan and Ishme-Dagan. The chief goddess was Astarte, whose worship was perpetuated by the Philistines; originally a goddess of procreation and fecundity, she was later confused with the goddesses Asherat and Anat, the latter being the leading character in the old myth of Ba'al and Aliyan Ba'al. The myth, which epitomizes the agrarian nature of the Syrian cults, describes the struggle between Aliyan Ba'al as lord of the springtime growth and his opposite, the god Mot, spirit of the summer harvest.

It is the war of the two seasons. High summer reigns and Aliyan Ba'al has been banished to the underworld and the temple of Ba'al exists no longer. Anat calls upon the help of Ba'al, and the god reconquers for her the mountain heights of Lebanon; then she conducts a mass-sacrifice of human children and with their blood rejuvenates the old god El and secures from him the rebuilding of Ba'al's temple which, at the beginning of winter, is opened with a holocaust of sheep and cattle, and Ba'al promises 'to fatten gods and men and to make to live again the multitudes of the earth'. But as the hot suns strike on the olives and the fruit trees Ba'al must yield up his throne; he descends into the underworld amid universal mourning in which even Mot joins, and Anat performs his funeral rites. She begs of Mot, now again enthroned, to restore her brother from the dead, describing the horrors of the drought due to his death—'Life abandons the sons of men'—but Mot refuses, relying on that higher dispensation which 'put into the hands of Mot, the divine Son, the lowlands that lack the rain which falls from heaven'. Since prayers are unavailing Anat has recourse to force. 'She seizes Mot, the divine Son. With a blade she cuts him, with the winnowing-fan she winnows him, with the fire she parches him, with the quernstone she grinds him'; the harvest is in, and the new year begins with the winter rains—'the heavens will rain down fatness and the rivulets will run with honey'.

The myth, recited in the mystery-plays performed in the Syrian temples, is in its essential nature-worship identical with that of Ishtar and Dumuzi (Tammuz) in Mesopotamia and that of Isis and Osiris in Egypt: indeed, according to tradition, Egypt got the story from Syria, just as Greece derived from it the legend of Adonis, 'Adoni', 'My Lord', as Ba'al Aliyan is called upon a Phoenician altar from Byblos. In religion as in other things the Phoenicians were the middlemen for international exchange, and of the many Asiatic elements in Greek mythology not a few must have been introduced by Phoenician merchants of the Early Iron Age visiting the harbours of Greece.

But while the Syrians might cast the legends of their gods in a picturesque and dramatic form which commended them to foreign hearers, there was nothing in their religion that could help to advance man's conception of the divine. The myth of Aliyan Ba'al is as savage and brutal as the natural phenomena personified in it, and the Syrian cults faithfully reflected that savagery. The Hebrew prophets who brought against them the accusation that 'they sacrificed their sons and their daughters to idols, and the land was defiled with blood' did them no injustice, for with the Phoenicians at least the custom of sacrificing the first-born persisted long after neighbouring peoples had learnt to substitute an animal for a human victim; the story of Jephtha's daughter and the child-sacrifices which were practised in the valley of Tophet outside the walls of Jerusalem show that even the regions east of the mountain range long observed the same barbarous rites. Whereas most of the peoples of the Middle East held the simple view that sacrifice was necessary because the gods, man-like, were hungry and must be fed, for the Syrian it was a magic rite; through the blood of the victim the offrant has access to his god, and therefore he anoints his hands with the blood before he makes his prayer. Even the animal victim is only a substitute for the offrant; by the laying-on of hands he identifies the beast with himself and by the proper ritual charges it with his own sins, making it a 'scapegoat' by whose death he is freed from all guilt before god. Undoubtedly the formal religion of the later Jews borrowed much from the old Semitic ritual, just as Christianity was to borrow from contemporary paganism; but it was the adaptation of outward forms only. So far as we can see—and the Ugarit tablets afford evidence enough—the religion of the coastal Semites was singularly lacking in moral and ethical content and contributed nothing to later human thought.

CRETE

It has been stated above (p. 66) that in the first half of the second millennium BC Cretan civilization was in many ways the finest of the old Mediterranean world, and on the strength of that it might be expected that its contribution to the history of man's religious beliefs would be proportionately great. But such is not the case. We possess many cult figures, many religious symbols and, on intaglios and seal-impressions, a vast number of illustrations of what seem to be religious characters and of unmistakable ritual; but in the absence of documentary evidence the interpretation of all this is arbitrary and subjective. Almost every scholar (and there are many such) who has written on the subject of Cretan religion has on almost every point arrived at conclusions different from those of the others. Nor is this divergence confined to details; it is fundamental. One writer declares that the religion was a dual monotheism, the Supreme Principle being personified as a woman to whom was subordinate a young male—'there is no evidence for more deities than these'; for another there was a plurality of gods and goddesses having special functions; for some, the head of the Cretan pantheon is the Great Mother, to be identified with Cybele, Isis and Astarte; for others, the ubiquitous symbol of the Double Axe bespeaks a Great God like the Hurrian Teshub, later to become Zeus Labrandeus, whose double axe, the *labrys,* accounts for the name of the Labyrinth of Knossos. The uncertainty of interpretation is increased by the fact that the evidence on which all arguments are based is mixed, some being definitely Minoan and some Mycenaean; we cannot be sure that the two peoples had the same religion, and even where there seems to be continuity there can be no assurance that the Mycenaeans, while taking over from their predecessors the forms of religion, necessarily preserved the content of those forms unchanged. In a history such as this it were best to keep, so far as possible, to the few facts about which there can be no doubt.

No excavation has yet brought to light anything that deserves the name 'temple'; it is fairly safe to say that such did not exist. Numerous sacred caves, rock shelters and hill-top shrines have been identified and examined. These were places of pilgrimage, at which offerings were made—the character of the offerings being noticeably different at different sites; essentially natural features, they might be distinguished by a *temenos* wall, an altar of rough masonry, and by a little building which may have been a sanctuary. With the caves we can associate a pillar cult, for in some of them, e.g. in the cave of Eileithyia at Amnisos, and in that of Psychro, there are stalagmitic pillars into the cracks in which the worshippers thrust their votive offerings; that the cult was not confined to these natural baetyls is shown by intaglios where a pillar standing in the open has a bird perched upon it to witness to the immanence of the deity.

With such rustic shrines again must one associate the tree cult. This is amply vouched for by the intaglios, which show the little *temenos* wall, the altar and (sometimes) the aedicule built against or round the tree, while the worshipper grasps one of the tree's branches and a divine figure may sit beneath the shadow of the foliage or may issue from the branches; it is the epiphany of the Tree goddess.

Within the same category of nature-deities must come the well-known figure of the Lady of Beasts. On a seal from Knossos she stands upon a mountain-top, flanked by lions, with a worshipper on one side and a shrine on the other; here she is unmistakably the goddess and the mistress of wild creatures. More often she appears heraldically set between two animals, grasping them by the head or by the foot; or she may grapple with a single beast, or walk accompanied by one, or she may be the huntress armed with spear or bow. Occasionally her place is taken by a male figure, and the latter is manifestly a god,[35] but the Lady of Beasts is far more common than the Lord of Beasts; here, as in other cases, the male deity exists indeed, but plays a subordinate part.

In the palaces and houses of the Minoan period that have been excavated it has generally been possible to recognize cult-rooms or 'chapels' or, at least, a corner or a niche of an ordinary room where an altar, with cult objects, shows that some religious ritual was practised. Such rooms are always very small, and it is not easy to reconcile them with the shrine façade represented in silhouette and repoussé work on certain gold-leaf ornaments from Mycenae; these show a building in three sections, of which the central one stands up high above the side compartments, all alike crowned by horns of consecration; in each compartment a sacred pillar stands upon horns of consecration while, over the side compartments, a bird is perched to symbolize the presence of the deity. Very similar buildings are represented on a gold-leaf plaque from Volo, and also on fragments of a miniature fresco from the Knossos palace; undoubtedly the picture is correct, but the ground-plans of the cult-rooms so far discovered do not correspond with it; it has even been suggested that what is represented is not the exterior façade of the shrine but its interior—the reredos, as it were, with horns of consecration in front of it very much as we see them in the Shrine of the Double Axes at Knossos.

On the altar-ledge of the Shrine of the Double Axes (which is of LM. III., i.e. of Mycenaean, date) there were four crude bell-shaped terra-cotta figures of goddesses or attendants and one of a male worshipper holding a bird; similar cult figures occur regularly in other house—and palace—cult-rooms, but the most famous are the late Middle Minoan III faience figures found in the Central Palace Sanctuary deposit at Knossos (Pl. 41). The distinguishing attribute of these goddesses, as of the fine chryselephantine statuettes such as those now in Boston, is the snakes which they hold in their hands or have coiled about their bodies; elsewhere, as at Gournia, the bell-shaped altar figurines are encircled by or grasp snakes, and a common feature of shrine furniture is a tube-shaped clay vessel decorated with snakes in relief; the domestic cult carried on in palace and house is the cult of a Snake goddess.

It has generally been urged that the snake is the proper attribute of a chthonic deity; therefore the Cretan goddess must be the goddess of the underworld, of the earth beneath whose surface is the realm to which the dead go down and from whose surface the plants and the crops grow up; she is worshipped in the household chapel as the protectress of the house's dead. This may be so, but another view, put forward first by Evans[36] and adopted by Nilsson, would appear preferable. In ancient and in modern folk-lore, including that of Greece, the snake is the guardian and genius of the house—an actual snake is welcomed and respected and may even be fed with milk and bread-crumbs; therefore the Snake goddess is the protectress not of the dead but of the living members of the household. Certainly this accords better with the archaeological facts; the 'snake-tube' sanctuaries go back to the L.M. I period, i.e. are definitely Minoan, and so far as is known the Minoans did not greatly concern themselves with any after-world, and it was only the Mycenaeans who lavished labour and money on great tombs and splendid offerings to the dead.

In the cult-rooms no other deity seems to have been worshipped, for the birds, to whatever species they may belong, probably do no more than symbolize the presence of the divine power. The intaglios give us an astonishing range of what may be called demonology, creatures compounded of man and beast and bird, but whether these are anything more than exercises of the craftsman's fancy it is impossible to say. There is no evidence for anything in the nature of a bull cult; the horns of consecration may well originate from the bucranium (with which they are sometimes associated) but the bucranium stands for the sacrifice, not for the god. The case for the double axe is doubtful; we may see in it the special aniconic form of the supreme deity, or we may regard it as simply the sacrificial instrument which by virtue of its function has come to be considered holy; certainly it is never seen in the hands of a male god, but only in those of women.

Our actual knowledge regarding Minoan religion is, then, limited to this, that there were, on the one hand, the rustic deities of caves and trees and hill-tops and, on the other, the domestic deities who looked after each individual house and were worshipped within its walls; there were gods as well as goddesses, but the latter played a far more important role. Apparently there were no proper temples, and apparently no professional priesthood, for neither the family cult nor the pilgrim's offering called for such. Animal sacrifices were offered to the rustic gods, for these are represented on the intaglios; libations were poured out of vessels of prescribed form and offerings were made of fruit and flowers; above all, the gods were honoured by dances, and we are shown the worshippers reeling in an orgiastic ritual.

Generally speaking, the scenes upon the intaglios suggest that the Minoan religion was in keeping with the character of Minoan art, picturesque, humane and cheerful. The Snake goddesses protect the house, the Lady of Beasts is man's ally, and the divinity immanent in baetyl and tree is not likely to be nocuous; the approach to the gods is by feasting and dancing, and if they show themselves in answer to the adorant's prayer their epiphany is awe-inspiring, of course, but with a joyful excitement. This is something utterly unlike the beliefs and practices of Egypt, of Mesopotamia and of Phoenicia. Whether any element of it was to survive and influence later societies, whether the 'fair dancing-place which Daedalus made for Ariadne' may have helped to mould the Dionysiac choruses of the Attic stage it would be rash to say; but at least we may grant to the Minoans a conception of the gods which was neither slavish nor savage but innocently gay.

THE HEBREWS

The family from which the Hebrew nation claimed descent belonged to the western branch of the Semitic people, the Amorites of the Old Testament, which contrasts these inhabitants of the north-eastern steppes stretching from the Jordan rift northwards to the Anatolian foothills with the Canaanites of southern Syria. According to Hebrew tradition the proper home of the family was at Harran, but a branch of it had established itself at Ur, in which city Abraham was said to have been born.[37] Those two cities, Harran and Ur, were the capitals of the two earthly realms whereof Nannar, the Moon god, was the king, and it was inevitable that anyone living in either of the cities should acknowledge the supreme authority of the divine ruler. Whatever relics of the original Semitic religion of his house Abraham may have retained, his real religion was that of Ur, with the cult of the Moon god as its principal element. In later days the Jews were well aware that 'your fathers worshipped strange gods beyond the River' and to that tradition added the legend that Abraham's father, Terah, was by trade a maker of images; we may dismiss the legend, but the truth of the tradition is proved by the fact that the name Terah is taken from the northern (Hurrite) name of the Moon god who was worshipped as Terah in Harran and as Nannar in Ur. Hebrew religion, therefore, is rooted in that of Sumer.

Although there is no evidence sufficient to fix any precise date for Abraham (see note 37) the various chronologies that have been attempted so far agree that his time of residence at Ur can safely be assigned to the Larsa period, i.e. between 1920 and 1800 BC. Now, as has been explained in the section dealing with Sumerian religion (p. 458) this is exactly the period in which the cult of the family god reached its full development, when every house possessed its domestic chapel beneath whose pavement lay the graves of the family's forebears and when family worship filled the void left in man's religious consciousness by the growing exclusiveness of temple ritual and by Nannar's failure to protect his kingdom against foreign enemies. That the household of Terah followed the example of his neighbours at Ur in this respect also could be safely assumed, but no assumption is necessary; when Jacob made a covenant with his cousin Laban he invoked the sanction of just this family god, 'the God of Abraham and the God of Nahor, the God of their father'; this is no personal deity but that unnamed divine being which personifies the family throughout its successive generations and is for its members the operative power in all their family affairs.

The removal of Abraham's household from Ur to Harran had no significance so far as its religious observances were concerned. Here, too, the state worship centred upon the Moon god as Lord of the City; much, at any rate, of the popular mythology had been borrowed from Sumer; that the cult of the family god was practised here also is evidenced by the Hurrite law which laid it down that possession of the figures of the family god (the teraphim of the Book of Genesis xxxi. 19, 30) constituted a claim to primogeniture. At Harran, then, Abraham would have been completely at home; it was when he migrated thence into the relatively barbarous surroundings of Palestine[88] that the first step was taken which led to the isolation of the Hebrews as a 'peculiar people'.

Wherever he went Abraham would take with him the traditions of civilized life with which he had been imbued at Ur; on the intellectual, ethical and moral sides the change of country would mean no change of character. It is, indeed, made quite clear by the Old Testament narrative that the patriarchal family did in fact continue to observe the Sumerian social standards to which the elders were accustomed. But in the matter of religion migration into Canaan involved a complete break with the past. The supreme authority of the Moon god naturally ended at the frontiers of his kingdom, and it could be extended beyond them only by conquest; Nannar could not accompany the most devoted of his subjects into a land in which he would be at best but a stranger admitted on sufferance. But apart from this, the Moon god had to be properly housed; for his residence on earth he required a temple, the 'house of God', served by his accredited priests, and that was something that no wanderer could supply. The Moon god, therefore, had to be left behind. And the same was true of the other major gods; they had to have their temples; they were all localized deities, whether they bore rule in kingdoms of their own or, as at Ur, formed part of the court of the locally supreme god and so had their own 'houses' built for them in his territory and at his expense. Even those minor powers, exercising a strictly limited jurisdiction, whose little shrines we have seen wedged in between the private houses in the streets of Ur, needed a dwelling, however simple—and in any case they were far too numerous and far too seldom invoked to be exported *en masse*. The only god whom Abraham could take with him, of all those whom he had known and worshipped, was the nameless family god who *was* the family and, if the family moved, could not be left behind.

It is, of course, true that every traveller at that time was faced with the same predicament; the gods were local and could not go with him on his travels. But the normal solution was simple enough. A man passed from the territory of one god to that of another. Naturally he was bound to accept and acknowledge the established government of each land that he entered; where the government was exercised by a god he would automatically recognize that god's local supremacy, and on his return home he would resume the worship of his native deity without any consciousness of past disloyalty. This political-religious shift of allegiance would, under normal conditions, have imposed itself upon Abraham, and the story of his paying tithe to the priest-king of Salem suggests that he was prepared to practise it; but conditions were not normal. As a pastoralist accompanied by his flocks Abraham was obliged to avoid as far as possible the little Canaanite towns ringed about with their agricultural domains and to keep to the open country which was more or less no-man's-land; there the writ of the gods of the city states did not run, there were no temples of the sort to which he had been accustomed, and such crude 'high places' as he may have passed would not appeal to him as being in any sense 'houses' of gods. Admittedly it was difficult not to be affected in some degree by the opinions and beliefs of the people whom he met, and who presumably knew what was right in their part of the world; the proposal to sacrifice his first-born, Isaac, was an unwilling concession to local practice. But the town-bred family of Terah had a supreme contempt for the barbarous peoples of Canaan (Rebekah thought that life was not worth living if she had to associate with 'the daughters of the land'),[39] and the civilized traditions of Ur were strong enough to make the patriarch reject the demands of Canaanite ritual. There was no denying the existence of the great gods. The growing clan had brought with them the mythological legends which were current equally in Ur and in Harran (it was the northern version that they had made their own), and these were passed down from father to son to form the background of faith; but for practical purposes it was the family god that mattered because with him alone they could be in contact, and inevitably he tended to assume for himself the powers which really belonged to the great gods; the mediator tended to become the giver and the source of giving. The head of the clan conducted the worship of the family god—the God of Abraham, of Isaac and of Jacob—in the traditional manner, sacrificing to him not in any temple but upon a makeshift altar set up wherever the camp might be pitched, and although, by means of intermarriage with native women, 'strange gods' did find their way into the hands of the clansmen, yet such were regarded as unorthodox (Gen. xxxv. 2) and had to be given up; it would seem that throughout the period of the patriarchal residence in Canaan the cult of the family god remained unadulterated.

It was different in Egypt. The Hebrews were still shepherds, and were living only on the outskirts of the Nile valley, but they were associated with and subject to a people whose civilization they could not despise, governed by a king who was himself a god, and settled in the proximity of towns where magnificent temples housed the gods in whose territories they dwelt. It was a fortunate thing for them that the Egyptians, for whom shepherds were 'an abomination'—the prejudice reflects their national hatred of the Hyksos conquerors—kept the Hebrews at arm's length; but even so the process of assimilation went far, and the faith of the patriarchs was very nearly swamped by the organized religion of Egypt. Persecution emphasized their racial identity, but the peculiar beliefs and practices of their forefathers were largely forgotten.

According to Hebrew tradition, as set out in the book of Exodus, the flight of Moses, a prominent Hebrew,[40] into the land of Midian proved to be the salvation of his people. In the tent of Jethro, whose daughter he married, he could take part in the domestic ritual conducted by his father-in-law and recover the knowledge of Semitic religion which Egyptian influences had almost obliterated. In the hill pasturages of Midian he could forget the temples of the Nilotic towns and fall back upon the cult of the God of Abraham, of Isaac and Jacob. This old nameless god he now identified with the Yahweh whose worship had been widespread long since amongst the Western Semites and whom he now rediscovered in the wilderness where Jethro pastured his flocks; by this identification the family god of the patriarchal clan gained in stature and, without any change of character, could be the god of what had become a considerable tribe.

Although Moses' demand to Pharaoh that he should let the Israelites go in order that they might hold a feast in the wilderness implied to Pharaoh—and probably to the Israelites—that theirs was, like others, a local deity who could be worshipped properly only in his own domains, the conception of a tribal god was manifest from the outset. When the migration from Egypt began 'Judah was His sanctuary and Israel His dominion', so that 'the sea fled' before the face of a new power and 'the mountains shook' at the coming of a god who was not their local lord. To the Israelites the idea of a god whose sphere was not a place but a society must have been difficult to grasp, even though it was visibly symbolized by the fire and cloud that accompanied their march; when they entered the district in southern Sinai where Egyptian miners had set up their temple of Hathor they reverted to the beliefs they had acquired in Egypt and fashioned the golden calf in honour of the Cow goddess who was the prescriptive mistress of the land.[41] Only after a lapse of time during which those to whom the Nilotic customs had become second nature had died, and a new generation had grown up in the isolation of the desert and under the instruction of Moses, could the idea of a peripatetic tribal god untrammelled by space be accepted as fundamental.

The creed that Moses taught was not, properly speaking, monotheistic, but it was uncompromisingly monolatrous. The heterogeneous crowd of refugees that came out of Egypt had somehow or other to be hammered into a national unit, failing which they would be submerged in the population of Canaan and disappear, and the birthright of the patriarchs would be lost with them. The one thing that could weld them together was the patriarchal faith, and that must be exclusive. The Israelites must acknowledge allegiance to no other god; in that they would be a peculiar people distinguished from all others; but their god must be exclusively the god of Israel, the champion of them alone and the enemy of all other peoples and all other gods. The continuity of tradition must be upheld, but at the same time a new dispensation must be recognized; the tribal god was 'the god of your fathers, the god of Abraham, of Isaac and of Jacob', but no less emphatically was he 'the god that brought you out of the land of Egypt'; that deliverance marked the beginning of a new era. What may have been the custom in patriarchal times was now formalized into an ordinance—there was to be no material representation of the god who was immanent in the tribe—'thou shalt not make to thyself any graven image . . . thou shalt not bow down to them nor serve them'; but in order that men might not forget that their god was present amongst them a special tent was prepared for him and an order of priests established for his service.

Considering how large a part the preparation for the next world played in the religion of Egypt, with which the Israelites were familiar, it is curious that the Mosaic creed has nothing whatever to say about any life after death; the incentive to virtue is 'that thy days may be long in the land which the Lord thy God giveth thee'. The whole of the moral code is based upon the divine sanction, but it does not attain any high level; its ordinances are such as would naturally be observed by the members of a nomad tribe towards one another. Murder is forbidden, but the law of the blood-feud is allowed; adultery is forbidden, but this applies only to adultery with a married woman whereby the line of descent is broken and the right of heritage endangered; theft is forbidden, but god promises to his followers all the wealth of Canaan provided that they faithfully exterminate its present owners. Granted, however, that the laws which can be attributed to Moses do not in substance rise above the level of the ethics of a primitive society, they possess one unusual quality; they are not put forward as the codification of traditional custom but claim to be the direct orders of the tribal deity. Consequently any infraction of the laws is not merely a social offence but a sin against god. The laws dealing with man's relations to god are put on the same footing as those that regulate his behaviour to his 'neighbour'; the mere form of the decalogue brings everyday life and religion into closer contact than had been effected by any other established creed.

The traditional forty years of wandering in the wilderness was none too long a time to inculcate the new faith in the hearts and minds of a people accustomed to the splendours of Egyptian ritual, but that faith was likely to be exposed to yet greater dangers in Palestine. The social legislation of Moses, and many of his religious ordinances, were expressly designed for a nomad tribe[42] and might well prove ill-adapted to a people settling down to a sedentary life in villages and towns. But in fact that danger was minimized by the character of the settlement in its earlier phases, and it would seem that the course followed was not fortuitous but deliberately planned to avoid the risks of too sudden social change.

It is true that the Israelites had been promised 'great and goodly cities which thou buildedst not, and houses full of all good things which thou filledst not, and wells digged which thou diggedst not, vineyards and olive trees which thou plantedst not';[43] but they were warned that that was the time when their allegiance to their god would be most imperilled. Events proved that this was indeed so. The initial victories over Sihon and Og won for the Israelites a considerable territory in Moab; they settled down in the Moabite 'cities' and promptly adopted the worship of the Moabite gods; it was because of this apostasy that when Midian in its turn was conquered Moses 'burnt all their cities wherein they dwelt, and all their goodly castles, with fire' and pitilessly slaughtered all the inhabitants except the unmarried girls.

But the main promise, constantly repeated to the tribe, was of a very different sort; they were to be brought into 'a land flowing with milk and honey'. The prospect offered to them was not of agricultural land, for which their whole experience made them unsuited, but of the rough uplands of the Judean hills, where there was all-the-year-round grazing for their sheep and goats and, thanks to the exuberant flowers of springtime, the wild bees furnished plenty of that sweetness which otherwise life lacked. It was a miserably poor land if judged by the standards of civilized man, but a veritable paradise for shepherds accustomed to the scanty pasturage of the Sinaitic desert. The prospect was quite understood, and for the bulk of the Israelites was the best that they could desire; only the tribes of Reuben and Gad, because they possessed numbers of cattle looted from the Midianites, demanded, and were allowed, to settle in Gilead, east of Jordan 'which is a land for cattle'; the other tribes asked nothing better than the hill pastures. This accorded well with what was clearly the deliberate policy of their leaders; for as long as possible the Israelites were to remain a pastoral community living apart from the more civilized Canaanites who might corrupt them. The capture of Jericho was essential, in that it blocked the road into the promised land, but the city was promptly laid waste and a curse invoked on anyone who should try to rebuild it; in the same way the town of Ai was burnt 'and made a heap for ever'. The towns and villages of the petty 'kings' who opposed the invaders were destroyed and their inhabitants exterminated, but the larger centres, with the exception of Hazor, escaped, not only because their defences were too strong for the undisciplined forces of Israel but also because they lay in the lowlands and therefore were not coveted by the shepherds. The policy is made evident by what is said concerning the Anakim; those were cut off 'from all the mountains of Judah and from all the mountains of Israel', and their settlements there 'utterly destroyed', but their main lowland cities, Gaza, Gath and Ashdod, were left in their hands unmolested. Joshua's aim was the occupation of the hill country, where his followers should remain nomad, isolated by their manner of life from the temptations of Canaanite civilization. To some extent the policy was followed, and even as late as the reign of Merneptah of Egypt (1225–1215 BC) the Pharaoh, in his song of triumph over his Syrian campaign, while he boasts of the capture of cities like Gezer and Askalon, uses of Israel an expression which does not necessarily refer even to a settled agricultural people.

The plan of isolation was not carried out systematically. Not nearly all the old inhabitants could be slain by the sword—even Jerusalem remained an enemy outpost until the days of the kingdom; many were put to tribute or admitted as allies, and, on the plea of blood-brotherhood, accepted as fellow-Israelites. Such may have been the origin of the tribes of Dan, Zebulon and Asher, seeing that in about 1430 BC, before the invasion under Joshua, King Idri-mi of Alalakh took refuge with the Habiru[44] who then occupied the territory assigned in the Old Testament to those tribes; indeed, Asher and Zebulon are mentioned by name in the legend of Kereth[45] and must therefore have been in Palestine—though not necessarily in the same area—at a still earlier date. The Book of Judges describes the constant apostasy of sections of the Israelites, generally of the more northerly tribes; it was due to their intercourse with the various races surrounding them, and in many cases may have been but a relapse from a conversion prompted more by political motives than by any rooted belief; so can we explain the final apostasy of the northern kingdom of Israel instigated by the rebel king Jeroboam. In the south country, however, the tribes of Judah and Benjamin, together with the priestly house of Levi, concentrated in the inhospitable tangle of the Judean hills, could better preserve themselves from contact with their neighbours.

It is remarkable that in spite of the important part played by the Philistines in later Hebrew history the Old Testament is completely silent about their arrival in the coastal plain; the great invasion of the Peoples of the Sea which threatened the existence of Egypt and changed the whole complexion of the Middle East seems to have passed unnoticed by the Hebrews. The invaders advanced generally along the coast and turned inland only if it were necessary to crush some city that otherwise might threaten their flank; obviously the Hebrew tribes presented no danger, and if so it was because they were still largely a pastoral people in the process of settling down to agriculture with the village as the largest unit of society. In this conservative existence, when even the Ark of the Covenant was kept not in a builded temple but in the tent that recalled the desert wanderings, the pure doctrine of the Mosaic teaching could be maintained intact. None the less, there was a marked development of the Mosaic conception. In Sinai the God of Abraham, of Isaac and of Jacob had become the God of Israel, and since Israel was a nomad and a landless folk his dominion had been not territorial but personal, over the tribe as an entity and over the individuals composing it. Now the Israelites possessed a land of their own, and that a considerable one, for all its poverty; in theory at least the 'Twelve Tribes' were united, and by common action they had defeated recognized kingdoms and had maintained their independence. All this was god's doing, and with the growth of his people their conception of god grew likewise; Yahweh was becoming a national god, and the spirit was astir which in due time would make Jerusalem 'the place where men ought to worship'.

THE INDUS VALLEY

The excavation of the ruined cities of Harappā and Mohenjo-daro brought to light an ancient civilization which was at first sight as puzzling as it was unexpected; for it appeared as an isolated phenomenon having no roots that could be traced back into the past and no connection with anything that was to follow it; it seemed wholly alien to India in its character and unrelated to the development of Indian history. We can now see that in part at least its character was formed by contacts with the west (Chapter II) and we can begin to realize that it was not so sterile as its dramatic end made it appear.

It is true that the Aryan invaders completely destroyed[46] that urban civilization which was so much at variance with their own ideas of life. Indra was 'the destroyer of cities', and with the overthrow of the cities the arts and crafts which had ministered to their splendour and depended on the wealth of the citizens for patronage perished also; Aryan victory seems to have involved wholesale massacre—the bodies of women and children lie amongst the ruins of the houses—and there was no chance of any trade revival under the rule of the barbarians. In the light of history it is only natural that the material evidence which archaeology can produce implies that the entire culture came to an abrupt end; the great cities were wrecked and long remained desolated; in the course of time poor squatters camped upon the ruined sites, and the odds and ends of domestic furniture which bear witness to their presence seem to show clearly enough that the old arts of the Harappā civilization had been forgotten.

On the other hand, the mass of the Harappā populace were agriculturalists living not within the city walls but scattered over the countryside; and these people, who constituted no danger to the conquerors, but were economically indispensable, were not massacred but were enslaved. They were not skilled in the arts and crafts of the townsman, but they did share the townsman's religious creeds and practices, and those they would—and obviously did—preserve, perhaps the more faithfully because the only liberty left to them in their serfdom was that of belief.

Of the many buildings excavated at Mohenjo-daro and Harappā not one can be identified with any certainty as a temple or shrine. The many inscriptions found, which might well have been of great value as giving the names of gods and goddesses, are still undeciphered and therefore help us not at all. Our sources of information regarding the religious ideas of the Indus valley people are therefore limited to a few small stone figures which may represent gods; clay figurines, some of which are merely toys, some votive, but some certainly religious ikons; the very numerous seals and amulets of which again some give religious motifs or figures of deities; and, lastly, baetylic stones and phallic symbols. This material evidence, if taken by itself, would tell us little more than that there was, in the Indus valley, a religion that recognized gods in human form, venerated and possibly worshipped various animals, and made a cult of the phallus as representing the reproductive powers of nature, a religion, in short, so uniformly characteristic of any primitive agricultural society as to have no particular interest. Fortunately, however, our evidence is not altogether isolated. Because the religion of Harappā did not die out, but was handed down by successive generations of servile peasants, it is possible to link it up with the known beliefs of later ages and thereby better to estimate not only its intrinsic character but also its historical importance.

The outstanding object is a seal on which is carved the figure of a three-faced god seated on a low Indian stool with knees bent double beneath him, heel to heel, and toes turned down, his arms outstretched and his hands, with the thumbs to the front, resting on his knees, a typical attitude of *Yoga*; he is flanked by animals, an elephant and a tiger on his right, a rhinoceros and a buffalo on his left, and two deer at his feet. This Mohenjo-daro figure can be recognized at once as the prototype of the historic Siva; Siva is represented with three (or with four, or five) faces; he is the *Mahayogi,* the prince of *Yogis,* so that the attitude is proper to him; he is Lord of beasts; and the deer is sacred to him, and two deer, in exactly the pose that we have on the seal, are portrayed on many mediaeval images of Siva, just as, beneath the throne of Buddha, they symbolize the deer-park at Gaya. This is the most convincing, but by no means the only, representation wherein we can recognize the god Siva; a deity in the same *Yogi* attitude figures upon a faience seal and is accompanied by Nagas, one on either side of him, kneeling with hands uplifted in prayer; on another seal the god is again in the same posture but has only one face.

Now Siva was not a member of the early Aryan pantheon; his introduction into it comes later, when the Aryan conquerors had settled down and by association with their subjects absorbed much of their old faith. Similarly the Nagas are still unknown in the literature of the Vedic Age but are prominent in the later literature from the time of the Sutras onwards. Even in modern India the worship of aniconic stones, both natural and worked, plays an important role; the phallic form, the *linga*, is the embodiment of Siva, the vulva form that of his consort Mahädevi; ring-stones, having the same significance, are connected with the goddess of fertility and have many magical properties. None of these would seem to have any place in Aryan cults; all are characteristically Dravidic, but all of them are found in great numbers on the sites of the Indus valley cities. Of the terra-cottas, the hand-modelled female figure with high head-dress, usually nude except for belt and elaborate necklace but sometimes wearing a short kilt, is surely a deity and can safely be identified as the Earth goddess or Mother goddess; another, or perhaps the same, divinity, is represented on seals as in, or issuing from, a *pipal* tree, with a worshipper kneeling before her and seven ministrants or votaries below, an epiphany of a tree spirit like the *Yakshī* of the Bhārhut and Sānchī sculptures; incidentally one may notice that the sanctity of the *pipal* tree does not begin with the Bhodi tree of Gaya; rather because it was and had always been sacred was it chosen for the scene of the Buddha's illumination. Where animals are represented, as they constantly are, it is generally difficult to say whether they are objects of worship at all—they may be symbols or vehicles of an anthropomorphic god, and they may be sacrificial victims; the fact that they are often shown feeding out of a special vessel or associated with such things as lamps, which presumably are cult objects, gives them a ritual significance but does not necessarily mean that they are gods. On the other hand, when the bull (the commonest animal on the seals) is represented as wearing a wreath of flowers, the parallel afforded by modern Indian custom cannot be a mere coincidence.

Without going farther into the details of the archaeological evidence—and much more could be cited—we can safely assert that the religion of classical India is a combination of two very different creeds, that of the Aryan invaders being superimposed on that of the conquered race. An enslaved people is always apt to cling tenaciously to its faith, for the simple reason that belief is the only liberty left to it. The Aryans formed at best a minority, and the disproportion would become more marked as fresh conquests spread their dominion eastwards and southwards. The result was that in time the indigenous faith assumed the leading role; as Sir Mortimer Wheeler has put it, Indra had won the battle, but Siva won the war. But the continuity which we must recognize as a historic fact further implies that the religion of the Indus valley before the Aryan invasion was the religion of Dravidic India, not the special creation of the Harappā culture. It is true that the nude female figurines which represent the Mother goddess are akin to those found in countries to the west, in Elam, Mesopotamia, Syria and Egypt, and that both in their character and in their technique (e.g. the pellet eyeballs inserted in hollow sockets) they bear a remarkable resemblance to the terracottas of Sumer; and since the dominant class in the Harappā state was composed of people who had come into the Indus valley from the west (Chapter I) it might be thought that the figurines belong to a non-Indian cult which those people brought with them from their original home. But an art form can be adapted to an existing tradition without altering its content, and a native idea can be expressed in a foreign technique and still remain fundamentally native; granted that the Harappā figurine-makers were influenced by western models, yet the Mother goddess certainly belongs to the Indian pantheon—in no country is her worship so deep-rooted and ubiquitous as in India. A single representation of a double-headed Janus-like figure has been compared with a Sumerian stone carving of the Gudea period; the figure of the Sumerian demigod Gilgamesh has been more plausibly identified on four or five Mohenjo-daro seals; the dove as a sacred symbol is common at Mohenjo-daro and appears in Mesopotamia also; but none of these gives proof that there was a mixture of western and Indian elements in the Harappā religion. It is, of course, certain that over a long period there were close commercial relations between the Indus and the Euphrates valleys; during the earlier part of that period the Gilgamesh motif was one of the most popular subjects for Sumerian seals, and if it reappears on an Indian seal it can have been borrowed for its decorative value just as well as for its religious significance; in Mesopotamia we find seals with Indian designs which were unquestionably cut by Sumerian craftsmen—they are Mesopotamian cylinders instead of being Indian stamp-seals—and the Indian gem-cutters may in the same way have adopted Sumerian designs. On the evidence that we possess it is safest to assume that the people of Harappā and Mohenjo-daro, while enjoying a material civilization which was peculiar to the Indus valley and its immediate neighbourhood, shared the religion of the Dravidic population of India generally. That assumption justifies our interpretation of the Harappā monuments in the light of later Hinduism; it also makes the ultimate victory of Siva over Indra far more easy to explain than would have been the case had the non-Aryan elements in Hinduism to be attributed to the religion of the Indus valley alone. None the less it is to the Indus valley that the credit should be given for the survival of the religion. The high civilization of the Harappā people could not fail to influence not necessarily the content but the artistic expression of the common faith, producing something unattainable by the other Dravidic peoples, whose culture, as illustrated by archaeological discoveries, was of a relatively very low order. This is obviously true of the Mother goddess figurines with their western technique, and in the same way it needed the refined skill of the Mohenjo-daro gem-cutters to render in glyptic form the attributes and character of Siva. While their more barbarous kinsmen were perforce content with the *linga* and the baetylic stone, the artists of Harappā could translate ideas into visual shapes which would survive the political annihilation of the Harappā state. If by the analogies of later iconography we are able to trace back some of the religious conceptions of Hinduism to the dark ages of the Early Bronze period it is because the art of the Indus valley had represented in inevitable forms the vague persons of the Dravidic gods.

CHINA

In the religions of latter-day China a very prominent part is played by ancestor-worship. Since ancestor-worship is wholly alien to Buddhism in its pure form as taught by Buddha, and since it is not included in the teaching (which is more philosophical than religious) of Lao Tzu, the founder of Taoism, its origin has to be sought elsewhere, and recent discoveries have proved that it is far older than any one of the systems which have been engrafted on it and must be accounted as a survival from the earliest days of Chinese civilization.

The literary evidence available for the Shang period consists in the inscribed oracle-bones found in the Anyang district, and to this must be added the archaeological evidence provided by the tombs. Since the oracle-bones refer almost if not quite exclusively to the king and his family they deal only with the ancestor-worship practised by the royal house, and that may have been peculiar; out since the ritual of burial proves to be essentially the same for all classes—the difference being one of degree only, corresponding to the varying importance of the individual dead—one may take it that ancestor-worship was the common practice of Chinese society as a whole. The ritual was not simply a matter of pious sentiment, though affection might be an extra motive for the recently bereaved; when a king names over forty dead kinsmen, covering twenty-six generations, his offerings do not express a personal affection for each and all; they betoken a religious belief which, if we may judge from the the number of inscriptions which refer respectively to ancestors and to gods in general, was in the Shang creed more practically important than belief in the gods.

According to that belief a man's real power began when he died. Death transformed the mortal man into a spirit, possessed of undefined but vast powers where his descendants were concerned. While not quite omniscient or omnipotent the spirits could grant, or withhold, success in hunting, in agriculture, in war or in anything else, and they could punish those who failed to please them with famine, defeat, sickness or death; so awful were they that it was dangerous even to pronounce the personal names they had borne in life, and they were best designated by their relationship and the day on which they were born or died, as 'Grandfather Tuesday', 'Elder brother Saturday', and so on.

To the dead, then, offerings had to be made, both at the time of burial and afterwards, so long as the family remained. The dead man, wrapped, apparently, in matting, was laid in the grave with such furniture as his relatives could afford—in the case of the very poor a few pottery vessels and perhaps a bronze dagger-axe, while an official of high rank might have a profusion of beautifully cast decorated bronze vessels. These were genuine objects, not the crude copies which in later times were specially manufactured for burial purposes, nor like the flimsy paper imitations of still more recent days; the Shang people seem not to have evolved the idea that spirits can be satisfied as much by the 'ghosts' of things as by the things themselves; for them the spirits were real and the offerings made to them must be real also. In the case of the kings realism was carried to the farthest extent. A pit was dug which might be 60 feet square and over 40 feet deep, with on each side a sloped passage or stairway leading down from ground-level. In the pit, and covering the greater part of its area, there was constructed a tomb-chamber of wood finely carved or adorned with designs in polychrome lacquer; in this was laid the body of the king, and in and around it an astonishing wealth of objects, including such things as chariots with their horses, and the bodies of attendants, women wearing elaborate head-dresses of turquoise or soldiers with copper helmets; then the pit was filled with earth pounded into a solid mass as was done for house foundations, and in the filling more human victims were buried, so that the total number might run into two or three hundred.

After this elaborate ritual of burial, which bears in details a remarkable resemblance to the Sumerian ritual of the Early Dynastic period and may, like the use of metal, be due to western influences,[47] there was still need for the regularly recurrent sacrifices which furnished nourishment for the spirits and won their favourable response to prayer. The spirits of the ancestors dwelt with and were under the rule of Ti, the great god, and they acted as mediators and intercessors between him and their human descendants; prayers to the ancestors take the form of imploring them to ask god to do this or that. This mediation would be forthcoming only if the spirits were satisfied by the proper offerings. The character of these can be gathered from bone inscriptions. Drink offerings of spirituous liquor seem to have been the only product of the soil that was presented to the dead, or to the gods; of such things as bread or fruit there is no mention—in fact, according to a story of the Chou period, when a high official directed in his will that during the first year after his death his favourite delicacy, water-chestnuts, should be sacrificed to him, his strait-laced son decided that filial duty must give way to orthodox tradition and refused to carry out so irregular an order. The normal sacrifices were of men and animals—cattle, sheep, pigs, dogs, and occasionally horses and birds. The total number of victims sacrificed at a time was usually small, from one to ten; but for an important ceremony might be very large—'one hundred cups of liquor, one hundred sheep and three hundred cattle'; and in several inscriptions a hundred and even three hundred human victims are mentioned. The human victims of a tomb sacrifice performed after the actual burial, either as the last act of the ceremony or at a later date, were decapitated and buried in pits, ten to a pit, sometimes with their hands tied behind their backs, furnished each with a uniform outfit of small bronze knives, axe-heads and grinding-stones, and their skulls were buried separately, in small square pits close by. With reference to these victims the bone inscriptions use different words: sometimes 'men', sometimes 'captives', but most often, and always where large numbers are concerned, 'Ch'iang' which, as written, combines the signs for 'men' and 'sheep' and is said to mean 'barbarian shepherds of the West'.

Clearly then the sacrificial victims were not Shang but 'foreigners' and prisoners-of-war; and since on the oracle-bones the question repeatedly asked is 'Shall we be successful in capturing Ch'iang?' it would appear that military expeditions were sent out for the express purpose of collecting offerings for the altars of gods and ancestors. Isolated cases of human sacrifice, usually performed in connection with the death of an emperor or after a military campaign, occur not infrequently down to the sixth century BC, after which time the practice gradually died out as being contrary to the teaching of Confucius. But in the Shang period it was an essential part of Chinese religious ritual.

All sacrifices other than those in the tombs of the kings were celebrated in temples, in 'the House of the Spirits'. About the ritual very little is known. The liquor was poured out on the ground as a libation; animals, or special parts of the animals, were generally burnt by fire, but sometimes buried in the earth or thrown into water; the last two methods were employed for offerings to human ancestors, while the burnt offerings, according to the oracle-bones, were destined for the gods; but how far this distinction really held good it is impossible to say, and it may even be that for the Shang people the distinction was too vague to be consistently observed.

In the bone inscriptions two signs are used for 'spirits'; the first is taken from the human figure and should therefore apply only to ancestors; it might be translated 'ghosts'. The second sign, 示, may represent 'the spiritual forces streaming down from the heavens to men below'; one would therefore expect it to apply only to the gods, but in fact its reference is not always unambiguous, e.g. it forms part of the sign for 'temple', 宗, 'House of Spirits', but the temple is associated with ancestor-worship as much as with the cult of the gods. But there were gods. Some of these were powers of nature or natural features; one oracle-bone records 'a burnt offering of four cattle to the sources of the Haan river', the river on which the city Shang stood, perhaps an offering made because of a drought such as that of *c.* 1190 BC when the river ceased to flow. The earth was a deity which later, and probably in Shang times also, was symbolized by an earthen mound ('the Earth of the region') piled up in the centre of each village; possibly this is the 'Queen Earth' of after ages. Mention is made of the 'Dragon Woman' and of the 'Eastern Mother' and the 'Western Mother' and of the 'Ruler of the [Four?] Quarters'; sacrifices are offered to the east, west and south, and to the wind, the 'King Wind' and 'the Wind, the Envoy of Ti'. Ti, or Shang Ti, 'the Ruler Above' seems to have been the chief god. He was specially concerned with war, and the king of Shang would not open a campaign without consulting Ti; he was asked about the prospects of the year's crops, he was one of the powers who could assure sufficient rain, and generally he could allot good or bad fortune to men. War was, perhaps, his peculiar province, but his other atttributes were shared by the other gods and by the ancestors; at best he ranked as *primus inter pares*. It has, indeed, been suggested that he was himself but a deified ancestor, the progenitor of all the Shang kings, or that he embodies all the royal ancestry; that is possible, but the argument adduced in support of the theory, namely the fact that certain of the Shang kings bear such names as Ti I and Ti Hsin, could just as well be urged against it, seeing that theophoric names, i.e. names compounded with the name of a god, of the sort common in Sumer and in other lands of the ancient Middle East, imply the recognition of an already existing deity. Another explanation of Ti, perhaps more plausible, is based on the fact that in Shang Dynasty Chinese the word *Ti* is almost (and sometimes absolutely) identical with another word *liao* which means 'to present a burnt offering'; on the oracle-bones, in a sentence such as 'present as a burnt offering five bulls to Ti', the words *liao* and *Ti* are written identically. The theory, therefore, is that Ti was originally the ritual of sacrificing to the ancestors or to other gods and that men gradually confused the sacrifice with the deity sacrificed to, and so came to think of it as itself a separate god, just as in India the Aryans who poured clarified butter into the sacrificial fire known as Ani (this being the means for obtaining favours from the gods), attributed such potency to the means that in due time they deified it and Agni became a High God. Both theories may contain an element of truth; but no one logical explanation is likely to be exclusively true; the religious conceptions of the primitive Chinese were so vague, not to say muddled, that any attempt to rationalize them runs the risk of misrepresentation. The Shang people were thoroughly convinced of the survival of their human ancestors and of their supernatural powers; in addition they might imagine a deity behind any natural phenomenon, but such a deity seems to have been strangely impersonal; the nature of their religion did not call for any closer definition or differentiation of the gods.

Both the gods and the ancestors existed; they had knowledge and they had power, power for good and for evil. The purpose of religion was therefore twofold: to secure by offerings the favour of the gods, so that they might grant to the suppliant not evil but good, and to wrest from the gods the knowledge that would guide his actions in this world. The sacrifices have been described; the knowledge was to be gained by divination.

One method of divination was, probably, by mediums, in Shang as in later days, but naturally no material evidence for that remains. The other method, for which we have evidence in plenty, was the interpretation of the cracks produced by heat in tortoise-shell or in bone. Of the two materials the former seems to have been the original and the most efficacious, for there are frequent references to consulting 'the tortoise', or 'the Great Tortoise', whereas bone is never mentioned as such. When, in 1395 BC, P'an Keng shifted his capital to Anyang he reminded his discontented subjects, 'You did not presumptuously oppose the decision of the Tortoise'.

Archaeology shows that this was a method inherited by the Shang people from the Neolithic 'black pottery' peoples of north-eastern China; in the Shang practice (which was in the hands of a small college of diviners, though the king himself might conduct his own divining) the scapulae and leg bones of oxen—probably the victims of sacrifice—and the shells of tortoises, which certainly had been sacrificed, were trimmed and polished, and then oblong pits about three-quarters of an inch long were sunk in them, each pit serving for one consultation, the number of pits being determined by the area, so that a large tortoise-shell might have upwards of seventy pits. The enquirer put his question, and the diviner then applied heat, probably by pressing a red-hot bronze point against one side of the pits; the heat caused two cracks, one intersecting the pit, the other running through the point of application, and it was from the angle taken by the second crack that the answer of the spirit was made known. The answer could only take two forms, 'yes' and 'no', or 'fortunate' and 'unfortunate'; the question therefore had to be put in a form admitting of so simple an answer and, if the problem was at all complicated, a whole series of questions might be required so that the final reply was obtained by a process of elimination. Fortunately for the modern student, in about 10 per cent of the consultations the question and the answer were engraved upon the bone or shell; why this was done in some cases and not in others it is impossible to say, but the inscriptions that do appear are the source of nearly all our knowledge about the Shang period.

The questions are severely practical. Some deal with sacrifice, to whom it should be made—it was, of course, essential to find out which deity had to be propitiated—and when, and with what kind of offerings. A very common subject is war;

the king enquires of the oracle when to declare war, how many men to engage, whether to attack or remain on the defensive, and what prospects were there of booty and prisoners? The crops—the outlook for each kind of grain and for the output of liquor; the weather, not only the general forecast but the immediate—'Will it rain tonight?' (and in a few cases we are given not only the official answer 'No' but the comment 'It really didn't rain!'); illness—will the patient recover?; dreams—does such and such a dream portend good or evil?; and the astrologer's usual gambit, 'Will next week be lucky or unlucky?'; and finally, and very often, 'Will the Powers help?' 'Shall I receive aid?' 'Will the spirit of Grandfather aid the king?' Such is the information that man in ancient China desired to obtain from the spirit world, and to obtain it was the whole purpose of religion.

This primitive and materialistic creed is important not for its content but for the enduring influence it has exerted upon China. Because ancestor-worship, looking ever to the past, is above all things conservative, it has helped to secure for Chinese civilization a continuity such as no other people have enjoyed, a stability proof against military defeats and political upheavals which otherwise would have broken the thread of tradition and obliterated the country's past. It may at first appear strange that the world's longest-lived culture, one distinguished from the outset by intellectual ability and extreme refinement of art, should for more than three thousand years cling to a religion so barbarous as that suggested by the Shang documents. The Shang creed was indeed purely materialistic in its aims and it had nothing whatsoever to do with morals or ethics; its spirits were neither good nor evil, and of its followers it required nothing but the sacrifices whereby the spirits were placated. What must be noted is that China never produced any substitute for it; Lao Tz'u and Confucius alike taught not a religion but a philosophy; they supplied what had been wanting in the national religion, i.e. a system of ethics,[48] and thereby so reinforced its hold upon the national conscience that when the foreign religion of Buddhism was introduced in the early years of the Christian era, its adoption did not involve the jettisoning of the spiritual side of the old faith. For crude as that old faith was in its outlook and barbarous in its ritual, ancestor-worship as such has its spiritual side and makes a peculiarly human appeal; with its bloody sacrifices reduced to a more or less poetic symbolism and its ignorant magic either dropped or relegated to a secondary place, the simple Shang belief that men lived after death and became sources of guidance and protection for their descendants and proper objects of worship satisfied a natural craving in man and did more than anything else to form the ideals of Chinese civilization.

NOTES TO CHAPTER VIII

1. This name of the Earth goddess, which we find in the time of the First Dynasty of Ur, seems not to have been used in the Jamdat Nasr period; it certainly does not occur on the numerous tablets of that date found at Ur.
2. According to Professor I. M. Diakonoff there were fields belonging to individual patriarchal families. These fields could be bought and sold. Sometimes the ruler bought them. Some fields, therefore, were not the property of the theocratic state.
3. The absolute autonomy of Sumerian cities in religious affairs was in fact perhaps not quite so absolute; see M. Lambert, 'Polythéisme et monolâtrie des cités sumériennes', in *Revue de l'Histoire des Religions,* 157 (1960), pp. 1–20.
4. *SAKI*, p. 37, No. 1–7.
5. Professor I. M. Diakonoff points out that a city state was governed by a ruler together with a Council of Elders and an Assembly, while the kings of Ur were autocrats.
6. J. B. Pritchard, 'The Death of Gilgamesh', *Ancient Near Eastern Texts Relating to the Old Testament* (Princeton, 1950; 2nd ed., 1955), p. 51.
7. E.g. the Sargonid cemetery at Ur; one might compare with the mediaeval cemetery inside the Bab en-Nasr at Aleppo.
8. This is the accepted view, but the texts quoted in its support do not always bear the desired meaning. Thus when Urukagina lays the blame for the sacking of Lagash on Lugalzaggisi 'and on his goddess Nidaba', the translation 'his personal goddess' begs the question. In this, as in other cases, the expression 'his god' or 'the god of my father' would apply just as well to the family god as to any personal god.
9. In the opinion of Professor J. Leclant, stress should be laid on the local aspect of Egyptian religion. The very numerous local gods all along the Nile valley were, of course, manifestations of the same universal divine force. These gods preserved their geographical personality; they were attached to the localities of which they were the respective 'lords'. They were the 'gods of the cities', worshipped and solicited by the populace; the temple inhabited by the city god is sacred soil, where the local demiurge is believed to have inaugurated creation. Thus at Hermopolis, whatever great dynastic god may have been dominant at one time or another, it is always to Thoth that texts make constant reference.
10. See *supra*, p. 103, n. 18.
11. The categorical form of this and the following sentences may be challenged by some authorities. Professor John A. Wilson objects as follows: 'the term "totemism" has two levels of applicability; first, the totem is emblematic of the group; secondly, the group is descended from or related by blood to the totem; Egyptian totemism is only of the first level. A bull was the totem of Hermonthis, and a single, specially marked bull was maintained by the community as the seat and sign of this divinity of the group. Other bulls in that community had no essential sanctity, before the confusion of Graeco-Roman times. In other words, there was no blood-relationship of the people of Hermonthis to bull as bull.

There is no evidence that the native of Hermopolis, city of the ibis god Thoth, believed that he was descended from an ibis. Men were not in the lineage of Atum and the later gods.'

As against this view Sir Leonard Woolley asks how the totem animal came to be identified with a god, or to be emblematic of the group. Also it must be pointed out that Pharaoh, at any rate, called himself Horus, the falcon. The generally accepted view credits the Egyptian with a fine-drawn and logical definition of his religious beliefs which is entirely lacking in his mythology as a whole.

12. In the prehistoric cemetery at Badari there were found graves of cows, dogs (or jackals), sheep and goats. E. J. Baumgartel comments as follows: 'thus animal worship in Egypt goes back as far as the Badarian age, never to die out as long as Egyptian religion was practised; but the burial of animals does not prove the worship of them. The fact that the animal graves occur in the cemetery merely implies that these were funerary sacrifices for the benefit of the human dead.
13. Scenes of this kind are sometimes found on cylinder seals; see G. Godron, 'Notes d'épigraphie thinite', *Annales du Service des Antiquités de l'Egypte,* Vol. 54 (1957), pp. 191–206.
14. It may perhaps prove necessary to qualify slightly the author's conviction that the Egyptians were unable to conceive of any existence other than the physical.
15. The absence of any general study of the psychology of the Ancient Egyptians is greatly to be regretted.
16. Professor J. Leclant draws attention to the fact that the reliefs are also for the living. The splendour shown is also meant to invite the visitors to accord consideration to the dead man, to make a rich offering or, better still, pronounce the funerary formula in favour of the dead man.
17. Yet the dead man does not remain entirely outside the scene represented: he is shown walking among the figures portrayed on the walls of the tomb, thus taking some part in their activity.
18. Professor J. Leclant emphasizes the fact that certain individual prayers, on the contrary, were addressed to the sun: they were the solar hymns sung by those who had themselves portrayed in the act of offering a stele to the glory of the Sun god.
19. Professor J. Leclant emphasizes the importance of not losing sight of the Bull (or Falcon) god Mentu, whose name was honoured in those of the Eleventh Dynasty (Mentuhotep). It is, moreover, important to specify that Amon, about whose true nature (in spite of K. Sethe's essay *Amon und die Acht Urgötter*) we are still very ill-informed, was assimilated to Rê, the Sun god, forming the composite god Amon-Rê.
20. Sir Leonard Woolley was doubtless thinking of Mry-Ptah. It is, however, considered that this 'chief treasurer' (or rather 'director of the treasury') was merely a homonym of the contemporary high priest [see A. Varille, *Annales du Service des Antiquités de l'Egypte,* Vol. 40 (1940), p. 647; W. Helck, *Zur Verwaltung des Mittleren und Neuen Reichs* (1958), p. 405].
21. The elements of the mounting attention given to Aton are already discernible in the time of the predecessors of Amenhotep III.
22. It should not be forgotten, however, that a great temple of Aton had been constructed at Karnak itself at the beginning of the reign. The excavations of H. Chevrier have brought to light the colossal Osiric statues of the king in the eastern sector of Karnak. Innumerable small blocks of sandstone ('Talatates') coming from

30

(a) *Ur-Nammu stele. Philadelphia, University Museum*

(b) *The heading of Hammurabi's Code. Paris, Louvre*

(c) *Warka: gypsum vase (3 feet / 0.90 m in height), Berlin, Voderasiatisches Museum*

(b)

[*photo Chuzeville*

(a)

[Penn

(c)

[O.I.

31 *Sumer: group of figures from the Square Temple of Abu at Tell Asmar*

(a)

[B.M.

32

(a) *Sumer: statue of a woman. London, British Museum*

(b) *Sumer: Statue of a man. Copenhagen, Ny Carlsberg Glyptotek*

(b)

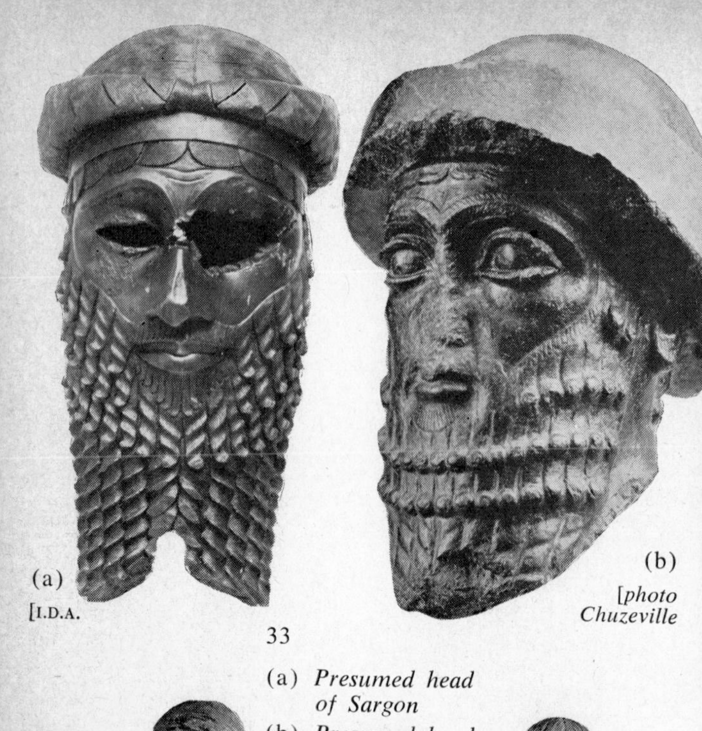

(a) [I.D.A.

(b) [photo Chuzeville

33

(a) *Presumed head of Sargon*

(b) *Presumed head of Hammurabi. Paris, Louvre*

(c) *The Mari 'Chorister'*

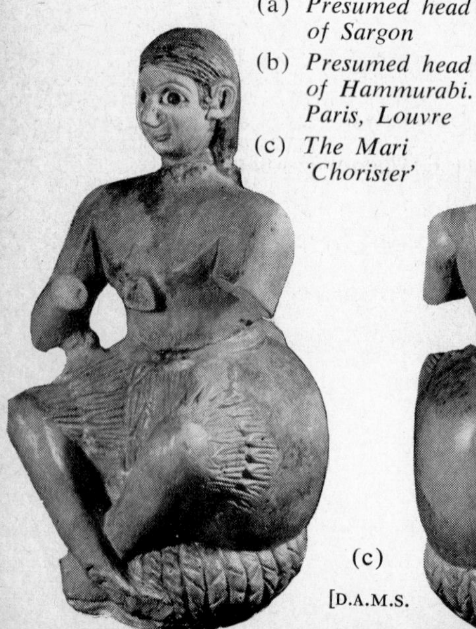

(c) [D.A.M.S.

[*photo Chuzeville*

34 *Statue of Gudea. Paris, Louvre*

(a)

[*photo Josephine Powell*

35

(a) *Boğazköy: the King's Gate figure*

(b) *Yazilikaya reliefs*

(b)

[*photo Josephine Powell*

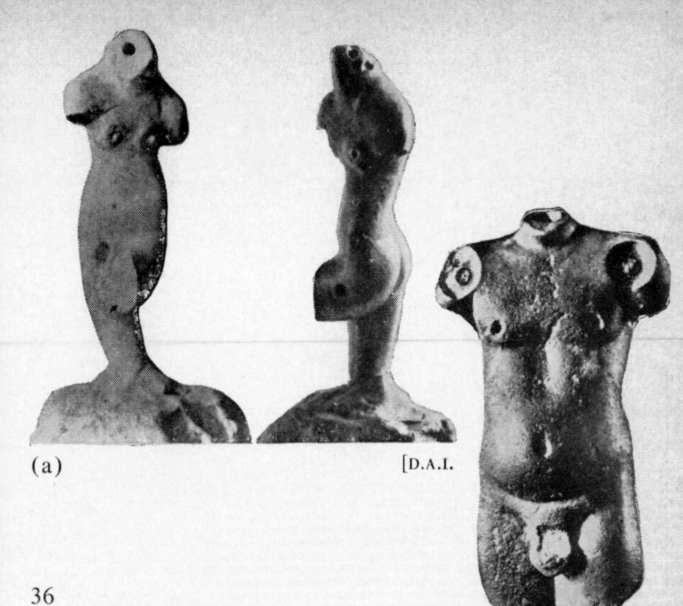

(a) [D.A.I.

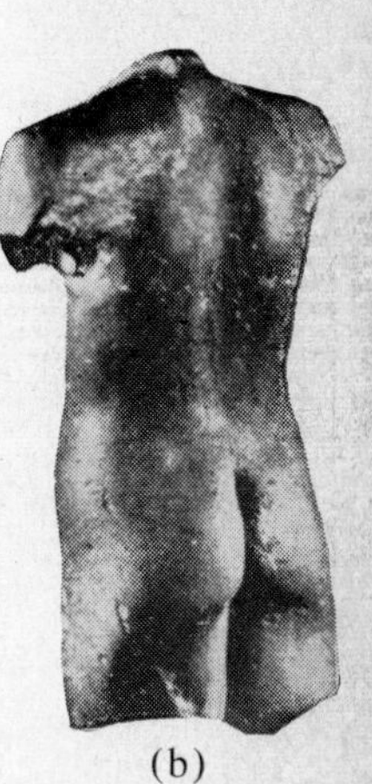

(b) [D.A.I.

36

(a) *Harappā: dancing youth*
(b) *Harappā: standing youth*
(c) *Mohenjo-daro: bronze dancing girl*

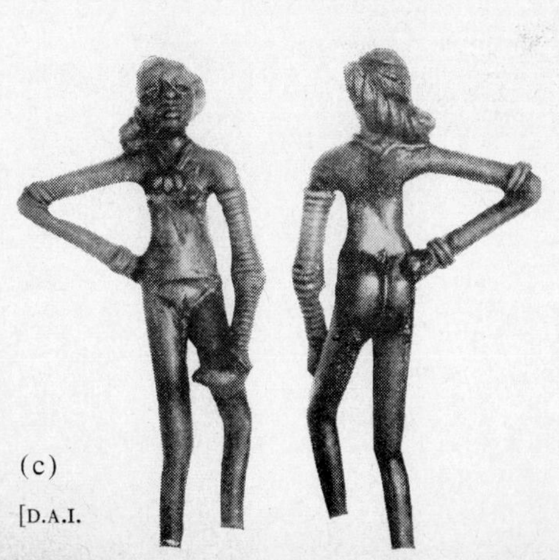

(c) [D.A.I.

[*photo Josephine Powell*

37 *Mohenjo-daro: bearded man*

[D.A.I.

38 *Mohenjo-daro: steatite seals*

[CHEN

39 *China: Marble statue of Yin Shang (6 inches / 0.15 m in height)*

40 *China: bronze elephant in the Shang tradition. Paris, Musée Guimet*

[M.G.

[photo Josephine Powell

41 *Crete: Snake Goddess*

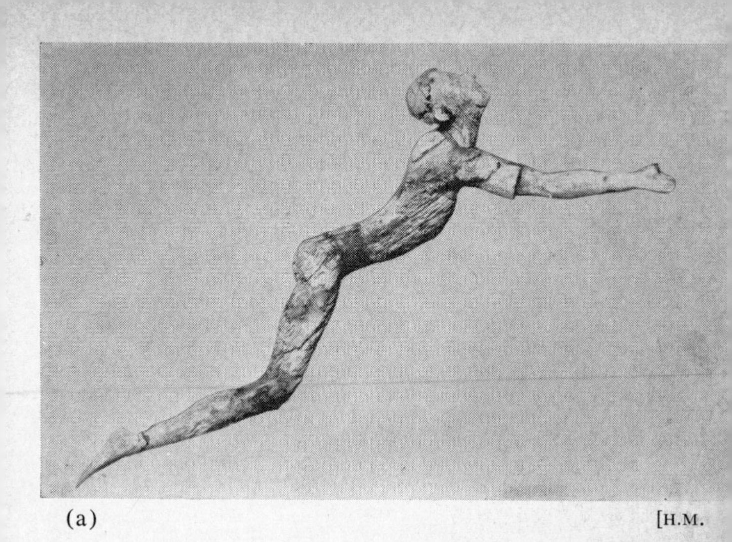

(a) [H.M.

42 (a) *Crete: ivory youth*
(b) *Crete: Minoan bull with baiter,* c. *1600 B. C.*

(b)

[Spencer-Churchill

43 *Crete: Vaphio gold cups. Athens, National Museum*

[Schaeffer

44 *Ugarit (Ras Shamra): gold bowl*

this sanctuary have been discovered in re-use particularly as filling for the foundations of the Hypostyle Hall or, again, as filling for the second and ninth pylons of the Great Temple of Karnak itself.

23. It is, however, essential to the study of the religious psychology of Ancient Egypt to note that the Amarnian revolution, though the best known, was not the only religious revolution of Ancient Egypt.
24. From a certain viewpoint, monotheism may be regarded as basic to the religious conception of the Ancient Egyptians, as is contended by H. Junker and E. Drioton in their well-known works on this subject.
25. Professor I. M. Diakonoff considers that it was very profitable for the priests of Amon and for the governing classes to picture Amon as the god of the poor.

    Sir Leonard Woolley, however, maintains that profit was not the motive; this picture of Amon does not originate with the official priesthood. Exploration of the social background of evidence should never be neglected. The most personal prayers come, of course, from the necropolis quarry workers living in the workers' village of Deir-el-Medineh.
26. Professor J. Leclant observes that the tradition of the Wisdoms is continuous throughout Egyptian literature, remaining always the basis of education.
27. E. A. Speiser, 'The Hurrian Participation in the Civilizations of Mesopotamia, Syria and Palestine', *Journal of World History,* I, 2 (October, 1953), p. 312.
28. No doubt the present exposition could be completed by the recent research on this subject. An Anatolian (partly Hittite) and a Hurrian (northern Mesopotamia, Syria) pantheon prior to the famous Mitannian symbiosis (2000–1700 BC) are now clear. The intrusion of the Hurrians into the Anatolian pantheon did not take place until after the Hittite expeditions into Syria (1600–1500 BC).
29. Many scholars think that the Mithras of Hellenistic and Roman times was almost certainly a newcomer from Iran in Achaemenian times, not the descendant of the Mitannians. The date of the Mithraeum of Alalakh is also open to discussion.
30. Professor E. Laroche observes that several texts explicitly state that the Hittite king was the delegate of the gods, charged with the administration of the countries belonging to these gods; see H. G. Güterbock, in 'Authority and Law in the Ancient Near East', American Oriental Society, *Journal,* Supplement 17 (1954).
31. Professor I. M. Diakonoff points to the existence of a Hurrite (or Hittite?) seal depicting a human sacrifice. In his view, the Hurrians and the Hittites were no more humane than their neighbors.
32. In the opinion of Professor E. Laroche, the small remaining fragment of the Hurrian version of the Gilgamesh is practically unintelligible. There exists, on the other hand, a Hittite version of the Gilgamesh of which Otten, in particular, has made a study.
33. Dr D. C. Baramki observes that the Moabites, Edomites and Arameans make their appearance as settled folk only after the Amarna Age, and after the onslaught of the Habiru and Sa Gaz. The evidence seems to indicate that these peoples did not settle in Syria until the Iron Age. They seem to be partially descended from the Habiru; Canaanites and Amurru were already settled in the Near East at that time. They had come as a single wave in the twenty-second century BC. There were already Semites in the area who had come at the beginning of the third millennium BC. The Phoenicians referred to here were, of course, slightly different from the later folk of the twelfth century BC.

34. Professor A. Caquot points out that Philon of Byblos provides the only evidence that Elyon's consort was an Earth goddess. Bêl (one of Marduk's titles) plays no role among the Western Semites at this time and figures as a 'Sun god' only in Hellenistic times.
35. On a seal from Kydonia he stands between the horns of consecration.
36. *Palace of Minos,* IV, pp. 152 sq.
37. Sir Leonard Woolley wrote the following note: 'My treatment here of Abraham has been most strongly opposed by my Russian critics, who say that I make "no difference between history and myth; the latter is presented as history"; they allow that, thinking that Abraham was historical, I have a right to my own opinion, but think that I should not disregard other well-founded opinions on the subject, and urge that all Soviet scholars will insist on such opinions being brought to the notice of the reader.

 'I was, of course, aware that Abraham has been dismissed as a myth. The theory was propounded by German scholars of the nineteenth century; they were admirable textual critics, but they had (and could have) no archaeological knowledge, and they were bad historians. Today their extreme views are rejected by most scholars, who are ready to place more reliance upon ancient tradition as distinguished from myth; if they are approved by all Soviet scholars it is because they agree with Marxist principles, which were formulated when the "Higher Criticism" still held the field.

 'I do not hold that the Hebrew tradition is impeccable, but am convinced that it has a historical basis. Abraham I believe to be a conflation of at least two (and probably three) historical individuals; allowing for that (quite understandable) confusion, the incidents related are likely to be correct on the whole—some of them, indeed, reflect contemporary conditions so accurately that they could not have been invented at a later date when those conditions no longer existed. I have put forward at length the evidence on which my conclusions are based in my book *Abraham* (London, 1936); in this History detailed argument would be out of place, and I have simply assumed the historical basis of tradition.'

 For the past two decades the Bible has been shown tc be a *useful* guide to archaeological research though not to be a *reliable* one. Some critics of Sir Leonard Woolley's book, *Abraham,* consider that it remains uncertain whether Abraham resided in Ur or another city of the same name. The similarity of Abraham's father's name, Terah, to the name of the Moon god might be a coincidence, the critics say. On the other hand, unhewn altar stones like those used by the Jews but not used in the Sumerian tradition have been found at Ur. Sir Leonard Woolley has dated Abraham as *c.* 1920–1800 BC by reference to the Old Testament record and has supported this by identifying the word 'Habiru', in use at the time, as a reference to the Hebrews. He concluded that the god whom Abraham took with him was an unnamed family deity and that his god became the Hebrew Yahweh. At present this construction remains a hypothesis not accepted by all scholars. See W. F. Albright, *From the Stone Age to Christianity* (Baltimore, 1940), pp. 179–82; S. W. Baron, *A Social and Religious History of the Jews, I, Ancient Times* (2nd ed., New York, 1952), p. 34. In order to obtain a clearer idea of the real position concerning Abraham, attention should be given to the nomad life of the period; see J. R. Kupper, *Les nomades en Mésopotamie au temps des rois de Mari* (Paris, 1957), and J. Bottéro, 'Le problème des Habiru à la

4ème Rencontre Assyriologique Internationale', Société Asiatique, *Cahiers,* XII (Paris, 1954).

38. Dr D. C. Baramki considers that the excavations at Ras Shamra, Byblos, Megiddo, Beisan and Gezer show that these cities were at this time well fortified with strong walls. During this period civilization reached heights not again achieved by this area until the Hellenistic Age. Abraham seems, according to the Bible, to have been a roving nomad. The peculiarity of the followers of Abraham is therefore much better explained as a contrast between the nomadic barbarism of Abraham and his followers, who may have been the 'Terahites' of the Ras Shamra tablets, and the settled and more civilized city communities of Canaan.
39. Genesis xxvii. 46.
40. Sir Leonard Woolley wrote the following note in response to objections formulated by Russian scholars: 'Prof. I. M. Diakonoff has challenged my treatment of Moses as a historical character in the same way as he has challenged that of Abraham. Again, I believe that there is a basis of truth in the tradition, though imagination has been more active in colouring the various incidents or, in some cases perhaps, in inventing them. It would be impossible to discuss the origins of the Hebrew religion without mentioning Moses; the part played by the Mosaic tradition is too important to be omitted. If, as Professor Diakonoff maintains, Moses was a figment of the Hebrew imagination, his creation was an astonishing feat, for his "history" symbolizes to perfection the gradual change in Hebrew religion, and that implicitly, as if his creators were unaware of what they were doing. Actually in my account of the religion I have treated Moses as a symbol without insisting on his historical character as an individual, citing those incidents which, perhaps in a poetic form, throw light upon religious ideas. I should have thought it obvious that when I quoted from a psalm "the sea saw that and fled", I was not relating a historical fact, or when I said that the presence of the tribal deity was "symbolized by the fire and cloud that accompanied their march", I was not accepting a miracle without comment. I believe that to most readers "this uncritical and quite unhistorical narrative" will present no difficulty.'
41. Professor I. M. Diakonoff contends that the golden calf was an image of a male animal; it is therefore doubtful that it could be made in honour of the goddess Hathor.

    Sir Leonard Woolley thinks that the fact that the editor of Exodus used a masculine word is probably due to a mistake in the 600-year-old oral tradition; in his view, a male calf would be difficult to explain.
42. According to a scholar on behalf of the National Commission of Israel, 'the sabbatical year' seems to show that Mosaic legislation was not entirely designated for a nomad tribe. Sir Leonard Woolley, however, considers that the sabbatical year is a late institution.
43. According to a scholar on behalf of the National Commission of Israel these promises are enumerated in Deuteronomy and can hardly be used as illustrative of the Bronze Age religion of Israel.
44. Sidney Smith, *The Statue of Idri-mi* (London, 1949).
45. This is one of the Phoenician legends recorded on tablets found at Ugarit. It must, however, be remembered that the original interpretation proposed for these texts no longer meets with complete acceptance.
46. See discussion, p. 107, note 38.
47. Professor I. M. Diakonoff suggests that the burial ritual described

here can be found where every human society has reached a certain stage of development. There is, therefore, no reason to think that it was borrowed from the Sumerians who lived some 1,500 years earlier and thousands of miles away.

48. Professor Shigeki Kaizuka *et al.* point out that sections of the Book of History, *Shu Ching*, dating from the early Chou era show that the concept of Heaven was given a definite moral interpretation—Heaven aids the good ruler and punishes the bad. At least among the ruling class religious ideas and moral concepts had become fused long before the time of Confucius or Lao Tz'u. Confucius seems to have been anxious to preserve these earlier moral concepts which, in the social and political upheaval of his own time, were being spurned. In attempting to do so he modified and broadened them, of course.

CHAPTER IX

THE FINE AND APPLIED ARTS

THE FINE ARTS

THE distinction between the fine and the applied arts is largely artificial. Although sculpture and painting may serve no more than purely aesthetic ends and be judged as works of art wholly on their own merits, yet both sculpture and painting are equally liable to be called in for the decoration of useful objects, so much so that between them they cover the entire field of applied art, where judgement must needs be based on functional criteria in the first place, with aesthetic values relegated to the second. The line is indeed difficult to draw. The applied art reflects more or less faithfully the 'fine art' of its period, and often, lacking other evidence, we can deduce the character of the fine art only from the surviving examples of the more commercial product; this is pre-eminently the case with early China, where we have to rely on little but the decorative bronze castings for our knowledge of artistic styles, and with prehistoric India, where the material—painted pottery and engraved seals together with half a dozen figurines in the round—is again sadly inadequate. But although the boundary between fine and applied art be indeterminate, the two provinces are none the less really different. Excavation in Egypt has furnished us with an endless variety of examples of the applied arts of the finest quality and in every sort of material; but if from those alone we were to conjure up a picture of Egyptian art it would be astonishingly unlike that presented by the statues, the reliefs and the paintings which come from the temples and the tombs. Egypt is indeed unique in the conspectus of its ancient art which it affords, illustrated at every stage by masterpieces, so that our first study should be of Egypt and, in Egypt, of the course of the major arts.

In a history of man's cultural progress any discussion of the fine arts of painting and sculpture might seem to be out of place. A great work of art results from the genius of an individual and may reflect only in a very small degree the conditions of contemporary society;[1] thus the astonishing pictures of Altamira and Lascaux were painted at a time when man's manner of life and his moral and intellectual outlook were those of the primitive savage, and if sculpture were to be accepted as a criterion then a comparison of the 'Venus of Willendorf' with one of the statues of Mr Henry Moore might lead to the conclusion that for thirty thousand years civilization had been stagnant.

On the other hand, our understanding of a people or of a period will be sadly incomplete unless the art of that people or period be taken as an essential element of its culture. But from that point of view what really matters is not the production of a masterpiece but the public reaction to art in general. Most people, at most times, have demanded, though for very different reasons, the representation in plastic or pictorial form of natural objects; their demand has been met by men who may be either artists or craftsmen. The latter, possessing no more than technical ability, are inspired only by the tastes of their clients —they follow the current fashion, make what the public wants, and so reflect faithfully the spirit of their time. The artist expresses himself in his work, but will seldom lose sight of his public, and in so far as he is a child of his generation the self which he expresses is germane to his people and period; he may be an innovator, breaking new ground, but if he succeeds in winning popular approval then his work can fairly be said to represent the spirit of his age and country, not as he found it but as he has helped to mould it.

But here a *caveat* is called for. In the ancient Levant the artist's public, to which he had to appeal and which he might influence, was for the most part strictly limited. Not only were his patrons confined to the aristocracy, but very little of his work would ever be seen by the people at large; the 'spirit of the age' which he represents is in fact that of a numerically small *élite*.[2] Strictly limited also was the sphere in which the artist might work, at least in those countries, Egypt and Mesopotamia, which afford us the best material for study; he was not at liberty to give free rein to his imagination, to make his own choice of subject or even to strike out a new line in technique. His patrons did not regard a work of art as something having an independent value, something to be judged by aesthetic standards; it was utilitarian, a means to an end which had nothing to do with art as such, and if they required it to be beautiful that was because by its beauty it better fulfilled its useful function. That was not the point of view of the artist, who was interested in his work as such; but he was obliged to accept its limitations on the whole and could even profit by them, much as the poet may profit by the discipline of the rigid sonnet-form, so that on the rare occasion on which he flouts convention the modern spectator is almost shocked into disapproval.

Egypt

Egyptian art was from the outset representational and, subject to certain conventions, realistic. For the earliest stages of its development there is no good evidence, but from the beginning of the Dynastic period we have an ivory statuette of a king (Pl. 21, a) which, though isolated, is enough to show the natural bent of the Egyptian sculptor untrammelled by convention. It is amazingly naturalistic; the attitude and gestures are imposed from within, not dictated by any stylistic tradition; this weary and disillusioned old man, having none of the aloof assurance of the later Pharaohs, is a living organism; we have here not a monument but a human presence.

Something of the same sort, though technically cruder, can be seen in the carving in relief on the so-called 'Lion palette' (Pl. 21, b); in it a number of figures, men, birds and a lion, combine to make a realistic group in which all are related together by action or by interest; it is a picture intended to produce a three-dimensional effect, an illustration of a single event in time and place, not a statement of a general truth. When we turn from this to the famous mace-head of Khasekhamui (Pl. 3) the change is evident, for though the background incidents are pictorially treated and though the king's figure retains a certain vigour and lively tension yet its hieratic pose suggests a symbolic conception; the relief illustrates not any one event but a recurrent function of royalty. Still more is this the case with the palette of Narmer (Pl. 19, a); the minor figures bear no spatial relation to the main group so that their presence has to be explained by reading rather than by visual apprehension, and the king slays his enemy by a symbolic gesture that is without movement or emotion. Pharaoh inevitably overcomes his foes, and the palette is a monumental work stating that general truth.

Thus early was there imposed on Egyptian art the convention which was to last almost throughout its history.

The convention results from the uses to which the fine arts were dedicated, i.e. to the furnishing of temples and of tombs. In the private houses there were no statues of any sort. In the house of a rich man stone door-jambs or lintels might bear carved inscriptions, but scenes in painting or in relief found a place only in the private chapel in the garden; the walls were indeed painted, but only with some decorative scheme based on architectural or floral motifs, not with pictures in which men or animals played any part. The sculptor and the painter were not decorators, nor was it their aim to appeal to the aesthetic sense of the spectator; their purpose was far more serious, on the one hand to assert the divinity of Pharaoh, on the other to secure the well-being of a man's soul. Temple art and tomb art were thus differently inspired, but both were essentially religious and both could express the ideas inherent in them only by the help of a style which removed their subject from the realm of normal life, from all considerations of space and time.

By the time of the Fourth Dynasty the style had been fully developed and was set for good and all. The exquisite wooden reliefs of Hesire (Pl. 19, b) and the tomb paintings of Rahotep in the Third Dynasty, the magnificent diorite statue of Khafra (Pl. 22, a), the triads of Menkau-ra and the famous 'Sheikh el Beled' of the Third Dynasty, these embody all the principles which later artists, even allowing for the deviations of the Amarna revolution, were faithfully if not slavishly to observe. It is not true that Egyptian art stagnated, or that its history is simply one of slow degeneration; changes were made and innovations were introduced, such that a statue or a relief can be dated with tolerable accuracy on internal evidence alone; but none the less, there is an astonishing continuity, and for the most part changes, when they occur, are not due to any novel aesthetic but reflect some modification of religious belief.

In Egyptian painting and relief—and the two are almost identical in so far as the relief is invariably low[3] and was generally enhanced by colour—the formed style involves certain conventions which to the modern European eye may appear primitive and almost puerile; it is indeed the permanence of these features that induces the mistaken idea of the 'changelessness' of Egyptian art. In the carved or painted scenes there is no perspective and no illusion of depth;[4] generally speaking the human figures, identical in size, are aligned along a single base, in profile, with no background to suggest their setting; even when, as in the hunting scenes, animals may be shown scattered over the field at different levels, each is normally given a separate ground-line which tends to join up with others and to divide the figures into separate registers. The principal character—the king in a temple relief, the dead man in a tomb—is represented on a very much larger scale, commensurate with his importance, and always with what has been called the 'paratactic' convention whereby the head and legs are drawn in profile and the torso frontally; the smaller figures may be treated in the same manner or may be entirely in profile; in either case they are little more than silhouettes with a minimum of internal detail. All this sounds primitive, and indeed the Egyptian artist did perpetuate the naïve conventions of his proto-Dynastic forebears, but he did so deliberately. He was quite able to draw a human figure in any position—in the tomb of Rekhmirê (early Eighteenth Dynasty) there is a three-quarter back view of a naked girl, admirably done; he could draw figures not all on one plane but grouped one behind another, witness the wailing women on the funerary barge in the tomb of Neferhotep of the same date (Pl. 25, a); he could draw figures full-face instead of in profile, as we see in the tomb of Nekht, and could even, by decreasing the size of figures so that they seem to recede in space, suggest perspective; true linear perspective he did not recognize any more than did the artists of China (there is one possible attempt at it in the el Amarna period); all the rest he understood but with such rare exceptions as have been cited above rejected as alien to his purpose.

The ancient Egyptian tomb was designed and furnished with one end in view, the continued life and the assured well-being of its occupant. The portrait statues hidden in the *sirdab* of the Early Dynastic *mastaba* were not in any sense memorials; they were the man himself, and took the place of his flesh-and-blood body, should that decay, and guaranteed his personal immortality. The tomb-chapel reliefs served the same function, and further promoted his happiness;[5] he is represented as standing or sitting to 'watch' (that is the term used) the scenes of agriculture, hunting, feasting, industry and so on which are painted or carved on the tomb walls; he is not dead, but as an inhabitant of another world he takes pleasure in watching the activities of the world he used to know (Pl. 26, a). There is in this something of magic; the pictured offerings of food do, like the actual foodstuffs offered in the tomb, provide sustenance for the soul, the ostentatious display of wealth may secure wealth in the after-world, and the funerary rites depicted may be a lasting guarantee of life as well as a source of satisfaction; but the tomb's owner plays no part in these vivid scenes; he simply watches them. The tomb portrait then is not that of the dead man; it is that of the man as he lives in the hereafter, and therefore it must represent him as the same man indeed, but divorced from human life. The primitive convention whereby the limbs are composed inorganically does just this; it sets before us all that makes up the body but removes it from actuality; the man that we see is isolated, takes no part in the life spread out in front of him and is rid of the trammels of space and time; the curious feeling of awe that assails the modern European confronted with such a tomb relief testifies to the success of the Egyptian sculptor's use of a primitive convention. Of that success the sculptor was fully conscious, and every care was taken that the formula for it should not be lost.

In a number of Egyptian tombs the carving is so far incomplete that the figures—sometimes mere sketches—still show the 'grid' by which the artist was guided in making his drawing. Until lately it has been assumed that this was a *mise aux carreaux,* the squaring of the ground to assure the accurate enlargement of a small-scale sketch. Now Dr Eric Iversen has pointed out that to square a sketch for reproduction you make the squares arbitrarily, as big or as small as you may think fit, but in the hundred or so Egyptian grids preserved the squares always intersect the bodies, whatever their scale, at exactly the same points and divide them into exactly the same parts; the squares, then, were not originally imposed arbitrarily upon the figures but the figures are composed deliberately upon a system of squares. The system is based on the theory that each part of the human body has a fixed ratio to the other parts; for the artist the constructional proportions represent a standardization of the objective proportions, i.e. the real ones as they exist, not as they happen to be seen in perspective by the human eye. The units, identified with the human arm and its parts, represent a series of ratios independent of their values as actual measures of length. Thus the smallest unit is the width of the fist (= 4 fingers plus the thumb, reckoned as 1⅓ fingers, total 5⅓ fingers), and this makes the side of a square; the total height of the figure from sole to forehead will then be 18 squares, the length from wrist to elbow 3 squares, the foot 3 squares, from the sole to the top of the knee 6 squares, sole to base of buttock 9 squares, to elbow of hanging arm 12 squares, to arm-pit 14½ squares, to shoulder 16 squares; this is the canon of the Third Dynasty relief of Hesire, and it is scrupulously maintained down to the Twenty-sixth Dynasty, and even then, when a new canon was introduced, it was due not to any artistic refinement but to a change in metrology.

The canon, which applied to sculpture in the round equally with relief or painting, is clearly an idealization of the human body, far removed from the realism of the ivory statuette of early times. But the evidence of realism induced by the whole conception of tomb sculpture went much farther; the virtual elimination of all muscular development counteracts what may in outline seem an active pose; the planting of both feet firmly on the ground regardless of the position of the legs nullifies all physical tension; if the dead man lives and moves it is with a life and a movement not of this world.

The same principles were applied to temple sculpture, though for a different reason. Pharaoh was in very truth a god, and therefore he, too, must be represented *sub specie aeternitatis,* unconfined by time or space; his statues must be monuments embodying superhuman majesty; with such an idea any naturalistic rendering of momentary activity would be out of keeping. That the 'other-worldliness' of the Pharaoh's statue was an effect at which the artist consciously and deliberately aimed is proved by a striking exception to the rule. On certain wall reliefs, e.g. one of Seti I at Abydos, the king is represented as offering to the temple god (in this case Osiris) a statuette of himself prostrate in adoration before the deity, and one such statuette survives, a figure (now in the Cairo Museum) of Ramses II (Pl. 22, c). In the whole range of Egyptian art there are very few things more alive and more realistically human than this royal portrait. The explanation surely is that here, for a moment, Pharaoh renounces his divinity in self-abasement before the greater Power; it is his mortal nature that must be emphasized for the purpose of this momentary act; but at all other times an inorganic rigidity becomes the god in human form just as it does the 'life-in-death' pictured on the wall of a tomb.

In the tombs the dead man 'watches' scenes of life in the normal world; in the temples—i.e. in the mortuary chapels of the kings—there are reliefs illustrating the functions of royalty. Obviously here the artist has more opportunity for freedom, for his subjects are taken from life and the majority of the characters he represents, peasants, craftsmen, sailors and servants, shown in dramatic and often in trivial action, have in themselves no claim to other-worldliness. But even here there is no spatial illusion and the figures are incorporeal and non-functional.

The first impression made on the modern spectator by many of these scenes of agricultural labourers at work, boat-builders, huntsmen and the like is that of extreme vivacity, as for example in the case of the fighting boatmen in the tomb of Ptahhotep (Fig. 33), the musicians and dancer in the tomb of Djeserkaresonb or, for the Eighteenth Dynasty, the wailing women from Neferhotep's tomb (Pl. 25, a). It is perfectly true that sometimes the artist (who, as has been urged already, was quite capable of drawing in the most realistic fashion) did let

FIG. 33. *Fighting boatmen from the tomb of Ptahhotep.*

himself go, overriding the conventions, but even when he observed them faithfully we find a variety of posture and significant gesture which scarcely needs the snippets of recorded conversation (interpolated as on a modern 'strip') to bring the picture to life. None the less, the more we look at even the gayest of them, the more do we realize, almost uneasily, how remote these pictures are from our world. The figures, whether drawn in true profile or with the 'paratactic' distortion, do not suggest—and are not intended to suggest—three-dimensional figures; their gestures are imposed upon them by the scheme of the picture and are not muscular activities inspired by their will; they are, at their best, pleasing silhouettes thrown upon a flat screen. When the artist has to represent animals he is less inhibited, for they are not subject in the same degree to religious taboos; but even so, although the treatment of the individual beasts may be lifelike and their actions appear spontaneous, there is still no spatial illusion and little or nothing in the way of related grouping.

The tomb pictures are not biographical (except in the hunting and boating scenes the tomb owner plays no part other than the onlooker's) and they are not incidental; they illustrate, sometimes in successive phases, the typical and regularly recurrent events of life and in that sense they are removed from actuality and become symbols. The tomb paintings and reliefs were not meant to instruct the modern spectator (and when once the tomb was finished no Egyptians saw them at all) but were for the dead man to watch; they were not records of his life but glimpses of the still surviving and constant life of earth, and those glimpses had to be brought into harmony with the changed personality of the one onlooker. The gay and lively subjects must not only be generalized; they must be so treated as to lose all suggestion of transcience, of functional corporeality, of space and time. So, too, in the temple reliefs Pharaoh himself is represented as taking part in the scene pictured; but his acts are those recurrent and symbolic acts which manifest the royal godhead—many of these are really magic—and where, as in the mortuary chapel of Sahurê (Fifth Dynasty), a royal victory is recorded there is no battle scene (for Pharaoh was *ex officio* victorious) but the gods of Egypt lead in the foreign captives. 'What was aimed at was not to stress the lasting significance of transient events but to show static perfection revealed in acts.'[6] The same convention as prevails in tomb sculpture serves the not very dissimilar purpose of the temple reliefs. Not until the Nineteenth Dynasty, when Egyptian art was declining and the religion of imperial Egypt had warped the old ideas, do we see Pharaoh in the forefront of battle playing the part of captain of the host rather than of god (Fig. 36).

Up to this point our study has emphasized the consistency with which the Egyptian artist subordinated his style to the religious or at least unworldly nature of his subject. But the beliefs which he so scrupulously interpreted had another side which introduced a curious anomaly into art, at any rate so far as sculpture in the round was concerned.

Pharaoh was a god; but at the same time he was himself, one Pharaoh of a line of divine ancestors, an individual in his own right. The owner of the tomb was no longer of this world, and the statue which the mourners placed in the hidden *sirdab* or in the tomb chamber was meant to be the lodging for his soul should his actual body no more serve as such; but the lodging must be one that the soul—*his* soul—would recognize as familiar, and when the soul entered it the living thing that resulted must be no changeling, but himself. The statue, therefore, must recall the man that he had been.

The realistic art which we saw in the proto-Dynastic ivory (Pl. 21, a) was perpetuated in Egyptian portraiture, and in this branch of art the Egyptian sculptor proved himself a supreme master. But here again he was working for other than aesthetic ends; his portraits were carved not for their own sake, not as memorials of the dead, like Roman portrait busts, but for tombs and temples, and hence arose that extraordinary contradiction inherent in every Egyptian statue. In obedience to the formula described above the body is lifeless, inorganic and immobile, the limbs have no separate function, the arms hang limply or are stiffly arranged—in a seated figure generally held against the sides with the lower arms resting on the thighs—with no purposeful gesture; and in a standing figure the legs suggest no muscular energy but, with the soles of both feet planted solidly upon the ground, seem to be no more than massive pillars supporting the trunk, and if one leg be advanced it is but a diagonal prop reaffirming immobility. And crowning this rigid negation of life is a face whose lifelikeness is unmistakably individual. The combination should be ludicrous, but such is the art of the sculptor that we today are conscious only of a personal presence superbly dignified and in some way awe-inspiring.

That a clash of opposites could be so successfully resolved is due to the sculptor's deliberate choice of what should be the content of his portraits. That they should represent individuals was essential to their religious function; there must be a likeness, but that need not be confined to physical resemblance, and what the artist attempts to render is the character of his subject. Obviously such insight and such skill were not at the disposal of every maker of images, and there are plenty of Egyptian statues whose blank faces, though not all of a pattern, betray nothing of the inner man. But where a really great artist is concerned—sometimes in the Old Kingdom, more often in the Twelfth Dynasty, occasionally in the Eighteenth and as late as the Saitic period—his work leaves no doubt as to the general aim of his art. The heads of Khafra (Pl. 22, a), of the Sheikh el Beled, the obsidian head of a nameless Twelfth Dynasty Pharaoh (Pl. 23, b), that of Thutmose III (Pl. 23, c), and the unknown Saitic head in Berlin, to mention only a few, are amongst the most sensitive character-studies ever expressed in stone. But never is there any suggestion of mood. Character is real and constant, but moods are transient; character, suitably idealized and sublimated, is a necessary element in a true portrait, but the passing mood could not possibly accord with the static body to which even gesture has been denied; the artist's task was to leave out the ephemeral and the accidental and to retain that absolute character which, in so far as it is independent of time, has that much in common with the body. It was indeed a case of abstraction. In the sculptor's workshop which was excavated at el Amarna there was found a series of stucco heads modelled with such exact verisimilitude that they gave the impression of being death-masks moulded on the human face; they were studies for heads to be carved in stone, but even in the 'revolutionary' el Amarna period no sculptor carved a head at all like them. The first sketch reproduced faithfully the man as he looked at a given moment, the finished work was meant to immortalize what he was.

The continuity of Egyptian art was interrupted by the religious changes brought in by Akhenaton. The suppression of all the old gods involved the abandonment of the stock themes hitherto employed for temple reliefs; the only subject now allowed was that of Akhenaton and his family worshipping the sun's disk, a scene repeated with wearisome monotony on walls, columns and stelae. In the case of tombs, a changed belief in values set aside all tradition; the dead man no longer 'watches' the activities of a world in which he can himself play no part; on the contrary he proudly puts on record the leading incidents of his own life on earth, his devotion to Pharaoh and the honours that Pharaoh has bestowed upon him. The divine and the mystic elements are thus eliminated and art becomes wholly human. This was true even for Pharaoh himself. Since Akhenaton was not a member of a divine hierarchy and therefore a being of another world, but was none the less divine, everything about him was godlike, not only his ceremonial acts but all the intimacies of his family life, and where a former king of Egypt might be suckled by a goddess, the el Amarna artist could show Akhenaton embracing his wife (Pl. 24, a). Akhenaton talked much of *Ma'at*, 'Truth'; what precisely he meant by the term is uncertain, but the artist was at liberty to interpret it as 'realism', and delighted to prove that even the physical deformity of a Pharaoh was an attribute of godhead. The new creed insisted on 'life', and art therefore becomes more lively.

In subject, therefore, and in treatment, the art of the el Amarna period departs widely from precedent; symbolism has given place to straightforward representation of real people and of actual scenes. To achieve this figures tend to be drawn in true profile instead of in the old paratactic convention, gestures become natural and significant, buildings in the background tie the scenes down to a definite place; once at least an artist makes an attempt at linear perspective and once, in the famous wall-painting of the little princesses seated at the foot of their father's throne (Pl. 25, b), he tries to produce a three-dimensional effect by the use of shadows and highlights. It would be easy to exaggerate the extent of the change in techniques. Already, in the preceding reign, the influence of Cretan art had led to a greater naturalism, to a more pictorial arrangement and to an appreciation of the scenic value of the wide spacing of figures; the caricatures of Akhenaton are in direct descent from the deliberately comic figure of an emaciated cowherd in a Middle Kingdom tomb at Meir and akin to the starving peasants in the Old Kingdom pyramid of Unas (Fig. 34); the artists were innovators in so far as they aimed at dramatic effects, but their means were for the most part not original. The portrait head of Nefertiti, and the even finer head of Akhenaton (Pl. 23, a), prove that there was at any rate one great master of sculpture at el Amarna, but most of the work is second-rate—perhaps because of the haste with which everything had to be done rather than of the lack of skilled artists; thus the best reliefs in the el Amarna style are those in the tomb of Harmhab, done after Akhenaton's death, when life had returned to the normal and there was time to work properly.

Because the style resulted from a religious revolution which collapsed with its founder's death and its tenets became anathema, Egyptian art promptly reverted to the old tradition. But the 'revolution' was not without lasting effect. In the case of tomb reliefs direct influence was confined to an occasional dramatic touch, but it was soon nullified by a new religious attitude towards the after-life. Instead of 'watching' the scenes of man's activities the dead man is now shown taking part in them. The whole conception on which tomb art had been based is now altered, and though the scenes may be superficially similar the spirit has gone out of them; in the old days they had been designed to give pleasure to the dead man, but henceforward they were routine pieces meant to act as charms. The priests of Amon had discovered and popularized the mechanism of sal-

FIG. 34. *Starving peasants from the tomb of Unas.*

vation and the tomb walls reproduced the formal vignettes of the Book of the Dead; the elaborate funerary rites, the perils of the passage to the next world, the weighing of man's soul, such scenes repeat *ad nauseam* the phantasmagoria of robot gods and demons, but all life has gone and with it all the pleasure of life.

On the other hand the sense of drama, which can already be detected in the art of the early Eighteenth Dynasty but has free play in that of el Amarna, did not disappear with Akhenaton; it was to inspire all the royal reliefs of the future. A magnificent painted casket from the tomb of Tutankhamen (Pl. 26, b) gives us scenes of Pharaoh in battle with the Syrians and again hunting lions which are altogether in the el Amarna spirit —incidentally they show, especially the lion-hunt scene, how strongly el Amarna art has been influenced by that of Crete. These are still 'typical' scenes, though the details are treated with a naturalism that is quite new; but when we turn to the huge monumental reliefs of Seti I at Karnak (Pl. 24, b) and of Ramses II and III we can see at once how the episodic actuality of el Amarna has been adopted as the starting-point for a more ambitious essay. The artist chooses for his subject a unique event (very different from the regularly-repeated functional acts figured on reliefs from Narmer's palette onwards) which occurred at a definite time and in a definite place; it is therefore an episode, to be treated with as much realism as he may choose to employ for the setting and for the details of his picture. But on the other hand he is executing a royal monument the purpose of which is to manifest not the casual but the permanent triumph of the divine ruler; realism therefore must be counterbalanced by symbolism. The old convention whereby Pharaoh is figured on a much larger scale than anyone else shows his superiority and concentrates the onlooker's attention on him; as himself the conqueror he must appear in the thick of the battle, but attitude and expression must imply not the effort but the inevitability of victory, the unique exploit illustrating a cosmic rule. This equipoise between the actual and the symbolic which is the secret of monumental art and, for the Egyptian, was a new departure, was attained by the artists working for Seti I, but it was too elusive to be reduced to a formula, and the sculptors of the next reigns were not sufficiently endowed with imagination to dispense with formulae. The vast compositions that sprawl over the walls of Thebes and Abu Simbel, celebrating the doubtful victory of Kadesh, exhibit a curious mixture of the formal and the pictorial, monotonous registers of identical figures alternating with a wild tangle of bodies which at least suggests the confusion of battle; but, although some of the detail is clever and lively enough, yet the whole is impressive for little more than its size. The sculptor, working strictly to the rule of the traditional canon, was still able to create, as in the seated figure of Ramses II now in Turin (Pl. 22, b), portrait statues almost worthy to rank with the masterpieces of old; but where, as in the reliefs, the link with the past had been broken, he is at a loss, having no ideal of his own.

Mesopotamia

When we turn from Egypt to Mesopotamia the first thing that strikes us is the relatively small amount of material available whereon to base our judgement of art. Of reliefs and of sculpture in the round only a few score examples, covering the whole of the long history of the country down to 1200 BC, contrast sadly with the thousands which Egypt can boast. None the less, there are amongst these few some which are outstanding in the whole range of ancient art and prove that the Mesopotamian sculptor amply played his part in the development of his country's civilization; and since the great majority of the works that have come down to us belongs to the early stages in that development we can trace with some confidence the genesis and nature of his contribution.

Of painting scarcely anything survives. At Warka a few traces of colour do no more than prove that the faces of the inner walls of the Jamdat Nasr period were adorned with paintings *in tempera,* but the designs of them are lost. At Tell Uqair, in the 'Painted Temple' dated by the excavators to the Uruk period, i.e. to the late fourth millennium BC, two more or less complete animals and human figures preserved only as high as the waist show that the wall decoration was of an elaborate pictorial nature.[7] For the time of the First Dynasty of Babylon, *c.* 1750 BC, we have the paintings in the palace at Mari[8] which alone are in fairly good condition. These show a curious mixture of styles. The main scenes are formal and stereotyped; the rectangular framed picture of the king's investiture (Pl. 27) might be an enlargement from a cylinder seal; on the long frieze the sacrifices by water and by fire look like different copies of the stelae of Ur-Nammu and of Gudea, and the gryphons, sphinxes and human-headed bulls are in a convention long since stale. On the other hand, the minor figures, a fisherman, a soldier, a man leading a bull to the sacrifice and men gathering dates from the tall palm-trees, are naturalistic, free and vivacious. It may be significant that two techniques are employed; the freely-drawn figures were sketched in outline in black paint with a surety that bespeaks a practised skill, but in the investiture scene the outlines were impressed with a point in the wet plaster, and seem to have been the work of an engraver rather than of a painter.

Interesting as are the Mari wall-decorations neither their number nor their date—for they must be regarded as works of the decadence—would justify us in basing on them any general appraisal of Sumerian painting. For any idea of style and treatment in earlier times we have to fall back on the circumscribed evidence of cylinder seals (a comparison which the Mari drawings seem to warrant) and of engraved shell plaques. Of the latter the Ur cemetery has supplied a large number belonging to the close of the Early Dynastic period, *c.* 2600–2500 BC, small rectangles of polished white shell engraved and enriched with niello (Pl. 28). They have not, of course, the colouring of wall paintings (though as such colours were always flat, without shading, they matter comparatively little) and lines cut into a hard substance cannot be expected to have the quality of the free-hand lines of the draughtsman;

they could be compared rather with the wood-blocks of the mediaeval German artists. But in their often naturalistic drawings of animals and in their calculated balance of black and white—which can even achieve a colouristic effect—they are admirable in themselves and surely imply that the lost paintings were of no mean order of art.

More than once in my earlier chapters it has been necessary to describe Sumer as a country in which stone is lacking, and that feature must here be emphasized again because of the effect it undoubtedly had upon sculpture. The Mosul area, it is true, yields that soft 'alabaster' which was regularly used by later Assyrian palace-builders for their wall-reliefs, but in the early days the knowledge of this seems not to have reached the craftsmen of the south, where civilization was most advanced; although the artists of Tell Asmar employed it freely, in the delta towns it occurs but seldom as an alternative to the rather rough limestone which could be got from the high desert bordering the valley. For important sculptures the Sumerians imported diorite (and sometimes trachyte), a hard stone capable of taking a fine polish, which was brought overseas in ships of the 'Magan' line, probably from Oman; it would appear that this was not quarried but came in the form of boulders, and the size and shape of such could not but influence the sculptor's work. The stone was expensive, and had to be used to the best advantage. Rarely would a block be long enough to make a life-size standing figure; much more often it lent itself better to one in a seated or a squatting position, and it is curious how frequently a seated Sumerian statue suggests the shape of the natural boulder from which it was economically carved. Further, because as will be seen later all statues were portraits,[9] and because the artist had very little interest in the anatomy of the body, only the facial features being important, the head is in most cases too large for the body; rather than reduce the scale of the portrait head to the dimensions demanded by his inadequate block of stone the sculptor was prepared to do full justice to the head at the body's expense. This naïve disproportion which we see even in the splendid statues of Gudea (in one of them the head is one-fifth of the total height) results directly from the lack of stones big enough to satisfy the requirements of sculptor and client.

Yet another consequence of the dearth of stone was to drive the artist to the use of other materials; reliefs and statues in the round were freely made of copper or bronze and sometimes of gold. Because the metal could always be melted down and re-used the chances of such works surviving are small, but enough is preserved to prove that from the Early Dynastic period onwards they were produced in great numbers.

From the al'Ubaid period we have nothing more than the carefully modelled and highly stylized terra-cotta figurines of goddesses found at Ur; these, while scarcely deserving the title of sculpture, must none the less be taken into account, for they are the sole forerunners of the art in which the next (Protoliterate) period was to show itself inexplicably confident and mature. Such qualities are most obvious in the magnificent gypsum vase from Warka (Pl. 30, c), belonging to the Uruk period; it stands about 3 feet (1 metre) high and is decorated with three bands of relief, the width of these diminishing from top to bottom to conform to the slightly tapered shape of the vase. The reliefs—in the top register the ritual workshop of the goddess Inana, then a procession of men bringing gifts, and below a row of rams and ewes—are shallowly cut but with a delicate surface-modelling which makes the figures stand out in sharp contrast with the background; the whole effect is austere, with dramatic action and even variation of pose reduced to a minimum, and yet astonishingly alive; the squat and plumply built gift-bearers are really carrying their burdens, are organic and individual, and in the upper register the figures are not merely juxtaposed but are related one to another in intention and in space. Much the same thing can be seen on the cylinder seals of the period. These may be schematically composed with, for instance, groups of animals antithetically arranged, or may be more pictorial, scenes of adoration or cult ritual, but always the figures are alive and in motion and, particularly in the scenes, the spatial relation is strongly emphasized; the artist—and the best of these seals are genuine works of art—aims not at a pattern but at concrete representation. This combination of lively observation and stylistic restraint is continued in the better works of the Jamdat Nasr period, such as the stone bowls decorated with figures of bulls in high relief or the little steatite carving of a wild boar found at Ur; in some degree it survives in the dedicatory limestone plaques which, in the temples, served as supports for offerings, but these are as a rule technically poor and wholly uninspired, mere records of some pious act performed. It might have been assumed that, with the beginning of the Early Dynastic period, the sculptor's art was in a decline if the evidence of the plaques had not been contradicted by that of such an outstanding work as the stele of Eannatum in which hieratic symbolism, formal and severe, is skilfully combined with the realistic battle scenes wherein not only violent action is portrayed but there is even an attempt, naïve but not unsuccessful, at spatial perspective.

Eannatum's stele, primitive though it be, yet possesses those monumental characteristics which find their full expression in the stele of Naram-Sin (Pl. 6, b). Here a single historic occurrence, individualized by its setting, is so treated as to acquire permanent significance. 'The topography, though partly formalized, has convincingly concrete details, and both it and the incidents of the battle hold a subtle balance between the decorative and the dramatic. The roughly triangular grouping, for instance, fits the shape of the stone, but it also underlines the climax of the action; and the upward surge of the conquerors is balanced by the falling and collapsing figures, halted by the rigidity of the four doomed survivors on the right. The smooth cone of the mountain top, rising well above the impressive figure of the king, does not dwarf him in any way but seems to emphasize his human stature and at the same time check the impetuosity of his stride. For the king's posture epitomizes the movement of the soldiers, yet he appears almost immobile at the moment of his triumph, holding the enemy transfixed with fear, and though his towering figure has a symbolical quality, the spatial relation between him and his prospective victims has been made more concrete by the tilting of their heads at different angles, the lower ones looking increasingly upwards. The king is thus not only the symbolical and decorative but also the actual dramatic centre of the whole composition, and the empty surface surrounding him emphasizes his spatial isolation. This aloofness is enhanced, not minimized, by the divine symbols at the top of the stele.' [10]

This detailed appreciation of the Naram-Sin stele is not out of place because, although it is the only monument of the kind to have survived, it may none the less well have been typical of its time. Even in the cylinder seals of the Sargonid Age (Pl. 29), whether the subject be the traditional antithetically opposed animal group or a mythological scene pictorially treated, we find 'the subtle balance between the decorative and the dramatic', the violent action held momentarily in suspense, and the spacing of the figures so that each is isolated against a clear background and by its detachment gains enormously in value. In the glyptic art of Sargon's day there are qualities which distinguish it altogether from the Early Dynastic wherein the dramatic was sacrificed to the decorative and the crowded figures gave a pattern rather than a picture, and distinguish it also from that of the Third Dynasty of Ur and all succeeding periods. In those later times the monotony of subject, giving no scope for imagination, reduced seal-cutting from an art to an industry. But in sculptural relief also the high-water mark had been reached by the upsurge of Sargonid art, and thereafter the ebb sets in. The stele of Ur-Nammu (Pl. 30, a) is indeed a striking monument whereon the dignified symbolism of the adoration scenes, enlivened by the floating figures of 'angels' pouring heaven's waters on the earth, contrasts but does not clash with the pictorial realism of the workmen who built the Ziggurat of Nannar; but the value of this as an artistic creation becomes less significant when we realize that it is almost identical with the stele of Gudea; the apparent originality of the Ur-Nammu relief is due to the accidents of survival, and in truth it is but one of a traditional series from which life was bound to fade progressively. In precisely the same way the relief that caps the text of Hammurabi's Code of Laws (Pl. 30, b) has won the highest praise; 'transcendent power and majesty on the one hand, dignified humility on the other, have been expressed with an economy of means and a convincingness never surpassed in ancient art', writes Groenewegen-Frankfort,[11] and it is indeed a dignified piece of sculpture and admirable in its technique; but the group is no other than an adaptation of that on Ur-Nammu's stele, nor is there here any invention but only a successful variation of a conventional theme.

If up to this point only reliefs have been considered, to the exclusion of sculpture in the round, it is because this was the field in which the Sumerian artist had the freer hand. The major reliefs at any rate were monuments intended to be seen by and to impress the public; it was a challenge which the sculptor had to meet as best he could, and the dramatic element which has been noticed in these works was one of his means to that end. Where reliefs were used for the adornment of buildings—in which case again they were meant to be seen—realistic representation could be combined with decoration; this can be seen in the bronze and copper reliefs of A-anni-pad-da's temple at al'Ubaid, in which the naturalism of the recumbent heifer (Pl. 11, a) is remarkable, whereas the great heraldic slab of the eagle grasping two stags is becomingly formal, symbolism prevailing over representation. But with statues in the round conditions were wholly different.

In Sumer statues were of two sorts only. In the first place there were the statues of the gods which were set up in the sanctuaries of the temples; these naturally had to conform with tradition and, though in human shape, must betray none of the passions or weaknesses of human beings; each deity must be identified by his or her attributes (which might be an animal supporting the throne or base of the image) but not by features or expression, nor must any hint of action impair the god's effortless omnipotence. Clearly here the sculptor's scope was limited. Statues of men, the second category, were needed not for public exhibition but for temple use. The pious Sumerian knew that there could be no well-being except by the favour of god, and that favour must be won by faithful attendance and prayer. Life was too short and too full for such constant devotion, but it could be managed by proxy; just as the deity was represented by an image made by man, so his worshipper might be symbolized in like fashion. Therefore he would have a statue of himself set in the temple, in the presence of the god's statue, and the effect would be the same as if the worshipper were present in person; obviously, if the statue was to fulfil its purpose, it must be a portrait of himself, since it was for himself that the divine blessing was asked, and the safest course was to show him in the attitude of humble prayer. This meant that while Sumerian statuary was strictly limited in range, confined to one or two conventional poses, the demand for portrait sculpture gave the artist boundless scope. But the client wanted something more than crude realism. He must be shown not quite as he really was but as he would wish the god to see him; he must appear at his best, and also must express the awe and the devotion that the sight of god should inspire; to that extent there must be idealization.

The earliest examples of such temple statues that we possess, the remarkable group from Tell Asmar (Pl. 31), illustrate very well, despite their archaic crudity, the ideal at which the artist aimed. The worshippers are shown standing upright with their hands clasped before their breasts in the attitude of prayer; their long skirts are simple sheaths, the upper part of the body together with the arms is schematized in a curiously geometrical fashion, but the heads, however grotesque they may appear, are individual and full of expression; there is an unmistakable awareness of the god's presence. The group includes one figure of a different sort, apparently a piece of temple furniture like the bronze wrestlers from Khafaje, a naked man kneeling; in this the treatment of the body is so lifelike and sensitive as to prove that the geometric stylization of the 'worshippers' is due not so much to the sculptor's lack of skill as to some established convention imposed upon him. Similar statuettes in gypsum and in bronze which were discovered at Khafaje, of a slightly later date in the Early Dynastic period, show that convention losing force; the drapery is for the most part still formless, but the torsos are almost realistic, the angular contour of the arms is modified to a natural attitude and there is a new variety of pose, as when one foot is advanced in the act of walking instead of both being planted stolidly in line as props for an immobile body; and now too there are seated as well as standing figures. Before the Early Dynastic period came to an end the Sumerian sculptor, without departing from the formal tradition, had advanced so far that out of the almost comic 'worshippers' of Tell Asmar there had developed real works of art. Naturally, where the demand was great (and the little temple statues are found on any site from Ur in the south to Mari in the north-west) quality is uneven, so that even in the portrait faces the intense piety of early days may degenerate into trivial and unmeaning smugness; but in the better examples the original religious significance is combined with an artistic appreciation of form and texture which is wholly admirable. Thus a female figure (Pl. 32, a) (e.g. one in the British Museum) may wear a cloak draped over the left shoulder and covering the upper arm which, though broadly treated, does suggest the form of the body and is interesting in itself; a male figure in Copenhagen (Pl. 32, b), seated cross-legged, which for dignity and expression is one of the most striking pieces of the series, wears a short fringed skirt and the musculature of the legs as seen below it is rendered with surprising realism; a seated figure of a woman temple-chorister found at Mari (Pl. 33, c) is so instinct with life that it is hard to recognize in it the traditional 'worshipper'. As his technique improved with experience the sculptor was no longer forced to rely on the adventitious aid invoked by his predecessors, paint and inlay; when working in limestone or alabaster he might still have the eyes, and perhaps the eyebrows, set with shell and lapis lazuli, but this was probably because the client had ordered a polychrome statue with black hair and coloured flesh-tints; but when he worked in diorite his sensitive modelling, to which the high polish of the stone did full justice, was far more expressive than any painted image. The Gudea statues are the latest examples preserved to us of the 'worshipper' series, and the finest; in their dignity of conception, in their delicacy of execution and in their emotional appeal they surpass anything that we have of earlier date and must be reckoned amongst the great works of art of the ancient world.

For the immense advance in artistic performance which is signalized by the Gudea statues some at least of the credit must be given to the sculptors of the Sargonid period. We have already seen that in work in relief they were innovators to an almost revolutionary extent; two heads sculptured in the round, one of a woman (found at Assur) and one of some local kinglet or governor from Adab, portraits but not necessarily 'worshippers', are strangely different in character from the ordinary run, and the male head in particular is strikingly individual. But the real art of the time is summed up in the magnificent bronze head from Nineveh, probably a portrait of Sargon himself (Pl. 33, a); this is a masterpiece in which the qualities of the metal are utilized with sympathetic understanding while a profound insight into human character sets upon an idealized head the unmistakable stamp of individuality. The art of portraiture in which the Sumerian thus excelled had reached its zenith by the time of the Third Dynasty of Ur (Pl. 34) (Gudea is now known to have been contemporary with Ur-Nammu) and flourished for some time after that; a diorite head found by the French at Susa, believed to be a portrait of Hammurabi (Pl. 33, b) in his later years, is tragic in its intensity and yet beautifully restrained in its rendering of old age.

Syria

The Mesopotamian monuments on which our judgement must be based are few and far between, and for the Kassite period there is nothing of import. But even if the school dwindled and perished it was a great one while it lasted, and it cannot but have influenced artists in other lands. From Alalakh, far away to the west, comes a diorite head, probably a portrait of Yarim-Lim, king of Yamkhad in the first half of the eighteenth century BC, which while not actually carved by a Sumerian at least owes much to Sumerian art; and it is difficult not to recognize some trace of Sumerian influence in the unique warrior who flanks the King's Gate at Hittite Bogazköy (Pl. 35, a). Syria and Anatolia, however, throughout the Bronze Age contributed little to the development of the major arts. The local schools of northern Syria and of the Phoenician coast were certainly productive, but did not attain a high level of performance; as Professor Frankfort has well put it, 'they lack cultural continuity; their art shows a succession of more or less promising starts which lead nowhere'.[12] Much of their work was imitative, based upon foreign originals; this is particularly true of the southern Phoenician towns. Where, as happens more often in the north, we find an art of a more indigenous sort, Hurrite art, its interest is local rather than general. Ugarit has yielded numerous statuettes in bronze and in silver which, though not without traces of Sumerian or occasionally of Aegean influence, are yet markedly individual; but in themselves they are far inferior to what was being produced in Egypt or in Mesopotamia, and it is difficult to maintain that from them arose any later art of intrinsic value. Alalakh has produced a few stone carvings which deserve mention here only because they seem to illustrate the beginnings of the Syro-Hittite school which was to dominate north Syria in the early Iron Age; it is possible that some reliefs from Carchemish belong to the Bronze Age (a point on which authorities are not agreed) and if so they must be taken as examples of that Hurri art which otherwise is deduced from cylinder seals and from later monuments.

Hittite

Closely associated with Hurri art is that of the Anatolian Hittites. This, so far as is known, was a late development, none of the monuments being necessarily earlier than the fifteenth century BC, and, considering the political importance of the Hittites, a disappointing one; as a recent writer on the subject has said, 'In actual fact it should not be assumed that the art of the New Kingdom offers any unexpected display of beauty, profusion and sophistication. The sculpture of the period is rather inferior, and the other artistic remains are conspicuously rare. When mention is made of Boğazköy, Alaca Höyük, the rock-carvings of Yazilikaya and of a number of scattered finds here and there in central Anatolia, nearly all has been said.[13]

The gate sculptures of Boğazköy, apart from the King's Gate warrior, are modelled on north Syrian precedents. The Yazilikaya reliefs (Pl. 35, b), a complete picture-gallery carved in the living rock, are an astonishing *tour de force* if only for the immense scale of the whole thing; from the point of view of Hittite religion they are of supreme importance; from the point of view of art they certainly represent the highest attainment of the Hittite sculptors. In the best of them (for not all are by the same hand, and the quality is uneven) the technique is excellent, and there is a delicate modelling of the surface combined with the deliberate intention of keeping the figures to a single plane and accentuating the outline so as to produce the effect of silhouettes isolated against their background; the flat two-plane relief is characteristic of Hittite art in general—we see it at Alaca Höyük and in the earlier reliefs at Carchemish—and it can be childishly inept, but the Yazilikaya artists have refined it with surprising success. But for all their incidental virtues these rock carvings can hardly be ranked as masterpieces of the world's art. Here, in what was probably their holiest sanctuary, close to the capital of the empire, a powerful Hittite monarch would undoubtedly employ the best native artists of his day, but their performance will not stand comparison with what was being done in Egypt; theirs is an art essentially provincial, here seen at its best, and apparently unable to advance beyond the Yazilikaya level. For the Alaca Höyük reliefs, which compared with Yazilikaya are almost comically crude, are the direct ancestors of the Syro-Hittite reliefs of the early Iron Age, some of which are artistically admirable; but the development is not along the lines of Yazilikaya; it results from influences wholly alien to the Bogazköy school. In a study of the ancient art of the Middle East it would be impossible to omit that of the Anatolian Hittites, but it would be wrong to over-estimate its merit or its importance.

India

In lands farther to the east the paucity of evidence baffles the historian of art. There is no stone in the Indus valley, all had to be imported, as was the case in Sumer also, and for that reason stone sculpture was likely to be relatively rare and on a small scale. This seems to be confirmed by excavation, for there have been found at Mohenjo-daro (apart from inconsiderable fragments) only one human bust, one head and a small headless seated figure, and at Harappā two fragmentary statuettes; from Mohenjo-daro comes also one bronze figurine of a dancing girl.

The Harappā figures, one of a standing youth and the other of a dancing youth (Pl. 36, a and b), are masterpieces of sculpture. The red stone torso of the standing youth (Pl. 36, b) is a direct transcript from nature in so far as anatomical truth is concerned and is definitely Indian in type;[14] but a certain idealization which removes it from mere realism, and the wonderfully sensitive modelling of the surface, might have been due to a Greek sculptor of the fifth century BC. The grey stone dancer is, by contrast, of a more effeminate type; the complicated poise and the swing of movement are rendered with consummate skill, and if, as Sir John Marshall inferred from the abnormal thickness of the neck (the head, in this as in the first figure, was made separately) the dancer was three-faced, this was as beautiful a representation of the youthful Siva Natarāja as India was to produce in any subsequent age. Of the Mohenjo-daro figures the bust of a bearded man wearing a cloak (Pl. 37) with trefoil decoration, is a remarkable piece of work; the inlaid pattern of the dress might both in technique and in motif have been derived from Sumer, but about the head there is nothing Sumerian; not only is the type of face different, but the half-closed eyes concentrated on the tip of the nose seem to proclaim this to be a *Yogi* and therefore essentially Indian. Because all emotion and virtually all expression are deliberately eliminated (deliberately, the subject being what it is) this head is perhaps less striking than the other which, though of more summary workmanship, is more in the nature of an individual portrait, that of a bearded man with plaited hair, in which character is suggested with the utmost economy of means. The seated figure, simply but well modelled, is perhaps of interest chiefly as proving that the sculptor had a fairly wide range. The bronze figure of a naked nautch girl (Pl. 36, c), in spite of the conventional elongation of the arms (there is the same exaggeration in a similar but much rougher example also from Mohenjo-daro), is a charming little *jeu d'esprit,* beautifully modelled and instinct with life.

The two main Indus valley sites have, then, between them yielded no more than half a dozen incomplete examples of sculpture to serve as criteria for the artistic output of as many centuries. Yet these few do enable us to glimpse an art of a very high order and of great originality. If to their evidence we add that of some of the engraved seals (Pl. 38) we can with but little hesitation affirm that the Harappā art was not sterile but motivated and made possible the Dravidian art of later ages.

China

For China the evidence available is even less than that for India. A few fragments of worked marble found in the town ruins of Anyang prove the existence in the Shang era of large stone sculptures but tell us nothing about their character or quality; for that we must look to the carvings in marble or limestone, mostly of very small size, which come from the tombs. These figurines would appear to have been decoration attached to articles of furniture so that they would be more correctly described as objects of applied art and judged in the same way as the zoomorphic bronze vessels of the same period, but they may at least give some idea of the major works which have disappeared. For the most part they represent animals—tigers and elephants, pigs and owls, but one shows a man seated upon the ground, dressed in a garment the embroidered patterns on which recall the incised decoration of the bronzes (Pl. 39); the little figure (it is only 6 inches—0.15 metre—high) is boldly sketched, with no attempt at realistic detail but with a highly skilled appreciation of form and a three-dimensional rendering which is eminently sculpturesque. From such a figure as this, and from the bronzes—particularly the famous elephant in the Musée Guimet (Pl. 40), may be of the Chou period but certainly is in the Shang tradition (the circumstances of its discovery are unknown)—

it is fair to conclude that the enduring character of Chinese art had been formed as early as the fourteenth century BC and that the technical excellence of the Shang bronzes was paralleled by the artistic quality of Shang sculpture.

Crete

The only other country which has yielded evidence of noteworthy performance in the fine arts during the Bronze Age is Crete. No large-scale sculptures have been found there, but small bronzes and ivory carvings, coloured stucco reliefs and fresco paintings illustrate an art completely different from anything that Egypt or Mesopotamia can show. Granted that Crete borrowed the technique of fresco-painting from Asia and granted, too, that the one recognizable design on the scanty fresco remains from Alalakh does anticipate the motif of windblown grass which occurs at and is characteristic of Knossos, it is none the less true that the Cretans evolved an art entirely their own, inspired with a spirit alien to all Middle Eastern thought, aiming, one is driven to suppose, not at any magical or symbolic use but at a purely aesthetic satisfaction. Some of the subjects such as those of bull-fighting, boxing-bouts and dances may be drawn from 'games' which were in the nature of religious ritual, but it is the spectacular and not the religious aspect that is emphasized, and for the underwater scenes with their rocks, fish and nautili, for the 'landscapes' with their riot of wild flowers, the birds, the hunting cat or the leaping deer, there is no religious basis at all, only the desire for decoration and the love of nature.

The desire for decoration does not show itself only in the frescoes which covered the palace wall; it extended also to pottery. It is a commonplace of history that a primitive people may produce clay vessels painted with elaborate art but, with increasing wealth, will prefer table-services of metal-bronze, silver or gold, caring nothing for mere crockery, so that the potter can find a market for no more than the plain vessels intended for kitchen use. The Cretans of the Middle Minoan period made the exquisite egg-shell wares adorned with patterns in red and white on a black ground which were even exported as luxury goods to Egypt (Pl. 22, b); it is more surprising to find that in the Late Minoan II period, when the metal-workers were fashioning in gold and silver the splendid jugs and goblets pictured on the walls of Egyptian tombs, clay vessels were still held in honour and were decorated with painted designs which for painstaking artistry are in no way inferior to the frescoes (Pl. 12).

The love of nature is unmistakable, and the observation of

nature is equally manifest, but all this is, in the frescoes, subordinate to decorative effect. Not only will the artist combine the leaves of one plant with the flowers of another, but he never treats his scene realistically as a 'landscape'; the whole ground of the painting may be divided into bands and patches of colour—red, pink, yellow, blue and grey—whose sinuous outlines bear no relation to anything in nature, and against it the plants are drawn regardless of the changes of background and, if they happen to come high up in the composition, may be drawn sideways or upside down; it is 'landscape' only in terms of decoration, and the effect is curiously alive but not lifelike.

'Aliveness' is indeed the peculiar feature of Cretan art, alike in painting and in sculpture. The Sumerian sculptor portrays his client in the absorbed quietude of worship, the Egyptian figures him as 'life in death' or, in the case of Pharaoh, as a being of another world for whom action is only symbolized by attitude. The Cretan artist had no use for such suspended animation. The famous bronze showing the athlete in the middle of his somersault over the back of the galloping bull (Pl. 42, b), the ivory youth leaping forward, his head down, also from a bull-fighting group, these are as vigorous in action as sculpture can be; but even where no violent movement is involved, as in the ivory statuette (Pl. 42, a) or in the faience Snake goddesses (Pl. 41), there is a tension and an alertness giving the same impression of potential vigour. 'Überhaupt Leben', 'life absolute', is Ludwig Curtius's description, and Groenewegen-Frankfort comments, 'The phrase might well serve as a motto for any treatment of Cretan art, for movement, organic movement, seems of its very essence; movement in beast or man, in wind-blown flowers with petals dropping, in the writhing stems of creepers clinging to rocks, even in the rocks themselves, which seem a substance barely solidified'; but she goes on to say that the movement here is of a peculiar kind, effortless, unhampered, and self-contained in that it is balanced by a counter-movement which makes it appear self-centred yet never at rest.

Without doubt Cretan art, even when the subjects chosen by the artist are such as bull-fights, dances or harvest processions, had a religious basis. With the details of that—about which much has been written—we are not concerned, but we may summarize the matter by saying that the Cretan artist interpreted his religion as the complete acceptance of the grace of life. If we turn from the island to the mainland of Greece we shall see that, although Mycenaean art is technically identical with Cretan, so that one even suspects that the best of its works were made by Cretans in the service of Mycenaean patrons, yet it is in a measure secularized and has lost something in the process. The Vaphio gold cups (Pl. 43) show men fighting bulls, but it is a real fight, not a ritual, and in the design there is none of that antithetical movement which renders a phase of action complete in itself; the Mycenaean dagger-blades with their magnificent polychrome inlay have hunting scenes—i.e. purely secular scenes—but the violent action pictured so skilfully has not that compensating balance on which the Cretan at home would have insisted. The technique could be practised far afield, but the spirit was not for export, and only in its native island did Minoan art attain the level at which it must rank as the most inspired of the ancient world.

THE APPLIED ARTS

The major arts have been dealt with regionally because sculptors and painters, working as they did in nearly every case either for temples or for the rulers of the state, were profoundly influenced by the religious conceptions and by the political structure of their own countries; and because these were very different the inspiration of the artists manifested itself in different ways; the fine arts were, strictly speaking, local and national.

But with the applied arts the conditions are not the same. Obviously, the technique is identical. The Sumerian artist who carved the reliefs on the great gypsum vase of Inana found at Warka could turn his hand to the decoration of a toilet-box for a lady of the king's court; the Egyptian who made portrait statues for the tombs of Eighteenth Dynasty nobles could in his spare time fashion the handle of an ivory spoon in the form of a swimming girl. Obviously, too, the canons which had been formulated for sculpture proper would be followed in these minor works also—the professional artist was too habituated to them to think of departing from them, and the craftsman naturally copied what everybody knew to be good and right. Superficially, therefore, the distinction between the fine and the applied arts might seem unwarranted.

But the toilet-box and the spoon-handle have no serious background. The man who makes any such thing is not doing honour to a god, manifesting the glory of a divine Pharaoh or securing the well-being of a man's soul; he is making a pretty thing which will take people's fancy by its prettiness and ingenuity and will sell at a fancy price. He is not bound by any conventions other than those which have become for him second nature; he can give free rein to his imagination and his whimsy, can appeal as profitably to the humour as to the aesthetic taste of his public but, if he is to command a market, he must make full use of his technical skill. The applied arts, therefore, are imbued with a totally different spirit from that of the fine arts, and they enjoy a vastly greater freedom of subject and of treatment; moreover, they circulate far more widely. Sculpture in the round, reliefs and wall paintings were for home consumption. It is true that a victorious Pharaoh might build an Egyptian temple in a Syrian town which he had added to his dominions, and would send statues of himself to stand in the temple or, more often, would send an Egyptian court artist to carve such statues on the spot; but relatively few of the Syrian townsmen would enter the temple to see Pharaoh's statue, and if they did it would be for them not an object of art but a symbol of their own enslavement. When, in an upsurge of patriotism, the citizens of Ugarit smashed the sphinxes of Amenemhet III, the statue

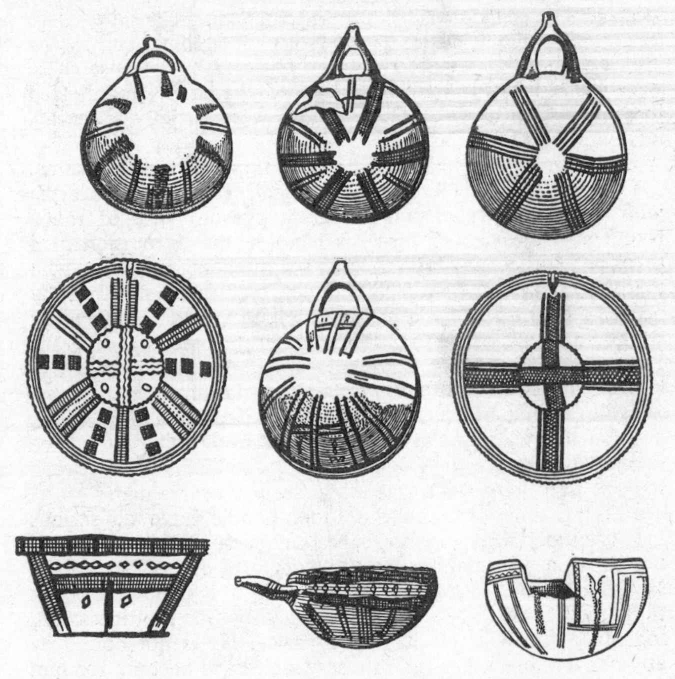

FIG. 35. *'Cypriote White-slip ware' (after Walters).*

of the wife of Sesostris II and that of the Egyptian governor of the town, they were destroying the evidence of foreign domination; but the same people would not in the least object to using—and treasuring—an unguent-vase of ivory or alabaster carved in the characteristic style of Egypt. The minor works of art were valued for their own sake; they were freely exported and they, not the great masterpieces, spread abroad the knowledge of the art of any one of the ancient civiliza-

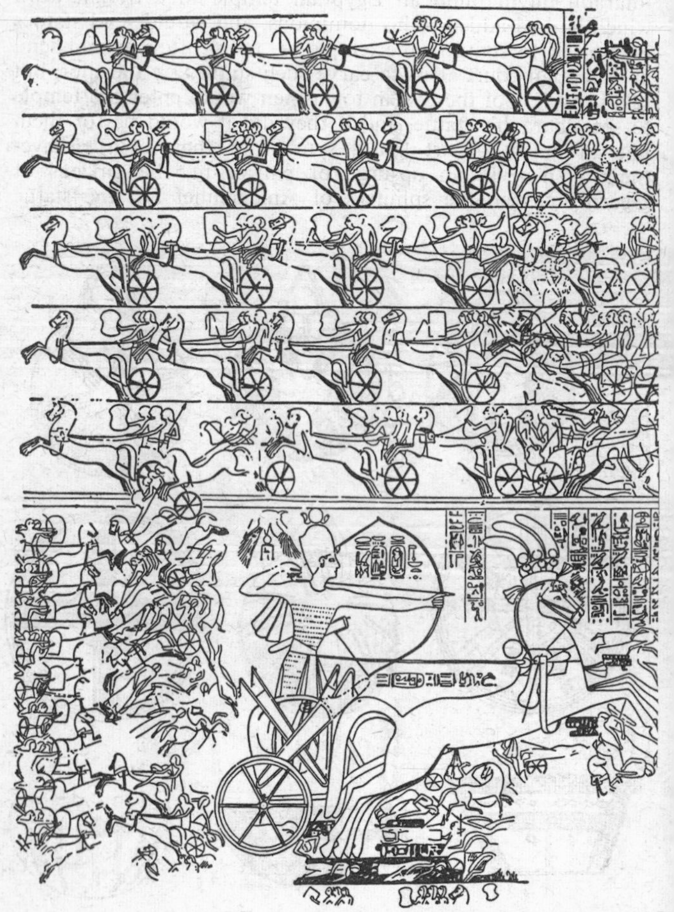

FIG. 36. *'The Battle of Kadesh' (after Frankfort).*

tions. Where they found favour they would be copied by local craftsmen or would influence local styles. When, in the eighteenth century BC, Alalakh had control of the elephant reserve in Niya and so monopolized the north Syrian ivory supply,[15] the Alalakh craftsmen carved ivory objects in the styles of Egyptian, Hurrite and Aegean art indiscriminately (Pl. 16). At Ugarit were found a bowl (Pl. 44) and a patera of beaten gold, dated between 1450 and 1350 BC, in whose

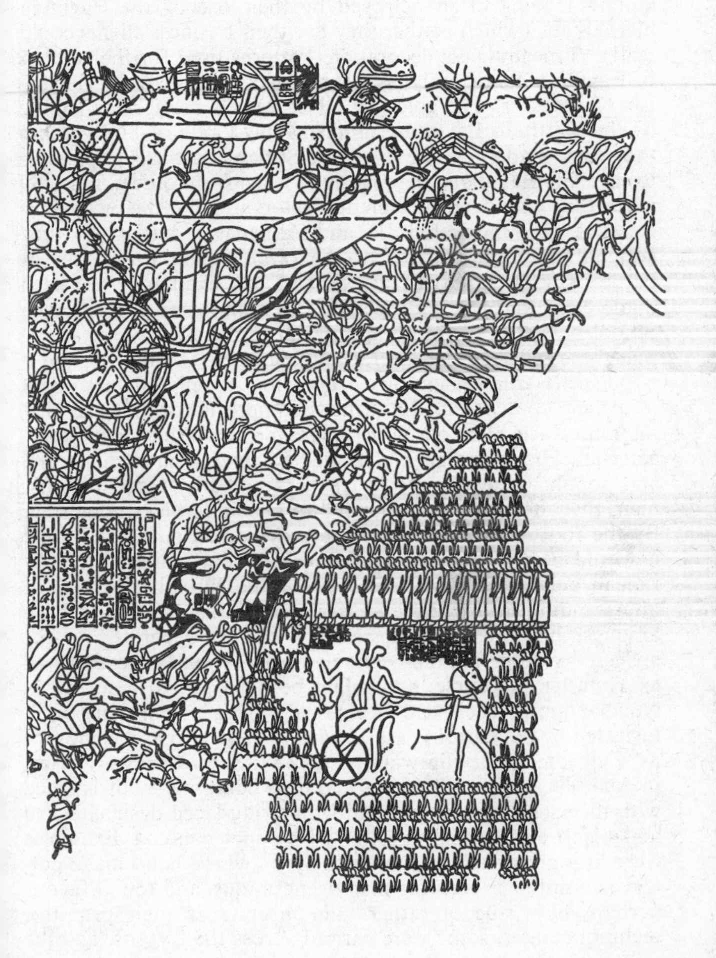

decoration the styles of Egypt, of the Aegean and perhaps of Mesopotamia are inextricably fused together with the rather naïve local Syrian art as solvent. From Enkomi in Cyprus comes a bowl of gold, silver and niello of which it is hard to say in what country it was made, so various are the possibilities suggested both by its technique and by its design. The craftsmen of the Phoenician coast towns industriously copied or adapted Egyptian motifs, their otherwise successful imitation being often betrayed by their use of the Egyptian hieroglyphs (which neither they nor their business clients could read) as meaningless decoration. Patterns used for the ceilings of Egyptian Twelfth Dynasty tombs were borrowed by the artists of Knossos. The gold and silver vessels brought as tribute by the Keftiu to Egypt are unmistakably Cretan—but whether they were made in Crete or on the Syrian coast it is impossible to say. The Egyptians were ready to learn from others, not only when they employed Aegean decorators to paint the pavement-frescoes of Amenhotep III and Akhenaton but when they adopted the Cretan motif of the *galop volant* for scenes of battle or hunt. In the earlier part of this chapter it has been made clear that the leading countries maintained each its own school of art in sculpture and painting, necessarily so, seeing that these reflected the several religions of the countries; and it is perfectly true that motifs originating in religious art might lose their content and be turned to mere decoration, so that the minor arts also to a large degree preserve their local character; but the interchange of traded goods was on such a scale, and popular designs were so freely imitated by foreign craftsmen, that the applied arts tended to become internationalized. By the fourteenth century BC the process had gone far. While it would be an exaggeration to speak of an 'eastern Mediterranean culture' at that time, we may be sure that a man of any standing in any eastern Mediterranean town would have amongst his household possessions objects decorated in the styles of various national schools of art, would take them all as a matter of course, and might be hard put to it to say in which country each had been made. This promiscuity is illustrated by the curious case of what is known to archaeologists as 'Cypriote White-slip ware' (Fig. 35). Some backward tribe, in Anatolia, apparently, made and used hand-made bowls faced with meerschaum clay, painted with string-laced designs in red and black and furnished with 'wish-bone' handles. Examples were brought down into northern Syria, where hand-made pottery had not been seen for many generations, and found favour perhaps by virtue of rather than in spite of their primitive technique; later, some were carried across the Cyprus, and the always imitative Cypriotes, seeing that they were popular, began to manufacture very passable copies and, expanding a successful industry, exported them all over the eastern Mediterranean. A Syrian of about 1400 BC might, if asked, have said that his 'milk-bowl' came from Cyprus, or might have attributed it to some Syrian coast factory, possibly manned by Cypriotes; he would probably have had no idea that this fashionable and exotic object had anything to do with a barbarous Anatolian tribe.

The common familiarity with and acceptance of foreign art forms, an important factor in man's artistic and intellectual advance, was based on the active exchange through trade channels of the products of commercial studios and also, to some extent, on the work of peripatetic guildsmen travelling in search of employment. The process was interrupted by the catastrophic events that marked the beginning of the twelfth century BC, but it had already done much to widen men's minds and to prove to them that art has no frontiers.

NOTES TO CHAPTER IX

1. In the opinion of Professors I. M. Diakonoff and J. S. Gasiorowski, an artist may outgrow the limitations of his surroundings and of his time, but his work will all the same reflect the conditions of contemporary society. The relation between art and the constituent factors of society is undoubtedly complicated and not always easy to apprehend.
2. According to Professor J. S. Gasiorowski, culture and civilization are primarily the expression of an élite, consisting of the intellectual, social and political leading elements in a given society. The opinion that the art of the ancient Orient has been exclusively destined for the élite is, for him, untenable. The colossal figures of Ramses II hewn in rock in Abu Simbel in Nubia, and the colossal figures at the doorways of the Assyrian palaces, even the lions of enamelled brick lining the walls of the procession street at Babylon in the time of Nebuchadnezzar were not for the élite only.
3. Professor J. Leclant draws attention to the technique of recessed relief and points to the existence of fairly deep relief work such as that of Ramses III at Medinet Habu.
4. Professor J. Leclant feels that the whole problem of Egyptian methods of rendering depth and even, perhaps, perspective deserves further study.
5. See note 16 on p. 512.
6. H. A. Groenewegen-Frankfort, *Arrest and Movement: An Essay on Space and Time in the Representational Art of the Ancient Near East* (Chicago, 1951), p. 50.
7. *Journal of Near Eastern Studies,* II, No. 2.
8. A. Parrot, 'Les Peintures du palais de Mari', *Syria* XVIII (1937), p. 325.
9. Professor I. M. Diakonoff has contested the claim that pre-Sargonic Sumerian statues were portraits. Sir Leonard Woolley, however, maintained his opinion in face of this objection.

10. H. A. Groenewegen-Frankfort, *Arrest ana Movement*, p. 164.
11. *Ibid.*, p. 168.
12. *The Art and Architecture o, the Ancient Orient*, p. xxv.
13. M. Vieyra, *Hittite Art, 2300–750* BC. (London, 1955).
14. In front of each shoulder there is a deep depression made with a tubular drill. Sir John Marsnall suggests that the holes were intended to take inlay in the form of rosettes such as appears on a terra-cotta from Baluchistan. To Sir Leonard Woolley it seems almost certain that they were to take a second pair of arms (the first pair also were made separately and fitted into sockets) in which case we have a (standing, not dancing) figure of the Siva type.
15. On the presence oi elephants in north-west Syria, see *supra*, pp. 306, 319, n. 31; 547; also R. O. Barnett, *Journal of Hellenistic Studies*, 68 (1948), pp. 6–7.

CHAPTER X

MUSIC AND LITERATURE

MUSIC

IT might well be said that of all the arts music contributes most to man's culture, if only because its appeal is direct, emotional and universal, requiring for its appreciation no intellectual effort and no sophisticated training: 'Give me the making of a people's songs and I care not who makes their laws' is a scarcely exaggerated tribute to the power of music. A history of human progress, therefore, which left music out of account would be sadly imperfect.

Unfortunately there is little that can be said about music itself. It is possible to describe at length the various instruments used for music-making; it is possible also to see on what occasions and for what purposes they were used and to judge therefrom the part which music played in the life of the people; and again, from casual references in the texts, it is possible sometimes at least to learn what emotional response the several instruments were supposed to elicit; but of the character and quality of the music we know nothing.

In 1915 Dr Ebeling published a tablet from Assur of the eighth century BC which gives in parallel columns the text of a Sumerian hymn on the Creation of Man and the Assyrian translation of it; in a third column on the left-hand side of the tablet there are, corresponding to each line of the hymn, groups of cuneiform signs which are no part of the text and might be the musical notation. Traces of similar signs used in the same way have been found on a tablet from Sippar which is not later in date than the sixteenth century BC.

Dr Curt Sachs, working upon this Assur tablet, arrived at the conclusion that the Babylonians (which term should include the Sumerians also) had a non-chromatic pentatonic musical system, but that their melodies were not bound to one rigid five-tone scale; they could range freely within four inter-related five-tone scales. He supported this view by an argument based on a seventh-century Assyrian relief showing seven 'Elamite' harpists who are welcoming the king with music; they are all playing on different strings; the numbers of the strings follow in intervals of five (the 5th, 10th and 15th, and the 8th, 13th and 18th) and, on the assumption that the Assyrian sculptor represented the scene with photographic exactitude, this must mean that the genus was pentatonic, either with major thirds and semitones, or with minor thirds and whole tones. On the basis of this, Sachs reviews other pictures of harpists in which the strings and plucking fingers are equally clearly shown, pictures not uncommon in Egyptian tomb reliefs, and comes to the conclusion that in Egypt, from the early third millennium BC, fifths and fourths, octaves and unisons, can all be found: 'It proves', he says, 'the use of pentatonically tuned instruments, although this in turn does not necessarily imply pentatonic melodies.'

Canon Galpin also deals at length with the 'notation' signs on the Assur tablet, and goes so far as to reconstruct the air of the Creation Hymn, but he rejects Sachs's theory entirely. Sumerian and Babylonian music, he maintains, was not pentatonic at all but heptatonic. While a five-note scale was widely circulated amongst primitive peoples in east Africa, the southern parts of Asia and Indonesia, the seven-note scale is the basis for Mesopotamian, Indian, Korean and Chinese music.[1] He does not accept the pictures of harpists as evidence, holding that sculptors and artists often omitted strings if space were limited, and confines himself to actual instruments or to names denoting a certain number of strings, e.g. the Akkadian *sabîtu* with its seven strings, i.e. three series of seven-note scales such as are found in the Chinese system also.

That two diametrically opposed theories should be deduced from the same evidence, namely the Assur tablet, is proof that the evidence is insufficient. Moreover, Professor Landsberger not only condemns Sachs's interpretation of the signs in the first column as pure assumption, Babylonian culture never having attained so high a pitch as Sachs's very intricate scale formation would imply, but further affirms that the signs have no connection with music at all.

Giving up, therefore, all hope of recovering from the material at present available the character of Bronze Age music, we can turn to the consideration of the instruments. In these Babylonia was extremely rich, and most of the types illustrated either by surviving examples or by representation in sculpture, etc., can be traced at least into the Early Dynastic period, early in the third millennium.

Instruments of Percussion

Clappers. These are curved flat pieces of metal or of wood, sometimes mounted on handles, which were held one in each hand and beaten together. Such can scarcely be called a musical instrument; it is simply a more effective version of the hand-clapping universally employed to accentuate the rhythm of dance or song.

Drums. These differ from the clappers in being not merely rhythmic but tonal and tunable. There were several types. The commonest was a small instrument with a wooden body, circular, either straight-sided or bowl-shaped over which the leather was stretched and fixed, probably, by wooden pegs; a variant is hour-glass-shaped, and yet another had a terra-cotta body of a shape rather like that of a champagne glass on which the leather was made fast by a cord. These drums, which were played horizontally with both hands, could stand upright on the ground or be carried by means of a strap round the player's neck; in size they vary from 6 inches to a foot (0.15 to 0.30 metre) in diameter. Representations show us a larger kettle-drum standing some 3 feet (1 metre) high, played by one player. The little drums might be used on any occasion, secular or religious; for temple use there were big drums whose note is compared to 'the bellowing of a bull'; these might be as much as 5 feet (1.60 metre) in diameter and were either suspended from poles or were stood on edge and were played by two men with drumsticks.

Timbrels. These might be either circular or rectangular, with shallow frames and normally one head only; they were used in temples to accompany certain hymns and liturgies. The square type may have been of copper.

Sistra. The spur-shaped sistrum is represented on the inlay of an Early Dynastic harp from Ur and an actual (but fragmentary) example was found there of which the 'jingles' strung on the wires were of white shell and therefore can have made but little noise. We have no later record of it, and it may have dropped out of use in Mesopotamia. It was at all times common in Egypt, and thence passed into Crete in Minoan times and is represented on the Harvesters' Vase.

Wind Instruments

Flutes. The vertically-held simple reed tube, sounded by blowing across one of its open ends, was from very early times a favourite instrument, especially for joyful occasions—Gudea of Lagash (*c.* 2150 BC) tells the Director of Music in the temple 'to cultivate diligently flute-playing and to fill the fore-court of Eninnu with joy'. It had three finger-holes, equidistant from each other, and according to Galpin could, by the help of the first and second registers of the harmonic series, produce a diatonic scale of seven notes with a sharp or tritone fourth; this scale could be extended into a second octave. One of the names of the flute was 'the seven-tone'; another was 'the long flute' or 'the large reed', and the names alone suffice to give its character. Besides its temple use it was a regular accompanist to love songs and was even thought to exercise a lascivious influence upon the hearer, so that according to a Jewish tradition the angel who warned Lot of the fate impending over Sodom said, 'There are flute players in the land, and the land ought to be destroyed'—a very different reason from that for which the flute was condemned by Alcibiades.

Pipes. The single pipe held at an angle, or horizontally, with the vibrating tongue of the reed between the lips, appears very early and is soon followed by the double pipe, actual examples of which were found in an Early Dynastic grave at Ur. It might be made of wood or reed, but was more often of metal, silver or copper; the pipes were about 10 inches long, slender, and with four finger-holes giving the octave. It is probable that even in the early period there was in use a variant in which the pipes were bent and had an upturned bell—or horn-shaped top opening; such 'bent pipes' are mentioned in a Sumerian list of objects brought to a temple. A tapered pipe (both single and double) was perhaps Syrian rather than Sumerian in origin, but it may be referred to in the Ishtar epic; it was a high-pitched instrument and the pipes being conical would sound an octave above the ordinary double pipe with cylindrical reeds. The double pipe is represented on a painted coffin of late Minoan date from Hagia Triada.

Horns and Trumpets. There is in the British Museum a conch-shell trumpet from Nineveh, and presumably such were in use from an early date. The bull's horn trumpet is mentioned on the cylinders of Gudea (*c.* 2150 BC), but before that time metal trumpets were being made. This seems to have been pre-eminently a temple instrument (for which its crescent form would further recommend it); in combination with the big drum it constituted 'full music' and, like the drum, was described as making a noise like the roaring of a bull. Akin to this was the straight trumpet used by the army, a wooden instrument sometimes overlaid with gold which was built up from several parts bound together. The oldest examples are votive miniatures in gold found at Tepe Hissar and at

Astarabad and dated to the seventeenth century BC; three hundred years later Egypt is receiving such trumpets from Dushratta, king of Mitanni; so that a Caucasian rather than a Mesopotamian origin is suggested for the instrument.

Stringed Instruments

Harps. The harp is one of the oldest and most characteristic of Mesopotamian musical instruments, so much so that its invention was ascribed directly to the great god Enlil; and the description given of that mythological original corresponds very closely to the actual examples preserved to us. There are two main types, the bow-shaped (which is the more primitive) and a more or less rectangular type which was never very large and could be played either in an upright or in a horizontal position; it is this latter form that is the ancestor of the modern harp.

A small bow-shaped harp is represented on a vase-relief from Bismya of the fourth millennium BC and on a rather later relief from Khafaje; an actual third millennium example comes from Ur, a large standing instrument (it is 3 feet long by 3 feet 6 inches high) with a deep and wide sound-box decorated, as was the harp of Enlil, with the head of a calf in gold; it had eleven strings which passed over metal guides and were twisted round the upright arm to be tightened or loosened by hand; the number of strings varies in different instruments from 4, 5, 7 to 11, and up to 21, giving three series of seven diatonic notes to the scale; this last, which we see in the Elamite 'orchestra', may be an Assyrian development and occurs at a late date in Egypt. The instrument used by the Elamite orchestra is the upright harp, in which the strings are set more vertically than in the bow harp, where they form a triangle with the sound-box and the arm; it was played with the fingers, whereas for the bow harp the Sumerians had used a long plectrum.

Lyres. These popular instruments were made in many sizes and with a good deal of variety in ornament if not in shape. The lyre is distinguished from the harp by having two uprights with a cross-bar between them, and the strings, attached to the cross-bar, instead of passing down into the sound-box are stretched over a bridge placed on the side of the sound-box and are tuned by short rods set on the cross-bar; these were for fine tuning, the twisting of the rod altering the tension of the string. The number of the strings varies from 4 or 5 (these are pictured representations and not necessarily true to life) to 7, 8 and 11 on actual examples, the last being apparently the most favoured number.

Where we have illustrations of lyres being played on what seems to be civil or domestic occasions the instruments are mostly small and are simply fashioned. The big lyres found in the tombs of the Early Dynastic period at Ur correspond to those described in various texts as dedicated to or used in the service of the temples in that they are adorned with animal heads in copper, silver or gold; in some cases the sounding-box is a schematized rendering of the animal's body; in one the animal, a stag, is shown standing in a boat and merely supports one of the uprights. In the dedication-texts the animal connected with the lyre is normally the bull, and stress is laid on the fact that the sound of the lyre is like the bellowing of the bull. If that association of form and sound generally held good, it is interesting to remark that in one royal burial at Ur there were in the death-pit three lyres which had clearly all been played at the same time (the fingers of the players were on the strings) and which represent three different animals, the bull, the heifer and the stag, so that they may well have been instruments of different tones.[2] The lyre was especially favoured as the accompaniment to the human voice. On the 'Standard of Ur' a musician with a bull-shaped lyre is shown accompanying a woman soloist at the solemn banquet celebrating the Sumerian victory; in a hymn to Ishtar of about 2100 BC it is written, 'I will speak to thee with the lyre [*AL-GAR*] whose sound is sweet'. The Minoans used a lyre made of ibex horns.

Lutes. The lute, with its small (generally circular) sounding-box and long neck on which the strings can be 'stopped' by the fingers, is almost certainly a northern instrument. It may have originated in the Caucasus area or beyond that, in Russian Asia in the neighbourhood of the Caspian Sea; in Mesopotamia there is no early reference to it, and the earliest examples date from the Kassite period. In the course of the second millennium it becomes fairly common there and soon reaches Egypt also; but the fact that it does not seem to have been used in Mesopotamian temple ritual even in Assyrian times would tend to show that it was a foreign instrument introduced only at a late date.

It is indeed tantalizing to know the character of so many different instruments and yet to be unable to deduce from them any certain conclusions about the music itself. It must be remembered, however, that only too often the information even as regards the instruments is indecisive, e.g. in the case of reliefs, etc., the number of strings shown may have no relation to the facts; that the stringed instruments could be tuned to any progression; that the wind instruments are not in a condition to be played and reproductions of them are unreliable, seeing that so much depends upon the strength and thickness of the reeds: even in the case of the pipes found at Ur different authorities arrive at totally different results. However interesting it may be to try to trace back the nature of the music played from the synagogue chants of the Jews through Late Babylonian to Sumerian, such deduction is too problematic to find a place in the history of early music.

The actual structure of the Egyptian instruments seems to show—what indeed our knowledge of their mathematics would lead us to expect—that the Egyptians never of themselves advanced beyond the arithmetical progression of the equipartition system. It was the Mesopotamians, with their better mathematical understanding, who decided on a geometric progression whereby in music the distances of stopping are increased proportionately. Having observed that stopping at ½, ⅓ and ¼ of the entire length resulted respectively in the three principal intervals they logically went a step farther and accepted the stopping at ⅕ as producing the major third and that at ⅙ as producing the minor third. It was the divisive principle, which would not have occurred to the Egyptians.

Another point showing Egyptian backwardness in music seems well established. In early times the variety of instruments illustrated is very small. There are plenty of scenes carved or painted on tomb walls in which music is prominent; we see players on the little kettle-drum, on the sistrum (the stirrup-shaped type is more common than the spur-shaped Babylonian type), on the vertical flute, on the upright harp and with castanets; it is a very simple assortment. It is doubtful whether there was any instrumental music as such; it was essentially an accompaniment, even were it only to hand-clapping—*hsi,* the Egyptian word for 'sing', has as its determinative the hand sign, and that sign may be used by itself as an abbreviation for *hsi.* In nearly every picture the instrumentalist is seen accompanying singers or playing for dancers (and the dancing might be accompanied by song), and the scenes are almost invariably secular, showing the entertainment of the nobleman in his own house. Music for the early Egyptian was pre-eminently a social art, and it made use of the limited range of instruments which were either native to the Nile valley or had been introduced to it in the remote past and had become traditional.

This age-long tradition was broken when, in the Eighteenth Dynasty, the Syrian campaigns of the Pharaohs acquainted the Egyptians with the far more developed and complex art of the

Asiatic musician. They had, indeed, learnt a little by more casual contacts at an earlier date; thus in a Twelfth Dynasty tomb at Beni Hassan there is a picture of a lyre, but it is an alien instrument carried by Semites from Syria; the Eighteenth Dynasty saw an artistic revolution. The tomb of Nekht, fifteenth century BC, gives the first Egyptian representation of a finger-board, and it was in that century that 'stopped' instruments were introduced; the old flute was replaced by the shriller pipes, the standing harp became larger and had a greater number of strings, and several new types of harp came into fashion; lyres and lutes of the long-necked Kassite sort make their appearance, together with Asiatic types of drums. As Professor Sachs says, 'A new kind of noisy, stimulating music seems to have taken possession of the Egyptians', and we may perhaps recognize an anticipation of modern experience when the Nile dweller, who had despised the Asiatic as a barbarian and a creature of a lower order, suddenly succumbed to the exciting polyphony of the barbarian's orchestra. Just as in the other arts we have seen throughout the Middle East at this time a mutual interchange of ideas which went far towards establishing if not a Middle Eastern civilization at least a common understanding and appreciation of civilization in general, so too in the province of music there was an internationalization which meant that the same instruments if not the same harmonies were everywhere in use.

LITERATURE

In our last chapter the fine arts were treated upon a regional basis and the attempt was made to trace in each country the historical development of the arts. In the case of literature this method would be unprofitable and to a large extent impossible. It would be unprofitable because in none of the countries concerned does the material preserved to us cover the whole field; the type of literature most characteristic of one people may be entirely lacking from the repertory of its neighbour, so that the literary achievement of the ancient world can be assessed only by disregarding frontiers and dealing with categories in whichsoever country they may occur. It would be impossible for the simple reason that there is no evidence to guide us. Much of what is known about Sumerian literature comes from the Assyrian versions found in Assurbanipal's library at Nineveh, much comes from versions of the Kassite period found at Nippur; but recent discoveries prove that the best works go back two thousand years before Assurbanipal's time, and that with little or no variation, while of none of them can it be said that it is necessarily a later composition. Meissner summed up the matter when he wrote: 'Owing to its anonymous nature and its relatively small variation it is impossible to write a history of Babylonian-Assyrian literature connected with names of authors and displaying its development by period. We must for the time being be content to occupy ourselves with the various categories of its literary output group by group, and to examine them from the point of view of form and content.'[3] Weber was even more emphatic: 'We are thus, in fact, faced with the phenomenon that in Babylonian literature there is, broadly speaking, neither archaic nor modern, nor any transition stages leading from one to the other; the period of nearly 3,000 years through which the monuments carry us shows in all essentials an unvarying picture of intellectual life.'[4] Similarly in the case of Egypt the date of an actual text is no criterion for the age of its contents. Down to the close of Egyptian history the exercises set for schoolboys were drawn from the ancient classics, and, be it noted, only from the ancient classics, never from contemporary or recent literature. Quite a number of Egyptian works are known to us only from late copies, but more and more does the evidence tend to demonstrate that the originals are to be assigned at least to the Twelfth Dynasty and perhaps to the period between the Sixth and the Fourth Dynasties; it is possible that that period, 2800 to 2200 BC, was the greatest in Egyptian literature; and it is certain that in the Middle Kingdom, beginning in 2000 BC, most of the literary forms had reached their highest development. After that date, early though it was in Egyptian history, literary invention appears to have been nearly exhausted. A few hymns of the Eighteenth and Nineteenth Dynasties—such as the Akhenaton hymns—do attain a really high level of poetry, but even those are modelled on, and owe not a little of their quality to, older poems; in the story of Wenamon, which dates to the eleventh century BC, we have an excellent composition, but it stands alone; for the most part the late works, in so far as they are not mere copies, are but literary exercises whose aim is only to give some new stylistic turn to a familiar original.

Until more evidence is forthcoming we must accept the surprising conclusion that, so far as our period is concerned, the fountain of inspiration in Mesopotamia and in Egypt alike virtually dried up about eighteen hundred years before Christ.[5] In neither case can the earlier literary development be traced in detail. Since in both countries the ancient classics were treasured as the staple literature of all succeeding periods we can best treat them not as the products of any one particular dynasty or century but as the literary possessions of Egypt and Mesopotamia during the Bronze Age.

Any attempt to assess the artistic value of that literature on the grounds of its form and content is from the outset beset with difficulties. In the first place, the amount of material upon which judgement can be based is small.[6] In Chapter VI, it was shown that writing was invented to meet the practical demands of business and, in a secondary degree, of religion, not at all as a medium foı literature; so it is that of the vast stores of ancient documents preserved to us, written on stone, on clay or on papyrus, most are business records, letters, dedications, omens, funerary inscriptions, religious formulae, and only a very small percentage can be classed as literature, even though that term be used in its widest connotation. Considering that we have to do with a number of important civilizations over a space of nearly two millennia the material is indeed scanty.

Secondly, there is the difficulty of language. Only too often the texts are fragmentary, and the key word to the sentence may be missing; we cannot be sure that the gloss introduced by the modern scholar is necessarily correct or gives the meaning intended by the author. But even when the text is complete translation may be largely guess-work; it is true that the ordinary temple- or grave-inscriptions, or the trade documents, can be read quite accurately—they are stereotyped formulae of the simplest sort; but it is quite another matter where poetical or imaginative writing is concerned, for then the vocabulary employed is entirely different, words commonly occur for which there is no parallel and therefore no explanation, and familiar words may be used with alternative or metaphorical values. The result is that we may find two translations by modern scholars of the same ancient text in which not only is the expression varied but the entire subject and meaning are different. If then, owing to linguistic problems, we are occasionally in doubt as to the content of a 'literary' document, the likelihood of our recovering anything of its form and style is small indeed. Generally we can, from the sense, assign the document to its proper category as hymn or secular poem, myth or romance, proverb or aphorism from a 'book of wisdom', but it is extremely difficult to judge the extent to which the subject is treated in what we should call a literary manner and so to assess the value of the writing as a work of art.

This is, of course, a difficulty inherent in all translation from one language to another. A literal rendering of the original words will result in a caricature in which all the beauty of language is lost and all the undertones of meaning are missed, and it needs a profound knowledge of both languages to re-create in the idiom of one not only the sense but something corresponding to the artistic form expressed in the idiom of the other. But that familiarity cannot be acquired in the case of languages which have been in disuse for two thousand years and were those of peoples whose methods of thought and modes of expression, unknown to us directly and probably very different from our own, can be surmised only from those very documents, few in number, whose translation is in question. The scholar, aware of the pitfalls, naturally tends towards a strictly literal rendering; but in so far as he departs from this it is his own personal taste and not necessarily that of the author that is reflected in his version. Even the form of the original text may be doubtful. If only because poetry is more easy to memorize than prose a great deal of the literature of any people for whom writing is either unknown or known only to an educated minority is likely to be in verse, and this is certainly true of the ancient Middle East. But it is not always easy for the modern scholar to decide whether a Sumerian or Egyptian text is in poetry or prose. On an Egyptian papyrus the ends of lines may be marked by red dots, in which case no difficulty arises; but where the scribe has omitted the dots the identification of a text as poetry may be hazardous. None of the Middle Eastern languages made use of rhyme. The normal characteristic of a poem is its strophic arrangement, i.e. the division of the text into couplets in which there is generally a parallelism of form or of thought, the second member either carrying on and expanding the sense of the first or standing in exact antithesis to it. This type of versification is familiar enough to us because it is that of the Hebrew writers of the Old Testament; and because Hebrew is not a dead language in the sense that Egyptian and Sumerian or Babylonian are dead, but has been handed down by an uninterrupted tradition, the translators of the Old Testament were able to produce an English version in which rhythm and metre are used with an effect similar to that of the original. Influenced by the partial parallel the translator of an Egyptian poem almost inevitably attempts to justify the strophic couplet (which is often, though not always, recognizable) by the introduction either of metre or, at any rate, of rhythm, that being an artistic form in his own idiom. But a scholar as acute as the late Professor Peet has put in the *caveat* that 'our ignorance of Egyptian vocalization and accentuation forbids us to say that there was any metrical parallel in the original couplet; and it may be that for the ancient Egyptian the artistic value of his poem depended on some quality which escapes us altogether'. In fact, the analogy with

Hebrew must not be pushed too far. The parallelism (or antithesis) within the strophe is less uniformly binding in Egyptian than in Hebrew, and although both languages employ the strophe, that does not imply anything further; moreover, in an Egyptian hymn the same line may be repeated several times, but where one line has the simple name of a god it may, when repeated, be lengthened by the addition of epithets which would completely destroy the metre if metre existed and were at all strict. We must therefore reconcile ourselves to the fact that whereas the sentiment or the imagination expressed in an Egyptian poem should be duly credited to its author, much of the phraseology and any charm of rhythm or metre must be attributed to the translator.

The form of Mesopotamian lyric poetry is less dubious. The text is divided into lines (each of which again may be separated into two half-lines); each line contains a more or less fixed number of stress accents and is a complete sentence; the lines are grouped into strophes consisting generally of two pairs of lines or into half-strophes consisting of only one pair; each strophe is a complete unit of thought. On the other hand it is more difficult to appreciate the content. All the lyrics are religious, and a few of them are extremely fine, rivalling the noblest of the Egyptian hymns and of the Hebrew psalms, but the majority are dull and almost unintelligible. This is because they are liturgical, hymns sung in 'the elaborate daily services of the most formal and musically intricate religion of antiquity'[7] or mythological legends meant to accompany the ritual of special festivals; they are therefore not independent works of art but only one of several elements composing a work of art in which an equal and perhaps a major part was played by music and drama; and lacking such accompaniment they cannot fairly be judged on their own merits. Were we asked to decide on the artistic value of Wagner's *Ring* on the basis of the libretto alone, and that printed as a continuous text with nothing to show that different parts are spoken by different characters, and with no stage directions, we should refuse to attempt anything so impossible; but the Sumerian hymns confront us with just this problem. If, in the pages which follow, anything is said about the form and style of Mesopotamian or Egyptian verse, the reader should bear in mind all these disabilities which qualify our judgement.

Perhaps the best of the Babylonian hymns (and we are concerned with the best only) is that in honour of Shamash the Sun god:

The mighty hills are surrounded by thy glory,
  The flat lands are filled with thy brightness.
Thou hast power over the mountains and lookest over the earth;
  Thou dost hang up the hems of the land in the innermost part of heaven.
The men of the lands, thou watchest over them all;
  Thou dost watch over all that King Ea the Adviser hath created.
Thou givest pasture to all living creatures,
  Yea, thou art the shepherd of all that is above and beneath.

. . . .

Men's designs in the speech of all lands
  Thou knowest, and observest their goings.
The whole of mankind looketh up to thee.
  O Shamash, the universe longeth for thy light.
Thou destroyest the horn of him who deviseth evil;
  Thou overturnest the place of him who planneth oppression.
Thou causest the unjust judge to see confinement,
  And punishest the corrupt and evil leader.
But he that is incorruptible and maketh intercession for the weak
  Is well pleasing to Shamash, and his days are lengthened.
The conscientious judge that giveth just judgement
  Prepareth for himself a palace; his habitation is a dwelling of princes.
He that oppresseth the dependant is marked down with the pen:
  They that do evil, their seed shall not abide.
They whose mouth is full of lies, thus dost thou unto them,
  Thou burnest and dissolvest the words of their mouth.
Thou hearest the oppressed as thou passest over them and searchest out their rights;
  Each and all are in thy hand.
Thou guidest their oracles, thou freest what was bound;
  Thou hearkenest, O Shamash, to prayer, to entreaty and praise,
Prostration, kneeling, whispered prayer and bowings-down.
  From the depth of his throat the wretched crieth to thee;
The failing, the feeble, the tormented, the poor,
  Cometh ever to thee with song of woe or petition. . . .
Them that kneel to thee thou absolvest and makest clean:
  Thou acceptest the praise of them that praise thee.
But they fear thee and revere thy name,
  Men bow them down ever before thy greatness.
Them that are foolish of tongue and speak that which is ungodly,
  That which hath neither front nor back, like clouds
That pass over the face of the wide earth
  And rest upon the high mountains,
The god Lakhmu shall overwhelm them, even the lord of terror.

The harvest of the sea, all that cometh out of the deep,
The tribute which the stream payeth, O Shamash, lieth before thee.
What mountains are not covered by thy gleam?
What places are not warmed by the beams of thy light?

The tablets upon which the cuneiform text is written are sadly damaged so that its reconstruction and translation were difficult and in places uncertain; but through the rather pedestrian rendering quoted above there can be seen a really fine poem, rich in imagery—the comparison of foolish and godless speech to clouds is beautifully done and for its loftiness of thought not inferior to the Hebrew psalms. Certainly the Mesopotamian poet, here at his best, is the equal of the Egyptian. The Hymn to the Nile, which is at least as old as the Hyksos period, is relatively unimaginative and naïve:

Praise to thee, O Nile, that issuest forth from the earth and comest to nourish Egypt;
Of hidden nature, a darkness in the daytime;
That waterest the meadows, which Rê hath created to nourish all cattle;
That givest drink to the desert places which are far from water, it is his dew that falleth from heaven;
Beloved of the Earth god, director of the Corn god, that maketh to flourish every workshop of Ptah;
Lord of fish, that maketh the water-fowl to go upstream. . . .
That maketh barley and createth wheat, so that he may cause the temples to keep festivals;
If he is sluggish, the nostrils are stopped up and all men are brought low;
The victuals of the gods are diminished and millions of men perish.

It is the New Kingdom that gives us the finest of the hymns to the gods. Akhenaton's Hymn to the Sun, although it borrows somewhat from the older Hymn to Amon-Rê, breaks altogether with the tradition which insisted on the dreary enumeration of titles and attributes as necessary to the praise of the deities; it is a spontaneous outpouring of gratitude for the beauty of the world, and while it has nothing corresponding to the spiritual profundity of the Babylonian hymn it possesses a light-hearted charm which the other cannot rival.

Thy dawning is beautiful in the horizon of heaven
O living Aton, Beginning of life!
When thou arisest in the eastern horizon of heaven
Thou fillest every land with thy beauty;
For thou art beautiful, great, glittering, high over the earth;
Thy rays, they encompass the lands, even all thou hast made.

Thou art Rê, and thou hast carried them all away captive;
  Thou blindest them by thy love.
Though thou art afar off, thy rays are on earth;
  Though thou art on high, thy footprints are the day.
When thou settest in the western horizon of heaven
  The world is in darkness like the dead.
They sleep in their chambers,
  Their heads are wrapt up,
Their nostrils stopped, and none seeth the other;
Stolen are all the things that were under their heads,
  While they know it not.
Every lion cometh forth from his den,
  All serpents, they sting.
Darkness reigns [?], the world is in silence,
  He that made them has gone to rest in his horizon.
Bright is the earth
  When thou risest in the horizon,
  When thou shinest as Aton by day.
The darkness is banished
  When thou sendest forth thy rays;
The Two Lands are in daily festivity,
  Awake and standing upon their feet,
  For thou hast raised them up.
Their limbs bathed, they take their clothing;
  Their arms uplifted in adoration to thy dawning,
Then, in all the world, they do their work.
All cattle rest upon their herbage,
  All trees and plants flourish;
The birds flutter in their marshes,
  Their wings uplifted in adoration to thee.
All their sheep dance upon their feet,
  All winged things fly;
They live, when thou hast shone upon them.
  The barques sail upstream and downstream alike,
    Every highway is open because thou hast dawned.
  The fish in the river leap up before thee,
    And thy rays are in the midst of the great sea.
Thou art he who createst the man-child in woman,
  Who makest seed in man,
Who givest life to the son in the body of his mother,
  Who soothest him that he may not weep,
  A nurse even in the womb;
Who givest breath to animate every one that he maketh;
  When he cometh forth from the body
  . . . on the day of his birth,
Thou openest his mouth in speech,
  Thou suppliest his necessities.
    When the chicklet crieth in the egg-shell
    Thou givest him breath therein, to preserve him alive.
  When thou has perfected him
    That he may pierce the egg,
  He cometh forth from the egg

To chirp with all his might;
He runneth about upon his two feet
When he hath come forth therefrom.
How manifold are all thy works!
They are hidden from before us,
O thou sole god, whose powers no other possesseth.[8]

The unmistakable resemblance to the Hebrew Psalm civ does not in itself concern us here because of the latter's late date; but it is worth noting that the literary form which is common to the poetry of both countries (and also to that of Sumer) is not necessarily, in the case of the Hebrews, derivative. The strophe with its parallel or antithetic balance of thought goes back with them to very early times, as can be seen from fragments of songs, incorporated in the text of the Old Testament, but taken over by the compilers of the books from oral tradition; such as is the song of the desert wanderings:

Spring up, O Well,
Sing ye unto it!
The princes digged the well,
The nobles of the people digged it,
By the direction of the Lawgiver,
With their staves.

or the far older song of the 'antediluvian' Lamech

Hear my voice, ye wives of Lamech,
Hearken unto my speech;
For I have slain a man for my wounding,
A young man for my hurt.

The Ras Shamra tablets show that a similar form was used for Phoenician poetry; it was indeed the common property of the Middle Eastern peoples, and the use of it by any one of them does not imply any lack of originality. It was not the only form employed, but it is the one that can be most easily recognized as verse; in some other cases, the repetition of a 'burden' or (in Egypt) such a trick as the starting of every line with the same word implies a verse form, but the rhythm or metre escapes us.

There is no doubt that the beauty of thought and imagery which is apparent to us even in a translation of such work as the Aton hymn was, for the ancient Egyptian, matched with a beauty of language which literal translation cannot recapture. The Egyptian poet was a conscious stylist. Khakheperre-Snb, in the Twelfth Dynasty, begins his 'Complaint' with a frank statement of his aim: 'Would that I had words that are unknown, utterances and sayings in new language that hath not yet passed away, and without that which hath been said repeatedly—not an utterance that hath grown stale, what the ancestors have already said.' The Proverbs of Ptah-hotep are entitled, 'The beautifully-expressed utterances spoken by the prince . . . Ptahhotep while instructing the ignorant in knowledge and in the rules of elegant discourse', and in the Prophecy of Neferti the Pharaoh calls for someone 'that will speak to me some beauteous words, choice speeches, in hearing which my majesty may find diversion'. Obviously, style was prized for its own sake. We do not find in Meso-potamia any explicit reference to such a purely literary quality, but that their style also was valued in literary composition can safely be assumed.

Akin to the hymns in praise of the gods, in so far as they also were employed in religious services (probably in anniver-sary celebrations of the events they commemorate) were the Sumerian hymns of lamentation over the downfall of cities. Owing to the vicissitudes of Sumerian political history there were few cities which had not at some time or another suffered destruction at the hands of the enemy, and such disasters were a regular theme for Sumerian poets. The collapse of the Third Dynasty of Ur and the capture of its king, Ibi-Sin, by the Elamites, is thus celebrated:

> When they overthrew, when order they destroyed,
> Then like a deluge they consumed all things together.
> Whereunto, O Sumer, did they change thee?
>
> The sacred dynasty from the temple they exiled,
> They demolished the city, they demolished the temple,
> They seized the rulership of the land.
>
> By the command of Enlil order was destroyed;
> By the spirit of Anu hastening over the land it was snatched away;
>
> Enlil turned his eyes towards a strange land,
> The divine Ibi-Sin was carried to Elam.

Even in the English version the expression here is markedly different from that of the Shamash hymn. The stark simplicity of the language, the short bitter sentences, are in keeping with the finality of Ur's ruin; here style is deliberately harmonized with subject. If, in the later part of the poem, the destruction of one temple after another is catalogued in identical terms, so that for us the effect is monotonous in the extreme, it must be remembered that for the citizen of Ur these names of temples, evoking his city's past history, were poignant symbols; each temple had its individual character and unique associations, and the contrast between that diversity and the dull sameness of the formula describing their common doom is, in its way, an artistic triumph.

There are a few comparable Egyptian pieces, belonging to (or referring to) the disastrous days of the First Intermediate Period (prior to the Middle Empire), which bewail the anarchy of the time and the upsetting of all that ordered existence which for the conservative Egyptian meant well-being:[9]

Behold, the poor of the land have become rich;
  The possessor of property is now one who has nought.
Behold, servants have become masters of butlers;
  He who was a messenger now sends another.
Behold, he that had not a loaf is the possessor of a granary;
  His magazine is equipped with the goods of another.
Behold, noble ladies go hungry;
  What was prepared for them now goes to sate the king's men.

So the sage Ipuwer; so too the scribe Neferti:

I show thee a land in lamentation and distress;
  That which never happened before has happened.
Men shall take up weapons of war,
  That the land may live in uproar.
Men shall fashion arrows of copper
  That they may beg for bread with blood . . .
I show thee the son as foeman and the brother as adversary,
  And a man murdereth his own father.

As literary compositions these may rank reasonably high, but they are artificial exercises. Juvenal's phrase, *facit indignatio versus*, 'indignation is the inspiration of the poet', would apply to the Sumerian Lamentation but scarcely to the work of such as Neferti and Ipuwer; these, writing after the event, have merely found, in a disaster known to them only by tradition, an apt subject for pessimistic verse. The Egyptian poet succeeded infinitely better where his pessimism is genuine. The finest example of this 'contemplative' poetry is the Twelfth Dynasty work now known as 'The Man weary of Life', written partly, it would seem, in prose but partly in verse. The first poem describes his sorry state:

Behold, my name stinks
More than the odour of carrion
On days in summer, when the sky is hot.

The second laments his solitude in an evil world:

To whom do I speak today?
Brothers are evil;
The friends of today love not.

To whom do I speak today?
Hearts are covetous;
Every man plundereth the goods of his fellow.

and in the third poem he sings the praises of death:

Death is in my eyes today
As when a sick man becomes whole,
As when one walketh abroad after sickness.

Death is in my eyes today
Like the scent of myrrh;
As when one sitteth under the boat's sail on a windy day.

Death is in my eyes today
Like the smell of water-lilies;
As when one sitteth on the bank of drunkenness.[10]

Death is in my eyes today
Like a well-trodden road,
As when one returneth from the war unto his home.

Death is in my eyes today
Like the unveiling of heaven
As when one attaineth to that which he knew not.

Death is in my eyes today
As when one longeth to see his house again
After he hath spent many years in captivity.

There is a simplicity and a restraint in these verses which assuredly entitles them to a very high place in the poetry of the world. They are not the outburst of a man driven to desperation, nor of a pessimist, but are drawn from the real beliefs which the Egyptian might disguise but could not forget. It is true that the harper at the banquet might regularly invite the guests to eat, drink and be merry, 'for tomorrow we die'; in a New Kingdom version:

Spend the day merrily. Put unguent and fine oil together to thy nostrils, and garlands and lotus-flowers on the body of thy beloved whom thou favourest, as she sitteth beside thee. Set singing and music before thy face. Cast all evil behind thee and bethink thee of joy, until that day cometh when one reacheth port in the land that loveth silence.

but facing this in the Theban tomb we find another poem in which the dead man, rebuking the light song, attains a far higher level of poetry:

I have heard those songs that are in the ancient tombs, and what they tell extolling life on earth and belittling the region of the dead. Wherefore do they thus concerning the Land of Eternity, the just and fair, which has no terrors? Wrangling is its abhorrence, and no man there girds himself against his fellow. It is a land against which none can rebel; all our kinsfolk rest within it since the earliest day of time. The offspring of millions are come hither, every one. For none may tarry in the land of Egypt, none there is who has not passed yonder. The span of earthly things is as a dream; but a fair welcome is given to him who has reached the West.

The Egyptian poet, in short, is at his best where he can be most personal and where sincerity absolves him from the literary artifices which tickled the fancy of his Egyptian auditors but too often ruined his verse—the elaborate puns upon words, the stringing together of short songs each of which must begin and end with its actual number in the sequence, the tedious clichés borrowed from and perhaps intended to recall favourite old poems. Some of the New Kingdom love songs (they are few in number and for the most part sadly incomplete) are charming in spite of their artificiality:

Seven days from yesterday I have not seen my beloved,
And sickness hath crept over me
And I am become heavy in my limbs
And am unmindful of mine own body.
If the master-physicians come to me
My heart hath no comfort of their remedies,
And the magicians, no resource is in them;

. . . .

Better for me is my beloved than any remedies,
More important is she for me than the entire compendium of medicine
My salvation is when she enters from without
When I see her, then am I well;
Opens she her eyes, my limbs are young again,
Speaks she, and I am strong.
And when I embrace her, she banishes evil,
And it passes from me for seven days.

This cannot be claimed as poetry of the highest sort, but it is a very pleasant conceit and in the original must have sounded far better than in the translation; and even the repetition of 'seven days' at the beginning and end is no more artificial than what we have in a roundel or a triolet.

Outside Egypt the 'contemplative' or introspective type of poetry is comparatively rare. A people whose chief prayer was always for long life upon earth could not fail to be shocked by man's transient state, and at least one poem (the text, found in Assurbanipal's library, is late, but seems to be based on an earlier original) harps upon this very much in the manner of the Hebrew psalmist or of the earlier parts of the Book of Job:

> He who in the evening was yet alive
>   in the morning was dead;
> Suddenly was he cast down,
>   quickly was he brought to naught.
> For the twinkling of an eye he sings and plays;
> In a moment he howls as one voicing his wrongs.
>
> Day and night men's moods change;
>   If they be hungry, then are they like corpses,
>   If they be filled, then they deem themselves equal with their god.
>   If things go well with them, they talk of mounting to Heaven,
>   If they be in trouble, they speak of going down into Hell.

More characteristic, however, are the 'penitential psalms' of Mesopotamia and of Palestine, which are inspired not by pessimism but by the consciousness of sin and the hope of god's mercy:

> In the wrath of his heart the lord hath looked banefully on me,
> In the fierceness of his heart the god hath smitten me with his enmity;
> When I sought help none took me by the hand,
> When I cry aloud no man hearkens to me.
> I turn me to my merciful god, I cry aloud to him;
> I embrace and I kiss the feet of my goddess.
> O Lord, cast not thy bondman down;
> Seize him by the hand as he lies in the miry water.
> The sin that I have committed turn into good,
> Let the wind bear away my transgressions;
> Take from me like a garment the multitude of my iniquities;
> My god, though my sins be seven times seven; yet wash away my sins.

There is, indeed, little to choose between the best of the Babylonian and the Hebrew psalms, regarded purely as religious poetry, and the thought also can be curiously alike. When the Hebrew psalmist says:

> Who can tell how oft he offendeth?
> O cleanse thou me of my secret faults.

he seems to be echoing the words of the earlier Babylonian writer:

> The sin which I have done know I not,
> And I am not aware of my transgression.

The few Egyptian parallels belong to a time just outside the scope of this volume; found on the tombstone of quite humble people of the Nineteenth Dynasty, however, they are likely to be based upon earlier poems which have not been preserved in their original form but may well have rivalled in quality those of their neighbours:

> Though the servant was disposed to do evil
> Yet is the Lord disposed to be merciful.
> The Lord of Thebes spendeth not a whole day wroth;
> His wrath is as the passing of a moment and naught is left;
> His wind is turned to us again in mercy.

What we miss in Egyptian literature is the mythological epic which figures largely in that of Mesopotamia, as also of north Syria and of Phoenicia. The epic poem seems to have been the natural mode of expression for the genius of the Sumerian people; in this form they enshrined not only the complicated and generally savage legends of mythology proper, the theogony of the gods and their rivalries for the overlordship of heaven, but the story of man's advance in culture and art, the exploits of the divine or semi-divine heroes who led that advance, and finally, coming to more modern times, the great deeds of human kings and conquerors. It is clear that the composition of such was spread over many centuries, and while some epics relate to incidents in historic times others must go back to the very earliest days of Sumer; they may have been edited and rewritten, as is manifestly the case with the Deluge story, incorporated in the Gilgamesh myth in the third millennium BC but extant in more versions than one, yet their content at least is ancient. Only when men still dimly remembered the miracle that had supplanted the chipped or ground flint by metal tools could they have invented the myth of the Creation of the Axe. Enlil, immediately after he has 'moved away heaven from earth, moved away earth from heaven', proceeds to make the pickaxe which the Anunnaki, the Judges of the Nether World, give to the 'black-headed' Sumerian people:

> The pickaxe and the basket build cities,
> The steadfast house the pickaxe builds;
> The steadfast house the pickaxe establishes,
> The steadfast house it causes to prosper.
>
> The house which rebels against the king,
> The house which is not submissive to its king,
> The pickaxe makes it submissive to the king.
>
> Of the bad plants it crushes the head,
> Plucks out the root, tears at the crown;
> The pickaxe spares the good plants.
> The pickaxe, its fate decreed by Father Enlil,
> The pickaxe is exalted.

So, too, must we assign to an early date the poem which, like the Hebrew story of Cain and Abel, describes the beginning of the pastoral and the agricultural modes of life and the rivalry that divides them. The great gods, En-ki and Enlil, fashion and send down to earth the rustic deities Lahar and Ashnan:

> For Lahar they set up the sheepfold,
> Plants and herbs they present to him;
> For Ashnan they establish a house,
> Plough and yoke they present to her.
> Lahar standing in his sheepfold,
> A shepherd increasing the bounty of the sheepfold is he;
> Ashnan standing among the furrows,
> A maid kindly and bountiful is she.

The actual theogonies are coarse and barbaric, and the narrative is too often held up by long word-for-word repetitions, as when a god announces at length his intention of doing something and is immediately and at equal length represented as doing it, or when a message is given to a messenger and reproduced by him verbatim; but even so there is gold in the dross. A myth of the creation in which, for sweet water to be created and for the soil to become fruitful, the god En-ki has to marry his own daughter and then his granddaughter, to eat the eight plants to which the last gives birth, to be cursed by her grandmother Nin-khursag, and to be smitten with eight plagues than can be cured only by Nin-khursag's giving birth to eight gods and goddesses whose names are puns on the afflicted parts of En-ki's body—this is as poetically valueless as it is artificial; yet it does contain a description of Dilmun (Telmun) as the yet unfinished Garden of Eden which is authentic poetry:

> The land Dilmun is a pure place, the land Dilmun is a clean place;
> In Dilmun the raven uttered no cries,
> The kite uttered not the cry of the kite,
> The lion killed not,
> The wolf snatched not the lamb;
> Unknown was the kid-killing dog . . .
> The sick-eyed says not 'I am sick-eyed',
> The sick-headed says not 'I am sick-headed',
> The old woman says not 'I am an old woman.'

The great poem on Inanna's descent into hell contains much that is for us dull and hardly intelligible, but sometimes, as in the dirge for Inanna, the metre enables us almost to hear the chant of the chorus:

> My Lady abandoned heaven, abandoned earth
> To the nether world she descended.
> Inanna abandoned heaven, abandoned earth,
> To the nether world she descended;
> Abandoned lordship, abandoned ladyship,
> To the nether world she descended.

while the appeal made on her behalf well illustrates the richness of Sumerian metaphor, even though all beauty of language is lost in translation:

> O Father Enlil, let not thy daughter be put to death in the nether world!
> Let not thy good metal be ground up into the dust of the nether world!
> Let not thy good lapis-lazuli be broken up into the stone of the stone-mason!
> Let not thy boxwood be cut up into the wood of the carpenter!

The Gilgamesh epic would seem to have taken shape not before the time of the First Dynasty of Erech, one of whose kings was named Gilgamesh, and the same should be true of the charming poem 'Inanna prefers the Farmer to the Shepherd', since again the shepherd god Dumuzi is synonymous with a king of Erech. From these half-mythical times and characters we come to what at least purports to be history with 'The Legend of Enmerkar and the Lord of Aratta', a real heroic epic in which the protagonists are mortals and the gods, as in Homer, intervene on behalf of their favourites. The final stage is reached when an actual event in history is celebrated on a purely human level and Sargon of Akkad tells the tale of his military adventure in Anatolia.

In this literary *genre* the Sumerians did not stand alone. The Hurri also were writers of epic poetry of the mythological sort and, while they might in some cases borrow Sumerian tales, in others they dealt with their own legends the scenes of which were laid in Hurri territory; thus the Kumarbi legend, of which the text was found at Boğazköy, locates the battle between El and Kumarbi at Mount Hazzi, i.e. Mount Kasios, at the mouth of the Orontes river. From Ugarit there have been recovered numerous texts of Phoenician mythological poems such as that of 'Môt and Aleyn-Baal', and the 'Birth of the gracious and fair Gods', the 'Death of Baal', etc., while with the 'Legend of Kereth' we pass into the heroic world where tribal tradition is mixed with religious myth as it is in the Sumerian legend of Enmerkar and as it was in the Arabian saga on which the stories in the Book of Genesis are based. Interesting and important as are the contents of these poems, their literary merit is difficult to assess, if only because of the fragmentary condition of the texts and the uncertainty of their translation; but the popularity of the epic over so much of the Middle East compels us to regard the Sumerian examples as typical of Bronze Age achievement in an art form which was to be that of some of the world's greatest poetry.

That the Egyptians should not have employed this form for mythological themes is curious, considering how many such themes must have offered themselves to the poet; if there were heroic legends, no trace of them survives. The nearest approach to epic is the long poem celebrating Ramses II's doubtful victory at Kadesh; it comes late in time and the narrative form now used for, apparently, the first time in Egyptian verse may have been modelled on some foreign original; but the style is wholly Egyptian, with all the Egyptian faults of bombast and cliché grievously exaggerated.

Common to the Middle Eastern countries was the 'Wisdom' literature familiar to us from the Book of Proverbs in the Hebrew Old Testament. This consists of short aphorisms which may be written in verse or in prose; collectively they represent the nearest approach to philosophy of which the ancient mind was capable; but they are not informed or inspired by any philosophic system or any general principles of thought or ethics; they are disconnected 'wise sayings' of a more or less didactic character tersely expressed and readily memorized. Such were immensely popular. In Mesopotamia the earliest collection (found at Nippur) is Sumerian and dates from the first third of the second millennium BC, but some of the proverbs in it occur earlier and on other sites, while the latest redaction, in Neo-Babylonian, comes from Assurbanipal's library in the seventh century BC. The Sumerian 'Proverbs' are anonymous and were arranged in groups merely by their initial signs—those beginning with *šà* (the heart), or *uru* (city), being put together regardless of their sense. The Egyptian preferred to attribute authorship of the different collections to one or other of the great sages of the past, Ptahhotep, Kagemne and Hordedef, just as the Hebrews attributed their proverbs to Solomon, and in both cases there may be reason; Ptahhotep was a vizier of the Fifth Dynasty and two of the papyri containing his proverbs go back to the Twelfth Dynasty, by which time already they were recognized as classics and were popularly accredited to him. Certainly the vogue of these 'wise saws' begins very early, and goes on until the end of the second millennium BC, when the proverbs of Amenemope were first published.

The form of a proverb is as important as its content, if it is to be remembered and quoted. The Sumerian was satisfied if it was terse and epigrammatic and on the whole preferred the literal to the metaphorical expression:

> The wealthy are distant, but poverty is close at hand.
> He who eats too much cannot sleep.
> The heart has not spawned hatred, but speech has spawned hatred.

and only later did the Babylonian favour the verse form:

> Slander not, but speak kindliness;
> Speak no evil, but say that which is good.

But the Egyptian was from the first a stylist, and for the prose proverbs of Ptahhotep it is claimed that they are 'beautifully expressed . . . in the rules of elegant discourse'. For the old court official etiquette was as important as morality, and his sayings are a curious mixture of pious reflections and practical rules of behaviour:

> If thou wouldest that thy conduct be good, keep thee from evil.
> Beware of covetousness; it is an evil sickness, incurable.
> Be not arrogant because of thy knowledge, and have no confidence in that thou art a learned man. Take counsel with the ignorant as with the wise, for the limits of art cannot be reached, and no artist fully possesseth his skill. Goodly discourse is more hidden than

the precious green-stone, and yet it is found with slave-girls over the mill-stones.
If thou art a guest at the table of one who is greater than thou, take what he may offer thee as it is set before thee. Fix thy gaze upon what is before thee, and shoot not many glances at thy host, for it is an abomination to get upon his nerves. Cast down thy countenance until he greeteth thee, and speak only when he hath greeted thee. Laugh when he laugheth; that will be pleasing in his heart, and what thou doest will be acceptable.

It is not easy to recognize any literary quality in such aphorisms, apart from their studied naïvety, but in the original, for the Egyptian, they were 'elegant discourse', and we can see the sense of style maintained by the proverb-maker down to the time of Amenemope:

God is ever efficient
But man faileth ever.
The words that men say are one thing,
The things that God doeth are another.

Or again, with an elaborate use of metaphor:

Be resolute of heart, make firm thy mind,
Steer not with thy tongue;
The tongue of a man is the rudder of the boat,
But the Lord of all is its pilot.

What does appear in Ptahhotep, as also in the satire on the professions quoted above in Chapter III, is a sense of humour which is peculiarly Egyptian. We find it again in the story of Sinuhe. One must needs suppose that the whole of the Middle East, in ancient as in modern days, was familiar with the prose romance, the sort of story with which some wandering entertainer enlivened the evening gatherings in court or cottage. Perhaps because they formed the stock-in-trade of professional reciters, who would have regarded any written publication as an infringement of their interests, none of those romances survives in Mesopotamia; but in Egypt a few of the most famous were copied out at one time or another, and serve as examples of what must have been a widespread popular art. In the tale of the 'Shipwrecked Sailor', thrown ashore on a desert island where he is befriended by a giant serpent, we have a foretaste of the *Arabian Nights*, as also, though in a more sophisticated vein, in the story of King Cheops and the Magicians; in this, indeed, the Pharaoh takes the place of Haroun al Raschid and the stories are told to beguile his leisure and have just that admixture of court splendour, bawdiness and magic that was to enchant Baghdad. The best of them is the Story of Sinuhe, an Egyptian official who, hearing of the murder of King Ammenemes I, fled to Palestine. There he was made sheikh of a tribe and captain of the host of the prince of Retenu and when a jealous rival challenged him to single combat ('at dawn, when Retenu came, it had gathered together its tribes, it had planned this combat. Every heart burned for me; the men's wives jabbered and every heart was sore for me. They said, "is there another mighty man who can fight against him?" ') he slew him and seized his goods; but, rich and honoured in Syria, in his old age he bethought him of his former position at the court of Pharaoh and longed for burial in his own land, in 'the cities of Eternity'. Recalled by Sesostris I, he presents himself before Pharaoh, bearded and travel-stained, in Beduin garments, and is graciously received. 'Then the royal children were caused to be ushered in. Said his Majesty to the Queen, "Behold Sinuhe, who has come back as an Asiatic, an offspring of the Beduin." She gave a great cry, and the royal children shrieked out all together. "It is not really he, O king, my Lord!" And His Majesty said, "Yes, it is really he." ' The princesses plead for him, and he was bathed and shaved and dressed in fine linen ('I slept on a bed, and gave up the sand to them that be in it'), appointed court chamberlain and given a house, and a pyramid was built for him near that prepared for the king; 'and so live I, rewarded by the king, until the day of my death cometh'.

This is story-telling at its best—Sinuhe himself is a piece of real character drawing, the narrative is vivid, there is poetry and there is humour—the description of the little princesses' incredulity is quite delightful—and it is not surprising that it was immensely popular; but that does not mean that it was a folk tale. On the contrary, it is a highly sophisticated work of art, composed partly in prose and partly in verse, in which the form is more important than the matter, consciously stylized throughout and with every effect carefully thought out; for the ancient Egyptian it was a masterpiece of literature, and modern critics have not shrunk from ranking it as a world-classic.

Even if the story of Sinuhe be not founded on fact, as it very well may be, yet its narrative form purporting to be autobiographical sets it in a class almost by itself. The only other Egyptian composition to which the term 'historical' is in any way appropriate is the Carnarvon writing-tablet in which the Pharaoh Kamose describes how he launched the campaign which was to drive the Hyksos out of Egypt.[11] But while that campaign was a historical fact, yet the account of a single historical incident is not, properly speaking, history. No Egyptian, Sumerian or Babylonian man of letters ever wrote history as we conceive it today, in terms of unfolding processes and underlying principles. As we have seen in the case of the exact sciences, these peoples knew nothing about the psychological techniques of definition and generalization which the modern historian, in his field, takes for granted; with their world view, events came about not by any natural process of cause and effect but through the incalculable whims of the gods who had ordered everything from the beginning. Events as such were, of course, noted and written down, as in the case of the date-formulae in Mesopotamia, where each year was named after some important happening, and even a sequence might be recorded, as in the King-lists of Sumer and the tables of the royal ancestry at Abydos in Egypt; historical data might be inserted incidentally and even used as themes, as in the Kamose story or in that of the Anatolian campaign of Sargon of Akkad, 'The King of Battles'; but this did not lead to the writing of connected and meaningful history. The extent to which such history was incompatible with the psychology of the ancient world is curiously illustrated by the long inscription in which Entemena, ruler of the city of Lagash in the twenty-fifth century BC, records the restoration of the boundary ditch between Lagash and the neighbouring city of Umma, which the Ummites had destroyed. As this was a question of legal rights precedents had to be cited, and Entemena therefore passes in review the political relations of the two cities over a space of a hundred and fifty years; but instead of giving a factual narrative he fits known events into a framework of theocratic theory, and gods and men are so entangled as to be indistinguishable one from another, the actual incidents become insignificant and it is the apparent will of the inscrutable gods that must decide the case. But that is as near to history as the Sumerian could come. An Egyptian general like Thutiy might record on the walls of his tomb the campaigns in which he served, but only to boast of the prisoners he took and the honours he won; Ramses II expatiates at length on his heroism at Kadesh, but the poem is a paean, not a history.

At least one of the essential qualities of history, the orderly sequence of events, is present in the military annals of the Hittite kings. For each year of the king's reign there are recorded the campaigns in which he was engaged, the country in which he fought, the kings or chieftains whom he encountered, the names of the cities which he captured or burned; there is a great deal of historical information to be got out of these annals, but there is in them nothing of the science of history, and their literary merit is very small. In the account of every campaign the same stereotyped phrases recur and an identical formula assigns to the gods the credit of victory; it is for the most part dull reading; and yet when Mursilis II prefaces his list of wars with the explanation that his father's death, quickly followed by that of his elder brother, and his own accession to the throne as an untried youth, had together been responsible for a general revolt of all the vassal states which he had to bring back one by one into subjection, he does give to that list a certain logical unity. Every now and then the bare record is relieved by a human touch. He was advancing on Karkiša when its king offered his submission; Mursilis curtly reminds him that he had betrayed him who had set him on the throne, 'and now am I to receive you as my servant?' But when the terrified king sends his mother to intercede for him and the old lady throws herself at Mursilis's feet then, 'because this lady had come to meet me and had kissed my feet I had pity upon her', and he broke off his march and accepted the rebel's surrender. Again, there is a graphic account of a successful manœuvre—he was attacking a ruler named Pittaggatallis, and was anxious for a decisive victory but 'as they had scouts out, if I had advanced straight upon him then, his scouts seeing me, he would not have stood his ground but would have slipped away. So I turned my eyes aside and faced towards Pittaparash. And when it was night I changed direction and marched on Pittaggatallis; all night I marched, and was in his territory by dawn. When the sun arose I advanced on to the field, and the nine hundred men under Pittaggatallis came forward to give battle.'

The studied moderation of the Hittite annals does give them something of the objectivity at which the historian aims. In still more striking contrast to the braggadocio of a Pharaoh such as Ramses III is the curious apologia put out by the Hittite king Hattusilis III. Although it is couched in the form of a thanksgiving in honour of the goddess of Samuha that has not much more bearing on the text than has the dedication of a modern book; it is really an autobiography, covering all the early years of the king's life. Hattusilis's motive was to defend himself against the charge of treachery and rebellion against his nephew whom he had supplanted on the throne of Hattusas; his method was to set in order the events that led up to his action in a record which has all the air of being straightforward, objective and truthful, and its effect as propaganda is immensely strengthened by the modesty and moderation of its tone. The apologia, which might have served as a model for Julius Caesar's *Commentaries*, is a real historical essay, something which no Mesopotamian or Egyptian writer ever thought of attempting; the only parallel to it is the much shorter autobiography of Idri-mi, king of Alalakh, written about a century earlier, in which again we are struck by the royal writer's moderation and objectivity, very unusual in the ancient Middle East. While we may hesitate to assert, as some authorities have done, that Hattusilis's apologia is a definite expression of the Indo-European character of the Hittites, we must agree that it belongs to a category of literature which is peculiar to the Hittites and the Hurri. 'Here,' says Moortgat, 'for the first time in the ancient Orient, a man reveals a capacity for regarding his own life and the life of the nation in a meaningful relationship, for interpreting from a particular viewpoint a series of important events and actions, his own as well as those of others—in short, the capacity for thinking historically.'[12] To this we must add that the simplicity of Mursilis's language is not artlessness but a calculated literary style suited to his propagandist aims; his history is tendentious but convincing.[13]

In China, in the year 213 BC, the first emperor of the Ch'in Dynasty ordered the destruction of nearly all books written before that time, and made their preservation by private persons a political offence involving severe penalties.[14] Actually some works did survive, but today there is no piece of literature that can be assigned to a date earlier than Chou, and even then the attribution is to some extent arbitrary, though the Shang oracle-bones and inscriptions on early Chou bronzes now afford standards for judgement. It seems probable that the parts of the *Shu Ching,* the Book of History, which record details of the rulers of Hsia, Shang and Chou, belong in substance to the periods with which they deal, though there has certainly been later re-editing. Similarly in the *Shih Ching,* the Book of Poetry, the Five Sacrificial Odes of Shang, which the later Chinese attributed to the Shang period but modern scholars prefer to assign to Chou, nevertheless do probably incorporate much Shang material. Clearly there is here nothing that would justify an attempt to estimate the literary quality of Hsia and Shang writings.

On the other hand, it is worth while to note something about the general character of early Chinese literature. We have seen that in Egypt writing was confined for the most part to the priestly class and used mainly for temple purposes, and that in Sumer it was employed primarily for business purposes and was practised mostly by priests and to a limited extent by merchants. In China, in the earliest period for which we have detailed information, the ability to read and write was expected of every member of the privileged aristocratic class, and the young nobles would study treatises on poetry and music, history and rhetoric, and writing was itself regarded as a fine art.

If we go back farther, though treading then on more doubtful ground, we can yet see something of the uses to which writing was put. The omen bones from Anyang show its connection with religion, though whether there was anything that could be called religious literature, corresponding to the hymns and psalms of Egypt and Mesopotamia, it is impossible to say. But the quotations incorporated in the *Shu Ching* and the *Shih Ching* do mean that the Chou period inherited from Shang the tradition of historical writing and of poetry, forms of literature of which the first is rarely to be found in Mesopotamia and was unknown in Egypt. It was a Chou soldier who voiced his homesickness in the poem:

> When we went away
> The millets were in flower.
> Now that we are returning
> The snow falls and the roads are all mire.
> The king's business was very difficult
> And we had not leisure to rest.
> Did we not long to return?
> But we were in awe of the orders in the tablets.

But the directness and the simplicity might well, we think, reflect the qualities of China's earliest verse.

NOTES ON CHAPTER X

1. Galpin is here referring to the ancient music of China. Since the Ming period the five-note scale has been that officially observed, but the sixteenth-century authority, Prince Tsai-yü, maintains that the old music was heptatonic and cites in support this a vertical bronze flute of the second millennium BC which he has seen and of which he gives detailed measurements. Dr Moule remarks that it seems unreasonable to doubt that the great classical instruments existed in the second millennium BC in possibly as perfect a form as they have today.
2. It is tempting to see in this fact, as well as in various representations of different instruments being played together, e.g. lyre, sistrum and timbrel, or psaltery, timbrel and double pipe, evidence for some definite theory of harmony. It is not, however, safe to make that assumption unconditionally. Miss Schlesinger notes that, 'if the musicians were only providing a number of notes in unison in timbre, i.e. in the composition of their masschords, the result would be an impressive and greatly enriched accompaniment of harmonic overtones, a natural harmony sounding above the melody and independent of theoretical knowledge'.
3. B. Meissner, *Die Babylonisch-Assyrische Literatur* (Potsdam, 1927–28), p. 2.
4. O. Weber, *Die Literatur der Babylonier und Assyrer* (Leipzig, 1907), p. 2.
5. As Professor I. M. Diakonoff points out, the 'Warnings to the

Kings' in Mesopotamia and the vivid Assyrian royal inscriptions ('Letters to the God') were written during the eighth and seventh centuries BC. Furthermore, Professor Diakonoff avers that many major Babylonian literary works were created in the Kassite and post-Kassite periods, i.e. *after* the eighteenth century BC. (The cosmogonic epic, 'Enuma elis', 'The Poor Man of Nippur', 'The Righteous Sufferer', 'The Babylonian Theodicy', 'Surpu', 'The Man and His Slave'.) See also the works of W. Lambert.

6. Professor I. M. Diakonoff is of the opinion that this material is not so much inadequate as insufficiently explored. We have philological editions of the different texts and fragments but we have no words devoted to their historical or aesthetic evolution. But see W. Lambert, *Babylonian Wisdom Literature* (Oxford, 1960).
7. S. H. Langdon in *The Cambridge Ancient History*, I, p. 443.
8. Breasted's translation.
9. The texts of Ipuwer and Neferti are certainly compositions but betray clear signs of the disorders of all kinds characterizing the First Intermediate period; see J. Spiegel, *Soziale und Weltanschauliche Reformbewegungen in Altaegypten* (Heidelberg, 1950).
10. i.e. at a picnic on the Nile bank.
11. Professor I. M. Diakonoff points out that the story of General Thutiy belongs to this class. There are also several stories after 1200 BC.
12. Anton Moortgat, *Die bildende Kunst des alten Orients und die Bergvölker* (Berlin, 1933).
13. On the subject of historical literature and the religious philosophy of history which it implies, cf. R. C. Dentan (ed.) *The Idea of History of the Ancient Near East* (New Haven, 1955).
14. Professor Shigeki Kaizuka *et al.* point out that the first emperor of the Ch'in Dynasty ordered the destruction of private copies of the classics and works of philosophy. Copies were kept at the capital but these were later destroyed inadvertently by rebels when the dynasty fell. The list of proscribed books excluded works on medicine, divination and agriculture. The emperor was mainly concerned with the suppression of the chronicles of the feudal states which contained uncomplimentary references to his ancestors. It is in the field of the chronicles of the Chou period that there were the most serious losses.

CHAPTER XI

THE LIMITS OF CIVILIZATION IN THE BRONZE AGE AND THE CONDITION OF CIVILIZED LIFE AT THE END OF THE THIRTEENTH CENTURY BC

If this History had been planned as a World History, with no hint of the limitations of its scope, the author of this record of the Bronze Age would have been the first to admit that it was partial, disjointed and inadequate. In the foregoing chapters only passing reference has been made to the vast areas comprised within the territories of the Union of Soviet Socialist Republics, and to Europe in general, including the British Isles; nothing at all has been said regarding Africa, apart from Egypt, or the American continent. But this seeming partiality is explained and justified by the fact that our History is that of the scientific and cultural development of mankind, and its interest is necessarily centred upon those regions in which development can be observed, and that within the time-limits of the Bronze Age.

In the first section of the volume the multifarious peoples of Asia, Africa and America were all alike discussed, and that with good reason. Up to the close of the era with which that section dealt all those peoples alike shared in the comparatively uniform culture of Neolithic man: in the sixth millennium BC an onlooker would have seen them all more or less equally equipped, aligned at the starting-point of real development, and would have found it impossible to foretell which of the competitors was going to make genuine progress, and when. Of the African tribes many never advanced at all, others only at a date far outside the scope of this volume; the inhabitants of Central and South America who ultimately produced the Maya, the Peruvian and the Aztec civilizations were, so far as we know, at much the same cultural level in 1200 BC as they had been in the fifth millennium—at least we have no proof of any change as yet. With such countries, then, we are not here concerned. In so far as they did in the course of time achieve civilization or make some noteworthy contribution to science or art, they will be dealt with by other writers; but the background from which they will be seen then first to emerge will still be the Neolithic prehistory described in the first section of this volume.

Our purpose has been to mark the outstanding features of man's cultural advance in the formative period of the Bronze Age, and the fact is that the advance was for the most part local, confined to the few communities which developed an urbanized civilization. Logically, therefore, our attention has been concentrated on such communities, passing over those which, occupying the greater part of the earth's surface, remained for the time being in the primitive state of barbarism and, at best, borrowed from their more inventive neighbours such techniques and practices as might ultimately equip them to contribute in their turn to general progress. But even within those limits equality of treatment is denied to us, for only in the case of certain peoples do we possess the written records without which it is impossible to examine in detail and to follow with assured accuracy the steps whereby man arrived at the arts and institutions which constitute material civilization. Even where the material remains bear witness to intellectual advance and to a high order of culture, the total absence or the sparse survival of literary evidence may make the real character of the culture problematic. When, as in the case of India, we are thrown back upon purely archaeological evidence, we can indeed draw a picture of civilization, but cannot trace its genesis or its outcome; we are presented with facts in a historical vacuum, and our interpretation of the facts is only too liable to be arbitrary and subjective. When, as in the case of China in the Shang period, there are written documents but those are strictly limited in range and character, then our natural inclination to interpret them in the light of our knowledge of later China may well lead to an anachronistic falsification of history. Thus in the Anyang bone-inscriptions there recurs the sign *yi* meaning a settlement of people; at a later date the character denotes a town, a territory or a possession, and from this it has been argued that the rural community played a very important role in the constitution of the Yin state; again, the *ching* sign representing a well is used to mean 'fields', and from this, and from the data of later literary sources, it is concluded that in the Yin period land-cultivation was in common and was organized on the so-called 'well-fields' system. Such conclusions *may* be right, but they remain assumptions which ought not to be cited as history, and it is better to confine ourselves to the objective view which may appear less scholarly but does at least avoid the risk of reading our own prejudices into the remote past.

In other areas, especially in Europe (Map IX), the case is

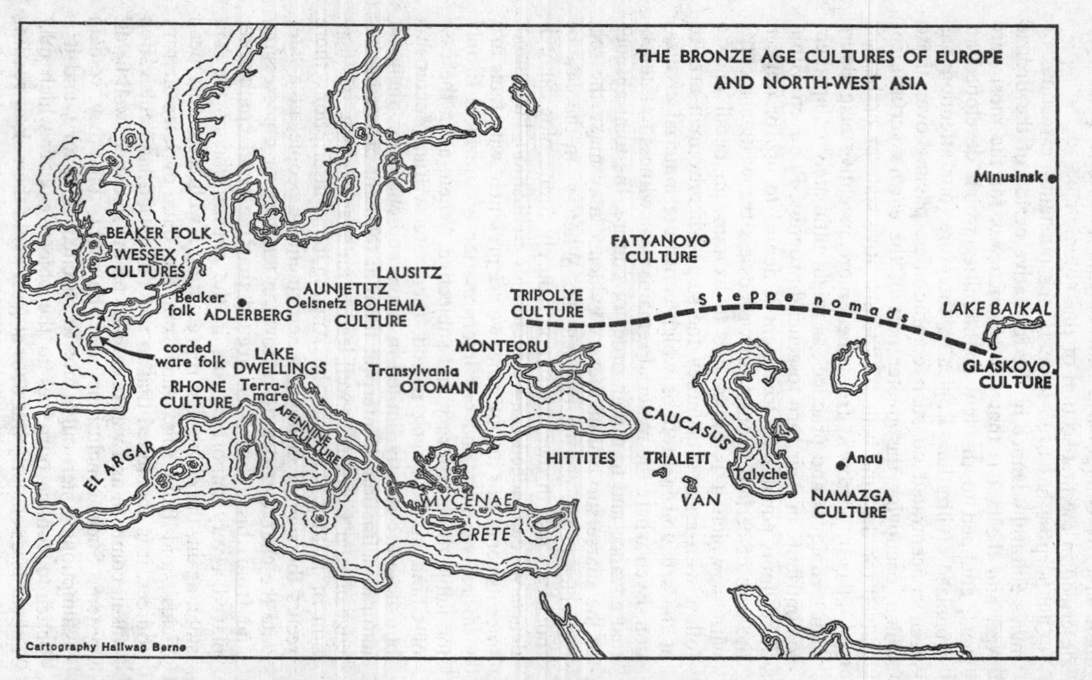

THE BRONZE AGE CULTURES OF EUROPE
AND NORTH-WEST ASIA
Minusinsk
BEAKER FOLK
WESSEX CULTURES
FATYANOVO CULTURE
LAUSITZ
AUNJETITZ
Oelsnetz
BOHEMIA CULTURE
Beaker folk
ADLERBERG
TRIPOLYE CULTURE
Steppe nomads
LAKE BAIKAL
corded ware folk
LAKE DWELLINGS
MONTEORU
Transylvania
OTOMANI
GLASKOVO CULTURE
RHONE CULTURE
Terra-mare
APENNINE CULTURE
CAUCASUS
EL ARGAR
HITTITES
TRIALETI
Talyche
Anau
MYCENAE
VAN
NAMAZGA CULTURE
CRETE
Cartography Hallwag Berne

MAP IX

different. Whereas in India excavation has thrown a spotlight upon a single phase of history, virtually isolated in the surrounding darkness, in Europe the archaeological evidence is relatively abundant, so that it is possible to trace everywhere innovations and improvements in the technical field and, by the evidence of man's handicrafts, to follow the intercourse between different ethnical or cultured groups and the migrations of tribes from one part of the continent to another. But on the moral and intellectual sides we have no evidence at all. Of the thoughts and ideals of those tribes we know nothing, and for Europe and north-west Asia the whole Bronze Age belongs to prehistory.

None the less is it true that in the course of the Bronze Age great changes took place throughout those regions, changes which we can observe sometimes in considerable detail, and that in 1250 BC conditions in Europe and the territories of the USSR were altogether other than they had been in 3000 BC.

The change was in its origin, as Professor Hawkes has said, 'an affair of Oriental influence, the West receiving, tardily and in comparative poverty, what the East was only giving after long familiarity within its own borders. But we have never found it possible to call this reception merely passive. The peoples of Europe had already developed cultural traditions within the limits imposed by their Mesolithic economy, and the spontaneity and adaptive vigour with which they took to themselves the elements of Oriental culture that reached them typify not passive reception but positive reaction. From the Danubian Neolithic to the Mycenaean Bronze Age, the result was characteristically not second-hand reflexion of Eastern achievement but integration of Eastern with native elements in something essentially new."[1] To this should be added that in each region the cultural tradition was so far peculiar that when the eastern elements were introduced the resultant amalgam was not the same; throughout the length and breadth of Europe, and again in the lands east of Europe, we see a diversity of Bronze Age cultures which may tend to compose itself into a consistent pattern but preserves none the less the individual character of each of them.

As we have seen already, it was the development of metallurgical techniques which, advancing along the trade-routes and concentrating upon those areas where prospectors could recognize the presence of metal ore, gave birth to the local Bronze Age cultures. In Europe the most important, and one of the earliest, was the Aunjetitz culture of the Bohemian-Middle German region. There copper ore was abundant, and tin was found both in association with it (in the Oelsnetz district) and independently in the area from the Erzgebirge westwards to the Thuringian hills, round the upper waters of the Saale; there, then, the old workers in copper could turn their practised technique to good account by the use of the superior alloy whose merits had been discovered by the east. The presence amongst their manufactures of the torque and the knot-headed pin proves that Oriental influences had been brought to bear upon the native founders, and further dates the introduction of true bronze to eastern Europe to about 1900 BC. Within a century, by 1800 BC, the Aunjetitz culture of Bohemia was fully developed and its products, serving as patterns for imitation, had been carried far afield, spreading its influence through Thuringia and Saxony right up to the Rhineland (where the Adlerberg culture is within the Aunjetitz orbit) and eastwards across the Carpathians to give birth to the Monteoru, Otomani and Witenburg cultures of Transylvania.

The Rhône Bronze Age culture is proved by its torques and knot-headed, roll-headed and trefoil-headed pins to be an offshoot of that of Aunjetitz, but it was still a fairly individual development; it was interrelated with the Italian, and it gave rise to the Swiss lake-dwellings culture, but its ramifications extended westwards to Languedoc and the Gironde, and northwards to the Franche-Comté. The latter area, together with Alsace and Lorraine, was at the beginning of the millennium being settled by a pastoral warrior group distinguished by their burial customs (single graves under round barrows) who as the 'Corded Ware' people had previously overrun much of central Europe and were now moving west; about 1750 BC they invaded and occupied Brittany, displacing or subjugating the old builders of the Breton megalithic monuments. The northern elements of these tribes came into touch with the Adlerberg culture, and this contact reinforced the influence upon them of Aunjetitz metallurgy.

Spain is one of the richest metal-bearing regions of Europe, and the Iberian copper-mines were from early times exploited by Aegean prospectors. The first landings were made on the Almerian coast, a fact which suggests that the approach had been by way of the African shores of the Mediterranean, and, judging from the female stone figurines found on the Spanish sites, the settlers had come from Cyprus; but the corbelled tombs which they introduced are more closely paralleled in Crete, and Cretans were perhaps more likely to travel far afield in search of copper than Cypriots who possessed resources of their own. Early in the third millennium Almeria could show big fortified trading-citadels, as at Los Millares, and was extending its culture northwards along the Spanish coast; later on the same culture is found spreading up the coast of Portugal also, to Cintra and beyond, so that the Los Millares people were opening up the Atlantic sea-ways, eventually reaching Britain, and popularizing along their route the megalithic tombs of Iberia.

From its beginning this was a mixed culture in which the impetus was derived from the Aegean but the development was mainly due to native genius, its roots being traced to the arts of the local Neolithic Age. Undoubtedly a certain measure of urbanization did result from the concentration of mine-owners and industrialists, but for that we have little contemporary evidence; we may accept the fact, but we cannot visualize it. No very great advance had been made in the days which saw the wide expansion of the south Iberian culture; the adventurers who crossed the Pyrenees into southern France and those who voyaged overseas to Brittany exported to those lands the tomb customs which had originated in the Aegean and the pottery beakers inherited from their Stone Age ancestors, and in so doing they made an important contribution to the primitive cultures of their trade customers; but they could offer nothing of a higher order. They were themselves still in the Chalcolithic stage. Tin is virtually confined to the northern districts of Spain, and it would seem to have been neglected by the more backward local population, for the metallurgists of the south of the peninsula, the Los Millares people and their immediate successors, long continued to use only the unalloyed copper of their own mines.

It was probably through trade connections with Bronze Age Italy (and perhaps southern France also) that the importance of the Spanish tin deposits was recognized—certainly there are types of Spanish implements such as the halberd which suggest a connection with Italy; but for the most part Iberia was thrown back upon its own resources. The old sea-route used by the Aegeans could not stand against the competition of the overland trade routes that had now been opened up across Europe, so that Spain became a backwater, and there is evidence to show that a period of relative poverty set in. The newly discovered metal alloy resulted in the development of a culture more or less peculiar and indigenous, the El Argar culture, which arose about 1700 BC and lasted into the second half of the millennium; but it did not diverge in any marked respect from the general European pattern, and was really but a rather backward branch of the continental culture. But it is at least possible that Iberia, in spite of its isolation, maintained certain trade relations with Ireland, clinging still to a centuries-old tradition, and that the Irish halberd is derived from Spain.

The old Amber Route, which had brought the Baltic into touch with the Mediterranean, ran north by south through Aunjetitz territory. But the amber merchants used also a western route, through Scandinavia and by sea to Britain and across north Britain to Ireland, where amber could be exchanged for gold. A third trade-route, branching off from the first, ran from Saxo-Thuringia by way of the Lower Rhine to the North Sea coast; this brought the Aunjetitz culture into relation with north-west Europe and also facilitated the export of Irish gold and bronze to the continent, the Irish boats sailing up the Channel and over to the mouths of the Rhine. The distribution of metal types bespeaks a remarkably close intercourse between the different and often distant areas. There were, of course, regions remote from the trade-routes where the old Neolithic or Chalcolithic cultures persisted with but little change; but the greater part of the continent came in time to enjoy a Bronze Age culture which, though ultimately inspired by the Orient and though varying to the extent that it is possible to distinguish the products of particular areas, was yet so far uniform that it may properly be called European.

That it should be European and not merely pseudo-Oriental was the necessary result of conditions. Contacts with the ancient civilizations of the Middle East were indirect, and what the east contributed to Europe was not so much models as skills. The old metal-prospectors and travelling smiths who had first followed the Amber trade-route and then branched off wherever business might lead them—itinerant merchants such as the 'torque-wearers' who made their way into Alsace (see pp. 292–93)—took with them ingots or half-finished goods to be worked up to suit the taste or the needs of their barbarous clients. Later in time the Mycenaeans, whose colonies dotted the Mediterranean coast, had to pay for what they bought with goods acceptable in the local market and the easiest way of doing that was to train local craftsmen. In many parts of the thinly-populated continent hunting was still as important as agriculture, and in many parts agriculture was still of the Neolithic type according to which crops would be grown on land cleared of undergrowth by burning and after two or three years, when the soil was exhausted, the farmer would move elsewhere; nowhere was there that concentration of organization which makes possible the development of cities, and nowhere those stable conditions which are expressed by the great Oriental kingships. The foreign merchant, therefore, had no central mart where he could sell his goods, but had to go in search of clients;[2] and his clients were not wealthy monarchs who would buy luxuries wholesale but petty chiefs and their followers, of small means and fastidious tastes. Instead of being the servant of a royal despot, working to order, he was a free agent using his ingenuity to meet the varying demands made upon him, and it was to his interest to learn from his customers; thus it was that while his technique was altogether in the Oriental tradition the things he and his pupils made tended to assume a character of their own.

Several times in this history emphasis has been laid on the spread of ideas. New ideas can be spread only by human carriers. In the case of Bronze Age Europe this traffic is admirably illustrated. Here the techniques elaborated in the Orient are seen to be diffused far and wide by the wandering merchant-smiths; but there result from them not mere copies of the Oriental models but modifications of them, or new creations, which foreshadow a distinctly European civilization.

Trade was the normal medium, but as well as trade, war and folk-migrations spread the knowledge of styles and techniques; thus it was that the invasion of Wessex by the 'bell-barrow' people, aristocratic immigrants from Brittany, made of western Britain an entrepôt of the Aunjetitz culture. Moreover, such movements gradually resulted in a change in the ethnic character of Europe which foreshadowed something of the continent's future. The westward advance of the 'bell-barrow' culture signalizes the emergence of the people afterwards known to us as the Celts. In the latter part of the Bronze Age the backward tribes of northern Europe were coalescing, in their relatively undisturbed forest-tracts, as the ancestors of the Germanic peoples. The founders of the Apennine culture, who had poured across the Alpine barriers, by-passing the Terramare hut-builders of the Po valley, secured Italy for the Italic peoples. In central Europe the old Aunjetitz culture had lost the momentum of its creative period, and about the middle of the second millennium BC was replaced by the Lausitz culture, originally an offspring of the Aunjetitz but remodelled by a northern people (perhaps members of the Slavo-Baltic tribes), who cremated their dead and preferred barrows to the flat graves of the Aunjetitz folk; Lausitz influence spread westwards as far as the British Isles, while in the south it would seem to have been responsible for the development and, to some extent, the re-population of Illyria and Thrace.

Progress in north-western Asia began later and was less consistent than in Europe. Much of this was steppe country where cattle-breeding was the main industry and the people therefore nomads or semi-nomadic; such people are more likely to import than to manufacture metal implements or weapons. Importation was easy. It has been remarked that the Otomani and Monteoru cultures were indebted to Aunjetitz; but cultural influences came rather from the south, from the Caucasian area which was the home of the earliest metal-working industry. In Transcaucasia, where ore was available, even a predominantly pastoral people were bound to borrow the metallurgical techniques practised by their neighbours. The crop-raising peoples of southern Turkmenia (the pioneers of culture in what are now the USSR territories) certainly manufactured their own metal instruments and ornaments, as is proved by the discovery of furnaces and copper slag in ruins of the big village settlement at Namazga Tepe. There, in the Namazga IV level, which corresponds roughly to Anau III, all the evidence points to Iranian influence being particularly strong in the second half of the third millennium BC; the painted pottery shows contacts with Tal-i-Bakun in southern Persia, with Susa and with Sialk III, and the Russian excavators emphasize its resemblance to that of the Quetta culture of Baluchistan. It must, however, be remarked that most of the locally made metal objects from Namazga Tepe are of copper, though bronze does also occur.

The general character of the Namazga culture is relatively simple, that of a community living on a backwater rather than on any important stream of progress, whereas in Caucasian Georgia the barrows of the tribal chiefs yield bronze weapons and gold and silver objects, excellently made by local smiths, which show that early in the second half of the second millennium BC this Trialeti culture had reached a high level. It was a curiously mixed culture. Some of the metal types recall those of such as Talyche, on the northern borders of Persia, others are paralleled as far afield as Mycenae, others again come from the Lake Van area; the most remarkable are bowls with repoussé decorations, scenes of animals and men, which are indisputably of native inspiration, and these are by far the most barbaric. At the very end of our period, i.e. in the thirteenth century BC, sites such as Gandja-Karabakh and Kuban show a later but not dissimilar culture in which, though the pottery is local—and incidentally very fine—the metal-work betrays the inflence of foreign schools. Only by slow degrees did the knowledge acquired by the southern tribes of Transcaucasia penetrate to the forest regions of the north, where men lived by hunting and fishing in purely Neolithic conditions, and it was only in the second millennium that invaders introduced there the arts of husbandry, cattle-breeding and metallurgy and a Bronze Age culture (known as the Fatyanovo culture) arose in the valley between the Oka and the Volga rivers.

Another outpost of bronze-working technique was established about 1200 BC in the neighbourhood of Minusinks, but it was an outpost only; Siberia remained Neolithic, and so far from progress being made tribes in the Baikal region preserved into the nineteenth century AD the Glaskovo culture which archaeology has brought to light from the second millennium BC.

Even from this brief survey it must be obvious that archaeological research has supplied us with an immense amount of information regarding the prehistory of Europe and northwestern Asia. But just as obviously are the limits of our knowledge implied by the terms which we are driven to use. We talk of the 'Beaker' people, the 'Bell-barrow' people, the 'Terramare' people, and of the 'Aunjetitz' culture, the 'Adlerberg', the 'Lausitz', the 'El Argar' and the 'Apennine' cultures, thus identifying a people by some peculiar product or feature, a culture by its habitat or, more often, by the name of the place in which the relics of it were first found. The fact is that we do not know who any of these peoples were; we know scarcely anything about them, only about the things they made and used. But the more we study their material remains, which are the sole basis for our judgement, the more are we forced to recognize that none of these tribes or groups concerns our present purpose, for at this stage of their existence none of them made any original contribution to the progress of mankind. Starting as savages, they did indeed better themselves by means of borrowed arts, but they invented nothing that was new or to the general good. In our summary account the term 'culture' has recurred with wearisome iteration; its constant use merely emphasizes the fact that here the term 'civilization' is quite inapplicable. It is, of course, true that, whereas some groups were to stagnate or to disappear, the occupants of some of these great regions were in after times to play a part in man's advance no less important than that of the Sumerians, the Egyptians or the Babylonians. But for us their prehistory only acquires significance after they have achieved historic stature; and by that time they are no longer 'the Beaker folk' or 'the corded ware people', nor even, perhaps, the linear descendants of such, but a mixed stock which directly or indirectly owed something to the one or the other of those prehistoric cultures, or perhaps to both. Within the time-limits of the Bronze Age we can attribute to the various and shifting 'groups' and 'cultures' those shadowy creations of the archaeologist—promise, perhaps, but not performance.

It is, therefore, within the narrow field of the literate peoples alone that we have tried to show how there were developed the early phases of civilized life. In treating of the elements that go to make up civilization—agriculture, law and trade, sciences and crafts, religion and art—it has seemed necessary to consider each in turn, abstracted from its context, merely observing how in each community they were affected by local conditions, took varying shapes, were furthered or hindered, sterilized or made fertile, by the different patterns of society. By the detailed analysis in the abstract of what are in fact indivisible parts of a greater whole we may lay the foundations of the study of that whole; but it must not be forgotten that such isolation of the component elements is essentially artificial. Civilization is not merely the sum total of the arts and sciences, the performances and the beliefs of an accomplished people; civilization is a manner of life. Our analysis of the means to civilization has touched only parenthetically on the ends which they served; it is time therefore to assess, so far as possible, the effect which the astonishing progress made by man after the invention of metallurgy exercised upon his life.

For this purpose we cannot deal with society as a whole. Civilization did not result in an impartial distribution of benefits. The material progress achieved by man could not have been made without forced labour, nor maintained without it; in the most enlightened state, therefore, there were still slaves for whom civilization did not spell liberty, still serfs whose rights were limited and their opportunities for the better life but little enlarged; and these classes inevitably formed the bulk of the population. Progress has always originated from and been developed by the superior intelligence—and the more favourable conditions—of the minority, and has ministered primarily to the well-being of a social élite. If we ask what effect the changes wrought in the Bronze Age had upon the manner of man's life we must not consider the case of the slave, whose condition had been relatively unaffected, any more than that of the king or ruler, whose splendour was in any case exceptional, and from the point of view of man's history may well have proved ephemeral and inconsequent. It was the citizen, the free man, priest or merchant, landowner or skilled artisan, who reaped the benefits of civilization, and his normal life is the standard by which progress should be judged.

But because our history is that of the advance of man in general our summary must not be regional; it is not a case of portraying the life of an individual citizen of Egypt or of Mesopotamia, of China or India, of the Hittite or the

Phoenician states; rather is it to mark how the combined or separate experience of all those countries had opened up to man as such the possibilities of a liberal existence. No citizen of any of the states enjoyed all the rights and privileges of his contemporary world, but those which he did enjoy, whether shared by others or peculiar to his own society, did help to enrich the human heritage. If, therefore, we disregard regional accidents and weave together threads drawn from diverse sources, our resultant pattern will not indeed reproduce that of any one society but should represent not unfairly the dynamic concept of civilization which man had now evolved and was handing down to future generations.

None the less is it true that regional differences, though they may be explained as the accidental results of local conditions, bear witness to one of the most important social changes that took place in the course of the Bronze Age. The accidents of physical surroundings—of soil and climate—naturally led to differences in the manner of life of the various groups; but with the perpetuation of such differences and with the induration of tradition there were evolved distinct mentalities. With, on the one hand, the centralization of government tending to crystallize tradition and, on the other, foreign wars not only emphasizing the contrast between one group and another but also picturing everything alien as inimical, there was born the local self-consciousness which makes for nationalism. At the beginning of our period we found social groups distinguishable more readily by their geographical location than by their cultural idiosyncrasies; at its close we are confronted by nations. In the thirteenth century BC an inhabitant of the Nile valley regarded himself primarily as an Egyptian, a member of that social order which was based on and maintained by the divinity of Pharaoh; he despised anyone who did not share that status; his whole outlook was peculiar to the land of his birth; the man and his country were indissoluble; to live away from Egypt was exile; to die away from Egypt was damnation.[3] The citizen of Babylonia, a man of very mixed blood, with far wider interests and a less intense love of the soil, although a narrower patriotism devoted him to the city state of historical tradition was still in the broadest sense a Mesopotamian. The yet more mixed members of the confederation which was the Hittite empire held themselves aloof from their neighbours and in spite of internal jealousies defended the formidable unity of Hattusas. The Phoenicians tolerated for commercial reasons the outsiders with whom they trafficked, but clung to their independence with passionate tenacity; their centres of government were separate and individual—Ugarit, Byblos, Sidon and Tyre—but each of them was Phoenician first and foremost. Lastly, the Hebrews were a 'Chosen People', a nation set apart.[4]

In 1250 BC then, any man in the civilized countries of the Middle East was a citizen or a subject of one of a number of recognized national states.[5] But this particular allegiance constituted no threat to his personal security. It is true that the birth-pangs of the states had generally meant wars between rival rulers, with the resultant risk of ruin to the individual citizen; but at this date he profited by what must have appeared to him an assured stability; his world was a world at peace,[6] and it was difficult to imagine that any serious breach of the peace could occur, or anything upset the seemly order of international coexistence.

Admittedly, one great power had disappeared. But it was now a century and a half since Minoan Knossos had gone down in flames, and for peoples outside Crete that had really made but little difference: the Mycenaean heirs of Knossos carried on the old traditions, and that in a more cosmopolitan spirit, for they were keener and more accessible traders, and with their merchant colonies established on the Asiatic mainland, as at Ugarit, they brought the Aegean into closer touch with the rest of the Middle East than the Minoan Cretans had ever done. It was true that one heard tales of far-off troubles, that 'the isles were unquiet', that the attitude of the ruler of Libya seemed rather menacing, and that Assyria was growing formidable; and everybody knew that the Hittite king had a campaign every year—but these were mere border affairs, which were the concern of the regular army, and the troops were engaged in maintaining the peace, not in disturbing it. What really mattered were the relations between the great powers, and those were excellent. Egypt, Babylon, Hattusas, the Syrian states, seemed to have renounced all their old enmities. The dynasts were linked together by political marriages; even a minor ruler like Niqmad of Ugarit had espoused an Egyptian princess, while the Great King of the Hittites had visited Egypt in person[7] to attend the marriage of his daughter to Ramses II; another daughter of Hattusilis was the wife of Bentesina, prince of the Amurru. Regular embassies attached to the different courts assured the smooth settlement of minor difficulties, and so anxious were the rulers to have their interests represented in palatable form that they would even employ foreigners in the diplomatic service; thus Amenophis III had sent a Hurrite, Irshappa, as his envoy to Arzawa and Tili-Sarruma, prince of Carchemish, employed an Egyptian who was so thoroughly naturalized that he wrote his name in Akkadian form and in Hittite hierglyphs upon his seal. Whereas the wars of former days had so often been occasioned by disputes regarding the ownership of some frontier town or province, these important questions were now peacefully settled by diplomacy, and for negotiations of the sort the ambassador might be granted plenipotentiary powers and entrusted with a facsimile of the Great Seal of the Hittite king; there could be no stronger evidence of the wish to avoid war at all costs, which, after the indecisive battle of Kadesh, governed the policies of the exhausted Middle Eastern powers.

A world at peace gave to the individual not only a feeling of stability which made effort worth while, but also the leisure and inclination for self-expression. Frontiers were open, so that a man could travel freely, and the governments encouraged trade, so much so that a royal treaty might secure the rights of merchants or artisans of one country to pursue a seasonal occupation in another, returning home for the unprofitable part of the year, while, on the other hand, the local merchants were protected against unfair competition by foreign rivals. The personal safety of travelling traders was guaranteed, and we even find the Hittite queen paying compensation for the sinking of a Ugarit merchant vessel outside its territorial waters allegedly due to Hittite sabotage. A well-organized system of credit enabled the merchant-adventurer to finance his expeditions with funds provided by private bankers, by the temple or the palace at a fair rate of interest, and both sides were protected by the legal conditions specified in the contract. International trade not only brought foreign goods and luxuries into a country, but also opened men's eyes to new inventions and their minds to new ideas; whether a man voyaged abroad or stopped at home his horizon was not circumscribed by the frontiers of his state, but he could feel himself to be, in a measure, a fellow-member of a wider community, of a union of states which together made up the civilized world.

In fact, of course, the 'union of states' was simply the mutual tolerance of autocrats anxious not to be involved in war. The citizen who profited by his country's foreign policy had nothing to do with the framing of it. He could boast of being a freeman, but for him 'freedom' meant only that by law he was absolved from certain unpleasant obligations and was licensed to live his own life after his own fashion within the limits of the law. But that happy state of affairs was a fortunate accident; the absolution and the license had been granted and could be revoked by something wholly outside his control. Man had not yet evolved the idea of 'freedom' in a democratic sense, the sense in which the Athenians were to use the term seven centuries later: a citizen of the Middle East in the Bronze Age lived under the law and might approve of the law, but he had no say in the making of it.

Any suggestion that the code of law might be drawn up by the people, or in consultation with the people, would in those days have been condemned as paradoxical and impious.[8] Law emanated ultimately from a god, and was enunciated either by the god himself (as in the case of Pharaoh) or by his official mouthpiece, king or priest; its authority therefore was absolute and unquestionable. The administration of the law was a different matter in that the officials were human; the citizen might complain of injustice or corruption, but his appeal was to the gods, for the correction of abuse, not for any amendment of the code. However hardly the terms of the law might bear upon the individual he was obliged to accept it as it stood.

Nowhere, in the course of the Bronze Age, had man attained that moral outlook which would make him see an anomaly in the fact that all men were not equal before the law. The gods had so designed the world; men were not equal, and the divine law accorded with the will of the gods. It was therefore no injustice, but a frank recognition of the facts, that distinction was made even amongst freemen, that there was one law for the rich and another for the poor, one law for the nobleman and another for the man of the middle class; rather was it a proof of the essential justice of heaven that the nobleman's privileges were counterbalanced by heavier punishment for any misdoing and that middle-class inferiority found compensation in lighter dues. In any case the free citizen had his measure of freedom guaranteed to him—indeed except when by his own fault or by the accident of war he forfeited freedom—and although he served an autocratic government he was not a slave.

The institution of slavery was traditional, universal and essential to social life and progress, nor was any man's conscience (not even the slave's) hurt by it. Custom and law alike vacillated uncertainly between the two incompatible theories, that a slave was a mere chattel, and that a slave was a human being in sorry circumstances but not altogether without claims upon his fellow-men. In practice the second view seems to have prevailed most often. When slavery was incurred for debt it was difficult to maintain that the temporary sentence[9] deprived the debtor of all human rights, and even when the slave was a foreigner, bought and sold as merchandise, he was a valuable possession whose worth might be increased by decent treatment. In practice, therefore, slavery was of a mild type, and the slave-owner might pray that he receive from god as much clemency as he extended to his slaves; there is no reason to think that the owner was necessarily brutalized by the institution which all regarded as part and parcel of the divine scheme of things. On the other hand the gulf that separates the freeman from the slave, and the fact that the private citizen could possess slaves of his own, emphasized his free citizenship; the privilege that he enjoyed, and the sense of mastery, profoundly affected his view of the relation in which he stood *vis-à-vis* the state.

He accepted readily the fact that the government of the state was autocratic and absolute; its power over him was unquestionable and its demands upon him might be exigent. But that did not make him the slave or the victim of a tyrant. The head of the state was either himself a god, or represented a god; its demands upon him were made in the name of a divine being upon whose goodwill depended the welfare of each and all; the service that one rendered to the god was, as it were, an insurance premium which no man could grudge. Some people believed that man had been created for no other purpose than to produce food for the gods; however that might be, it was certainly true that the gods expected and enjoyed the sacrifices which men offered to them, and would miss their accustomed meals if through the slackness or the penury of their worshippers such were to fail. The god who was Lord of the state depended on his subjects for his own well-being, and since their offerings must be according to their means their prosperity was to his own advantage. Granted that the state required of its citizens blind obedience, this was not a rule of brute force; it was no case of a human tyrant dragooning his fellow-men; enlightened self-interest recognized the benefits of a divine autocracy, and the dignity of the individual did not suffer because he acknowledged the absolute supremacy of god.

So far as can be gathered from the documents of an age when philosophic thought found no expression, the burden of state authority sat very lightly upon men's minds. They believed that they enjoyed a freedom which in fact did not exist, but the illusion satisfied them. The political history of the time recounts innumerable attempts by conquered peoples to shake off a foreign yoke, but there they were rebelling against the enforced rule of a human master; but there is no record of the citizens of a state trying to upset the state régime,[10] for that would have meant fighting against god. Even when Akhenaton disowned the Egyptian pantheon and dishonoured their temples his apostasy, however unpopular, aroused no violent opposition even from the powerful priesthood of Amon, so that only after his death could the counter-revolution take place; and that because of the divinity of the Pharaoh himself. The Hittite king could be tried and executed by the *pankus,* the General Assembly of his warriors, but only if he himself offended against the divine law which as a man he was supposed to maintain; the *pankus* in such a case was not in revolt against the state but was defending it. The subject of a theocratic state acquiesced automatically in the inviolability of the state and in its absolute rule, and saw in that no infringement of his personal liberty; he was, under god, a freeman and a master of men.

Undoubtedly the idea had been born that the state was run for the benefit of its citizens.[11] Of course, the intention of the god might be thwarted by the incompetence or the dishonesty of his ministers, but the humblest man, such as the 'Eloquent Peasant' of the Egyptian tale, need not hesitate to appeal to the god—in this case Pharaoh—or to his mortal vice-regent; the freeman, in fact, had his rights, which the government could not disregard without giving offence to heaven. However unmoral might be the behaviour of the gods themselves, they had yet ordained for men a social code which corresponded more or less to morality; it overrode human values in so far as it encouraged slavery, but the personal value of the individual free citizen was established by it, and such a one could, although he had no say in the shaping of the laws, none the less claim to be a responsible member of the state.

The individualism of the citizen was symbolized by his right to hold private property, especially in land. The two primitive systems whereby land was either communal or was temple property, i.e. owned by the god, were gradually breaking down in all the more civilized countries. It may be that the communal system still persisted in China in the Shang period, but elsewhere it had vanished long before the end of the Bronze Age.[12] The temples still possessed enormous estates (and in Egypt were even adding to these) but the fiefs granted to soldiers and to courtiers, originally on conditions of feudal service, in the course of time were freed from those encumbrances and were held in fee simple. The Middle East never developed a comprehensive feudal régime such as we may suspect to have prevailed in China under the Chou Dynasty, but grants of land were on a scale sufficient to build up a class of landowners, many of them small landowners, who acquired hereditary and, finally, absolute rights; and, as property changed hands freely, there resulted a mixed system with the great domains of king or temple neighboured by the fields and gardens of private landlords, even of small-holders. More than anything else does landed property persuade a man that he is independent and has a real stake in the country. When then we find, as we do in Babylonia, that apart from the regular farming class the townsman was prone to possess a vegetable plot or a field or two somewhere outside the city walls, we may fairly conclude that society was strongly individualistic and, at the same time, satisfied with its form of government. A Babylonian, and still more an Egyptian, would have regarded with incredulous horror the right of the Hittite community to sit in judgement on its sovereign; the conception of a limited monarchy was wholly alien to his experience and to his beliefs, nor would it have seemed to him to imply any higher social ideal; his own government was very properly autocratic, it exacted from him such dues as were necessary to the state's welfare, and it allowed him all the personal liberty that a man could ask.

It is well to remember that the immense progress in culture and in technical knowledge which has been described in our foregoing chapters had been crowded into a relatively brief space of time. In the Stone Age, although the sum total of advance had been revolutionary, its pace had been very slow, so that millennium had succeeded to millennium with barely perceptible change in man's estate. But in the Bronze Age a few centuries saw the world of the Middle East transformed. Material advance outstripped the growth of thought. Provided that a man was free to enjoy the comforts and advantages that ever-new inventions spread before his eyes he asked nothing more; he grasped at the 'bread and circuses' and cared not at all for political theories and ideals.

The good things of life were indeed manifest. The citizen was well lodged, after a fashion undreamed of in the preceding age. The Mesopotamian, even one of very moderate means, had a solidly built house adapted to his manner of life (*v.* Chapter II, p. 120–23), reasonably spacious, which guaranteed privacy and comfort and enabled him to entertain his friends; a permanent home, it enshrined the traditions of his family, and the setting enhanced his dignity as the head of the household and the high priest of its ancestral cult. The Egyptian man of rank lived in more palatial conditions, a walled garden surrounding the great house with its open loggias, its gaily-painted walls and columns, its bathrooms and separate quarters for the womenfolk; no one, in those flat and rainless lands, could have the channelled water that flushed the closets of Minos's palace, but the mere fact that such an amenity had been invented showed how keenly men appreciated the sophistications of domestic life. As early as the Twelfth Dynasty the Egyptian country house, though it might be flimsily built, aimed at civilized comfort, and its formal garden, its pergolas and ornamental tank where one could bathe were a delightful setting for the *al fresco* entertainment of guests. The Egyptian house, indeed, was not the family shrine which the more serious-minded Babylonian made of his home, but a place in which he could enjoy himself and to which he could invite his friends. The tomb paintings show us the banquets which in his life the dead man had loved to give; the tables are heaped with rich foods, fish and birds and joints of meat, cakes and fruit, and there are jars of wine whose seals bear the name and date of the vintage—'House of the High Priest of the Sun, year 9'—and perhaps its quality, 'very good'; the guests, both men and women, well dressed and finely perfumed, decked with jewels and with garlands of flowers hung round their necks, are not ashamed to drink to the point of intoxication, while musicians play and sing and naked girls amuse them with dances or acrobatic feats. It was such luxury as this that for the Egyptian constituted 'the good life'. Obviously it could be enjoyed only by the wealthy; but wealth and all that it brought depended upon the favour of Pharaoh, and there was no saying on whom that capricious favour might fall; even a slave might be raised to rank and riches, and a high officer of the court could declare, 'I was one whose family was poor, and whose town was small, but the Lord of Two Lands recognized me; I was accounted great in his heart'. Education opened the door to public service, and the humblest Egyptian of the middle class might warm himself with the dream that he would one day catch the eye of Pharaoh and rank amongst the great ones of the earth.[13]

In other countries of the Middle East, where the form of government depended upon law and precedent rather than on the untrammelled caprice of the ruler, such opportunities of advance were limited, and the individual citizen found other means to self-expression. On the whole, this meant that a man relied more upon his own efforts and abilities than on the accidents of patronage, and he could choose various ways of employing them. He had to equip himself for success. A freeman of the lower class who followed a craft had, of course, to be a member of a guild; but when once he had served his apprenticeship he could set up as his own master, not wholly dependent upon any patronage as was the Egyptian, and in competition with his fellow-craftsmen profit by his skill. A boy of a better-class family would be sent to school—not necessarily a temple school—where the education would be of a fairly general type; he might be trained for the priesthood, or for the public service; he might even become a research scholar or a schoolmaster in his turn, but he might equally well look forward to a business career. Business and trade were, indeed, the main preoccupation of the townsman; they should bring him wealth, but in any case they were an outlet for his energies and a means of asserting his personality. Trade was regulated by the state, but the regulations were ultimately in the merchant's interest, and provided that he observed the law he was encouraged and protected by them; even where the state, i.e. the king or the temple, embarked on trade, the private dealer could compete with it on fair terms and not be overborne by official rivalry. In Babylonia—and the same was probably true in the essentially commercial Phoenician states—the merchant enjoyed a remarkable degree of freedom and displayed a corresponding initiative; the same man would speculate in business of many sorts and in the goods of many countries. He could travel freely and with reasonable safety, and in foreign parts had the backing of his own government, to whose resident political envoy he could appeal for such help as in modern times would be given by a consul;[14] it was to his interest to appreciate the arts and to learn the ways of lands other than his own, and since at every stage of his journeys he was bound to recognize and respect the local gods, he was likely to develop a broad-minded cosmopolitanism corresponding to the free cultural exchanges which, in the thirteenth century BC, seem to make for a Middle Eastern unity.

The liberty accorded to the merchant, and the liberal outlook with which we may credit him, did not intrude into the sphere of politics; engrossed in the exploitation of the resources open to him he had no time for abstractions and could recognize no conflict between individualism and divinely constituted authority. In the ancient civilizations, there could be no place for that rebellious protest ascribed by the Old Testament to the lawless horde of Hebrew runaways when 'the princes of the assembly, men of renown, gathered themselves together against Moses and against Aaron, saying, "Ye take too much upon you, seeing that all the congregation is holy, every one of them" '. Such independence of spirit, which is the germ of the democratic idea, could be given to the world only by a young people, not hidebound by the old traditions which civilized man took for granted. Experience had proved to him the value of those traditions; they had indeed worked amazingly well. Observing them, man had in the course of the Bronze Age created a new world wherein a decently ordered society could live, and even live in peace, enjoying wholly new standards of comfort; he had produced in sculpture and painting works of art which still command the admiration of the world and in literature poetry and prose worthy to survive—and which did survive because he had also invented the art of writing; in architecture he had discovered all the basic principles and had employed them in masterpieces. It is characteristic that in what we call the sciences his advance was purely pragmatic; his observations and experiments aimed at practical results, and if he could compile a calendar, dye his textiles, manufacture metal alloys, dose for a fever, calculate the area of a field or the cost of a building in materials, labour and time, he was satisfied; questions of cause and effect did not interest him—they simply were not his affair, for the processes of science were miraculous, and his success in them was due as much to prayers, charms and magic as to method. Similarly, he did not question the gods. As gods, they were not bound by the rules of conduct which social life necessarily imposed upon men; it was their indisputable power for good or evil that impelled man's obedience and worship, and for averting their anger sacrifice was better than obedience. They did demand of man the social virtues, because on society depended their own well-being—such was the natural explanation of the divine sanctions against crime; but even at this early stage an individual, or a generation, might occasionally glimpse a moral aspect of deity and in a penitential psalm invoke the forgiveness of god. But introspection of that kind was rare, little more than the morbid outcome of misfortune. While it would be unjust to condemn as grossly materialistic an age in which the love of beauty is an unmistakable feature, it must be recognized that, on the one hand, the tyranny of accepted and authoritarian religion closed the door on any true philosophy or any independence of thought, and, on the other, the adventure of re-shaping the world engrossed man's mind and afforded him full scope for self-development.

We have seen with what success Bronze Age man took advantage of his opportunities, and it may well be that by the end of the thirteenth century he had exhausted all the possibilities of his new material, working within the limitations of his society. New materials and new men, uninhibited by the old traditions, were needed for further advance. The Harappā civilization had collapsed in ruins and the future of north-west India was in the hands of the semi-barbarous Aryan invaders. The glories of Knossos had long since vanished. The rise of the warrior state of Assyria had reduced Babylonia to the rank of a second-rate power and although it had not destroyed its traditions had for the time being at least sapped its virility. Now the Hittite empire was to be wiped out. Egypt, after the final effort that saved her frontiers, could do no more;[15] she ceased to count as a pioneer of civilization and, nursing her memories, long stagnated in a world of progress to which she contributed nothing until such time as Babylonian and, later, Greek instructors put her in touch with modernity. All the great centres of Bronze Age civilization perished from foreign attack or fell behind through internal decadence, all save China only. There civilization was so deeply rooted in the land of its origin that wave after wave of savage invaders only brought in new blood and fresh energy to carry on the old traditions and to build upon the old foundations. At no moment of time did the accidents of history breach the continuity of Chinese culture; but in the western world, about 1200 BC, dramatic happenings were to mark the end of one age and the beginning of a new.

NOTES TO CHAPTER XI

1. C. F. C. Hawkes, *The Prehistoric Foundations of Europe,* p. 381.
2. E. Herzfield in *Iran in the Ancient East* (Oxford, 1941), pp. 158 sq., suggests that these old prospectors, because of their value to the peoples through whose territories they passed, must have enjoyed some kind of safe-conduct. An exact analogy to this is provided by the *Solubiyeh,* an itinerant non-Moslem tribe of smiths in Syria and Arabia; they are despised as unclean, but travel freely over the different tribal areas and enjoy complete immunity.
3. Professor J. Leclant emphasizes the fact that the Egyptian was essentially defined by his religion, his integration into pharaonic society: it was the Pharaoh who realized the participation of the Egyptians in cosmos, the Pharaoh who made them, and them only, 'men' (*rmt*).
4. Professor I. M. Diakonoff doubts that the citizens of Babylonia thought of themselves as belonging to a Mesopotamian nation. The Phoenicians did not even have a common name in their own language; they were 'Tyrians', 'Sidonians', etc., but never 'Phoenicians'. The tribal connections of the Hebrews were stronger than their intertribal ties; they began to call themselves a 'chosen people' only later, and then exclusively on religious and not on 'nationalistic' grounds. Professor I. M. Diakonoff considers that what was important was that a man belonged to a certain community, and to a certain local or tribal cult. There were no 'nations' as we define them.
5. Professor I. M. Diakonoff here renews his doubts as to the existence of national states at this time. The Hittite kingdom was not a national state nor was the Kassite kingdom. What united Babylonia and to a certain extent Egypt was a common system of irrigation, not national feeling; the small states of Syro-Phoenicia were not national states; Assyria had a mixed population and its kings, beginning with Tiglatpileser I (twelfth century BC), having conquered a territory, used to count the population among the people of Assur, disregarding the ethnic and linguistic character of the conquered.
6. At least this is what he thought. But the peace did not last. See pp. 604–05.

7. According to the Egyptian story, which is not necessarily true.
8. Professor I. M. Diakonoff observes that in Mesopotamia the law at this time consisted of *(a)* customary law developed in the legal practice of the courts and as councils of elders, assemblies, etc., or *(b)* royal ordinances which might be collected in such documents as the 'Laws of Ur-Nammu' and the 'Laws of Hammurabi'. If citizens felt that the customary law was unjust they could appeal to the king who might issue an ordinance for the particular case concerned or promulgate a new law.
9. Professor I. M. Diakonoff notes that Hammurabi had limited slavery for debt to a term of three years. However, both before and after Hammurabi, slavery for debt was practically slavery for life.
10. There were periods of anarchy in Egypt, but these were due not to any rising of the proletariat against the régime but either to foreign invasion or to the ambition of hereditary nomarchs anxious to become Pharaohs. The upsetting of social ranks which the poets bewail (cf. Ch. X, p. 568) resulted from the favouritism shown to 'new men', the adherents of a successful upstart, at the expense of the old official class. None of these changes affected the constitution in any way.
11. Professor I. M. Diakonoff considers that the state was run for the benefit of the ruling class and sometimes for the benefit of a tyrant, whatever the ideological justification. Society was divided into freemen and slaves. But the freemen themselves belonged to different classes and the class division was perpetuated by the state. An Egyptian of these times was a responsible member of the state in a limited sense only: he had many duties and few rights.
12. Professor I. M. Diakonoff observes that the communal system still persisted in many countries such as, for instance, Assyria. The rights of the proprietor were restricted, i.e. they were combined with duties toward the community such as keeping up the irrigation system. The land of the small owners was land granted by the community, not land granted by the king or temple.
13. Professor I. M. Diakonoff remarks that education cost money and was in most cases practically inaccessible to the poor. Professor Ralph Turner points out, however, that during the Middle Kingdom and New Kingdom education increasingly became a means of climbing the social ladder, even for the poor; see H. Brunner, *Altägyptische Erziehung* (Wiesbaden, 1957), pp. 40–2.
14. Professor I. M. Diakonoff points out that the risks were sometimes great. Even the envoys of the kings in El Amarna times were subject to assaults on the way. Such envoys were often mere hostages in the hands of the foreign king.
15. Professor J. Leclant does not consider that Egypt ceases to make a contribution to civilization after the second millennium. In the eighth and seventh centuries BC Egypt enjoyed a magnificent renaissance. During the Ethiopian and Saite periods and in late Egyptian times, even under the Macedonian and Roman Pharaohs, Egypt produced much that is worthy of admiration. This was the Egypt in which Herodotus stayed and Plato studied.

SELECTED BIBLIOGRAPHY

CHAPTER I

THE BRONZE AGE

GENERAL

J. B. BURY *et al.*, eds., *The Cambridge Ancient History* (Cambridge and New York, 1923–27), Vols. I and II.

C. F. C. HAWKES, *The Prehistoric Foundations of Europe to the Mycenean Age* (London, 1940).

MESOPOTAMIA

V. G. CHILDE, *New Light on the Most Ancient East* (4th ed., New York, 1953).

L. W. KING, *A History of Sumer and Akkad: An Account of the Early Races of Babylonia from Prehistoric Time to the Foundation of the Babylonian Monarchy* (London, 1910).

C. F. A. SCHAEFFER, *Stratigraphie comparée et chronologie de l'Asie occidentale IIIe et IIe millénaires* (London, 1948).

EGYPT

A. J. ARKELL, *A History of the Sudan from the Earliest Times to 1821* (London, 1955).

J. H. BREASTED, *A History of Egypt from the Earliest Times to the Persian Conquest* (2nd rev. ed., London, 1905).

E. DRIOTON and J. VANDIER, *Les peuples de l'Orient méditerranéen. L'Egypte. II* (3rd ed., Paris, 1952).

E. OTTO, *Ägypten: Der Weg des Pharaonenreiches* (Stuttgart, 1953).

J. A. WILSON, *The Culture of Ancient Egypt* (Chicago, 1956). (First published in 1951 under title: *The Burden of Egypt.*)

PALESTINE

W. ALBRIGHT, *The Archaeology of Palestine* (Harmondsworth, Middlesex, 1949).

CRETE

F. MATZ, *Kreta, Mykene und Troja, die Minoische und die Homerische Welt* (Stuttgart, 1956).

J. D. S. PENDLEBURY, *The Archaeology of Crete: An Introduction* (London, 1939).

GREECE

H. R. H. HALL, *The Civilization of Greece in the Bronze Age* (London, 1928).

F. SCHACHERMEYR, *Die ältesten Kulturen Griechenlands* (Stuttgart, 1955).

ASIA MINOR

K. BITTEL, *Grundzüge der Vor- und Frühgeschichte Kleinasiens* (2nd ed., Tübingen, 1950).

A. GOETZE, *Kleinasien* (2nd ed., Munich, 1957).

HITTITES

G. CONTENAU, *La civilisation des Hittites et des Hurrites du Mitanni* (Paris, new ed. 1948).

L. DELAPORTE, *Les Hittites* (Paris, 1936).

O. R. GURNEY, *The Hittites* (Harmondsworth, Middlesex, 1952).

SETON LLOYD, *Early Anatolia: the Archaeology of Asia Minor before the Greeks* (Penguin Books, London and Baltimore, Md., 1956).

INDIA

S. PIGGOTT, *Prehistoric India to 1000* BC (London, 1950).

CHINA

H. G. CREEL, *The Birth of China: A Study of the Formative Period of Chinese Civilization* (New York, 1954).

H. G. CREEL, *Studies in Early Chinese Culture* (First Ser., Baltimore, 1937).

E. ERKES, *Geschichte Chinas von den Anfängen bis zum Eindringen des ausländischen Kapitals* (Berlin, 1956).

J. NEEDHAM, *Science and Civilisation in China* (Cambridge, 1955), Vol. I.

CHAPTER II

THE URBANIZATION OF SOCIETY

MESOPOTAMIA

W. ANDRAE, *Das Wiedererstandene Assur* (Leipzig, 1938).

H. FRANKFORT, 'Town-Planning in Ancient Mesopotamia', *Town Planning Review,* XXI, 2 (July 1950).

SIR C. L. WOOLLEY, *Excavations at Ur; A Record of Twelve Years' Work* (London, 1954).

EGYPT

H. W. FAIRMAN, 'Town-Planning in Pharaonic Egypt', *Town Planning Review,* XX (1949).

J. D. S. PENDLEBURY *et al.*, 'City of Akhenaten' in Egypt Exploration Society *Memoirs,* Ser. No. 44 (Oxford, 1951), 2 vols.

J. D. S. PENDLEBURY, *Tell el-Amarna* (London, 1935).

CRETE

SIR A. J. EVANS, *The Palace of Minos; a Comparative Account of the Successive Stages of the Early Cretan Civilization as Illustrated by the Discoveries at Knossos* (London, 1921–35), 4 vols.

SYRIA

SIR C. L. WOOLLEY *et al.*, 'Alalakh: an Account of the Excavations at Tell Atchana in the Hatay, 1937–1949', Society of Antiquaries of London, Research Committee *Reports,* No. 18 (London, 1955).

INDIA

E. J. H. MACKAY, *Further Excavations at Mohenjo-daro* (Delhi, 1938), 2 vols.

SIR J. H. MARSHALL *et al., Mohenjo-daro and the Indus Civilization* (London, 1931), 3 vols.

S. PIGGOTT, *Prehistoric India to 1000* BC (Harmondsworth, Middlesex, 1950).

SIR R. E. M. WHEELER, 'Harappā', in *Ancient India,* 3 (January 1947).

CHAPTER III

THE SOCIAL STRUCTURE

LAW AND JUSTICE

Code of Ur-Nammu. 'Code of Ur-Nammu', *Orientalia,* XXIII (1954).

Code of Libit-Ishtar. F. R. Steele, 'Code of Libit-Ishtar', *American Journal of Archaeology,* LII (1948), pp. 425 ff.

Code of Hammurabi. Hammurabi, *The Oldest Code of Laws in the World Promulgated by Hammurabi, King of Babylon,* BC *2285–2245* (translated by C. H. W. Johns, Edinburgh, 1903).

Tomb of Rekhmiré. R. O. Faulkner, 'Tomb of Rekhmiré', *Journal of Egyptian Archaeology,* XLI (1955).

A. BAKIR, 'Slavery in Ancient Egypt', Service des Antiquités de l'Egypte, *Annales* Supplement No. 18 (Cairo, 1952).

G. CONTENAU, *La civilisation des Hittites et des Hurrites du Mitanni* (Paris, new ed. 1948).

F. HANCAR, *Das Pferd in prähistorischer und früher historischer Zeit* (Vienna, 1956).

J. R. KUPPER, *Archives royales de Mari,* VI (1954).

L. A. LIPINE, 'Les anciennes lois de la Mésopotamie', *Receuil de Palestine,* I (1954), p. 63.

B. MEISSNER, *Babylonien und Assyrien* (Heidelberg, 1920–25), 2 vols.

J. M. MUNN-RANKIN, 'Diplomacy in Western Asia', *Iraq,* XVIII, I (1956), p. 68.

E. SEIDEL and A. SCHARFF, *Einführung in die Ägyptische Rechtsgeschichte bis zum Ende des Neuen Reiches* (2nd ed., New York, 1951).

J. A. WILSON, 'Authority and Law in Ancient Egypt', American Oriental Society, *Journal,* Supplement 17 (1954).

CHAPTER IV

TECHNIQUES, ARTS AND CRAFTS

AGRICULTURE

V. G. CHILDE, *What Happened in History* (Harmondsworth, Middlesex, 1943).

H. G. CREEL, *The Birth of China: a Study of the Formative Period of Chinese Civilization* (New York, 1954).

R. J. FORBES, 'The Fibres and Fabrics of Antiquity', *Studies in Ancient Technology* (Leiden, 1955).

R. J. FORBES, 'Food in Classical Antiquity', *Studies in Ancient Technology* (Leiden, 1955).

H. R. HALL and SIR C. L. WOOLLEY, 'Al'Ubaid; a Report on the Work Carried Out at Al'Ubaid for the British Museum in 1919 and for the Joint Expedition in 1922–3', in Joint Expedition of the British Museum and the Museum of the University of Pennsylvania to Mesopotamia, *Ur Excavations,* I (London, 1927).

S. N. KRAMER, *From the Tablets of Sumer; Twenty-Five Firsts in Man's Recorded History* (Indian Hills, Colo., 1956).

SIR J. H. MARSHALL *et al., Mohenjo-daro and the Indus Civilization* (London, 1931), 3 vols.

B. MEISSNER, *Babylonien und Assyrien* (Heidelberg, 1920–25), 2 vols.

W. M. F. PETRIE, *Social Life in Ancient Egypt* (London, 1923).

J. WIESNER, *Fahren und Reiten in Alteuropa und im Alten Orient* (Leipzig, 1939).

ARCHITECTURE

I. E. S. EDWARDS, *The Pyramids of Egypt* (Harmondsworth, Middlesex, 1949).

SIR A. J. EVANS, *The Palace of Minos; a Comparative Account of the Successive Stages of the Early Cretan Civilization as Illustrated by the Discoveries at Knossos* (London, 1921–35), 4 vols.

C. M. FIRTH and J. E. QUIBELL, *Excavations at Saqqarah; The Step Pyramid* (Cairo, 1936), 2 vols.

H. FRANKFORT, *The Art and Architecture of the Ancient Orient* (Harmondsworth, Middlesex, 1954).

SIR J. H. MARSHALL *et al., Mohenjo-daro and the Indus Civilization* (London, 1931), 3 vols.

J. D. S. PENDLEBURY, *Tell el-Amarna* (London, 1935).

SIR C. L. WOOLLEY *et al.*, 'Alalakh; an Account of the Excavations at Tell Atchana in the Hatay, 1937–1949', Society of Antiquaries of London, Research Committee *Reports,* No. 18 (London, 1955), 4 vols.

SIR C. L. WOOLLEY and T. E. LAWRENCE, *Carchemish; Report on the Excavations at Jerablus on behalf of the British Museum* (London, part 3, 1953).

SIR C. L. WOOLLEY, *Excavations at Ur; A Record of Twelve Years' Work* (London, 1954).

SIR C. L. WOOLLEY, *Ur Excavations* (London, 1927).

METALLURGY

V. G. CHILDE, *What Happened in History* (Harmondsworth, Middlesex, 1943).

H. G. CREEL, *The Birth of China: a Study of the Formative Period of Chinese Civilization* (New York, 1954).

C. F. ELAM, 'Some Bronze Specimens from the Royal Graves at Ur', Institute of Metals, *Journal,* XLVIII, I (1932).

R. J. FORBES, *Metallurgy in Antiquity; a Notebook for Archaeologists and Technologists* (Leiden, 1950).

B. A. KUFTIN, 'Prehistoric Culture Sequence in Transcaucasia', *Southwestern Journal of Anthropology,* II, 3 (Albuquerque, New Mexico, 1946).

H. MARYON, 'Metal Working in the Ancient World', *American Journal of Archaeology,* LIII, 2 (April–June 1949).

G. MOELLER, *Die Metallkunst der alten Ägypter* (Berlin, 1925).

H. J. PLENDERLEITH, 'Metals and Metal Techniques' in Sir C. L. Woolley, *Ur Excavations,* II, ch. xiv, p. 284.

F. SCHACHERMEYR, *Die ältesten Kulturen Griechenlands* (Stuttgart, 1955).

C. F. A. SCHAEFFER, 'Porteurs de Torques', *Ugaritica II; Nouvelles études relatives aux découvertes de Ras-Shamra* (Paris, 1949–50).

C. F. A. SCHAEFFER, *Stratigraphie comparée et chronologie de l'Asie occidentale* (London, 1948).

CRAFTS AND INDUSTRIES

H. C. BECK, 'Glass before 1500 BC', *Ancient Egypt* (June 1934).

H. G. CREEL, *The Birth of China: a Study of the Formative Period of Chinese Civilization* (New York, 1954).

R. ENGELBACH, 'Mechanical and Technical Processes' in S. R. K. Glanville, ed., *The Legacy of Egypt* (Oxford, 1942).

SIR A. J. EVANS, *The Palace of Minos; a Comparative Account of the Successive Stages of the Early Cretan Civilization as illustrated by the Discoveries at Knossos* (London, 1921–35), 4 vols.

R. J. FORBES, *Studies in Ancient Technology* (Leiden, 1955–58).

P. FOX, *Tutankhamun's Treasure* (Oxford; Toronto, 1951).

C. F. C. HAWKES, *The Prehistoric Foundations of Europe to the Mycenean Age* (London, 1940).

E. J. H. MACKAY, *Further Excavations at Mohenjo-Daro* (New Delhi, 1938), 2 vols.

B. MEISSNER, *Babylonien und Assyrien* (Heidelberg, 1920–25), 2 vols.

M. A. MURRAY, *The Splendour that was Egypt; a General Survey of Egyptian Culture and Civilization* (New York, 1949).

S. PIGGOTT, *Prehistoric India to 1000* BC (Harmondsworth, Middlesex, 1950).

C. G. SELIGMAN and H. C. BECK, 'Far Eastern Glass', Museum of Far Eastern Antiquities, *Bulletin,* No. 10 (Stockholm, 1938).

SIR C. L. WOOLLEY *et al.*, 'Alalakh; an Account of the Excavations at Tell Atchana in the Hatay, 1937–1949', Society of Antiquaries of London, Research Committee *Reports,* No. 18 (London, 1955), 4 vols.

CHAPTER V

THE ECONOMIC STRUCTURE

TRADE

J. H. BREASTED, *Ancient Records of Egypt; Historical Documents from the Earliest Times to the Persian Conquest* (Chicago, 1920–23), 5 vols.

J. H. BREASTED, *A History of Egypt from the Earliest Times to the Persian Conquest* (2nd rev. ed., New York, 1909).

L. DELAPORTE, *Mesopotamia; the Babylonian and Assyrian Civilization* (New York, London, 1925).

R. DUSSAUD, *Prélydiens, Hittites et Achéens* (Paris, 1953).

G. DYKMANS, 'La Vie économique sous l'ancien empire', *Histoire économique et sociale de l'ancienne Égypte,* Tome II (Paris, 1936).

C. F. C. HAWKES, *The Prehistoric Foundations of Europe to the Mycenean Age* (London, 1940).

F. M. HEICHELHEIM, *An Ancient Economic History from the Palaeolithic Age to the Migrations of the Germanic, Slavic and Arabic Nations,* I (tr. by J. Stevens, rev. and complete Eng. ed., Leiden, 1958).

H. KEES, 'Aegypten', *Kulturgeschichte des alten Orients,* Abschnitt I (Munich, 1933).

B. MEISSNER, *Babylonien und Assyrien* (Heidelberg, 1920–25), 2 vols.

A. L. OPPENHEIM, 'The Seafaring Merchants of Ur', American Oriental Society, *Journal,* Vol. 74, I (January–March 1954).

L. PERNIER, *Il Palazzo minoico di Festòs; scavi e studi della Missione archeologica italiana a Creta dal 1900 al 1950* (Rome, 1935–51), 2 vols.

A. J. B. WACE, *Mycenae; an Archaeological History and Guide* (Princeton, 1949).

J. A. WILSON, *The Culture of Ancient Egypt* (Chicago, 1956). (First published in 1951 under title: *The Burden of Egypt.*)

C. ZERVOS, *L'art de la Crète néolithique et minoenne* (Paris, 1956).

CHAPTER VI

LANGUAGES AND WRITING SYSTEMS: EDUCATION

LANGUAGES AND WRITING SYSTEMS

W. F. ALBRIGHT, in *Basor,* No. 110 (1948), pp. 6–22.

L. BLOOMFIELD, *Language* (London, 1935).

M. COHEN, *La grande invention de l'écriture et son évolution* (Paris, 1958), 3 vols.

H. G. CREEL, ed., with Chang Tsung-Ch'ien and R. C. Rudolph, *Literary Chinese* (Chicago, 1938).

G. R. DRIVER, *Semitic Writing from Pictograph to Alphabet* (rev. ed., London, 1954).

SIR A. J. EVANS, *The Palace of Minos; a Comparative Account of the Successive Stages of the Early Cretan Civilization as Illustrated by the Discoveries at Knossos* (London, 1921–35), 4 vols.

J. G. FÉVRIER, *Histoire de l'écriture* (Paris, 1948).

SIR A. H. GARDINER, 'Writing and Literature', in S. R. K. Glanville, ed., *The Legacy of Egypt* (Oxford, 1942).

I. J. GELB, *Study of Writing; the Foundations of Grammatology* (Chicago; London, 1952).

R. GHIRSHMAN, *Iran from the Earliest Times to the Islamic Conquest* (Harmondsworth, Middlesex, 1954).

H. U. HALL, 'A Buffalo-Robe Biography', *Museum Journal*, XVII, I (Philadelphia, 1926).

S. H. HOOKE, 'Recording and Writing', in C. Singer *et al.*, eds., *A History of Technology* (Oxford, 1954).

O. JESPERSEN, *Language: its Nature, Development and Origin* (7th ed., London, 1947).

B. KARLGREN, *Ordet och Pennan i Mittens Rike* (Stockholm, 1918).

B. KARLGREN, *Sound and Symbol in Chinese* (London, 1923).

R. LABAT, *Manuel d'épigraphie akkadienne, signes, syllabaire, idéogrammes* (Paris, 1948).

P. LACAU, *Sur le système hiéroglyphique* (Cairo, 1954).

L. LEGRAIN, 'Archaic Seal Impressions' in Sir C. L. Woolley, *Ur Excavations*, III.

G. MALLERY, 'Picture Writing of the American Indians', U.S. Bureau of American Ethnology, *Tenth Annual Report*, 1888–89 (Washington, 1893).

E. SAPIR, *Language, an Introduction to the Study of Speech* (New York, 1921).

S. SCHOTT, *Hieroglyphen; Untersuchungen zum Ursprung der Schrift* (Wiesbaden, 1951).

E. H. STURTEVANT, *An Introduction to Linguistic Science* (New Haven, 1947).

M. VENTRIS and J. CHADWICK, *Documents in Mycenaean Greek; Three Hundred Selected Tablets from Knossos, Pylos and Mycenae* (Cambridge, 1956).

M. VENTRIS and J. CHADWICK, 'Evidence of Greek Dialect in the Mycenaean Archives', Society for the Promotion of Hellenic Studies, *Journal of Hellenic Studies*, LXXIII (1953).

H. A. WINKLER, *Rock Drawings of Southern Upper Egypt*, Vol. I (London, 1938).

EDUCATION

H. BRUNNER, *Altägyptische Erziehung* (Wiesbaden, 1957).

C. J. GADD, *Teachers and Students in the Oldest Schools* (London, 1956).

S. N. KRAMER, *From the Tablets of Sumer; Twenty-Five Firsts in Man's Recorded History* (Indian Hills, Colo., 1956).

SIR C. L. WOOLLEY, *Excavations at Ur; a Record of Twelve Years' Work* (London, 1954).

CHAPTER VII

THE SCIENCES

MATHEMATICS

W. F. ANDERSON, 'Arithmetical Computations in Roman Numerals', *Classical Philology* 51 (1956), pp. 145–150.

R. J. GILLINGS, *Mathematical Gazette*, Vol. XXXIX, No. 329 (September 1955), p. 187.

O. NEUGEBAUER, 'Arithmetik und Rechnentechnik der Ägypter', *Quellen und Studien zur Geschichte der Mathematik, Astronomie und Physik*, B. 1, p. 301 (March 1929–September 5, 1938).

O. NEUGEBAUER, *The Exact Sciences in Antiquity* (2nd ed. Providence, R.I., 1957).

O. NEUGEBAUER, 'Mathematische Keilschrifttexte', *Quellen und Studien zur Geschichte der Mathematik, Astronomie und Physik*, A 3 (1930–36).

B. L. VAN DER WAERDEN, *Science Awakening* (tr. by Arnold Dresden, Groningen, 1954).

THE CALENDARS

B. RICHMOND, *Time and Measurement and Calendar Construction* (Leiden, 1956).

Babylonian

F. CORNELIUS, 'Die Chronologie des Vorderen Orients im 2. Jahrtausend v. Chr.', Institut für Orientforschung, *Mitteilungen*, XVII (1954–55).

B. MEISSNER, *Babylonien und Assyrien*, II (Heidelberg, 1920–25).

Chinese

M(ASUKICHI) HASHIMOTO, *The Astronomical Divisions of Time in Ancient China* (1943).

LIU CH'AO-YANG, 'Chronology of the Late Yin Period', *Studia Serica Monographs*, Series B, No. 3 (West China Union University, Chinese Cultural Studies Institute, Chengtu, 1945) (in Chinese).

LIU CH'AO-YANG, 'Calendar of the Early Chou Period', *Studia Serica*

Monographs, Series B, No. 2 (West China Union University, Chinese Cultural Studies Institute, Chengtu, 1944) (in Chinese).

LIU CH'AO-YANG, 'Fundamental Questions about the Yin and the Chou Calendars', *Studia Serica,* IV (Chengtu, 1945).

CHINESE ASSOCIATION FOR THE UNITED NATIONS, *A Symposium on the World Calendar* (Taipeh, 1951).

Egyptian

SIR A. H. GARDINER, 'The Problem of the Month-names', *Revue d'égyptologie,* X (1955), p. 11.

O. NEUGEBAUER, 'Die Bedeutungslosigkeit der Sothisperiode für die älteste Ägyptische Chronologie', *Acta Orientalia,* XVII (Copenhagen, 1939), p. 169.

R. A. PARKER, *The Calendars of Ancient Egypt* (Chicago, 1950).

A. SCHARFF, 'Die Bedeutungslosigkeit des sogenannten ältesten Datums', *Historische Zeitschrift,* fol. 161 (1940), pp. 3–32.

J. W. SEWELL, 'The Calendars and Chronology', in S. R. K. Glanville, ed., *The Legacy of Egypt* (Oxford, 1942).

H. E. WINLOCK, 'The Origin of the Ancient Egyptian Calendar', American Philosophical Society, *Proceedings,* Vol. 83 (1940), p. 447.

ASTRONOMY

F. X. KUGLER, *Sternkunde und Sterndienst in Babel: Assyriologische, Astronomische und Astralmythologische Untersuchungen* (Münster in Westfalen, 1907–24), 3 vols.

O. NEUGEBAUER, 'Ancient Mathematics and Astronomy', in C. J. Singer *et al.,* eds., *A History of Technology* (Oxford, 1954).

O. NEUGEBAUER, *Astronomical Cuneiform Texts; Babylonian Ephemerides of the Seleucid Period for the Motion of the Sun, the Moon and the Planets* (London, 1955), 3 vols.

O. NEUGEBAUER, *The Exact Sciences in Antiquity* (2nd ed., Providence, R. I., 1957).

B. L. VAN DER WAERDEN, 'Babylonian Astronomy II and III', *Journal of Near Eastern Studies* (Chicago), VIII, p. 6, and X, p. 20.

MEDICINE AND SURGERY

R. CAMPBELL THOMPSON, *The Assyrian Herbal . . . a Monograph on the Assyrian Vegetable Drugs* (London, 1924).

R. CAMPBELL THOMPSON, 'Assyrian Medical Prescriptions against

Simmatu Poison', *Revue d'assyriologie et d'archéologie orientale,* XXVII.

R. CAMPBELL THOMPSON, *A Dictionary of Assyrian Chemistry and Geology* (Oxford, 1936).

H. GRAPOW, *Grundriss der Medizin der alten Ägypter* (Berlin, 1954–56), 3 vols.

R. LABAT and R. CARATINI, 'La science antique et médiévale des origines à 1430', *Histoire générale des sciences,* I (Paris, 1957).

G. LEFEBVRE, *Essai sur la médecine égyptienne de l'époque pharaonique* (Paris, 1956).

B. MEISSNER, *Babylonien und Assyrien* (Heidelberg, 1920–25), 2 vols.

CHAPTER VIII

RELIGIOUS BELIEFS AND PRACTICES

EGYPT

J. H. BREASTED, *A History of Egypt from the Earliest Times to the Persian Conquest* (2nd rev. ed., New York, 1909).

J. H. BREASTED, 'Ikhnaton, the Religious Revolutionary', *Cambridge Ancient History,* II (Cambridge, 1924).

J. CERNY, *Ancient Egyptian Religion* (London, 1957).

H. FRANKFORT *et al., Before Philosophy, the Intellectual Adventure of Ancient Man; an Essay on Speculative Thought in the Ancient Near East* (Harmondsworth, Middlesex, 1951).

T. E. PEET, 'Contemporary Life and Thought in Egypt', *Cambridge Ancient History,* II (Cambridge, 1924).

T. E. PEET, 'Life and Thought in Egypt under the Old and Middle Kingdoms', *Cambridge Ancient History,* I (Cambridge, 1923).

MESOPOTAMIA

B. W. ANDERSON, *The Living World of the Old Testament* (London, 1958).

E. DHORME, *Les religions de Babylone et d'Assyrie* (Paris, 1945).

B. MEISSNER, *Babylonien und Assyrien* (Heidelberg, 1920–25), 2 vols.

J. B. PRITCHARD ed., *Ancient Near Eastern Texts Relating to the Old Testament* (2nd ed., corr. and enl., Princeton, 1955).

THE HITTITES

G. CONTENAU, *La civilisation des Hittites et des Hurrites du Mitanni* (Paris, 1934).

L. DELAPORTE, *Les hittites* (Paris, 1936).

R. DUSSAUD, 'Les religions des hittites et des hourites, des phoeniciens et des syriens', in E. Dhorme, *Les religions de Babylone et d'Assyrie* (Paris, 1945).

A. GOETZE, *Kleinasien* (2nd ed., Munich, 1957).

H. G. GUETERBOCK, 'The Hurrian Element in the Hittite Empire', *Journal of World History,* II, No. 2 (Neuchâtel, 1955), p. 383.

O. R. GURNEY, *The Hittites* (London, Baltimore, 1952).

F. B. HROZNY, *O nejstarším stehováni národu a o problému civilisace protoindické* (Prague, 1940).

E. MEYER, *Reich and Kultur der Hethiter* (Berlin, 1914).

E. A. SPEISER, 'The Hurrian Participation in the Civilizations of Mesopotamia, Syria and Palestine', *Journal of World History,* I, No. 2 (Neuchâtel, 1953).

SIR C. L. WOOLLEY, *Abraham; Recent Discoveries and Hebrew Origins* (New York, 1936).

SIR C. L. WOOLLEY, 'The Iron-Age Graves of Carchemish', Liverpool University College, Institute of Archaeology, *Annals,* XXVI, 1–2, p. 11.

INDIA

E. J. H. MACKAY, *Further Excavations at Mohenjo-Daro* (New Delhi, 1938), 2 vols.

SIR J. H. MARSHALL *et al., Mohenjo-daro and the Indus Civilization* (London, 1931), 3 vols.

S. PIGGOTT, *Prehistoric India to 1000* BC (Harmondsworth, Middlesex, 1950).

R. E. M. WHEELER, *Five Thousand Years of Pakistan; an Archaeological Outline* (London, 1950).

CHINA

H. G. CREEL, *The Birth of China: a Study of the Formative Period of Chinese Civilization* (New York, 1954).

H. A. GILES, *The Civilization of China* (London, 1911).

W. C. WHITE, *Bone Culture of Ancient China; an Archaeological Study of Bone Material from Northern Honan dating about the Twelfth Century B.C.* (Toronto, 1945).

CRETE

SIR A. J. EVANS, 'The Mycenaean Tree and Pillar Cult', Society for the Promotion of Hellenic Studies, *Journal of Hellenic Studies,* XXI (1901).

M. P. NILSSON, *The Minoan-Mycenaean Religion and its Survival in Greek Religion* (2nd rev. ed., Lund, 1950).

CH. PICARD, 'Les religions préhelléniques', *Les religions de l'Europe ancienne,* Tome I (Paris, 1948).

CHAPTER IX

THE FINE AND APPLIED ARTS

J. CAPART, 'Egyptian Art', in S. R. K. Glanville ed., *The Legacy of Egypt* (Oxford, 1942).

L. CURTIUS, 'Der Klassische Stil' *Die Antike Kunst, Handbuch der Kunstwissenschaft,* II (Potsdam, 1931–35).

SIR A. J. EVANS, *The Palace of Minos; a Comparative Account of the Successive Stages of the Early Cretan Civilization as Illustrated by the Discoveries at Knossos* (London, 1921–35), 4 vols.

H. FRANKFORT, *Cylinder Seals; a Documentary Essay on the Art and Religion of the Ancient Near East* (London, 1939).

H. FRANKFORT, *Sculpture of the Third Millennium B.C. from Tell Asmar and Khafājah* (Chicago, 1939).

H. A. GROENEWEGEN-FRANKFORT, *Arrest and Movement; an Essay on Space and Time in the Representational Art of the Ancient Near East* (Chicago, 1951).

E. IVERSEN, *Canon and Proportions in Egyptian Art* (London, 1955).

SIR J. H. MARSHALL *et al., Mohenjo-daro and the Indus Civilization* (London, 1931), 3 vols.

F. MATZ, *Kreta, Mykene und Troja; die Minoische und die Homerische Welt* (Zürich, Stuttgart, 1956).

M. A. MURRAY, *The Splendour that was Egypt; a General Survey of Egyptian Culture and Civilization* (New York, 1949).

E. POTTIER, *L'art hittite* (Paris, 1926–31).

H. SCHMÖKEL, *Ur, Assur und Babylon; drei Jahrtausende im Zweistromland* (Stuttgart, 1955).

M. VIEYRA, *Hittite Art*, 2300–750 BC (London, 1955).

O. WEBER, *Die Kunst der Hethiter* (Berlin, 1922).

SIR C. L. WOOLLEY, *The Development of Sumerian Art* (London, 1935).

CHAPTER X

MUSIC AND LITERATURE

MUSIC

F. W. GALPIN, *The Music of the Sumerians and their Immediate Successors, the Babylonians and Assyrians* (Strasbourg, 1955).

F. W. GALPIN, 'The Sumerian Harp of Ur', *Music and Letters*, X, No. 2 (London, 1929), p. 108.

H. HICKMANN, 'Instruments de Musique', *Catalogue générale des antiquités égyptiennes du Musée du Louvre* (1949).

A. C. MOULE, 'A List of the Musical and other Sound-Producing Instruments of the Chinese', Royal Asiatic Society, China Branch, *Journal*, Vol. 39 (1908).

New Oxford History of Music, I (London, New York, 1957).

C. SACHS, *The Rise of Music in the Ancient World, East and West* (New York, 1944).

C. SACHS, 'Zweiklänge im Altertum', *Festschrift für Johannes Wolf* (Berlin, 1929).

K. SCHLESINGER, 'The Significance of Musical Instruments in the Evolution of Music', *Oxford History of Music* (2nd ed., Oxford, 1929).

LITERATURE

J. H. BREASTED, *A History of Egypt from the Earliest Times to the Persian Conquest* (2nd rev. ed., New York, 1909).

E. CAVAIGNAC, 'Les annales de Mursil II', *Revue d'assyriologie et d'archéologie orientale*, XXVI (1929).

E. CAVAIGNAC, *Les annales de Subbiluliuma* (Strasbourg, 1931).

A. ERMAN, *The Literature of the Ancient Egyptians; Poems, Narra-*

tives, and Manuals of Instruction, from the Third and Second Millennia B.C. (tr. by A. M. Blackman, London, 1927).

A. H. GARDINER, 'Writing and Literature', in S. R. K. Glanville, ed., *The Legacy of Egypt* (Oxford, 1942).

A. GOETZE, 'Die Annalen des Mursilis', Vorderasiatisch-Ägyptische Gesellschaft, *Mitteilungen* (1933).

A. GOETZE, 'Hattusilis', Vorderasiatisch-Ägyptische Gesellschaft, *Mitteilungen*, XXIX, 3 (1924).

E. I. GORDON, 'The Sumerian Proverb Collections', American Oriental Society, *Journal*, Vol. 74, No. 2 (New Haven, Conn., April–June 1954).

S. N. KRAMER, *Emmerkar and the Lord of Aratta; a Sumerian Epic Tale of Iraq and Iran* (Philadelphia, 1952).

S. N. KRAMER, 'Sumerian Historiography', *Israel Exploration Journal*, III, No. 4 (1953).

S. N. KRAMER, *Sumerian Mythology; a Study of Spiritual and Literary Achievement in the Third Millennium B.C.* (Philadelphia, 1944).

A. C. MACE, *Egyptian Literature* (New York, 1928).

B. MEISSNER, *Die Babylonisch-Assyrische Literatur* (Potsdam, 1927–28).

T. E. PEET, *A Comparative Study of the Literatures of Egypt, Palestine and Mesopotamia; Egypt's Contribution to the Literature of the Ancient World* (London, 1931).

T. E. PEET, *Mesopotamia* (London, 1931).

O. WEBER, 'Die Literatur der Babylonier und Assyrer', *Alte Orient* (Leipzig, 1907, 1911).

W. C. WHITE, *Bone Culture of Ancient China; an Archaeological Study of Bone Material from Northern Honan dating about the Twelfth Century B.C.* (Toronto, 1945).

INDEX